Resistance to Empire and Militarization

Resistance to Empire and Militarization
Reclaiming the Sacred

Edited by
Jude Lal Fernando

SHEFFIELD UK   BRISTOL CT

Published by Equinox Publishing Ltd.

UK: Office 415, The Workstation, 15 Paternoster Row, Sheffield,
South Yorkshire S1 2BX

USA: ISD, 70 Enterprise Drive, Bristol, CT 06010

www.equinoxpub.com

First published 2020
First printing in paperback 2020

© Jude Lal Fernando and contributors 2020

All rights reserved. No part of this publication may be reproduced or transmitted in any form or by any means, electronic or mechanical, including photocopying, recording or any information storage or retrieval system, without prior permission in writing from the publishers.

ISBN-13   978 1 80050 020 4   (paperback)
          978 1 78179 995 6   (hardback)
          978 1 78179 996 3   (ePDF)

British Library Cataloguing-in-Publication Data

A catalogue record for this book is available from the British Library.

Library of Congress Cataloging-in-Publication Data

Names: Fernando, Jude Lal, editor.
Title: Resistance to empire and militarization : reclaiming the sacred /
   Jude Lal Fernando.
Description: Sheffield, South Yorkshire ; Bristol, CT : Equinox Publishing Ltd, 2020. | Includes bibliographical references and index. | Summary: "The main focus of this work is militarization without which empire cannot sustain itself; but we would interrogate militarization as part of the cultural, religious, economic and (geo)political forces which are unique to and constitute the modern empire. In other words, it is not only military hardware that is destructive. In our times, militarization encompasses multiple levels of cultural, religious and sociopolitical relations within a state, a geopolitical region and the world imperialist order"—Provided by publisher.
Identifiers: LCCN 2019054700 (print) | LCCN 2019054701 (ebook) | ISBN 9781781799956 (hardback) | ISBN 9781781799963 (ebook)
Subjects: LCSH: Militarism—Religious aspects—Christianity. | Militarism—Religious aspects. | Capitalism—Religious aspects—Christianity. | Capitalism—Religious aspects. | Imperialism—Religious aspects. | Religion and politics. | Religion and culture. | Holy, The. | World politics—Moral and ethical aspects.
Classification: LCC BT736.2 .R465 2020 (print) | LCC BT736.2 (ebook) | DDC 261.8/73—dc23
LC record available at https://lccn.loc.gov/2019054700
LC ebook record available at https://lccn.loc.gov/2019054701

Typeset by JS Typesetting Ltd, Porthcawl, Mid Glamorgan

*Dedicated to
our beloved brother
Vuyani Shadrack Vellem (South Africa)
(1968–2019)
black liberation theologian
and to
our beloved elder
Kinhide Mushakoji (Japan)
(1929–)
lifelong peace scholar/practitioner*

Contents

Foreword by Collin Cowan — xi
Preface by Sudipta Singh — xiii

Introduction — 1
Jude Lal Fernando

PART I
EAST ASIA, SOUTH ASIA, WEST ASIA AND BEYOND

Empire, Globalization and Militarization

1. Wars Beyond the Armed Forces: Colonialism and Militarization of Ethno-national Conflicts in Contemporary South Asia — 25
   Radha D'Souza
2. Contemporary Globalization and Militarization: From Speculation Blitz to the "War on Terror" Rampage — 45
   Haluk Gerger
3. Peoples against a New Cold War: Nuclear Imperialism or Dialogue for Reconciliation — 64
   Kinhide Mushakoji

The Geopolitics of Conflict and Peace: Japan, Korea and Sri Lanka

4. Contesting Pasts, Presents, Futures: East Asia's "Japan Problem" and "Korea Problem" — 81
   Gavan McCormack
5. The Geo-politics of Imperialism and the Unitary State of Sri Lanka: Militarization and Structural Genocide of the Eelam Tamil Nation — 97
   Athithan Jayapalan and Gajendrakumar Ponnambalam

Resistance in Kashmir, Korea, Okinawa and Palestine

6. Militarization and Everyday Struggle: A Case of Families of the Victims of Enforced Disappearances in Kashmir — 114
   Farrukh Faheem

7 "Enemies of the Nation, Heretics of the Church": Conscientious Rejection of State Authority 127
   Nami Kim

8 Okinawan People's Philosophy of Direct Action against Capitalism and Imperialism from Post-World War II to the Present 141
   Kozue Uehara

9 Understanding Non-feminist Groups through the Necessity to Resist Feminist Hegemony: The Palestinian Women's Movement versus Hamas 158
   Sara Ababneh

De-imperializing Religious Narratives in an Interreligious Mode

10 God versus Goliath: Theological Challenges to Empire in South Asia 178
    Francis Gonsalves

11 The Empathetic Power of Suffering: The Memories of Killing and Feminist Interfaith Spiritual Activism 198
    Keun-Joo Christine Pae

12 The Qur'an, the Bible, and the Indigenous Peoples of Canaan: An Anti-Colonial Muslim Reading 213
    Shadaab Rahemtulla

13 Counter-imperialistic Features in Biblical Israel 233
    Youngseop Lim

PART II
AFRICA, LATIN AMERICA, THE CARIBBEAN AND THE PACIFIC ISLANDS, AND BEYOND

The Neocolonial Empire and Necropolitical Capitalism

14 Colonialism Still Matters: Militarization and Imperial Grand Strategy in the Era of US versus China 251
    Andy Higginbottom

15 New Imperialisms and Struggles for Peace 270
    Napoleón Saltos Galarza

16 Necropolitical Capitalism, the State of Exception and Accumulation by Dispossession 288
    Luis Arizmendi

Islands as Imperial Assets or Centers of Peace?

17 Hawaiʻi: A Pivot of Empire or Piko of Aloha ʻĀina? 306
    Kyle Kajihiro

18 Existential Threats to the Pacific Islands: Oceania Resists the Long Reach of Empire 323
    Vanessa Griffen, Gordon Nanau, and Maureen Penjueli

Theologies of Resistance in Africa, Latin America, and the Caribbean Islands

19 Knowledge Militarized in Africa: On Crushing Ubuhlanti to Advance Pseudo-democratic and Economic Imagination in the Context of Empire 339
V. S. Vellem

20 Resistance, Peoples' Rights and the Role of the Churches in Latin America 354
Javier Giraldo Moreno

21 Empire, the Caribbean Church and the Gospel of Resistance 369
Garnett Roper

Index 383

Foreword

Collin Cowan

The chapters of this book are the fruit of two consultations organized by the Council for World Mission (CWM) to resist the deadly imperial designs of militarization of our world. We are living in a scandalous world. Global military spending today has reached its highest peak when millions of our children are dying of hunger. CWM, an international mission organization, is continually discerning how to be relevant in a time of increasing war and militarization, how to proclaim fullness of life at a time when life around the globe is threatened, and how to decolonize mission, its theology and praxis.

The two conferences that were held in Seoul and Mexico City in 2018 under the title "Resistance to Empire and Militarization: Reclaiming the Sacredness of Lives, Lands and Seas" are initiatives through which CWM continues its prophetic engagement with the present political and social landscapes and denounces the power of militarized might on behalf of the social movements of the masses or the multitudes.

How do we reconstruct our theological reflections informed by the murdered, tortured, raped, displaced and mutilated victims of war and conflict? What is the theological significance of the memories of tormented peoples in bearing our public witness in the midst of bloodshed and displacement? Dangerous memories, according to Johann Baptist Metz, are "memories which make demands on us. These are memories in which earlier experiences break through to the center-point of our lives and reveal new and dangerous insights for the present." I agree. Dangerous memories are subversive memories, memories that make demands on our way of being in relation to lives, lands and seas. So, our remembrance of those tormented lives are political, spiritual, and subversive, inviting and challenging us to witness to the God of life in the public sphere through our active resistance to all imperial forces and systems that propagate death.

Jesus was radically opposed to every form of militarization because he believed in the dignity of life for all creation (Jn. 10.10). The movement he led was a system-threatening movement. He fiercely confronted the political and religious forces of death and destruction. The cross he endured was the consequence of his public stand which exposed and challenged the sinfulness/selfishness of the prevailing order. Acts of the Apostles presents the early Church as a community engaged with public witness through "turning the world upside down" (Acts 17.6). Speaking to Truth to power and empowering the powerless is the Christian praxis of our times despite the cost. It involves constructing transformative alternatives of our social and political relations that embody our faith in the God of life.

Through this publication, CWM enters into solidarity with partners from different faith communities and resistance movements who uphold the sacredness of lives and lands and are engaged with various struggles across the globe to dismantle the deadly empire. The writers of this collection of essays come from many countries and continents in the world. They belong to different faith traditions as well as secular humanist traditions. They have listened to the voices of victims of militarization, reflected on their hope-filled unwavering resistance to the empire and helped us to see the interrelatedness of militarization, capitalism, colonialism, imperialism and various religious fundamentalisms. They vehemently oppose imperial cults of death that are couched with various sectarian ideologies and call us to proclaim our faith in life, life in abundance, for us and for generations to come. Together, they announce the dawn of the "Beloved Community" (Martin Luther King) of humanity that overcomes the darkest nights of various borders of exclusion while embracing a new consciousness of our common home, the planet Earth (Greta Thunberg).

The words of these essays reveal to the reader the audacious hope in action in a context numbed by human and structural cruelties. Walter Brueggemann's notion of "prophetic imagination" beckons, even demands of us the audacity of hope; the refusal to accept the present social landscape as normal and adequate. Hope as subversive activity is what this book agitates and advocates for in the midst all imperial forces.

Rev. Dr. Collin Isaiah Cowan is the general secretary of the Council for World Mission. He is originally from Jamaica and was the general secretary of the United Church in Jamaica and the Cayman Islands. Known for his courage, passion and commitment to justice, peace, integrity of creation and building of life affirming communities, he has inspired many socially engaged groups and communities across the globe through his preaching and writing. He challenges the churches to move away from Christian triumphalism associated with empire and promotes a new understanding of Christian witness and praxis that speaks truth to the power and empowers the powerless. His contribution towards developing capacities of churches to resist all imperial forces is immense.

Preface

Sudipta Singh

War and conflict have proliferated in our time to the extent that they have become normative in several parts of the world. There is an entire generation of people who do not know what it is like to live without the constant noise of gunfire and the fear of being bombed. Around the world small- and large-scale conflicts kill and maim people, recruit young boys into armed groups, perpetrate violence against women and girls, and destroy the environment. The proliferation and advancement of weapons has meant that we have literally reached the edge of the world, having now the capability of destroying the earth several times over, as though one time is not enough! Nuclearization has been reinforced threatening the whole world only to serve a global imperial system. The geopolitics of the atom has split nations. On an individual state level there is increasing violence by the state against its own people, mostly with the overt and covert support provided by external powers. Dissent is quickly and firmly thwarted by coercive means and the propaganda machine, quelling freedom of expression and restricting debate. We are being seduced into a state of numbness, inured to the pain of the violence around us.

Militarization causes poverty, hunger, malnutrition, sickness, and destruction of environment as defense expenditure around the world is increased by slashing public spending on all welfare systems. The obscene amounts of money being invested in this immoral cult of violence serves to impoverish vast populations while at the same time generating wealth for those involved in the manufacture and trading of weapons. It is no coincidence then that the warmongers are also business leaders. The political parties and leaders who are dependent on them ask the people for a mandate to morally justify war. The global patriarchal war machine legitimizes hierarchy, glorifies and justifies violence, and increases the gap between the rich and the poor in the world while dividing the peoples along various ethno-religious fault lines. It is the way in which the modern empire consolidates its centers and expands its margins.

In the midst of this rampant deification of power, it is the God who is wounded for our sake (Isaiah 53.5) that calls out to us from the cross. In the cross, we find an alternative strategy of resistance to the empire. The cross is not a site where violence and suffering are glorified, but is a place which calls for active confrontation of the empire through solidarity and struggle with the wretched of the earth. God's call in history has always been a celebration of bearing witness in confronting the empire. Mission in the context of the empire demands our unwavering allegiance to the blossoming of life by exposing and confronting the imperial forces. It is an invitation to resist the temptation to be co-opted by the empire and the nerve to come out of the empire by creating counter-imperial alternatives. In this politics, we experience profound spirituality.

With this renewed vision, Council for World Mission (CWM) began to search for new expressions of Christian public witness in a broken world. Its Theological Statement identifies multiple resistances to the empire as the context in which we are called to be partners with God in transforming the world. When we resist the power of the empire, we are reclaiming our sacred agency to liberate our lives, societies, lands, seas, and the whole of cosmos. The hope that sustains us in the context of the empire is the possibility to live in opposition to the logic of the empire. When we live out our faith rejecting the claims of the empire on our lives and our world, we witness the God of life.

The politics and spirituality emerging from the social and political movements of the multitudes in different parts of the globe provide us new possibilities to live out our faith in the context of an undeclared emergency. As the multitudes continue to contest the claims of absolute sovereignty of the powers and principalities of our times, their movements become the new sacred scriptures that reveal the Divine presence in our midst. The annunciation that reverberates in the movements of the multitudes is the prophetic proclamation of alternatives. It is not the waiting for a new messiah; rather it is the discernment of the community that "we are the ones we've been waiting for." Creative attempts of these communities of blessed unrest, defying the logic of the prevailing order through their direct action, talk, writing, dance, art, movies, communes, search for just and eco-friendly sustainable alternatives, and self-rule are the embodiments of a new politics and spirituality in our midst.

This book is a collection of deep reflections on the struggles of all those "modern prophets" who are fighting against the empire in their own contexts through multiple ways. They are academics, activists, artists, theologians, and common people from the margins of the society.

I take this opportunity to thank all the contributors, reviewers of papers and participants from both the conferences held in Seoul and Mexico in 2018 under the theme of this book for their valuable thoughts and insights emerging from various liberative practices. Peachy from CWM who assisted in coordinating the conferences deserves a very big thank you. We could not have brought out this volume without the help of those who engaged in translating, proofreading, editing and indexing. Among them are Freya Dasgupta, Jacqueline Díaz, Radha D'Souza, Ari Fogelson, Jose Antonio Gutierrez, Andy Higginbottom, Hamish Ironside, Amanda Latimer, Jenny Padgham, Andrew Pierce, John Robinson and Jill Sweet. I would like to thank them immensely for their assistance. The managing director of Equinox, Janet Joyce, and her colleagues, Valerie Hall and Sarah Lee, have been super-efficient in bringing out this publication on time. Thank you very much Equinox. The whole project would not have been possible without the deep commitment to critical scholarship and activism of my friend Jude Lal Fernando. Kudos to him and to his wife Nadee, and their son Raveesh, who as a family have lived a life of exile for over a decade because of their resistance to militarization in their country of origin. The colleagues at the Irish School of Ecumenics, School of Religion, Trinity College Dublin where Jude teaches need our appreciation for supporting him in many ways to accomplish the editing of this book.

We pray that these testimonies of resistance will inspire all of us and strengthen our common struggle against the empire. We urge that through this work our global network of anti-war and anti-militarization will be strengthened.

Sudipta Singh is presently serving as the mission secretary for research and capacity development of the Council for World Mission. Originally from India he is a renowned social activist involved with a range of people's movements around the globe. One of his key activities is to explore how different faith traditions could come together to resist the empire and religious fundamentalisms. He has organized many international conferences and promoted a range of publications on this theme.

"A nation that continues year after year to spend more money on military defense than on programs of social uplift is approaching spiritual death."
—Martin Luther King Jr.

"You are not to be so blind with patriotism that you can't face reality. Wrong is wrong, no matter who does it or says it."
—Malcom X

Introduction

Jude Lal Fernando

After all, there are conditions under which war is waged, and we have to know them if we are to oppose war. Indeed, the opposition to war has to take place, in part, through remaking the conditions of its possibility and probability. Similarly, if war is to be opposed, we have to understand how popular assent to war is cultivated and maintained, in other words, how war waging acts upon the senses so that war is thought to be an inevitability, something good, or even a source of moral satisfaction.
—Judith Butler, *Frames of War* (2016: ix)

Our strategy should be not only to confront empire, but to lay siege to it. To deprive it of oxygen. To shame it. To mock it. With our art, our music, our literature, our stubbornness, our joy, our brilliance, our sheer relentlessness—and our ability to tell our own stories. Stories that are different from the ones we're being brainwashed to believe.
—Arundhati Roy, *An Ordinary Person's Guide to Empire* (2013: 61)

And as a pastor I refuse to separate the reality of this world from the reality of the Bible by preaching a "cheap Gospel" that neither challenges reality nor is challenged by it... For me as a Palestinian Christian, Palestine is the land of both my physical and my spiritual forefathers and foremothers. The biblical story is thus part and parcel of my nation's history, a history of continuous occupation by succeeding empires. In fact, the biblical story can best be understood as a response to the geopolitical history of the region.
—Mitri Raheb, *Faith in the Face of Empire* (2014: 3)

Hence our unique contribution to inter-faith dialogue is to confess ... that Jesus is God's defense-pact with the poor—not by mere words but by actively joining God's own defense of the poor. Such activity could never be a threat to other religions, because its main thrust is *not* conversion of other religionists to Christianity *but* the conversion of the chaos of induced scarcity into the order of shared abundance through greedless living. All religionists can join this struggle without compromising their faith.
—Aloysius Pieris, *The Genesis of an Asian Theology of Liberation* (2013: 182)

Empire building, as a high concentration of cultural and political power in one single domain, and its imposition across borders through various means ranging from brute force to subtle forms of assimilation, is not new in human history. It has had different phases, with many driving factors and actors. At the heart of the modern empire and its colonialist designs lies capitalism, upon which Britain built the most expansive empire in human history. The inseparable relationship between the modern empire and capitalism has enabled an unprecedented level of militarization of the globe. The empire's technologies of control range from psychological warfare (winning hearts and minds) to advanced technological warfare (creating a wasteland with maximum destruction), leaving an intergenerational impact. Even though direct colonial rule has ended in most parts of the world, indirect domination through cultural, religious, economic, political and military means continues unabated. We live in an era of the neocolonial empire, a term that seems to be not *politically right* in some academic circles.

The main focus of this work is militarization, without which empire cannot sustain itself; but we would interrogate militarization as part of the cultural, religious, economic and (geo)political forces which are unique to and constitute the modern empire. In other words, it is not only military hardware that is destructive. In our times, militarization encompasses multiple levels of cultural, religious and sociopolitical relations within a state, a geopolitical region and the world imperialist order. Militarization is accompanied by militarism; the mobilization of cultures and societies in morally justifying militarization: without recognizing these multiple levels in the militarized imperial project, effective resistance to empire and militarization is not possible.

This work does not enter into a lengthy theoretical debate surrounding either the use of the terms empire, imperialism and imperial, or those concerned with the argument that the era of imperialism is over and what remains is "Empire" (Hardt and Negri 2000: xii). Instead, the term empire is understood as a set of principles, mechanisms and modes of governance. Imperialism is used to refer to the hegemony of the Euro-American political economy in the world since the emergence of capitalism and its understanding of modernity in Europe. The capitalist logic of the modern empire is intrinsically interwoven with the logic of expansion, which necessitates militarization. We would identify the key drivers and multiple dimensions of the capitalist empire, while specifically interrogating the impact of its militarization on different geopolitical locations and peoples across the globe.

Why "the Sacred"?

Resistance emerges from a specific people at a particular location, mostly against the visible actors; but it needs to be further contextualized within the specific histories and geopolitics of imperialism and colonialism associated with that particular location. This calls for a geo-historical consciousness. The chapters in this collection have adopted this broad perspective, which resources developing interrelationships among resisting peoples across the globe. The driving force behind resistance is not simply opposition, but also the alternative liberating cosmovisions of life and world. Resistance should not "simply reciprocate the language of the conquerors in order to authenticate the terms of its resistances" and "the language of resistance must be domestic and definitive to the people who do the resisting" (Dabashi 2008: 60). The subtitle of this work highlights the sacredness of life and of the whole cosmos, which is being destroyed by the modern empire and its imperialism. One of the positive effects of our modern age is the growing conviction of the value of secularity, which is the material dimension of reality, which we call "world." Raimon Panikkar uses "*sacred secularity*" and "*secular sacredness*" interchangeably while distinguishing secularity from secularism:

> What I mean is this: The sacred, with whatever name we may express it, is a constitutive dimension of reality and an essential character of the human being ... Secularism, as distinct from secularity, is antinatural and antihuman: It denies transcendence and becomes an ideology which pretends to organize life by means of rationally planned structures. A mere socio-economic peace is not only impossible; it would not be peace at all. Human life is sacred, and so is society, and so is the world, the *saeculum*, and reality.
>
> (Panikkar 1999: 193–194)

This work recognizes the multiple ways of expressing sacredness among many peoples across the globe. The cosmovisions enshrined in major religious traditions and in numerous indigenous traditions in multiple cultural settings, proclaim a sacredness that sustains life and its continuity. Some versions of religious traditions that embrace the imperial logic will be resisted as part of reclaiming the sacredness of life and cosmos. Non-religious humanist traditions' emphasis on the dignity of human beings and on the care for the earth reflect this sense of sacredness in a secular language. Sacredness is inseparable from empathy (liberating love) and the realization of interrelationships (liberating knowledge or wisdom) of eco-humanity. When we resist with liberating love and knowledge we reclaim the sacredness of our will to freedom.

The Neocolonial Empire and Religious Fundamentalisms

Let us turn to the geo-historical positioning of the contemporary empire, its ambivalent relationship with religions, and to the multiple sites of resistance. The imperial world order, in which we live today, is mainly a result of the post-World War II politics. After World War II, the USA, in alliance with the UK, has been the main driver of this empire, which was countered by the USSR. After the Cold War, it is the USA that has emerged as the predominant imperial power, reinforcing militarization as its key feature and maintaining around 800 small and large scale military bases across the globe (Vine 2015: 4). With the sale, development and deployment of advanced weaponry, entire economies have been formed on the basis of investments in warfare. This is the hardware of the empire. However, the empire cannot maintain its physical structures of militarization without making hearts and minds conform to its ideology. This it achieves through a belief system in security, a new creed that idolizes such structures, and which forms the software of the empire (Raheb 2014: 24). The global "war on terror" and "national security" have become new creeds that are being recited in the name of imperial peace:

> The military-political doctrine of national security has replaced the older political values and convictions of democracy, freedom of the press, and human rights; instead, "national security" has become the foundation of policy. A threat to national security is the greatest risk, and its betrayal is a capital crime.
> (Soelle 1990: 109)

Often the language of this belief system is a modern secular one, but it is also supported and justified by a religious language that mobilizes societies and thereby promoting militarism.

The neocolonial empire has built a close relationship with certain fundamentalist strands of major religions. Both within the USA and its allied states across the globe (e.g., Guatemala, Brazil, India, Israel, Japan, Saudi Arabia, Sri Lanka and South Korea), these strands have gained the upper hand in determining politics. In Afghanistan, the USA forged militant groups that followed a fundamentalist interpretation of Islam to counter the USSR during the latter part of the Cold War (Mamdani 2004). Likewise, while aiding repressive regimes in Latin America, the USA relied on its support of conservative strands within the Roman Catholic Church led by the Vatican (Berryman 1987) and its promotion of fundamentalist strands within Christian evangelicalism. In this process, the liberative strands within Christianity in Latin America, Philippines, South Korea, and those within Islam in the Middle East and places like Indonesia were brutally suppressed. A similar trend can be seen with regard to all other major religious traditions. In this way, the neocolonial empire has suppressed strands within religions that emerge out of liberative praxis and that unite peoples of different faiths. This strategy relies on both direct attack and on creating conditions in which religious fundamentalist forces can gain the upper hand, thereby creating milieus of hate and suspicion in which diverse faith communities are pitted against one another. Belief in militarization and militarism is driven by a particular "spirit" of fear, and a desire for vengeance and supremacy, which is falsely couched in heroism. Unlike in the past, there is no longer one religious altar of imperialism. Now, there are multiple religio-national altars of militarism, all serving the one empire, which is in constant conflict with critically reflective secular reasoning, as well as the counter-imperial ethical/liberative practices of all religious traditions.[1]

Therefore, the end of the Cold War—allegedly marking the dawn of a new world order—proves to be nothing more than another name for a single empire, furthering the militarization of the globe as never before in our history, while causing deep polarizations between nations, and ethnic and religious communities across the world. Communist-phobia has been replaced with Islamophobia. China has emerged as an economic empire competing with the USA, while individual states and regions have been drawn into these new battle lines: in Africa, Asia, the Caribbean and the Pacific Islands, the Middle East, and Latin America. The USA, as a military empire, today attempts to reduce the number of its own soldiers on the ground. Instead, the security forces of its allied states fight imperial wars in the name of the national security of their own states, with this security often aligned to a majority ethno-religious identity, which in turn often overlaps with fundamentalist versions of religion. The empire and its allies project themselves to be all-powerful: "We have seen that a will which takes itself to be all-powerful, or which aspires to that condition, tends to wreak an exceptional amount of chaos and misery" (Eagleton 2005: 118).

Even though the empire claims that militarization is for peace, it is in a constant state of war due to its inherent logic of expansion and control, and so thwarts any peaceful negotiations to resolve conflicts while criminalizing and destroying progressive social and political movements in the name of security. Ideas of democracy and human rights, too, have been militarized and have become tools for the empire to propagate its insidious agenda (Suh 2014). Invasions are justified in the name of restoring democracy and in ushering in global security and peace (e.g., Afghanistan, Iraq, Libya, Kashmir, Syria, Tamil Eelam, or Yemen), and they are being proposed for those states that do not obey the imperial orders (e.g., Venezuela, North Korea). The most fundamental rights to food and medicine have been snatched away from millions of people through sanctions imposed in the name of human rights. Faith communities have been prohibited by international sanctions and national security laws to practice their most fundamental ethic of care for the other by organizing humanitarian aid across the borders.

The Imperial Peace that Bleeds

Millions perish at the altars of the idol of imperial peace and security. Many are maimed and raped. Millions have been expelled from their homes, fertile lands and shores, which have been converted into minefields. The people who are caught up in these wars are forced to flee their beloved homelands. Sometimes, to save their lives, they are herded onto dangerously overladen boats, many of which never reach the far shore. The political borders of the countries that lead the empire have been tightened. For strategic reasons, battle lines have been drawn on the ever-changing waves of the seas to secure the boundaries of the empire. Islands have been turned into strategic assets. Their peoples have been terrorized and forcibly evacuated. When the imperial expansion cannot be sustained through land and seas, the empire begins to exert its dominion from the skies, through aerial bombing, drones and satellites (Hippler 2017). An oral poem by an unnamed Tamil youth in northern Sri Lanka—who, as a child, survived an attack carried out by the Sri Lankan air force using an Israeli-made Kafir jet—expresses the ongoing deep trauma of modern-day aerial warfare: *As a child I loved the sky and birds, but now I look at the skies with fright and hate those birds.* The empire unleashes a "constellation of oppressions" (Santos 2016: 18). It is not only genocidal, but also epistemicidal and spiritualicidal. It not only physically destroys ethnically, racially and religiously distinct peoples, but also subjugates and crushes their liberative collective consciousness and alternative knowledge forms. It manufactures certain locations and societies across the globe into its likeness and image, while at the same time reducing a vast population on earth to the status of non-persons and treating the earth as a disposable commodity.

Images of refugees, widely disseminated by mainstream media outlets, depict them as helpless victims, not in order to evoke an empathetic response, but so as to hide imperial involvement in the wars that are the cause of their victimhood in the first place. The media tries to project these wars as internal strife or as butchery intrinsic to the "underdeveloped" world. Not only that, but victims are also categorized as worthy or unworthy. Lives are classified as grievable or ungrievable, based on what the empire determines as peace, security, and democracy. "Ungrievable lives are those that cannot be lost, and cannot be destroyed, they are ontologically, and from the start, already lost and destroyed, which means that when they are destroyed in war, nothing is destroyed" (Butler 2016: xix). But that is not the end of our story.

In response, we also witness uncompromising resilience and resistance of many groups and peoples who have been inspired, both by different faiths and various non-religious humanist strands. The voices of those who are afflicted across the world are not only voices of despair, but also of hope (Roy 2004). This collection of chapters is a response to the ever-increasing urgency of spreading transformative, liberating knowledge that can reinvigorate resistance and inspire the vision of an alternative world beyond the empire. The chapters were originally papers presented, discussed, reviewed and later revised at two conferences—in Seoul, October 20–23, 2018, and in Mexico City, December 10–12, 2018—under the name "Resistance to Empire and Militarization: Reclaiming the Sacredness of Lives, Lands, Seas and Skies," organized by the Council of World Mission (CWM). The belief that truth shall make us free prompted the CWM to this endeavor, as part of the member churches' mission in building life-affirming and liberating communities through an interdisciplinary, intercultural, interreligious, and internationalist approach. Around 70 participants, who together represent three generations of survivors of imperial invasions and genocidal massacres across the globe, were present at both events, each three days long. They refuse to be mere helpless victims of war and militarization. Despite genocidal onslaught, they survived epistemicide and spiritualicide. They believe that they are one with the affected peoples who exercise the creative agency of resistance, despite continuous death, destruction and division.

The Dual Role of Resistance

The authors have embraced people's cries against mass killings, starvation, rape, militarized prostitution, torture, forced disappearances, land grabs, and the destruction of nature caused by modern warfare, as well as people's inherent collective aspiration for liberation of their lives and lands. In that sense, the chapters reflect the dual role of resistance: speaking truth to power, and speaking truth to the oppressed. The first challenges the belief system that idolizes militarization for its promise of absolute security for humanity (minus nature). It exposes the sinister agendas of the empire, which *prima facie* profess to bring peace and security to the world, while insidiously waging incessant war against lands and their peoples to maintain its dominion and expand its power. It is necessary to expose the multifaceted destructive effects (past, present and future) of militarized imperial relationships that have dehumanized lives and desecrated the earth in the name of security. This means revealing the implicit intentions of the empire and their impact on the lives of people and the earth, while also challenging the ways in which societies have been made to think about security so as to make the empire an absolute imperative. Such a task requires robust political analysis, involving concrete facts and figures undertaken by a range of political analysts who come from secular, humanist, and non-religious standpoints.

Speaking truth to power, in the Abrahamic traditions, is the prophetic task of denouncing imperial designs that dehumanize people and desecrate the earth. In the Indic traditions, this means interrogation of collective greed. What is needed is not only critical studies, but also self-reflective practices which ask the question *where am I and where are we in all these?* Theologians/scholars of religion emerging from faith communities who uphold a sense of the Ultimate (whether expressed as God in the Semitic traditions or Enlightenment in the Indic traditions), engage in critical self-reflection that challenges the absoluteness of the empire and its claims as the provider and sustainer of humanity's security (*Baals* are resisted in the Bible, *al- Jahiliyya* is overcome in Islam, and *maya* and *mittcha ditti* shunned through Hinduism and Buddhism respectively).

The other task of resistance is speaking truth to the oppressed, which reminds the victims of war and militarization that they are not helpless objects, but subjects of history who carry the greatest potential to overcome imperialism. This is the truth of the oppressed; the truth of their collective dignity, their resisting power, and their liberating destiny. They are not insignificant individuals who are being forced by the empire to abandon their collective struggles and fight for their mere survival, but members of an oppressed community, from wherever they are, who retain dignity, honor, and the will to freedom, and who have the power to unite with oppressed communities beyond imperial divisions. Their liberative agency is sacred. Such an awareness is necessary at a time when entire societies have been reconstructed as part of counter-insurgency warfare aimed at exterminating resistance, destroying people's collective liberating consciousness, reducing them to bunches of individuals by combining post-war neo-liberal development with securitization, or by herding them into religiously fundamentalist blocs. This liberating awareness is pertinent when millions of people who flee their lands become dry statistics detached from their collective aspirations and power of resistance. They are not mere victims of war, but survivors and symbols of resistance. They are messengers of just peace. To that end, the authors have combined political analyses of the modern empire and militarization with an effective awareness of the death and destruction they cause, so as to elaborate upon the transformative practices/knowledge that have emerged out of their concrete engagement with people's liberative praxis.

A Critically Self-Reflective Practice

The chapters undertake the task of recognizing the agency of affected communities, both from faith and non-faith perspectives, of those who are engaged in liberative politics of interpreting their scriptures, popular narratives, traditions, doctrines, rituals, popular beliefs and indigenous traditions, in opposition to imperial ideologies of militarism. Such exercises of interpretation are necessary to resist the empire as well as the reactionary religious fundamentalist currents that serve the empire. The need to rethink interreligious dialogue from a counter-imperial decolonial liberative perspective is reiterated. Without it, such dialogue becomes not only futile, but also a cover-up for imperial designs.

The participants in the conferences and writers of these chapters are scholar/activists from Africa, Latin America, East Asia, South Asia, the Middle East, Latin America, and the Caribbean and Pacific Islands, who are renowned for their critical thinking and principled, ethical position against empire and militarization. They represent two distinct disciplinary strands that need to be brought into deep conversation with one another to form new interdisciplinary intersections in problematizing the empire and envisioning a liberated eco-human future. On the one hand, it was a gathering of secular activist-scholars and theologians/scholars in religions who engaged in dialogue with one another to help different faith communities broaden their vision and mission in resisting the empire within the context of militarization. On the other hand, the gathering also helped secular activist-scholars in the field of the humanities to appreciate the potential in different faith traditions to contribute to the resistance against empire. In this endeavor, the following insights from a pioneering liberation theologian/sociologist of religion proved helpful:

> The human being is indivisible: spirituality presupposes matter that, on the one hand, has no sense without the spirit ... Spirituality, with or without reference to a supernatural, gives sense to human life on the planet. How it may be expressed is conditioned by the social relations in each society, but it can also give direction to these relations. A change of paradigm cannot be carried out without spirituality, which has many paths and multiple expressions.
>
> (Houtart 2012: 50–51)

Critical reflections on faiths need to be grounded in robust socio-political analyses, without which the liberative cosmovisions enshrined in the primoridal experience of religious traditions "cannot make any sense to or have any impact on contemporary society" (Pieris 2013: 18). Theology and other religious insights have to play a crucial role in critiquing the belief system and imperial consciousness that are associated with the militaristic empire. The majority of the world does not think in a highly secularist (as distinct from secular) conceptual framework based on a Eurocentric capitalist modernity. Many continue to imagine reality through religious lenses, interpreted with different ideologies. These chapters recognize distinctions between liberating ideologies and enslaving imperialist and fundamentalist ideologies through critical theological and religious analyses.

This task is absolutely necessary at a time when religion, in general, has been portrayed in some quarters of the Western hemisphere, as inherently fundamentalist. Such a simplistic, reductionist and politically motivated Eurocentric portrayal not only suppresses liberative religion, but also promotes its conservative and fundamentalist currents while contributing to a false civilizational conflict that hides profound socioeconomic and geopolitical injustices. The theological/political task has to involve an analysis of the empire in the scriptures and history of religions, while also identifying counter-imperial currents in these sources. This publication attempts to overcome the politicized dichotomies between socio-political studies and theological/religious studies that only impede holistic analysis.

Methodology

Engagement, evocation, and envisioning formed the methodology that was adopted in the writing of these chapters. The chapters interlink different disciplines in humanities, themes, and regions, so that the knowledge produced has global resonance. The chapters proclaim faith in an ultimate reality (expressed in radically different ways) as well as in eco-humanity. Faith is understood here as the liberating language of the spirit, both divine and human. The core of this exercise is a concrete *engagement* with people's struggles, prophetic articulation, and proclamation of liberating truths that *evoke* and sharpen the alternate consciousness among people in furthering resistance, and in *envisioning* and building a non-imperialist future for us, for our children, and for the planet earth.

This collection of chapters is an appeal to our basic human capacity to love and think. It demands that we resist the empire, its structural militarization, as well as its belief system of militarism, which makes us rely on deadly armament. Instead it seeks to reclaim the sacredness of lives, lands, seas and skies through a dialogical approach in languages that are both religious and non-religious.

Structure

Part I covers chapters on East Asia, South Asia and West Asia and connects these regions to the wider world beyond their physical territory. Part II reflects on Africa, Latin America and the Caribbean and the Pacific Islands, while identifying the significance of these regions to the rest of the world. Both parts start with chapters that conduct an in-depth analysis of the empire and militarization, providing the reader with the analytical tools and perspectives needed to understand subsequent chapters that examine particular local and regional experiences of being subjected to the empire. Often, issues generated by militarization have been analyzed by adopting a single-state lens and an ahistorical approach without undertaking an overall critique of the empire. Individual states and international relations do not exist in a historical vacuum. Empirical data on militarization is necessary. However, such facts need to be accompanied by a robust political analysis of the ways in which diverse social classes, religious and ethno-nationalist groups, and states are formed by and hardwired to imperial system of politics.

The authors of the global analysis develop their insights through their concrete engagement with the realities of their home countries and regions. The authors who focus on local contexts do so within the broader global context, suggesting that local resistance should take on board the broader reality of empire and militarization.

Part I

The first part begins with three articles of broad analysis. Radha D'Souza, an Indian-born political activist and an expert on South Asian politics, examines the ways in which imperialism continues through state structures, ethno-religious identities and the associated militarization of the South Asian states after British rule ended. Since World War II, which introduced "total war," the victors have established a new imperial order. A new warfare has thus been introduced which involves more than the armed forces by encompassing economies, societies and politics. The South Asian states, which were initially carved as part of the colonial project along ethno-religious lines, have been integrated into the new geopolitics of warfare, which unfolds locally in ethno-nationalist conflicts. As a result, one finds not only a process of militarization of the dominant states against resisting oppressed nationalities, but also the mobilization of entire societies of numerically majority ethnic groups with militarism. It is necessary that social and political movements who resist militarization in the region develop a common understanding of this bigger picture in their search for justice and peace. D'Souza's insights prompt us to raise a fundamental question: What does peace mean when entire economies are militarized, or when politics becomes defined by ethno-nationalist identities and entire societies embrace militarism? This is also not only a political question, but also an ethical and spiritual question. What kind of a human being is being shaped in the shadow of the neocolonial empire? This self-reflective question is necessary to form a genuinely liberative praxis.

Haluk Gerger, who was once imprisoned for his stand against the Turkish state's oppression of the Kurds, and is a staunch opponent of the global war on terror, raises the following question: What is present day globalization and why is militarization an essential factor? He argues that, at the heart of the present *modus operandi* of globalization, lies capitalism. The modern empire is a capitalist empire. Capitalism cannot operate without exploiting men, dehumanizing women, and destroying the cosmos. Moreover, it cannot advance itself without expansion, which necessitates empire building. Both capitalism's operation and advancement require the repression of resistance arising from peoples (and their lands) who think and live differently from the imperial way. Militarization is a necessary outcome of the generation of capital. Capital accumulated through exploitation is being continuously reinvested in the advancement of technological warfare, so as to bring the whole globe under one imperial domination by causing maximum destruction of those who resist. In the advancement as well as destructive growth of capital, it is the social being in us that is being destroyed. In this sense, for Gerger, the resistance to empire is essentially a struggle to reclaim our humanity.

For more than half a century, Kinhide Mushakoji, one of the most prominent Japanese public intellectuals, has dedicated his life to demilitarization and denuclearization. His chapter shows how the hegemonic character of Atlantic Liberalism—which arose to resist the Nazis and was later utilized against the communists—has manipulated human rights discourse through the so-called humanitarian interventions in maintaining and expanding the USA's imperial agenda across the globe, preparing the ground for a new Cold War. This manipulation has created false polarizations (e.g., Islam versus West), conditioned the way we think about human dignity, and justified wars, like the war on terror. The definition of modernity is associated with this agenda. Nuclearization has not ended after the Cold War, but has been has accelerated. Mushakoji highlights the need for a post-modern emancipatory discourse, grounded on multiple voices of various subaltern groups, which he calls "class-based and identity-based epistemic communities," particularly indigenous communities in Asia-Pacific, The Middle East and Latin America, in averting a new Cold War and journeying towards a non-imperialist future. The author identifies a range of sites of resistance across the globe.

The next two chapters consider specific cases of militarization; one in East Asia and the other in South Asia. Gavan McCormack, a political analyst and chief editor of *Japan Focus*, undertakes a revealing study of the ways in which Japan, contrary to its Peace Constitution, has served the USA's military dominion over East Asia for decades. At the dawn of the second millennium, with the USA's pivot towards Asia to encircle China, Japan moved to remilitarize itself to solidify the USA's position. This has had a drastic impact on the Korean peninsula, the people of Okinawa, and on the whole of East Asia, more broadly. While the Japanese electorate is conditioned by this neo-imperialist agenda, the Okinawan people, who bear the heaviest burden of militarization in East Asia and have suffered immensely, both under the USA and Japanese regimes, have emerged as the most formidable force against the strong military build-up in the region.

In a joint chapter, Athithan Jayapalan, whose parents had to flee the war in Sri Lanka, and Gajendrakumar Ponnambalam from Sri Lanka, whose father was assassinated by "an unknown gunman," demonstrate the importance of the island of Lanka for the imperial powers (like the islands of Okinawa and Jeju in East Asia) in controlling the Indian Ocean and the subcontinent. Contrary to the general perception that Sri Lanka has been one single country for centuries, they show how a unitary political structure on the island was created by the British Raj to be used as a military strategic foothold in the Indian Ocean—thereby privileging the numerical majority Sinhalese and laying the foundations for discrimination against the Eelam Tamils. The two authors take forward Radha D'Souza's analysis (Chapter 1) on South Asian states, and add a crucial geopolitical perspective. The war that was waged against the Eelam Tamils, despite the 2002 peace process that gave an opportunity to transform the colonially carved oppressive state structure, is nothing but a move to reconsolidate the unitary state to aid USA/

UK/India's attempts to encircle China in the region. The discourse on the war on terror (critically analyzed by Haluk Gerger in Chapter 2), was heavily utilized in the war against the Eelam Tamils. Like the Okinawans in East Asia, the Eelam Tamils in South Asia have contributed to a non-imperial consciousness and polity in Asia. As political analysts, all the above writers do not represent or invoke a particular faith perspective, but appeal to the human spirit of resistance based on secular humanism.

The next set of chapters have emerged from Kashmir, Korea, Okinawa and Palestine, four of the most formidable locations of resistance to highly militarized imperial security in Asia. The key feature of the resistance in these places is the role of women against occupation and the problematization of militarized masculinity. Farrukh Faheem from the University of Kashmir takes us to one of the most militarized zones in the world, the Kashmir Valley, and points out how women have taken to the streets every day after men have been made to disappear. Through a range of interviews he captures the creative resistance and resilience of Kashmiri women who have transformed patriarchal cultural traditions and religious boundaries. They have formed the frontline of the protests that demand the Indian military to quit Kashmir and have dismantled the oppressive space between the private and public domains.

Nami Kim challenges the Protestant Right's justification of compulsory military service in South Korea that upholds militarism, while giving voice to the conscientious objectors who problematize hegemonic masculinity. By representing a distorted idea of masculinity, militarization emphasizes, if not encourages, the subjugation of anyone who does not fit its narrow definition of what it means to be a man, making women the most oppressed and vulnerable group. This dominant idea of masculinity marginalizes women even within the military where both women and men serve as compatriots. The male imperial logic of dehumanizing anyone who is "not the same as us" has been adapted to utilize rape as a weapon of war (Bosnia-Herzegovina) and to justify wars to "liberate" women (Afghanistan). Is not conscientious objection, as Kim asks, a radical response on the part of some men to the hegemonic masculinity that leads to wars and oppression of women?

Kozue Uehara, a scholar/activist from Okinawa, gathers testimonials from islanders whose resistance to US–Japanese imperialism is shaped not only by their opposition to military bases, but also by their alternative vision of socio-political relations. Uehara draws our attention to the creative power of indigenous peoples, particularly Okinawan women, who teach us how to organize an affected community by attending to the basic needs of each other on a daily basis and sustaining continuous resistance in a formidable way with great resilience.

Sara Ababneh from Jordan, who conducted a series of interviews with women living in Gaza, invites us to go beyond the feminist framework in identifying the empowerment of women by the Palestinian liberation struggle, particularly in Hamas-administered areas. She problematizes the stereotypical portrayal of Islam as patriarchal and highlights the role of Muslim women in resisting the occupation of Palestine. The four authors above testify to how their distinct communities have empowered themselves in multiple ways in resisting militarization and militarism.

The last four chapters of Part I invite us to consolidate resistance with a theological and interreligious orientation. Such an approach is essential when interreligious relations have been colonized and imperialized through militant religious fundamentalisms, which are themselves pitted against one another and are aided directly or indirectly by the main drivers and allies of the empire. It is not possible to unite diverse local communities for resistance against imperial designs—where poverty, oppression and military occupation are lived realities in religiously pluralist societies and regions—without retrieving the liberative core of faith traditions in a dialogical way.

The Indian theologian Francis Gonsalves challenges the unholy nexus between religions that exercises dominance over others due to numerical majority and militarization that has become a key feature of many allies (e.g., Burma, India, Pakistan, Sri Lanka) of the neocolonial empire, causing the oppression of many distinct groups of peoples in South Asia. Following on from Radha D'Souza's critique (Chapter 1) of the South Asian states and of their national identities as colonial constructs, Gonsalves reminds us of the need to undertake a critical reflection of one's faith, particularly through the eyes of the oppressed peoples. The need to build solidarity among the oppressed—which Gonsalves calls the "Jesus movement"—regardless of their religious backgrounds, as resistance to religious majoritarianism and militarization has been reiterated. Such a task has to be seen as overcoming imperial politics that leads to the polarization of distinct communities. A Christian theological language has been used to awaken Christian communities to join this solidarity of selfless action, but the author reminds us that in the South Asian context, any such liberative action has to be interreligious, including not only Buddhists, Hindus, Muslims and Sikhs but also indigenous peoples. He is grounded in his faith and goes beyond it by embracing other faiths in his region in a dialogical mode.

Keun-Joo Christine Pae, utilizing insights from liberation/feminist theologies and engaged Buddhism (Dorothee Soelle and Sister Chan Khong respectively), emphasizes an empathetic response to the suffering caused by war. Drawing from the collective memories of wars in her native Korean peninsula, Pae invites readers to reinterpret their faiths within the context of militarized prostitution by the US military empire in East Asia, which she refers to as a form of genocide, as distinct from sexual violence. Her chapter probes what interfaith dialogue and resistance can mean to those who are most dehumanized by the military empire.

In the next chapter, Shadaab Rahemtulla, an Islamic liberation theologian—whose works have explored how religious texts can be (re)interpreted to challenge systems of domination, including poverty, patriarchy, and racism—makes a daring appeal to Christian liberation theologians. He challenges the epistemic might of the grand narrative of Israelites' conquest of Canaan, a narrative that has functioned as a religious justification in building the modern-day empire and its allied states through settler colonies. Rahemtulla, who reads the Qur'an through the eyes of the oppressed, points out how such a conquest of land is absent from the Qur'an, and invites his Christian counterparts to read the Biblical texts from an anti-colonial, Muslim perspective that embraces indigenous people's struggle for land.

In the final chapter, Youngseop Lim, a biblical scholar and a Christian pastor from South Korea, clearly identifies biblical counter-imperial currents in early Israel and challenges the oppressive character of modern Israel. These currents were obliterated during the Solomonic times which forged a religion of eminence based on the politics of oppression by subduing the religion of liberation that proclaimed the politics of justice. The empire cannot hold ground simply on oppressive socio-political structures and military hardware. It has to be justified rationally and morally through the software of narratives that we are taught to internalize. Lim invites the faith groups who depend on the narrative of chosen-ness of Israel to make an ethical hermeneutical choice between the politics of liberation and oppression.

Rahemtulla's problematizing of the Biblical narrative of the conquest of Canaan and Lim's retrieval of counter-imperial currents in ancient Israel open a pathway towards an alliance between progressive Christian and Muslim forces in resisting the empire. Since Christians and Muslims constitute the largest faith groups on earth, and since a lethal imperial narrative— Islam versus Christianity, or Islam versus West, or Islam versus the rest—has been forged by the main drivers of the empire and their allies, it is necessary that both communities enter into a relationship of trust and cooperation that adopts anti-imperial and anti-colonial perspectives. Interreligious dialogue cannot envision just peace among nations without a liberative perspective.

Part II

After identifying multi-faceted ways of resistance in distinct locations of Asia in Part I, we move to Africa, Latin America, and the Caribbean and the Pacific Islands in Part II. The first three chapters engage in a broad analysis by using the concepts of neocolonialism, new imperialisms and necropolitical capitalism, which enables us to interconnect Asia with these regions and identify commonalities and specificities among them.

Andy Higginbottom, who leads international solidarity campaigns for the rights of peasant communities in Colombia, oppressed Eelam Tamils in Sri Lanka, and miners in South Africa, identifies a number of key shifts in the USA's military initiatives, aided by the UK after the Cold War, in countering China, the Middle East and Russia. The USA's military interventions in the Middle East, its pivot towards Asia, the US Africa Command and Washington's economic warfare against Venezuela have concretized such moves. In the name of security cooperation, the USA has entered into military pacts with a wide range of states across the globe, forming thereby a neocolonial condition. These states, which have been dressed up in the garb of national sovereignty, are in fact directed by the might of the empire. They are neocolonial allied states. New modes of militarization have been introduced through informatics, a global system of aerial monitoring and rapid deployment power projection, which make the USA the most powerful military power on earth. This imperial militarism threatens and destroys non-compliant states, and aids and abets the repression of a vast array of resisting social and political movements, and ensures the genocide of distinct nationalities by the rentier and neocolonial allied states. Conflicts are formed and "resolved" according to the imperial designs. Higginbottom's penetrating analysis contextualizes particular wars and conflicts within a global setting; this approach provides a solid foundation for movements of solidarity beyond borders, inviting the reader to realize the interrelationships among diverse collective struggles. In other words, the author invites the reader not to treat particular local realities of militarization in isolation from what is happening elsewhere. This chapter helps connect Asia with Africa and Latin America.

The next chapter is authored by a prominent Ecuadorean scholar/activist, Napoleón Saltos Galarza. Latin America is one of the first places outside Europe reached by the modern empire; it is also the place where resistance to that empire inspired many other liberation movements across the globe, and was one of the first places in modern times to capture the liberative ethos of the Christian faith. Galarza perceptively points out how, after the Cold War, geopolitics has become more complex with a reconfiguration of the international system of states. He uses the term imperialisms in the plural, as new global power blocks like Russia and China have emerged. He reminds us, however, that with the weakening of the Westphalian system of state—which has sharpened civilizational and religious differences—the USA has taken up the role of global custodian, continuously issuing threats of invasion and war, while setting new trends in the arms race, and reinforcing ethno-religious conflicts and geopolitical disputes. The author stresses on the need to strengthen democracy which the "progressive governments" in Latin America failed to accomplish, creating thereby space for far-right forces to gain power. This is intrinsically connected with the failure to find alternatives to capitalist modernity, which justifies not only an anti-humanist phase, but also post-humanist dystopias managed by a technocracy without the workers, peasants and nature. Militaristic games are part of this process. Democracy is resistance to a dehumanizing order, which has transmuted brute force into biopower. Citing his personal encounter with a popular indigenous leader, Galarza presents resistance as taking ethical responsibility for the oppressed other, to the extent of risking one's life by transgressing systemic limits. In defining democracy in this way, the author blends his political analysis with a deep ethical sense—based on Enrique Dussel's ethics of liberation—treating such a task as a civilizational issue.

Luis Arizmendi, from Universidad Nacional Autónoma de México, a prolific writer and political activist, shows how Mexico has been on a historical trajectory towards becoming one of the most powerful criminal economies in the world as a logical outcome of the capitalist empire. The politics of such an economy is called necropolitics or the politics of death. The liberal state that mitigated the structural inequalities through social welfare has been dismantled to aid the inordinate increase in private capital, which translates as accumulation through dispossession. Such a process does not need a military invasion like that of Iraq.

It has been achieved by the crippling subordination of the Mexican economy to the USA's private capital, where not only energy, but also babies and human organs, are commodified. Criminality has been heightened across society, both in the formal and informal economic sectors, and has strong links worldwide through investments and other means. In other words, the relationship between capitalism, and death and destruction has been intensified. There is no separation between the political elite, big businesses, and criminal gangs who promote a neo-authoritarian state. This tendency is growing across the world as a necessary outcome of the very logic of the capitalist system.

Arismendi embarks on his highly critically reflective account by referring to the massacre of forty-three college students by the local police in 2014 in Ayotzinapa for opposing the status quo. Ayotzinapa is not only a cry for justice, but also of the hope for an alternative future. It has given rise to one of the most pluralist social movements in Mexico. The movement is a convergence of the most diverse groups in Mexico: students from public and private universities, workers, peasants, artists, feminists, Catholics, nuns, Hare Krishnas, agnostics, and indigenous people. It is death-defying and has given rise to a life-giving movement that has challenged not only the political elite of the country but also the very rationale of the system that generates nothing but death and destruction. There are many solidarity groups beyond Latin America who have been awakened to the criminality of the capitalist empire through the Mexican reality. Without such a pluralist movement, the planetary power of the politics of death cannot be overcome. Arismendi emphasizes the need for self-managed social forces and movements in globalizing the resistance against necropolitics.

Authors who have written the next two chapters are from the Pacific Islands who contextualize the ways in which neocolonial empire operates in the Pacific region. Many islands across the globe have been utilized as strategic locations in modern empire building, which has left them highly militarized. Without gaining political/military control of these islands, or annexing them fully to imperial centers of power, it is not possible to maximize the strategic usability of these locations. Some islanders, like the people of Diego Garcia, have been fully and forcibly evacuated so as to convert the archipelago into a USA's military complex in the Indian Ocean. Most of these islanders uphold centuries-old indigenous traditions, which promote harmony between human beings, the earth, and the seas, as well as with their neighboring communities. The authors of this section challenge the dominant portrayal of the Pacific as a vast empty space with no historical and political significance. With their deep commitment to overcome the neocolonial empire that has turned the islands into operational theatres of war and deep seas into mining fields, the authors invite us to embrace the deep cultural wisdom of the islanders that upholds the integrity of the cosmos, and promotes a sustainable living. The ongoing multiple struggles of these islanders against the empire are not only for their independence, but also for building peace between the East and the West, wherein the Pacific is pivotal.

Kyle Kajihiro, from the University of Hawai'i at Mānoa, who campaigns for the end to USA's military occupation of the island, gives us an illuminating historical account of how the Pacific islands were targeted as the USA moved from continental territorial imperial formations to sea-based archipelagic conquests. It is in the context of this imperial expansion that the Hawaiian kingdom was annexed. The anti-base movement in Hawai'i is inseparable from its independence movement, which resists the USA's military agenda in the Asia-Pacific. Kajihiro demonstrates how this movement is deeply imbedded in the Kanaka Maoli indigenous traditions, and makes connections with other movements in the Pacific Islands in forming a broader alliance against the USA's military adventures in the region. Often undisclosed by the dominant media to the rest of the world, these movements give us inspiration, courage, and hope amidst the death and destruction of wars. The Pacific, Kajihiro reminds us, is not an "American Lake," but a bridge of peace between the East and West. The indigenous Pacific struggles generate a new imagination of the region as the great ocean that builds cordial relationships rather than animosities.

In a jointly written chapter, Vanessa Griffen, Gordon Nanau and Maureen Penjueli, who campaign for the demilitarization and denuclearization of the Pacific islands, describe the ways in which the imperial powers have converted these islands into colonial assets, causing death and destruction of human lives and natural habitats. The islands, such as the Marshall Islands and French Polynesia, were converted into nuclear testing grounds by the major powers like the USA, UK and France. This has caused an intergenerational radioactive impact on the communities. One of the most vibrant anti-nuclear campaigns of the twentieth century emerged in this region, with the churches playing a significant role. This led to the containment of the proliferation of nuclear weapons, forming a broad level of solidarity across the colonized islanders in the region, from Papua New Guinea to the Solomon Islands, Vanuatu, Fiji, Tonga, Samoa, the Cook Islands, Kiribati and the Micronesian Trust Territory islands. The islands which have gained independence have, however, been following the colonial commodification of land. This has radically altered the relationship between the land and its people. In such a setting, even without the nuclear tests, the islands have been militarized, as they have been carved out as strategic locations by the imperial powers. Furthermore, the writers point out how the expansion of capitalism has necessitated expansion of mining the deep blue sea, in what can be called Blue Colonialism. Under these new conditions, where climate change has posed a common threat to humanity, the authors urge us to regroup ourselves based on the centuries-old values of sharing among the communities of the islands, of love for the land and sea, and the interrelationships between the island communities in resisting the plunder of islands.

The next section comprises three chapters that further substantiate the global analyses of the first three chapters of Part II, with evidence from local realities identifying various sites of resistance in Africa, Latin America and the Caribbean Islands. They have been written by theologians/human rights activists who probe the theological resources for resistance in their specific cultures and histories.

Higginbottom's economic and political analysis of the neocolonial condition (Chapter 14) is extended by V. S. Vellem, a South African public theologian, into cultural, spiritual and theological levels in his reflections in Africa. Vellem reminds us that the former Apartheid state was also a highly militarized state. Its strategy of winning hearts and minds through "Low Intensity Warfare" has created deep socio-political and psychological effects in the post-Apartheid society. The colonial matrix of power continues to wound Africa. The USA's close alliances with some African countries have reinforced the role of the military in the democratization of regimes. It is essentially a Eurocentric view of democracy that has destroyed the creative spirituality of the oppressed masses by stifling their broader participation in humanizing their own polity and society. Vellem brings to light *ubuhlanti*, the black African cosmovision, which sees power as relational and that does not dissect and fragment every sphere of life by forces of subjugation. In Africa, Low Intensity Warfare, a distinctive paradigm of liberal counter-insurgency and neocolonialism, has subjugated every sphere of life to a pseudo-democracy. Borrowing insights from black liberation theology, Vellem sees the biblical Exodus and covenant-making as a journey of remaking life relationally, as in *ubuhlanti*, in opposition to the fragmentation of life offered by the currently prevailing pseudo-democracy. He reiterates the need to blend together biblical faith and black African spirituality in resisting false promises of democracy, security, and economic prosperity. In fact, the relational power of *ubuhlanti* encompasses all life, human and non-human, as opposed to the brute force that displaces, maims, rapes and kills human life, and also destroys the earth.

Vellem passed away due to a sudden critical illness after completing his chapter. In fact, he gave his last bit of energy to work on this prophetic articulation. He was an embodiment of liberating black consciousness whose life radiated fullness of humanity. He was filled with deep love for the marginalized and relentless zeal for justice and human dignity. He lived what he wrote and wrote what he lived. His sudden death is an unbearable and irreplaceable loss. Yet, his burning desire for freedom and unwavering commitment to the wretched of the earth lives on.

Javier Giraldo Moreno, one of the most prominent human rights activists in Colombia and the vice president of the Permanent Peoples' Tribunal, joins our conversation with his life-long commitment to the protection of human rights in Colombia. With an unsurpassable historical consciousness, he deeply probes the relationship between the USA and the militarization of Latin America, and the role of the Roman Catholic Church, highlighting the ideological foundations of the politics of death in Colombia and the resistance to it. With great clarity and lucidity, he writes about the ways in which Colombia was incorporated into the USA's capitalist system after World War II, through imperial domination and military might, and in opposition to the USSR, thus repressing the local masses. Giraldo reminds us of the worldwide implications of the Cold War. Many Colombian soldiers perished fighting in the USA's war in the Korean peninsula. The Roman Catholic hierarchy in Latin America supported this process through its anti-communist ideology. This ideology is a result of Christianity's close relationship with the European colonial conquests and empire building for a large period of its history, as well as its relationship with the modern capitalist empire. Giraldo demonstrates how, with the reforms of Vatican II, the Latin American churches embarked upon a journey of converting themselves to the plight of the poor and the oppressed. Some even embraced a new form of martyrdom, which proclaimed an inseparable relationship between the Gospel and justice, thus opposing the repressive policies of capitalist states and USA's imperialism. Giraldo combines an historical analysis of USA's imperialism in Colombia with his own church's critically self-reflective practice in presenting to us spiritual, theological, and ecclesial resources for resistance.

The last chapter written under this section draws our attention to the people in the Caribbean Islands, who have experienced slavery, extermination, repression and militarization under the modern empire-building project. Garnett Roper, a public intellectual who combines his roles as a pastor, biblical scholar, and radio preacher in Jamaica, narrates how, after the Cold War, particularly in places like Africa and the Caribbean, the domestication and distribution of massive military arsenals increased exponentially. This has led to the endemic enforcement of structures of marginality, dispossession and disenfranchisement, generating an unbearable collective trauma that is expressed in many disorders affecting individuals and the society as a whole. Roper, as a preacher, undertakes a prophetic reading of Jesus' exorcism of a legion of evil spirits in Mark's Gospel and applies it to socio-political conditions in the Caribbean that have deprived people of their full humanity through the processes of demonization. The legion in the Gospel refers to the striking force of the Roman Empire, and Roper presents Jesus' act of exorcism as a powerful narrative to overcome the demonizing socio-psychological conditions that the modern imperial forces impose, thereby taking away the humanity of the Caribbean people. With conviction, clarity, and courage, he tells us that the way we interpret religious narratives is crucial in the empowerment of the oppressed masses and their journey towards a liberated future. The chapters of Vellem, Giraldo and Roper complement Luis Arizmendi's (Chapter 16) pluralist approach to resistance in Latin America, by identifying the ways in which a particular faith community can participate in a wider movement by critically engaging with its faith through an anti-imperial liberative lens.

Conclusion

The authors of this collection have allowed themselves to be moved by the cries and hopes of victims, both cognitively and affectively. The oppressed are seen not as helpless victims, but as bearers of a collective hope of a new eco-humanity. We are told that only by listening to their voices with empathy can we enter into a creative imagination of the future with them. The authors recognize these voices locally, regionally, and globally in highlighting critical perspectives on militarization and the empire, so that a new spring of knowledge is generated to inspire the struggle for an alternative world.

The chapters are not only the outcome of an exercise of listening to victims, but they also connect peoples, thereby initiating a process of listening to the liberating truths of one another's struggles for freedom. They not only expose the multifaceted onslaughts of the empire against lives, lands, seas, and skies across the globe, and attend to the ways in which resistance has been consolidated, but also highlight the need for horizontal solidarity among diverse peoples of the world to further strengthen this resistance. In this sense, the chapters invite the readers to be truly global with a sense of interconnectedness while recognizing both the commonalities and specific features in each region and context. The authors have signaled that the two most fundamental features in building solidarity are the recognition that there can be multiple ways of resisting and that each resistance has to be interlinked with the other.

As a way of conclusion, let me mention how the participants ended the two conferences. In Seoul, it was concluded with a prayer that pleaded with God for help to "find the ways and connections to create a better world, come up with alternative discourses, and ways to resist and defeat imperial aims, and to find ways in which we can govern ourselves in love, justice, and equality." In Mexico City, our prayer took the form of Arundhati Roy's words, comprising a prophetic command (included among the epigraphs at the head of this introduction) and a testimony, both of which were recited by all those who were present:

> Our strategy should be not only to confront empire, but to lay siege to it. To deprive it of oxygen. To shame it. To mock it. With our art, our music, our literature, our stubbornness, our joy, our brilliance, our sheer relentlessness—and our ability to tell our own stories. Stories that are different from the ones we're being brainwashed to believe.
> Another world is not only possible; she is on her way.
> On a quiet day, I can hear her breathing.

Jude Lal Fernando is assistant professor and coordinator of the M.Phil. in Intercultural Theology and Interreligious Studies Programme in the Irish School of Ecumenics, School of Religion, Trinity College Dublin (University of Dublin), and director of the Trinity Centre for Post-Conflict Justice. He was the coordinator of the Peoples' Tribunal on Sri Lanka.

Note

1. Aloysius Pieris, borrowing an insight from Raimon Panikkar, notes that every religious tradition has three phases of progression: the primordial Experience of Liberation, the Collective Memory of that Experience and the Interpretation of that Memory. It is necessary to "sustain this collective memory by interpreting it in such a way as to make it accessible to each generation in the cultural, linguistic, social and political idiom of that generation." There are also, however, ideologically enslaving and liberating interpretations. In that sense, interpretation is both necessary and dangerous (Pieris 2013: 18).

References

Berryman, Philip. 1987. *Liberation Theology: Essential Facts about the Revolutionary Movement in Latin America and Beyond*. Philadelphia, PA: Temple University Press.
Butler, Judith. 2016. *Frames of War: When is Life Grievable*. London: Verso.
Dabashi, Hamid. 2008. *Islamic Liberation Theology: Resisting Empire*. London: Routledge. https://doi.org/10.4324/9780203928387

Eagleton, Terry. 2005. *Holy Terror.* Oxford/New York: Oxford University Press.
Hardt, Michael and Antonio Negri. 2000. *Empire.* Cambridge, MA: Harvard University Press.
Hippler, Thomas. 2017. *Governing from the Skies: A Global History of Aerial Bombing.* New York: Verso Books.
Houtart, François. 2012. "From 'Common Goods' to the 'Common Good of Humanity'." In *A Postcapitalist Paradigm: The Common Good of Humanity,* edited by François Houtart and Birgid Daiber, 11–56. Brussels: Rosa-Luxemburg Foundation.
Mamdani, Mahmood. 2004. *Good Muslim, Bad Muslim: America, the Cold War and the Roots of Terror.* Princeton, NJ: Princeton University Press.
Panikkar, Raimon. 1999. "Religions and the Culture of Peace." In *Religion, Politics and Peace,* edited by Leroy S. Rouner, 185–204. Notre Dame, IN: University of Notre Dame Press.
Pieris, Aloysius. 2013. *The Genesis of an Asian Theology of Liberation: An Autobiographical Excurses on the Art of Theologizing in Asia.* Gonalwala-Kelaniya: Tulana Research Centre.
Raheb, Mitri. 2014. *Faith in the Face of Empire: The Bible through Palestinian Eyes.* Maryknoll, NY: Orbis Books.
Roy, Arundhati. 2004. *Public Power in the Age of Empire.* New York: Seven Stories Press.
Roy, Arundhati. 2013. *An Ordinary Person's Guide to Empire.* Haryana: Penguin Books
Santos, Boaventura de Sousa. 2016. "Epistemologies of the South and the Future." *From the European South* 1: 17–29.
Soelle, Dorothee. 1990. *The Window of Vulnerability.* Minneapolis, MN: Fortress Press.
Suh, Bo-hyuk. 2014. "The Militarization of Korean Human Rights: A Peninsular Perspective." *Critical Asian Studies* 46(1): 3–14. https://doi.org/10.1080/14672715.2014.863575
Vine, David. 2015. *Base Nation: How US Military Bases Harm America and the World.* New York: Metropolitan Books.

Part I
East Asia, South Asia, West Asia and Beyond

1

Wars Beyond the Armed Forces: Colonialism and Militarization of Ethno-national Conflicts in Contemporary South Asia

Radha D'Souza

> The killer begets a killer;
> One who conquers, a conqueror.
> The abuser begets abuse,
> The reviler, one who reviles.
> Thus, by the unfolding of karma,
> The plunderer is plundered.
> —Gautama Buddha, *Sutta Pitaka*

Introduction

We live in the epoch of imperialism, which is a distinct historical stage of capitalism that is contingent on militarization and sustained by it (D'Souza 2018: ch. 3). In such an epoch, militarization encompasses all levels of socio-political organization—the domestic state, the geopolitical region and the wider world imperialist order. Struggles against militarization, anywhere and in any form, must necessarily locate the specificity of the struggle which occurs in the domestic state within the wider imperialist characteristics of the epoch, the specific histories and geopolitics of imperialism and colonialism in a specific region, as well as the characteristics of the states that are the visible actors in militarization. The objective of this chapter is to be the under-laborer for the struggles against militarization in South Asia by delineating the characteristics of militarization in the epoch of imperialism and identifying the specificities of imperialist histories and geopolitics in South Asia as the context for understanding militarization in each state. These conditions include the formation of institutions, including the armed forces, which were shaped by the exigencies of colonial rule and continue to characterize the structural features of South Asian states.

Whereas South Asia has a shared cultural heritage, the formation of modern states, the visible actors in contemporary militarization, was a quintessentially colonial project. Colonialism also provides South Asian states with common genealogies of governance as they were all part of the British Empire. As a result of the shared colonial roots of state formation, institutions and governance, in South

Asia at least, political struggles for freedom, justice, equality, dignity, and participation in governance plays out as struggles between different nationalities or ethno-national groups within states. The ethno-national lens obscures imperialist hands and logics behind militarization as well as the demands for justice and freedom by the people.

The primary target of militarization in South Asia is internal to the state and directed against segments of its own citizens who are distinct nationalities. These state-nationalities conflicts are shaped by and feed into imperial Anglo-American geopolitics in the present as they did historically in British colonial geopolitics. At the same time, the peoples of the Indian subcontinent have a shared history of anti-colonial resistances, and cultures that transcends modern nation-state formations. In South Asia more than anywhere else, struggles against militarization must pay close attention to the numerous economic, political, and military linkages and connections between militarization of political conflicts within states and imperial interests and rivalries in the region. Such an understanding demands that South Asian struggles against militarization must develop common understandings of the big picture of global and regional militarization and the ways in which they feed into the struggles for freedom and justice within each state.

The Epoch of Imperialism: War and Peace after the World Wars

In popular imagination, wars occur when the armed forces of two or more states target each other with missiles and weapons. Equally, popular understandings of peace anchor it to moral and ethical imperatives and appeal to human beings as bearers of social conscience. Militarization, since the beginning of the twentieth century, has transformed the meanings of war and peace far beyond inter-state conflicts and moral imperatives. Modern states are juristic entities that centralize and concentrate economic and political power in the institutions constitutive of the state. The two most important of these institutions are the armed forces (including police) and the bureaucracy. The centralization of authority authorized by law gives the juristic entity the capacity to act as a single, unified body politic (D'Souza 2019). The modern state, including modern professional armies, provided the institutional support for capitalism, and continues to do so (Lovering 1987). Beyond these general features of capitalist modernity, the modern state underwent qualitative transformations during the world war years.

The end of World War II established a new kind of imperial order (D'Souza 2018). The characteristics of the new type of state can be gauged from the two inaugural events that mark the beginning of the post-World War II world order: (i) the Holocaust, and (ii) the nuclear bombings of Hiroshima and Nagasaki. The scale and scope of the two events presuppose certain institutional, legal, scientific, technological, political, and ideological preconditions (i.e., a certain type of state/governance apparatus). Both events were made possible because of the integration of the state (i.e., its bureaucracy and armed forces) with corporate and scientific bureaucracies and cultural and ideological apparatuses (D'Souza 2019). Mainstream accounts of the events typically omit the fact that the Emperor of Japan had already made an offer of surrender three months before Hiroshima and Nagasaki, but diplomatic responses to the offer was delayed until the deadly new scientific innovations co-produced by the emerging military-industrial-finance-media complex were trialed (Uberoi 2002). Likewise, the Holocaust was the result of the participation of scientific and corporate interests alongside bureaucracy, armed forces, and state propaganda (Bauman 1989; Halebsky 2014). These inaugural events mark the emergence of a new type of imperial state and a distinctive era in militarization and imperialism.

The two world wars introduced the concept of *total war* (Chickering, Forster and Greiner 2005). Total war organizes the entire society beyond the armed forces for warfare. During the world wars, the idea of total wars was used to induct industries, manufacturing and trade, banking and finance into the apparatuses of the state alongside the traditional armed forces and bureaucracy to provide the state with a third limb as it were. It was during the world wars that nominees of Wall Street and defense contractors became part of the state apparatus in the US for example. (Koistinen 1980; Waddell 1994; 1999, 2001; Whitman 1991). Total war included new legal infrastructures. The establishment of an intelligence apparatus outside political authority of the elected representatives was one such apparatus. In most Western countries, national security laws shield the secret intelligence services from public scrutiny (D'Souza 2019). The institutional conditions for total war were most well established in the United States during the world war years (Waddell 1994, 1999, 2001). Total war established what scholars have called "warfare state" (Edgerton 2005; Waddell 2001). Contemporary empires comprise a handful of warfare states. The institutional architecture of these states and societies are such that the survival of workers and citizens, industry and finance, media and humanitarian organizations as much as weapons manufacturers and arms traders depend on militarization.

Warfare states wage total wars by waging war on economic, political, cultural, ideological, scientific, legal, and humanitarian fronts such that the line between civilian and military, wartime and peacetime fades away. On each front, total war is fought with different types of weapons: the economic wars with sanction regimes that target entire populations and monetary manipulations that "take down" economies, the ideological wars waged by media misinformation while racial profiling sows discord among ethnic, linguistic and religious groups. Deployment of armed forces (i.e., boots on the ground) is typically the last step. When military force is used, the technologies of war destroy civilian infrastructures, displace entire nations, and cause lasting damage to public and ecological health of future generations. For example, new born babies in the city of Fallujah where US troops waged intense battles, suffer from birth abnormalities because of the use of depleted uranium by the troops in the war against Iraq (Fisk 2012; Jamal 2013), and victims of Agent Orange, a deadly chemical used by the United States in the Vietnam war, continue to suffer from exposure to it (Nguyen and Hughes 2017; Staff Reporter 2005).

The world wars necessitated large scale scientific innovations. Aerial warfare innovated during World War I necessitated scientific inventions on an industrial scale by integrating the work of universities, states, corporations, and civil society organizations (Edgerton 2005). Aerial warfare transformed the nature of warfare. All wars, ever since, have targeted entire populations, making the legal distinctions between civilians and soldiers redundant at best. Warfare states turned scientists into wage-workers, cogs in the wheels of a gigantic scientific establishment (Werskey 2007). Industrial scale science enabled industrial scale wars and mobilization for politics as Hiroshima and the Holocaust demonstrate. Since then, scientific research has been driven by militarization as the engine powered by corporations (D'Souza 2010). Most modern technological innovations were designed initially for warfare and later adapted for civilian uses (Kulve and Smit 2003). The internet was invented as a weapon of war in the 1960s under the name APRANET and later became available for civilian use (van Loon 2006). The US Army's Engineering Corps was instrumental in the innovation of large dams (Tarlock 2004) made possible by the invention of earth-movers by the military scientific complex to build roads and bridges, and to move equipment and troops (Teclaff 1967). Large dams operate as weapons of war and are used against nationalities and indigenous nations. For example, the Ilisu dam built by the Turkish state, ostensibly for electricity, submerges Kurdish lands adding another dimension to the Turkish state's war on the Kurdish nation (Kurdish Human Rights Project 1999). Even everyday technologies like food packaging were developed using military budgets by the military-scientific establishment and later made available to private corporations for civilian uses (King and Salathe 1946). That is win-win scenario for the defense establishment as well as corporations.

Total war includes ideological warfare using scientific methods. PSYOPS or psychological warfare is a technique innovated during the world wars that wages war on domestic populations to mobilize popular support for war as well as enemy populations to incite them against their own governments. PSYOPS uses scientific methods including psychology and communication technologies (Narula 2004; van Loon 2006). Wars today are conducted by exacerbating, fanning, and arming differences and dissent within societies as we are witnessing in Syria, Yemen, Iraq, Somalia, Turkey and elsewhere.

International treaty regimes, even after the formation of the United Nations (UN), recognize treaties imposed by imperial powers on colonies long after their formal independence. The continued operation of colonial treaties has created, what legal scholars have called, "legal black holes" in the international system. Legal black holes create spaces where no law—domestic or international—applies, as is revealed in the use of Guantanamo Bay, a territory where neither Cuban, American or international law applies, for the incarceration of prisoners of the "global war on terror" (Strauss 2009). International law allows agreements between warfare states and newly independent colonial states to establish military bases around the world. The legal infrastructures for these bases were also established during the world wars close on heels of Montevideo convention on statehood in 1933 which internationalized the idea of modern states as formal juristic entities with legal personality. The UN Charter itself was written by the victors of the world wars. Contemporary military planners and strategists speak about "war ecology" or "military platforms" as a total system that includes "gaming" the economy, polity, society and culture (van Loon 2006).

The world wars have transformed legal frameworks for public and private institutions in qualitative ways. The old imaginaries of war and peace, public and private actors, do not fit contemporary realities. In the context of the world order that I have very briefly sketched, what is the meaning of empire and militarization? What do social movements mean when they say they wish to resist empire and militarization? Within this wider global context, what does it mean to resist empire and militarization in South Asia?

State Formations in South Asia: The Internal/External Lens

Modern state formations in South Asia are the outcomes of rivalries between European states over colonial expansion, trade routes, and territorial conquests that followed the rise of capitalism in Western Europe. Inter-European wars established modern empires (Lenman 2014). The Congress of Vienna in 1815 which "settled" the Napoleonic Wars between European states was an important turning point in Empire building (Bowie 1989). The conceptual genealogy for the contemporary international order such as sovereignty, veto powers, special prerogatives of European powers, balance of powers, and spheres of influence (i.e., mutual recognition of colonial conquests) may be traced back to the Concert of Vienna. (Simpson 2004). The truce between European powers lasted until the end of the nineteenth century. Renewed inter-European wars by the end of the nineteenth century led to the Scramble for Africa, the Anglo-Dutch Boer wars in South Africa which culminated in the two world wars. The world wars dismembered the Austrian and Ottoman empires and brought their colonies under the newly established League of Nations led by Allied powers as mandate territories, a new form of colonial hegemony (Smuts 1918). The world wars redrew the political boundaries of colonial states, including states in South Asia, and made way for the US as the new imperial power.

The territorial boundaries of contemporary South Asian states were consolidated by the outcomes in the inter-European rivalries in the subcontinent and remain contingent on imperial geopolitics in the region. In southern India, the state of Mysore under the leadership of Tipu Sultan aligned with the French East India Company while the Nizam of Hyderabad sided with the English East Indian Company (Gott 2012: ch. 17). The defeat of Tipu-French alliance brought the east coast of the Indian subcontinent, except Puducherry/Pondicherry, under the British Indian Empire. The northern frontiers of the British Indian Empire were "settled" in an extended series of four Anglo-Afghan wars which were part of the larger Anglo-Russian rivalries in Central Asia (Fremont-Barnes 2014). The Anglo-Russian wars had formative influence on the rise and consolidation of the British Empire in South Asia (Lobanov-Rostovsky 1948). The southern frontiers were settled by the Treaty of Amiens which briefly paused the Napoleonic wars. Britain took over the Dutch colony of Ceylon to pre-empt the colony falling into French hands in the Napoleonic wars in 1796 and later formalized the acquisition under the Treaty of Amiens in 1802 (Peiris and Arasaratnam 2019; Encyclopaedia Britannica 2019). The eastern frontiers of the British Empire were formed by Britain's arrangements with its ally, Portugal. Even before the Napoleonic wars, Britain had become the dominant partner in the Anglo-Portuguese relationship (Sideri 1970). The Portuguese and British were allies in the Napoleonic Wars. Under attack from France, Portugal sought, and Britain provided military assistance to defend Goa from the French from 1797 to 1798, and again from 1802 to 1813 (Encyclopaedia Britannica 2018; Wanmali and Lodrick 2019). As a result of the Anglo-Portuguese alliance, even after the defeat of Napoleon, the small territory of Goa remained a part of the Portuguese empire alongside the vast British Empire which spread across the subcontinent.

Of course, there were internal factors that played into the external wars over empire-building between European powers. The victory of the Nizam of Hyderabad in the proxy war enabled the East India Company to consolidate British rule in the subcontinent. Having India as its operational base and source of war-finance enabled Britain to expand its empire in other parts of South Asia (Onley 2009) such as Nepal (Michael 2012; Marshall 2004), Bhutan (Gupta 1974; Marshall 2004), Burma (Cobden 1853; Ramachandra 1977), Tibet (Addy 1984; Lamb 2018; Marshall 2004) and Maldives (Panton 2015; Robinson 1989). After Ceylon was secured from the Dutch, it was used as the base for the incorporation of the kingdom of Kandy (Godden and Casinader 2013). In the drawing and redrawing of the political maps of states, imperialist geopolitics has been as formative, if not more, than local political conflicts.

Political independence in the subcontinent ended British Rule and indeed became the beginning of the end of the British Empire. However, it did not end imperialism in the region. Once more internal conflicts were congealed politically by the trajectory of imperial geopolitics in the subcontinent. The waning of British power widened the opportunities for anti-colonial struggles in the region. However, the anti-colonial struggles occurred against the backdrop of the world wars which were fueled by new inter-imperialist wars. The most formative influence in state-formation in Asia and the Middle East was the forging of the "special relationship" between Britain and the US. The "special relationship" formed when the Atlantic Charter was signed in 1941 between the US and Britain was founded on simultaneous conflict and cooperation between the collapsing British Empire and the emerging American empire (Louis 1985; Herring 1971). Britain led the world wars militarily but became economically bankrupted by them (Milward 1970). It turned to the US for financial help. In turn the US through the lend-lease agreements leveraged the financial support to take over the reins of the empire from Britain (Herring 1971; Kimball 1971). By the time the world wars concluded Britain was unable to hold on to its colonies. Britain traded its colonies for economic reconstruction of its war-torn economy (Milward 1970).

The US stayed on the fringes of the world wars for most part. Soon after the end for the world wars, the US prioritized saving capitalism and liberalism from the other victor in the world wars: Russia and socialism. Containing the Soviet Union became the primary focus of US foreign policy and a justification for expansionism around the world, a focus driven by the newly established CIA and the emerging military-industrial-intelligence-media complex (Talbot 2015). The more immediate and pressing concern for the US after World War II ended was to contain the spread of communism in Europe. Britain conceded its inability to govern Greece and Turkey, a vacuum that the US stepped in to occupy (Kux 2001: 15). These overarching developments in the Anglo-American "special relationship" forged during the world wars played out in particular ways in South Asia.

Unlike Southern Europe, China, Korea and Southeast Asia, there was no communist threat in the South Asia. US imperatives in the subcontinent were to secure its geopolitical reach in the Middle East and Far East. The US considered India to be within Britain's sphere of influence until the attack on Pearl Harbor when the Japanese army reached close to Calcutta (now Kolkata). The US deployed 350,000 American troops in Eastern India, the first US military involvement in the region, taking care to reassure Indian nationalists that "the American forces were in India [i.e., British India] only to fight the war against the Axis" (Kux 2001: 15). The partition of India occurred against the wider backdrop of US expansion in the region. Without doubt the Hindu–Muslim hostilities were the internal causes of the partition. However, it was only one of the causes occurring as it did when Britain passed the baton of empire to the US. Britain rushed to a recklessly hasty conclusion of the terms of independence and partition within months because it was unable to govern India or lead the negotiations to bring the nationalist parties together for a solution acceptable to all (Kux 2001). Likewise, Britain's inability to manage the Middle East, in particular Palestine, left a gaping power vacuum in a strategically vital region.

Pakistan's proximity to the Soviet Union and the Middle East together with its economic vulnerability and political isolation after partition gave the US the opportunity to expand its military reach in the region where it had been absent (McMahon 1988). The defense treaty with the newly formed Pakistan in 1954 followed by the CEATO (Central Treaty Organization or the Baghdad pact) and SENTO (South East Asia Treaty Organization) agreements secured American bases for overt and covert operations targeting the Middle East as well as the Soviet Union (McMahon 1988). The military and economic aid and political recognition came at a serious cost to the people of Pakistan who were perforce forcibly uprooted from their historical and cultural roots in South Asia, and forced into a difficult political marriage with the Arab world. The uprooting of Pakistan from its historical home in South Asia, as well as the forced marriage with the Arab world, continues to play out in the militarization of the state and its internal wars against different ethno-national groups, beginning with the Bengalis, and continuing wars against Baluchis, Kashmiris, Sindhis and non-Sunni Muslim denominations in the country like the Ahmedias. The voluminous literature on the partition of India focuses on the partition riots and atrocities committed by Hindus and Muslims in northern India, which of course did happen. A holistic reading of the partition of India invites us to consider the internal sectarian conflicts as well as the external imperial geopolitics as part of the same historical moment.

Less than two and half decades after independence, the partition of India was followed by the partition of Pakistan. If the partition of India occurred during the onset of the Cold War, the creation of Bangladesh occurred at the height of the Cold War compounded by the defeat of the US in the Vietnam War, the Sino-Soviet rift, and the US–China rapprochement, all of which contributed to the way the independence war in Bangladesh played out. The US administration stood firmly behind its ally Pakistan even after intimation by the US diplomatic mission in Dhaka about the genocide of Bengalis by Pakistan's army using US weaponry (Bass 2013). In addition, the support for Pakistan is understood to have been a payback for its role as the conduit for US–China rapprochement following new opportunities opened-up by the Sino-Chinese rifts. The US not only opposed the independence of Bangladesh, but also made secret efforts to intervene and disrupt the independence movement from within (Riaz 2006). Not to be outdone, India signed a friendship treaty with the Soviet Union. The US moved its naval ships to the Bay of Bengal, all of which not only escalated the Cold War brinkmanship in South Asia, but also conditioned the context for political independence within Bangladesh, most notably the genocide by the Pakistani army. As the Cold War moved to a conclusion, Bangladesh moved away from the Russo-Indian alliance towards China. In this Bangladesh was not different from Pakistan.

The colonial wars were proxy wars between different native rulers aligning with different European powers. The Cold Wars were proxy wars between new states that emerged from the end of the British Empire and the Anglo-American and Soviet blocks after World War II. The Cold War subsumed internal conflicts between states and nationalities, pushing them to the background. After the end of the Cold War, as South Asian states became more vulnerable to US domination in politics and economy, the internal conflicts between nationalities and states in South Asia came under the direct geopolitical gaze of Anglo-American foreign policies in the form of the "war on terror." Anglo-American states leveraged internal conflicts under the guise of the "war on terror" to fill the vacuum left by the implosion of the Soviet Union in the region. Not long after the end of the Cold War, new rivalries emerged between China and the Anglo-American bloc. The Anglo-American geopolitical strategy of containment of China after the end of the Cold War continues to have profound consequences in terms of militarization for South Asian states and the struggles against it. Scholars attribute the outburst of internal conflicts against South Asian states to the rise of ethno-national consciousness after the end of the Cold War leaving out of account the changed imperial geopolitics in the region (Wallensteen and Sollenberg 1998). Once more, the ethno-national lens diverts attention from the new imperialism after the Cold War, as it had done with the numerous partitions in the past. The ethno-nationalist lens severed the conflicts from the longer history of imperialism, state formations, and militarization in the region. Everywhere, the new militarization brought older internal conflicts generated by colonial state formations under the lens of the new global "war on terror" waged by Western powers led by the US and NATO. South Asia was no exception. The end of the Cold War exposed South Asian struggles against militarization of political conflicts to new geopolitical vulnerabilities.

The end of the Cold War had profound consequences for internal conflicts within South Asian states and between them. The single most important change was India's decisive shift to the US security sphere. Together with opening-up the economy, India and the US began joint naval exercises for the first time in the 1990s after India joined the Indian Ocean Region security complex of Western allies. Since then a series of defense agreements with the US, notably the Joint Framework Agreement for India–US Civilian Nuclear Cooperation which exempts India from the international Nuclear Non-proliferation Treaty (known as the 123 Agreement) signed as quid pro quo for purchasing materials for nuclear plants from US suppliers, the Henry J. Hyde United States–India Peaceful Atomic Energy Cooperation Act 2006 which commits India to align her foreign policy to the US; the Joint Statement on India-US Strategic Partnership, the Logistics Support Agreement (LSA) in 2010 updated in the Logistic Exchange Memorandum of Agreement (LEMOA), Communications Interoperability and Security Memorandum of Agreement (CISMOA) in 2010, Basic Exchange and Cooperation Agreement (BECA) among the more important agreements, have put India firmly as a junior partner in the US military-security strategy for South Asia. Since the end of the Cold War India's defense budget has soared, the supplies coming mainly from the US and Western allies, replacing the Soviet Union as the main supplier, and opening the public sector to collaborations in arms production (Vombatkere 2010, 2012, 2017; Winner 2011).

These changes have brought India back into its old colonial role as sub-regional empire (see below). It is no longer possible to understand the "internal" conflicts within South Asian states, including India, let alone develop strategies for resistance against militarization of the states, without considering these wider geopolitical developments. These geopolitical developments have a profound impact on the relationships of the diverse nationalities of the region within the states, the defense and international relations policies of the South Asian states, and the geopolitical and military strategies of the Anglo-American states. In the struggles of different nationalities for freedom, justice, equality, dignity, and participation in governance, whether it be the Tamils in Sri Lanka, the Kashmiris in India and Pakistan, the Baluchis in Pakistan and Iran, the Chakmas in Bangladesh to name a few, the regional and global contexts are precisely the missing elements in the strategies of resistance to militarization.

Colonialism, Imperialism and the Ethno-nationalist Lens

Turning from the "external" in the framings of imperial geopolitics to the "internal" (i.e., the institutions of state and governance in South Asia), the British Empire was divided into five administrative categories: the mother country, the dominions, the protectorates, the crown colonies, and India (Voigt 1987). Crown colonies were administered directly by the colonial office in Britain (Ward 1976). In the British protectorates, native rulers administered their countries according to customary laws and practices after ceding authority over defense, foreign affairs and international trade to Britain. Protectorate systems established indirect rule, a form of governance where formal independence could co-exist with a hierarchy of states within the British Empire (Holdsworth 1930). Indirect rule, as a form of governance, provided the model for the League of Nations and later the United Nations (D'Souza forthcoming). The dominions were the most autonomous among the colonies. The elite leadership of the Indian National Congress during the early phases of the nationalist movement demanded dominion status for India within the empire comparable to Australia, Canada, New Zealand, and Ireland (Nehru 1928: ch. 7) which was rejected by Britain (Gandhi 1930). British India was a distinct administrative category and a sub-empire within the larger British Empire. British India's special jurisdictional status allowed Britain to develop forms of governance, including laws and institutions, that were exported around the Empire. J. S Mill famously said that India was the great experimental laboratory for the British Empire. The tools of colonial governance developed in British India were later internationalized in the UN Charter (D'Souza forthcoming). Within India, there were at least nine different administrative categories, of which the protectorates (also known as Princely or Indian states) were the most autonomous, and the Presidency States were the least as they were governed directly by the British-Indian representatives in India (Keith 1961). These differences in the constitutional and legal models of colonial governance provided Britain, the foremost imperial power, wide flexibility and adaptability in modalities of imperial governance that had profound influence on institution building. The institutions established by the British colonial administration remained more-or-less intact after the dissolution of the British Empire.

South Asia was the backbone of the British Empire for three reasons. First, South Asian soldiers were the pillars of the British imperial armed forces. Within South Asia, the British Indian army was the foundation of the imperial armed forces. Britain relied on deployment of South Asian troops around the world to expand its empire in the Middle East, Africa and Southeast Asia. Without South Asian foot-soldiers, the British Army on its own was incapable of building such a vast empire. More significantly, the troops were financed from revenues generated in South Asia. Secondly South Asia, a populous continent, was a perennial source of cheap labor and lower-level administrators to service the empire and keep its nuts and bolts oiled. Thirdly, South Asia supplied agrarian goods and services, food, raw materials, timber and such which in turn freed Britain's productive capacities to focus on manufacturing, including that of arms. South Asian labor and natural resources continue to be important in the geopolitics of imperialism even after independence. For the purposes of this chapter on militarization, the discussion has been limited to military significance of South Asia for contemporary imperialism and its historical and structural roots.

Whereas the trading companies, notably the East India Company, raised the early European armies in the subcontinent, after the First War of Independence in 1857 in which the soldiers of the British-Indian army and peasants joined forces against the East India Company, the East India Company was dissolved and the British parliament took charge of the governance of British India which was, as already noted, an empire within an empire. Reorganizing the British Indian army became a priority for Britain after 1857. Based on anthropological racial profiling studies, the colonial government classified certain nations of the subcontinent as "martial races," and military regiments were based on these. Thus, the Sikh Regiment, Punjab Rifles, Madras regiment, Maratha regiment, Mahar Regiment, the Gurkha battalion, each formed a distinct group within the army in which mixing of nationalities was not permitted (Barkawi 2012; Rand 2012; Roy 2012). The reorganized British Indian army institutionalized ethnic differences in the very core of the state apparatus.

The British Indian army was used largely against the people of the subcontinent, deploying one nation (i.e., an ethno-national regiment) to put down people of other nationalities. The British Indian army was also used against anti-colonial movements around the empire (D'Souza 2014). Likewise, in the late nineteenth century, Britain raised a light infantry force in Sri Lanka/Ceylon in which commanding officers of the armed forces were overwhelmingly Christians—Burghers, Tamils, and Sinhalese—who comprised only a small percentage of the population, to the exclusion of Buddhists, Hindus, and Muslims (Global Security 2019). Britain deployed the Ceylon regiments in the Boer Wars initially, and later in the two world wars. The state of Punjab dominates the Pakistani army for the historical reason that Punjab regiments dominated the British Indian army (Soherwordi 2010). The institutional architecture of the military in South Asia was, from its inception, designed to pit one nationality against others as strategy of imperial governance. After independence, the powers and privileges of the ethno-nationally constituted armed forces were retained in the state apparatus. The ethno-national structure of the armed forces has profound implications for political claims to justice, equality, dignity, freedom, and participation in governance in contemporary politics.

Anecdotally, even today, in India, the Naga battalion is frequently deployed in various situations of military conflicts around the country including the highly militarized conflicts in Jharkhand and Chhattisgarh, but never in Nagaland. The Assam rifles are deployed in Manipur but not in Assam where there has been large-scale military deployment for decades as well. The Madras regiment is frequently deployed in Kashmir, the Bihar regiment was deployed in Punjab during Operation Blue Star (although the regiment was commanded by Major-General Brar, a Sikh officer). State-centric approaches to militarization in India has clouded the ways in which ethno-national divisions are used to maintain the authority of the Indian state and suppress resistance against militarization. In Pakistan, the Punjabi dominated army is deployed against peoples of Baluchistan, Sindh and the North-West provinces. In Sri Lanka the rise of Buddhist nationalism after independence transformed the armed forces into a Sinhalese force. State repression of Tamils manifested as Sinhalese repression against Tamils internally within Sri Lanka, and as war against terrorism in interstate relations internationally.

Independence did not take away the military involvement of the Anglo-American states in South Asia. The partition of India also partitioned the armed forces between India and Pakistan pre-empting a newly independent country from inheriting a large professional army. If the partition of India divided the Indian army between India and Pakistan and opened the spaces for military bases in South Asia, the terms of continued British presence in Sri Lanka was negotiated in ways that distanced Sri Lanka from India in the post-World War II era (Sivasundaram 2013). These factors cast a shadow on many struggles against militarization of political conflicts in South Asia during the Cold War, most notably in Kashmir, Tamil Eelam, the Chittagong tracks, and Afghanistan.

As a Crown Colony directly ruled by Britain, Sri Lanka was used as a garrison post for the East India Company because of its geostrategic location in the Indian Ocean. At the time of independence, Britain negotiated continued control over the military bases and alliances including the military base in Trincomalee in the Tamil Eelam areas (Ratnapalan 2016). The geostrategic importance of Sri Lanka as a garrison post returned once more after the end of the Cold War and the beginning of the "war on terror" in the Tamil conflict over proposals for US military bases in the Tamil area of Trincomalee. The Anglo-American alarm over Sri Lanka's tilt to China, the rise of India as an important regional US ally in the encirclement of China, and the Anglo-American maneuvers for a military base in Trincomalee situated in the Tamil Eelam region played out in important ways in the Tamil struggles for freedom, equality, justice, dignity, and participation. Trincomalee, an important garrison town since Portuguese colonialism continues to be an important military garrison/military base issue for Anglo-American imperialism in Sri Lanka (Anderson and Wijeyesekera 2019; Staff Writer 2019). The military offensives against Tamils over the years have undergone changes that reflect imperialist realignments in the region.

Archival sources unearthed in 2014 revealed correspondence between British Prime Minister Margaret Thatcher and Indian Prime Minister Indira Gandhi disclosing Britain's support for Operation Blue Star against the Sikh nation in return for arms purchases by India from Britain. *The Guardian* newspaper wrote:

> A secret Foreign Office briefing dated 22 June 1984, which was sent to Downing Street, stressed that British "commercial interests" in India were "very substantial. It is a large and growing market for both commercial and defence sales. British exports in 1983 exceeded £800m and since 1975 India has bought British defence equipment worth over £1.25bn," the document claims.
>
> (Syal and Miller 2014)

At the same time, Britain and other Anglo-American states gave asylum to large numbers of Sikh victims of Indian military offensives. The same could be said about British military support to Sri Lanka for its war against the Tamils (Miller 2014). In May 2018, *The Guardian* newspaper reported that Britain's Foreign Office destroyed almost 200 files on Sri Lanka from 1978 to 1980 regarding a Tamil Tiger uprising during which the MI5 and SAS secretly advised Sri Lanka's security forces (Miller 2018). At the same time, Britain gave asylum to large number of Tamil asylum-seekers fleeing the war. Britain's asylum policies provide the government with levers to pursue their strategic geopolitical interests in the subcontinent. South Asian soldiers may have been the backbone of British Empire in the past and deployed against anti-colonial struggles around the Empire. What about now? If we forget the national boundaries that exist for a moment, throughout the post-World War II era, South Asia—India, Pakistan, Bangladesh, Sri Lanka, and Nepal—remains the largest supplier of UN peacekeeping troops deployed in conflicts around the world (Kirk 2015) as it was during colonial times.

The above account is a very broad one involving selected South Asian states where political demands for freedom, equality, justice, and participation in governance have become heavily militarized. In international law and international relations, the militarization of political conflicts within the states are viewed through the lens of ethno-national conflicts. The ethno-national lens for viewing political struggles for freedom, autonomy, dignity, equality, and justice obscures how imperialism shapes and structures the conditions for the conflicts and the avenues for their resolution. Equally, the ethno-national lens erases memories of solidarities among the peoples of South Asia in their struggles against imperialism in the past.

There is need for far more nuanced analysis of each political struggle that has become militarized than what is sketched in the space of this chapter. The militarization of the conflicts in Afghanistan or the militarization of political struggles in Kashmir, Nagaland, Mizoram, Assam, Manipur by the Indian state or that of Baluchi struggles by the Pakistani state or the emerging Madhesi conflicts by Nepali state or the Chakma conflict by Bangladeshi state, or the Rohigyna and Karen conflicts by the Myanmar state have not been touched upon. The Anglo-American geopolitics of the encirclement of China, and how it plays out in each of these ethno-national conflicts in South Asia have also not been discussed. The point is that if internal conflicts become levers in wider imperial geopolitics, then resistance to those conflicts must respond by building regional alliances against militarization, even to intervene effectively against militarization of political conflicts within South Asian states. It is not that there are no serious tensions between the Sikh, or Kashmiri or Naga or other nations and the Indian state, or between the Eelam Tamils and the Sri Lankan state. Rather, the point is that the ethno-national lens for understanding these conflicts diverts attention from the justness of the struggles. More importantly, interventions against militarization based on a state-centric understanding of conflicts cloud understandings of how total wars are conducted, and obscure the continued role of imperial powers in keeping South Asian states, as well as movements for freedom and justice, vulnerable. The international order establishes the legal and institutional conditions for such vulnerability.

The International Order: Continued Colonization

The UN Charter privileges the Big Five or the veto countries in the Security Council. They are the victors from the world wars who have the powers to manage conflicts around the world, and negotiate war and peace issues (D'Souza 2017). The genealogy of the veto can be traced back to the Concert of Vienna (Simpson 2004). In contrast, the powers of the General Assembly of the UN, a body that represents all states, is limited. The General Assembly's powers are limited to making recommendations and it must refer all decisions about war and peace, including deployment of peacekeeping troops, to the Security Council. The model for the General Assembly can be traced back to the Chamber of Princes established by Britain in 1920 after World War I, ostensibly to "democratize" indirect rule in British India (Legg 2013). Like the General Assembly, the Chamber of Princes had deliberative, consultative, and advisory status (Holdsworth 1930). The UN Charter internationalizes the institutional model of the Chamber of Princes. The international institutional conditions under which South Asian troops are deployed by the Big Five in peacekeeping missions around the world demonstrate how the military hierarchy in contemporary epoch of imperialism is not qualitatively different from the military hierarchies under the British Empire. And much like during colonial rule, the costs of raising and maintaining the troops come from revenues raised within South Asian states.

Revisiting the debates on the establishment of the League of Nations and the UN reveals that the international legal and institutional arrangements were deliberate and well considered (D'Souza forthcoming; Smuts 1918). Jan Smuts, a Boer War veteran who later became a member of the British Imperial War cabinet and played a prominent role in shaping the League of Nations, was clear about the contribution that the British experience of colonial governance had to make in the emerging international order. Smuts wrote: "Where the British Empire has been so eminently successful as a political system ... the League, working on somewhat similar lines, could not fail to achieve a reasonable measure of success" (Smuts 1918: 29).

In the post-World War II era, the UN Charter made genocide—the systematic use of armed forces by the state to eliminate a people or a nationality—an international crime. South Asian states escape the net of the genocide definition even when the states used one nationality against others because the ethno-national armed regiments are now embedded in the institutions of the state and recognized as the national military of an independent state by international law in which states are the primary units. The UN Charter made preservation of the institutional and territorial integrity of the colonial state a condition for transition to independence (Lyon 1993). The recognition of the juristic state as a legal entity abstracted from history or ethno-nationalistic characteristics in international law means that the ethno-national composition of the armed forces became a part of policing as an integral component of state functions, operating as a constitutional entity. On one hand, the interstate UN order and international legal frameworks insist that the states are the primary subjects of international law. At the same time the UN Security Council, dominated by the Big Five veto powers, retain the rights to humanitarian interventions within states (Mamdani 2010). Many scholars see this as a tension or contradiction or a weakness in international law and the UN system.

Many South Asian movements protesting deployment of armed forces against people's struggles appeal to international organizations such as the UN High Commissioner for Human Rights, or the UN People's Permanent Forum on Indigenous Issues, and wonder why the responses of international organizations are so unpredictable or inconsistent. In fact, it is precisely the linguistic ambiguities in international law that enable imperial powers to make strategic interventions or non-interventions depending on their interests or to use linguistic ambiguities to leverage their negotiations with the South Asian states. A new people-centered regional framework for understanding militarization of political conflicts in South Asia opens the pathway to situate each conflict within the concentric circles of historical state formation, regional interstate rivalries, and the global imperial geopolitics. By doing so, resistance movements against militarization can develop strategies to escape manipulations by imperial and state powers, and avoid becoming pawns in imperial and interstate geopolitics. To avoid becoming a pawn in the games of imperial and state powers requires new thinking on regional solidarities and nuanced understandings of interstate, as well as geopolitical, relationships in South Asia.

Conclusion

At the end of the day, the "nationalities" question dominates South Asian politics. The struggles of different nationalities in South Asia are political struggles for greater freedom, dignity, equality, justice, and participation in institutions of the state. This chapter has focused on providing a rough sketch of the problems in the existing frameworks for understanding militarization in South Asia which views the conflicts from the ethno-nationalist lens of identity politics, and its flip-side, the state-centric "internal/external" lens, in an interstate global order. These lenses make the apparently dominant groups entrenched within the institutions of the state, as well as those marginalized in it, vulnerable to imperial manipulations. This chapter has focused on the ways in which the British Empire shaped state formations in the subcontinent and the common features of military institutions and governance. It has shown that militarization in South Asia embeds and privileges certain ethno-national groups. The chapter has also drawn attention to the continuities between certain patterns of relationships within and between states today that resemble colonial relationships. What might a framework that is not ethno-nationalist and not based on the state centric "internal/external" conceptual divide look like? What might the key elements of a new framework be? How might a framework that is centered on freedom, justice, and dignity for all people look like? Such questions are precisely the ones that resistances to militarization in South Asia must address as a matter of urgency.

Radha D'Souza is professor of law at the University of Westminster. She is a critical scholar, activist, barrister and writer who has worked with a range of social movements around the world. Her recent book *What's Wrong with Rights? Social Movements, Law and Liberal Imaginations* (Pluto, 2018) maps, for the first time, the transformations in the regime of international rights to the transformations in post-World War imperialism.

References

Addy, Premen. 1984. *Tibet on the Imperial Chessboard: The Making of British Policy Towards Lhasa, 1899-1925*. Calcutta: Academic Publishers.

Anderson, David and Anton Wijeyesekera. 2019. "US Naval Basing In Sri Lanka?" Retrieved from https://smallwarsjournal.com/jrnl/art/us-naval-basing-in-sri-lanka (accessed June 1, 2019).
Barkawi, Tarak. 2012. "Army, Ethnicity and Society in British India." In *The Indian Army in the World Wars*, edited by Kaushik Roy, 419–443. Leiden: Brill. https://doi.org/10.1163/9789004211452_016
Bass, Gary J. 2013. *The Blood Telegram: India's Secret War in East Pakistan*. New Delhi: Random House.
Bauman, Zygmunt. 1989. *Modernity and the Holocaust*. Cambridge: Polity Press.
Bowie, John. 1989. *The Empire at War*. London: Batsford.
Chickering, Robert, Stig Forster and Bernd Greiner, eds. 2005. *A World At Total War: Global Conflict and the Politics of Destruction, 1937-1945*. Cambridge: Cambridge University Press. https://doi.org/10.1017/CBO9781139052382
Cobden, Richard. 1853. *How Wars Are Got Up in India: The Origin of the Burmese War*. London: William & Frederick G. Cash.
D'Souza, Radha. 2010. "When Unreason Masquerades as Reason: Can Law Regulate Trade and Networked Communication Ethically?" In *Handbook of Communication Ethics*, edited by George Cheny, Steve May and Debashish Munshi, 475–493. Abingdon: International Communication Association Routledge/Lawrence Erlbaum.
D'Souza, Radha. 2014. "Revolt and Reform in South Asia: Ghadar Movement to 9/11 and After." *Economic & Political Weekly (Special Articles)* 49(8): 59–73.
D'Souza, Radha. 2017. "Victor's Law? Colonial Peoples, World War II And International Law." *International Comparative Jurisprudence* 3(1): 67–84.
D'Souza, Radha. 2018. *What's Wrong with Rights? Social Movements, Law and Liberal Imaginations*. London: Pluto Press. https://doi.org/10.2307/j.ctt1zk0mmx
D'Souza, Radha. 2019. "The Surveillance State: A Composition in Four Movements." In *Activists and the Surveillance State: Learning from Repression*, edited by Aziz Choudry, 23–52. London: Pluto Press. https://doi.org/10.2307/j.ctv893hzw.5
D'Souza, Radha. Forthcoming. "International Law and Development: From Company Raj to Network Governance via Indirect Rule." In *On International Law and Development: From Colonization to Globalization*, edited by Abdul Paliwala and Samuel Adelman, 20. London: Routledge.
Edgerton, David. 2005. *Warfare State: Britain, 1920-1970*. Cambridge: Cambridge University Press.
Encyclopaedia Britannica. 2018. "Portuguese India." Retrieved from www.britannica.com/place/Portuguese-India (accessed March 23, 2019).
Encyclopaedia Britannica. 2019. "Treaty of Amiens." Retrieved from www.britannica.com/event/Treaty-of-Amiens-1802 (accessed March 23, 2019).
Fisk, Robert. 2012. "The Children of Fallujah: The Hospital of Horrors." *The Independent*.
Fremont-Barnes, Gregory. 2014. *The Anglo-Afghan Wars 1839-1919*. Oxford: Osprey Publishing
Gandhi, Mohandas K. 1930. "Letter from Gandhi to the Viceroy, Lord Irwin, 2 March 1930." Indian Independence: Nationalism Source 3 [MSS EUR C152/24], British Library archive.
Gibbs, David N. 1997. "Is Peacekeeping a New Form of Imperialism?" *International Peacekeeping* 4(1): 122–128. https://doi.org/10.1080/13533319708413655
Global Security. 2019. "History of Sri Lankan Army: Post Independence." Retrieved from www.globalsecurity.org/military/world/sri-lanka/army-history-4.htm (accessed May 31, 2019).
Godden, Lee and Niranjan Casinader. 2013. "The Kandyan Convention 1815: Consolidating the British Empire in Colonial Ceylon." *Comparative Legal History* 1(2): 211–242. https://doi.org/10.5235/2049677X.1.2.211

Gott, Richard. 2012. *Britain's Empire: Resistance, Repression and Revolt*. London: Verso.

Gupta, Shantiswarup. 1974. *British Relations with Bhutan*. Jaipur: Panchasheel Prakashan.

Halebsky, Stephen. 2014. "Corporate Practices and Harmful Consequences: Learning from the Holocaust." *Humanity and Society* 38(3): 237–267. https://doi.org/10.1177/0160597614537797

Herring, George. 1971. "The United States and British Bankruptcy, 1944–1945: Responsibilities Deferred." *Political Science Quarterly* 86(2): 260–280. https://doi.org/10.2307/2148010

Holdsworth, William. 1930. "The Indian States and India." *Law Quarterly Review* 46: 407–446.

Jamal, Dahr. 2013. "'Falluja Babies' and Depleted Uranium: America's Toxic Legacy in Iraq." *Al Jazeera*, March 18.

Keith, Arthur. 1961. *A Constitutional History of India: 1600-1935*. Allahabad: Central Book Depot.

Kimball, Warren. 1971. "Lend-Lease and the Open Door: The Temptation of British Opulence, 1937-1942." *Political Science Quarterly* 86(2): 232–259. https://doi.org/10.2307/2148009

King, C. G. and Ole Salathe. 1946. "Developments in the Science of Nutrition during World War II." *American Journal of Public Health* 36: 879–882. https://doi.org/10.2105/AJPH.36.8.879

Kirk, Ashely. 2015. "UN Peacekeepers: How Many Personnel Does Each Country Contribute?" *The Telegraph*, February 6.

Koistinen, Paul. 1980. *The Military-Industrial Complex: A Historical Perspective*. New York: Praeger Publishers.

Krishnasamy, Kabilan. 2001. "'Recognition' for Third World Peacekeepers: India and Pakistan." *International Peacekeeping* 8(4): 56–76. https://doi.org/10.1080/13533310108413920

Kulve, Haico and Wim Smit. 2003. "Civilian-Military Co-operation Strategies in Developing New Technologies." *Research Policy* 32: 955–970. https://doi.org/10.1016/S0048-7333(02)00105-1

Kurdish Human Rights Project. 1999. "The Ilisu Dam: A Human Rights Disaster in the Making." Retrieved from www.thecornerhouse.org.uk/resource/ilisu-dam-human-rights-disaster-making (accessed March 17, 2019).

Kux, Dennis. 2001. *The United States and Pakistan, 1947-2000: Disenchanted Allies*. Washington DC: Woodrow Wilson Centre Press/Baltimore, MD: Johns Hopkins University Press.

Lamb, Alastair. 2018. *British India and Tibet 1766-1910*. London: Routledge. https://doi.org/10.4324/9780429445378

Legg, Stephen. 2013. "An International Anomaly? Sovereignty, the League of Nations and India's Princely Geographies." *Journal of Historical Geography* 43: 96–110. https://doi.org/10.1016/j.jhg.2013.03.002

Lenman, Bruce, ed. 2014. *Britain's Colonial Wars 1688-1783*. New York: Routledge. https://doi.org/10.4324/9781315837864

Lobanov-Rostovsky, Aleksey. 1948. "Anglo-Russian Relations through the Centuries." *The Russian Review* 7(2): 41–52. https://doi.org/10.2307/125518

Louis, William. 1985. "American Anti-colonialism and the Dissolution of the British Empire." *International Affairs* 61(3): 395–420. https://doi.org/10.2307/2618660

Lovering, John. 1987. "Militarism, Capitalism, and the Nation-State: Towards a Realist Synthesis." *Environment and Planning D: Society and Space* 5: 283–302. https://doi.org/10.1068/d050283

Lyon, Peter. 1993. "The Rise and Fall and Possible Revival of International Trusteeship." *The Journal of Commonwealth and Comparative Politics* 31(1): 96–110. https://doi.org/10.1080/14662049308447651

Mamdani, Mahmood. 2010. "Responsibility to Protect or Right to Punish?" *Journal of Intervention and Statebuilding* 4(1): 53–67. https://doi.org/10.1080/17502970903541721

Marshall, Julie, ed. 2004. *Britain and Tibet 1765-1947: A Select Annotated Bibliography of British Relations with Tibet and the Himalayan States Including Nepal, Sikkim and Bhutan*. London: Routledge.

McMahon, Robert. 1988. "United States Cold War Strategy in South Asia: Making a Military Commitment to Pakistan, 1947–1954." *The Journal of American History* 75(3): 812–840. https://doi.org/10.2307/1901531

Michael, Bernardo. 2012. *Statemaking and territory in South Asia: Lessons from the Anglo-Gorkha War (1814-1816)*. London: Anthem Press.

Miller, Phil. 2014. *Britain's Dirty War Against The Tamil People: 1979-2009*. Bremen: International Human Rights Association.

Miller, Phil. 2018. "Files on Tamil Tigers and MI5 in Sri Lanka Erased at Foreign Office." *The Guardian*, May 23. Retrieved from www.theguardian.com/world/2018/may/23/files-on-tamil-tigers-and-mi5-in-sri-lanka-erased-at-foreign-office (accessed December 19, 2019).

Milward, Alan. 1970. *The Economic Effects of the Two World Wars on Britain*. London: Macmillan. https://doi.org/10.1007/978-1-349-00731-8

Narula, Sunil. 2004. "Psychological Operations (PSYOPs): A Conceptual Overview." *Strategic Analysis* 28(1): 177–192. https://doi.org/10.1080/09700160408450124

Nehru, Motilal. 1928. *The Nehru Report: An Anti-Separatist Manifesto: The Committee Appointed by the All Parties" Conference 1928*. New Delhi: Michiko & Panjathan.

Nguyen, Viet Thanh and Richard Hughes. 2017. "The Forgotten Victims of Agent Orange." *The New York Times*, September 15.

Onley, James. 2009. "The Raj Reconsidered: British India's Informal Empire and Spheres Of Influence in Asia and Africa." *Asian Affairs* 40(1):44–62. https://doi.org/10.1080/03068370802658666

Panton, Kenneth. 2015. *Historical Dictionary of the British Empire*. Lanham, MD: Rowman & Littlefield.

Peiris, Gerald and Sinnappah Arasaratnam. 2019. "Sri Lanka." Retrieved from www.britannica.com/place/Sri-Lanka/British-Ceylon-1796-1900 (accessed March 23, 2019).

Ramachandra, Gangadharan P. 1977. "Anglo-Burmese Relations 1795–1826." PhD thesis, University of Hull.

Rand, Gavin. 2012. "Allies to a Declining Power: The Martial Races, the Second World War and the End of the British Empire in South Asia." In *The Indian Army in the Two World Wars*, edited by Kaushik Roy, 445–460. Leiden; Boston: Brill. https://doi.org/10.1163/9789004211452_017

Ratnapalan, Laavanyan M. 2016. "Britain and the Politics of Ceylon, 1948–1961." *The Historical Journal* 59(2): 541–565. https://doi.org/10.1017/S0018246X15000151

Riaz, Ali. 2006. "Beyond the 'Tilt': US Initiatives to Dissipate Bangladesh Movement in 1971." *History Compass* 4(1): 8–25. https://doi.org/10.1111/j.1478-0542.2005.00169.x

Robinson, Francis. 1989. *The Cambridge Encyclopedia of India, Pakistan, Bangladesh, Sri Lanka, Nepal, Bhutan and the Maldives*. Cambridge: Cambridge University Press.

Roy, Kaushik, ed. 2012. *The Indian Army in the World Wars*. Leiden: Brill. https://doi.org/10.1163/9789004211452

Sideri, Sandro. 1970. *Trade and Power: Informal Colonialism in Anglo-Portuguese Relations*. Rotterdam: Rotterdam University Press.

Simpson, Gerry. 2004. *Great Powers and Outlaw States: Unequal Sovereigns in the International Legal Order*. Cambridge: Cambridge University Press. https://doi.org/10.1017/CBO9780511494185

Sivasundaram, Sujit. 2013. *Islanded: Britain, Sri Lanka, and the Bounds of an Indian Ocean Colony.* Chicago, IL: University of Chicago Press. https://doi.org/10.7208/chicago/9780226038360.001.0001

Smuts, Jan. 1918. *The League of Nations: A Practical Suggestion.* New York: Hodder and Stoughton.

Soherwordi, Syed. 2010. "'Punjabisation' in the British Indian Army 1857–1947 and the Advent of Military Rule in Pakistan." Retrieved from www.pol.ed.ac.uk/_data/assets/pdf_file/0011/48674/WP24_Shaheed_Hussain.pdf (accessed May 31, 2019).

Staff Reporter. 2005. "Agent Orange Case of Millions of Vietnamese Is Dismissed." *The New York Times,* March 10. Retrieved from www.nytimes.com/2005/03/10/nyregion/agent-orange-case-for-millions-of-vietnamese-is-dismissed.html (accessed December 19, 2019).

Staff Writer. 2019. "Concerns Raised on the Possibility of a US Base in Trincomalee." Retrieved from www.newsfirst.lk/2019/01/28/concerns-raised-on-possibility-of-a-us-base-in-trincomalee (accessed June 1, 2019).

Strauss, Michael. 2009. *The Leasing of Guantanamo Bay, Cuba in Transition Papers and Proceedings of the Twentieth Annual Meeting of the Association of the Study of the Cuban Economy.* Westport, CT: Praeger Security International.

Syal, Rajeev and Phil Miller. 2014. "Margaret Thatcher Gave Full Support Over Golden Temple Raid, Letter Shows." *The Guardian,* January 15. Retrieved from www.theguardian.com/world/2014/jan/15/margaret-thatcher-golden-temple-raid-support-letter (accessed August 4, 2019).

Talbot, David. 2015. *The Devil's Chessboard: Allen Dulles, The CIA and the Rise of America's Secret Government.* New York: HarperCollins.

Tarlock, A. Dan. 2004. "A First Look at a Modern Legal Regime for a Post-Modern United States Army Corps of Engineers." *University of Kansas Law Review* 52: 1285–1325.

Teclaff, Ludwik A. 1967. *The River Basin in History and Law.* The Hague: Martinus Nijhoff. https://doi.org/10.1007/978-94-015-1025-7

Uberoi, Jit Pal Singh. 2002. *The European Modernity: Science, Truth and Method.* New Delhi: Oxford University Press.

Van Loon, Joost. 2006. "Network." *Theory Culture Society* 23: 307–314. https://doi.org/10.1177/0263276406062696

Voigt, Johannes. 1987. *India in the Second World War: A History with Problems.* New Delhi: Arnold-Heinemann.

Vombatkere, Sudhir. G. 2010. "Deepening India–US Strategic Ties: Evidences and Repercussions." Retrieved from www.countercurrents.org/vombatkere220910.htm (accessed March 30, 2019).

Vombatkere, Sudhir. G. 2012. "US Special Forces in India: Sovereignty Issues and the Military." Retrieved from www.countercurrents.org/vombatkere050312.htm (accessed March 30, 2019).

Vombatkere, Sudhir. G. 2017. "India's Sovereignty: Have We Lost It?" Retrieved from www.mainstreamweekly.net/article7094.html (accessed August 20, 2019).

Waddell, Brian. 1994. "Economic Mobilization for World War II and the Transformation of the US State." *Politics and Society* 22(2): 165–194. https://doi.org/10.1177/0032329294022002004

Waddell, Brian. 1999. "Corporate Influence and World War II: Resolving the New Deal Political Stalemate." *Journal of Policy History* 11(3): 223–256. https://doi.org/10.1353/jph.1999.0007

Waddell, Brian. 2001. "Limiting National Interventionism in the United States: The Warfare-Welfare State as Restrictive Governance Paradigm." *Capital and Class* 74: 109–139. https://doi.org/10.1177/030981680107400106

Wallensteen, Peter and Margareta Sollenberg. 1998. "Armed Conflict and Regional Conflict Complexes, 1989–97." *Journal of Peace Research* 35(5): 621–634. https://doi.org/10.1177/0022343398035005005

Wanmali, Sudhir and Deryck Lodrick. 2019. "Goa." Retrieved from www.britannica.com/place/Goa (accessed March 23, 2019).

Ward, John Manning. 1976. "The Crown Colony System." In John Manning Ward, *Colonial Self-Government*. Cambridge Commonwealth Series. London: Palgrave Macmillan. https://doi.org/10.1007/978-1-349-02712-5_4

Werskey, Gary. 2007. "The Marxist Critique of Capitalist Science: A History in Three Movements?" *Science as Culture* 16(4): 397–461. https://doi.org/10.1080/09505430701706749

Whitman, James. 1991. "Of Corporatism, Fascism, and the First New Deal." *American Journal of Comparative Law* 39(4): 747–778. https://doi.org/10.2307/840740

Winner, Andrew C. 2011. "The United States, India, the Indian Ocean, and Maritime Elements of Security Cooperation." In *India's Contemporary Security Challenges*, edited by Michael Kugelman, 99–118. Washington, DC: Asia Program: Woodrow Wilson International Center for Scholars.

2

Contemporary Globalization and Militarization: From Speculation Blitz to the "War on Terror" Rampage

Haluk Gerger

As a fully-fledged imperialism, globalization is an integrated system of economic, political, military and ideological powers and geopolitical arrangements supervised by real people in real board rooms.
—Aijaz Ahmed, *A Reflection on Our Times* (2004: 60)

Introduction

Globalization implies capital's mobility, internationalisation, and virtually unhindered penetration into all corners of the world as if it were a single market. The recent wave of globalization, starting in the 1980s in response to the general crisis of capitalism, had a distinctive character: International domination of a mode of accumulation which is, to a large degree, divorced from production, paving way for a decaying parasitism with inherent destructiveness. In 1988, an observer discerned the destructive tendency of finance capital at the time:

> When economic conditions are prosperous and stable, financial capital flows help support and even foster productive investment. But when the economy has become stagnant and unstable, investors tend to move their capital out of productive investments ... The investment climate becomes increasingly speculative. The past fifteen years appear to have illustrated the latter dynamic. As the rate of return on fixed investment in plant and equipment has declined and as global economic conditions have become increasingly volatile, firms and banks moved toward paper investments.
>
> (Gordon 1988: 59)[1]

In time, surplus capital's dissociation from production for human need reached such a point that it "inevitably [became] speculative capital geared solely to its own self-expansion" (Sweezy 1994: 2).

Ronald Reagan led and personified the aggressive policies of monetarist counter-revolution. Reaganomics started at home. Corporate profit margins expanded, real wages fell, social spending cut, and military expenditures increased. Millions in the rust belt were rendered superfluous.[2] Reagan also unleashed the Second Cold War, militarized international relations, weaponized outer space. After the home front was quieted, a destructive wave of global de-regulation thrust was initiated. The monetarist offensive of international capital then overwhelmed the whole world. Ronald Reagan's arrogant remarks were indeed true: "We have meant to change a nation, and instead we changed a world" (Bello et al. 1999: 105).

The Violence of Capitalist Globalization

In the South, the "Globalization of Adjustment" preceded globalization (Bello et al. 1999: 28). Due to the imposition of structural adjustment programs by the World Bank and the IMF, most Third World countries had to set aside large amounts of their already meagre foreign currency earnings for debt servicing. This siphoning was so massive that the former director of the World Bank said, "not since the conquistadors plundered Latin America has the world experienced a flow in the direction we see today" (Bello et al. 1999: 68). As a result, "nearly all of the Third World countries' already low income levels have declined severely" (Hayter 1992: 8). Third World's share of world income fell from 5.6 percent in 1978 to 4.5 percent in 1984. The income gap between the rich and poor countries widened, income ratio going up to 60:1 in 1989 from 20:1 in 1960 and 46:1 in 1980 (Schuurman 1993: 10). The disparagement of poor countries created a state of global apartheid. The new international caste system produced its own untouchables; "If God gave it [Africa] to you and made you its economic dictator, the only smart move would be to give it back to him" (Thurow 1993: 216). The ensuing worldwide destitution contracted world markets limiting productive investment opportunities.[3] Growth was curtailed, global stagnation was aggravated. With these developments, the global network of financial markets in the deregulated world capitalist market where national barriers were demolished started eagerly to receive idle surplus capital looking for profit and expansion. Speculation and globetrotting usurer money dominated the system. Every state and government in the world was rendered vulnerable to the whims of financial markets. The privatization craze contributed to the plunder.

Between the sixteenth and eighteenth centuries, mercantilism, as an economic policy and activity, "overemphasized ... the process of exchange versus production, exchange value versus use value, accumulated money versus consumable commodities, and international sources versus national ones for capitalist development" (Szentes 1988: 11). What emerged, in this period, was a corporate mercantilism with enrichment reminiscent of primitive accumulation that was based upon "a process by which producers were deprived of their means of production, and also the process of the accumulation of capital in money form ... and ... a process of robbing and commercially exploiting other countries" (Szentes 1988: 9). Under the wave of globalization, humanity was dragged into the world of expropriation of social production through privatization, worldwide plunder through institutionalized unequal exchange, and the erosion of the world's productive base through financial extortion.

During the 1970s, the amount of money circulating daily in currency markets was about $18 billion, and that corresponded to the money value of almost 90 percent of the world trade in goods and services. In the mid-1990s, every 24 hours, 1 trillion dollars were being traded in currency exchanges which was the "equivalent of all the gold and foreign currency reserves of all countries belonging to the International Monetary Fund" (Singer 1994: 92). The situation was illustrated in a 1994 publication:

> The Global Financial Network is a constantly changing maze of currency transactions, global securities, mastercards, euroyen, swaps, ruffs, and an ever more innovative array of speculative devices for repackaging and reselling money. This network is much closer to a chain of gambling casinos than to the dull grey banks of yesteryear. Twenty-four hours a day, trillions of dollars flow through the world's foreign exchange markets ... no more than 10 percent of this staggering sum has anything to do with trade in goods and services.
>
> (Barnet and Cavanagh 2002: 2)

By the end of the decade, the daily transactions exceeded 1.5 trillion dollars. In the year 2002, the German President complained; "today, 90 percent of the money circulating around the world every day has nothing to do with the exchange of goods and services. More than 2,000 billion euros keeps changing place daily for speculative reasons" (quoted in *Frankfurter Allgemeine Zeitung*, May 14, 2002). To this gigantic amount, about $5 trillion of daily trade in financial derivatives should be added to get a clearer picture of the gambling spree in the world financial markets:

> More significant is the trade in derivatives. The Triennial Survey indicates that the average daily volume of exchange-traded derivatives amounted to $4.5 trillion in 2004. In the OTC derivatives market, the average daily turnover amounted to $1.2 trillion at current exchange rates. The OTC market section consists of "non-traditional" foreign exchange derivatives—such as cross-currency swaps and options—and all interest rate derivatives contracts. Thus, total derivatives trading stood at $5.7 trillion a day, which together with the $1.9 trillion daily turnover in the foreign exchange market adds up to $7.6 trillion. This exceeds the annual value of global merchandise exports in 2003.
>
> (Chandrasekhar 2004)

At the end of the 1990s, "some $25 trillion in currency is moved daily in global financial markets, and the daily turnover at the largest stock markets has surpassed $1 trillion, compared to a daily world trade of only about $10 billion (so that real trade is only one percent of fictitious trade)" (Robinson and Harris 2000: 24). In the early 2000s, the total sum of the bubble of speculation was estimated to be close to 100 trillion US dollars!

The volume of international financial transactions has exceeded world trade in physical goods, and in developed economies "intangibles," rather than production of physical goods, have become the real sources of wealth. The trend has continued unabated:

> Capital flows amounted to about 21 percent of global GDP in 2007 up from 6 percent in 1996 ... While in 1980 daily currency exchange turnover amounted to about

0.7 percent of global GDP during the entire year, as of April 2007 it had increased more than nine-fold to 6.6 percent.

(Guillen and Suarez 2015: 129)

The implications and results of these developments have been tremendous. All over the world, while the share of world GNP, represented by manufacturing, declined in relative terms, the service sector was greatly expanded everywhere.[4] Unemployment soared world over[5] and the share of laboring classes in the social wealth declined universally. For billions of people, those years have been a period of utter desolation. Globalization has turned the world into a seamless market network within which billions were trapped in the maelstrom of hunger, war, repression, disease, and death.

Although, as the United Nation's Human Development Report in 2001 points out, "human development has historically shown sustained improvement, especially when measured by the human development index" of income, life expectancy, and literacy, it fell in 21 countries during the 1990s:

> Some 54 countries are poorer now than in 1990. In 21, a larger proportion is going hungry. In 14, more children are dying before age five. In 12, primary school enrolments are shrinking. In 34, life expectancy has fallen. Such reversals in survival were previously rare.

(United Nations 2001)

The telling triumph of modern finance capital, on the other hand, has created conditions under which "a very small number of persons, often single individuals, are becoming rich in a manner without precedence at least since the times of feudal society" (Hobsbawm 2000: 88). The balance sheet even during the earlier stages was horrifying:

> By the early 1990s the top twenty-five multinational corporations all had sales over $25 billion. The largest (in 1992), General Motors, had sales larger than the gross domestic product of all but twenty-one nations. Lists of countries by GDP and companies by sales showed Toyota's sales exceeding the GDP of Portugal and Poland, IBM larger than Venezuela, and Unilever exceeding New Zealand.

(Tabb 2001: 148)

The process of globalization created obscene inequalities within and between countries.

All these, in and by themselves, represent violence par excellence. And this panorama of globalization could only be created and maintained through systematic application of sheer violence, and coercion of all sorts. The "New World Order" (NWO) was constructed to be the legal, political, ideological superstructure of globalization. The ultimate aim was to impose, facilitate, safeguard, and deepen the globalization process. The concept was the answer to the strategic need of global governance. These twin processes were laden with violence, aggression, brutal imperialist interventions, wars, and ferocious upheavals. For billions of people, normal conditions of life have become violent. Violence was intrinsic to globalization and a *sine qua non* component of the NWO. Both processes were introduced, managed, and sustained with continuous application of an amalgam of various forms and means of violence. In a more profound sense, violence was more than a means for both globalization and the NWO. Both are organically violent in their very essence for they comprise physical and non-physical forms of structural violence.

To realize its penetration and squeeze on a regular basis, financial capital needs to destroy independence and sovereignty of its prey, and through imposed deregulation measures, does away with local laws, customs, central banks, finance ministries, the bureaucracy and other regulatory bodies; it either renders them utterly impotent or reduces them into instruments of oppression against their own people. To do this, all means of pressure, including violence, are applied and all schemes of intrusion are utilized. In other words, deregulation is enforced through intervention. When all rules and norms are done away with, and regulatory and control mechanisms are shattered thus, excess in financial markets that are prone to instability by their nature, become rampant. Integration of financial markets, by corollary also means incorporation of excess, volatility, flux and crises. Then, even marginal markets begin to deeply affect imperialist centers in the seamless integration of the world market.

Endemic Intervention and Inevitable Militarization

Globalized financial markets and global speculative capital, therefore, signify globalized instability and crisis. Imposition of deregulation requires intervention; deregulation in turn lets speculation loose, and requires intervention again to restore order and alleviate crisis. Inevitable resistance further aggravates the need for intervention. Therefore, intervention is endemic in, and intrinsic to, the very dynamics of globalization itself. Imperialists must intervene to impose deregulation for speculative financial transactions and for obscene rates of profits for global plunder. Then they need to intervene again to manage mishap, to protect home markets, to quell resistance, to ensure the future functioning of the system and to restore "global governance."

Memoirs of the former Treasury Secretary of the Clinton administration testifies to this "intervention imperative" created by the very dynamics of globalization:

> Financial markets are driven by human nature and have a propensity to go to excess. This means that periodic financial crises of one sort or another are virtually inevitable ... The global crisis underscored the reality that in an economically integrated world, prosperity in faraway countries can create opportunities elsewhere, but instability in a distant economy can also create uncertainty and instability at home. One country's success can enrich others, and its mistakes put them at risk ... In my career, I have been concerned mostly with the economic and financial links that tie our interests to those of other nations ...
> (Rubin 2003: 213–215)

Management of speculation, global loot, parasitical world economy, and crises has its own set of regulations. Unabashedly, Thomas Friedman enumerated the rules of the canons of globalization:

> [A] country must either adopt, or be seen as moving toward, the following golden rules: making the private sector the primary engine of its economic growth, maintaining a low rate of inflation and price stability, shrinking the size of its state bureaucracy, maintaining as close to a balanced budget as possible, if not a surplus, eliminating and lowering tariffs on imported goods, removing restrictions on foreign investment, getting rid of quotas and domestic monopolies, increasing exports, privatising state-owned industries and utilities, deregulating capital markets, making its currency convertible, opening its industries, stock and bond markets to direct foreign ownership and investment, deregulating its economy to promote as much domestic competition as possible, eliminating government corruption, subsidies and kickbacks as possible, opening its banking and telecommunications systems to private ownership and competition, and allowing its citizens to choose from an array of competing pension options and foreign-run pension and mutual funds ...
>
> (Friedman 2000: 105–106)

This means that a country's political choices get reduced to Pepsi or Coke—to slight nuances of taste, slight alterations in design to account for local traditions, some loosening here or there, but never any major deviations from the core golden rules. The imperial order also presupposes certain well-defined and ruthlessly enforced "principles" like

> large, long-term interest payments on external debt; massive transfers of profits derived direct and portfolio investments; buyouts and takeovers of lucrative public enterprises and financially troubled national enterprises; as well as direct investments in sweatshops, energy resources, and low-wage manufacturing and service industries; collection of rents from royalty payments on a wide range of products, patents and cultural commodities; and favourable current account balances based on the dominance of US corporations and banks ...
>
> (Petras and Veltmeyer 2001: 78)

Enforcing of all this is no easy matter. So, Thomas Friedman too was well aware of the fact that imperialism needed an apparatus of governance more worldly than Adam Smith's fictitious "invisible hand":

> Sustainable globalization requires a stable power structure, and no country is more essential for this than the United States ... The hidden hand of the market will never work without a hidden fist ... Indeed, McDonald's cannot flourish without McDonnell Douglas, the designer of the US Air Force F-15. And the hidden fist that keeps the world safe for Silicon Valley's technologies to flourish is called the US Army, Air Force, Navy, and Marine Corps.
>
> (Petras and Veltmeyer 2001: 78)

In the NWO, not only mockery is made of sovereign equality and the principal of non-interference in internal affairs, state sovereignty itself is being questioned. Within the framework of globalization, sovereignty of most states becomes a burden for capitalism that hinders free flow of speculative capital, for it demands absolute autonomy to circulate internationally. In other words, Capital itself wants to be above the law, that is, to be sovereign. Therefore, sovereignty denial is an integral part of the NWO, and it is to be put into effect by the sovereign representatives of International Capital, namely, the US and her imperialist allies.

The corporations controlled by the financial oligarchy eclipse the modern state and replace the legal framework within which even the most authoritarian state operates with its sole law—the urge for profit. The shareholders displace citizens who grant life and meaning even to the most totalitarian state. The inevitable friction between the legally controlled, and politically accounted for, policies of the states and the unstable, capricious, deregulated requirements of the speculative financial markets was in the end resolved at the expense of the public domain. As a result, millions of disenfranchised working people and indeed whole societies have been condemned to total irrelevance. Since sovereignty-denial is an essential component of Pax Americana under the NWO, the Director of the Policy Planning Staff of the US Department of State Richard Haass claimed that "sovereignty is not a blank check ... Non-intervention is no longer sacrosanct" (Haass 2003).

The main norm of the NWO pertains to a new right, namely, the right bestowed upon the imperialist block under the leadership of the United States to intervene, if need be militarily, in any part of the globe. This new "Law of Intervention" was designed to form the basis of the system. The new order could have been fully instituted only when this norm became an established rule of international law. International law is mainly based upon tradition and custom. Those actions and relationship patterns in international relations that take place habitually and accepted routinely, in time, turn into established rules of international law. In other words, a political category itself, international law develops out of international practice and therefore is a product of the operation of the system itself within which repeated and accepted practices take place. The norms of international moneylenders were to become the law of the world and the US the global super sheriff. She becomes the prosecutor; she accuses. Then she is the judge; she condemns. She assumes the role of the police; she enforces. She is the executioner; she administers the verdict. She is the undertaker; her companies take care of what she has destroyed.

A wave of military and non-military interventions has already invigorated this creeping process of creating a new rule of intervention and adding it to the corpus of the law. The sinister objective to lay down the pseudo-legal basis of "international colonialism" through the legalization of the right to intervention was, however, effectively obstructed by worldwide resistance, which in turn was answered by the US "war on terror." The "New World Disorder" would soon give way to "creation through chaos" in the Middle East. All this, however, was not the only sources of the rampant militarization built into the globalization process.

An Onslaught on the Social Solidarity

As the new economic order reigned supreme, the values and ideology sprung from it strengthened their domination. Even scientific-technological advances, information and communications revolutions, shifts in social-cultural attitudes, in a manipulated and twisted form, were all used by corporate money power and propaganda machine to reinforce the hegemonic assault. Minds had to be set first to passive acceptance, and in time to active adulation, of the "rising values of our age." Whatever stood in the way had to be rolled back and the helplessness of whole societies before the power of money and violence needed to be reinforced by psycho-sociological enslavement of minds and hearts. As the world went tabloid, societies, states and governments not only faced the danger of losing the levers of economic control but also ideological penetration and cultural decadence of invading financial dogmas. Values that embrace social solidarity and participation were rejected by the new culture. Social human and collective will were defeated by the new individual hell-bent on making money. As they lost the future, millions everywhere became devoted followers of the financial gurus of the religion of getting rich.

The ideological gist of neo-liberal aggression can be detected in its totality in the "end of history" idea articulated by the American diplomat, Francis Fukuyama (Fukuyama 1989: 3–18; Fukuyama 1992). In his writings, Fukuyama contended that humankind was witnessing the final triumph of liberal capitalism that has defeated all rival social projects. Since history in the last instance is the struggle between contending ideologies, each forwarding its own model of socio-economic organization, then, with the final victory of one of them, history must have also ended. Therefore, humanity has entered an era of eternal (and, by definition, motionless and hopeless) reign of International Capital. The intellectual terror and the wholly totalitarian bent here are obvious: The idea behind the NWO purports to terminate the eternal search for a better world that perhaps started with the advent of Homo Sapiens. This is nothing less than imposing eternal servitude on humanity. The assault started with the manipulation of democratization to hide concentrated exploitation, repression, and totalitarianism. Democratization was linked to "a kind of generalised offensive for the liberation of 'market forces,' aimed at the ideological rehabilitation of the absolute superiority of private property, legitimation of social inequalities and anti-statism of all kinds, and so on" (Amin 1993: 59).

Accompanying this offensive was the rehabilitation, re-legitimatization, and moral justification of colonial/imperial ideology coupled with the demonization of the Third World and the criminalization of most of its political movements (Furedi 1994: 98–119). In the process,

> the public space has shrunk ... The steering capacity of each of the modern states is more and more subject to external conditions beyond its control. The content of politics has been further displaced by symbolism, conducted mainly through the largely corporate controlled, international, visual media. When politics is stripped of its content, when the political human gives way so completely to self-interested, competitive, economic human, both democracy and human rights are stripped of their contents as well. They become part of an ideology used to justify their very negation.
>
> (Fields and Narr 1992: 19)

This cultural-ideological offensive represented one of the worst kinds of violence against human society. Tampering with the social fabric and debasing the collective is indeed a crime against humanity. Corrupting culture, values, norms and mores, deforming social institutions, imposing spiritual death were some of the ways chosen to acquire permanent, institutionalized hegemony. Hegemony of values thus constructed was to ensure "voluntary servitude." This is indeed militarization par excellence.

Although outright physical aggression and war represent the routine embedded in imperialistic thought and reflex, such latent forms of systemic violence to condemn societies to structural dependency are no less real or violent than manifest physical means used to bring about servitude to international capital. The ideology of the monolithic NWO, therefore, is not only totalitarian in nature, it is also inevitably militaristic in practice. It is only natural at the "end of history" to view any alternative to—or any rejection of—the promises of liberal capitalism as archaic time bombs laid at the very foundations of the eternal order. Therefore, any opposition or alternative is construed as irrational and unnatural, and treated as a vital threat to be destroyed immediately at any cost and by any means.

The "War on Terror" Rampage Begins

In 1991, Saddam's invasion of Kuwait offered the first golden opportunity to the Bush administration to create alibis en route to global mastery. The Middle East was chosen as the launching pad in this offensive for global hegemony. It took forty-two days of constant bombardment resulting in over 100,000 Iraqi deaths for George Bush to proclaim in 1991 a "New World Order" and boast "the specter of Vietnam has been buried forever in the desert sands of the Arabian Peninsula." That was the proclamation of the NWO.

Yet Saddam was no match for America's need for an enemy that would act as a pretext in a whole range of circumstances. In the year 2000, the Project for the New American Century, an influential think-tank, released a report called *Rebuilding America's Defenses: Strategy, Forces and Resources for a New Century*. Among its authors were Dick Cheney, Donald Rumsfeld, Paul Wolfowitz, Francis Fukuyama, and W. Bush's brother, Jeb Bush. The report conceded that:

> in the Persian Gulf region, the presence of American forces, along with British and French units, has become a semi-permanent fact of life. Though the immediate mission of those forces is to enforce the no-fly zones over northern and southern Iraq, they represent the long-term commitment of the United States and its major allies to a region of vital importance. Indeed, the United States has for decades sought to play a more permanent role in Gulf regional security. While the unresolved conflict with Iraq provides the immediate justification, the need for a substantial American force presence in the Gulf transcends the issue of the regime of Saddam Hussein.
>
> (Project for the New American Century 2000: 14)

The report also called for wholesale militarist reorganization in the United States to add momentum to the push for the global hegemony they sought, comparable with what the notorious NSC-68 demanded in 1948 for the Cold War drive. The authors were yearning for a congenial domestic atmosphere: "the process of [such a militaristic] transformation ... is likely to be a long one, absent some catastrophic and catalyzing event—like a new Pearl Harbor" (ibid.: 51). The pretext for "justification" descended on New York and Washington DC on September 11, 2001. The new, much-needed, elusive enemy was christened "terrorism." It would become the blanket term to denigrate all resistance to imperialism. Every shade of opinion, every center of democratic opposition, any political movement or Third World leadership would be branded as terrorism or accomplices of terror.

In October 2001, the "war on terror" was unleashed. The richest country in the world started bombing Afghanistan, home to one of the poorest people on earth (Gerger 2008). In 2002, the then White House Counsel Alberto Gonzales advised the president; "as you have said the war against terrorism is a new kind of war. The nature of the new war places a high premium on other factors, such as the ability to quickly obtain information from captured terrorists and their sponsors in order to avoid further atrocities against American citizens." Gonzales concluded: "In my judgment, this new paradigm renders obsolete Geneva's strict limitations on questioning of enemy prisoners and renders quaint some of its provisions." He argued that by dropping the Geneva Convention, the president would "preserve his flexibility" in the war on terror (quoted in *Newsweek*, May 24, 2004). Again, similar to the precursory Cold War schemes, a new "ruthless" and "dehumanized" enemy had to be invented to paralyze the world with fright and to vindicate imperialist terror. Now, the "baby-eating Chinese communists" of the Cold War era gave way to the "blood-thirsty Arab-Moslem terrorists." Once again, to justify imperialist aggression devoid of moral or legal restraints, and to delude the people to support it, "a new kind of war" had to be contrived. A new militarization was needed through which Capital could indulge itself in global plunder and full-spectrum dominance. The first strike hit the US itself when, on October 26, 2001, Bush signed the Patriot Act. Matthew Rothschild enumerated some of the provisions:

- The government is monitoring your phone calls and can read your e-mails and open your snail mail.
- The government can access records of your large financial transactions, such as buying a house.
- Law enforcement officers can bust into your home when you're not there, riffle through your belongings, plant a recording device on your computer, and leave without notifying you for at least thirty days, and may be a lot more.
- You no longer have the right to protest where the president or vice president can see you, or at major public events when they aren't even present.
- Law enforcement officers can now monitor you in public if you are merely exercising your political rights.
- They can infiltrate your political organizations.

- And they can keep track of you at your place of worship.
- The government can find out from bookstores and libraries the material you've been reading, and the bookstore owner and the librarian can't talk about it, except to their lawyers, for a whole year or more.
- The government can hold you in preventive detention for months on end as a "material witness."
- If you are not a citizen, the government can depart you on a technicality or for mere political association.
- If you are not a citizen, the government can label you an "enemy combatant" and send you to secret prisons around the world, where you may never see the light again, much less a lawyer or a judge.
- And even if you are a citizen, the government can label you an enemy combatant and hold you in solitary confinement here in the United States.

(Rothschild 2007: 5–7)

And later two Americans summarized the frightening practice:

The Nazi government also operated in secrecy ... defending its abuses of power in the name of national security ... The systematic violations of law and civil liberties in America—the operations of secret prison camps; the president's claimed right to torture prisoners of war ... ; the warrantless eavesdropping on phone conversations and e-mail messages; the assumed power of the president to declare martial law and turn America into a police state; the claim that the entire nation is a "battlefield in the war on terror" so that ordinary legal protections don't apply; the president's use of signing statements to nullify legislative constraints on executive power; the threat to prosecute journalists for treason if they reported information that endangers "national security" (as determined exclusively by the president and company); the cancelling of habeas corpus; the labelling as "unlawful enemy combatants" anyone the president deems "hostile" to the interests of the United States; the suspension of legal protection for whistle-blowers who expose government corruption; the attempt to control judicial outcomes (from firing federal prosecutors and intimidating state and federal judges to stocking the Supreme Court with right-wing conservatives)—these and many other antidemocratic, authoritarian activities make the analogy with Nazi Germany not only fitting but compelling ... [T]he quest for money and power has created a dangerous, unholy alliance between big business and government, crushing the American dream, snuffing out civil liberties, and leaving us stranded in a media sea of propaganda and lies ... [T]he American people ... have been shocked and awed into submitting to a megalomaniac government that has made the war on terror a pretext for keeping us all on a short leash ...

(Cohen and Fraser 2007: 292–293)

A category called "enemy combatant," that strips a person of his or her humanity, was legalized. Government-sponsored abduction was called "extraordinary rendition." Legionnaire armies were created through hired private contractors authorized to torture and kill.

On March 2003 the invasion of Iraq unleashed the militaristic dynamics intrinsic to globalization/NWO. In the wake of empire building and faithful to his motto ("You are either with us or against us"), President Bush pushed aside the United Nations, the world public opinion, and even NATO and traditional allies like France and Germany. Any semblance to international legitimacy, let alone international legality, was treated with utter contempt and arrogance. The message was clear: The US was dead-set to go it alone if need be. As a matter of fact, international rules, instruments and alliances were seen as obstacles to be dispensed with. Unrestrained unilateral militarism was the rule of the day. In the name of the "New Order" the capitalist colossus was set to wreak havoc.

The Vietnam Syndrome in Reverse

This was a peculiar type of "Vietnam Syndrome" in reverse (i.e., inflicting upon the rest of the world fatal fear of dreading the ire of the powers-that-be and thus effectively forfeiting its humanity). The United States targeted the region also to rob the region of its important resources for a protracted anti-imperialist struggle. The Region's rich cultural heritage and human potential together with oil wealth formed the moral and material basis for sustaining a prolonged struggle and this challenge was countered with Bush's "preventive war" lawlessness. "If you confess you will be damned and condemned. If you do not confess, you will be damned and condemned, this time for perjury." The inquisitor Bernard Gui spoke these words in Umberto Eco's novel *The Name of the Rose*. This was how the Bush administration approached Saddam. Saddam would be damned and condemned whether or not he confessed to the existence of weapons of mass destruction. In the end, the Inquisition justice was meted out to him; the country was incinerated. In the Middle Ages, it was permissible to keep the relatives of a fugitive as hostages. From 1991 onwards, the Iraqi people—old, young, sick, healthy, men, women, and children—were effectively taken hostage and punished in lieu of Saddam. In the Middle Ages, it was tradition to display the corpses of the vanquished enemy for all to see, just the way the images of the bodies of Saddam's sons and grandson were aired on TV. Another medieval tradition of plunder and pillage after occupying enemy territory was also repeated by the US in Baghdad as the marines lay siege to the city.

In the twenty-first century, the United States began to impose an "Inquisition justice" on the peoples of the Middle East. Under the aegis of the omnipotent and omnipresent prince-president, the guardians of the universal truth, together with the sword of the capitalist faith and acting under the guidance of Capital, started waging holy wars, excommunicating and punishing the heretics who dared to question the liberal dogma, plundering their assets, profaning their land, punishing blasphemy, torturing the infidel, enslaving the pariah. The new church in Washington DC was spreading out the sacred scriptures of the IMF and the World Bank. The US was set to recreate the world after its own image and realize her divine "manifest destiny." The blasphemous Middle East was to pay the price. The original sin of the targeted Middle East was unabashedly explained by the Senior Researcher at the US Naval War College, Professor Thomas P. M. Barnett who wrote in 2004 that those states, which are not "connected" to globalization, should be punished and forced into the current of globalization. He called those "non-integrating" regions that are "disconnected" from the "functioning core" of the globalizing world, "ozone zones" (Barnett 2004: 4). The theoretician of the Pentagon and the ideologue of globalization, identified the "true enemy" in the Middle East: "That enemy is neither a religion (Islam) nor a place (the Middle East), but a condition-disconnectedness" (ibid.: 49). For Barnett, this was also the real crime of Saddam Hussein:

> Saddam Hussein's outlaw regime was dangerously disconnected from the globalising world—from our rule sets, our norms, and all the ties that bind the Core together ... He was the Demon of Disconnectedness, and he deserves death ... If America can enable Iraq's reconnection to the world, then we will have won a real victory in the globalization struggle, and the transformation of the Middle East will begin in earnest.
>
> (Barnett 2004: 286)

Barnett's strategic outlook clarified US policy: "connecting the Middle East to the outside world in not about replacing leadership, by and large, but about expanding connectivity in any form possible" (ibid.: 215). Therefore, "we are never leaving the Middle East until the Middle East joins the Core (ibid.: 289)." "America ultimately does not transform the Middle East to defeat terrorism, contain Islam, secure oil, or defend Israel. We seek to transform the region to end its disconnectedness" (ibid.: 330). Therefore, no region or country could feel safe anymore:

> America is prepared to wage war in Southwest Asia, defined as Central Asia and the Persian Gulf, because the energy that flows out of these regions is a global connectivity worth protecting ... [Ready to fight everywhere] although we will seek to limit our exposure there until our efforts to export security to the Persian Gulf bring about lasting changes not just for Iraq, but for Iran, Syria, Lebanon, and Saudi Arabia itself ... Finally, we bring war against the entities that threaten global economic stabilisation ... We are prepared to bring war anywhere in the world, but our focus in terms of frequency lies inside the [disconnected] gap.
>
> (Barnett 2004: 334)

In the whole process, however, the twisted logic of imperialism fell prey to momentous blunders. First, it misread a lesson of history. Blinded by their technological superiority in the means of violence and by the capacity for "overkill," American imperialists assumed the enduring supremacy of machines over humankind. They thought of themselves as capable of eradicating once and for all notions of human dignity, free spirit, and innate antagonism to exploitation and oppression. In their inherent racism, they anticipated from the toiling masses of the desolate East obedience to their mastery and awe in the face of their terror.

The Iraqi Resistance and the American Moral Defeat in Abu Ghraib

The Iraqi resistance coupled with outspoken defiance of hundreds of millions all over the world changed the equation. Bertrand Russell once observed; "when the defensive is strong, civilization makes progress, and when the offensive is strong men revert towards barbarism" (Coates 1984: 154). The aggressors put their faith in the barbarism of the offense. The Iraqi resistance showed to the chagrin of the oppressors the endurance of human values, human dignity, and the ascendancy of man over the machine, in short, supremacy of civilization over barbarism. So, the Greater Middle Eastern Project (GMEP) was announced as a policy shift and reaction to the American predicament in Iraq. The grandiose scheme of military dominance in the Middle East to be pursued by the invasion of Syria, Iran, and even Saudi Arabia, so arrogantly espoused by the Neoconservative ideologues was to be modified.

The Bush administration, entrapped in the quagmire of its own creation, had to change track in Iraq. For, indeed, the GMEP was not only a break with American strategic unilateralism in its Middle Eastern policy signified by the Bush administration's pleading to the Europeans, the NATO, and even the despised United Nations to give a hand to the ailing USA but also, in a more profound sense, a timid confession of mortifying failure and admission of military incapacity to subdue the peoples' resistance. Thus, on May 12, 2004, speaking in the US Senate, Chairman of the Joint Chiefs of Staff General Richard Myers said, "There is ... no way to militarily win in Iraq." He also provided his prescription: "This process has to be internationalized." Joseph Cirincione and Anatol Lieven, both senior associates at the Carnegie Endowment, wrote in the May 17, 2004 issue of the *International Tribune*, "The American position in Iraq is untenable ... To this military defeat has been added the moral defeat of Abu Ghraib prison ..." The authors recommend putting together a "regional coalition" that would allow an "eventual US withdrawal." And, in *Washington Post* of May 10, 2004, Sebastian Mallaby articulated the new solution which he called "internationalist imperialism": "What's needed is a new style of imperialism, legitimised by international institutions and to some extent enforced by them."

The new initiative meant a methodological change in aggression. The US was now initiating a new mode of hegemony in the region—one of cultural hegemony, dominance over values to alleviate military impotence. For the time being, "soft power" would complement physical variants of militarism. This type of governance depends on deceit and corrupting the culture, values, social mores of a people and their indigenous institutions. It relies on more latent, structural violence instead of manifest military violence. It depends on importation of the dehumanized values of capitalism and on the treacherous destruction of other, traditional ways of life. The masters would, then, solve the "clash of civilizations" by destroying the vanquished and by assimilating the victims into their fold! One of the main aims of this arduous process was to integrate, especially the elites, into the value system as defined by the United States and international Capital. This was intended to create an "organic dominance" by transforming the US into an organic element, an integral component, a constituent ingredient of the established order; in other words, fusion with the order of things and all aspects of the daily lives of the people. Thus, US would exert its hegemony and reproduce itself structurally within the "domestic system" itself. This was a peculiar variant of nation-building and a method to conquer from within by becoming a fifth column in its own right and to break the will of the people for eventual assimilation. The final aim was to insure American hegemony and enslavement of the people in the collective mind of the very society under control. Thus, the subjugated peoples themselves would maintain American dominance.

As indicated earlier, this naturally necessitated extra tools in addition to sheer military violence. A factsheet prepared by the White House Office of the Press Secretary on June 9, 2004 for the G-8 summit included a "Plan of Support" enumerating bribes to be distributed in the form of education assistance, scholarships, literacy campaigns, teacher training, funds for small businesses, financial support for employment, sponsorship of young and women entrepreneurs, and other schemes such as "Network of Funds to coordinate the work of development institutions and international financial institutions working in the region, and a Task Force on Investment to assist the region's efforts to improve the business climate" (University of Toronto G8 Information Centre 2004). The military adventure was in disrepute under the rubble of war and resistance. After the reverberations of popular defiance, the American imperialists have become disoriented and begun to wander off after another hopeless goal. To squeeze social complexity into the straight jacket of cultural standardization, and to impose a single "hegemony of values" on humanity was doomed to failure. It certainly did not succeed in Iraq. The United States failed miserably to turn the people of the region into one soulless and slavish flock.

The Arab Spring and ISIL as a Handy Imperial Instrument

The rejection of the United States project by the peoples of the region was already a fact of life and resistance at its peak when the 2007-2008 crisis struck at the heart of the neo-liberal globalization project. In many countries hit by the crisis the emergency was met by another type of violence; trillions of dollars were siphoned from the public to buy "globalization junk" from failed corporations and banks. This was more than an ordinary cyclical crisis of capitalism, but a profound cataclysm of the accumulation mode itself. Massive state intervention making a mockery of liberal pretensions saved the day only to pave the way for more crisis. In the meantime, the Arab masses taking their freedom into their own hands rose up against local tyrants and foreign masters. After the initial shock and hesitation, the first reaction to the "Arab Spring" unfolded in Egypt. General Sisi would soon be welcomed in power centers as a great statesman. The Egyptian coup was followed by the Saudi action in Bahrain who were mandated to crush the uprising there. Then came direct Western intervention in Libya.[6] In the end, the West has become, directly or by proxy, the principal opposition in the Syrian civil war.

Two years after the civil war Edward N. Luttwak who at times has served as consultant to the US Department of State and the National Security Council, the US Navy, Army, and the Air Force advocated keeping Syria in stalemate:

> There is only one outcome that the United States can possibly favour: Indefinite draw ... Maintaining a stalemate should be America's objective. And the only

possible method for achieving this is to arm the rebels when it seems that Mr. Assad's forces are ascendant and to stop supplying the rebels if they actually seem to be winning.

(Luttwak 2013)

More importantly, he claimed that "[t]his strategy actually approximates the Obama administration's policy so far" (ibid.). In the meantime, another useful tool emerged from the bloodshed. The Islamic State of Iraq and the Levant (IS) harvested its lethal fruit from the land prepared by the American aggression in the Middle East. Seeds of militarization were sowed copiously in the arable land. The selected fields were cultivated by despair, helplessness and anger. They were fertilized by hatred and violence, watered by the blood of the innocent. To think that it came out of nowhere, developed in a vacuum, or that it is solely a local phenomenon is fallacious. Oppression, degradation and dehumanization breed all sorts of reactions, protests and resistance. To divorce the emergence of IS from Abu Ghraib and Guantanamo or from the terror of the "war on terror" may even lead to the Islamophobic variant of racism. Although local sources and dynamics do play a definitive role in its operations, to evaluate IS purely as a regional phenomenon would be misleading. Irrespective of its seemingly local socio-cultural underpinnings, IS is a demon created by externally imposed conditions. Fundamentally, it is an implant rejected by the body politic of the Islamic world. At any rate, it was indeed a handy instrument.

Reagan called the Taliban "freedom fighters"; the CIA educated its cadres, and provided them with weapons. Then the US Army occupied Afghanistan to rescue the Afghans from the Taliban. Similarly, the Western forces under US command entered the Middle East en masse from the land, sea and air to protect and save it from the IS. For the United States, the IS threat provided the perfect pretext for the long-sought desire to re-design the Iraqi regime without Maliki, not only to check Iran, but also to use the country once again as a military post for further incursions into the Middle East. It terrified and cornered Iran. It also terrorized and disciplined many others in the region and elsewhere, turning them into malleable material for the ominous American alchemy. The "American shield," like its "nuclear umbrella" in the Cold War, provided the Empire's plebeians with shelter. The two militarisms fed upon each other, trapping millions in a vicious cycle of mutual hatred and ever-escalating violence.

Conclusion

The anti-terror hysteria and the new "terror laws" have created new prejudice and persecution, one of the main victims of which are immigrants from the Middle East. The witch-hunt is globalized as well. Pariahization follows the Middle Eastern in immigrant life too. In many Western countries, if one's speech sounds like Arabic, if a person looks "foreign" or his/her attire appears "Islamic," the already demonized victim instantly becomes easy prey for the racist predator. No end is in sight for the tragic story of the Middle East. On the contrary, the deluge is overwhelming the whole world. Now the populist-nationalist militarists as a sui generis amalgamation of the neo-liberal globalization process and the neoconservative project of the NWO are taking over the unfinished task of the War on Terror for world domination. And, trapped within the Empire's domestic and foreign predicament, the world is passing through multifaceted crises, drifting on the edge of abyss into Armageddon. Amidst appalling poverty, disheartening inequalities, daunting injustices, the terrifying global ecological disaster, agonizing societal moral breakdown, and tragic human spiritual death create a dark hole of diabolical emptiness into which our blue planet is bound to be sucked if resistance fails.

Haluk Gerger is former assistant professor at the University of Ankara, Turkey and an author of articles and books on the Middle East, US imperialism, Turkish foreign policy, and nuclear weapons. His teaching post was terminated after the 1980 coup and he was twice imprisoned for his human rights activism.

Notes

1. See also Gerger (2000).
2. For disturbing statistical evidence concerning the US see Brouwer (1988).
3. In the 1990s the share of manufacturing in direct foreign investments in the Third World fell to 50 percent (Miller 1993: 16–19).
4. While the services accounted for about a quarter of all foreign direct investment stock in early 1970s, their share doubled to 50 percent by the late 1980s (Horsman and Marchall 1994: xii, 51).
5. According to the estimates of The International Labor Organization, "30 percent of the world's labor force of about 2.5 billion people is either unemployed or underemployed" (Broad 1995: 24).
6. For the linkages see Prashad (2012).

References

Ahmed, Aijaz. 2004. *A Reflection on Our Times: Revolution, Restoration and Resistance*. Hyderabad: Prajasakti Book House.
Amin, Samir. 1993. "The Issue of Democracy in the Contemporary Third World." In *Low Intensity Democracy: Political Power in the New World Order*, edited by Barry Gills, Joel Rocamora and Richard Wilson, 59–79. London: Pluto Press.
Barnet, Richard and John Cavanagh. 1994. *Global Dreams: Imperial Corporations and the New World Order*. New York: Simon and Schuster.
Barnett, Thomas P. M. 2004. *The Pentagon's New Map: War and Peace in the Twenty-First Century*. New York: G. P. Putnam's Son.
Bello, Walden, Shea Cunningham and Bill Rau. 1999. *Dark Victory: The United States, Structural Adjustment and Global Poverty*. London: Pluto Press.
Broad, Dave. 1995. "Globalization versus Labor." *Monthly Review* 7(47): 20–31. https://doi.org/10.14452/MR-047-07-1995-11_2
Brouwer, Steve. 1988. *Sharing the Pie: A Disturbing picture of the US Economy in the 1980s*. Carlisle/ PA: Big Picture Books.

Chandrasekhar, C. P. 2004. "The World of International Finance." *Frontline* 21(23). Retrieved from www.countercurrents.org/econonmy-061104.htm (accessed January 16, 2019).
Coates, Ken. 1984. *The Most Dangerous Decade*. Nottingham: Spokesman.
Cohen, Elliot D. and Bruce W. Fraser. 2007. *The Last days of Democracy: How Big Media and Power-Hungry Government are Turning America into a Dictatorship*. New York: Prometheus Books.
Fields, A. Belden and Wolf-Dieter Narr. 1992. "Human Rights as a Holistic Concept." *Human Rights Quarterly* 1(1419): 1–20. https://doi.org/10.2307/762549
Friedman, Thomas. 2000. *The Lexus and the Olive Tree—Understanding Globalization*. New York: First Anchor Books.
Fukuyama, Francis. 1989. "The End of History?" *The National Interest* 16: 3–18.
Fukuyama, Francis. 1992. *The End of History and the Last Man*. London: Hamish Hamilton.
Furedi, Frank. 1994. *The New Ideology of Imperialism: Renewing the Moral Imperative*. London: Pluto Press.
Gerger, Haluk. 2000. "Globalization, the Highest Stage of Imperialism." Retrieved from www.assmp.org/spip.php?article133 (accessed October 5, 2019).
Gerger, Haluk. 2008. "On the US 'War on Terror'." Retrieved from https://ilps.info/en/2008/06/18/on-the-us-qwar-on-terrorq (accessed October 6, 2019).
Gordon, David M. 1988. "The Global Economy: New Edifice or Crumbling Foundations?" *New Left Review* 68: 24–65.
Guillen, Mauro and Suarez, Sandra L. 2015. "The Global Financial and Economic Crisis: A Drama in Three Acts." In *Globalization: The Critical Phase*, edited by Brian Spooner, 115–142. Philadelphia, PA: University of Pennsylvania Museum.
Haass, Richard N. 2003. "Sovereignty: Existing Rights, Evolving Responsibilities." Retrieved from www.state.gov/s/p/rem/2003/16648pf.htm (accessed July 21, 2019).
Hayter, Teresa. 1992. *The Creation of World Poverty*. London: Pluto Press.
Hobsbawm, Eric. 2000. *In Conversation with Antonio Polito*, trans. Allan Cameron. London: Abacus.
Horsman, Mathew and Andrew Marshall. 1994. *After the Nation-State: Citizens, Tribalism and the New World Disorder*. London: HarperCollins.
Luttwak, Edward N. 2013. "Keep Syria in a Stalemate." *International Herald Tribune*, August 24.
Miller, Robert. 1993. "Determinants of US Manufacturing Investment Abroad." *Finance and Development* 30: 16–18.
Petras, James and Henry Veltmeyer. 2001. *Globalization Unmasked: Imperialism in the 21st Century*. Delhi: Madhyam Books.
Prashad, Vijay. 2012. *Arab Spring, Libyan Winter*. Edinburgh: AK Press.
Project for the New American Century. 2000. *Rebuilding America's Defenses: Strategy, Forces and Resources for a New Century*. Washington, DC: Project for the New American Century.
Robinson, William I. and Jerry Harris. 2000. "Towards a Global Ruling Class? Globalization and the Transnational Capitalist Class." *Science and Society* 64(1).
Rothschild, Matthew. 2007. *You Have No Rights: Stories of America in an Age of Repression*. New York: The New Press.
Rubin, Robert E. and Jacob Weisberg. 2003. *In an Uncertain World: Tough Choices from Wall Street to Washington*. New York: Random House.
Schuurman, Frans J. 1993. "Introduction: Development Theory in the 1990s." In *Beyond the Impasse: New Directions in Development Theory*, edited by Frans J. Schuurman, 1–48. London: Zed Books.

Singer, Daniel. 1994. "Europe's Crises." *Monthly Review* 3(46): 86–100. https://doi.org/10.14452/MR-046-03-1994-07_7
Sweezy, Paul M. 1994. "The Triumph of Finance Capital." *Monthly Review* 46(2): 1–7. https://doi.org/10.14452/MR-046-02-1994-06_1
Szentes, Tamas. 1988. *The Transformation of the World Economy: A New Directions and New Interests.* London: Zed Books.
Tabb, William K. 2001. *The Amoral Elephant: Globalization and the Struggle for Social Justice in the Twenty-First Century.* New York: Monthly Review Press.
Thurow, Lester. 1993. *Head to Head: The Coming Economic Battle among Japan, Europe, and America.* New York: Warner Books.
United Nations. 2001. *United Nations Human Development Report.* Cary, NC: Oxford University Press.
University of Toronto G8 Information Centre. 2004. "G8 Plan of Support for Reform (Sea Island)." Retrieved from www.g8.utoronto.ca/summit/2004seaisland/reform.html (accessed January 20, 2019).

3

Peoples against a New Cold War: Nuclear Imperialism or Dialogue for Reconciliation

Kinhide Mushakoji

> I have been oppressed a lot over the past forty years. However, no oppression could break my will to devote my life to inter-Korean reconciliation, cooperation, and unification. I have cherished the passionate desire to dedicate my life to a peaceful reunification of our fatherland, which is also the sincere wish of 70 million Koreans. For this task, Chairman Kim and I would like to unite our hearts in laying the foundation for mutual trust and peaceful co-existence and co-prosperity of the South and North. Let us all gather our strength and wisdom to drive out the fear of war from our land and open the new age of interchange and cooperation.
> —Dae-jung Kim, *Conscience in Action* (2019: 650)

Introduction

We are entering into a new Cold War. The first phase of the post-Cold War period was marked by an age of exogenous human rights interventions led by the trilateral hegemony of Atlantic Liberalism. We are now entering the second phase of the post-Cold War complex reality. In that, we find the emergence of two subaltern trends, one developed by subaltern states, especially in North-East Asia, and the other among subaltern peoples, animated by post-modern global citizens in close alliance with indigenous peoples and minority identity communities. These states and peoples are post-modern in the sense that they are part of a reaction to the modernism of the first phase of the post-Cold War world. This phase was marked by a "modern" attempt to materialize the Kantian global community of nation states with "eternal peace,"[1] based on the Westphalian state system with an inter-state institution created by the Atlantic Liberals who were founders of the League of Nations and the United Nations. It is they who control the inter-state or inter-national community composed of the UN member-states. After the defeat of the Soviet bloc, in the first post-Cold War phase it was hoped that the dream of trilateral hegemony of the Atlantic states (plus non-Atlantic/non-Western Japan) "at last" would be materialized. This "liberal" power-bloc remained the unique hegemonic state bloc, which was composed of the so-called "industrial democracies" led by the liberalists of the West, with Japan as a non-Western partner (after World War II) forming the American-European-Japanese trilateral global hegemony. The Anglo-American powers took the first steps towards it on the basis of the

Atlantic Charter adopted before World War II. This was forged to fight Hitler and his axis allies. Its "liberalism" gradually became democratic and welfare-oriented in its fight against the Communist bloc, and subsequently developmentalist in the face of North–South gaps. It was an anti-communist Atlantic Liberalism formed by the industrial democracies who adopted a universalist policy to spread democracy and human rights throughout the non-Western regions. This exogenous human rights approach was accentuated with the fall of the Communist bloc, which left the United States and its Atlantic trilateral bloc supreme in the post-Cold War world (Gill 1990).[2] However, this supremacy could not be maintained for long as relatively powerful states outside the Atlantic trilateral bloc (China in particular) have gained confidence as active participants in the global neo-liberal economy. This has contributed to an emerging new Cold War. This chapter argues that the way to overcome this war lies among the post-modern global citizens who align with a multitude of subaltern communities across the world. In that, the importance of treating denuclearization as an anti-colonial project, reconsideration of the One Belt One Road project as an anti-imperialist program and the recovery of the liberative cosmovisions of the major religious traditions and indigenous traditions are reiterated.

The War on Terror, East Asian Occidentalism and Nuclear Imperialism

The turn of the new millennium was characterized by the start of the "war on terror" in the Middle East and the emergence of Occidentalism in the Far East, to use a Euro-centric division of the world. Nuclear weapons continued to be a burning issue in the post-Cold War world. We propose here a new concept, "nuclear imperialism." Nuclearization as a hegemonic regional project took place in both the Middle East and the Far East. In both regions, the Western powers exercised their imperialist interests in accordance with the pre-existing geo-historical dynamics. In the Far East, a made-in-Japan Orientalism was at the root of Japanese imperial and imperialist aggression, colonization and occupation. Japan legitimized its intrusion into Korea and China by the need to modernize (i.e., Westernize the two neighbors while "resisting" Westernization). Japan's role, perceived by its rulers, was to resist Western imperialism by modernizing itself and its neighbors by annexing them into its imperialist "lebensraum." Japan experienced, in Hiroshima and Nagasaki, how its easy-going imitation of Western imperialism led to nuclear retaliation. This nuclear traumatism is still dividing its citizens into those who repent the Japanese imperialist aggression and those who believe that it was Japan's opposition to the United States that spelt disaster and that Japanese imperialist aggression could be repeated if it is done under the nuclear umbrella of the United States.

The nuclearization of imperialism does not necessarily imply the use of nuclear weapons by imperialist nations. It began as an anti-fascist move to prevent Hitler's Germany from inventing a nuclear bomb. Once invented by the Atlantic Alliance, its first use in Hiroshima and Nagasaki was to penalize imperial Japan and warn the Soviet Union. In Las Palmas, a monument representing Article 9 of the Japanese Constitution declares that Japan, responsible for its imperialist expansion, renounces the use of military forces for aggression and repents for the violation of rights of all peoples of the world to live in peace. The citizens of the Canary Islands who were fighting against the Spanish government's decision to join NATO built this monument in Plaza de Hiroshima y Nagasaki. It links Japan's repentance about its imperialist aggression with the tragic nuclear attack by the United States on Hiroshima and Nagasaki. The close link between imperialism and nuclearization is well represented by this monument in Plaza de Hiroshima y Nagasaki.

The citizens of Japan should indeed repent about Japanese aggression. And then they should criticize the United States for retaliating by a nuclear attack on the people of Hiroshima and Nagasaki who were not responsible for the imperialist aggression of Japan. The nuclear weapons cannot be separated from the historical context in which they were invented which includes Japan's aggression against its neighbouring countries and its participation in the imperialist race to avoid becoming a colony of the Western powers. Nuclear weapons were invented as part of this historical period of colonialist competition between major powers, and this caused imperialism to become nuclear. The abolition of nuclear weapons would be a total negation of the twentieth century colonial expansion. Instead, the twenty-first century is becoming the age of full-fledged nuclear imperialism, inaugurated officially by the Trump administration's 2018 *Nuclear Posture Review*, which turned the US nuclear weaponry simply into the key component of its military panoply enabling it to cope up with any foreign attack on any level of intensity. This was called "flexible" response and is combined with the world-wide spread of US military bases, "forward deployment." The new treaty on the abolition of nuclear weapons is, in a sense, the target of the Nuclear Posture Review which does not want to recognize the ethical reason of its ban. It is crucial to establish the unambiguous relationship between the abolition of nuclear weapons and the right to live in peace. This is why, within the Japanese context, Article 9 of its Constitution has to be proclaimed incontrovertible with respect to the abolition of nuclear weapons.

From the point of view of post-modern global citizens, the modern Atlantic Liberalism—and its exogenous efforts to spread Westminster democracy and Westphalian human rights—has to be replaced by a post-modern age of endogenous democracy and human rights. In other words, the Atlantic Liberal process of globalization-from-above—which is meant to maintain the nuclear weapons in the hands of the hegemonic powers—has to be checked by a globalization-from-below through a non-proliferation of nuclear weapons and stopping today's nuclear imperialism. We will review the different aspects of such a major shift in international political economy including the anti-imperialist program of One Belt One Road, which should integrate de-nuclearization based on popular participation from below in lieu of focus on Westphalian states, thus opening the global arena to indigenous peoples and multi-livelihood migrant diaspora communities.

Anti-Terror Self-Protective Atlantic Liberalism: Opening the Second Phase of Post-Cold War Globalization

During the first phase of post-Cold War globalization the most important attempt to eliminate any resistance to the monopoly of violence by the Atlantic Liberal hegemonic states was humanitarian and human rights-based intervention in the other parts of the world. This kind of intervention has been presented as an important obligation for all human rights defenders. Humanitarian intervention became the main tool of implementation of international human rights. There was, nevertheless, an attempt to define, unambiguously, and restrict the conditions of legitimate humanitarian intervention using human security as the basis for critical analysis. This was done by a group of European experts chaired by Mary Kaldor who presented the Barcelona Report on humanitarian intervention to the European community (Kaldor 2007).

Notwithstanding, humanitarian intervention became a typical tool for the exogenous imposition of human rights by the West on the Rest. This exogenous imposition of human rights and humanitarian intervention by the United States with European support has kicked off a new kind of civilizational conflict, though not one due to the reasons Samuel Huntington has underlined (Huntington 1993).[3] An anti-terrorist movement in Europe and North America helped develop a new racism against non-Western peoples, like the "Je suis Charlie" ("I am Charlie") movement begun in Paris, on the basis of the right to freedom of expression. There is a very thin line of demarcation between this kind of narrow perception of human rights and the ideologies of the emerging neo-fascist groups in Europe. Nevertheless it is important to point out that this European xenophobic reaction—based on human rights and a liberal right of self-expression—gave not only an occasion for a large sector of the European north-Atlantic Liberals to manifest the Euro-centric exclusivist view of human rights, but also made space for a diversified group of intellectuals who declared that they were not "Charlie" and were opposed to the disrespecting of Islam and its Prophet (Barrett 2015). This is a "clash within" (Nussbaum 2009).[4]

Trump's Opposition to Atlantic Liberalism and Far East Occidentalists

Atlantic Liberalism has made Europe and the United States into targets of "Arab" and "Muslim" attacks. More generally, Atlantic Liberalism, including the exogenous imposition of human rights, has become the target of intellectual criticism of "Occidentalism." Ian Buruma and Avishai Margalit have given this term to the denial of the positive aspects of Atlantic Liberalism (Buruma and Margalit 2005). They propose this concept to refer to the discourse associated with the total denial of all the universal values proposed by the human rights discourse presented by the West. For Occidentalism, the exogenous imposition of universal values, beginning with human rights, is believed to be the tool of the colonialist West to force the Rest of the world to follow the West. In fact, Occidentalism is a mirror image of Orientalism, which creates stereotypical images about the

West and East respectively while dividing and combining the geopolitical spaces at the same time. It is a result of the Western colonial practice. This can be called "Orientalist–Occidentalist divide and combine."

The Abe government, representing Japanese Occidentalism,[5] simply denies all the colonialist atrocities committed by Japanese imperialism and its invasions in the East and Southeast Asian countries (Mushakoji 2015). Japan strengthened this position in the face of increasing demands for apologies and state compensation made by the victims of military sexual slavery of comfort women and of the Nanjing massacre. China's Occidentalism started with the Tiananmen incident and labor camps for human rights supporters. The issue of abduction of Japanese citizens combined with the questions of internments of foreigners in labor camps by the North Korean regime (DPRK) defined its Occidentalism. In Myanmar, the Rohingya Muslim issue has become a case where the human right stance of Aung San Suu Kyi is now criticized by the liberal industrial democratic states who had previously supported her fight against the military regime of Myanmar. In Sri Lanka, the USA/UK axis which supported the Sri Lankan state's military victory over the Liberation Tigers of Tamil Eelam (LTTE) at the expense of thousands of lives later went on raising issues of violation of human rights by the Sri Lankan security forces in the last phase of the war. These criticisms have come to the fore as Chinese–Sri Lankan economic relationships increased. In this way, human rights issues which are seen in the case of the Middle East as questions of Christian–Muslim or Euro/American–Muslim conflict, are defined, especially in the three Occidentalist states, China, DPRK and Japan, as a conflict caused by the West's imposition of universalist human rights exogenously on the Far East and the latter's endogenous reaction to it.

Trump's Integral Nuclear Imperialism and Kim Jong-un's Challenge

Occidentalism is closely associated with the fight against nuclear imperialism. The effort of President Trump to keep the "American Lake" solely open to US nuclear submarines became recently the cause of an Occidentalist reaction by the DPRK whereby it attempted to develop across the Pacific a nuclear strategic situation of "mutually assured destruction" (MAD) with the United States (Hayes 1987). Chairman Kim Jung-un wants to prove that MAD can be built between a non-Western nation and the United States. Trump is making Atlantic Liberalism openly meaningless by his "America first" policy, which does not try to cover up the close relationship between its human rights and humanitarian intervention in the name of world peace and the US hegemonic national interests hidden behind pretentions of universalist values. In this sense, the most conspicuous manifestation of Trump's America First policy has been its nuclear policy. The *Nuclear Posture Review* of 2018 is a very revealing document, which justifies a radical shift from the previous Nuclear Strategic Posture, which was based on an attempt to treat nuclear weapons strategically (i.e., as weapons not used in open conflicts). This strategic posture was adopted by the United States together with the Soviet Union. It was a system controlling the building up of each other's nuclear arsenal so that they would mutually cancel-out in such a way that even if one side attempts to annihilate the opponent by an unexpected nuclear strike, the other side would be able to strike back and annihilate the first striker by a second strike. Nuclear weapons were considered so deadly that they were never treated together with the non-nuclear conventional arsenal. Under President Trump, this distinction has been entirely eliminated by a logic justifying a radical shift of the nuclear strategy. The logic is based on nuclear imperialism, which aims at preparing the ground to use nuclear weapons in the face of all possible attacks on all levels of military intensity, from space wars to low-intensity conflicts, including non-violent demonstrations.

The DPRK special unit which conducted all the experiments, both nuclear and ballistic, was the Nuclear Strategic Unit. This unit was clearly instructed in secret by some Russian experts. It was an entirely meaningless effort to prove to President Trump the DPRK's capacity to develop a second-strike capability, making any first US strike a meaningless suicidal action. Trump had already dropped the MAD strategic "rationale." Kim Jong-un, nevertheless, succeeded in convincing the military and intelligent services that the young technocrats of his generation sent to Europe, Russia and Ukraine by him were not potential traitors siding with the Western diplomats and economic planners. They were hailed by the DPRK military as national heroes who proved the military parity between North Korea and the United States. The DPRK leader's move succeeded in convincing President Trump, that the demonstration of the US's overwhelming military might by the US–Republic of Korea joint military maneuver should be interrupted at least during their negotiations about the de-nuclearization of Korea, which would mean for the Koreas, including the Republic of Korea, the renunciation of the United States' deployment of nuclear divisions in the Korean peninsula. By these moves Trump is contradicting his 2018 *Nuclear Posture Review*, which presupposes a forward deployment of US nuclear forces in all regions of the world including the Korean peninsula.

The negotiations between the military command of both the DPRK in the North and the RK in the South already reached an agreement on partial de-nuclearized zones on land and in the sea. Their approach is an example of the creation of denuclearized regions preparing for the full application of the treaty on the abolition of nuclear weapons. It implies the revision of the US's forward deployment strategy into a strategy of forward disengagement,[6] which needs to be applied all around the world to stop the present trend leading to a second Cold War.

The One Belt One Road Program as an Answer of the Rest to the Colonial Expansion of the West

One typical case of a nationalist subaltern state project can be mentioned here as a program based on a historically shared belief. It is the One Belt One Road (OBOR) project proposed by China. To define China as a subaltern neoliberal state needs some explanation. It is based on the fact that China does not share the historical background of neoliberalism, which finds its origin in Atlantic Liberalism.

China, since Deng Xiaoping's liberalization of the economy, has participated in the 1980s' global neoliberal "production capitalist" competition and the 1990s' neoliberal "financial capitalist" competition. It was forced to do so by the G7/G8 trilateral hegemony, and it profits now from its successful competition with the hegemonic states through the foundation of the Asian Infrastructure Investment Bank and the OBOR project, which are both a strange mixture of neo-liberalism and anti-colonialist Occidentalism.

The OBOR project has two faces. It is a short-run plan to develop an international network of development poles where China can build diaspora communities to give jobs to its excess labor force who settle down in China Towns of the diaspora. However, OBOR has another face. It has been projected by Xi Jinping as a long-range civilizational vision to start a process of endogenous development in the opposite direction of the Western colonization process, reversing the road that the West took through the Pacific and Indian Ocean reaching China at the time of the Opium War, after having colonized India and the South East Asian states. China wants to use its financial wealth to contribute to the development of the Eurasian continent and Africa by linking the two silk-roads in the arid zone and the maritime passage.

To oppose OBOR, Japan supports India, which wants to have a free and open Pacific/Indian Ocean development program reaching Africa. The OBOR program counteracting Western-led neo-colonialist development may become a new kind of Chinese colonialist expansion if the short-term Chinese diaspora network becomes the objective of colonial concessions absorbing the Chinese excess working population. However, if it can combine with the Pacific/Indian Ocean development project, it can become an Afro-Asian project. To do so, China and India will have to return to the Nehru–Zhou Enlai declaration which includes the two principles of peaceful coexistence and equal mutual benefit. Such a long-range project may become an occasion for Japan to play a positive role, together with China and India, as a repentant colonial expansionist state which joined the North Atlantic countries. With these two possibilities, negative or positive, the second phase of the post-Cold War globalization is characterized by the activities of two Occidentalist states. One of them, Japan, has been working within the conditionalities of the OECD countries including human rights performance of the developing countries. The other is the OBOR program. China is a complete outsider to trilateral hegemony and Atlantic Liberalism. The OBOR program may develop, in the near future, a certain number of Chinese diaspora communities in the Eurasian continent. This will become a source of insecurity with both negative and positive alternative possibilities in the second phase of post-Cold War globalization.

The OBOR program is not a developmentalist project based on exogenously defined universalist principles. It is proposed as endogenous multi-national participatory activities of workers and planners with a variety of religious and cultural backgrounds and ethnic identities. This is where new sources of discrimination and/or of promotion of human rights will have to be monitored and become the focus of UN human rights activities. This makes the mere continuation of existing

Western-led human rights discourse unsatisfactory for the protection and promotion of human rights in the Pacific/Indian Ocean region, in the Eurasian continent and in Africa. Besides, there is a human rights concern; a necessity to develop a systematic program to minimize cultural conflicts and to maximize the possibility for positive processes of rights to peace and cultural development.

The OBOR program of China should be well coordinated with the "One Road" needs of the Pacific/Indian Ocean region through a dialogue between Chinese Confucianism, the diverse cultural traditions in India, the arid "One Belt" Turkic Islamic cultures, the Oceanic indigenous traditions and universal human rights. OBOR should not be simply a civilizational project of China. It should be a cooperative and pluralist project owned by all the above-mentioned partners whose major civilizations and indigenous traditions embody the greatest spiritual and religious riches of humanity.

We must return to the 1954 Nehru–Zhou Enlai *Five Principles of Peaceful Coexistence*, especially the last two principles of "peaceful co-existence" and "equal mutual benefit" which declares that China and India agree on renouncing their claims on civilizational supremacy and want to build together an egalitarian world within each country and between both of them. In both civilizations there are spiritual and religious resources that promote a just rule that adopts egalitarian anti-imperialist principles. They both need to declare their will to build both domestically and internationally societies where equality exists, including Dalits and Adivasi in India, Eelam Tamils and Sinhalese in Sri Lanka, Burmese, Rohingya the other ethnic communities in Myanmar, and equality between the Han civilization and the minority endogenous cultures in China, including the Uyghur people. Chairman Xi Jinping's thought has a key identity concept of the Zhonghua Minzu, which is composed of equality between Han Minzu and the other minority Minzus. Domestically, it treats all the nationalities, Han and non-Han as equal nations. The concept of equal mutual benefit has to be a key value both inside China, in all the OBOR regions, and among the countries of the region. All the Muslim Turkic nations in the One Belt, and all the maritime nations, especially the indigenous nations in the One Road, will have to share the OBOR civilizational project in mutually beneficial equality.

The OBOR project has been discussed by international press as a Chinese project proposed by Chairman Xi Jinping. It is necessary to criticize it in terms of the political-economic interest of China. However, this project is primarily a civilizational project involving historical interactions linking the arid land, One Belt, and the maritime region, One Road. The project will develop new interactions between the countries and peoples involved. It will become a new historical reality that counters the exogenous manipulations of Western colonialist expansion, and if successfully conducted, will develop an example of endogenous collective development and democratization. In this sense, the OBOR project is a positive new reality, particularly meaningful in the second phase of post-Cold War globalization. However its counter-imperialist content cannot be capitalized without the active participation of the various subaltern groups. The Western overemphasis on political rights at the expense of economic and cultural rights can be overcome by enhancing economic and cultural development with the wide participation of subaltern groups based on a broad understanding of human rights. In this way, there is a way beyond Occidentalist–Orientalist divide and combine.

The Post-Modern Peoples' Endogenous Libertarian Initiatives: The Post-Modern Left in the United States

It is important to study the formation of a post-modern left (libertarianism as a post- Atlantic-Liberal utopianism) which will play an important role in the second phase of the post (first) Cold War left. In the US, we must study the People's Congress of Resistance (PCOR) formed in September 2017 which attempts to unite the diverse energies of the US left against the racist, sexist, xenophobic and capitalist system. It tries to combine organizations based on various marginalized social classes and identity-based organizations. The class dimension is reflected in Occupy Wall Street representing the "99 percent." It includes also the Women's March and the LGBTQ community who work with all classes of the society. It has its network among the Latino, African and the Native Americans. The People's Congress adopts a libertarian position believing that poverty is racialized and feminized, and all opposed to any sort of discrimination should seek to form a movement of the many for a society of the many. The Rojava Revolution in Kurdistan adopts the same approach. It is also shared by the Zapatista Revolution in Mexico. In Japan, the Okinawa/Ryukyu indigenous people are united for a united action, "Shima-Gururmi" (All Islands Together), accepting all diverse cultural trends under one identity of Ryukyu people. On the global level, the World Social Forum started in Porto Alegre, Brazil, is also a libertarian coalition of different identity communities.

These organizations and movements are basically different from the modern citizens' networks supporting Atlantic Liberalism of the United Nations during the first phase of the post-Cold War which rejected both class and identity by taking a de-contextualized universalist position on human rights. This position will be replaced in the second phase by a libertarian pluralist unification of class-based and identity-based epistemic communities. On the state level this post-modern libertarian approach of civil society will be partially adopted by the subaltern states, which are excluded from the hegemonic Atlantic Liberal coalition of the first phase. They will tend to strengthen their "identity" prerogatives as Westphalian nation states. This is how the discourse on individual rights can be complemented by Bandung principles of the Cold War period, which emerged as an Afro-Asian state coalition based on domestic and cross-national alliances among different identity communities.

The global economic pressures of migration from the Global South to the Global North will generate a short-term racist effect strengthening the exclusivism of the nation states in the North.[7] However, in the long-run, the tidal wave of migrant workers, including refugees and victims of trafficking and other forms of exploitative migration will contribute to the development of de-facto multi-culturalism in the industrialized "democracies." The migrant workers, male and female, live a *multi-local livelihood*. Their minds are not feeling separated from their loved-ones and their neighbors in their home communities as well as their friends and enemies in the cities they lived. They live in in-between spaces and are in a migratory voyage between their home communities and the receiving communities where they live and work now. They develop multiple identities. This process of formation of pluralist identities and the experience of exploitation as a social class will blend together with one another on the basis of the collective experience of human insecurities of the migrant workers which will enable them to join liberatarian politics.

Endogenous Human Rights Development in Latin America and the Contribution of the Indigenous Nations

The 1970s was a Cold War period when the United States supported the military juntas in Chile, Argentina, Brazil and other Latin American countries. This helped the development of a series of new concepts by the Latin American community of human rights defenders. They were fighting against Pinochet in Chile, who was a hero for the United States, for his violent control of the possible success of a democratically elected socialist regime; the Allende government, which could have become a stronghold of anti-Americanism. Pinochet was also a typical example of a military elite building a neoliberal economy, an invaluable ally of the United States. The anti-Pinochet fight developed a world-wide trend of anti-military governments. The Argentinian and Brazilian military juntas were also precious neoliberal supporters of the US-led economy. They were following Chile's bloody elimination of opponents, including the human rights defenders in the region. Within such a context human rights gained a creative new endogenous meaning associated with democracy and civil liberties that galvanized many groups in opposition to authoritarian and military governments during the first phase of the post-Cold War era of the 1990s. This endogenous innovation in Latin America included the concept of people's security. The military violence against human rights defenders had led to chronic states of insecurity of the people. This was caused by the rulers who were charged to protect their country's national security. This is why the fight against military juntas' barbaric suppression and repression defined itself as a fight for "people's security." This concept spread since the 1980s and was renamed "human security" when it was introduced to the United Nations through Canadian and Japanese initiatives.

The original concept of people's security was enriched in Latin America by the indigenous communities for whom peace was not only freedom from fear, but implied the building of good societies caring for the rights not only of peoples but also of Mother Earth, *Pacha Mama*. Human communities have to develop a good life, *sumak kawsay*, in harmony with the joyful universe. These two endogenous concepts of the Latin American indigenous civilization became part of the Latin American peace and human rights culture. As the late François Houtart notes, "these are two of the founding concepts of indigenous peoples which, in concrete historical conditions, signified a specific cosmovision and practices regarding respect for nature and for shared collective life. As such they can inspire contemporary thinking and social organization and can revitalise the symbol," while combining the best of ancestral and modern wisdom (Houtart 2012: 23).

Pacific/Indian Ocean Indigenous Traditions and the Global Emergence of Indigenous Civilizations

The contribution of the indigenous peoples to the Latin American endogenous development of human rights regarding peace and people's security needs to play a special role in the elaboration of a creative way to cope with the failure of Atlantic Liberalism to build a sustainable future in the second phase of Post-Cold War globalization. We propose to add a concept which has been occluded by the predominant developmentalist idea ignoring the richness of the original stage of human creativity, preceding the Axial religions (i.e., the indigenous civilizations, especially the maritime indigenous civilizations of the Pacific and Indian Oceans) deserve special attention. The Durban Racism Conference opened a way to understand the important role of the Pacific (and the Indian Ocean) maritime indigenous civilizations as a product of Asian descendants. Clearly enough, the Latin Americans are the earliest Asian descendants who crossed the Baring Strait and migrated into the Americas, North, and South, and the Caribbean region. We must broaden our field of search for endogenous development of human rights as a response to decadent Atlantic Liberalism by recognizing the occluded sources of intellectual creativity of the indigenous peoples indispensable to overcome the emerging new Cold War.

The second phase of the post-Cold War period is entering an era where global neo-liberal competition becomes increasingly violent. This is indeed a typical feature of the new Cold War. The global post-modern civil society has to organize campaigns to support the indigenous communities who have been attacked in their conflict with the neo-liberal investors and exploiters of their land who are strongly backed by the neo-liberal states. In this case, right to peace should be applied to protect the indigenous communities from continuous attacks. International solidarity should be, nevertheless, based on the autonomous activities of the indigenous communities and nations. This is where the examples in Mexico are of special interest, in terms of the endogenous activities of indigenous communities for the promotion of their right to peace. The Zapatista movement in Chiapas can provide a model relevant to all regions of the world. *Zapatismo* wants to build a world where "all worlds" have a place. What are these worlds? They are guided by liberative cosmovisions. They put at the center of their activities their traditional liberative wisdom and practices. Through *Mujeres por la Dignidad* and the *Aguas Calientes*, Zapatista communities develop a system of self-organized citizenry and enhance people's right to peace. This was in a way the first post-modern revolution. The initial stage of armed uprising of the Zapatistas was meant to make in a formidable way the indigenous cosmovision visible to the world. Its leader Subcomandante Marcos says:

We don't want to impose our solutions by force, we want to create a democratic space. We don't see armed struggle in the classic sense of previous guerrilla wars, that is as the only way and the only all-powerful truth around which everything is organized. In a war, the decisive thing is not the military confrontation but the politics at stake in the confrontation. We didn't go to war to kill or be killed. We went to war in order to be heard.

(Quoted in Nail 2012: 104)

Also in Mexico, the collaboration between the indigenous communities such as the city of Taran in Michoacán and the indigenous philosophy faculty of the *Colegio de Michoacan* has brought about an increased awareness of the city's long historical roots among the local Tarascan people (Zavala 1988). As a result, the Mexican government decided to give the city a special autonomous status. Professor Hacinto Zavala who teaches indigenous philosophy, is developing a comparative study of Mexican indigenous philosophy and Japanese philosophy. It is important for the endogenous non-Western civilizations to have a comparative study of their philosophies, which may prove that they have a common root in the Pacific Oceanic indigenous civilization.

The new Cold War is taking two distinct paths in Latin America and the United States. The movement to protect *Pacha Mama* has gained greater visibility across Latin America where there are continuous protests against cooperate interests despite some setbacks due to regime changes in the region. In the United States, the contradictions within Atlantic Liberalism has led the poor belts of the Mid-West to return to the belief in American Manifest Destiny that applauds an America First President. The new Cold War has accentuated both a negative right wing and a positive left wing! The Pacific region is a maritime region where US Manifest Destiny and the Chinese Great Maritime traditions collide. In the Pacific, Aotearoa is a land where reconciliation between the Western migrants and the indigenous Maori nations contributes to a harmony between humans and Mother Nature. This was clearly manifested in the decision of the Waitangi Tribunal, which used the British Common Law tradition to introduce a new legal practice to accept a Maori request to give a legal personality to rivers, which are sacred to some of their communities.

Like the Latin Americans subverted the human rights language of the Atlantic Liberalism in resisting dictatorships that were aided by the United States, the indigenous peoples' movements in the Pacific have succeeded in subverting the British legal tradition to protect their rivers. In a similar vein, the Ecuadorian Constitution has enshrined the right of nature, broadening our understanding of eco-human rights. These new legislations have been widely acclaimed in the other parts of the world. Some civil society groups in India want to imitate Aotearoa/New Zealand and consider the possibility of demanding that their government give legal personhood to their sacred rivers.[8] Timor-Leste has become known for its beliefs surrounding the close relationship between humans and nature. The film *Canta Timor* presents how the Mother Earth is sad about all the violence of the Indonesian occupying armed forces. Mother Earth is not angry, but she just shares this sadness. The Roman Catholic lay people and priests in the country share this indigenous sensitivity which is widespread in the Pacific. This sensitivity seems quite acceptable to the Christians who believe in the omnipresent Trinity in nature through the Spirit who animates all living creatures as taught by the Franciscan vision of the universe (Boff 1997). It is our hope that the second phase of the post-Cold War world may cease to impose Atlantic Liberalism and listen to indigenous communities so that the human rights heritage of our modern civilization can be enriched by accepting indigenous endogenous wisdom.

The Right to Peace as a New Social Contract and a Fourth Generation Human Rights

The right to peace was developed in Latin America, as we saw already, as a summarized articulation of the anti-militaristic and anti-imperialist endogenous movement in support of the fight of human rights defenders against military regimes. This initiative of the Latin American citizens received the support of the Spanish citizens dedicated to human rights who have been eager to compensate the peoples of the Americas who were the victims of the Spanish colonialist conquests and expropriation. This solidarity between the descendants of the victims and offenders gave birth on 10 December 2010 to the Declaration of Santiago de Compostela on the Human Right to Peace. This declaration included in its text both the concept of the Asian Charter of Human Rights defining all human rights to find their origin in the *right to life* as well as the Japanese concept of *human security* based on the *right to live in peace* enshrined in the Japanese Constitution. The latter gives testimony to Japan's repentance over violating this right by its colonialist invasions during World War II. The declaration designates the *right holders* of the *right to peace* as all the citizens of the global community, with special attention to the victims of the violation of their right to peace. The sovereign states were defined as the *duty holders* of this new social contract (Transconflict 2017).

The right to peace is an example of endogenous human rights progression, which is opposed to the exogenous processes led by the Atlantic Liberalism of the first phase of post-Cold War globalization. The endogenous process aims at stopping the omnipotence and omnipresence of the Westphalian states under the hegemony of the Atlantic Powers while upholding human security and human rights for peace as the basis of a new social contract and thereby going beyond the third generation of human rights. The latter insists on collective rights but does not relativize the sovereign states by rejecting the hegemony of the industrial democracies that generates conflict after conflict through exogenous human rights interventions. The existing dominant international political order is meeting the goal of the civilizational project of the right to peace. For this project to come true it is indispensable to develop an endogenous egalitarian process on the basis of mutual respect accorded to the Mandala, Zhonghua civilizations, the Islamic Ummah, and the Maritime indigenous civilizations. Peaceful coexistence arises out of mutual cultural empathy towards each other.

Western universal values will have to cease being exogenously imposed, and become well-integrated as a multi-cultural hybridization into post-modern civilization. This has to be done on the basis of parity of esteem accorded to different civilizational eco-human values. The first phase of post-Cold War globalization developed a human rights culture exogenously propagated whereas the second phase has to develop mutual respect between the universal values of human rights, and the equally universal values of the Pacific/Indian Ocean indigenous civilization and of all the Axial civilizations which need to agree to disagree in working for the "common good" of eco-humanity.[9] An inter-civilizational dialogue needs to be developed by all the post-modern citizens and multitude of marginalized communities.

Conclusion

Our discussion on a few aspects of the difference between the first and second phases of the post-Cold War democracies leads us to the following practical conclusion. It is indispensable for the achievement of the UN Sustainable Development Goals, and broadly to avoid a potential World War III and a second Great Depression, to convince the subaltern neoliberals who are also subaltern neoconservatives that their best interest lies not in the ranks of the hate-crime supporters hoping to return to the past White or Japanese supremacy. Their occlusion of the existence of so many alternative possible "worlds" (cosmovisions) must be replaced by a belief to change the present world by a nonviolent struggle of all the subaltern groups of post-modern peoples.[10] In Asia, it is indispensable to convince the Occidentalist subalterns about the radical distinction between the positive modern discourse of universal human rights that emerged as a result of wars and revolutions in the West, and the negative colonialist and neo-colonialist Western political interventions in the name of human rights. It is only through this recognition that Orientalist–Occidentalist discourses can be overcome. These two discourses reinforce each other while contributing to deep polarization within the subaltern groups within the individual states, regional politics and world political order.

It is also necessary to have a civilizational dialogue between the different subaltern groups including the indigenous communities who rely on their traditional livelihoods and the diaspora communities of migrant workers living their multi-local livelihoods. The Durban UN Conference against Racism defined two new concepts, Afro-descendants and Asian decedents. The first concept was easy to understand because it simply included all the descendants of the victims of slave trade who were forced to migrate to North and South America and the Caribbean region especially between the sixteenth and the nineteenth centuries. The second concept should be defined clearly because there were migrants from Asia to different other world regions, at different times, with a variety of purposes and socioeconomic statuses. In any situation, the Diasporas of Asian descendants should not exclude any Asian person, be they indigenous or modern migrants. On the other hand, it is useful to define each sub-category of Asian descendants in terms of their geo-historical origin. The Asian descendant must be understood in their multi-local and multi-generational identities. The same applies to the Afro-decedents. These two concepts should help us to explore the possibility to form the alliance of a group of human actors who share a common identity in terms of their historical position as victims/defenders of their endogenous right to live in peace free from fear and wants. Theirs should be the largest common identity group in history. Specificities of their historical backgrounds should enrich and strengthen their common struggle toward justice and common security.

Exchanges of views and sharing of experiences among multitude of subaltern groups should develop a pluralistic common-sense of mutual empathy that envisions the common good permitting a subaltern self-liberation from the enslaving dreams of neoliberal competitive zero-sum mutual rejection of each other which is embodied in fascism. These groups carry the greatest potential to resist the *destructive trilateral hegemony* of Atlantic Liberalism as well as the *limitations* of the counter-imperialist One Belt One Road program led by China. They carry the power to avert a new Cold War and stop nuclear imperialism as part of the unfinished decolonizing project.

Kinhide Mushakoji is professor emeritus of Sophia University, Japan and a leading analyst of international affairs in East Asia. He is a founding member of the International Movement Against All Forms of Discrimination and Racism (IMADR), and the *Journal of Human Security*, and a senior specialist at the East–West Centre in Hawaii and Consultant to the Committee on Society, Development and Peace in Geneva.

Notes

1. A tomb epithet chosen as title by the humorous Kant, who was aware that his plans were time-bound.
2. The author was one of the key members of the preparatory meeting of the Trilateral Commission in 1971 which was organized by Zbigniev Brzezinski from North America, Max Kohnstam of the Netherlands from Europe, Toshiyoshi Miyazawa from the Liberal Democratic Party of Japan, late Japanese premier Saburp Ohkita who was a renowned economist, and the late Japanese foreign minister Tadashi Yamamoto who was the secretary of the America-Japanese Shimoda Conference. The author knew personally Max Kohnstam, who was active in development cooperation activities led by the World Council of Churches. The European and Japanese participants were interested in influencing the United States to support North–South international development cooperation activities. We wanted Japan to be a non-Western member in this North Atlantic coalition of so-called industrial democracies.
3. Huntington lays emphasis on civilizational differences as cause of conflict, while undermining geopolitical dynamics generated by the hegemony of the Atlantic Liberalism, which imposes a Euro-centric understanding of modernity on the rest of the globe that subjugates knowledge forms of other civilizations.
4. Nussbaum argues that the real clash is not between Islam and West, but within each modern state between those who respect diversity and those others who uphold homogeneity.
5. The present prime minister of Japan, Shinzo Abe is an ambiguous Occidentalist who embraces neo-conservative and neo-liberal Western practices, but refuses

the application of Occidental critique of imperial Japan's colonial aggressions of neighbouring countries. His rejection of accountability of Japan in World War II as "Western values" is a reaction to the long period of Orientalism in Japanese politics ranging from 1950 to 2000 which insisted on taking responsibility for the past Japanese colonialist atrocities occluding the Western colonialist history with comparable atrocities.
6. The author of this article discussed this with Matthew Ridgeway, who succeeded MacArthur as the UN Military Commander, at a meeting of the Trilateral Commission and told him that forward deployment was much costlier than forward disengagement, but Ridgeway did not accept this argument. Now the Korean nation, both North and South, demands the application of forward disengagement for a denuclearized Korean peninsula.
7. We use the term "subaltern" as understood by Antonio Gramsci, but adapt it to the post-Cold War international situation. All the political and economic groups who do not identify themselves with the Trilateral Power Bloc are included into the subaltern sector. There are many groups of subalterns, even in the United States who are excluded from the regime. Some follow Martin Luther King and Malcolm X, and others Donald Trump. Many non-Atlantic nations are subaltern, but accept the neo-liberal rules of the game, because they are unable to find an alternative to survive in the neo-liberal global market.
8. India has adopted an aggressive developmentalist approach in building many dams across the rivers that have displaced thousands of indigenous communities destroying their traditional livelihoods and the liberative knowledge forms associated with the rivers and valleys. Giving the rivers a legal status can guarantee this close relationship between the indigenous communities and nature (Roy 1999).
9. In conceptualizing and identifying concrete actions for the Common Good of eco-humanity through multi-religious, multi-cultural and indigenous perspectives the seminal work of François Houtart and his colleagues from Asia, Africa and Latin America is worth noting. Houtart points out that we have to go beyond multiculturalism and adopt "open interculcuturalism" which promotes "dialoguing between cultures and opportunity for exchanges" (Houtart 2012: 48).
10. Stephen Gill suggests a search for a post-modern Prince following the Gramscian concept of Modern Prince. For Gramsci, the Prince cannot be a concrete individual person. It has to be an organism of complex social interactions that challenge the hegemony of the world order (Gill 2008: ch. 12).

References

Barrett, Kevin J., ed. 2015. *We are not Charlie Hebdo: Free Thinkers Question the French 9/11*. Lone Rock, WI: Sifting and Winnowing Books.
Boff, Leonard. 1997. *Cry of the Earth, Cry of the Poor*. Maryknoll, NY: Orbis Books.
Buruma, Ian and Avishai Margalit. 2005. *Occidentalism: The West in the Eyes of its Enemies*. London: Atlantic Books.
Gill, Stephen. 1990. *American Hegemony and the Trilateral Commission*. Cambridge: Cambridge University Press.
Gill, Stephen. 2008. *Power and Resistance in the New World Order*, 2nd edition. London: Palgrave Macmillan. https://doi.org/10.1057/9780230584518
Hayes, Peter and Lyuba Zarski. 1987. *American Lake: Nuclear Peril in the Pacific*. London: Penguin.

Houtart, François. 2012. "From 'Common Goods' to the 'Common Good of Humanity'." In *A Postcapitalist Paradigm: The Common Good of Humanity*, edited by François Houtart and Birgid Daiber, 11–56. Brussels: Rosa-Luxemburg Foundation.

Huntington, Samuel P. 1993. "The Clash of Civilizations?" *Foreign Affairs* 72(3): 22–49. https://doi.org/10.2307/20045621

Kaldor, Mary. 2007. *Human Security: Reflection on Globalization and Intervention*. London: Polity Press.

Kim, Dae-jung. 2019. *Conscience in Action: The Autobiography of Kim Dae-jung*, trans. Jeon Seung-hee. Singapore: Palgrave Macmillan. https://doi.org/10.1007/978-981-10-7623-7

Mushakoji, Kinhide. 2015. "Ethno-Politics in Contemporary Japan: The Mutual-Occlusion of Orientalism and Occidentalism." *Proto Sociology* 32: 36–58. https://doi.org/10.5840/protosociology2015323

Nail, Thomas. 2012. *Returning to Revolution: Deleuze, Guattari and Zapatismo*. Edinburgh: Edinburgh University Press. https://doi.org/10.3366/edinburgh/9780748655861.001.0001

Nussbaum, Martha. 2009. *The Clash Within: Democracy, Religious Violence and India's Future*. Cambridge, MA: Harvard University Press.

Roy, Arundhati. 1999. "The Greater Common Good." Retrieved from https://frontline.thehindu.com/static/html/fl1611/16110040.htm (accessed October 15, 2019).

Transconflict. 2017. "Santiago Declaration on the Human Right to Peace." www.transconflict.com/2017/11/the-santiago-declaration-on-the-human-right-to-peace-021 Retrieved from (accessed August 15, 2019).

Zavala, Augustin Jacinto. 1988. *Mitologia y Modernizacion*. Michoacan: El Colegio de Michoacán.

4

Contesting Pasts, Presents, Futures: East Asia's "Japan Problem" and "Korea Problem"

Gavan McCormack

You may be the smallest village in the land
Yet peace across this land will emanate from you
You may be the smallest village in this land
Yet peace across this land will emanate from you
We won't forget when you break and shatter
When you collapse and fall down we will stand with you
You may be the smallest village in this land
Yet peace across this land will emanate from you.[1]

Introduction

In thinking about contemporary militarism and militarization, Japan does not immediately spring to mind. It has a "peace constitution" and "three non-nuclear principles," and its soldiers enjoy the enviable record of having killed no one in the past sixty-three years. They are commonly seen within Japan as a disaster relief force and outside it as part of various UN peacekeeping forces. And yet Japan accommodates and subsidizes a major US military presence (hosting over one hundred bases), thereby supporting wars on many fronts, and it accumulates its own fighter aircraft, battleships and submarines, and recently committed to acquire its own aircraft carrier(s) and establish a specialized unit modelled on the US Marine Corps. How do these apparently contradictory aspects cohere?

Inter-state relationships as they exist today in East Asia remain set in the frame developed seventy years ago, in the wake of the cataclysmic World War II and subsequent San Francisco Treaty (1951) (Hara 2014). Then, the US was undisputed master of the world, China was divided and excluded, Korea divided and at war, Japan divided (Okinawa severed from it) and occupied, and the apparatus of occupation, bases, and US hegemony was assumed to be crucial to maintaining regional and global "security." The San Francisco Treaty was the blueprint for incorporating Japan's "peace state" within the US's "war state."

No historical settlement or framework of alliances lasts forever and it is surely time this one was re-negotiated. Apart from the steady rise of China over the past several decades, from 2018 events unimaginable even a year earlier on and around the Korean peninsula (not discussed in this chapter) shook the system.

Koreans, of south and north, began to seize the initiative and to negotiate their way towards a Korea at peace, de-nuclearized and subject to multilateral security guarantees. Paid much less attention but nevertheless highly significant and at the very heart of the San Francisco Treaty system, the people of Okinawa challenge it. If the Cold War knots around the Korean peninsula can indeed be untied and foreign troop occupations ended, in Japan as well as Korea, the door could be opened upon a comprehensive, post-San Francisco Treaty, post-Cold War, even post-US hegemonic era.

Japan, however, resists any such change. It appears set on deepening dependent militarization. How and why should that be so?

Peace State versus Militarism

In the wake of its decade and a half of twentieth-century war that left its cities levelled and its people, soldiers and civilians exhausted and impoverished, Japan in 1946 adopted a fresh constitution that entrenched the three democratic principles of popular sovereignty, fundamental human rights, and pacifism. The last of these, to which the famous Article 9 was devoted, was unambiguous:

> Aspiring sincerely to an international peace based on justice and order, the Japanese people forever renounce war as a sovereign right of the nation and the threat or use of force as means of settling international disputes.
>
> In order to accomplish the goal of the preceding paragraph, land, sea, and air forces, as well as other war potential, will never be maintained. The right of belligerency of the state will not be recognized.

It has to be remembered that the San Francisco settlement—commonly seen as a "soft peace"—actually divided Japan into a mainland, constitutional "peace state" and a Okinawa/Ryukyu "war state" under direct US control. Both were integrated in functionally complementary ways under US hegemony. Control over Okinawa was only returned to Japan, albeit nominally, in 1972, after which mainland Japan's "peace state" status has become more and more nominal. Re-establishing military forces under the title of "self-defense forces" during the Korean War, Japan gradually rose to become today's world number eight on the scale of military power, spending around $42 billion annually on weapons and weapons systems for its own forces (247,000 strong and therefore larger than the forces of the UK, Germany or France) and subsidizing the Pentagon to the tune of an additional $6.76 billion annually (as of 2016) (McCormack 2018c: 186). US forces hosted by Japan in its lavish system of bases came to host 50,000 US troops who have been dispatched at will to battlefronts from Korea and Vietnam from the 1950s to the 1970s and to the Middle East and North Africa since then.[2] Japan not only builds and furbishes the base facilities for the US but it turns a blind eye to the danger, noise and nuisance they inflict on base neighborhood communities, especially in Okinawa.

Under Prime Minister Abe during his second term (from 2013), defense expenditure has been steadily raised (six years in a row), the ban on arms exports softened and the long-self-imposed expenditure limit of one percent of GDP dropped in March 2017. Japan's air force and navy are second to none (save the United States itself) in the Western Pacific. Japan under Abe Shinzo has *de facto* revised the constitution by the adoption of legislation making possible recourse to war, and it steadily increases military spending and purchases of US weaponry. In 2018 the LDP called on government to double defense expenditure to reach the NATO (nominal) level of 2 percent of GDP (Sankei Shimbun 2018a).

Visiting Tokyo in November 2017, US President Trump spoke in the following terms to Abe:

> So one of the things, I think, that's very important is that the Prime Minister of Japan is going to be purchasing massive amounts of military equipment, as he should. And we make the best military equipment, by far. He'll be purchasing it from the United States. Whether it's the F-35 fighter, which is the greatest in the world—total stealth—or whether it's missiles of many different kinds, it's a lot of jobs for us and a lot of safety for Japan and other countries.
>
> (White House 2017)

Abe responded, saying, "We will be buying more from the United States. That is what I'm thinking." He then lost no time in showing that he would be as good as his word. Weeks later, Cabinet confirmed the Japanese purchase of several dozen F-35 fighters, two Aegis Ashore missile defense systems (a prodigiously expensive system,[3] not to come into operation until 2023, and probably not effective against the new generation hyper-sonic Soviet or Chinese missiles) (Kataoka 2018: 5; Guardian 2018), and one, or more likely two, aircraft carriers.

Japan denounces North Korea's attempt to develop nuclear weapons and has been loudest and most uncompromising in urging strict sanctions against it. In 2017 it began sending self-defense force units to join multilateral, US-led exercises rehearsing a new Korean War. However, it rests its own national defense on (US) nuclear weapons, resists global pressures for denuclearization, and sits on an enormous stockpile of plutonium (36 tons of it in Britain and France, 11 tons in Japan), enough for about 6000 nuclear bombs, with the prospect of increasing the stockpile as more reactors are switched back on and in the absence of any plans for shrinkage or disposal (Associated Press 2018). Vociferous about the threat of North Korean nuclear weapons, Japan has no ears for North Korea's complaint that it has labored under US threat of nuclear annihilation for seven decades. For Japan, those same US weapons are its defensive "umbrella."

From 1969, Japan was party to secret understandings with the US as to how its so-called "Three Non-Nuclear Principles" (adopted in 1967) might be evaded. In a February 2009 document, headed "Japan's Perspective on US's Extended Deterrence," the then Aso Taro government urged the United States not to cut back but to diversify and reinforce its nuclear weaponry and to reserve an entitlement to their preemptive use.[4] It found "persuasive" the idea of storing nuclear weapons, again, at Futenma (and at the US Air Force base at Kadena). Nine years later, when the Trump administration published its "Nuclear Policy Review" in February 2018, insisting on the right to develop "flexible," "credible" (i.e., usable) nuclear weapons (Department of Defense 2018), Foreign Minister Kono expressed Japan's "high appreciation."

Part of the base construction works under way at Henoko today is the expansion and upgrading of the Ordnance Depot, one of the very places where nuclear weapons were stored in the past. However, the non-nuclear countries of the United Nations General Assembly (UNGA) have been mobilizing to have the nuclear states meet their obligation under the Non-Proliferation Treaty to take steps to abolish nuclear weapons. In 2017, the General Assembly majority (122 states) adopted a treaty declaring everything to do with nuclear weapons—possession, manufacture, threat, or use—illegal. Despite its unique nuclear victim status Japan stood together with the nuclear states and against the small and middle powers of the General Assembly on this issue. Through 2018, the process of formal ratification, country by country, proceeded, in the face of intense opposition from nuclear powers plus "umbrella" states, especially Japan and Australia. Once the requisite number of countries has adopted and ratified the ban treaty it becomes law, most likely some time in 2020. Thereafter, to the extent that Japan (or other countries such as Australia) continues to base its security on the "extended deterrence" of American nuclear weapons, along with their patron, the US, they are set to become outlaw states.

Sovereignty Fudged: Japan's "National Policy" Priorities

That peculiar declaration of support by nuclear victim state Japan for US nuclear weapons can only be understood in the context of what I refer to as its "client state" nature.[5] Post-1945 leaders from Hirohito (emperor 1926–1989) to Abe (prime minister 2006–2007 and 2012–present) fudged national sovereignty by adopting as core national policy submission to the United States, becoming its "client state" (or *zokkoku*). Submission to the global superpower sat uneasily with Japanese pride and identity but made some sense on the assumption that the US global dominance of 1951 would continue and that the US would maintain a benevolent disposition towards Japan. The provision of a chain of military bases throughout the Japanese archipelago (and to 1972 complete control over the strategically important Okinawan islands) seemed a modest price to pay for Japan's privileged position within the US-dominated world system. Today, however, the economic underpinnings of that relationship have been rudely shaken: the US, now 16 percent of global "purchasing power parity" (PPP) GDP, is expected to decline to 12 percent by 2050, while China, already 18 percent in 2016, having grown by an astounding fifteen-fold in the two decades from 1995, is expected to continue rising, to reach, according to the OECD, about 27 percent during the 2030s before slowly declining to around 20 percent in 2060 (OECD 2018). In comparative terms, China's GDP grew from being one-quarter that of Japan in 1991, to *surpassing* it in 2001 and trebling (or even quadrupling) it in 2018 (Terashima 2018: 42–47).[6]

It is that shift in *relative* weight vis-à-vis US and China that disturbs and challenges Japan, especially because for about 1350 years it has stood aloof from any Sinic world order, only periodically, in the sixteenth and twentieth centuries (under Hideyoshi and Hirohito), attempting to impose its own instead. The worry begins to spread in Japanese government circles that the two centuries of Anglo-Saxon hegemony on which Japan has staked its future for more than half a century may be coming to an end. The more that the United States grows feeble and flounders, the closer, it seems, that its Japanese client state wants to cling to it. Prime Minister Mori's 2000 reference to Japan as "the emperor-centered land of the gods" and Abe and his clique's attachment to the "glorious Japan" myths of *Nihon kaigi* reflect that desire.[7] The bitter truth is, however, that Japan cannot be simultaneously "glorious" and "servile." The phenomenon sometimes described as Abe "nationalism" is actually non- or anti-nationalism, resting the nation's fate in the hands of Japan's supposedly all-powerful and benevolent, yet actually erratic and unreliable, patron.

The paradox of today's Japan is that the Japanese electorate chooses a government that prioritizes military build-up and alliance service, over peace-oriented or climate change sensitive policies. One reason for this is simply that half the people do not exercise their right to vote, so that a parliamentary contest can be won with a relatively small proportion of votes.[8] The electoral reforms of the early 1990s had the effect of entrenching the LDP to the point where in October 2017 a mere 17.9 percent support from the electorate (48.2 percent of the vote) was sufficient in the small seat electorate division for it to gain 61.1 percent of the parliamentary seats (or 74 percent when combined with its partner Komeito).

The Japanese term "*ikkyo*" or "one strong" captures the concentration of state powers in the hands of Prime Minister Abe and his close associates. From such a narrow electoral base, in his second term of office following the general elections of December 2012, Abe moved to concentrate an unprecedented measure of control over the levers of state, nominating his cronies to special policy advisory committees and to head the Cabinet Legislative Bureau, the National Security Council, the Bank of Japan, the Nuclear Regulatory Commission, and the national broadcaster (NHK).

His agenda of neo-liberal economic policies, military build-up and alliance reinforcement, secrecy laws, constitutional reform and nuclear energy generation, lacks majority support and the package may also lack coherence. But it is backed by formidable state resources. Abe's Liberal-Democratic Party, originally (1955) a US project, enjoys multiple benefits from more than six decades of US patronage.

Roughly half the Japanese people do not support the Abe government in general and most also oppose Abe's core concern, constitutional revision, especially of Article 9.[9] With smaller, right-wing-inclined parties included, the pro-revision forces as of late 2018 constituted a block of 80 percent strength in the Diet but in the public at large 53 percent opposed revision and an even higher figure, 67 percent, saw no need to rush it (Utsunomiya 2018a).

Alongside Japan's insistence on prioritizing US military objectives may be noted its commitment to nuclear power, a policy adopted at US advice more than half a century ago, despite the fact that no country on earth is so ill-suited, because of its inherent geological and climatic instability, to housing a nuclear complex as Japan. The government clings to its belief in nuclear greatness, refusing to allow the record of catastrophic quake-tsunami-meltdown at Fukushima in 2011 to stand in the way. Although the government is committed to reviving (and expanding) much of the national nuclear grid by 2030, one leading nuclear authority says that "the Japanese public has lost faith in nuclear safety regulation, and a majority favors phasing out nuclear power" (Suzuki 2017). As of 2016, 57 percent of people opposed the restart of nuclear generating plants "*even if* they satisfied new regulatory standards" (ibid.). As the nuclear tide ebbed globally following Fukushima, Abe committed the country, contrariwise, to fostering nuclear power as a core domestic industry and a major export sector. Japan found itself increasingly out-of-step with global trends, and struggling to cope with crippling reverses as country after country (United Kingdom, Vietnam, Lithuania, Turkey) moved to cancel nuclear industry plans tied to Japanese cooperation.[10]

The two-thirds Diet majority Abe and his government enjoyed in 2018 (in theory sufficient to adopt constitutional revision, which would then have to be submitted to a referendum) thus did not mean high level of support for their policies, but the lack of a viable alternative.[11] The Abe state's centralized and undemocratic character was evident from the steady stream of revelations of high-level corruption and influence-peddling that rocked it in 2017–2018. Suffice it here to mention the cases of Moritomo and Kake: in the former a plot of national land was sold at one tenth its value to close allies and personal friends of the Prime Minister and his wife who shared the *Nihon Kaigi* world view and promoted, inter alia, the values of the 1890 Imperial Rescript on Education—according to which the greatest glory came from sacrifice in the imperial cause; in the latter (Kake Gakuen veterinary school) the "Prime Minister's will" was said to have been a key factor in determining the success of the Kake group in securing national recognition as a veterinary school. The government in this latter case seems to have been successful in fending off charges of impropriety not least because it deliberately (and, of course, illegally) destroyed documents that might have thrown light on the negotiations (McCormack 2018c: 210–216). In general, over 80 percent of people disbelieve the Prime Minister on the great scandals of his government, Moritomo and Kake, and it seems probable that a similarly high proportion do not share the government's religious/ideological inclination expressed by *Nihon Kaigi* or Komeito. Another pointer to Abe government priorities was the adoption in July 2018 of an "Integrated Resort" (i.e., gambling) law almost without debate and at strong LDP insistence despite the fact of opposition levels running at around 64.8 percent.[12] Yet Abe was returned in September 2018 for a third term as LDP party leader and therefore Prime Minister, and with he and his colleagues dominating the Diet the likelihood of constitutional revision, despite a majority popular opposition, is high.

Potentially of much greater significance than the Moritomo and Kake affairs, or even the gambling law, is the case of the JR Tokai's project for the construction of the linear (magnetic levitation) super express rail link between Eastern and Western Japan (Tokyo and Osaka). It appears to be rooted in the same phenomenon of close personal and ideological ties and economic advantage. Construction commenced early in 2016 on a deep, mostly underground (at depths to 1400 meters) route along which the linear vessels would travel at speeds up to 505 kph. The project is to cost at least 9 trillion yen (over $80 billion). The first part, Tokyo to Nagoya, is not scheduled for completion until 2027, after being brought forward from 2045 following grant of a national government credit of three trillion yen low interest (0.8%) credit (with a 30-year period of grace before any repayment was required).

Such an arrangement would be unthinkable with any bank and appears to have been driven by political rather than economic considerations and to entail huge risk. The national economic daily, *Nikkei Bijinesu*, belatedly paying attention to the project in August 2018, referred to the Linear project as a "land-based Concorde" and pointed out that throughout the decision-making process JR Tokai's head, Kaneko Shin, had met with Prime Minister Abe on no fewer than 45 occasions,[13] thus suggesting the affair should be seen in the same frame as Moritomo and Kake, as cronyism rampant and to the *n*th degree.

Unlike Moritomo or Kake, however, the linear shinkansen is a gigantic, hubristic plan of such scale that its failure would plunge the state, the country—indeed the world—into crisis. In their rare, English language account, Aoki and Kawamiya conclude that it is "deficit-breeding, energy-wasting, environmentally-destructive, and technologically unreliable … a guaranteed fiasco" (Aoki and Kawamiya 2017). The Abe state's promotion of the linear project invites comparison with the project of the 1940s to build the world's biggest and most powerful battleship. In due course, the Yamato, launched in December 1941 sank in April 1945 with loss of almost all (3036 out of 3332) of its crew. Yet like the Yamato, today's linear project proceeds without serious national or (till the Nikkei analysis in August 2018) media attention.

As of late 2018, entering upon Abe's third term as head of the LDP and therefore of government, the policy priorities of the Abe state were plain: deepening militarization, nuclear weapon defense and nuclear power promotion, gambling promotion, restriction of human rights and expansion of state powers and civic duties. All were state policies that lacked national consensus and defied global trends in favor of disarmament, renewable energy sources and ecological sustainability. It was characteristic of Abe that in his Diet-opening speech in October 2018 he oriented his government towards a 2020 revision of the constitution that under Article 99 he was obliged to respect and implement.

Okinawa

Okinawa's confrontation with the Japanese nation state is rooted in its experience of incorporation by violence, into the "early modern" state in 1609 and the "modern" state in 1879 (McCormack 2018a), the overwhelming catastrophe of war in 1945, and the ensuing severance from Japan and occupation between 1945 and 1972 (McCormack and Norimatsu 2018). While Okinawa was under complete US control in the 1950s and 1960s, up to 1300 nuclear weapons were stored there, at a time when Pentagon planners assumed a major role for Okinawa in scenarios involving the destruction of *all* major cities in the then Soviet Union and China, killing around 600 million people and very possibly bringing human civilization itself to an end (Ellsberg 2017, 2018). Okinawan people of course did not know this in detail, but they knew enough to fear and to seek relief from military oppression and exposure to war risk. From the struggles against land appropriation (the infamous "bayonet and bulldozer" process) in the 1940s and 1950s, through the "Beggars March" of 1955 and prefecture-wide protests leading to (partial) "reversion" to Japan in 1972, the *raison d'être* assigned Okinawa within the Japanese state system has been that of subordination to military priorities. Its 0.6 percent of the national land is reluctant host to over 70 percent of US military facilities in Japan.

No single incident so outraged the Okinawan people and so threatened the US base system as the rape of a 12-year-old girl by three US servicemen in 1995. It was followed by the announcement in 1996 that Futenma Marine Air Station (located in the middle of Ginowan City, a short drive from the prefectural capital of Naha) would be returned, but only once a substitute had been constructed. When it was made clear that that substitute had to be in Okinawa, that proposal was rejected, first by a Nago City plebiscite in 1997 and then by numerous resolutions of the Okinawan parliament, blocking implementation of agreements made between the two governments in 2006, 2009, 2010, 2011, 2013 and 2017. The Abe state nevertheless kept insisting on its "unwavering commitment" to the Henoko construction project, declaring it "the only solution" to Futenma replacement.

In December 2013, then Governor Nakaima Hirokazu bowed to pressure from Tokyo and consented, despite his electoral pledge to the contrary, to reclamation of a site on Oura Bay for construction of a Futenma Replacement Facility (FRF). The prefecture was outraged and when he faced the electorate late the following year Nakaima was dismissed from office (by a margin of 100,000 votes). Elected in his stead was Onaga Takeshi, standing on the platform of opposition to any such construction.

Despite the clear expression of prefectural sentiment against it, preliminary site works were undertaken in 2015. They were delayed or blocked by various legal and administrative steps on the part of Governor Onaga, and completely halted through much of 2016. In December 2016, however, the Supreme Court ruled against Okinawa. Its judgement signified that where military priorities compete with climate change and species depletion policies, primacy inevitably attached to the former. Thus Japan in 2018 (which happened to be the International Year of Coral) attached its highest policy priority to reclaiming (filling) much of one of its most prolific and bio-diverse coastal coral reef zones, Oura Bay, its mini "Barrier Reef," killing off unique colonies of coral and other marine species including the highly protected dugong in order to construct a comprehensive military complex for the US Marine Corps.[14]

For Okinawa, in other words, Japan's clientelist national polity called for sacrifice of one of nature's treasure-houses to make it a fortress from which the United States could continue indefinitely projecting its power over East Asia in accord with the San Francisco formula. It was "counter to the moves towards regional peace, cooperation and community, counter to the principle of regional self-government spelled out in the constitution, counter to the principles of democracy and counter to the imperative of environmental conservation" (McCormack 2018c: 246–247).

In June 2018, the government made known its intention to commence the actual reclamation from August 17. That prompted Governor Onaga to declare, on July 27, his intent to initiate formal steps for revocation of the reclamation license. However, with the strain of constant pressure and confrontation with the national government a likely contributory factor, Onaga fell ill. After undergoing surgery for removal of a cancerous pancreatic tumor in April and a further brief spell in hospital, he died on August 8.

Weeks after his death, the revocation process he had initiated came into effect. As of August 30, its license for reclamation thereby cancelled, the state had to suspend work. Again, however, it moved quickly to strike down the prefecture's protest. The government's Okinawan Defense Bureau called on Ishii Kei-ichi, Minister of Land, Infrastructure, and Transportation, to review the revocation under the Administrative Appeal Act and to issue an order cancelling its effect. There could be little doubt of the outcome as one section of government was called upon to review and pronounce on the legitimacy of the acts of another. As the *Ryukyu Shimpo* put it (posting its own editorial on the web in English):

> To begin with, the Administrative Appeal Act was passed with the purpose of supporting citizens' rights and interests when a government agency acts illegally or inappropriately. Therefore, the government itself cannot use the same law in this way ... For the government to abuse the system made for a regular citizen by insisting that the ODB [Okinawa Defense Bureau, the Okinawan section of the Department of Defense] is a "private entity" is tantamount to fraud. The government is once again taking unthinkably tyrannical measures ...
>
> (Ryukyu Shimpo 2018)

A statement issued with the signatures of 110 administrative law specialists from throughout Japan declared the government to be acting "illegally ... lacking in impartiality or fairness," and that it "failed to qualify as a state ruled by law" (Okinawa Times 2018). Fraudulent or not, on 30 October Minster Ishii did as was required of him, finding the revocation "unreasonable" and "likely to undermine relations of trust with Japan's security ally, the United States" (Kyodo 2018b). He suspended the effect of the prefectural order, whereupon, brushing aside outraged Okinawan protests, the ODB (for the government) ordered works at the Henoko-Oura Bay site resumed. After a two-month suspension, they resumed on 3 November.

In the interim, Tamaki Denny—widely seen as Onaga's political heir, inheriting his commitment to stop the Henoko works—was elected Governor, despite an unprecedented level of national government intervention to try to defeat him and secure the election of a more amenable candidate. For Prime Minister Abe, it was undoubtedly a bitter blow that the people of Okinawa should have overwhelmingly rejected his candidate for Governorship of Okinawa immediately after his own triumph in being re-elected head of his party and de facto head of government for three more years.

However, even with the state's more or less assured victory in any suit that pits citizens against it, without Governor Tamaki's consent resumption of works at Henoko/Oura Bay seems improbable, for reasons now as much technical as political or ecological. Specialist engineers doubt that the massive concrete and steel structure planned, in its present design, could be stably imposed on the site. They insist (as did the prefecture in its formal statement of revocation of the Nakaima license, that for the project to proceed the original design would have to be fundamentally redrawn to take into account factors only recently come to light, such as the soft, "mayonnaise-like" floor of Oura Bay and the active fault line that bisects it (McCormack 2018c: 246–247).

It is generally assumed that Governor Tamaki will not consent to either the original or any revised plan. If Tamaki and the prefecture do indeed stick to that position and proceed to contest every step of the way, and court proceedings follow court proceedings, the project will be indefinitely disrupted or postponed and the US government may come to doubt its wisdom and viability. Such doubts may indeed already be spreading, as the editorial board of the *New York Times*'s unusually harsh denunciation of the base construction project as "an unfair, unwanted and often dangerous burden on Japan's poorest citizens" suggested (*New York Times*, October 1, 2018).

The remarkable fact is that all attempts over decades by the two governments to persuade, buy off, or intimidate the people of the Ryukyu/Okinawa islands into submission to the military-first prescription have failed. The Okinawan movement opposes not only the reclamation and construction works on Oura Bay but also the steady advance of militarization in the form of Osprey aircraft encroachment on Okinawan skies and SDF military and missile bases on the various islands of the East China Sea. Modern Japanese history has no precedent for the phenomenon of a prefecture saying no to the authorities of the world's two great powers over a period of decades.

However, a qualification has to be entered. Although he is commonly seen as avatar of the Okinawan anti-base popular sentiment, Tamaki takes a narrow view of the Okinawan "base problem," essentially confining his objections to the Henoko project. He takes no position on the helipad works in the Yambaru forest of the north or on the Abe government's rapidly advancing plans for the extension of military (i.e., Japanese Self-Defense Force) facilities through the Southwest islands adjacent to Okinawa island itself, notably Miyako, Ishigaki, and Yonaguni, and he inherits from Onaga support for the "return" of Naha Military Port, promised by agreement between the two countries in 1974, an astonishing 44 years ago. Such "reversion," like that of Futenma, was made dependent on construction of an alternative, for which the adjacent Urasoe City, like Nago in the case of Henoko, was designated. As "reversion" of Futenma Marine Air Station, meant construction of the much expanded and upgraded Henoko facility, so that of Naha Military Port was to mean major new base construction at Urasoe. On current estimates, that transfer might occur in 2028. But if Tamaki moves to lead the opposition to it, it could take much longer. It is fraught with potential for serious conflict.

Furthermore, Governor Tamaki was no sooner elected than he indicated a readiness to consider one of the key "Japan handler" demands for the Japanese client state: the transformation of military bases in Okinawa from single (US or Japan) management and use to "joint" facilities (Sankei Shimbun 2018b). His interview clarifying this stance appeared in the right-wing national newspaper, *Sankei Shimbun*, almost simultaneously with the Centre for Strategic and International Studies (CSIS) report making precisely that demand as part of a design to reinforce the US–Japan alliance. By signaling readiness to consider a demand long made by alliance managers in Washington, Tamaki was consenting to a key part of the clientelist agenda.[15] He confirmed this pro-Security Treaty, pro-base stance in speeches in Tokyo and New York in November 2018.[16]

Despite the bitterness of the confrontation, it is the Okinawans, ironically, who take Abe literally in seeking to go "beyond the post-war system" and to "take back" Japan. However, for them it is Okinawa that is to be taken back, and it is from the militarist designs of the Japanese and US governments that it is to be taken.

Conclusion

While, internationally, few find reason to quibble with the message that Prime Minister Abe presents to multiple audiences, including the United Nations and the US Congress, of Japan as a democratic, law-governed, constitutional state, one with "moral standing" as a "robust democracy" (Le 2017), my own work over several decades leads me to doubt such claims and to seek to understand by what alternative formulations it may be understood. Increasingly, I see evidence that my doubts are widely shared within Japan itself, where a critical, dissenting view gathers strength:

- Philosopher Takahashi Tetsuya of Tokyo University attaches the label "extreme right" to early twenty-first-century Japan (Takahashi 2015).

- Filmmaker and journalist Soda Kazuhiro sees what he calls a "fascism of indifference" in which the Japanese voters are like frogs in slowly heating fascist water (Soda 2015).

- Kagoshima University historian Kimura Akira believes that "Japan is already no longer law-governed or democratic and is moving towards becoming a dark society and a fascist state" (Kimura 2016).

- Kyoto University scholar of German literature Ikeda Hiroshi points to similarities between Abe and Adolf Hitler (Ikeda 2016).

- Hosei University political scientist Yamaguchi Jiro feels "a sense of crisis that Japan has begun a steep decline towards civilizational collapse" (*Tokyo Shimbun*, May 22).

- Author Yamaguchi Izumi sees a "fundamental corruption of politics" spreading through every nook and cranny of Japanese society (*Ryukyu Shimpo*, October 21).

- One group of intellectuals and writers calling itself "committee of seven appealing for world peace" declared (in June 2017) "the political system of this country has become entirely the private property of Prime Minister Abe ... Japan is in this way a fascist state" (Committee of Seven to Appeal for World Peace 2017).

- Kyoto Seika University's Shirai Satoshi argues that there is a close correlation between the emperor-centered *Kokutai* or national polity of pre-war (fascist) Japan and today's US-dominated Japan. He sees both polities as absolutist and in time becoming exhausted, plunging Japan into existential crisis (Shirai 2018).

- Onaga Takeshi, Governor of Okinawa in 2010–2018, refers to the Abe Government as: "condescending, unreasonable, outrageous, childish, depraved, [one that] ignores the people's will, and ... [is] completely lacking in ability to say anything to America" (all words taken from various statements and speeches by Onaga Takeshi; see McCormack and Norimatsu 2018: 279).

For the most part, all of these would agree that the Japanese state rests on unstable, contradictory principles.

Almost seventy years into the San Francisco Treaty/Cold War system, Abe concentrates on maintaining its frame, servile for the most part to Washington, while confronting China, Russia, and North Korea and steadily building up military readiness for war. Simultaneously, however, he shows keen interest in alternatives, contemplating positively the Xi and Putin designs for Eurasia.[17] He hedges his bets, and edges towards reconciliation and cooperation with Russia's Putin and China's Xi Jinping.

By 2019, the contradiction on which the Abe state formula rested was clear. It did not make sense to think of liquidating the post-war, American-granted regime and comprehensively revising the constitution to reflect the Shintoist, "beautiful," "new" and emperor-centered Japan while also declaring unqualified support ("100% *shiji*") for the Trump "America First" agenda. Unable to resolve the contradiction, Abe tended to concentrate instead on widening state prerogatives, circumscribing citizen rights, reinforcing national security, and on re-centering the state around the imperial institution and its sustaining Shinto myths of uniqueness and superiority. However, if one looks to the people rather than the state, one senses a strong and very different common sentiment, one that is universalist and civil democratic, one that embodies the wish to play a central, positive role in the struggle for the cause of humanity in an epoch of climate change, global warming, and species loss, for the outlawing of nuclear weapons and the substitution of renewables for nuclear and fossil fuel energy systems, and for maintaining, even reinforcing, the constitutional commitment to peace. How to get a government that will overcome the barriers of clientelism and advance these goals is the problem the Japanese people face.

Gavan McCormack is professor emeritus at the Australian National University. He is the co-founder of the electronic journal *Japan Focus* (now the *Asia-Pacific Journal—Japan Focus*). Much of his work appears in Japanese, Korean and Chinese, as well as English. His most recent work is *The State of the Japanese State: Contested Identity, Direction, and Role* (Renaissance Books, 2018).

Acknowledgements

This chapter draws on some material discussed in my book *The State of the Japanese State: Contested Identity, Direction and Role* (Renaissance Books, 2018).

Notes

1. This is the English translation of the song sung in Korean by the protesters of Gangjeong village who have been blocking the entrance to the naval base in Jeju island, Korea on every afternoon for over six years.
2. Japan is host to 109 of the roughly one thousand US military bases around the world, as well as home port (at Yokosuka) to the US 7th Fleet's nuclear-powered carrier USS Ronald Reagan with its 70 to 80 ships and 140 aircraft.
3. At 600 billion yen for two, ca three-times the original price (Sankei Shimbun 2018b). Putin claimed a speed of Mach 10, or 12,000 kph, for the newly unveiled Kinzhal missile (Guardian 2018).
4. That document is known as the "Akiba Memo" (from Akiba Takeo, then Minister at the Japanese embassy in Washington and as of 2018 Vice-Minister of Foreign Affairs). For photographic reproduction of the document, see Haruna (2018: 69–78). For discussion, see Kulacki (2018) and Zaha (2018). Foreign Affairs Vice-Minister Akiba denies making his 2009 statement that proposing nuclear storage site on Okinawa or Guam would be "persuasive," recorded in US Congressional memo" (Zaha 2018). And see interpellations in the Diet's Defense and Foreign Relations Committee on March 20 and 26, 2018, between the Japan Communist Party's Inoue Satoshi and Foreign Minister Kono Taro.
5. See my *Client State* (McCormack 2007), and subsequent essays in *Asia-Pacific Journal—Japan Focus*.
6. The *CIA World Factbook* (2017) has China already 4.5 times Japan, $21.27 trillion to $4.92 trillion.
7. On Nihon Kaigi, the ultra-nationalist organization to which Abe and his government are closely attached (all members of government as of late 2018 being members), see McCormack (2018c: 29–31).
8. Voting rate in 2017 was 52.66 percent, down from 69.28 percent in 2009.
9. Support LDP constitutional revision 36.7 percent; oppose: 49:0 percent ("Jiminto kaiken-an hantai wa 5-wari 9-jo ikasu koso ga taisetsu da"; Kyodo 2018a).
10. Inter alia the Mitsubishi Heavy Industries project for four reactors on the Turkish Black Sea started with an estimated cost of 2.1 trillion yen but by late 2018 that had blown out to 5 trillion yen (Mainichi 2018).

11. Had the main opposition parties, Constitutional Democrats (19.9 percent) and Hope (17.4 percent) joined forces in a single liberal party, the outcome might have been different.
12. Japan is already a gambling super-power, with the Welfare Ministry estimating 3.6 percent of people (3.2 million people) at some level of dependency. Public support for the bill adopted in July was 27.6 percent, opposition 64.8 percent (Utsunomiya 2018b). According to *The Economist* (2017), opposition to the casino bill was higher than 80 percent.
13. Forty-five occasions since formation of the (Second) Abe government in December 2012 (Kaneda 2018). See also McCormack (2018c: 183–184).
14. The extraordinarily rich biodiversity of the Oura Bay vicinity is not contested. The government's own Okinawa Defense Bureau puts the figure of 5334 on the bio-species of the Bay, of which 262 are endangered (Sakurai 2018).
15. See my discussion of the "Japan handler" pressures on Japan (McCormack 2018c: 31).
16. To the Foreign Correspondents Club of Japan on November 9 and to New York University on November 11. See discussion in Kihara (2018).
17. For further discussion of this point see McCormack (2018b).

References

Aoki, Hidekazu and Nobuo Kawamiya. 2017. "End Game for Japan's Construction State: The Linear (Maglev) Shinkansen and Abenomics." *The Asia-Pacific Journal—Japan Focus*, 15 June. Retrieved from https://apjjf.org/2017/12/Aoki.html (accessed August 15, 2019).

Associated Press. 2018. "Japan Pledges to Reduce Plutonium, but Doesn't Say How." Associated Press, July 31.

Centre for Strategic and International Studies. 2018. "More Important Than Ever: Renewing the US-Japan Alliance for the 21st Century." Retrieved from www.csis.org/analysis/more-important-ever.

CIA. (2017). "The CIA World Factbook for 2017." Retrieved from www.cia.gov/library/publications/download/download-2017/index.html (accessed August 15, 2019).

Committee of Seven to Appeal for World Peace. 2017. "The Parliamentary System of Japan is about to Die." Retrieved from www.worldpeace7.jp (accessed September 2, 2019).

Department of Defense. 2018. *Nuclear Posture Review*. Washington, DC: Department of Defense.

Economist. 2017. "Japanese Government Has Legalised Casinos, but They Are Not Popular." *The Economist*, February 2.

Ellsberg, Daniel. 2017. *The Doomsday Machine: Confessions of a Nuclear War Planner*. London: Bloomsbury Publications.

Ellsberg, Daniel. 2018. Interview, "Setting the World Alight." *Sydney Morning Herald*, 9 March.

Guardian. 2018. "Russia Says it has Successfully Launched Powerful New Missile." *The Guardian*, March 11.

Hara, Kimie. 2014. *The San Francisco Treaty and its Legacies: Continuation, Transformation, and Historical Reconciliation*. London: Routledge. https://doi.org/10.4324/9781315759012

Haruna, Mikio. 2018. "Akiba Memo—Amerika kaku senryaku e no Nihon no kakusareta Yokyu." *Sekai*, April: 69–78.

Ikeda, Hiroshi. 2016. "Hitler's Dismantling of the Constitution and the Current Path of Japan's Abe Administration: What Lessons Can We Draw from History?" *The Asia-Pacific Journal—Japan Focus*, 15 August. Retrieved from http://apjjf.org/2016/16/Ikeda.html (accessed August 15, 2019).

Kaneda, Shinichiro. 2018. "Zaito 3-cho en tonyu, rinea wa dai-3 no Mori Kake mondai." *Nikkei Bijinesu*, August 2.
Kataoka, Nobuyuki. 2018. "Chijo ijisu haibi wa fuyo!" *Shukan kinyobi*, August 31: 5.
Kihara, Satoru. 2018. "Okinawa, Bei sentoki FA18 no suiraku wa nani o shimesu ka." *Ari no hitokoto*, November 15. Retrieved from https://blog.goo.ne.jp/satoru-kihara/d/20181115 (accessed August 15, 2019).
Kimura, Akira. 2016. "Hatoyama seiken hokai to Higashi Ajia kyodotai koso: atarashii Ajia gaiko to ampo, kichi seisaku o chushin ni." In *Okinawa jiritsu to Higashi Ajia kyodotai*, edited by Shindo Eiichi and Kimira Akira, 202–231. Tokyo, Kadensha.
Kulacki, Gregory. 2018. "Nuclear Hawks Take the Reins in Tokyo." Union of Concerned Scientists, 16 February. Retrieved from https://allthingsnuclear.org/gkulacki/nuclear-hawks-take-the-reins-in-tokyo (accessed August 16, 2019).
Kyodo. 2018a. "Jiminto kiken-an hantai wa 5-wari 9-jo ikasu koso ga tasetsu da." *Ryukyu shimpo*, August 28.
Kyodo. 2018b. "Okinawa Governor Meets Top Gov't Official Over US Base Transfer." *The Mainichi*, November 6.
Le, Tom. 2017. "The Price of Abe's Pragmatism: It Has Hurt Japan's Moral Standing." *Foreign Affairs*, March 23.
Mainichi. 2018b. "Japan Must Ditch Nuclear Plant Exports for Global Trends in Renewable Energy." *Mainichi*, December 25.
McCormack, Gavan. 2007. *Client State: Japan in the American Embrace*. New York: Verso.
McCormack, Gavan. 2018a. "Ryukyu/Okinawa's Trajectory: From Periphery to Centre, 1600–2015." In *Routledge Handbook of Modern Japanese History*, edited by Sven Saaler and Christopher W. A. Szpilman, 118–134. New York: Routledge. https://doi.org/10.4324/9781315746678-9
McCormack, Gavan. 2018b. "Grappling with Clientelism: The Japanese State and Okinawa under Abe Shinzo." *The Asia-Pacific Journal—Japan Focus*, December 1. Retrieved from https://apjjf.org/2018/23/McCormack.html (accessed August 21, 2019).
McCormack, Gavan. 2018c. *The State of the Japanese State: Contested Identity, Direction and Role*. Folkestone: Renaissance Books. https://doi.org/10.2307/j.ctv8pzb71
McCormack, Gavan and Satoko Oka Norimatsu. 2018. *Resistant Islands: Okinawa Confronts Japan and the United States*. Lanham, MD: Rowman & Littlefield.
OECD. 2018. "The Long View: Scenarios for the World Economy to 2060." Retrieved from www.oecd.org/economy/growth/scenarios-for-the-world-economy-to-2060.htm (accessed August 29, 2019).
Okinawa Times. 2018. "Henoko shin kichi, gyoseiho kenkyusha 110 nin no seimeibun zenbun." *Okinawa Times*, October 31.
Ryukyu Shimpo. 2018. "The Japanese Government Suing to Allow Land Filling is a Reckless Trampling of Democracy." *Ryukyu Shimpo*, October 18.
Sakurai, Kunitoshi. 2018. "Oura-wan seibutsu ni shi no senkoku." *Ryukyu Shimpo*, 2 December.
Sankei Shimbun. 2018a. "Boeihi 'tai GDP 2%' meiki, jimin boei daiko teigen no zenyo hanmei." *Sankei Shimbun*, May 25.
Sankei Shimbun. 2018b. "Tamaki Deni-shi, Jieitai to Beigun no kichi kyodo shiyo kyogi mo, intabyu de hyomei, okinawa ken chijisen." *Sankei Shimbun*, October 2.
Shirai, Satoshi. 2018. *Kokutairon: Kiku to Seijoki*. Tokyo: Shueisha Shinsho. https://doi.org/10.1093/oso/9780198817314.003.0009
Soda, Kazuhiro. 2015. "Nekkyo-naki fuashizumu e no shohosen," *Sekai*, February: 81–95.
Suzuki, Tatsujiro. 2017. "Six Years after Fukushima, the Japanese Public Has Lost Faith in Nuclear Power." *The Conversation*, 10 April. Retrieved from http://the

conversation.com/six-years-after-fukushima-much-of-japan-has-lost-faith-in-nuclear-power-73042 (accessed September 1, 2019).

Takahashi, Tetsuya. 2015. "Kyokuu ka suru seiji." *Sekai*, January: 150–161.

Terashima, Jitsuro. 2018. "Noryoku no ressun." No 192. "Chugoku no kyodaika kyokenka wo seishi suru, Nihon no kakugo." *Sekai*, April: 42–47.

Utsunomiya, Kenji. 2018a. "Kaiken ni hatsugi o yurusanai arasoi o." *Shukan Kinyobi*, January 19: 9.

Utsunomiya, Kenji. 2018b. "Seiki no gukyo, kajino-ho kyoko." *Shukan Kinyobi*, August 10: 55.

White House. 2017. "Remarks by President Trump and Prime Minister Abe of Japan in Joint Press Conference," Tokyo, Japan." November 6. Retrieved from www.whitehouse.gov/the-press-office/2017/11/06/remarks-president-trump-and-prime-minister-abe-japan-joint-press (accessed September 20, 2019).

Zaha, Yukiyo. 2018. "Foreign Affairs Vice-Mnister Akiba Denies Making His 2009 Statement that Proposing Nuclear Storage Site on Okinawa or Guam Would be 'Persuasive,' Recorded in US Congressional Memo." *Ryukyu Shimpo*, 6 March.

5

The Geo-politics of Imperialism and the Unitary State of Sri Lanka: Militarization and Structural Genocide of the Eelam Tamil Nation

Athithan Jayapalan and Gajendrakumar Ponnambalam

> Can the readers who did not experience this imagine what it is like to watch the complete destruction of one's country: the physical destruction, the destruction of the governance structures, the complete dispersal of its people, and massacres on massive scale? Has there ever been such complete destruction of a country in history? The only reason why it is not seen as such is because my country was only in the minds of its people, but not recognized by the global system of states.
> —N. Malathy (2012: back cover)

Introduction

Raphael Lemkin defined genocide, in the aftermath of the systemic crimes of persecution which took place during World Wars I and II, as processes and plans of action which are designed to target the "life, liberty and property" of a particular national, racial or religious group. Hence, he coined the term genocide out of the Greek word for people or race (*genos*) and *cide*, which denotes killing (Lemkin 1946). Hence any coordinated schemes of actions aimed at dismantling the national characteristic of a people, be it their collective socio-economic and cultural institutions and life, demographic and territorial contiguity, and cosmological or spiritual relationship to their land, is considered part of the structural processes of genocide. It is not defined by the mere physical murder of a member of the group, the term also grasps the structural processes often sustained and designed through state power, to assimilate by breaking that group's collective relationship to their traditional territorial habitats and dismantling that group's collective practices, beliefs and cultural make-up as well, in order to politically subjugate a nation of people, within the fold of the social, political and cultural order of a nation-state. Many of the states of the present, as a brief perusal of history will show, were born out of the seeds of colonialism, imperialism and capitalism.

The course of history sheds light especially on how since the epoch beginning with the Industrial Revolution and the initial stages of colonialism, genocidal processes have accompanied imperialist policies seeking geo-political and geo-economic hegemony. Consequently, sovereign peoples have been subjugated and their future development dictated through the might of the imperial military and economic capacities. Hence militarization of peoples, lands, and seas have been components of the geo-political consideration of imperial powers from the colonial era up until the modern age. Since the fall of the USSR, the US has led its coalition of allies into an era of hegemony, which has in the recent decade and a half been challenged by China and Russia. As part of the processes of development of capitalism and imperialism, from the seventeenth century until the twenty-first century, the homelands and seas of native peoples and nations across the world have been militarized and occupied. Military-administered zones, are established by nation-states as well as world hegemons to enforce upon people valuing their collective life, their lands and seas, the (neo)colonial will of military aggression, exploitation and political and economic hegemony. This has manifested across the world, whether it is the militarization of Mayan homelands by the Guatemalan state, or the military occupation enforcing a structural genocide by the Sri Lankan state of Tamil Eelam and its populace, and from the oppression of the Kurds by NATO member state Turkey, to the Indonesian militarization and oppression of West Papua, or the Israeli state's settler occupation of the Palestinian homeland. The US maintains military bases in far off places such as Okinawa, South Korea, Guam, Djibouti and Guantanamo Bay. They are, however, locations crucial in allowing US military operation in littoral regions and seas along which the world economy is constituted with the nexus of maritime trade routes and supply lines. In short, strategic locations across the world are militarized either directly by world powers or through their allied states and dictated by imperial policy of world hegemons for the similar colonial-imperial logic of yesterday.

In this pattern, various alliances of elites governing partner-states of the imperial powers of today have opted to militarize territories under their states' jurisdictions to exert control and exploitation on behalf of their chauvinist and comprador interests as well to serve the geo-political considerations of external interests backing their governances whether it is imperial powers or corporate forces and world financial institutions.

Seeds of Conflict: British Colonialism

The island today known as Sri Lanka is located to the south of the southern tip of the Indian peninsula, at the heart of the Indian Ocean trading routes. The island was in ancient times known by many names among historical states and empires across the world. It was called Taprobane among ancient Greek and Roman sailors, Serendib in the Persian and Arab world, Eelam among Tamils, various names in the Indic and Chinese world and Ceylon among Europeans. The island due to its natural resources, and its strategic maritime areas and coastal locations, has attracted traders and adventuress from lore to the fledging imperial powers of the sixteenth to nineteenth centuries, which marked the birth of modern capitalism. In the latter context, the island was a forward operative base to secure primitive accumulation for the imperial-capitalist industrial mode of production in Europe through the acquisition of colonies and imposition of conditions of monopoly over trading routes and sources of production in the Indian Ocean.

During the early years of the nineteenth century, the British Empire, constituted by an alliance of the crown and the British East Indian Company (i.e., the conjunction of British state, monarchy, private capitalists and the bourgeoisie), waged a global war with the French Napoleonic Empire for control of colonies, trading routes, land and seas and other strategic assets. One of the disputed regions which witnessed such a rivalry was the Deccan and South of India as well as the island of Sri Lanka. In what became known as the Carnatic wars, the British and their native comprador allies, fought off indigenous monarchies and chiefdoms, who at times were supported by the French. This was complemented by the overall war with French forces aiming to secure trading posts and privileges in the region. The conclusion of the Napoleonic war, in favor of the British and their allies, signaled the unchecked, in terms of rival imperial powers, attempt by the British to secure their hegemony in South Asia and the Indian Ocean region. Initially the short-lived treaty of Amiens (1802) and finally the Congress of Vienna (1815) ceded the maritime regions of the island of Sri Lanka, which was formerly under colonial Dutch control, to the British, as well as the Indian sub-continent with the exception of minor areas which remained under French or Portuguese control.

The British consolidated their power under the above conditions and hence enjoyed supremacy in conditioning the global capitalist economy, but this was complicated by indigenous polities in South India and the island of Sri Lanka. In the twilight of the eighteenth century and early nineteenth century the Palaikarrar (Polygyar) rebellion, led by Tamil speaking chieftains known as the Palaikarrar, and other rebellions in Southern India, formed the first formidable anti-imperial and anti-British struggle. It was waged against the empire to maintain native sovereignty in this strategic region central to enforcing imperial influence over the Indian Ocean trading routes and supply lines.

The nation of Eelam Tamils from time immemorial cherished and inhabited their traditional homeland, Tamil Eelam in the north and east of the island of Sri Lanka. Their relation to the seas off their homeland was cherished, as it facilitated their livelihood, trade, and accumulation of wealth. Native sovereignty over large tracts of their homeland was initially lost to the Portuguese in 1616, when the nobility of the Jaffna kingdom capitulated to the Portuguese King following the death of their king in battle against the Portuguese and their native Lascarin forces (Abeyesinghe 1988; Tambiah 1992; Hensman 2010). In the Vanni jungles of the Tamil homeland and the regions bordering the Sinhala homelands in the south, the predominantly Tamil speaking chieftaincies known as Vannimai, maintained their independence for another two centuries and organized resistance against the Portuguese and later against the Dutch with at times the tacit support from the Kandyan kingdom. The peril of British colonialism crushed the remaining native resistance on the island—suppressing the Vanniyars led by Pandara Vanniyan in Eelam in 1803 and crushing the Kandyans in the Sinhala south (Somasundaram 2010). After the formal conquest of the Kandyan throne by the

British in 1815, the chieftaincy and people rose in a rebellion which was brutally crushed by the British in 1818. The British, in the aftermath of their military triumph, enforced counter-insurgency policies of scorched earth, displacement and militarization in the areas of rebellion, both in the Vanni and the Kandyan region (Lewis [1895] 1993). This rebellion by the Tamil and Kandyan Sinhala people was paralleled by the indigenous Veddah rebellion in the southeast. It was in the midst of such persistent resistance against imperial presence in the region, that the Island was made a crown colony directly under the British monarchy, and the entirety of the island was brought under the frameworks of a unitary centralized state centered in Colombo.

Once indigenous resistance to colonial expansion and imperial control was quelled, the British crown commissioned the Colebrook commission to submit a report on a proposed administrative arrangement for the island based on colonial considerations and the experience of conquering the region. Subsequently the empire oversaw the establishment in 1833 of the presently existent unitary state. Military fortifications and encampment remnants from Portuguese and Dutch projects were expanded and consolidated and new ones built, as militarization of the land was needed to ensure security of the colonial state in "alien" regions prone to revolt. Today the militarization processes in Eelam implemented by the Sri Lankan state and its armed forces reflect the similar colonial condition of military occupation, structural genocide and oppression. Creating the unitary state as a crown colony separated it from the administration of South India, which was controlled under the Madras presidency by the British East India Company.

Out of what has been discussed above, it should be seen that indigenous Tamil, tribal and Sinhala resistance against the British expansion of imperial influence and presence in the South Asian region constituted a formidable challenge. Any liaison and coordination between these groups of people across South India and Sri Lanka, would mean jeopardy for British imperial ambitions of control over the region and hence influence in the Indian Ocean region. Such considerations must have influenced the creation of a separate state unit for the island in a unitary form neglecting Tamil national existence, while placing South India in a separate administrative order.

Unitary State: Janus Face of Imperialism and Sinhala Chauvinism

We see also the creation of the ideology of Sinhala nationalism under British supervision and in reciprocity with the perpetuation of the unitary state of Sri Lanka, as a key mechanism in ensuring imperialist designs. It evidences an alignment whereby Sinhala chauvinist orientations and "patriotic" policies deployed by Sinhala elites of various political parties in effect call for stabilization of the unitary state, and thereby facilitate imperial ambitions of supremacy over global economy and maritime security.

Parallel to the creation of the unitary state upon a land which harbored two historical nations, the Eelam Tamils and the Sinhalese, the British colonial governors often gave patronage to the orientalist knowledge production of British and

European scholars associated with institutions such as the Royal Asiatic Society Ceylon Branch, the Theosophical Society and the Pali Text Society. Many of their publications up until the late colonial period, were published at the expense of the colonial government through the government's printer. In effect, a fair share of their production of knowledge revolved around creating authoritative historical narratives in which the Sinhala Buddhists were defined as the natives of the island, and the sole inheritors to the island civilization or archaeological heritage as found in the many ruins across the country. Hence the Sinhala Buddhists were denoted by colonial scholars in liaison with the colonial government as belonging to the "Aryan Race," ideologically creating a proximity to the European colonial power centers and their self-garlanded Aryan supremacy. It was such a state ideology which was created to devise legitimacy for the colonial state among the masses of Sinhala speakers (Rampton 2011; Tambiah 1992; Kapferer 1988; Jayapalan 2015).

The Western-educated Sinhala elite was groomed in this chauvinist ideology as well as in the savoir-faire of a national bourgeoisie connected with the global economy and imperial interests of the British and their allies. Hence, to date, the unitary state is identified as the upholder of Sinhala national existence in the state-centered discourses of Sinhala Buddhist nationalism. The relation between various Sinhala elite formations and the masses during elections, reflects how chauvinist rhetoric and invocations of patriotic sentiments by the Sinhala governing party and oppositional politicians, Buddhist monks, Sinhala elite business representatives, officials of the armed forces and state bureaucrats are intended to rally Sinhala public acceptance to pursue state oppression and suppression of Tamils. Battle cries are made to defeat the Tamil political struggle which is communicated as threatening to fragment their unitary state and hence the future of the Sinhala Buddhist. Hence the masses are oriented within the direction of the Sinhala elites who hold the power of the state in pursuit of chauvinist and genocidal policies, while the unitary state facilitates imperialist interests and intervention in the island and through it the region.

The ancient concept of Dhammadipa was extracted out of Pali scriptures by the orientalist and colonial officials and re-written so as to connote the colonial unitary state. Sinhala Buddhist revivalists and nationalists of the nineteenth century and onwards, the likes of James D'Alwis, Anagarika Dharmapala or monks such as Bhikku Kasappa or Walpola Rahula, based their discourses and ideologies upon such a colonial-orientalist epistemology. Hence Sinhala identity, as articulated by colonial interests, was fashioned to the existence and survival of the colonial-imposed unitary state through the coerced condition of recognizing only the Sinhala-speakers as a nation of historical continuity in the island while presenting Tamils as usurpers and aliens and hence as unentitled to exercise self-determination and sovereignty (Tambiah 1992; Kapferer 1988; Rampton 2011). A recognition of the latter would have meant the reality of a Tamil state in the northeast of the island, which would reduce the optimality of the unitary Colombo-based state and its mechanism as envisaged by external interests, hence fundamentally upsetting imperial geo-political and economic strategies in the region.

Even after the conclusion of the war, minimal Tamil demands to the right of self-determination and sovereignty in a confederal or federal mode, is vigorously opposed by the Sinhala civil leaders, the Sinhala Buddhist clergy, and opposition politicians. The leaders of the Sri Lankan state are unwilling to recognize the crimes of genocide, crimes against humanity and war crimes committed against Tamils by officials of the armed forces and members of the government. On the contrary, they pride themselves on never surrendering to pressures to persecute any member of the state or armed forces. The war criminals are often celebrated as "war heroes" and as protectors of the Sinhala nation, Buddhist religion and state. In 2019, former president Maithripala Sirisena stated that his government ensured that his predecessor and the present prime minister Mahinda Rajapaksa was not brought to the electric chair by the west, and referring to the armed forces, said that his regime has saved "war heroes" from trial. These claims hinted at the manner in which the UNHRC-led process, initiated by the US in Geneva in 2009 following the war, was fundamentally defused once Sirisena's US-friendly regime came in place in 2015. The regime with Mahinda Rajapaksa as president, which oversaw the annihilation of the LTTE and the de facto state of Tamil Eelam, tilted towards Beijing in the aftermath of the war. This created a liability for US ambitions for the Sri Lankan unitary state. Hence a regime change was supported, manipulating, among other factors, Tamil demands for accountability for crimes of the state. The resolution moved in the UNHRC did not address genocide and national oppression which were re-defined as individual human rights issues. A pressure was nominally kept through monitoring while nothing of an international commitment has materialized in arresting the state-orchestrated processes of structural genocide in Eelam. Similar tendencies are seen with the incumbent regime of Gotabaya Rajapaksa which came into power in November 2019, with the US manipulating conditional pressure on individuals in power rather than the state system itself, to ensure Colombo's circuit within Washington's orbit.

Once the regime change occurred in 2015, and a government in favor of US geo-political and economic ambitions in power of the unitary state was in place, the question of Tamil political rights was further defused by representatives of the US and their allies. At the UNHRC, the resolution was renewed every year as the "international community" admitted recognition of progress in the policies of the incumbent government. Tamil political demands of self-determination and statehood were deliberatively not addressed while the legitimacy of the unitary state was affirmed by default. Tamil political aspirations and grievances were not addressed, and pursuit of accountability and justice was tuned out as a domestic process.

From the colonial conquest and deprivation of sovereignty, the Eelam Tamils under the conditions of the colonial and post-colonial era have been subjected to structural genocide levied against them by a shifting matrix of comprador Sinhala bourgeoisie elites wielding state power along with their imperialists backers, be it global or regional hegemons. What we want to shed light on here are the fact that multifaceted processes and series of actions perpetuated over the course of nineteenth, twentieth and twenty-first centuries through the framework of the unitary state, has aimed at dismantling the national characteristic of the Eelam Tamils and their intricate connection with their homeland. Political protests from Tamils commenced in the backdrop of state-aided colonization in the Tamil homeland in the 1930s, revolving around the principles of recognition of Tamil national existence, their traditional homeland, and the right to self-determination in the form of a federal solution. This was during the period of late British colonialism, when they facilitated the Colombo- and unitary-state-centric "national bourgeoisie," which was dominated by leading members of the English educated Sinhala bourgeoisie classes, to experiment with self-government of the colonial state apparatus under imperial supervision (Kapferer 1988; Ponnambalam 1983; Tambiah 1992; Jayapalan 2015). Hence the State Council was formed in 1931 following the first ever election held in the island with universal suffrage, and was headed by D. S. Senenayake, who also became the first prime minister of the neo-colonial state in 1948. A progressive Gandhian social movement which formed around the Eelam Tamil progressive bourgeoisie, The Jaffna Youth Congress, boycotted the first election as a protest against colonial rule (Kadirgamar 1980).

One of the first major actions of the State Council was that it passed the 1931 Land Settlement Ordinance Act which legislated the right of the state to alienate lands for various purposes and for what were termed development projects (Peebles 1990; Manogaran 1987; Tambiah 1984). Under the guise of "irrigation development," Sinhala settlers from the wet-zone were settled along the sparsely populated but Tamil dominated dry zone of the eastern province. In 1948, by granting formal independence, the British Empire handed over full state power to the English-educated Sinhala bourgeoisie led by D. S. Senanayake which formed the government under the United National Party (UNP). D. S. Senanayake also initiated the US and International Bank for Reconstruction and Development (IBRD) funded Gal Oya multi-purpose project shortly after independence which largely targeted over 95,000 acres in the then Tamil and Muslim dominated Eastern Province for land alienation, irrigation and colonization by Sinhala settlers (Peebles 1990; Moore 1989; Manogaran 1987; Muggah 2008; Tambiah 1986). A local consultant of the IBRD had this to put on record regarding the nature of colonization and settlement practices undertaken during the Gal-Oya Project: "It would be correct to say that ... all public investment on irrigation in the Dry Zone has been exclusively for the (Sinhala) peasants or small farmer class in the past 50 years" (Iriyagolle 1978: 60). Some 80,000 Sinhala peasants were settled in the areas of the eastern province which was targeted for the Gal Oya scheme (Muggah 2008). The first riots against Tamils also occurred along the new colonies in 1956, which caused the few Tamil and Muslim farmers who were allotted lands in such schemes to be chased out by Sinhala colonists as well as many hundreds being murdered.

By the 1960s the Batticola district was carved in two, with the southern part established as a separate district named Amparai. Decades of colonization had ensured the growth of a Sinhala population and subsequently Sinhala constituencies, in the midst of a Tamil speaking region, and today the region is dominated by Sinhala settler communities (Manogaran 1987; Ponnambalam 1980). Similar moves to wedge the Tamil homelands through the creation of Sinhala constituencies through state-aided colonization, have also been under way in the regions connecting Trincomalee and Vauvuniya district, and as a result a Sinhala colony based district-division of Weli Oya was created, furthering the state project of wedging the territorial and demographic contiguity of the Tamil homeland. These processes unfolded through the state institution of Mahaweli Development Authority which is the statuary body authorized to manage, maintain, and expand the Accelerated Mahaweli Project. The Accelerated Development Project was initiated by the UNP in 1966, aiming to further irrigate and colonize the Tamil dominated dry zones in the Northern and Eastern Province. The Weli Oya project was part of the L-Scheme of the Mahweli Development, which will be detailed later in the essay. The massive-scale "irrigation" and colonization project was developed with crucial financing from USAID, the World Bank, UNDP as well other Western-based funds (Peebles 1990; Gerharz 2014; Muggah 2008). The location of the project was along the Manal'aaru and the adjoining dry zone the majority of which falls within the traditional Tamil homeland. As the name indicates, the Manal'aaru, as this river was known in Tamil regions, was called Mahaweli Ganga among the Sinhala populace of the island. The state opted for the Sinhala name in an irrigation project which went hand in hand with establishment of Sinhala settlement and military encampments against the protests of Tamil villagers and political movements. As the counter-insurgency was unfolding in 1979, these areas and the traditional Tamil villages which were scattered around, were increasingly targeted by state military actions. What resulted was the destruction and displacement of Tamil villages and their inhabitants in the areas of the projects, especially in Mullaithivu, Poloniruwa, Batticaloa, Anuradhapura and Trincomalee districts (Somasundaram 2010). Once the land was cleansed of its Tamil inhabitants, the state created Sinhala colonies coupled with military bases and encampments, as part of the project to dismantle the contiguity of the Tamil homeland across the Northern and Eastern provinces. These sites have subsequently been the basis for further expansion of such colonization schemes with state patronage.

Tamil Resistance to the Unitary State and Geo-Political Dynamics

Increased state-sponsored terrorism, rampant colonization of the Tamil northeast and the opting for a military solution to deal with the Tamil national question, conditioned the armed and revolutionary phase of the popular Tamil national struggle, so that during the 1970s many revolutionary Tamil militant organizations emerged. The organization with the broadest popular support and which evolved to become the Eelam Tamils vanguard organization were the Liberation Tamil Tigers of Eelam (LTTE). The course of the war crystalized the array of global and regional hegemons who opted to safeguard the unitary state and neutralize the Tamil struggle, chief among which was the US–UK led alliance of states. This was repeatedly mentioned by the LTTE leaders in events held in their de facto state addressing the Tamil masses. The consolidation of the US-led alliance of states aiding the Sri Lankan state and their facilitation of necessary military and diplomatic resources to the Sri Lankan state apparatus was crucial in making possible what was in essence an internationally abetted pursuit of a military solution to the LTTE and Tamil national liberation struggle. It was part of the new phase of US imperial geo-political drive phrased the "war on terror" doctrine and successive Sri Lankan governments designed their military efforts at crushing the LTTE within such a US orientation. The military phase concluded in May 18, 2009 with the state executing the genocidal massacres of tens of thousands of Eelam Tamil civilians and freedom fighters alike at Mulli'vaykal on the northeastern coast. The counter-insurgency and the structural processes aiming to eradicate the pillars of the Tamil national existence and neutralize their political struggle to resolve the national question have unfolded in an unprecedented manner since annihilation of LTTE. Military occupation, militarization of civic life, land alienation and state aided colonization accentuate the overall pauperization of the Eelam Tamils.

These processes have unfolded in their homeland in different and often more sophisticated and structural form than what was the case during the war, as the state is now unchallenged in exercising their authority in the northeast. In terms of the contemporary geo-political dynamics the last war and its massacres unfolded through the unitary state apparatus of the Sri Lankan state with the tacit support of global and regional hegemons. The Sri Lankan military occupation and state oppression of Tamils continues with the same logic. The US and their allies, as well as India and China, among others, despite their rivalries or strategic partnerships, have all been vying to secure their strategic interests in the south Asian section of the Indian Ocean region through negotiation with various ruling elites ensconced in Colombo. Such considerations effectuate actions aimed at the stabilization of the unitary state. Consequently, in return, economic and strategic concessions on the island are being handed over by Sri Lankan governments to their external backers. For instance, Chinese state firms were given a ninety-nine-year lease on the Hambantota harbor, which they built, and the massive Colombo port-city project manned by China is under way. In the North and East, there have been proposed projects to be granted to Indian private and state firms in terms of the development of KKS port, Palali airport and Sampoor coal power plant.

On the Eastern coast of the island lays Trincomalee, declared as the political capital of Tamils throughout their political struggle. The renowned Trincomalee harbor has been eyed by various imperialist powers since the colonial era, for constituting one of the finest natural deep water harbors in the world. During World War II, Trincomalee was utilized by the British Empire, as the base of the Eastern fleet and it was bombed by the Japanese Airforce in 1942. At present, India, the US and its ally Japan as well China have all expressed wishes to secure deals with Colombo. As we speak, the Sri Lankan naval installments at Trincomalee harbor are being expanded under the context of increased maritime defense ties and military engagement with the US Indo-Pacific Command (USINDOPACCOM) (Tamilnet 2018a). In 2016, there was established a Marine Corps of the Sri Lankan

Navy (SLN), stationed at the SLN Vidura base at Trincomalee. The unit was modeled on the US Marine Corps and has received extensive training by branches of the US Navy and Marines. From November 22 to November 25, 2016, US Marines and Sailors of the 11th Marine Expeditionary Unit (11th MEU) were in Trincomalee to conduct a "Theater Security Cooperation" training with the Sri Lankan Marine Corps. In the aftermath of the joint military exercise, the head of US Pacific Command, Navy Admiral Harry Harris Jr, stated that joint training with the US Marines reflected that "Sri Lanka" was being developed as a "significant contributor" alongside US efforts at ensuring security of the "maritime superhighways" of the Indian Ocean region (Marine Corps Times 2016). From October 2 to October 6, 2017, the US and its allies held the 23rd Cooperation Afloat Readiness and Training (CARAT) exercises in Trincomalee for the first time, with the Sri Lankan Navy (Sri Lanka Navy 2017).

Under the newly constituted "Eastern Naval Area" of the Sri Lankan Navy, the eastern coastal districts of the Tamil homeland have been subject to increased militarization as large tracts of land are alienated and previously occupied land have been used to establish military and naval installments. At Mullivaykal in coastal Mullaithivu district, along the eastern coastal line of Eelam facing the Bay of Bengal, the SLN Gothabhaya base was established following the last war, appropriating 300 acres of private lands of Tamils and 200 acres of public land (Tamilnet 2016a). In 2016, this base was further expanded with new installations and further land was appropriated for such militarization purposes. In Trincomalee District, the Sri Lankan Navy Vidura was relocated from the harbor to the Champoor region, a move involved further alienating around 300 acres of the agricultural and residential lands of Tamils speaking communities in the Champoor area (Tamilnet 2016b). Further expansion of the Vidura SLN base was undertaken so that it accounts now for over 3000 acres and has extended into the neighboring Moothor East, alienating lands from Tamil speaking communities living there (Tamilnet 2018b).

Such a massive scale of militarization and occupation in the aftermath of 2009 is alienating more lands from a people who have already been displaced, deprived and pauperized by state militarization through the course of the civil war. There is a clear linkage in the increased military to military coordination of the Sri Lankan armed forces, in particular the SLN and the USPACCOM. The expansion of bases upon occupied Tamil land, is part of the US ambitions to consolidate the co-operability of the USPACICOM and their regional allies such as Japan and India with the Sri Lankan maritime defense facilities and the Sri Lankan Navy. This year the newly established Sri Lankan Navy Marine Corps was enrolled in the US-led RIMPAC military exercises for the very first time (*Dailymirror*, August 11, 2018). On August 24, 2018, the amphibious transport dock-ship, USS Anchorage with the 13th Marine Expeditionary Unit (MEU) arrived in Trincomalee port. The mission is to train with the Sri Lankan naval and military forces in the area, and to conduct surveys and study other conditions of the location. The official website of the US Embassy in Colombo, the Charge d'Affaires and interim of the embassy, announced the arrival and purpose of the visit in the following:

This visit and training will build our shared capacity to respond to humanitarian emergencies in the Indo-Pacific region. We're also excited to try out the air logistics hub concept which utilizes Sri Lanka's strategic location in the Indian Ocean to ensure the quick availability of relief supplies, equipment and other material when needed by the US and partner militaries and humanitarian organizations.
(US Embassy Colombo 2018)

Rear Admiral Brad Cooper, the commander of Amphibious Force US 7th Fleet expressed the importance of Sri Lanka in US geo-strategic ambitions in the maritime region: "Our Navy and Marine Corps team is deeply committed to continuing to strengthen our partnership with the Sri Lankan armed forces" (US Embassy Colombo 2018). Similarly many naval and maritime defense joint exercises with the Naval forces of Japan and India have also taken place.

Hence in the post-Cold War scenario the rivalry between various alliances of hegemons, be it the US–UK axis, China or India, especially in the Indian Ocean region, seems to be principled not on ideological or moral opposition, but by a free-market logic. This can be argued as being reminiscent of fledging stages at the development of world capitalism, in which competition between the colonial enterprises of the Portuguese, Dutch, Danish, French and British did not materialize any principled support of indigenous political sovereignty. Any sovereign movement with its basis among a deprived and oppressed people, which values collective life, self-reliance, dignity of their land and seas, in other words their sovereignty over their national or collective life, their homeland and their seas, do not by the very factors mentioned before, facilitate the exploitation of their lands, seas or future development on behalf of externally situated interests of an imperialist and corporate nature. This very logic seems to have been a driving consideration during the era of colonialism and the rivalry between imperialist powers. The creation of modern bureaucratic-capitalist states in the image of the imperial powers reflects such strategic considerations—they are administrative frameworks established to secure the strategic and geo-economic interests of the colonial powers in regions of the world outside the centers of empire while also integrating the homelands and seas of indigenous nations and peoples and their economic and cultural life within the domains of the then-fledgling global capitalist political and economic order.

The trajectory of recent "international interventions" in Libya and Syria in comparison to the Sri Lankan context, is a prime example to highlight one of our arguments. The comparison illuminates the connection between certain states of colonial origin, the geo-politics of contemporary imperialist powers, and the modus operandi of the capitalist-liberal world order with global institutions like the UN and the West-based corporate media being its foremost champions. The regimes in power of these state-formations were in opposition to US geo-political ambitions in the region of Africa and the Middle-East and, in the case of Syria, projects by the US and their regional allies related to energy supply lines, the latter, along with the UN system over which they hold hegemony, engaged in a strikingly different manner then in the Sri Lankan context. The dominant political and armed opposition to the state was orchestrated and financed by the US and its regional allies. Corporate media painted the picture in a way friendly to this opposition, whereas the regimes in power were demonized. This quickened public opinion in the West in favor of US imperial policy, and the UN Security Council acted accordingly. This is in stark contrast to the concluding phases of the war in Sri Lanka. There, the unitary state being within the orbit of the imperial ambitions of the US and its allies, it was the challenge posed by the armed struggle of the Tamils and the LTTE to state power which was demonized and delegitimized. The state and its brutalities were whitewashed and corporate media silenced the voices of Eelam Tamils who were protesting in the tens of thousands across world capitals alerting that a genocide was unfolding. Hence, over 146,000 Tamils perished during the last war and are still unaccounted for, without any sustained effort by international organizations such as the UN or any global or regional hegemon to prevent it during its occurrence or, in its aftermath, to deliver justice for the genocide struck against the Eelam Tamils. Neither is there any will for the "international community" to facilitate Eelam Tamil self-determination and sovereignty to arrest the processes of national oppression. This brief illustration should elucidate the relation between geo-political interests of the US–UK axis and the viability of the UN organization. Similarly, it casts light on when and why "international intervention" occurs and the conditions of corporate media coverage and what happens with such coverage when such a concocted effort does not take place, when the so called "international community" appeals to non-intervention or when the genocidal processes are distorted or silenced. Subsequently, humanity witnesses genocidal massacres being unfolded without any "global outcry."

Militarization and Colonization: Military-genocidal Solution to Eelam Post-2009

In the aftermath of the annihilation of the LTTE and their de facto state, which had effectively arrested the genocidal processes levied by the state targeting the Tamils, these structural processes have been implemented unhindered. The systematic colonization of Tamil collective and private lands by a multiplicity of state apparatuses and corporate institutions, the deprivation and dismantling of Tamil economy and livelihood practices in the northeast are among the many manifestations of these processes. Chief among others are the systematic changes of demographic patterns and cultural landscape of the Tamil homeland, through state-aided colonization by Sinhala settlers from the south. This is complemented with systemic revision of history through the educational institutions as well the state machinery through official narratives of history constituted in accordance with the ruling ideology of Sinhala chauvinism and supremacy. These deny Tamils' historical presence in the island and present the contemporary Tamil formations as the result of invasions and immigration from South India, while the island is represented as the heritage of the Aryan Sinhala Buddhist from the beginning of civilization. In terms of representing the recent past, the Tamil political struggle is portrayed as terrorism which threatened this Sinhala nation, the state and Buddhism. Such efforts have the express aim of silencing Tamil collective memory and history. Venues and institutions which can cultivate Tamil literary, folkloric, artistic and scholastic traditions, reflecting the history of the Tamil-speaking peoples and their intricate relation to their homeland, as well as their experiences of militarization and oppression and that of resistance and struggle for liberation, are not made available. While memorials and structures built by the people to commemorate and pay homage to the LTTE and their martyrs during the course of the war have been systematically destroyed since 2009, and such remembrance prohibited by the Sri Lankan state, large monuments commemorating the Sri Lankan army, and projecting the state narrative of the war, have been erected across the Tamil homeland by the Sri Lankan armed forces.

As part of the militarization of the Tamil homeland there has also been the mushrooming of Sinhala Buddhist monastic institutions and shrines with the support of the state and the military apparatuses. In Kanniya, Kooni-theevu in the Trincomalee district, as well as in sites in north of Vauvuniya, lands upon which Tamil worship sites were located, at which customary rituals were conducted from time immemorial, have been usurped from the Tamil villagers displaced due to military operations of the state. In Kanniya and Kooni-theevu, Tamil Hindu worship sites have been subjected to alienation by the department of archaeology in conjunction with Buddhist monks and their institutions, backed by the state, who build new Buddhist temples on these sites. This has been aimed at altering the cultural make-up of the northeast, which is Tamil speaking and non-Buddhist in demography. The military presence and occupation in the Tamil homeland has been expanded since the end of armed conflict in 2009.

While it is the unitary state which is facilitating such processes, it is important to understand the roles played by global and regional powers as well as multi-national and Colombo-based corporations in service of both the global economy and these genocidal processes. Their roles can be seen from the resistance that has been organized against them. In the face of such structural dismantling, Eelam Tamil civil society and grassroots organizations backed by struggle-centric political representatives of the Tamils, have increasingly organized peaceful protests against a variety of state-aided processes. There have also been grassroots organizations formed by affected Tamil villagers to reclaim their occupied land from the security forces and state aided Sinhala settlements as well as from state departments and multinational as well as southern Sinhala firms, such as at Keppapulavu, Mullivaykal, Naay'aaru, Kokku'lay in Mullaithivu district, Vaalikamam, Navakula in Jaffna, Iranaithivu and Mullikulam in Mannar as well as Sampoor and Muttoor in the east, where a coal power plant was initially planned by an Indian state cum private firm but has been temporarily abandoned after local protest against environmental hazards. Incidentally, the US Embassy in Colombo, driven by a wish to keep India out of the Trincomalee Harbour region, backed a Colombo-based NGO in filing a court case against the Indian project. Despite their strategic partnership, the US seems to aim to keep India in a dependent-subservient position to the US ambitions vis-à-vis the island. Many of the maritime and lagoon water areas in the northeast Sri Lanka which are occupied or sealed off by military encampments of the Sri Lankan army and navy, are exploited commercially through military-run or southern business-run firms, who then export the produce to foreign markets. Similarly, agricultural lands occupied by the army in Mullaithivu, Killinochi, Mannar, Jaffna and Trincomalee district, have also been made into agro-business entities, in many cases employing former LTTE cadres who went through forceful "rehabilitation" and enrolled into the Ministry of Defense administered Civil Defense Force (CDF).

As mentioned, there has also been large scale increases in land alienated from Tamil-speaking communities by the state for the expansion of naval and military installments in regions surrounding the Trincomalee harbor, as part of the expansion of the military to military engagements between the SLN and the USINDOPACCOM. These developments show how land alienation along the eastern coast, afflicting Tamil-speaking communities, which grassroots organizations are protesting, places Tamil political protest at odds with militarization of the region and the exploitation of maritime resources by multinational firms. These become material manifestations or "local effects" of the imperialist geo-political and economic ambitions within which the Sri Lankan state engages with the US, the UK and their allies, whether that is their strategic partners such as India or traditional allies such as Australia and Japan. Recently the seas of Batticaola, maritime areas used by Tamils for their livelihood and held in dignity by the fishing population of the Tamil nation, are being surveyed for natural maritime resources. The surveyor is a subsidiary of the US oilfield service company Schlumberger, called Eastern Echo DMCC, and was granted the survey study project by the government of Sri Lanka to survey the eastern coast for petroleum resources. The Colombo government is paying 50 million dollars to Eastern Echo DMCC. However the vehicle used by the Eastern Echo DMCC for the seismic study is acquired through a contract with a Chinese firm (Tamilnet 2018c). Free-market logic driven by capital accumulation has produced some strange abominations that overcome rivalry between hegemons. Hence the national oppression and structural genocide executed by the unitary state against Eelam Tamils, is tied structurally to US-led imperialist ambitions of militarization and hegemony over maritime trading routes, maritime resources and strategic positions within the Indian Ocean region.

Tamil protests have revolved around protesting state-mediated development in the Tamil regions, as the former chief minister of Northern Province declined a membership in the central state controlled Presidential Task Force, supposed to regulate and facilitate internationally financed and supported development. In a letter to the Sri Lankan president, the former chief minister Wigneswaran highlighted that the development needs of Tamils are in community and local-controlled enterprises and not large scale industrial development (Tamilnet 2018d). Recently, a large and popular protest, one of few of its kind in the aftermath of the last war and the subsequent military occupation, was organized by the Tamil masses in Mullaithivu district to oppose the state-aided colonization, land alienation and erection of Sinhala Buddhist temples and shrines in the northeast. The practical mechanism through which this was pursued is the controversial

L-scheme of the Mahaweli Development Project. This project oversaw the creation of the Weli Oya. The Tamil protestors identified the Western-funded project as a means through which colonization, militarization and Sinhala Buddhization occurred and demanded the arrest of the processes of structural genocide. They ask that lands of Tamils alienated under this development be returned to their rightful owners, and the military to return the land occupied from Tamils during the course of war.

Conclusion

Imperial powers persist in opting to stabilize the unitary state and enhancing its diplomatic, financial and military capacities to achieve the larger ambitions of securing geo-economic and geo-strategic interests in and around the south Asian maritime region. In terms of strategic location Sri Lanka is situated at a central position at a juncture of the sea-trading and supply lanes from the Americas, Europe, the Mediterranean and Middle East through the Suez or the straits of Hormuz, from the west towards Southeast Asia, the Isthmus of Kra, the straits of Malacca and ultimately to China, Japan, the Philippines and Korea.

Tamil armed struggle was the foremost destabilizing factor in terms of the unitary state, and through it also posed liabilities to the US geo-economic and strategic ambitions for the region, and subsequently to the order of global economy under the hegemony of the US, the UK and allies. Recently we have witnessed how US-led imperialism in a unipolar free-market order is increasingly under challenge from a rival hegemon such as China. However, in material terms, such challenge has not meant that the competing rivalry between powers to secure their imperial ambitions translates into provision of political space or possibilities for oppressed nations and peoples' movements subjected to state terrorism or genocide. As in the case for the Eelam struggle, the nation-state in question, Sri Lanka is sustained by the support of regional and world hegemons. One can see how competing powers all opt to secure the unitary Sri Lankan state and groom a coalition of ruling elites as masters of state power. As in the colonial days, the modern imperialist powers view as a pre-condition to secure their interests through the unitary state the need for their allied Colombo elites to generate legitimacy internally among the Sinhala masses through canvassing Sinhala chauvinism and consequently intensifying the structural genocide against the Eelam Tamil nation. It is upon such a world, when humanity is sacrificed for the calculations of the geo-political and economic interests of world and regional powers, that there is a need for people to unite without the mediation of states and their interests. It is the principled collaboration and solidarity between grassroots formations representing political struggles of oppressed peoples and nations, which can provide a geo-political leverage anchored on respect for humanity, for land, for seas and independence. We, the Eelam Tamils, wish to place our struggle among the many of whom are represented here. We also hope that the solidarity between the wretched of the earth shall form out of such conventions which bring together representatives of resistors and victims of the global political and economic order of the day.

Athithan Jayapalan is a PhD candidate at the University of Oslo, Norway. Due to the war in Sri Lanka he was displaced from the Tamil homeland and was raised in Norway. He holds an MA from Bergen University, Norway, and has published articles on the geopolitical dynamics of the Tamil national struggle.

Gajendrakumar Ponnambalam is barrister-at-law from Lincoln's Inn and an attorney-at-law in Sri Lanka. After the assassination of his father by the paramilitary groups operating with the Sri Lankan security forces, he joined political activism. He served as a parliamentarian representing the Tamil National Alliance and campaigned internationally for a negotiated political settlement for the decades-long ethno-nationalist conflict in the country.

References

Abeyesinghe, T. 1988. *Jaffna under the Portuguese*. Colombo: Stamford Lake.

Gerharz, E. 2014. *The Politics of Reconstruction and Development in Sri Lanka: Transnational commitments to Social Change*. London: Routledge. https://doi.org/10.4324/9781315777214

Hensman, A. 2010. "The Malvana Convention of 1598 and Other Historical Conventions." *Dailymirror* (Colombo), February 15.

Iriyagolle, I. M. R. A 1978. *The Truth about the Mahawelli*. Colombo: Nuegoda.

Jayapalan, A. 2015. "The Sri Lankan National Left, Imperialism and the Tamil National Question." Paper presented at the centenary of A. Vaidyalingam, November, London. Retrieved from www.researchgate.net/publication/281937022_The_Sri_Lankan_National_Left_Imperialism_and_the_Tamil_National_Question (accessed May 28, 2019).

Kadirgamar, S. 1980. "The Jaffna Youth Congress." In *Handy Perinbanayagam: A Memorial Lecture, The Jaffna Youth Congress and Selections from His Writings and Speeches*, edited by A. S. Kanagaratnam and N. Sabaratnam. Jaffna: Handy Perinbanayagam Commemoration Society.

Kapferer, B. 1988. *Legends of People, Myths of State Violence, Intolerance, and Political Culture in Sri Lanka and Australia*. London: Smithsonian Institution Press.

Lemkin, R. 1946. "Genocide." *American Scholar* 15(2): 227–230.

Lewis, J. P. [1895] 1993. *Manual of the Vanni districts (Vavuniya and Mulattivu) of the Northern Province, Ceylon*. New Delhi: Navrang.

Malathy, N. 2012. *A Fleeting Moment in My Country: The Last Years of the LTTE de facto State*. Atlanta, GA: Clarity Press.

Manogaran, Chelvadurai. 1987. *Ethnic Conflict and Reconciliation in Sri Lanka*. Honolulu, HI: University of Hawaii Press.

Marine Corps Times. 2016. "Pride of the pacific trains new Sri Lankan Marine Corps." *Marine Corps Times*, December 4. Retrieved from www.marinecorpstimes.com/news/your-marine-corps/2016/12/04/pride-of-the-pacific-trains-new-sri-lankan-marine-corps (accessed 20 May 2019).

Moore, M. 1989. "The Ideological History of the Sri Lankan Peasantry." *Modern Asian Studies* 23(1): 179–207. https://doi.org/10.1017/S0026749X00011458

Muggah, Robert. 2008. *Relocation Failures: A Short History of Internal Displacement in Sri Lanka*. London: Zed Books.

Peebles, P. 1990. "Colonization and Ethnic Conflict in the Dry Zone of Sri Lanka." *Journal of Asian Studies* 49(1): 30–55. https://doi.org/10.2307/2058432

Ponnambalam, S. 1980. *Dependent Capitalism in Crisis: The Sri Lankan Economy 1948–1980*. London: Zed Books.

Ponnambalam, S. 1983. *Sri Lanka: The National Question and the Tamil Liberation Struggle*. London: Zed Books.

Rampton, D. 2011. "Deeper Hegemony: The Politics of Sinhala Nationalist Authenticity and the Failures of Power-Sharing in Sri Lanka." *Contemporary and Comparative Politics* 42(2): 245–273. https://doi.org/10.1080/14662043.2011.564476

Somasundaram, D. 2010. "Collective Trauma in the Vanni: A Qualitative Inquiry into the Mental Health of the Internally Displaced due to the Civil War in Sri Lanka". *International Journal of Mental Health Systems* 4: article 22. https://doi.org/10.1186/1752-4458-4-22

Sri Lanka Navy. 2017. "Cooperation Afloat Readiness & Training (CARAT) Exercise Begins Tomorrow in Trincomalee." *Sri Lankan Navy News*, October 1. Retrieved from http://news.navy.lk/eventnews/2017/10/01/201710011600 (accessed May 20, 2019).

Tambiah, S. J. 1984. *Sri Lanka: Ethnic Fractricide and the Dismantling of Democracy*. New Delhi: Oxford University Press.

Tambiah, S. J. 1986. *Sri Lanka: Ethnic Fratricide and Dismantling of Democracy*. London. L. Tauris and Co.

Tambiah, S. J. 1992. *Buddhism Betrayed: Religion, Politics and Violence in Sri Lanka*. World Institute for Development Economic Research (WIDER).

Tamilnet. 2016a. "Colombo Beefs Up Naval Installations along Eastern Coast." Retrieved from www.tamilnet.com/art.html?catid=79&artid=38280 (accessed May 20, 2019).

Tamilnet. 2016b. "Resettling Champoor Tamils Deceived, Hundreds Of Acres Seized for Militarization." Retrieved from www.tamilnet.com/art.html?catid=13&artid=38464 (accessed May 21, 2019).

Tamilnet. 2018a. "US Naval Partnership with Genocidal Sri Lanka Escalates with New Delhi's blessings." Retrieved from www.tamilnet.com/art.html?catid=79&artid=39171 (accessed May 21, 2019).

Tamilnet. 2018b. "SL Navy Erects New Buildings in Occupied Moohoor East." Retrieved from www.tamilnet.com/art.html?catid=13&artid=39016 (accessed May 25, 2019).

Tamilnet 2018c. "US Oil Firm Surveys Seas off North-East Using Chinese Vessel." Retrieved from www.tamilnet.com/art.html?catid=79&artid=39185 (accessed May 26, 2019).

Tamilnet. 2018d. "NPC CM Declines Participation in Colombo's Unilateral Task Force for So-called Development." Retrieved from http://t.tamilnet.com/art.html?catid=13&artid=39127 (accessed May 30, 2019).

US Embassy Colombo. 2018. "USS Anchorage & 13th MEU Arrive in Sri Lanka." Retrieved from https://lk.usembassy.gov/uss-anchorage-13th-meu-arrive-in-sri-lanka (accessed May 30, 2019).

6

Militarization and Everyday Struggle: A Case of Families of the Victims of Enforced Disappearances in Kashmir

Farrukh Faheem

> ... We know the pain of erasure.
> We, the poets of persistence.
> We, who outran our destiny.
> We, who cradle the ache of an unsung longing, a lingering history.
> We, who bear the burden of outliving our children.
> We, who survived a genocide of colours, a massacre of language.
> We, who enwomb within us evanescence.
> We, who have tricked forgetting.
> We, within whom, flows a dark river of impossible love.
> We, the wandering minstrels of hope. We the balladeers of dawn.
> We the elegists of night. We the bards of loss.
> —Uzma Falak (cited in Sinha undated)

Introduction

Like other communities in South Asia, in Kashmir men are recognized as primary upholders of the family. Traditionally Kashmiri women have remained confined within the four walls of their homes attached to a patrilocal household. They remained dependent on the male members of their families. This dependence was so deep rooted that even the personal issues of the women were decided by the eldest male member. Although women have been earning their living in the home-based handicraft industry for a long time and have been contributing to the family's income, the male members always maintained control over matters related to family's income and expenditure (Dabla et al. 2000).

However, the early 1990s uprising against the Indian state in Jammu and Kashmir had a deep impact on every aspect of Kashmiri society. Massive militarization, clampdowns on protesting populations followed by long curfews and violence influenced the everyday life in Kashmir. The enhanced presence of Indian armed forces and vulnerability of male family members to detention, disappearance and killings undermined and stretched the traditional roles occupied by women in the Kashmiri society. Consequently, the stretched roles of women had a deep impact on the social relations and familial obligations. In this chapter, I argue that in conflict zones, violence often influences the family organization and such influences are a part of the larger patterns of change witnessed in the socio-political order.

As political contestations increase the conventional lines of difference between the domestic realm of the family and the public domain of politics vanishes. In this chapter, I attempt to capture the tensions between the domestic realm of the family and the public realm of politics and how political contestations enter the domestic domain of the family and produce new contexts or social relations. The chapter is based on field experience of working with the victims of state violence and the families of the victims of enforced disappearances associated with the Association of Parents of Disappeared Persons (APDP) in Kashmir.

Militarization, Women and Everyday Life in Kashmir

Militarization in Kashmir is synonymous with a state of total war that is not confined to "public" military-militant encounters or extra-legal offensive against Kashmiri [people]; it breaches conventional civil military spatial distinctions and permeates domestic "private" spaces presumed to be beyond the realm of war/militarized conflict.

(Kazi 2009)

As five key elected members of Muslim United Front (MUF) offered their resignations to the Jammu and Kashmir Assembly in 1987, the socio-political landscape of Kashmir witnessed resurgence in protests and violent skirmishes in the same year. By the end of autumn huge Azadi rallies (Freedom Marches) mobilized thousands of men, women and children. A young boy named Ajaz Dar who had died in a violent encounter with the police became one of the first martyrs of the struggle. Such young men subsequently became cult figures in Kashmir. Although women played a significant role in these mobilizations, initially their roles were restricted around the domestic spheres of life. Women who watched such mobilizations in the vicinity of their homes would often show their reverence to the struggle by showering flower petals and candies on the marching participants. During the initial phases of the spontaneous mobilizations women would cook and distribute meals and drinks to the protestors. Such domestic activism played a crucial role in sustaining the struggle. In the later stages of organized Azadi rallies women openly participated in the marches. Women from diverse backgrounds, teachers, students and house-wives closely identified with the struggle and were at the forefront of such mobilizations. Family members marching with siblings and other relatives in the rallies became a common sight in series of Azadi rallies in subsequent years

Many scholars argue that while armed conflicts do inflict immense suffering on women, paradoxically, they also create spaces for them in the public sphere. Armed conflicts thus compel women to actively reshape their domestic relationships and political commitments. As massive clampdowns especially on the Azadi mobilizations and particularly on men increased, women took up roles in the public sphere. Thus, women would often come out of the four walls of their houses protesting against the atrocities committed by the Indian armed forces and would take attempts to shield men from getting hit by their rifle-butts. They would also participate in sit-ins outside military installations protesting against the arbitrary arrests of their loved ones. In several ways these instances of activism by women were rooted in the socio-cultural values of the society at large. According to one estimate, in 2004, there were around 500,000 to 700,000 Indian soldiers in Kashmir, representing "just under half of or 44 percent of total Indian army strength" with almost a soldier for every ten Kashmiris. This approximately is equal to fifty-seven soldiers per square mile making Kashmir the most heavily militarized place in the world (Bhinda 1994: 66; Jaudel 1993: 4).

Against the backdrop of such a high military presence in Kashmir, the sites of violent fights between the army and armed groups are often the spaces frequented by women and children, the most vulnerable sections of any society. Such spaces have been shifting and shrinking for these groups in the past twenty years of conflict. The shared spaces like Yarbal (village tank), farmlands, orchards or even shrines frequented by women and children are often sites of conflict between the army and armed groups. It shall be futile to reaffirm that the worst sufferers through these episodes are women and children. Since the start of the uprising, eight to ten thousand people have disappeared and there are around one thousand "half-widows" in Kashmir today (Kazi 2009).

The loops of long concertina wire and the olive-green army bunkers that dot the streets of Kashmir, organized, ordered and altered the social relations within Kashmiri society. The delineation of the spaces highlighted through military sign boards as "security zone," "VIP area," "no-headlight on zone," or as a "surveillance zone" reflects the physical architecture of the militarized space and the challenges faced by people in negotiating these spaces. As the number of Indian armed forces and their encounters with armed groups increased, the countryside of Kashmir also witnessed a significant change. The shared open spaces were closed up with boundary walls and locked gates. The new practice of constructing boundary walls and gates as a physical barrier around households was intended as a measure to delay the arrival of armed forces and to secure the private space of the home. As the political contestations between the people and Indian State increased, the private realm of the family and the public political domain merged, constituting a new social organization.

Women and Family: Shifting Roles

Violence perpetrated by the Indian armed forces during what came to be known as a "crackdown" has been a daily routine in Kashmir. A crackdown can be announced anywhere in Kashmir without a warning. A typical crackdown involves Indian armed forces cordoning off a village or a locality in the wee hours of the day. Armed forces make an announcement giving directions to the people from the mosque loudspeakers; they then round up men and boys to identify active participants to the movement. Women are asked to stay back inside their houses, while men are paraded in front of an informant for identification. The area under a crackdown is surrounded by armed forces and shops are closed and people are made to stand for hours. A group of soldiers then conduct house to house searches looking for underground men, arms and ammunition. At the end of every crackdown complaints of houses being ransacked, men being beaten up and women abused by armed forces are quite common (Crossette 1991: §A, 8). Thus, besides the everyday experience of violence the incidence of sexual abuse and enforced disappearances at the hands of armed forces have been specifically reported during such crackdowns. After any violent skirmish between the Indian armed forces and armed guerrillas the fear of crackdowns would make the entire village or locality run for safety. Fearing reprisals from the armed forces, the families often run away to their kinship networks in other "safer" localities or villages.

The notion of "home" as a space, safe and distant from violent conflict "outside" has been threatened by the increasing intrusions into the domestic home space through military crackdowns, mid-night search operations and sieges. Series of military operations like Operation "Tiger," "Shiva" and the "Catch and Kill" were launched by the Indian state in the aftermath of the 1990s uprising in Kashmir. It was essentially a campaign of "surprise raids" and was designed to "capture and kill suspected militants and terrorize civilian sympathizers." These operations often resulted in summary executions of detainees and indiscriminate attacks on civilians. There were frequent reports of arson attacks, burning of houses, shops, and entire neighborhoods during such operations. As civilian causalities started to mount, one of the indirect consequences of such violence in Kashmir was the increasing role of women in the public sphere. Almost every Kashmiri household has a story about the Indian armed forces barging into their houses in the middle of the night and picking up male members of the household. In many women's experiences, the experience of their sons or husbands being "picked up" in front of their eyes highlights their trauma of being a witness to an injustice and their sense of responsibility towards the victim and to the family.

Rubiya from the Bemina locality of Srinagar, whose husband was picked up by the Indian armed forces, recalls how they barged into her house at midnight:

> We were fast asleep and then we heard a knock on the door. Around 1.30 in the night forces from nearby camp of Rashtriya Rifles barged into our house. They asked me to leave the room and began questioning my husband. They started interrogating and beating up my husband. When I tried to intervene they pushed me out of the room. I could hear him screaming in pain. They continued to interrogate and beat him up till Fajar Namaz (morning prayers). In the morning they roughed him up in an armored vehicle and took him away. We tried to look for him. We went to every military camp and police station but were unable to trace him. We even filed a First Information Report ... Getting the news that your loved one is dead is a different thing compared to the trauma of waiting for a person who has been made to disappear ... I was thirty when my husband was picked up. It is just me and my son now ... I have spent all my money in tracing him. It is so difficult to meet family expenses ... In Islam one is supposed to wait for a certain number of years if one's husband is disappeared ... I was asked to re-marry, but I do not want to. What if my husband returns? What will I do then?

Rubiya's husband was picked up by the Indian army on 2nd September, 1995. For the last two decades she has been waiting for her husband's return. Over the years, thousands of women like Rubiya, while taking on the economic burdens of running a household continue to suffer from the trauma of waiting and the associated uncertainty regarding their conjugal status. Thirty-two-year-old Firdaus, whose husband was made to disappear by the Indian armed forces in the year 2000, runs a small make-shift tea stall on a handcart outside a hospital in Srinagar. She is one among hundreds of women who are associated with the Association of Parents of Disappeared Persons (APDP). Her everyday life reflects how women in Kashmir have learnt to negotiate the new challenges. She often faces harassment and threat of eviction from the police:

> I knew there would be problems in running a tea stall outside this hospital. But when the conditions at your home are bad and you have to earn a living, one has to prepare oneself to face anything that may come one's way ... Three days ago my shop was removed by the police. Initially I thought of calling Jiji [Parveena Ahangar, Chairperson of APDP] and seeking help from her, but when I realized that these problems would keep recurring in future too, I decided to deal with it on my own ... you see now here I am back in my shop ...

Studies have highlighted that the arrest or disappearance of a family member has implications for family functioning as well as family structure. Arrests or disappearances where the victim happens to be a child's father can have even deeper implications (Garbarino 1996). In the context of Kashmir, the prolonged conflict has compelled women into non-traditional social and family roles. The vulnerability of men to arrests, enforced disappearances, killings, torture and long incarcerations; the consequent need for women to augment the family income; and the increased political involvement of children in agitations and stone-pelting incidents are some of the instances that triggered the transitions in family roles and expectations. Narratives of families in Kashmir reflect psycho-social and economic costs of the searches; "the struggle to survive economically when father or husband is taken away competes for primacy with the search." Families travel long distances in search of their loved ones and seek information about them from detention centers, police stations and prisons. Some children whose fathers have been made to disappear end up in orphanages when mothers and families can no longer support them (Mathur 2015: 1).

In the cases of widows of Kashmir, it has been observed that a majority of women shift from their patrilocal households to the paternal family house (Dabla et al. 2000: 264). However, in cases of "half-widows" and their children, several have preferred staying in their patrilocal households, as one of our respondents observed:

> I live with in-laws at their house, with my mother-in-law, sister in law and my son. My two sisters and three brothers live far away from here at my paternal home. I am not in touch with them ... things are not very good between us ...

In the absence of the husband, the nature and extent of support extended by the patrilocal family members determines whether a "half-widow" will be accommodated in the patrilocal house or at her paternal house. As another respondent substantiates:

My parents live in Urdu bazaar but I don't live with them, my father in law was kind enough to provide us with a shelter where I could live with my daughters.

Although many "half-widows" in Kashmir experience kindness and support from relatives and neighbors they have to live with the constraints of societal norms that surround women without husbands within the close-knit communities. As one of the respondents observed:

Whenever people from outside come here for interviews it generates lot of gossip in my neighborhood. Some of them have even accused me of taking money from them. I don't give any interviews to people from outside. We can't trust everybody … and I have grown-up daughters … I do not feel comfortable, I have to be bit careful with things …

Violent conflicts are known to have considerable impact on the social fabric of the affected communities. From social relations between family members, neighbors and friends to intra-community relations, conflicts are known to impact communities significantly. Armed conflicts deeply affect the social interactions and community trust resulting in transformations of social norms around trust and cooperation (Justino 2012: 1).

The loss of a breadwinner due to death or disappearance creates immense gaps in the functioning of the family unit. The loss of "the essential unifying role of the [disappeared] member can cause disruption and disharmony within the family" (Somasundaram 2007: 8). The uncertainty involved in the fate of the disappeared family member may push "half-widows" into a "conspiracy of silence" where further inquiries may lead to more problems for the victim and to his family members (ibid.). The "half-widows" often find it difficult to respond to their children's questions about the absence of their father and uncertainty around his absence, having consequences for the children's behavior and overall child-rearing practices. As Nighat observes:

My husband was picked up by the Indian Army in August, 1992. I had just given birth to a baby boy and was recuperating … Bringing up a boy in absence of his father is always difficult. He would ask me questions about him. Initially I would pacify him by showing his pictures and I would tell him stories about him … When he started going to the school, every day he would see fathers accompanying his schoolmates … He would seek answers from me … He was so angry … I was worried … So I finally decided to put a stopper on his curiosities … I lied to him and told him "Your father was a very bad man … he never loved you … he was not a caring father …"

In collectivist societies like Kashmir, individuals are embedded within the family and the community and have close and strong bonds with the extended families. The families in Kashmir tend to respond to external crisis as a unit rather than as individual members. As the mother of one of the disappeared observes:

I have seen the worst. My family was falling apart when my son was disappeared. My younger son Ali was badly affected by his brother's disappearance. He could not study further and suffered from depression. He would cry and was afraid of going out. Deep inside me, I feel a constant pain deep... a pain of being separated from my son.

As individuals women have to cope with direct and indirect effects of conflict in families. They have the capacity to offer commitment to secure their family members in times of violence. They also struggle against all odds to make little income to support their families. In the context of Kashmir, women have suffered immensely to keep intact the institution of the family. As one of the respondents observes:

> Personally, I suffer much but I don't talk about it to my family. I have many ailments, which I ignore. Once a local doctor told me to visit a hospital in Srinagar for treatment, but I didn't go; I had no money. I bear it all for the family and with the hope that one day I might be able to see my son. I have not given up on him. And I never will. I will wait for him till I am dead.

Women not only have to deal with the absence and loss of the family member in terms of being disappeared, but they also have to compete with multiple commitments at home and outside the home. They are forced to engage in all these tasks, along with persistent efforts to find their loved ones, the agony and pain of dealing with the grief and raising children.

Families, Transitions and Collective Assertion

Besides leading street protests and shielding their loved ones from beatings and arrests, women in Kashmir have also made attempts towards sustained collective action. Parveena Ahanger, mother of 21-year-old forcibly disappeared Javaid Ahmad Ahanger, is the symbol of Kashmiri women's assertion and their increasing role in the public sphere. Parveena's 17-year-old son, a student of class 11, was picked up by the Armed Forces on August 18, 1990, in the middle of the night from his uncle's house in the Batmaloo locality of Srinagar. Married at the age of 12, Parveena had never been outside her house before her son was taken away by the army. From detention centers to prisons to court rooms Parveena left no stone unturned in her search for her son. She describes her struggle against enforced disappearance of her son at the hands of the armed forces:

> They took away my son for no reason. I have been doing all I can to find out the truth about him. One former inmate of Badami Bagh [military cantonment] said he had seen Javid there. I secured legal permission to visit Badami Bagh to see my son. I took clothes and food but when I reached there at the appointed time, the military authorities refused to allow me to enter ... I want the army officers responsible for the disappearance of my son to be punished ... Although Srinagar High Court has issued warrants against the culprits they have never been produced before the court or prosecuted ... The Indian army offered me ten lakh rupees not to file a case against the culprits, but I refused.
>
> (Kazi 2009)

In her search for her son Parveena met other women who like her were struggling to find their relatives disappeared by armed forces. During her visit to police stations, detention centres and court rooms she would often "bump into women seeking whereabouts of their husbands and children." As she observes:

> We would often share our stories of grief and gradually we started to organize ourselves. Initially we would meet at roadsides or outside the gates of the court. Police did not allow us to meet outside the main gate of the court. They even beat us up with lathis couple of times. After this incident, we shifted our gatherings to the compound of a shrine in Batmaloo locality of Srinagar. The shrine was in my locality and was very close to my house that gave some confidence to the women and assured them some safety. Gradually, people from other areas of Kashmir got to know about our gatherings and they started joining us ... Like many other women I realized that I am not the only one who is suffering in search of her son, there were thousands of others ... This realization gave birth to the Association of Parents of Disappeared Persons in 1994.

Her struggle to trace the whereabouts of her son is a biography of grit and courage. Her individual biography of determination finds expression in the collective biographies of thousands of women who have been looking for their children for the last twenty five years. The Association of Parents of Disappeared Persons was formed to fight against injustice and seek information on the whereabouts of the disappeared persons. The movement emerged out of the private sufferings of individual families and their struggle with the structures of Indian military and justice systems. APDP has been organizing regular sit-in protests on the 10th of every month in a centrally located public park in the city of Srinagar. In its last nineteen years of struggle the movement has been able to break the isolation of the individually struggling families and has played a key role in collectivizing such struggles. The isolated and privatized struggles of the individual families have been brought back into the public sphere. Twenty-nine-year-old Nusrat, whose husband was disappeared on July 21, 2000, is one among the thousands of women affiliated with the movement. As a mother of a 12-year-old school-going daughter, she observes:

> After my husband was disappeared my parents and my in-laws wanted me to re-marry. I simply refused. I told them that I have done so much for Choti (my daughter) how can I leave her ... I want to live for her ... they stopped being in touch long since ... I am a regular to the monthly protests ... even if I am busy with my daily chores I make it a point that I spare time for the monthly sit-ins ... It feels good to be a part of it ... you meet so many women ... we talk ... we inquire about each other's health, domestic problems ... about kids and life ... I want my daughter to be independent. She misses her father a lot and wants to be a lawyer when she grows ...

Women of the disappeared have unique experiences of loss in which, to paraphrase (Boss 2007), the status of the loved one as "there" or "not there" continues to remain ambiguous. Thus, thousands of women who live with this ambiguity perceive their husbands or sons to be present when they are physically gone, or perceive them to be gone when they are present. In their struggle to seek the whereabouts of their loved ones many women transform their privately "frozen grief" into public protest. As Rifat Azad from Rajbagh locality of Srinagar, a woman in her mid-thirties whose husband became a victim of enforced disappearances in the year 1999 observes:

> Sitting at home and thinking about my husband, I almost slipped into a depression. For four years after my husband was disappeared, I spent most of the time within the four walls of my house ... Had I continued to live in that state for some more days I may not have survived ... I realized that I have to take control of my life and live for my child. This realization helped me to convince my Abbu (my father) to allow me to take up some work outside ... out of his love for me and my son he allowed me to take up a job ...

Married at the age of eighteen, within one and a half years of her marriage Rifat's husband became the victim of enforced disappearance. During initial years after her husband's forced disappearance, she had to negotiate her right to property and inheritance with her in-laws. With the support and encouragement of her father and brother she managed to take up a job. She is the only earning member in her two-member household. She now supports her son's education and is a regular to APDP sit-in gatherings. The major challenges encountered by the families of the victims of the enforced disappearances revolve around unresolved grief and ambiguous loss. The families of the disappeared take recourse to diverse strategies in responding. Besides living with ambiguity about the presence/absence of their loved ones the families also experience their concrete absence in terms of lack of economic and emotional support.

Battles and Struggles in Curfewed Kashmir

Pitched street battles between young protestors and armed forces, curfews and night raids resulting in detention of teenage children have been a regular phenomenon in Kashmir. In recent years, in the aftermath of the 2008 and 2010 intifada-style uprisings, many parts of Kashmir once again witnessed month-long curfews evoking memories of months of unbroken curfew that Kashmir had witnessed during the 1990s phase of the conflict. A typical curfew is like a dawn to dusk siege by armed forces meant to force people indoors. The curfew completely shifts the everyday life of people in Kashmir. From household supplies, visits to neighbors or relatives to other daily chores, everything shifts to evenings. In Kashmir, women have always played a key role in managing families under siege. From domestic activism such as organizing and sustaining food supply lines, to shielding their children from getting beaten up by the soldiers in the street, to themselves participating in the street protests, women have been able to keep intact and sustain the socio-political fabric of the family and the larger community.

In the earlier phases of the struggle announcements from the loudspeakers in the mosques requesting women to come out in protest against the injustices in Kashmir was a norm. However, in the recent mobilizations women led the protests even when there were no urgent announcements from the mosques. Thousands of protesting women like Jana Begum, mother of a 22-year-old son who was picked up by armed forces for taking part in the street protests, came out in the 2008 and 2010 uprisings leading the protests on the street. Like Jana Begum, thousands of Kashmiri women felt strongly about the safety and security of their children, as she observes: "We will demolish every symbol of the state as our sons are being targeted by the forces" (Pandit 2010: 1). Likewise Firdaus Farooq, mother of 14-year-old boy Wamiq Farooq, who was killed in 2010 by a tear gas shell fired by the armed forces in Srinagar, decided to hit the streets after her son's killing. In many ways the struggle of women to protect their families moves beyond the domestic chores into the public sphere. As Firdaus observes:

> Why should I not protest? Why should I not pick up a stone? I am doing this in the honor of my martyred son. I am doing this for azadi (freedom) from subjugation and repression.

Women cutting across class and age, wearing colorful dresses, defying curfews, shouting slogans and even leading protests with their children, have now been a regular phenomenon in Kashmir (Biswas 2010: 74). Movements like APDP have been at the forefront of sustaining the collective assertion of women in Kashmir. In the last two decades of its struggle APDP has brought the "privatized" suffering of individual families into the public sphere.

The families and relatives of the disappeared associated with APDP have been able to form solidarity networks with individuals and other movements struggling for the cause of justice. They have received continuous support from students, academia and other professionals across the globe. Cutting across ethnic and national boundaries, many support groups in solidarity with APDP now commemorate the International day on Enforced Disappearances every year on August 30 in Kashmir. Inspired by the movement against enforced disappearance in the Philippines, popularly called the Filipino Desaparcidos, APDP initiated a campaign to build a monument in the memory of victims of enforced disappearance in Kashmir.

In 2004, as APDP began preparations for building a monument similar to Filipino desaparcidos, the foundation stone of the monument to be constructed was laid down on a piece of land donated by the locals close to the martyrs graveyard in the old city of Srinagar. The children from one of the families of the victims of enforced disappearance laid down the foundation stone in front of hundreds of families who had gathered on the occasion. The foundation stone for the monument that read "We Shall Never Forget" was soon removed by the police. On March 28, 2004, APDP led a protest march to the United Nations Military Observer Group (UNMOGP) over the state's clampdown against the move to construct the monument for the disappeared. This march was thwarted by police action. Recalling the incident, Parveena observes:

> As we were about to march, the police broke through our lines and started beating us. We were then dragged and taken to the police station, where we were detained for one day. They also filed cases against us.

The trauma of the parents and relatives of the disappeared in Kashmir is reflected in the uncertainty and long wait. As Parveena reflects:

> We still would want to have a monument because that will give us some solace, since we do not have a grave or remains of our loved ones where we would go and mourn. APDP wants to build a monument and soon, we are going to rebuild it. I also think that we should have an international monument for the disappeared so as to give solace to the families living across the world.

In context of enforced disappearances where no one is made accountable for what these families have suffered, where there are no reparations, no apologies; where remorse of course remains an ever-elusive idea, APDP's struggle has played a significant role in articulating the struggles of women and families in the public sphere. By collectivizing the individual struggles of the families and women, the movements like APDP have brought back the feelings and suffering of such families into the collective memory of Kashmiris and millions of others who stand in solidarity with them.

The Politics of the Family

Conflicts represent transitions in their most bewildering forms, as they cast shadows over both the physical and moral underpinnings of the society, which may be weakened or strengthened in the long term, having consequences for the families, for women and their locations within the family and the community (Mukarubuga and El-Bushra 1995: 16–22). Historically, women have not only been a part of underground armies but they have also played a major role in the execution of collective violence in totalitarian regimes (Tara 2007: 202–219).

In the dominant discourse on war or conflict, women have been essentially portrayed as the victims of violence. The portrayal of women merely as victims overshadows our attempts of capturing the real lives of the women and the creative negotiations they forge for the survival of their families and the communities (Manchanda 2001: 4737–4745). The gendered habitus assigns less violent roles to women having an impact on the nature and extent of their participation in the public sphere. Women's entry into the public sphere constitutes a rupture with the traditional roles taken up by them. Thus, women frequently use their "maternal" location to relate and legitimize their participation in the public sphere. The increased intrusion of armed forces through night-raids and crackdowns blurred the notion of home as a space distant from conflict. As mobilizations against injustices increased, the apparent distance between the domestic space of home and the conflict "outside" vanished over a period of time. Tradition-based obstructions to the women's role in the public sphere are eliminated by sheer necessity of taking up roles outside the domestic sphere. Many women thus used positive concepts of femininity and maternity to justify their entry in the public sphere.

Conclusion

My discussion on the processes of transition witnessed in the roles of women underscore the fact that mobilizations of women in the public sphere was both a catalyst and result of the larger socio-political realities of 1990s Kashmir. Like many Palestinian women, women in Kashmir, in the absence of their men, have strategically used the absence and the vulnerability of men to death and disappearance. These vulnerabilities gradually pushed them into the public sphere, taking up roles and responsibilities beyond the domestic realm. In many ways women's participation in the public sphere was justified and viewed as their commitment to their men and the families. Thus, for these women, to borrow an expression (Taylor 2001), "performing" motherhood has been crucial to their existence. For women like Parveena the performative role of mothering gave way to a political role of being the mother. This discourse is reflected in the emergence of women like Parveena Ahangar in the public sphere as the "Iron Lady" of Kashmir as well as beloved "Jiji" (Aunt). This simultaneity as mother of a son who became the victim of enforced disappearance, a caring Aunt for the larger oppressed Kashmiri community, and a woman with strength and resolve, can thus be played in the public sphere with equal ease. In many ways, Parveena strategically negotiates and deploys her mothering role into her larger political role, giving sanction to her role as a leader in the public sphere. The fact that one of the strongest attempts at collectivizing the assertion of women in Kashmir came in the form of the organization of the parents of the disappeared persons reflects that in many ways it is the "politics of family" that has defined and shaped the assertion of women in the public sphere.

Farrukh Faheem is assistant professor at the Institute of Kashmir Studies, University of Kashmir, Srinagar. He has written journal articles and book chapters on understanding the militarization and cyclic protest mobilizations in Kashmir. He has taught at the University of Delhi and has been closely associated with several inter-community dialogues on dispute resolution and reconciliation organized by the Delhi-based think tank, Centre for Dialogue and Reconciliation (CDR).

Acknowledgements

Editor's note: due to prevailing security circumstances in Kashmir the author of this article was not in a position to supply full details of some of his references. At the time of going to press the situation remained unchanged.

References

Bhinda, Nils. 1994. "The Kashmir Conflict (1990–)." In *The True Cost of Conflict*, edited by Michael Cranna, 55–80. London: Earthscan.
Biswas, Soutik. 2010. "The Angry Housewives Setting Kashmir Ablaze." Retrieved from www.bbc.co.uk/news/world-south-asia-10961577
Boss, Pauline. 2007. "Ambiguous Loss Theory: Challenges for Scholars and Practitioners." *Family Relations* 56: 105–111. https://doi.org/10.1111/j.1741-3729.2007.00444.x

Crossette, Barbara. 1991. "India Moves Against the Rebels." *The New York Times*, April 7.
Dabla, Bashir Ahmad, Nayak, S. K. and Khurshid-Ul-Islam. 2000. *Gender Discrimination in the Kashmir Calley: A Survey of Budgam and Baramulla Districts*. New Delhi: Gyan Publishing House.
Garbarino, James. 1996. "Effects of Political Violence on Child's Behavior Problems: A Risk Accumulation Model Child Development." *Child Development* 67(1): 33–45. https://doi.org/10.2307/1131684
Jaudel, Etienne. 1993. *Violations of Human Rights Committed by the Indian Security Forces in Jammu and Kashmir*. Paris: Fédération internationale des ligues des droits de l'homme (FIDH).
Justino, Patricia. 2012. *Shared Societies and Armed Conflict: Costs, Inequality and the Benefits of Peace*. London: Institute of Development Studies. https://doi.org/10.1111/j.2040-0209.2012.00410.x
Kazi, Seema. 2009. *Between Democracy and Nation: Gender and Militarization in Kashmir*. New Delhi: Women Unlimited.
Manchanda, Rita. 2001. *Women, war and Peace in South Asia: Beyond Victimhood to Agency*. New Delhi: Sage Publications.
Mathur, Shubh. 2015. *Human Toll of Kashmir Conflict: Grief and Courage in South Asian Borderland*. New York: Palgrave Macmillan.
Mukarubuga, Cecile and Judy El-Bushra. 1995. "Women, War and Transition." *Gender and Development* 3: 16–22. https://doi.org/10.1080/741921866
Pandit, Salim. 2010. "What is Making the Ordinary Kashmiri Woman so Angry that She Is Out on the Street, Throwing Stones at Police and Leading the Mob?" *Times of India*, August 8. Retrieved from https://timesofindia.indiatimes.com/home/sunday-times/deep-focus/What-is-making-the-ordinary-Kashmiri-woman-so-angry-that-she-is-out-on-the-street-throwing-stones-at-police-and-leading-the-mob/articleshow/6272622.cms? (accessed December 15, 2019).
Sinha, Chinki. Undated. "Resistance Poetry in Kashmir." Retrieved from www.kashmirlit.org/resistance-poetry-kashmir (accessed September 20, 2018).
Somasundaram, Daya. 2007. "Collective Trauma in Northern Sri Lanka: A Qualitative Psychosocial-ecological Study." *International Journal of Mental Health Systems* 1: article 5. https://doi.org/10.1186/1752-4458-1-5
Tara, McKelvey. 2007. *One of the Guys: Women as Aggressors and Torturers*. Emeryville, CA: Seal Press.
Taylor, Diana. 2001. "Making a Spectacle: The Mothers of Plazo De Mayo." *Journal of the Association for Mothering* 3(2): 97–109.

7

"Enemies of the Nation, Heretics of the Church": Conscientious Rejection of State Authority

Nami Kim

> The cardinal virtue of authoritarian religion is obedience; the cardinal sin is resistance—in contrast to a human religion, where the corresponding virtue and vice are, respectively, self-realization and misspent life. In terms of social history, this kind of authoritarian religiosity functions to affirm the society and stabilize its dominant tendencies ... God's justice and love are less important than God's power.
> —Dorothee Soelle, *The Window of Vulnerability* (1990: 87)

Introduction

Like all other elementary school students in the late 1970s in South Korea, I memorized and recited the Pledge of Allegiance to the National Flag every Monday morning before starting classes. The Pledge of Allegiance was first started by the board of education in a providence in 1968 and was enforced nationwide by the Ministry of Education in 1972. It was revised in 2007. The Pledge of Allegiance I recited from elementary school till high school was: "I firmly pledge, in front of the proud Korean flag, to loyally devote my body and soul to the eternal glory of my homeland and the [Korean] people." In this context, loyalty means "an uncritical and unquestioning acceptance of the myth of the nation" (Neocleous 2008: 135). This loyalty oath represented allegiance to the authoritarian state under military dictatorships. The Pledge of Allegiance was needed for the construction of the identity of the people of the Republic of Korea primarily through the creation of "the Other." Included among the "Other" are North Korean communists and those disloyal to the state, including conscientious objectors, against whom state violence can be and must be exercised.

By examining the public statements of conscientious objectors in South Korea, this chapter seeks to provide a critique of the normative understanding of national security as the priority of a nation-state that requires mandatory military service to protect the nation from "enemies." An organization called the World Without War compiled 53 conscientious objectors' statements, and the statements are organized into three different time periods: 2001–2005, 2006–2009 and 2010–2014 (World Without War 2014). The conscientious objectors' statements show how they challenge the ideology of national security as the most urgent matter of the nation by disclosing the destructive intersections of war, militarism, sexism, and violence against vulnerable people. Their statements also expose that the "sacralization of military duty" is not a religious value. In addition to these, the statements show how conscientious objectors contest hegemonic masculinity by rejecting mandatory military service that is one of the components of hegemonic masculinity in Korean society.

To talk about conscientious objection in South Korea is to engage in de-cold war process (Chen 2010). Although the Cold War "officially" ended when the Soviet Union fell down in 1991, the Korean Peninsula is still divided by Cold War politics. In his book *The Other Cold War*, Heonik Kwon argues that the Cold War is not a "single and globally identical phenomenon" and that there are "the diverse and locally specific ways in which the Cold War is coming to an end" (Kwon 2010: 25–26). Taiwanese cultural critic Kuan-Hsing Chen argues that to de-cold war is to "de-Americanize" and by that he means, "to examine the consequences of the United States' role as a central component in the formation of East Asian subjectivity" (Chen 2010: 120). Chen points out the continuing presence of the US military bases in South Korea and Okinawa as one of the "undeniable markers of the continuation and extension of the Cold War" (ibid.: 119).[1] The US has stationed military troops in Korea since 1957 and the history of US military occupation of Okinawa goes back to World War II. The US has also been at the center of the political and military tension between South and North Korea since the three years of US ruling (1945–1948) through the United States Army Military Government in the South until now. In this heavily militarized context, marking out a space in which stories and histories of conscientious objection can be told is to engage in the de-cold war process.

Mandatory Military Service and Conscientious Objection in South Korea

After experiencing the Korean War (1950–1953), South Korea maintained one of the largest standing armed forces in the world, ranking seventh in 2019 (Global Fire Power 2019).[2] It also has the world's eighth highest defense budget as of 2019 (Global Security.org 2018).[3] South Korea is also one of twenty-six countries that have compulsory military service. Male citizens are required to perform active military duty that is mandatory for a limited time period under the Military Service Act of 1949 that was implemented in 1951 (Han 2002). Military service is based on the Constitution of the Republic of Korea, which was declared in 1948. Military service is one of four constitutional duties (duties of national defense, taxation, education, and work) required for all citizens of the Republic of Korea, though the conscription has been applied only to male citizens.[4] This mandatory military service has been accepted by the public not only as a necessary citizenry duty to protect the nation from the enemy but also as an indispensable rite of passage, by which a young man becomes a "real" man who takes financial responsibility for the family as its head.

Regarding the origin of conscientious objection in Korea, some people consider the imprisonment of 38 Jehovah's Witnesses during Japanese colonial occupation as the first incident of conscientious objection in Korea (Cho 2007: 2; Han 2004).

Thirty-eight Jehovah's Witnesses who objected to bowing in the direction of the Japan's royal palace were arrested for the violation of the maintenance of the public security, and five of them died in prison in late 1930s in Korea. However, other scholars, like In-cheol Kang, argue that while some incidents of conscientious objection could have possibly occurred between 1944 and 1945 as Japan started officially conscripting Koreans, the first incidents of conscientious objection in Korea occurred right before and after the Korean War (Kang 2005: 111). For the past 70 years, over 19,000 conscientious objectors have served prison terms for refusing to serve in the military (Lee 2017). Since 1955, the Korean Supreme Court has maintained the position that "the so-called 'conscientious decision' to deny the legal duty of military service in the name of religious doctrine is not allowed under the freedoms of conscience and religion in the Constitution" (Cho 2007: 9).[5]

Until 1961, two types of conscientious objection were tried in different courts: one was tried in military court and the other was put on trial in the civil court. For instance, the Jehovah's Witnesses refused to take part in any of the armed forces in its entirety, whereas members of the Seventh-day Adventist Church opposed "manual exercises," that is, they refused to hold weapons after they were conscripted and entered the military. Thus, the Jehovah's Witnesses can be called "absolute" or "complete" conscientious objectors in their opposition to military service. While those (mostly the Seventh-day Adventists) who opposed manual exercises were tried for mutiny in military court for "the crime of disobedience under Article 44 of the Military Criminal Law," those (mostly the Jehovah's Witnesses) who refused the conscription itself were tried in the civil court for "the crime of evading military service under Article 88 of the Military Service Act" until the beginning of Park Jung Hee's military rule (Cho 2007: 9).

Since the establishment of Park's military dictatorship in 1961, both types of conscientious objection were tried in military court, and in most cases, the prison sentences they received were longer than the duration of their active military service would have been. This was primarily because most conscientious objectors were subjected to repeated imprisonment for opposing to serve not only in the active military but also in the reservoir forces. In addition to their regular service, men must further serve as reservoir forces for eight more years after completing their active military service. No alternative service was available to take the place of any military service. The Seventh-day Adventists finally decided not to object to the military service due to harsh punishment, whereas the Jehovah's Witnesses continue to hold onto their stance of "complete" objection to military service.

Although several groups have challenged the mandatory military service for different motives, they have remained a minority voice. Conscientious objection to mandatory military service did not draw much public attention, let alone public support. As noted, most conscientious objectors have been the Jehovah's Witnesses and the Seventh-day Adventists. Their objections were simply viewed as futile resistance from religious minorities. Despite the ordeals that conscientious objectors faced, they have garnered no support from the mainline Korean

Christianity because they not only refuse to serve in the military but they are also considered "heretical" and thus undeserving any sympathy.

The direct ties between conscientious objection and the Jehovah's Witnesses were first loosened when Tae-yang Oh came out publicly as the first Buddhist conscientious objector in the beginning of the twenty-first century. He based his pacifism on the Buddhist doctrine of no killing. Most conscientious objectors are still the Jehovah's Witnesses. However, as more men have publicly come out as conscientious objectors based on their stance against war and militarism, with or without religious backgrounds, conscientious objection began to draw public attention. Thus, resistance based on the anti-war and peace movement has become enlivened, slowly challenging the conventional understanding of conscientious objection solely as an issue of religious minorities. Conscientious objection is, as Cockburn argues, "one of the most meaningful, demonstrative and difficult forms of non-violent direct action in the repertoire of the world's anti-militarist, anti-war and peace movements" (Cockburn 2009: iiiv).

On November 1, 2018, the Supreme Court reversed the 2004 court decision (12:1) that found conscientious objectors guilty.[6] The Court finally ruled (9:4) for conscientious objectors, saying that conscientious objection cannot be punished because it is based on the "freedom of conscience" guaranteed in the constitution. While the court's decision was welcomed, critics pointed out that it was a late decision. Conscientious objection advocates also objected to the suggested alternative system as punitive because it will require conscientious objectors' public service twice as long as the mandatory military service (World Without War 2018).

Although the Supreme Court's ruling was in favor of conscientious objectors, the issue of conscientious objection is not yet fully resolved. The military and the government are still trying to figure out what kind of alternative system should be offered. Two main arguments that continue to be made against conscientious objection are that it is not acceptable because of the ongoing military tension with North Korea; and that no one will serve the military because of the poor conditions of military life. In relation to these, two other arguments against conscientious objection have garnered the public support recently: fewer men are available for conscription and it is unfair that only men have to serve in the military without any tangible benefits (Lee 2017).

National Security and Identity Interlocked

In his book *Critique of Security*, Mark Neocleous argues that national security and national identity are inextricably linked. He states that "the fabrication of national security goes hand in hand with the fabrication of national identity, and vice versa" (Neocleous 2008: 107). Though the primary context in which he discusses the ideology of national security and its operation is the United States, his points are pertinent to the Korean context. As Neocleous argues, "security against the enemy—be it the communist menace or global terrorism—becomes a reaffirmation of the historical burden of a distinctive identity around which the nation must unite" (ibid.: 126). Security functions as "a means for defining and claiming identity," and the national identity also becomes a "mechanism for the constitution of security" (ibid.). The national identity is defined in reference to an "Other" that is deemed a national security risk (ibid.: 108). What Neocleous calls "a security-identity-loyalty complex" is held together by "fear and violence" (ibid.: 141).

The specter of war has loomed over the region for the past 70 years, and the rhetoric of impending war or the bellicose military threat from North Korea has been deployed to quell any dissenting voices because "national security" surpasses any other national concerns. This militarized situation has often in turn brought about state sanctioned violence against those who are perceived to be the enemy, both external and internal, in the name of national security. National security has been a convenient and effective tool of disciplinary measure against any people who are disloyal or those who are perceived to pose threats to the state. It has worked powerfully as a scare tactic for more than a half century in South Korea. As was true in the United States during the Cold War era, South Korea's "Other" has been communism, more specifically North Korean communist regime and pro-North sympathizers. While this category of "Other" is still considered as a major danger on the national scene because the Korean War has not ended yet, the "Other," against which the national identity of [South] Korean is juxtaposed, has encompassed anyone or any organizations that are considered to be dangerous to South Korea and the values attached to them. This category of "Other" continues to shift or expand as shown in the case of condemning "gay soldiers" and (im)migrant Muslims as security threats in the Protestant Right's discourse (Kim 2016). Conscientious objectors have also been included in the category of "Other," and therefore they have been rendered as a risk to the national security. They have been punished for their "crime" against nation, that is, refusal to serve in the military, the most "sacred" duty of Korean (male) citizens. They are *not* "loyal Koreans," and therefore not deserving any protection from the state. Instead, they are subject to the state violence.

In the following, I turn to the conscientious objectors' statements that offer a critique of the ideology of national security in three interrelated ways. First, within the larger global geopolitical context of US War on Terror, the statements of conscientious objectors repudiate the justifications of war, militarism, mandatory military service, and state violence in the name of national security. Their statements further show that their resistance is not only against war and state sanctioned violence but also against (hetero)sexism, the neoliberal economic system, and various forms of violence against women and other vulnerable people. Such resistance is significant because it demands that "national security" should be reexamined considering the everyday struggles of ordinary people, especially women and other minorities. Second, the statements of conscientious objectors challenge Korean mainline Protestant Christianity, more specifically the Protestant Right's[7] view of "national security" as the protection of the nation from both internal and external "enemies," by showing that sacralization of military duty is not a religious value. Third, the statements of conscientious objectors directly and indirectly challenge hegemonic masculinity. Their refusal to enact hegemonic masculinity signals cisgender men's different ways of performing masculinities that are counter-hegemonic in a highly militarized, classed, and misogynistic society.

The Objection to Military Service Is Resistance to War, Sexism, and Violence against Vulnerable People

While the majority of the conscientious objectors are still the Jehovah's Witnesses, there have been conscientious objectors who publicly denounce military service based on other interrelated reasons since 2001. Among the twenty conscientious objectors' statements from the earliest period (2001–2005), many of them referred to the US war against Iraq as a defining moment of their rejection of military service. They believed that the war would bring about a more disastrous situation for the ordinary Iraqi people. They were also convinced that US wars in Iraq and Afghanistan not only were killing people, but were also destroying the environment, which would have long-term devastating effects on the lives of people and the surrounding areas. Thus, those who had seen the ravaging results of wars caused by US military invasion in Iraq and Afghanistan opposed military service out of conviction that military is a killing agent. Not convinced by the conventional notion that the purpose of the military is to protect people and the nation from enemies, they argued that the military has been the very instrument of killing.

Conscientious objectors expressed similar disappointment and rage at the South Korean government, which decided to dispatch troops to Iraq as an ardent US ally. For instance, one conscientious objector, Do-hyung Kim, stated:

> I remember the sleepless nights because of the US war against Iraq. It is so sad that there isn't much I can do for those who die only because they were born and live in Iraq. I really wanted to be part of the human shields to block the attacks from the US military. It is reproachful and shameful that our country supports the murder by dispatching soldiers to Iraq. This was the momentum causing me to firmly reject the military service.
>
> (World Without War 2014: 39)

Another conscientious objector, Jin Choi, who was an elementary school teacher, also said, "The students, and I were speechless after hearing that the Korean government passed the resolution to dispatch troops to Iraq in the name of the national interest" (ibid.: 58). He went on to point out the military culture prevalent in the school system.

As they condemned US bombings of Afghanistan since the 9/11 and the US war against Iraq in 2003, conscientious objectors unequivocally challenged such US-led actions as unjustifiable violence and also the complicity of Korean government as an unwavering US ally in perpetuating such violence. A few conscientious objectors even made explicit connections between the Vietnam War and the US war against Iraq, by pointing out Korea's subimperial status that has continued a subordinate relationship with the US (World Without War 2014: 130). As a "lower-level empire" (Chen and Wang 2000: 15) that depends on the larger structure of the US military imperialism, South Korea dispatched soldiers to Vietnam during the Vietnam War, who served as "class and racial surrogate labor, both within the domestic and global contexts" (Lee 2010: 45).

Many of the conscientious objectors who have shared public statements reject military service based on not only their opposition to particular wars, such as the Vietnam War and the US war against Iraq, but also from their broader anti-violence stance and their commitment to peace. They renounce the normalization of violence. One conscientious objector, Eui-min Chochung, criticized the routinized violence at home and at school, and the militarization of the entire society. Referring to the military as the epicenter of militarized culture, authoritarianism, and everyday violence (World Without War 2014: 70–71) he also commented how men internalize the military culture during their service in the military and then express violence and male-centeredness in everyday life after they return to civilian life (ibid.: 73).

Conscientious objectors have also been very critical of state violence and of the way the military forces them to use violence against ordinary citizens when they exercise their rights as citizens to protest. For instance, reflecting on what is called the "Yongsan Tragedy" during which five residents who had been forcibly evicted were killed and many were wounded including his junior colleague who was mired in the police violence during forced eviction, Ki-won Choi questioned for whom the police and military serve. He listed historically significant incidents in which the state has used ruthless violence against its own citizens and decided that he could not take part in a military that directly and indirectly supports state violence against its own citizens, particularly those who are not members of the privileged class (World Without War 2014: 212–213). Choi's refusal to "fight" the state's "enemy," be they from outside or its own citizens, and the state's response to such disobedience through imprisonment discloses "the full extent of the state's power" (ibid.). Choi's refusal to serve can also be described as what Cynthia Cockburn calls "a provocative act of class loyalty" because he was against the state deployment of the police-soldier to suppress its own people who are insubordinate (ibid.).

Mandatory military service is based on the premise that the military will protect the nation from outside aggressors and from any "disloyal" people inside who challenge the state's authority. In this scenario the military is perceived to be indispensable to bring and maintain "peace," and national security becomes the priority at the expense of other social matters. Conscientious objectors' statements challenge this narrow view of peace and national security, and argue that "peace" should indicate not only absence of war but also social conditions in which people can live without fear of their lives being impinged on by various forms of violence—state violence, economic violence, gender, sexual, and other forms of violence. These statements also remind us that when we talk about peace, security, freedom, we should not separate the fight to end sexism, heterosexism, economic injustice, racism, and ableism in the national landscape from the struggle to end US militarist imperialism. These are not disconnected matters. Conscientious objectors' statements show how militarism and the militarization of society reinforce patriarchy, misogyny, sexual objectification of women, authoritarianism, social hierarchy, and classification of citizens based on gender binary and able-bodiedness. In so doing, conscientious objectors challenge the well-orchestrated notion that military is intrinsic to keep the national security that is the nation's primacy. Furthermore, these statements indicate that conscientious objection is a feminist undertaking in that it challenges militarism as well as patriarchy, heterosexism, ableism, and class exploitation.

The Sacralization of Military Duty Is Not a Religious Value

Scholars argue that the reasons conscientious objection has not drawn public attention and sympathy for such a long time in Korea include "sacralization of military duty." Conscientious objectors were seriously criticized for being "unpatriotic" for refusing to fight for the country against the enemy. According to historians, conscientious objectors who opposed the manual exercises were labeled and stigmatized as "non-citizen," "acting to serve the interests of the enemy," "worse than the Red," "mentally ill," "war hater," "religious fanatic" or "heretic" (Kang 2005: 113). These kinds of labeling and stigmatizing continued from 1950 till 1958, during which time conscientious objection was solidified as a crime against the nation. However, some labeling has continued even these days as shown in the Protestant Right's calling of them as "heretics," "threats to national security," and "selfish" (Jin 2006: 191–217). The Christian Council of Korea (CCK), the largest Protestant Christian alliance in Korea, has criticized conscientious objections as a conviction based on false religious belief. For instance, in their 2004 statement against conscientious objection, the CCK claimed that the reason the Jehovah's Witnesses refuse to hold weapons and serve in military is that they see the state and government as "satan's organization." Contending that this view is false, the CCK argued that their appeal to freedom of conscience based on religious conviction could not be seen as conscientious (Hangichong 2004). The CCK attributed conscientious objection to the wrong religious belief held by religious minorities (Hangichong 2018). Strongly opposing the Supreme Court's most recent ruling for the conscientious objection in 2018, the CCK issued a statement that says, "The men of the Republic of Korea should complete the military service with the mindset that they will protect family, neighbor, and the nation" (ibid.). The CCK also based its opposition on the false assumption that conscientious objection is a way to avoid military service. It further stated that since most conscientious objectors are Jehovah's Witnesses, it should be called a "particular religion's avoidance of military service" instead of "conscientious objection."

As indicated, there are primarily two reasons behind the CCK's hostility toward conscientious objection. One is that conscientious objectors are irresponsible as men because Korean men should protect their family and the nation by performing the "sacred" military duty. The other is that most conscientious objectors hold a false belief system, that is, the Jehovah's Witnesses, and so they are not entitled to the freedom of conscience to be a conscientious objector. One of the main reasons for conscientious objectors not garnering support from either the Roman Catholic or Protestant Christianity is that mainline Christianity has deemed conscientious objectors mainly as "heretics," and therefore did not care about their ordeals (Cho 2007: 3). Such negative view held by the mainline Christianity against the Jehovah's Witnesses has affected the ways in which conscientious objection has been deemed by the larger society (Jin 2006: 196).

The statements by conscientious objectors who oppose military service based on their religious conviction but who are not Jehovah's Witnesses directly challenge the CCK's stance. Dong-ki Ha contested the CCK's stand as contradictory to what Jesus stood for. He stated:

> Jesus taught "love your neighbor," but CCK does not support, let alone love, conscientious objectors whose conviction is based on the belief that they cannot take part in the military because it destroys the neighbor instead of loving them.
> (World Without War 2014: 141)

Another conscientious objector emphasized Jesus' non-violent resistance against Roman imperialism.

Although he himself is not a Jehovah's Witness, Bo-Cheng (Seok-min Kim) was inspired by their struggles and became a conscientious objector. His decision came about after learning about the imprisonment of over 10,000 Jehovah's Witnesses as conscientious objectors since independence from Japan's colonial occupation. He added that although they are the ones who rejected military under the Japanese occupation, they have not been treated as the first-class citizen in the Republic of Korea. By bringing up Jesus' treatment of socially marginalized people, and through his stance against religious and political authorities, Soon-uk Kwon who works at the disability advocacy organization exposed hypocrisy of the mainline Christianity that reviles conscientious objection (ibid.: 131). Another conscientious objector, Deul-Kae (Sung-min Kim), said that violence is a spiritual question and his conscientious objection was the answer to that question. As a person who wants to follow Jesus in loving the enemy, he stated that the church had been the biggest obstacle in terms of sharing his thoughts on peace. The church turned away from conscientious objectors and treated them as heretics. Deul-Kae also stated that whenever he brought up conscientious objection at his church, the church would talk about national security, anti-communism, and just war instead. He urged that the church should critically reflect whether the state, military, and war in which Christians take part are indeed just and best way to achieve peace (ibid.: 253).

Mainline Korean Christianity, unfortunately, has sided with the state regarding conscientious objection, completely ignoring the plight of religious minorities who have been labelled as "heretics" and "unpatriotic." The Protestant Right in particular has opposed the efforts to provide alternatives to military service on the ground that it would privilege a certain religious group, and that it would also jeopardize national security. It is troubling to see how, with only a few exceptions, Korean Christianity has been a ferocious force in opposing the introduction of the alternative service when in fact pacifism is one of the traditions in Christian history that cannot be overlooked. The lack of public concern over conscientious objection is related to the marginalization of Christian pacifist tradition in Korea. Christian pacifism has been a minority voice in Korea largely because of the following reasons: the presence of strong Christian patriotism from the beginning of Protestant Christianity in Korea; the conjoining of anti-communist ideology and Christianity under the Rhee Syngman regime; and the sacralization of military duty during military dictatorships, which led to the militarization of the entire society (Kim 2000: 113; Jin 2006: 210; Kang 1999: 64–68). Instead of supporting the cause of conscientious objection, Korean Protestant Christianity in general, and the Protestant Right in particular, have been one of the most callous groups in their condemnation of conscientious objection.

The Refusal to Enact Hegemonic Masculinity

As military service is a mandatory requirement for men only, it has functioned as one of the core elements of hegemonic masculinity in South Korea. Men are granted first-class citizenship through their military service, and their masculinity is hinged on the completion of this rite of passage through which they become a "real" men. However, the statements of conscientious objectors show that they refuse to enact hegemonic masculinity, which results in being relegated into the second-class citizenship with material consequences. Conscientious objectors acknowledge the consequences of their objections, one of which includes the social stigma attached to "evading" military service as well as the additional loss of certain economic benefits because of legal restrictions imposed on them. As military service used to be directly related to men's economic capacity, conscientious objectors' refusal to serve in the military had affected their economic capability that is considered as one of the components of hegemonic masculinity in Korean context. Because conscientious objection has been regarded as a "crime," conscientious objectors have been prohibited from getting an employment in any state agency, public organization, and even in private sector. They have also been denied official business permits. In other words, they have been reduced to the condition of "civil death," that is being "unable to obtain decent employment, deprived of the services and support, even the basic human respect, to which they are entitled," for refusing to bear arms for the country (Cockburn 2009: viii).[8]

Despite the serious consequences of committing this "crime," quite a few of them problematized hegemonic masculinity by challenging the notion that a man becomes a "real" man upon the completion of military service. For instance, Min-seok Yoochung who identifies as a sexual minority rejected mandatory military service because, for him, the military reproduces hostile barrack culture and aggressive masculinity (World Without War 2014: 97). Hong-ryul Ahn stated that the myth of a "real" man that has been perpetrated by men who completed military service or who have embodied military culture glamorizes the sexual objectification of women and sexual violence against women (ibid.: 122–123). He continued by saying that the distorted sexual culture spread by men can further encourage such violence (ibid.: 123). Another conscientious objector, Nal Maeng (Myong-jin Moon) stated that his decision to become a conscientious objector allowed him to think more deeply about feminism and pacifism. His deeper reflection on the connection between these movements has led him to pursue a different lifestyle—become a vegetarian, consume less, ride a bike (ibid.: 200). These conscientious objectors' conscious refusal to enact hegemonic masculinity indicates their counter-hegemonic ways of performing masculinities in a highly militarized, stratified, and heteropatriarchal society. This is also clear in their statements rejecting male violence against women on the one hand, and the discrimination and exclusion of sexual minorities and people with disabilities, on the other hand.

While conscientious objectors have been critical of enacting hegemonic masculinity, some of them also pointed out how conscientious objection can fall into patriarchal heroism through the reinscription of the reversed ideal image of a male hero. One of the expectations of conscientious objectors is that they somehow hold higher moral standards compared to other "ordinary" men who complete their military duty. In other words, the ideal image of a "conscientious man" as a heroic male pacifist is juxtaposed against the ideal image of a heroic male warrior. Stating how military produces both victims and perpetrators, Hyun Min, a conscientious objector, made an insightful point about the danger of "sacralization of conscientious objection," which is the opposite of "sacralization of military duty." If "sacralization of military duty" can produce a male hero who would fight to death for national security, "sacralization of conscientious objection" can demand "strong morality" from conscientious objectors, placing them on a higher moral standard. What this implies is that an individual conscientious objector who does not show "high morality" can be viewed as someone who weakens the conscientious objection as a peace movement. When a conscientious objector shows "deviation" or a "past" history that is not "consistent" with the expected narrative of conscientious objection, then the entire movement is discredited (World Without War 2014: 161–162; Kang 2007). Hyun Min found the rigid binary of deserving and undeserving conscientious objector problematic. He himself did not wish to represent himself as a "moral subject" (World Without War 2014: 163). As Cockburn argues, "when represented as an alternative masculine heroism, sometimes explicitly compared to the heroism of the one who is prepared to die for his country, it retains familiar masculine khaki!" (Cockburn 2009: ix). In a similar vein, Cynthia Enloe cautions that the conscientious objection movement can carry "the risk of making heroes out of male objectors and reproducing the patriarchy endemic to militarism" (cited in Altinay 2009: 99). Whether it is a hegemonic notion of masculine, that is, a "real" man who completed military duty, or the ideal image of male pacifist, conscientious objectors' statements demonstrate that they reject such images produced and reproduced in patriarchal, militarist culture. They indicate the possibility of different modes of masculinities in the militarized, neoliberal, misogynistic, ableist and heteronormative Korean society.

Coda

As I watched the summits between two Koreas on April 27 and between North Korea and the United States on June 12, 2018, I was excited and at the same time anxious about what was unfolding in front of my eyes. Like other concerned people, I could not take my eyes off the live streamed news and other commentaries on TV; these summits could lead to the end of the Korean War or what people call the Forgotten War that has not officially ended yet. While watching the news, I constantly asked what kind of unified Korea are we envisioning. Are we envisioning a prosperous neoliberal capitalist, ethnonation? Will North Korea be "embraced" into the militarist, neoliberal capitalist global network? Will military service be no longer mandatory if two Koreas come to terms with "peace"? Will the ideology of national security lose its grip, or continue to wield its power against new enemies?

People say that things will get better once two Koreas agree on the peace treaty. I hope so. Living without the fear of war matters. But ending war shouldn't be the ultimate goal. Nor should the establishing a neoliberal, one ethno-nation be the final agenda. If we really want peace on the Korean Peninsula and in larger Asia, we need to start reconceptualizing and reenvisioning "peace." We also need to rethink and undo the "national security" that has suppressed all other matters intrinsic to everyday survival of ordinary people. Indisputably, this making of a "secure" nation has been done in the larger global geopolitical setting—Cold War, US War on Terror, and ongoing US military presence around the globe. Hence, Koreans or any concerned people who hail the state level-efforts to officially end the Korean War should be ever more vigilant about how the imperial and the sub-imperial powers strive to secure and solidify their force at the expense of people who, like conscientious objectors, suffer because of their stance against the state authority. The efforts to engage in de-cold war process needs to continue even after the end of the Korean War because the struggle to de-Americanize has not ended yet.

Nami Kim is associate professor of philosophy and religious studies in Spelman College, Atlanta, USA. She has co-edited (with Wonhee Anne Joh) *Critical Theology against US Militarism in Asia: Decolonization and Deimperialization* (New York: Palgrave Macmillan, 2016), and *Feminist Praxis Against US Militarism* (Lexington Books, 2019).

Notes

1. Nami Kim and Wonhee Anne Joh also mention this dynamic of the cold war in their "Introduction" to *Critical Theology against US Militarism in Asia: Decolonization and Deimperialization* (Kim and Joh 2016).
2. According to this information, North Korea is ranked 18th.
3. According to the report South Korea had the world's 10th biggest budget in defense in 2017 and showed the highest increase from 2017 to 2018 among OECD (Organisation for Economic Co-operation and Development) member countries.

4. The Article 39 of the Constitution states, "All citizens shall have the duty of national defense under the conditions as prescribed by Act." South Korean male citizens, aged between twenty and thirty with certain level of education, are required to serve military unless they are deemed unfit after physical examinations. Both the required education level and the duration of military service have varied.
5. The position of the Supreme Court was changed in 2018 (World Without War 2018).
6. In 2004, twenty-two Congressmen submitted a draft of the Military Service Act, which included provisions for alternative service for conscientious objectors (Cho 2007: 3).
7. The Protestant Right refers to a subset of Korean Protestant Christianity that "combines conservative evangelical/fundamentalist theology with social and political conservatism" (Kim 2016: ix).
8. The military service extra points-system was ruled unconstitutional in 1999, and was eventually abolished. However, negative social stigma attached to not fulfilling military service is still prevalent."

References

Altinay, Ayse Gul. 2009. "Refusing to Identify as Obedient Wives, Sacrificing Mothers and Proud Warriors." In *Conscientious Objection: Resisting Militarized Society*, edited by Ozgur Heval Cinar and Coskun Usterci. London: Zed Books.

Chen, Kuan-Hsing. 2010. *Asia as Method: Toward Deimperialization*. Durham, NC: Duke University Press. https://doi.org/10.1215/9780822391692

Chen, Kuan-Hsing and Yiman Wang. 2000. "The Imperialist Eye: The Cultural Imaginary of a Subempire and a Nation-State." *Positions: East Asia Cultures Critique* 8(1): 9–76. https://doi.org/10.1215/10679847-8-1-9

Cho, Kuk. 2007. "Conscientious Objection to Military Service in Korea: The Rocky Path from Being an Unpatriotic Crime to a Human Right." *Oregon Review of International Law* 9(1): 1–26.

Cockburn, Cynthia. 2009. "Preface." In *Conscientious Objection: Resisting Militarized Society*, edited by Ozgur Heval Cinar and Coskun Usterci, viii–xi. London: Zed Books.

Global Firepower. 2019. "2019 Military Strength Ranking." Retrieved from www.globalfirepower.com/countries-listing.asp (accessed July 5, 2019).

Global Security.org. 2018. "Defense Budget." Retrieved from www.globalsecurity.org/military/world/rok/budget.htm (accessed July 5, 2019).

Han, Hong-ku. 2002. "Chanranhan 'Byungyoung Gukgaa' eui Tansang" ["The Birth of a Glorious 'Garrison State'"]. *Hankyoreh 21* (397). Retrieved from http://h21.hani.co.kr/arti/COLUMN/44/4532.html (accessed August 21, 2018).

Han, Hong-ku. 2004. "Yeohowaeu Zeungin Apesuh Bukeurupda" ["I Am Ashamed in Front of the Jehovah's Witnesses"]. *Hankyoreh 21* (511). Retrieved from http://legacy.h21.hani.co.kr/section-021075000/2004/05/021075000200405270511062.html (accessed December 5, 2018).

Hangichong. 2004. "Yangshimjeok Byongyukguhbu, Gukgaanbo Wooruh" ["Conscientious Objection, Concerned about National Security"]. *Keuriseucheontudei*, May 21. Retrieved from www.christiantoday.co.kr/news/161537 (accessed February 10, 2019).

Hangichong. 2018. "Yangshimjeok Byongyukguhbu Gangreok Bandae" ["Strong Opposition to Conscientious Objection"]. *NewsNJoy*, November 5. Retrieved from www.newsnjoy.or.kr/news/articleView.html?idxno=220808 (accessed November 6, 2018).

Jin, Sang-Beom. November, 2006. "Hanguksaheo Yangsimjeok Byongyukguhbuae Daehan Gukgawa Jonggyoeui Daeeong" ["The Reponses of the State and Religion Against Conscientious Objectors in Contemporary Korean Society"]. *Journal of Religion and Culture* 8: 191–217.

Kang, Don-Gu. 1999. "Hanguk Geundae Gaeshingyo Minjokjueuieui Jaeyihae" ["The Re-understanding of the Modern Korean Christianity's Nationalism"]. *Journal of Religion and Culture* 1: 64–68.

Kang, In-cheol. 2005. "Hanguksahoewa Yangsimjeok Byongyukguhbu" ["Korean Society and Concientious Objection"]. *Journal of Religion and Culture* 1: 103–141.

Kang, In-hwa. 2007. "Hanguksahoeeui Byongyukguhbuwoondongeul Tonghae Bon Namsungsung Yeongu" ["The Study of Masculinity Through the Movement of Conscientious Objection in Korean Society"]. Master's thesis, Ewha Women's University.

Kim, Doo-shik. 2000. "Chongeul Homiro: Yangshimjeok Byongyukguhbuwa Ghidokkyo Pyonghwajueui" ["Hoe instead of Gun: Conscientious Objection and Christian Pacifism"]. *NewsNJoy*.

Kim, Nami. 2016. *The Gendered Politics of the Protestant Right in Korea: Hegemonic Masculinity*. New York: Palgrave Macmillan.

Kim, Nami and Wonhee Anne Joh. 2016. "Introduction." In *Critical Theology against US Militarism in Asia: Decolonization and Deimperialization*, edited by Kim, Nami, and Wonhee Anne Joh, i–xx. New York: Palgrave Macmillan. https://doi.org/10.1057/978-1-137-48013-2

Kwon, Heonik. 2010. *The Other Cold War*. New York: Columbia University Press. https://doi.org/10.7312/kwon15304

Lee, Jin-Kyung. 2010. *Service Economies: Militarism, Sex Work, and Migrant Labor in South Korea*. Minneapolis, MN: University of Minnesota Press.

Lee, Yong Suk. 2017. "Daechebokmujaeleul Doiphaja, Gundae Inkwonmunjaega Haegyoldaeda" ["With the Introduction of an Alternative System to Military Service, Human Rights Issues in the Military Were Solved"]. *Ohmynews*, October 11. Retrieved from http://m.ohmynews.com/NWS_Web/Mobile/at_pg.aspx?CNTN_CD=A0002366755 (accessed October 12, 2017).

Neocleous, Mark. 2008. *Critique of Security*. Montreal: McGill-Queen's University Press. https://doi.org/10.3366/edinburgh/9780748633289.001.0001

Soelle, Dorothee. 1990. *The Window of Vulnerability: A Political Spirituality*. Minneapolis, MN: Fortress Press.

World Without War. 2014. *Woorineun Gundaeleul Guhbuhanda* [*We Reject Military: The Statements by 53 Conscientious Objectors*]. Podobat: World Without War.

World Without War. 2018. "Nonpyeong: Yangsimjeok Byongyukguhbujaae Daehan Daebupwoneui Mujoi Chiji Pagiwhansong Pangyeol Whanyounghanda" ["Commentary: We Welcome the Supreme Court's Ruling in Favor of Conscientious Objector"]. Retrieved from www.withoutwar.org/?p=14780&fbclid=IwAR0B2HlLTURG26cu7pLRpHONcMu7npVxRBSM1XqujomtzOSy2zShrN0pHwA (accessed November 1, 2018).

8

Okinawan People's Philosophy of Direct Action against Capitalism and Imperialism from Post-World War II to the Present

Kozue Uehara

> We're a tiny island, and the community and bonds are strong here ... Okinawa has the treasure of nature, the ocean and mountains ... It's the future generations who will be greatly burdened with all the damage ... We have to stop accepting the base as a status quo. We have been protesting every day with the belief our actions will definitely stop them. We're not fighting because we think we might be able to block them. We know we will. I won't be beaten up until I collapse, I will keep on going. Even if I do collapse, I'll keep raising my voice. That's how strong my will is.
> —Kumiko Onaga (cited in Narang 2017)

Seventy-three years after the Battle of Okinawa and forty-six years of Japanese control of Okinawa (a political control based on Japan's largest concentration of US military bases on the island), Okinawans' struggle has entered into a new phase. Onaga Takeshi, who was elected as the governor of Okinawa prefecture in 2014, had opposed the excessive burden imposed by the US military bases and declared his intention to revoke the approval for landfill work associated with constructing a new US military base in Henoko Bay, located in a northern city of Nago. However, he died of pancreatic cancer in August 2018. The governor's death, along with the local government's confrontational stance against the central government, has further exposed the coercive, undemocratic nature of the Japanese government's forcible construction of a new US military base in Okinawa.

Post-war Okinawans, who practice the simple philosophy of *nuchi du takara* (life is a treasure),[1] protested the imperialist expansion of the US military bases and the economic dominance of foreign and Japanese companies as well as the political hegemony of the Japanese government, which provided financial support to the US and allowed it to station its troops under the Japan-US Status of Forces Agreement. The presence of US military bases has been the cause of accidents/violence and has threatened the lives of Okinawan people. One disaster occurred in August 2004, when the US military helicopter CH-53 crashed into the campus of the Okinawa International University. One of the buildings was completely destroyed and its debris, including propellers, hit neighboring residential houses. Later, we learned that the propeller contained radioactive substances, which burned at the crash site, thus most likely spreading radioactive contamination.

People in Okinawa protested and organized multiple demonstrations to remove the Marine Corps Air Station Futenma in Ginowan, a southern city that suffered enormous destruction during the Battle of Okinawa and where a refugee camp was built right after the war. However, the Japanese government used the danger of Futenma as a pretext to accelerate the construction of new bases in Henoko. The new base construction plan was approved in 1996 by the US–Japan Special Action Committee on Okinawa (SACO), which set out "to realign, consolidate, and reduce US facilities and adjust operational procedures" (Ministry of Foreign Affairs 1996). The committee was formed after a twelve-year-old girl was raped by three US service members in 1995, an incident that prompted huge protest rallies demanding a reduction of US military presence in Okinawa.

Opposition against the bases has been ongoing for more than twenty years, and Okinawans have remained steadfast in their efforts to delay their construction. Henoko, for many years a site of popular opposition against US-Japan militarization, has received many visitors who extend solidarity from Okinawa as well as from mainland Japan and abroad. It has become a primary node for activist self-organization and the current foundation of our collective experience of the Okinawan movement. In 2004 and 2005, I joined the movement and was fortunate enough to get a chance to listen to the older protesters who taught me about their involvement in the Okinawan struggle since the immediate aftermath of World War II. I heard their stories on scaffolds in Oura and Henoko Bays, which were set up for seabed research by the Naha Defense Agency. Protesters were trying to stop the research and even squatted around the clock because the research required the extraction of the seabed and would have eventually damaged the coral reefs. The Henoko struggle thus constituted not only a concerted opposition to US militarization, but a creation of self-valorized space where the movement's history and practice were shared.

The Henoko struggle engaged numerous creative efforts by various people to spend more time at the protest site. As a sociologist and ethnographer, Abe Kosuzu describes how women intervened in creating new methods of meeting their everyday needs. She recollects her experience of visiting and squatting in Henoko for the first time. Unlike the male participants who could just relieve themselves by hiding behind a cabin or urinating directly into the water, the women participants had to invent a temporary private space that functioned as a toilet (Abe 2005). In spaces created with blue tarp or straw mats (fixed to the frames with string), they set up a bucket tied to a string so that, after they had relieved themselves, they could lower the bucket above the sea level floor and let the water carry away the waste. Such practices embodied "agency" in the struggle; they not only command attention for their utilitarian creativity but also for bringing a sense of "actual living and subsistence" to the struggle. The activists also took turns and made lunch boxes with lots of vegetables for the squatters. Henoko hence became a place to learn about how to work together politically and how to—and what to—eat together by paying attention to individual, often gendered necessities. Through social movements, people learn how to coexist with each other and re-create social relations of greater equality.

Multiple direct actions and collectively organized movements against the US bases have delayed their construction. However, the Japanese government has accelerated landfill construction and is using coast guard officers and riot police to violently suppress protestors. Especially after April 2017, the Japanese government has sped up the construction of coastal defense structures, initiating a landfill operation, which involves dumping earth and dirt into the bay, on August 17, 2018 (Japan Times 2018). What was happening during the height of the struggle as the protestors were facing their biggest crisis in 2018? The activists' various direct actions during the summer of 2018 will be discussed below, written ethnographically from my perspective as a participant.

August 2018, Okinawa: "Stop Dumping Landfill in the Ocean"

August 5: The Eve of the Two Consecutive Week-Long Intensive Actions

On August 5, 2018, I rented a car and headed for Uruma City to join a gathering to discuss the beginning of two consecutive week-long actions to stop the planned August 17 dumping of earth and dirt in Henoko Bay. People who had organized direct action to stop transportation of landfill materials at Shiokawa Port in Motobu and other ports in northern Okinawa gathered together, planning activities to take place simultaneously with the demonstration in front of the Henoko Camp Schwab Gate in the following two weeks.

At the meeting, the organizers shared important considerations to keep in mind in practicing direct action. *Netouyo*, or online right-wingers, are known to record and distort the images and sounds of activists without their permission and then dispersed them online, defaming the movement to hundreds of thousands of viewers. We discussed how to avoid provocation by such *netouyo*. Advice was also given for dealing with uncomfortable behavior within the movement. First, when the participants faced such a behavior, they should say "no." If they could not say "no," they should just leave the place where the behavior is occurring. If they are unable to move, they should ask for help. Organizers explained that experienced counselors and lawyers who could be contacted for advice are available and, if people needed immediate help, they could consult the organizers, who wore yellow T-shirts to distinguish themselves. They also explained the purpose of our movement, namely that we were waging a struggle against power and hence we must not reproduce the structure of domination among ourselves. This critical self-awareness seeped into every aspect of our actions in the following days.

When people confront power, they often find themselves in conflict with each other for various reasons. In struggling against US military expansion during the 1950s, when the island-wide struggle resisted the second land acquisition after the Battle of Okinawa, it was necessary to overcome such divisions among the people. Mutual distrust was caused by the Battle of Okinawa, which forced residents into a state of misery and made them suspect each other as spies in the wake of the US military occupation, exerting on them the repressive power of imperialist conquest. The struggle to overcome mutual distrust among themselves constituted the beginning of Okinawans' self-organization. Even the simple act of physically showing up at demonstrations took enormous courage on an occupied island under constant military surveillance. Seishu Sakihara says people concealed themselves by wearing masks or squatting down in the grass in Nishihara Village when he made a speech supporting Kamejiro Senaga for his stance against the US military's authoritarian decision to disqualify Senaga's eligibility to run for mayor in Naha (Uehara 2017: 91–92).

Even when people could overcome distrust and create solidarity among themselves, the powers that be carried out a divide-and-rule strategy in various ways. When a person stands up against a formidable enemy, he or she tends to neglect individual pains or problems experienced by someone next to him or her. How can we truly deal with each other's problems and help one another? This also relates to our attitudes towards the guards and the riot police. How should we deal with people who are attached to the power of the police or military? In the Iejima land struggle, often considered the first popular action that triggered an island-wide movement, rules for petitioning were established, including a rule that said "do not raise [one's] hand above the shoulder when protesting against a US soldier" (Tanji 2006: 67–68).

"Struggle needs to be conducted by persuading others with reason," Shoko Ahagon says (Ahagon 1998: 132). Such a rational mind-set is necessary in a struggle that confronts power. A rational philosophy rooted in experience is genuinely respected and exercised through words and deeds, more so in the struggle of the movement than in policymaking, parliamentary, or classroom settings, etc., because lessons from previous struggles are urgently needed to support and guide the ongoing struggle, providing directions and suggestions to the protagonists to choose the right action and words. Such movement wisdom often takes the form of a key phrase, passed on from one generation to the next, such as "life is a treasure," and in the following days I observed how it informed people's action as they organized the Henoko struggle.

One organizer asked what actions should we take on the first day of the week. We addressed the following questions: why take alternative action while sit-in protests in Henoko are still taking place, which ports should we meet, what kinds of routes are near the port, what would we do if we cannot not stop a truck on the road? The organizer explained several possible direct actions we can take and discussed the meaning of each, explaining its reason and purpose. We organized our action through such careful, collective deliberation.

August 6—The First Day of the Two Consecutive Week-Long Intensive Actions

The bus left the first pick-up stop at 7:00 a.m. Although some individuals drove their own cars to the harbor, a mini bus was used to transport people participating from Uruma. The bus picked up people at several stops on the way to northern Okinawa. We shared information with each other on the bus until we arrived at the harbor. People took turns emceeing, and the emcees discussed the importance of taking multiple actions such as physically stopping the trucks and appealing to drivers to delay construction, while continuing demonstrations at the Camp Schwab gate. Mr. I shared a story about what happened during the direct action at Shiokawa Port in Motobu. People in Motobu sat on their knees in the dirt and protested in front of the trucks, asking drivers to drive slowly to delay the construction. He explained that it was important to convey to them the message that they were not the enemies.

The bus headed for Shiokawa Port after picking up more people in front of Ishikawa City Hall. Isamu Nakasone said the imminent issue that day was whether the Okinawan prefectural government would accept the Defense Bureau's request to postpone the hearing on the Henoko landfill (Ministry of Defense 2018). If the prefectural government refused and withdrew postponement, it would be possible to stop the construction before the governor's instruction to dump dirt and sand into Henoko is executed. However, it was also possible that the hearing might not go well. If the prefectural government accepted postponing the hearing, the dirt and sand will arrive on August 17. Okinawan local government was making a difficult decision. What kind of appeal should we make? The bus soon arrived at Shiokawa Port, and more than 80 people began discussing what actions to take that day.

One fact that we discussed was that there seemed to be no transportation of sediment that day. In light of this knowledge, we debated the proper course of action. A participant stood at the circle's center and expressed an opinion, as the people surrounding the circle considered it. Was it better for us to go to the prefectural government hall, voice our support to the Okinawan government, and demand that they refuse the postponement request? Or should we organize a protest demonstration against the Defense Agency? Should we stop US military vehicles from entering and exiting the bases? August 6 was the day when the prefectural government decided on the date of the hearing with the Defense Agency. We all agreed that we should not let the prefectural government postpone the hearing and headed in a hurry for Naha, where the prefectural government hall is located, via the Okinawa Expressway, from Shiokawa Port. It would have been impossible to change our destination flexibly at a moment's notice if we had relied on the service of company bus drivers. We thanked our peers who drove us and accommodated the changes in our schedule and destination, according to the decisions we made at the spur of the moment in the face of shifting circumstances.

The bus arrived at the prefectural government at 11:30 a.m. Several individuals talked to the prefectural officials to arrange a meeting room for us to make our demands. While we waited in the lobby, the prefectural officials came downstairs. One said they would set up a meeting for 2:00 p.m. We decided to have lunch first and reassemble at 1:30 p.m. I went outside with a few other female participants, sitting on a bench and eating our bento lunch together. A woman sitting on the opposite bench gave us delicious *tsukudani* (sweetly boiled *goya*, or bitter melon, with small fish and bonito flakes). On the other hand, another woman, who came all the way to Naha from Uruma, walked away and ate alone at a café. I was glad to observe these individuals giving each other space and respecting each other's ways of participating in the struggle while fighting together against the construction of the new base.

We reassembled at 1:30 p.m. and agreed on the meeting's purpose, which was to listen to the prefectural government's perspective while proposing our demand to not postpone the hearing with the Defense Agency. Yoshiyasu Iha, Masanori Okuma, Zenji Shimada, Isamu Nakasone, and Hidekazu Miyagi were seated, and meetings with the prefectural governor's office-based countermeasure supervisor started at 2:00 p.m. While we prioritized listening to the prefecture's perspective, we made our position clear in insisting on the refusal of postponement of the hearing. During the second half of the meeting other participants who were in the back of the room also demanded halting of the base construction.

The prefectural side generally repeated ambiguous statements in response to our questions. They did not tell us whether they would refuse to postpone the hearing. We returned to the lobby and summarized the day's actions. We changed the previous plan we had at Shiokawa Port and flexibly moved to the Okinawa prefectural government. Some people decided to stay until the government made its announcement, and then the mini bus returned to Uruma.

I would also like to mention the diverse approaches that people took in expressing their dissent. On the way back, we stopped at the Nakagusuku rest area. One participant brought delicious steamed cakes that his wife had made. A piece of galingale leaf was laid beneath the cakes and they smelled delectable. People brought food from their agricultural farms. One lady brought the squeezed juice of *goya*. She explained that she woke up early in the morning, put *goya* in a blender, poured it through a strainer, and carried it in a container. Okinawan *goya* is really bitter and thus represents a kind of energy for the struggle. As people took part in protest, they could become nervous or angry from their prolonged confrontation with power. But the way she behaved made people relaxed or laugh because when we were confronting the Defense Agency officials and riot police she was worried about where to buy ice and cider to mix with the *goya* juice. That kind of humor and laughter is necessary for sustaining a movement in the long run.

The bus dropped us at three different stops where we had boarded that morning. After I returned home I checked the news, which reported that the prefectural government had refused the Okinawa Defense Agency's request to postpone the hearing planned for August 9.

August 7—Day 2 of the Two Consecutive Week-Long Intensive Actions

On day 2 we were picked up again by the bus at 7:20 AM, where we discussed the previous day's action. Hidekazu Miyagi initiated the discussion and said it was good that everyone expressed an opinion and made decisions on what to do next. The woman who gave us *tsukudani* during lunch emceed that day. She said she had been involved in the protest with a "flexible and sturdy" attitude and a desire to "live better." She commented that it was somewhat sad to sing songs written during and after the war. They were still living the Okinawan people's past reality in the present. However, she said she cannot just give up, and, as long as she is alive, she will continue to fight with her comrades for the future generation.

On the bus, we discussed what action we should prioritize that day. For example, should we go to the Camp Schwab gate and join the morning gathering and move to the Defense Agency in Kandena in the afternoon, or should we go to the Defense Agency immediately in the morning and organize the demonstration there? The prefectural government already refused to postpone the hearing and the Defense Agency ignored the prefectural government's administrative guidance, so we decided to express our protest against the Agency. The bus headed directly to the Defense Agency in Kadena, which is in the central part of Okinawa. People who were already gathered at Shiokawa Port came on foot. The participant sitting next to me on the bus was a female knitting artisan who liked coffee and taught me about Christo, the Bulgarian packing artist who had visited Okinawa.

While we chatted, the bus arrived at the Okinawa Defense Agency in Kadena. We waited for everyone's arrival around the building's entrance. The purpose of the day's action was to demand the Defense Agency to not interfere with the prefectural government's withdrawal of the landfill approval prior to the central government's introduction of earth and stones into Henoko Bay. However, no one could enter the office without permission. Several organizers negotiated around 9 a.m, but the request was not heeded so we started a sit-in in front of the Bureau's gate around 9:50 a.m. While we sat at the Defense Agency building's entrance, various people such as merchants arrived. Some of us politely asked these visitors to wait and line up because there were a hundred of us already waiting.

After a while, Isamu Nakasone and Yoshiyasu Iha explained that the Defense Agency was negotiating to meet with only five representatives from the crowd. Iha asked everyone what to do next at the entrance. This was our movement practice: everyone participated in the discussion and considered the decision we made. Of course, it was important to ensure that some representatives passed the request form to the Defense Bureau; however, people raised their voices, saying "there is no representative!" Similar voices arose, one after another. Everyone was a representative, and everyone needed to be present in the negotiations. Iha explained that "I guess it will be a tough fight all day today." He said "I guess" because he knew how difficult it was to persuade government officials to listen to the people's demands. We agreed to continue the sit-in at the Defense Agency until they let all of us in the meeting room. This moment particularly impressed me because I thought I witnessed a moment when people actually practiced the movement proverb "everyone is a representative of the movement," which was rooted in the 1970s Kin Bay movement that I will discuss later. Our ongoing protest is organized with the belief that protest should not be conducted top-down but should be organized horizontally by all individual participants. Our relationship needs to be horizontal, not vertical. We exercise participatory democracy at the grassroots.

This was going to be a long sit-in. We could not continue our struggle if we felt hungry, so first we had lunch. I bought a cider at a convenience store and helped a woman make bitter melon cider. I ate bento lunch very quickly and went to an Okinawan soba restaurant.

The philosophy of "everyone is a representative of the struggle" was practiced in different ways. People took turns making speeches. When I returned to the demonstration at the Defense Agency's entrance around 12:40, Iha was talking. He explained what happened in the Kin Bay struggle he had helped organize forty years ago. When people organized a group protesting the construction of oil stockpiling tanks, construction of the ocean landfill was already completed by more than 70 percent. When they sued the Okinawa prefectural government for approving Mitsubishi, the business operator, to create a landfill in the publicly owned body of water, the people lost because the judge determined that "there [was] no profit in suing (because the fishery rights have been abrogated from the landfilled water area)." Iha also explained that after the US aircraft *Osprey* started flying over the Yanbaru forest, the Pryer's woodpeckers, one of Okinawa's endangered species, stopped singing and communicating with each other because of the aircraft's noise (Ryukyu Shimpo 2014). He also expressed, as a science teacher, that biodiversity in Oura Bay exceeds that of the Great Barrier Reef (Muzik 2015). He concluded that we should not allow them to create a landfill in Henoko.

People's speeches continued. The Henoko protest's ship captain suggested the Defense Agency's staff to visit the beautiful Henoko bay. A woman shared her memory of swimming in the ocean when she was a child. She said that when she was young, every child knew there were two types of seawater with different temperatures. Both seawater and freshwater from the rivers helped algae grow. The ocean's richness nurtured the islanders' lives. Environmental destruction was analogous to a human war against nature. She strongly asked the staff to listen to the islanders who were painfully oppressed by the Japanese government and the US military but who continued to fight against them.

Some criticized the Defense Bureau for its failure to speak to the US military even when the latter put the island's children at risk. A survivor of the Miyamori Elementary School jet crash said it was not a window frame but a jet aircraft F-100 that crashed and killed 18 people (Hook, Mason and O'Shea 2015: 170). He said he cannot forget the smell of his flesh burning with jet fuel. Today, the US military responds in the same indifferent way as it did in the 1950s. "We are fortunate that the aircraft did not fall [onto the] Kadena base, thanks to the skillful pilots," he said. Tsuneo Shiroma stated that his father and seven siblings were killed by Japanese and US soldiers. His younger sister was choked to death by a Japanese solider for crying (Shinjo Summers Robbins 2015). He survived had to live alone for the rest of his life after the Battle of Okinawa.

I am enumerating these people's experiences in order to show how each protestor had a personal reason to engage in the protest and how their individual wartime or post-war experiences inform their political engagement today. There are histories that can only be overcome through people's struggles. Those who experienced war trauma sublimated their suffering by participating in the peace movement. The Japanese government ignored their pains and desires, imposing the US military bases with the use of state power, violence, and money, and by marginalizing base issues as an isolated "Okinawan problem." People's suppressed feelings were manifest in their words and actions as they confronted the Defense Agency. Hidekazu Miyagi took the microphone and said these narratives proved that serious damages from military power were experienced by the Okinawan people.

The sit-in continued even after 2:00 p.m. Around 4:40 p.m., Defense Agency officials began trying to evacuate people from the entrance while we insisted that we would wait until we received any response from the Defense Agency staff. Around 6:00 p.m., police from the Kadena station arrived. As soon as the tense policeman started forcefully evacuating us, Tokushin Yamauchi, the former mayor of Yomitan Village, proceeded to deliver a message to the police and riot police officials through a microphone. He said he was a longtime friend of the Kadena police chief and they worked together preventing crimes in Yomitan and Kadena. He told the police to consider why these elderly people were doing a sit-in. He told them to make sure to treat us nicely, joking that "these elderly people's bones are fragile; please treat [them] politely." His tone was humorous, but at the same time his message was effective in reaching the ears of the antagonists. As if his words had the effect of easing the tension, the riot police started evacuating us carefully.

During the general assembly meeting, Iha spoke as follows: "The achievement of today's action is great. Let [us] keep it up through the hearing on August 9 with this same energy." We all pledged to gather at the Defense Agency again the next day and sang a protest song entitled "Suwarikome kokoe" ("Let's Do a Sit-In Here")[2] and wrapped up the day. When we got on the bus, it was already dark. The woman who had emceed in the morning said, "every day we are pushed to change the plan of action, but let [us] keep our pure intention in mind—we just want to protect the ocean. Let [us] remind ourselves of such genuine feelings, so that we will be able to accomplish something."

The Reality of "Everyone is a Representative of the Struggle"

We shared a feeling of accomplishment from the first and second days of our protest. However, it did not last long. The morning of the third day on August 8 started with turmoil with the Defense Agency agents and security guards at the Defense Agency building's entrance. They stood up and barricaded the entrance, and our demands were stonewalled.

In the evening, Governor Taksehi Onaga, who had just announced that he would start the procedure to withdraw permission to construct the landfill, passed away. He was fighting pancreatic cancer and his physically weakening condition was apparent. The Okinawan people were waiting for him to fulfill his campaign promise to withdraw permission to build the landfill. He showed how difficult it was for Okinawan politicians to simultaneously represent the voices of the Okinawan people and resist national policy. The degree of difficulty depended on how much we could recognize this reality and act on our own. How could each of us practice protests against the military and create a common power that no one could represent? When the security barricade turns into a barricade of direct action, the meaning of representation starts to change and overcome the limitation of representative democracy. This might be the significant question raised by the death of Governor Onaga.

This is exactly the moment of crisis that the current people's struggle in Okinawa is facing. Winning the election is important, but, in the long run, it is no less important to nurture our common power. The statement that "everyone is a representative of the struggle" that I heard at the Defense Agency building's entrance has been echoing in my ears. People's movements should not be organized top-down but should be constituted by individuals who can express their own will.

"Everyone is a representative of the struggle" has been long practiced in the people's movement, especially in the Kin Bay movement, in Okinawa from the 1970s through the early 1980s. The Kin Bay struggle was a protest movement on Okinawa's eastern coast, where communities organized the Kin Bay Protection Society and opposed the reclamation of Kin Bay and the construction of the Central Terminal Station (CTS) (including oil storage tanks and refineries) through rallies, demonstrations, petitions, and lawsuits against the Okinawan prefectural government and oil companies.

Kin Bay is an arc stretching from the coast of Kin Village, extending towards the Katsuren Peninsula (also known as the Yokatsu Peninsula), and reaching the islands of Henza, Miyagi, and Ikei. The districts of Yakena and Teruma, which are part of Yonagusuku Village and are separated by the districts of Yonagusuku and Chuo, lie on the upper half of Katsuren Peninsula.

During the reversion period, after 27 years of US occupation, various economic development projects were undertaken to reduce the economic "gap" between mainland Japan and Okinawa. This gap and the calls for increased economic development remain key issues in Okinawa. One of the economic development projects was the Kin Bay Area Development Base Project (Okinawa, Kin-wan Chiku Kaihatsu Kihon Koso) conducted by Okinawa Keizai Kaihatsu Kenkyujo in 1972, which proposed reclaiming the ocean between Henza Island and the neighboring island of Miyagi and building an oil stockpiling camp, thermal and nuclear power plants, an aluminum industry, a petrochemical complex, and more on Okinawa's eastern coast. After Gulf Oil, a US oil company, started operating on Henza Island in 1970, Mitsubishi, a private Japanese company, planned a massive ocean reclamation project to fill in the ocean and create new land connecting Henza and Miyagi Islands.

The companies proposed constructing oil storage tanks and a refinery—a Central Terminal Station (CTS)—on the reclaimed land. These industries were promoted during the reversion period by private companies and the governments of the US, Japan, Okinawa prefecture, and Yonagusuku Village as alternatives to the military-dependent economy that had pervaded Okinawa during the occupation. Repeated oil spill accidents covered Kin Bay with heavy oil, and black, glue-like balls of waste coated beaches in the Kin Bay coastal area. Fishermen had to leave the community because they could not make a living from the fish caught in Kin Bay, which reeked of petroleum. Kin Bay residents protested the economic development project, contending that it would pollute their environment and affect local industry. The residents' movement transformed ideological beliefs into action and enabled them to mobilize local supporters and external resources and develop a counter-narrative against their opponents.

To protest the developmentalist policy, the Kin Bay Protection Society first took radical action against the Okinawa prefectural government through rallies, sit-ins, and mass bargaining. From 1974, Kin Bay residents organized themselves and sued Governor Chobyo Yara, a prominent leader of the reversion movement. Yara was viewed as someone who would listen sympathetically to the claims of the fishermen. However, the reformist Okinawa prefectural administration forcefully promoted the development project in the name of "national interest" and became an opponent to the Kin Bay movement. In the CTS trial, the courts were exposed as an institutional power that enforced governmental and corporate decisions under the banner of "national interest." The Kin Bay Protection Society's chosen field of protest—the judicial court system—proved unfair. The Society realized that the court was functioning as Okinawa's mechanism of domination even after the US occupation.

This trial document was written at a time when people in Kin Bay were starting to talk about the importance of addressing individual experiences. From April 1945, as US troops arrived, Yonagusuku residents were captured and moved to internment camps in the Kin Bay coastal area because the US needed a labor force for constructing its military bases (Okinawa Prefectural Board of Education 1974: 419). Residents who evacuated to northern Okinawa were taken and forced to work at internment camps, eventually traveling back to their hometowns. People who moved to mainland Japan or who were sent to Asian-Pacific battlefields were shipped through several cities in mainland Japan and returned to Okinawa if they survived. Among the Kin Bay communities, the Yakena District, a major site of the Kin Bay struggle, has been called *nanyo gunraku*, or the "south sea community." More than half the residents of Hirata Village in Yakena were repatriated from Saipan or Tinian, where many of them lost their family members (Ryukyu Shimpo 1993).

A similar narrative is found in Seishin Asato's *Umi wa hitono haha dearu*, or *The Ocean is the Mother of the People*, where he asserts the experience of war and the loss of family lies at the very root of the protest against oil tank construction in Kin Bay. Asato writes about Fumi Oshiro, who composed the following *ryuka*, or Ryukyuan song. She migrated to the Palauan Islands twice during the 1920s and 1930s, then worked as a spinning-mill worker in Osaka during the late 1930s. She lost her husband on the battlefield in China.

> Putting our minds together,
> we shouldn't lower our guards;
> we want a bright future.
>
> Blinded by money
> who has made CTS
> bring suffering to so many people?
> (Asato 1981)

Asato was a teacher who was sent to teach at a school in Taegu, the capital of Korea under Japanese colonial rule. He was then drafted three times during the war and got involved in a very fierce battle on the Chinese continent. When he was discharged from the Japanese imperial army, he learned that his wife and child, whom he had brought from Okinawa, had committed suicide in Korea before the war's end because they feared for their lives at the enemy's hand. Therefore, he returned to his village with his two remaining children (Hanazaki 2010: 186).

Asato became one of the organizers of the Kin Bay movement, and in 1977, six months after the Okinawan governor approved constructing the oil tanks, he published the following comment in the magazine *Shin Okinawa Bungaku,* or *New Okinawa Literature*:

> Carrying bones of my wife on my back and holding the bones of my child in my arms; bearing the cross of fellow soldiers and Chinese people who had died in the war, I live like a specter in agony.
>
> (Asato 1981: 15)

According to Asato, this was the core reason that he and other Yakena residents fought for their community. At the same time, the experience of displacement and loss produced remorse that led them to participate in the resistance movement as well as a perspective in understanding their situation in the context of world history.

Kin Bay activists engaged in solidarity work with the anti-nuclear movements on the Micronesian Islands, such as Palau and Guam, during the late 1970s, as they learned about the Japanese government's plan to dump radioactive waste from nuclear power plants into the ocean near the Micronesian Islands. The Kin Bay movement also welcomed activists from Guam and Palau, such as Roman Bedor from Koror, Palau, and David Rosario from Guam. In a larger context, the Kin Bay struggle was part of a worldwide, indigenous peoples' struggle to regain the right of self-determination. Indigenous communities struggling globally against capitalism and colonialism for their independence or autonomy were identified as allies in the Kin Bay movement (Uehara 2011). Exchanging thoughts and experiences through grassroots network with fellow Pacific Islanders helped the Kin Bay Protection Society frame their struggle. It also showed how the experience of displacement and loss became the source of popular will to build a better relationship with the Mariana Islanders, who used to be under Japanese colonial rule, and Okinawans accepted their role as settler-colonialists before and during World War II as they themselves experienced displacement and loss and struggled against them.

Shoko Ahagon is a famous organizer of the land struggle on Iejima. He was born in Motobu in Okinawa and migrated to Cuba, moving to Peru during the 1920s and 1930s and to mainland Japan in 1934 and then back to Iejima. Ahagon, as an Asian migrant farmer in Cuba and Peru, experienced first-hand American imperialism and US state and corporate labor exploitation, an experience that later led him to become a ferocious campaigner against US land eviction in Iejima. By examining his transboundary experience, we see that the Kin Bay movement and its philosophy of "survival" articulated an essential voice in the postwar "Okinawan struggle," nurturing participants through the experience of trans-Pacific displacement, which makes their movement part of not just Okinawan but global indigenous people's history.

The diversity of the Okinawan people's experiences in the postwar period also led them to appreciate the strategy of mass bargaining, where "each resident is a representative of the struggle." Although the Kin Bay Protection Society had "contact persons" Seishu Sakihara and Seishin Asato, it always made decisions through the general assembly. Collective actions were determined by the consent of all participants in the general assembly, and these participants were encouraged to join subsequent collective action. Through this strategy of participatory democracy, individuals could argue directly with government officials rather than having just a few members represent the collective voice.

This identification of the movement's collective agency was enhanced by emphasizing the epistemological and cultural beliefs shared by residents and fishermen, who sustained their lives with abundant catches from the sea, further differentiating them from those in government and political parties (i.e., those who believed that "affluence" could only be attained through industries which might be environmentally destructive and cause harm to subsistent ways of life). Cultural practice became valuable because it represented islanders' resistance to depopulation and weakening of community ties which started in the era of US occupation. Revival of cultural practices in the Kin Bay movement also challenged the capitalist and colonialist incursion by mobilizing residents of local communities into the movement and localizing environmental protest as the residents' own struggle. Their struggle aimed to preserve their cultural values and practices within their natural environment.

The Kin Bay Protection Society sought to guard the ocean against oil spillage and conflagration caused by tankers and oil-related industries, which Governor Yara's reformist administration promoted as a "peace industry" for the future economy of Okinawa. Since even reformists could not criticize the governor's collusion with national policy, residents came to distrust the reformist political parties that could or would no longer represent their interests. Thus, they became the representatives of their own struggle, despite the Kin Bay Protection Society's lack of success in mobilizing either reformist political parties or labor unions. Seishin Asato describes the "resident movement" as follows:

> As a matter of course, the residents' movement is organized where people living in a particular place are forced to expose serious risks caused by the national government, discover themselves, and push their nature out into the open ... Thus, a representative is unnecessary for the residents' movement ... Thus, there is no representative in the "Kin Bay Protection Society." The Okinawan prefectural officials do not understand that ... World War II happened even when we had representatives. Even the governor of Okinawa destroy[ed] the nature and the land of Okinawa. So these officials say that "they cannot deal with the Protection Society" ... Residents' movement should not be organized on the basis of decisions made by the top.
> (Asato 1981: 41)

As we can see in this passage, the significance of the residents' movement for Asato was encouraging each resident to express himself/herself through collective struggle. His narrative indicates his belief that war erupted because of decisions made by leaders and that we must protect our own land from ongoing development projects and not repeat the same mistakes. Asato asserts that it is critical to listen to elderly people's experiences who worked in the Kin Bay movement and record them as an important part of our history. He believed that the movement should not have a single "hero" who spoke for the rest.

Asato's narrative, which saw the similarity between constructing an oil stockpiling base and the eruption of World War II, was not limited to expressing anger and assigning blame for war and development. He reflected on his own past by "surviving as wraith but in agony" and preached the need to manifesting his own will by acting intentionally to not repeat the same mistakes. Specifically, the Kin Bay movement was the process of "living again" for Asato after the death-in-life he experienced during the war.

As Asato explains, critics such as Kawamitsu Shinichi and Keitoku Okamoto raised issues concerning the experience of collective suicide and how communities were pressured into committing it under national, military, communal power (Doi 2009). They argued for the need to determine how community can improve individual lives, rather than killing them, in Okinawa during the reversion period. Okamoto notes that the "modernization" policy after the Meiji period tried capturing and dominating "community physiology" in Okinawa in order to transform it into an instrument of state/military power. He questions how we can reject the "sense of order" that accepts the domination of power, how we can make the best use of the "will to live together," and "what "self-reliance" means in that context" (Okamoto 1970: 159–160). Okamoto concurred with the organizational practices of the Kin Bay movement and its belief that "every resident is a representative of the struggle." Okamoto's later involvement in the anti-CTS campaign among journalists and scholars demonstrates his own commitment during the reversion period.

The "postwar generation," or those who have not experienced World War II, also questioned Okinawa's war responsibility. The anti-Vietnam War movement motivated the postwar generation that started to question Okinawa's war responsibility during World War II and its position on the frontline of US Cold War military policy in East Asia. Teruo Hiyane opined that: "it is noteworthy that after the war the demand for questioning its own war responsibility was not pursued in postwar Okinawa, but the postwar generation pointed out Okinawa's war responsibility as a result of the Vietnam War." He also noted that "when Okinawa's postwar generation pursues war responsibility, the postwar experience [and] the harsh US military occupation over 20 years after the war has been the basis of their belief" (Ishida, Tanigawa, Gabe and Hiyane 1970: 76). The postwar generation, which lacked direct war experience but experienced US military rule, had firm ideological grounds for protesting war and the presence of military troops.

The Kin Bay movement demonstrated how participants could discuss, make decisions, and negotiate horizontally, rather than entrusting their voices to a few delegates responsible for making decisions. Participants always asked the Okinawan prefectural government and Yonagusuku village officials to set up the venue for collective bargaining so all residents could express their opinions. Additionally, residents and fishermen conducted environmental research in Kin Bay and recorded actual conditions of pollution and damage caused by the oil industry from the residents' perspective. This is how the Kin Bay movement stressed the importance of the residents' own experiences and perspectives.

If we see matters this way, "residents" in the Kin Bay Struggle means "people who live there," widening but simultaneously limiting the scope of its meaning. In Masazumi Harada's description, "the people who suffered the most from environmental pollution are those who lived in nature and relied on nature" and are at the same time "socially vulnerable" (Harada 2006: 275), people in Okinawa after the reversion also suffered because of environmental damages and the loss of fishing areas due to pollution. The national government, prefecture, and villages promoted further development, and the residents contested the idea that the Okinawa prefectural government represented the Okinawan people. Rather, the residents viewed the Okinawan government's disavowal of the value of the natural environment and local industries as the direct byproduct of Japanese and US colonialism in Okinawa. Takashi Morine, a youth who participated in the Kin Bay Protection Society, cited Asato, stating that "the residents' movement depends on how the people who have to live in the community and engage in life, culture, and events make an assessment of their circumstances and participate in the struggle". Those practices, though originally mostly religious and celebratory in nature, had the potency to serve a political cause by symbolically uniting individuals in the common pursuit of resisting new forms of colonialism and helping them to attain or rather restore a sense of regional autonomy.

The practice of participatory democracy, flexibly forging direct action according to the changes in the political circumstance, has been an essential part of people's recent struggles in Okinawa. The power of the people grows through struggle. In the resistance movement, we encounter moments when people share their experiences of wartime and postwar Okinawa. Why do individual participants do sit-ins and continue to protest even after experiencing so many conflicts and defeats through the postwar period? Every participant in the movement can hold a microphone and talk about his/her own stories with the police, riot police, military guards, and security guards. At the same time, we see countless efforts and concerns among participants to protect one another. This was the "Sea, Land, and the Power of Commons" that saved people's lives from the infernal experience of the war. This is a phrase inherited from the everyday struggle of the Kin Bay movement. It precisely defines the conviction that the residents' movement has derived from their daily struggle. We should remember to resurrect and practice the "power of commons" again, especially in the current difficult circumstances we face in Okinawa, as elsewhere.

Kozue Uehara is a lecturer at the Tokyo University of Foreign Studies. She is originally from Okinawa Island where she participated in the popular movement against militarization.

Her research focuses on the anti-developmentalist struggle in Kin Bay in central Okinawa in the 1970s. She is a member of the editorial committee of *Ekkyo Hiroba*, a cultural and political magazine based in Okinawa.

Notes

This chapter was originally completed in September 2018. The landfill construction of Henoko Bay planned on August 17, 2018, was extended and imposed on December 14, 2018, amid continuous protests. The contract company Ryukyu-Cement Co. Ltd. has carried and dumped soil and dirt containing red soil. The use of red soil for landfill construction is prohibited by Okinawa Prefectural Ordinance for Prevention of Red Clay Outflow. Protest action to delay the construction continues.

1. The concept of *nuchi du takara* is explained in Mitchell (2013).
2. This song was originally written by Imamura Kazuo, a union worker of Niigata All NTT Workers Union of Japan in the 1970s. The lyrics were slightly changed and sung in the ongoing people's protest against the US military base construction in Okinawa.

References

Abe, Kosuzu. 2005. "Umi de kurasu teiko" ["Struggle of Living in the Ocean"]. *Gendai shiso* 33(10): 182–191.
Ahagon, Shoko. 1998. *Inochikoso takara, Okinawa hansen no kokoro* [*Life is the Treasure, the Okinawan Antiwar Spirit*]. Tokyo: Iwanami.
Asato, Seishin. 1981. *Umi wa hito no haha dearu* [*Ocean is the Mother of the People*]. Tokyo: Shobunsha.
Doi, Tomoyoshi. 2009. "Koseiteki na kyodotai: Okamoto Keitoku *suiheijiku no hasso* o chushin ni" ["Constituent Community: Focusing on Okamoto Keitoku's *The Conception of the Horizontal Axis*"]. *Machikaneyama-ronso/Niohngakuhen* 43: 19–37.
Hanazaki, Kohei. 2010. *Tanaka Shozo to minshu shiso no keisho* [*Tanaka Shozo and the Genealogy of People's Philosophy*]. Tokyo: Nanatsumori Shokan.
Harada, Masazumi. 2006. "Minamatabyo 50 nen no fu no isan to minamatagaku" ["A Fifty-Year Negative Legacy of Minamata Disease and Minamata Studies"]. *Kan* 25.
Hook, Glenn D., Ra Mason and Paul O'Shea. 2015. *Regional Risk and Security in Japan: Wither the Everyday*. Abingdon: Routledge. https://doi.org/10.4324/9781315742007
Ishida, Ikuo, Kenichi Tanigawa, Masao Gabe and Teruo Hiyane. 1970. "Zadankai senso taiken to sengo shiso." ["Round Table Talk: War Experience and Postwar Thought"]. *Kyōwakoku* 3.
Japan Times. 2018. "Work planned Okinawa US base site to start in August." *Japan Times*, June 13.
Ministry of Defense. 2018. "Press Conference by Defense Minister Onodera." Retrieved from www.mod.go.jp/e/press/conference/2018/08/07a.html (accessed September 12, 2018).
Ministry of Foreign Affairs. 1996. *The SACO Final Report*. Retrieved from www.mofa.go.jp/region/n-america/us/security/96saco1.html (accessed September 12, 2018).
Mitchell, Jon. 2013. "Nuchi do takara, Okinawan Resistance and the Battle for Henoko Bay." *The Asia-Pacific Journal* 11(35-3). Retrieved from https://apjjf.org/2014/11/35/Jon-Mitchell/4173/article.html (accessed September 12, 2018).

Muzik, Katherine. 2015. "Fear and Hope: The Henoko Base and the Future of Oura Bay." *The Asia-Pacific Journal* 13(4-4). Retrieved from https://apjjf.org/-Katherine-Muzik/4817/article.html (accessed September 12, 2018).

Narang, Sonia. 2017. "In Okinawa, Older Women Are on the Front Lines of the Military Base Protest Movement." Retrieved from www.pri.org/stories/2017-02-14/okinawa-older-women-are-front-lines-military-base-protest-movement (accessed March 25, 2017).

Okamoto, Keitoku. 1970. *Suiheijiku no hasso* [*The Conception of the Horizontal Axis*]. Tokyo: Mokujisha.

Okinawa Prefectural Board of Education. 1974. *Okinawa kenshi: Okinawasen kiroku 2* [*The History of Okinawa Prefecture: Records of the Battle of Okinawa 2*]. Naha: Okinawa Board of Education.

Ryukyu Shimpo. 1993. "Hirata District in Yonagusuku Village." *Ryukyu Shimpo*, May 23.

Ryukyu Shimpo. 2014. "Ospreys Drive Okinawa Woodpeckers from Takae: Watchers Warn." *Ryukyu Shimpo*, 29 October. Retrieved from http://english.ryukyushimpo.jp/2014/11/10/15822 (accessed September 12, 2018).

Shinjo Summers Robbins, Masako. 2015. "My Story: A Daughter Recalls the Battle of Okinawa." Introduction by Steve Rabson. *The Asia-Pacific Journal, Japan Focus* 13(8-4). Retrieved from https://apjjf.org/2015/13/7/Masako-Shinjo-Summers-Robbins/4286.html (accessed December 24, 2018)

Tanji, Miyume. 2006. *Myth, Protest and Struggle in Okinawa*. Abingdon: Routledge. https://doi.org/10.4324/9780203016121

Uehara, Kozue. 2011. "Keizaikaihatsu e no teiko to shiteno bunka jissen: Shiseiken henkan go no Okinawa ni okeru Kin Wan Toso" ["Cultural Practice as Way of Protesting against Economic Development"]. In *Cultural typhoon: Karuchuraru sutadiz de yomitoku ajia* [*Cultural Typhoon: Cultural Studies' Reading of Asia*], edited by Minoru Iwasaki, Kuan-Hsing Chen and Shun'ya Yoshimi, 132–150. Tokyo: Serika Shobo.

Uehara, Kozue. 2017. *Hitoribitori ga daihyo: Sakihara Seishu no sengoshi o tadoru* [*Everyone is a Representative: Tracing the Postwar Personal History of Sakihara Seishu*]. Naha: Ryukyu Kikaku.

9

Understanding Non-feminist Groups through the Necessity to Resist Feminist Hegemony: The Palestinian Women's Movement versus Hamas

Sara Ababneh

Introduction

In late spring of 2007 I travelled to the occupied Palestinian West Bank to conduct my PhD fieldwork on female Islamists affiliated with Hamas. I took the opportunity to also attend conferences and meetings of the women whose writings on gender in Palestine I had admired for years. I was shocked at the hostility with which most of the women I met and heard spoke about female Hamas activists. Statements too crude to repeat in an academic chapter were the norm when the discussion turned to the victory of Hamas in the 2006 parliamentary elections, and the fact that now an Islamist was Minister of Women's Affairs. Female Islamists were described as passive tools in the hands of the male elite of Hamas who reproduced their own subordination. There was no doubt in the audience about the fact that Hamas would suppress all Palestinian women and bring the "secular" and "open" Palestinian society back to the dark Middle Ages.

Not only were Hamas members missing from any academic conference on gender, there were also almost no women who wore the headscarf present. At one conference I attended the only *Muhajaba* (woman wearing the hijab/headscarf) immediately felt the need to declare that she was a member of Fateh.

This vilification of Islamists, believing that female Islamic activists are not agents who make their own choices, was at odds with the otherwise sophisticated analyses of these academics and practitioners. Coming from feminist backgrounds, many had previously spoken out against the tendency of mainstream academia to universalize the experiences of those who are powerful.

This experience left me deeply unsettled. Moreover, in the secondary literature on gender politics in Palestine, international academics often uncritically adopted the same views. An example of an earlier incident in which this was the case is Reema Hammami's (1990) article on the so-called hijab campaign.

Hammami (1990) writes that in the early years of the first Palestinian uprising (intifada) a campaign was waged to impose the headscarf on first the women of Gaza and then the women of the West bank.

> In Gaza it started with religious youths writing graffiti, then breaking into girls' schools and making speeches. Next, young boys (between 8 and 12) who were empowered by the intifada joined the campaign. If there were no soldiers to throw stones at, women without headscarves made good targets. Politically unaffiliated shabab [youth] who felt left out found harassing these women a safe way to express nationalist sentiment. ... What was most problematic for many women in Gaza was that this social pressure accompanied an attempt to "nationalize" the hijab. Original arguments ascribing the hijab with religious meaning were all but swept away by its new intifada signification. The hijab was promoted ... as a sign of women's political commitment, as women, to the intifada.
> (Hammami 1990: 26)

In Gaza the harassment got so bad, Hammami writes, that within one year, there were almost no women left who did not eventually started wearing the hijab (ibid.: 27).

A year after the attacks the Unified Leadership, which was composed of all Palestinian political factions except for Hamas, finally condemned the attacks. Graffiti soon appeared saying that those who threw stones at women will be treated as collaborators. Hammami writes that

> the statement of the Unified Leadership had an immediate impact. In a matter of days the atmosphere in the streets changed dramatically, and women without headscarves no longer felt so threatened. Few men dared tell a woman to cover her head, and those who did could be accused of considering themselves greater than the Unified Leadership. The women had the power of the intifada on their side.
> (Hammami 1990: 27)

Even though Hammami acknowledges the complex nature of the incident, arguing that "the forces of the hijab campaign are hard to delineate because multiple forces worked simultaneously (though not necessarily jointly) to confront women at every turn with demands to wear a headscarf" (ibid.: 27), Hammami as well as others clearly blame the Islamists, mainly Hamas, for being behind this campaign (Abdulhadi 1998; Roy 1993).

More so than in Hammami's article itself, her article is henceforth cited as the proof of what awaits women if Hamas were to come to power. None of the secondary literature is interested in hearing the version of Hamas leaders. Jaroen Gunning, in an unpublished chapter on Hamas and gender, which is based on primary research in Gaza, argues that Hamas leaders were not even aware that there was a campaign going on. He further shows that, except for one case, the youth were not in any way part of Hamas or affiliated to it. Rather, more than once, the youth turned out to be collaborators employed by the Israeli army. Furthermore, Gunning maintains that although Hamas leaders (women and men) certainly encouraged women to wear the hijab, they were quick to affirm that forcing someone to wear a hijab was absolutely against their principles and was to be rejected. Moreover, Hammami herself concedes that "Hamas ... issued a local bayan[1] disassociating itself from the attackers" (Hammami 1990: 26).

This example should not function to discredit Hammami's article or to imply that women were not pressured to wear the headscarf. I cite this example to shed light on a practice that has become increasingly commonplace in work produced on Palestine, namely, speaking from a presumed position of neutrality when judging and condemning Hamas on issues of gender, which would otherwise be unthinkable when conducting feminist analysis. Feminists have been among the first to underline the link between the speaker's subject position and the knowledge she/he produces. As a result many strands of feminism emphasize the importance of the author, clearly situating herself in her work, as part of the data. Moreover, silences are treated as indicative of wider power relations and structures (Belenky et al. 1986; Guha and Spivak 1988; Ramazanoglu et al. 2007; Said 1978; Young 2001).

In this chapter I will examine the relationship between the Palestinian Women's Movement and Hamas to attempt to contextualize the debate between the Palestinian women's movement and their Islamist counterparts and to think through how we can study Islamists from the perspective of women's empowerment. In the case of Palestine, women from the Palestinian women's movement and women's rights NGOs have defined women's empowerment. As a result, I argue that we must start with a clear understanding of the basic assumptions of these activists in order to avoid judging Hamas simply by concluding that the assumptions of female Islamists are not the same as those of the Palestinian women's movement, and therefore, that they do not empower women. Furthermore, the specific context of those who are speaking about empowerment needs to be examined before uncritically taking on their verdict on whether other groups empower women or not. Finally, judging whether a certain group's actions are beneficial to women or not should be based on an analysis of this group's actions instead of simply taking on what others say or write about them. It would be unthinkable to conduct a study of Democrats in the United States in which all the data is based on Republican accounts, unless it is clearly marked as a study of "Democrats through Republicans' eyes."

I argue that in order to understand the "secular"[2] responses of the Palestinian women's movement to Hamas's Islamism, we need to (a) contextualize both sides; (b) analyze the discourse of Islamists; and (c) analyze their practice.

This chapter starts by discussing some of the main assumptions of members of the women's movement in the West Bank, as well as the history of the women's movement in all of historic Palestine. In doing so, we can contextualize the response of the Palestinian women's movement to women in Hamas and discern the multiple dimensions that led to the various confrontations between women's rights activists and female Islamists. I argue that we must try to understand non-feminist groups by examining their own practice and discourse. This chapter examines one example of the discourse of women in Hamas and another case of the practice of some female Islamists. The first example deals with the work and vision of Dr. Mariam Saleh and Amal Siyam when they became Ministers of Women's Affairs after Hamas won the legislative elections in 2006. This example aims to shed light on the politicized relationship between the Palestinian women's movement and female Islamists and asks what this means in terms of the types of "feminist" knowledge which are often assumed to be true.

The second case I examine is the structure of the Birzeit Student Islamic Bloc as an example of Islamism in practice. In particular, I will use the context of this student group to think through whether only Islamic models which critically re-examine patriarchal attitudes can be empowering to women and what this means in terms certain practices which many feminists and women's rights activists in the Arab world would consider inherently patriarchal, namely, gender segregation.

Palestinian Feminist Critiques and Assumptions

Eileen Kuttab, a professor of women's studies at the University of Birzeit, is considered one of the leading voices in the Palestinian women's movement who is critical of the Palestinian women's movement and somewhat sympathetic to Hamas (Kuttab 1999, 2006, 2008; Kuttab and Abu Awwad 2004). Yet despite her relatively open-minded attitude to Hamas, she remains deeply suspicious of the Islamic movement with regard to its gender politics. As she put it in our conversation:

> It is part of [Hamas's] political agenda to disempower women, or to empower them in a specific way. It is empowerment in Hamas's own context and disempowerment in our context. It is empowerment because Hamas want women to be public citizens. Hamas really pushes women for higher education. They want women to become more involved in public life, [but] the issue is how and where. [The question of] "where" is based on the separation of men and women. ... What kind of roles? Only those which are an extension of women's reproductive roles, as teachers, etc. and not at all to leave that framework. I think in that context it is relatively empowering, but it is disempowering because Hamas is not giving women new opportunities to explore. Like "the political" for example, the political for Hamas is only to serve the patriarchal goals of the party, which are very masculine. Hamas does this through the tool of religion, as a tool to suppress women. On the other hand it is empowering, because at least Hamas is accepting women to become more involved in public life.
> (E. Kuttab, personal interview, Birzeit, July 4, 2007; my brackets and my italics)

Salam Hamdan, another women's rights activist I interviewed, did not believe that the framework of Islam necessarily disempowers women, but that the specific framework that Hamas chooses does.

> You know the aya [verse from the Qur'an], that men are qawwamun "ala al-nisa" [literally "men are guardians of women"].[3] I told them [female Islamists] there are 380 different interpretations; and that they take the most conservative one. They do not allow you to speak about the hijab [the female headscarf]. ... I stood up saying: "so we are not in agreement." They said, "no we agree on the main parts." They said, "the concept of dignity." I said "my opinion about dignity is different from yours. I believe that I should have equal rights in all. I have the same rights and duties." They said "no, you do not have the duty to pay for your own living." Then we talked about whether women are ever going to be adults [their own guardians] and they said "no never ever."
> (S. Hamdan, personal interview, Al Bireh, July 5, 2007; my brackets)

Compared to others from the Palestinian women's movement, both Hamdan and Kuttab were among the most sympathetic to Hamas. Unlike many of those active in the field of women's rights in the West Bank, they did not dismiss Hamas activists outright. Their tolerance clearly had its limits, however. Despite making different arguments, both Kuttab and Hamdan believe that it is necessary to prioritize the struggle for gender justice to empower women as a group. Certain practices, such as the separation of the sexes and confining women to certain roles, are believed to be inherently patriarchal. Through examining two examples, this chapter shows that in practice many women can be empowered in "women's only spaces," and that, in fact, mixed spaces might act to exclude a certain type of woman, mostly those of more conservative and less privileged socio-economic backgrounds. Thus "women only spaces" enable women from all backgrounds to participate in activities that might, while in theory being open to all, in practice only enable women from so-called open-minded families to use. Moreover, there is nothing inherently patriarchal about the idea of separate spaces. So long as the space of men is in anyway more privileged than that of women, the concept as such is not patriarchal.

Hamdan argues that Islam as a religion can in fact be empowering to women, but only when the key texts are interpreted in a non-patriarchal manner and androcentric readings are deconstructed along the lines of the works of reformist scholars, such as the work of Pakistani scholars Rifat Hassan (1990) and Asma Barlas (2002) and the American scholar Amina Wadud (1999), to name only a few examples. Thus, the question arises whether it is possible for movements acting in accordance with an ideology based on an interpretation of Islam that does not refute the "conventional andro-centric wisdoms" to be empowering for women. In other words, can organizations such as Hamas still empower women even without refuting patriarchal Islamic interpretations? This chapter intends to answer these questions.

The relationship between the Palestinian women's movement and women activists in Hamas shifted from largely ignoring each other to an open clash when the Islamist Dr. Mariam Saleh, following Hamas's victory in the 2006 parliamentary elections, was appointed Minister of Women's Affairs. The next section examines this crisis in order to highlight the antagonistic relationship between the women's movement and the women of Hamas. In addition, the discussion will underline the a priori refusal of the women's movement to engage with the women of Hamas in any way. The women's movement, like in its publications, had already made its condemning verdict of Hamas and its women. Neither the following attempts of Hamas women to communicate nor the practice that the two Islamist ministers engaged in played a factor in the women's movement's appraisal and judgment. This is only one example of what has become commonplace in academic writing concerning gender and Islamism in Palestine, namely: that (while it might be deemed totally unacceptable to do so in any other case) when it comes to women and Islamism, there is an academically unsubstantiated and pre-conceived negative judgement concerning women's empowerment through an Islamic framework.

The Palestinian Ministry of Women's Affairs

The Ministry of Women's Affairs was founded in November 2003 with Zahira Kamal, a former DFLP (Democratic Front for the Liberation of Palestine) activist, as its first minister. Kamal remained Minister until the legislative council elections of 2006 when Mariam Saleh was appointed in her place. On March 15, 2007, Amal Siyam replaced Saleh as an "independent candidate" in the newly formed unity government. Even though Siyam argued that she is not affiliated to Hamas, she has been perceived by many as an Islamist. Khulud Da'yebis—an independent candidate—replaced Siyam when Mahmoud Abbas singlehandedly dissolved the unity government on June 15, 2007.

Hind[4] worked in an NGO promoting legal reform and making the law more gender egalitarian. When I met her she told me how outraged she was that an "Islamist" was the Minister of Women's Affairs:

> We saw that there was a woman who has never worked on women's issues, so she did not know how to deal with this. They got a woman to fill the job, but not a woman who believes in the centrality of women's issues.
> (Hind, personal interview, Ramallah, June 20, 2007)

Marcel, who has worked at the Ministry for Women's Affairs under all four ministers, summarized the events as follows:

> When the government changed all the NGOs were against the new government. They prejudged that Hamas oppressed women. They said that they could not work with the Islamists on the issue of women.
> (Marcel, personal interview, Ramallah, May 30, 2007)

Upon assuming her responsibilities as Minister for Women's Affairs, Amal Siyam faced much opposition from the staff:

> They did not cooperate. In the three months I could not hire a head of office and an escort. ... We could have ratified all these laws, but the employees inside the Ministry did not cooperate with me. There was a plan not to work with me.
> (A. Siyam, personal interview, Bethlehem, July 3, 2007)

Prior to Siyam, Mariam Saleh had encountered a similar reaction:

> A month after taking over I called all women's organizations to come, from all the different factions. The general union boycotted this meeting. ... I was very keen to stop the marginalization that I myself had suffered from. The way they saw us as backward, ignorant women who will bring women back to the Stone Age.
> (M. Saleh, personal interview, Ramallah, July 8, 2007)

In order to understand the Palestinian women's movement's rejection of Hamas women it is essential to understand the history of the former. As the next section will show, rather than simply being the outcome of ideological differences concerning gender politics and women's empowerment, political factionalism and class politics have also played a central role in bringing about this hostile relationship between the two movements.

The Palestinian Women's Movement: Historical and Contextual Notes

Palestinian women have been politically active at least since 1917 when they mobilized alongside Palestinian men against the Balfour Declaration (Hout 1986). In 1921, the first exclusively female organization—the Palestinian's Women's Union—was founded (Ismail 1993). Two hundred Palestinian delegates attended the 1929 Arab Women's Congress of Palestine (Sayigh 1992: 4; Hout 1986). As would be the case for most of its history, apart from a few exceptions, in the early stages the Palestinian women's movement consisted mostly of upper middle class women.

While some branches of the Palestinian Arab Women's Union stayed active, the Nakbeh of 1948 and the loss of the majority of Palestine led to a period in which work came to an almost complete halt. This lasted until the establishment of the General Union of Palestinian Women (GUPW) in 1965 (Sharoni 1995: 61). The GUPW was founded alongside the Palestinian Women's Association (PWA) as part of the establishment of the Palestinian Liberation Organization (PLO). The goal of the GUPW was to "mobilize the efforts of Palestinian women and to organize a progressive political women's organization in order to represent Palestinian women everywhere" (Sayigh 1992: 4).

The second major change in the women's movement occurred in the late 1970s with the establishment of the women's committees, which many have claimed provide the backbone to what is now known as the New Women's Movement (Sharoni 1995: 65). On Women's Day in 1978, the Women's Work Committee (WWC) was founded by a new generation of women who were "university educated, politically aware and socially progressive" (ibid.).[5]

Before starting its work, the WWC activists decided to assess the needs of the women they intended to work with. Conducting a survey and making connections with the women they aimed to empower, the WWC women "were astonished to discover a population totally outside their experience" (Sturm 1993: 62). The upper and middle class backgrounds of the WWC activists had meant that few had knowledge of the lives of women in refugee camps, who were "illiterate, overworked, poor, economically dependent on men, [and] unaware of their legal rights" (ibid.). Sharoni writes that "this new awareness among middle-class Palestinian women activists and emphasis on grassroots projects and organizing had a great influence on the development of WWC and later the entire women's movement" (ibid.: 66). This awareness led to debates about the relationship between gender and other forms of discrimination. Despite seeking to "reach out to more ordinary women" (ibid.: 68) on the whole, awareness of their class privileges did not lead the women's movement to work aggressively on expanding the membership to include women from lower socio-economic backgrounds, however (I. Jad, personal interview, Ramallah, 2007).

As a result of factional loyalties among the members of the WWC, different groups emerged out of the WWC. Since the WWC became increasingly identified with the

DFLP (Democratic Front for the Liberation of Palestine), the PFLP (Popular Front for the Liberation of Palestine) established the Union for Palestinian Women's Committee (UPWC); the pro-Fateh group founded the Women's Committee for Social Work (WCSW); and the more pro-communist members the Union for Palestinian Working Women Committee (UPWWC) (Sturm 1993: 64). Despite this split along party lines, the women's committees continued working together and avoided rivalry, carrying out joint projects during the 1980s (Sharoni 1995: 67). Here it is important to note that despite their differences all these factions were part of the Palestinian Liberation Organization (PLO). Hamas, which was founded in 1987, never joined the PLO. The political rivalry between the PLO and Hamas is well known. This antagonistic relationship has to be kept in mind when considering that most women in the Palestinian women's movement are also cadres of the different PLO factions.

The eruption of the First Intifada in 1987 resulted in a change in the composition of the women's movement (Jad 2004: 90). Palestinian women who had previously participated in the illiteracy programs provided to them by the women's movement officially joined the ranks of the movement itself (Sharoni 1995: 69).

After the Oslo Peace accords in 1993, many of the successful women's grassroots organizations were transformed into NGOs. Islah Jad argues that (what she terms) the "NGOisation of the women's movement" has not been empowering for women.

> NGOisation ... [denotes] the process through which issues of collective concern are transformed into "projects" in isolation from the general context in which they are implemented and without taking into consideration economic, social and political factors affecting these projects....It also denotes a shift in women's activism from voluntarism to dependence on foreign funding; a shift in the personnel dealing with women's empowerment from grassroots rural and refugee cadres to middle class urban elites of professionals.
>
> (Jad 2004: 12)

Thus Jad argues the women's movement was transformed from engaging in political resistance to state building. Voluntarism and political resistance was transformed into paid labor and depoliticized. In the process the former members of the women's movement came under increasing pressure to accommodate the preferences of the donor countries.[6]

The lengthy discussion of the women's movement is necessary to locate politically the voices of those who have written about and defined women's empowerment in Palestine for the last thirty years and whose accounts have become synonymous with the truth about Palestinian women's empowerment. While they differ substantially on most issues, on the relation of Hamas and women most writers (with the exception of a handful, like Islah Jad) are in agreement that Hamas oppresses women. What is left unsaid, however, is the political and class background of the speakers.

It is important to note the partisan background of the women's committees as well as the link of the GUPW and the committees to the PLO to appreciate the deep suspicion that the members of the New Women's Movement had towards Hamas. Although the relationship varies, during the summer of 2007 the relationship between Hamas and most of the factions of the PLO was extremely hostile and politicized.

Moreover, there is also a class difference between members of the women's movement and Hamas. Women from the women's movement mostly come from middle class backgrounds. In contrast, the women of Hamas come from refugee and village backgrounds as well as the cities.[7] While the level of education of women from Hamas and the women's movement was often the same (Jad 2004), with many women in Hamas pursuing their PhDs, the type of education differed greatly and played an important role in determining the types of jobs available upon graduation.

Jad writes that while male elites were mainly educated in Arabic, female elites were educated in English schools. After three decades of British colonial rule, the percentage of educated rural women did not exceed 7 percent. This, Jad continues, was one of the main factors preventing bonds between urban and rural women from materializing (Jad 2004: 284). Jad also notes that education is an important facilitator of class mobility. While women affiliated to Hamas are often as educated as their counterparts in the women's movement, the type of education they have received mostly differs. The fact that most Islamist women are refugees and educated in Gaza or Arab universities limits, for example, their chances of employment in the NGO sector, a place of employment for mostly middle to upper middle class women. This sector, which is one of the main sources of employment for women, requires foreign language (predominantly English) proficiency. Thus, despite the high level of education of most female Islamists, the lack of fluency in English as well as their backgrounds re-inscribes socio-economic difference between them and the women of the women's movement (ibid.: 25).

As a result of ideological, religious, class and political differences the definition of empowerment is contested. What is at stake is the question of what type of political activism is considered empowering for women. In addition, the objectives and outcomes of political activism vary as well. When comparing the content of the different versions of empowerment, we need to keep the context of the lives of the two groups—the Women's Movement and Hamas respectively—in mind. More so than simply being at odds in terms of the definition of women's empowerment, the main difference concerned what type of politics to practice.

A New Vision?

So what did Saleh and Siyam accomplish when they were Ministers of Women's Affairs? Firstly, it has to be noted that these women were only ministers for about a year and three months, between the two of them. During this time the discourse of the two Islamist ministers can be categorized in four broad ways.

Firstly, both ministers argued that Islam, rather than the Universal Declaration of Human Rights, should provide the basic guiding principles. Although the new Islamic administration of the Ministry of Women's Affairs said that it appreciated the efforts of the previous administration, its members believed that the basic framework that the mission statement of the Ministry was based on should be revised. What kind of Islam Siyam was referring to and how that relates to women remained unclear, however.

> When we studied it from an Islamic perspective we found a lot of problems from an Islamic point of view, some were directly contradictory, so they made a few changes, from 40 pages, it was only 3 pages ... They had made the West the main source of legislation. How can I take the West only? We take from the West, yes, but only for what goes along with our traditions. If China, the Vatican, Israel have refused CEDAW [the Convention to Eliminate All Forms of Discrimination Against Women], [why can we not have reservations]? All countries have their specificity. They refused the adjustment.
> (A. Siyam, personal interview, Bethlehem, July 3, 2007; my brackets)

Saleh also tried to widen the mandate of the Ministry. She believed that legal change was important. However, she saw the previous work of the Ministry as not dealing with the main problem facing Palestinian women, namely, the occupation. After she became minister, Saleh argued that the occupation should be the first priority of the Ministry of Women's Affairs. While many in the women's movement agreed with that, they also believed that the struggle for Palestinian liberation should be coupled with the struggle for gender justice.

Saleh, and following her Siyam, politicized the issue of women's rights, arguing that Palestinian women should be seen as prisoners, fighters, wives of martyrs, and so forth. According to Marcel, the Ministry (under Fateh) "did not really handle issues that were directly related to the idea of women under occupation. They also did not work on executive issues, rather its main role was to change laws that exist" (Marcel, personal interview, Ramallah, May 30, 2007).

Saleh and Siyam attempted to change the mandate of the Ministry from only having a legislative function inside the Palestinian Authority to dealing with Palestinian women under occupation, and the economic and political problems stemming from it. To use Jad's terminology, this was an effort to reverse the "NGOization" that had dominated political life after the Oslo peace process. Both ministers started visiting women all around the West Bank. During the time of my fieldwork, Siyam toured the main Palestinian cities in the West Bank and met with parents of female prisoners, "an issue forgotten by most nationalists and secular women's organizations" (Jad 2004: 246). Siyam organized festivals for the relatives of female prisoners in which they were honored for their sacrifice for Palestine. She also met with women and discussed their problems with them. In doing so, Saleh and Siyam countered what they saw as the elitist policies of the previous administration.

To enable legal reform, the Ministry had previously focused on organizing workshops with female and male experts working in the field of women's rights. Islamists were not the only ones who critiqued the elitism of the previous Women's Ministry. Critical voices inside the movement made some of the same arguments. Eileen Kuttab, a veteran of the women's movement, believed that:

> Not only the Women's Ministry but all [women's rights efforts] were targeting the elite. ... ... I don't believe that the secular movement is really fruitful for women in general because it is not dealing with priority issues, women's issues that are issues of the majority, it is a class ideology. ... I really sympathize with the Islamic movement targeting the poor because they target the majority of the women, and they are targeting the real issues. We do not have a state, why are we speaking about legislation? ... The danger is only what kind of state we want. The dream of the seculars was that of a secular democratic state,
> (E. Kuttab, personal interview, Birzeit, July 4, 2007; my brackets).

Jad points to the economic dimension of the rift between Islamist and "secular" Palestinian activists. "The universalist discourse used by women in NGOs is alien not because it is 'Western' but because it was not founded on a thorough knowledge of the women's situation whose interests these organizations claimed to be representing" (Jad 2004: 250). Thus it was argued that the new Ministry should approach those who had been neglected by the previous Ministry. Saleh believed that the Ministry of Women's Affairs should base its mandate on a more realistic version of "the Palestinian woman": a woman who lives under occupation and whose most pressing problems stem from it. Saleh argued that most Palestinian women did not feel that the Women's Ministry represented them, an observation confirmed by a number of writers in recent years (Jad 2004; Rubenberg 2001).

> I said we should not only work on employed women, there are so many more women who do not work in the government or in firms...How can we help these women, women in the refugee camps, the wives of the prisoners? Now there are 12000 prisoners. If none of these people are married we are speaking about 12000 mothers, and how many of them are married? Have daughters? So this is a big sector. We have many who are disabled from the first intifada. Who takes care of them? Not women? The martyrs? Where are their wives?
> (M. Saleh, personal interview, Ramallah, July 8, 2007)

In other words, seeing women only in their capacity as individuals led the previous administration, due to its perceived liberal biases, to overlook the problems that Palestinian women face as a result of their roles in relation to their children, siblings, parents and husbands: as mothers, daughters, sisters and wives. Neglecting to address these problems, Saleh maintained, resulted in ignoring some of the central concerns facing women in Palestine. Feminists have shown the problems with seeing women only in their relational capacities to men. This example draws our attention to the fact that seeing women only as individuals may also be equally problematic. While women might have needs as individuals, they can also have needs as mothers, sisters and wives. If we are interested in women's empowerment we need to address women in both their relational and individualistic capacities.[8]

To think through whether only Islamic models which critically re-examine patriarchal attitudes can be empowering to women, the next case outlines an example of an Islamic model of activism which does not refute any of the attributes which many feminists and women's rights activists would regard as patriarchal and conservative. In particular I will examine the question of whether practices such as gender segregation necessarily disempower women.

The Birzeit Student Group

The Islamic student group which is now affiliated with Hamas, *Al Kutla al Islamia* (the Islamic Bloc) was founded at Birzeit University, one of the largest universities inside the West Bank and located in the village of Birzeit near Ramallah. The Islamic Bloc was established in 1978 by a small group of men and women who identified more with the Muslim Brotherhood than with the dominant left-wing parties of the time. This group found that there was no political student group to reflect the ideology of those who did not identify with a secular solution to the Palestinian–Israeli conflict. It was not until April of 1979, however, that they decided to enter the electoral race for the student council under the name of Kutlat al 'amal al tulabi (the Student Action Bloc). After a few months of Israeli closure of the university, the students came back in November 1979 as Al Kutla al Islamia (the Islamic Bloc) (Abu Yaqeen, personal interview, Al Bireh, June 11, 2007). Even though there was only one woman with a headscarf involved in the Islamic Bloc at the time, other women, among them a Christian woman, had been active in the foundation period (ibid.).

In 1979, the Islamic Bloc consisted of a few students who coordinated their work in an informal manner. However, by the summer of 2007 (nearly thirty years later) the Islamic Bloc was one of the strongest, best organized and most structured student groups on campus. More importantly for this research, the Islamic Bloc consisted of two equal bodies, one for women and one for men.

There were about 100 active female and 100 active male members who organize activities all year around. These students constituted what is called the base of the Islamic Bloc. In separate elections for women and men, in which anyone's name could be nominated by any member from the base using secret nominations, 23 female and 23 male students were elected for the shura council (governing body). While the "sisters" advertise their elections, the "brothers" did not for security reasons. Separately, the 23 female and 23 males elected the lajneh (the committee), which consists of 5 sisters and 5 brothers. It is from these 5 brothers and 5 sisters that the leaders who were called the prince and the princess (the Amir and the Amira) are finally chosen. The rationale behind having these two structures was the belief that gender mixing was *haram* (religiously prohibited).

The Islamic Bloc thus consisted of two equal structures—one for women and one for men. The structures are identical and the prince and the princess are equal in position. Unlike the women's committee in the Islamic Action Front in Jordan, for example, the female section of the Islamic Bloc at Birzeit did not report back to the male section, nor is it a subpart of it. Rather, it was an equal body. Coordination between the male and the female sections happens between the prince and the princess (S. Hamzeh, personal interview, Birzeit, May 28, 2007).

In the 2005/2006 academic year the Islamic Bloc won the student council elections, attaining seven seats. From these seven seats two seats were given to female

Islamists and five to male Islamists (L. Hassan, personal interview, Birzeit, May 28, 2007). The only other student organization which also had female representation in the student council was the left bloc. Two female students were among the representatives. All the other students were only represented by male students;[9] "The Fateh faction did not have a single female student despite having 21 seats [in the student council]. Only when we criticized them did they get two women" (M. Mariam, personal interview, Birzeit, May 29, 2007; my brackets).

The example of the Birzeit Islamic Bloc not only counters the commonly held belief that women are at best marginalized or at worst wholly absent in Islamic political parties, it is also an example of a structure that is gender sensitive and equal with few equivalents worldwide. The example also counters the belief that gender segregation is necessarily disempowering for women.

In practice, gender segregation often translates into men having the right to use public spaces, and women being barred from using them (in other words, a case of separate but not equal spaces, which is what many opponents would argue is always the case when there is segregation). The example of the Birzeit Islamic student group counters what has now become a conventional wisdom for most feminists and civil rights activists, most notably in the United States. Namely, that separate necessarily means unequal. The belief that separate gender spaces are inherently unequal has also been adopted by many women's rights activists in the Arab world. I am aware that I might be making a controversial argument against a long-standing view. However, given third wave feminists' efforts to avoid universalizing certain practices and norms which emerged in the global north (hooks 1982; Mohanty 1993; Roy 2004; Koopman 2008), I believe that this is a crucial point to examine. bell hooks, critiquing the American women's movement, argues that regarding the family as an inherently oppressive institution, for example, is an outcome of the experience of white feminists. For African American women, hooks maintains, the family was often the only source of refuge in a hostile society (hooks 1982: 20, 46, 75). Thus she argues against universalizing the experience of one group—in this case white American feminists—to claim that this is a problem which faces all women. The issue of whether segregated spaces are inherently oppressive to women or not also relates to the larger question of whether we can determine a priori that certain practices are disempowering to women.

Consider the following example. One of the projects that the female part of the kutla Islamiah worked on was to rent an apartment building in 2006, using it as a dormitory for female students. Since the dorm was led and managed by female Islamists, parents of female students who lived far were more willing to allow their daughters to live on campus,[10] which enabled some female students to attend university (Reem, personal interview, Birzeit, May 31, 2007). Reem told me that many parents would have refused to let their daughters study at Birzeit altogether had it not been for the assurances that the female students of the Islamic Student Bloc gave the parents when they visited them. It was the fact that parents knew that there were "women only spaces" at Birzeit that played the determining factor (ibid.).

It was not just the parents, however, who were appeased by the fact that there were "women only spaces." Female students, too, argued that they were more comfortable in these spaces. Again, this is a debate that second wave feminists in particular engaged in. One example is the debate about the merits and drawbacks of co-ed educational systems versus female only ones (Ewing 2006; Smithers and Robinson 2006; Sullivan 2009; Sullivan et al. 2010; Wills et al. 2006; Younger and Warrington 2006). The subject remains of great interest to many today, however, as is apparent from the two special editions published on this topic in the journal *Sex Roles* in 2011 in 2013.

Many of the students I met confirmed that they would not have been able to address problems which face women specifically if they had been part of a wider gender-mixed group (M. Mariam, personal interview, Birzeit, May 29, 2007). In a gender mixed group issues that are considered "gender neutral" often take precedence over "women's issues," which are believed to be secondary to the national liberation struggle (Jad 1990; Young 2001). Even without making the more extended feminist argument that women's issues are inherently linked to national liberation, de facto, the Islamist students at Birzeit were able to focus on exclusively women's issues due to the gender-segregated space they had developed.

In many countries, gender segregation indeed indicates separate and not equal. For the student group in Birzeit, however, the belief in segregation did not lead to a model that disadvantages women and made them bear the burden of such segregation. Rather, over the past 28 years, the students had developed a structure in which they created two equal spaces. This shows that Islamist thinking in general, and the belief in segregation more specifically, does not necessarily lead to depriving women of certain freedoms.

Conclusion

This chapter started by posing the question of whether non-feminist groups can empower women. The two examples examined show that, despite not actively working to empower women, and sometimes even maintaining notions of gender hierarchy, it cannot be argued that the work of the Birzeit student group or the two Islamist ministers worked against the interests of women. Moreover, many of the differences between the women's movement and Hamas activists had little to do with issues of gender.

Neither Mariam Saleh nor Amal Siyam were ministers for long enough to enable an evaluation of what a Ministry of Women's Affairs under "Islamic" leadership would look like or whether their policies empower Palestinian women. Nor of course would the actions of these two ministers stand for what is Islamic and what is not. Nonetheless, this case touches upon many important issues. Firstly, it brings to the fore the fear that those engaged in the women's movement have of "the Islamic framework." This confirms Saba Mahmood's statement concerning the piety movement in Egypt that "the depth of discomfort the pietistic character of this movement evokes among liberals, radicals, and progressives alike is extraordinary" (Mahmood 2005: 37).

The reaction of the Palestinian's women's movement uncovers assumptions that most feminists share, namely, that the realization of women's rights can only stem from a secular ideology and that religiously inspired frameworks will invariably oppress women.

In one way, it can be said that the entrance of Mariam Saleh, a religious woman who grew up in a refugee camp, is in itself an example of a woman reclaiming the space of decision-making that the women's movement seeks to achieve. However, the class difference and, following that, the level of Westernization and different worldview, makes the women's movement perceive the vision for which women like Mariam Saleh stood as the antithesis to their struggle.

The issue goes beyond the person of Mariam Saleh, however. Also at stake was the validity of a different political approach. The basic assumptions of the women's movement were challenged through the so-called "Islamic"[11] approach of Saleh and Siyam. This approach not only privileged fighting the occupation over addressing the social problems Palestinian women faced—precisely because of the intrinsic connection between the occupation and Palestinian women's experiences—but also used Islam and not the Universal Declaration of Human Rights as their guide. The fact that neither of the two Islamist ministers were able to articulate exactly what "Islam" here meant underlines the point that religion, or the lack of religion, was not really at stake.

Saleh and Siyam challenged the mandate of the Ministry to go beyond ensuring that legislation is gender equal to dealing with the problems that Palestinian women face as a result of living under occupation. Furthermore, they argued that seeing women only as individuals prevents us from recognizing many of the problems women face as mothers, sisters, wives and daughters. Rather than organizing workshops for women's rights activists, the Islamist ministers met with ordinary Palestinian women all over the West Bank. The disagreements were less about women's empowerment and more about what type of politics to engage in: legal reform and state-building or engaging with the problems caused by the occupation?

What was portrayed as a struggle over women's rights is in large part a struggle between different classes and political factions. Both sides tried to impose their own worldview as the only legitimate, objective form of women's empowerment. While both sides are guilty of this, the women's movement had the power of the hegemonic discourse of the international sphere on its side, as well as the privileges of their subject positions within Palestinian society. The *Islammiyyat* (Arabic for female Islamists), on the other hand, were supported by the power of the "hegemonic discourse of Islam" as well as being perceived as "more representative" of "true" Palestinian women.

Which vision is more empowering for Palestinian women is difficult to assess. However, the focus on women under occupation, as well as women in relational terms, helped Siyam and Saleh to widen the mandate of the Ministry. It has also enabled them to reach more women and to hear first-hand what kind of problems women all over the West Bank are facing. Thus it is enough to say that their actions certainly were not a threat to women's wellbeing in Palestine.

In the case of the Islamic bloc, the idea of segregation is neither refuted nor reinterpreted in favor of a version that does not prohibit the mixing of the genders. Despite the lack of a radical reinterpretation of what is seen by many as a patriarchal reading of Islam, adhering to the idea of segregation has not led to disadvantaging women. On the contrary, it helped students who came from rural and conservative backgrounds, since a gender-segregated atmosphere allowed female students to be active politically without jeopardizing their reputation or disobeying their parents. Indeed, for numerous students, segregation made it possible for them to live on campus.

Perhaps most significantly, segregation enabled female activists to focus all their activity on women. This way, female students were not just the target of a small part of overall activities. By having two groups the kutla is the only student organization in Birzeit that has the ability to focus completely on the problems facing female students while simultaneously addressing the problems of male students. The female section organized workshops to help female students with their university work, photocopied class notes and books (for both male and female students) and organized events dealing with the challenges female students face at university.

The way the students of Birzeit have set up the Islamic bloc demonstrates that segregation does not always lead to disadvantaging women. The student bloc was able to create a structure that was completely gender equal. As a result of upholding gender segregation women were not pushed aside, but were required to fill the roles on all levels. In the Birzeit Islamic bloc female Islamists constructed a different model of women's empowerment. Their ideal "Islamic" society was one in which women and men are segregated. Women's roles and duties are defined within these separate spaces. Many women's rights activists in the Muslim world have argued that segregation disempowers women. However, as the previous example shows, it can be another form of empowerment. This example thus urges us to refrain from making sweeping statements concerning the nature of "Islamic" political activists in regard to gender, in the same way that such statements would be misleading of any other political faction, Palestinian or otherwise. Indeed, the model developed by the students of Birzeit is not only useful for other Islamist groups to consider and learn from but also for secular political groups and student organizations in general.

Finally, I am not arguing here that these examples are representative of Hamas's work, nor that this is enough to make any kind of "verdict" about whether Hamas as a whole works to empower or to disempower women. Rather, I use the first example of the clash between the women's movement and the Islamist ministers to show the danger of uncritically taking on the account of the Palestinian women's movement without contextualizing these accounts. Despite the important work of the Palestinian women's movement with regard to gender justice, this article functions as a warning not to take the accounts of those who have become "stars" in the field of women's studies in relation to Islamists or other groups as truths. As readers we must be careful not to assume that what the "good guys" (or, in this instance, the "good gals") say about certain issues is necessarily the "right" analysis. The example of Hammami's account of the so-called hijab campaign, and the fact that almost all the literature produced on women in Palestine took her account of the story on without stopping to ask about the other side of the story, is only one example of our willingness to go along with what the "experts" have to say. We need to pay more attention to the political, socio-economic, and religious backgrounds of the speaker. As feminists we must be aware of the hierarchies and truths within our own discourses.

Sara Ababneh is assistant professor at the University of Jordan's Center for Strategic Studies and earned her DPhil in politics and international relations from St. Antony's College, University of Oxford in 2010. She wrote her dissertation on female Islamists in Hamas in occupied Palestine and the Islamic Action Front in Jordan. Her research interests include class, gender, and struggles for liberation and change.

Acknowledgements

This article was first published in 2014 by the *Journal of International Women's Studies* 15(1): 35–53. All names of students and participants have been changed for the security and safety of the respondents.

Notes

1. Arabic for declaration.
2. I use secular between quotation marks because many of the members of the women's movement are devoutly religious (be they Muslim or Christian). I simply use the term because these women disagree with Hamas's vision of Islamism and that they usually do not fight for a religiously inspired type of politics.
3. The interpretation of this verse (4.34) is contested by Muslim feminists. The translation that I give here is only one of many. Yusuf Ali for example translates it as "Men are the protectors and maintainers of women, because Allah has given the one more (strength) than the other, and because they support them from their means. Therefore the righteous women are devoutly obedient, and guard in (the husband's) absence what Allah would have them guard." Pickthal's translation reads "Men are in charge of women, because Allah hath made the one of them to excel the other, and because they spend of their property (for the support of women). So good women are the obedient, guarding in secret that which Allah hath guarded" Shakir translates the verse as follows "Men are the maintainers of women because Allah has made some of them to excel others and because they spend out of their property; the good women are therefore obedient, guarding the unseen as Allah has guarded." Ali Quli Qara'i's translation reads "Men are the managers of women, because of the advantage Allah has granted some of them over others, and by virtue of their spending out of their wealth. So righteous women are obedient, care-taking in the absence (of their husbands) of what Allah has enjoined (them) to guard."
4. Name has been changed for purposes of privacy.
5. Jad notes that the WWC was largely composed of women who worked in political organizations, especially left-wing parties and Fateh.
6. It has to be mentioned here that while this critique of NGOs is relevant in many contexts, there are also counter examples. There are many instances globally where NGOs provide the sole structure and opportunity for women's extrication from

extremely difficult situations (Alnoor 2003; Andrews 2013; Alvarez 2009; Brown 2008; Eade 2005; Kilby 2006; Kühl 2009; Thayer 2009; Watkins et al. 2012).
7. Mariam Saleh was born in a refugee camp, so were most of my other respondents. Samira Halayqa, an elected member to the Legislative Council was born and continues to live in a village near Hebron. Amal Siyam too is from a refugee background. Consequently, a class barrier is re-inscribed and the women from the two groups rarely move in the same circles.
8. It is important to note here that, despite the argument of Hamas members that the Universal Declaration of Human Rights and international human rights in general were individualistic in nature, Hamas and other Palestinian liberation groups in general have often turned to the same conventions in order to affirm their rights as a people to self-determination. Thus it is mostly in relation to women's rights that the question of individualism is raised. This can be seen as being part of the connection many in the Arab world make between women's rights, colonialism and more recently imperialism and the mistrust towards women's issues that stems from that (Young 2001).
9. Thus once back in a gender mixed space, the Islamists, like other student groups, went back to privileging male representation. There was no conviction concerning the necessity of equal gender representation, or of integrating women's issues into what is understood as wider political issues. This example urges us to be cautious about the lasting empowering effects of gender segregated spaces in absence of a wider discussion about incorporating some of the lessons learned from these segregated spaces into gender mixed spaces, in other words from seeing the mixed space as one which includes both the female and male side equally.
10. Even though all dorms are gender segregated, parents of women are often worried about their daughters' reputations being affected by living in a gender mixed campus. Female Islamists in general, and the student activists in particular were seen by many Palestinians as trustworthy and their reputation above critique (Ababneh 2009, 2010). This trustworthiness was extended to any project that these Islamic Bloc activists engaged in and those taking part in these activities (in this case living in the dorm supervised by the female section of the Islamic student bloc).
11. The examples given in this chapter show clearly that the work of Siyam and Saleh are as little "Islamic" in this case as the policies suggested by the women's movement were about "women's rights." Islam and gender justice have very little to do with the practical differences in approach to the Israeli occupation which were suggested.

References

Ababneh, S. 2009. "Islamic Political Activism as a Means of Women's Empowerment? The Case of the Female IAF Activists." *Studies in Ethnicity and Nationalism, Special Issue on Gender: Gender, Ethnicity and the Nation: Cross-Cultural Perspectives* 9(1): 1–24. https://doi.org/10.1111/j.1754-9469.2009.01026.x

Ababneh, S. 2010. "Islamic Political Parties as a Means of Women's Empowerment? The Case of Hamas and the Islamic Action Front." DPhil thesis, University of Oxford.

Abdulhadi, R. 1998. "The Palestinian Women's Autonomous Movement: Emergence, Dynamicsand Challenges." *Gender and Society* 12: 649–673. https://doi.org/10.1177/089124398012006004

Alnoor, E. 2003. "Accountability in Practice: Mechanisms for NGOs." *World Development* 31(5): 813–829. https://doi.org/10.1016/S0305-750X(03)00014-7

Alvarez, S. E. 2009. "Beyond NGO-ization?: Reflections from Latin America." *World Development* 52(2): 175–184. https://doi.org/10.1057/dev.2009.23

Andrews, A. 2013. "Downward Accountability in Unequal Alliances: Explaining NGO Responses to Zapatista Demands." *World Development* 54: 99–113. https://doi.org/10.1016/j.worlddev.2013.07.009

Barlas, A. 2002. *Believing Women in Islam: Unreading Patriarchal Interpretations of the Qur'an.* Austin, TX: University of Texas Press.

Belenky, M, Blythe Clinchy, Nancy R. Goldberger and Jill M. Tarule. 1986. *Women's Way of Knowing, The Development of Self, Voice and Mind.* New York: Basic Books.

Brown, L. D. 2008. *Creating Credibility: Legitimacy and Accountability for Transnational Civil Society.* West Hartford, CT: Kumarian Press.

Eade, D. 2005. "Editorial." *Development in Practice* 15(1): ?. https://doi.org/10.1080/0961452052000321523

Ewing, E. T. 2006. "The Repudiation of Single-Sex Education: Boys Schools in the Soviet Union, 1943–1954." *American Educational Research Journal* 43(4): 621–650. https://doi.org/10.3102/00028312043004621

Guha, R. and G. C. Spivak. 1988. *Selected Subaltern Studies.* Oxford: Oxford University Press.

Hammami, R. 1990. "Women, the Hijab and the Intifada." *Middle East Report*, May-August: 24-28. https://doi.org/10.2307/3012687

Hassan, R. 1990. "An Islamic Perspective." In *Women, Religion and Sexuality: Studies on the Impact of Religious Teachings on Women*, edited by Jeanne Becher, 93–128. Philadelphia, PA: Trinity Press International.

Holmes, Oliver and Sufian Taha. 2018. "Ahed Tamimi—'I Am the Freedom Fighter. I Will Not Be the Victim.'" Retrieved from www.theguardian.com/world/2018/jul/30/ahed-tamimi-i-am-a-freedom-fighter-i-will-not-be-the-victim-palestinian-israel (accessed October 20, 2019).

hooks, b. 1982. *Ain't I a Woman: Black Women and Feminism.* London: Pluto Press.

Hout, B. 1986. *Political Leadership and Institutions on Palestine 1917-1948.* Beirut: Institute for Palestine Studies (in Arabic).

Ismail, N. 1993. *The Palestinian Women's Struggle for Independence: A Historical Perspective.* New York: Women of Color Press.

Jad, I. 1990. "From Salons to the Popular Committees: Palestinian Women, 1919–1989." In *Intifada: Palestine at the Crossroads*, edited by J. A. Nasser and H. Roger, 125–142. New York: Praeger Publishers.

Jad, I. 2004. "Women at the Cross Roads: The Palestinian Women's Movement Between Nationalism, Secularism and Islamism." PhD thesis, School of African and Oriental Studies, University of London.

Jad, I. and R. Hammami. 1992. "Women and Fundamentalist Movements." *News From Within* 8: 17–21.

Kilby, P. 2006. "Accountability for Empowerment: Dilemmas Facing Non-Governmental Organizations." *World Development* 34(6): 951–963. https://doi.org/10.1016/j.worlddev.2005.11.009

Koopman, S. 2008. "Imperialism Within: Can The Master's Tools Bring Down Empire?" *ACME: An International E-Journal for Critical Geographies* 7(2): 283–307.

Kühl, S. 2009. "Capacity Development as the Model for Development Aid Organizations." *Development and Change* 40 (3): 551–577. https://doi.org/10.1111/j.1467-7660.2009.01538.x

Kuttab, E. 1999. *Feminism and Nationalism: The Palestinian Case.* Ramallah: MUWATEN (in Arabic).

Kuttab, E. 2006. *New Challenges for Palestinian Women's Movement.* Ramallah: Palestine this Week in Palestine.

Kuttab, E. 2008. "Palestinian Women's Organizations, Global Co-option and Local Contradiction." *Cultural Dynamics* 20(2): 99–117. https://doi.org/10.1177/0921374008094283

Kuttab, E. and N. Abu Awwad. 2004. *Palestinian Women's Movement: Problems and Dialectic Issues*. Birzeit: Review of Women Studies.

Mahmoud, S. 2005. *Politics of Piety, The Islamic Revival and the Feminist Subject*. Princeton, NJ: Princeton University Press.

Mohanty, C. 1993. "Under Western Eyes: Feminist Scholarship and Colonial Discourses." In *Colonial Discourse and Post-Colonial Theory: A Reader*, edited by P. Williams and L. Chrisman, 196–220. New York: Columbia University Press.

Ramazanoglu, C. and J. Holland. 2007. *Feminist Methodology, Challenges and Choices*. Los Angeles, CA: Sage Publications.

Roy, A. 2004. "Do Turkeys Enjoy Thanksgiving?" *The Hindu*, January 18. Retrieved from http://sentient.mentabolism.org/snippets/Do_Turkeys_Enjoy_Thanksgiving.pdf (accessed 20 July 2013).

Roy, S. 1993. "Gaza: New Dynamics of Civic Disintegration." *Journal of Palestinian Studies* 22: 20–31. https://doi.org/10.2307/2538078

Rubenberg, C. A. 2001. *Palestinian Women, Patriarchy and Resistance in the West Bank*. London: Lynne Rienner Publishers.

Said, Edward. 1978. *Orientalism*. London: Penguin Books.

Sayigh, R. 1992. "Palestinian Women A Case of Neglect." In *Portraits of Palestinian Women*, edited by Orayb Aref Najjar and Kitty Warnock. Salt Lake City, UT: University of Utah Press.

Sharoni, S. 1995. *Gender and the Israeli-Palestinian Conflict: The Politics of Women's Resistance*. Syracuse, IL: Syracuse University Press.

Smithers, A. and P. Robinson. 2006. *The Paradox of Single-sex and Co-educational Schooling*. Buckingham: Carmichael Press.

Sturm, P. 1993. *The Women Are Marching: The Second Sex and the Palestinian Revolution*. New York: Lawrence Hill Books.

Sullivan, A. 2009. "Academic Self-concept, Gender and Single-Sex Schooling." *British Educational Research Journal* 35(2): 259–288. https://doi.org/10.1080/01411920802042960

Sullivan, Al, H. Joshi and D. Leonard. 2010. "Single-Sex Schooling and Academic Attainment at School and through the Lifecourse." *American Educational Research Journal* 47(1): 6–36. https://doi.org/10.3102/0002831209350106

Thayer, M. 2009. *Making Transnational Feminism: Rural Women, NGO Activists, and Northern Donors in Brazil*. London: Routledge. https://doi.org/10.4324/9780203869888

Wadud, A. 1999. *Qur'an and Women: Rereading the Sacred Text from a Woman's Perspective*. Oxford: Oxford University Press.

Watkins, S. C., A. Swidler and T. Hannan. 2012. "Outsourcing Social Transformation: Development NGOs as Organizations." *Annual Review of Sociology* 38: 285–315. https://doi.org/10.1146/annurev-soc-071811-145516

Wills, R., S. Kilpatrick and B. Hutton. 2006. "Single-Sex Classes in Co-educational Schools." *British Journal of Sociology of Education* 27(3): 277–291. https://doi.org/10.1080/01425690600750452

Young, R. 2001. *Postcolonialism: A Historical Introduction*. London: Blackwell Publishing.

Younger, M. R. and M. Warrington. 2006. "Would Harry and Hermione Have Done Better in Single-Sex Classes? A Review of Single-Sex Teaching in Coeducational Secondary Schools in the United Kingdom." *American Educational Research Journal* 43(4): 579–620. https://doi.org/10.3102/00028312043004579

10

God versus Goliath: Theological Challenges to Empire in South Asia

Francis Gonsalves

If the history of religions in India is seen as the articulation not only of ideas and rituals but also the perceptions and motivations of social groups, the perspectives which would follow might be different from those with which we are familiar.
—Romila Thapar, *History and Beyond* (2000: 87)

The people who can truly purify a religion of communalist ideology are not the theologians or the exegetes or the religious hierarchs, but only the conscientized victims of that ideology. For only the oppressed know and speak the language of liberation, the language of true religion.
—Aloysius Pieris, *Fire and Water* (1996)

Introduction: South Asian Lights and Darkness

The south Asian countries—Afghanistan, Bangladesh, Bhutan, Maldives, Nepal, India, Pakistan, and Sri Lanka—are arguably among the most culturally colorful, linguistically rich, religiously diverse, demographically dense, politically intriguing, and economically worst-off of the world's nations. On the one hand, when one thinks of the dazzling diversity of cultures, languages, tribes, ethnicities and religious traditions born and blooming upon south Asian soil, one has reason to rejoice; but, on the other, when one sees how most of these countries are swiftly deteriorating in terms of the quality of life of their citizens, especially the poorest among them, one cannot but feel alarmed and ashamed. Since it is almost impossible to do justice to all of south Asia, I shall limit myself to focusing upon just three countries: Pakistan, Sri Lanka, and that of my birth and work, India.

In this chapter, I will first briefly clarify basic concepts, highlight traces of militarization, nuclearization and Empire in south Asia, and state consequences of the same. Then, inspired by Christian scripture and tradition, I will develop the "God versus Goliath" image as paradigmatic of divine power, with Jesus—of the lineage of David—providing another portrait of prophetic power against Empire of his time. It is a Christian interpretation of resistance formed in an intercultural and interreligious mode. Citing cases of the involvement of south Asian Jesuits in promoting peace and animating initiatives of protest and resistance, and throwing light on some insights of Pope Francis, I will finally trace trajectories for evolving what could be an effective Christian response to counter Empire, militarization and nuclearization.

Christian Call to Authority, not Power: Conceptual Clarifications

Power, a central concept in our discussions, has been defined by many thinkers. According to Weber, "'Power' [*Macht*] is the probability that one actor within a social relationship will be in a position to carry out his [*sic*] own will despite resistance, regardless of the basis on which this probability rests" (Weber 1968: 53). Though this definition is popular, it merely stresses the individual's will, which need not be the prime reason for exerting power. Anyway, beyond definitions of power (see Sykes 2006: 1–11), the following words used for "power" in diverse languages indicate what it implies. For example, the English "power" can be translated as *Macht* and *Kraft* (German), *pouvoir* and *puissance* (French), *poder* and *fuerza* (Spanish), *potere*, *potenza* and *forza* (Italian), which can be equated with the Latin *potestas*, meaning, (a) the potential to do something, and, (b) the control or domination over something or someone. This is similar to the Greek *exousia* and *dynamis*—roughly understood as potential energy and works of power, respectively.

Power is exerted from various quarters and appears in many avatars. We often say "God is Almighty and Omnipotent" referring to the original, ultimate and absolute power from "up above," so to say, attributable to God alone. Moreover, power can be wielded by individuals and groups who have been elected by the public or "*have*" resources like money, land and familial-tribal influence. This segment is usually equipped with political, social and economic capital. Additionally, we speak of the power of the people. Referring to India, Arundhati Roy writes, "In India, the word *public* is now a Hindi word. It means *people*. In Hindi, we have *sarkar* and *public*, the government and the people. Inherent in this use is the underlying assumption that the government is quite separate from 'the people'" (Roy 2004: 6).

Related to the idea of power is "*authority*"—from the Latin *auctoritas*—which, though often used synonymously with power, can be differentiated from power in some ways. For instance, one can say that, when and "if power is acknowledged and thereby legitimized and institutionalized, then authority emerges" (Hengel 1977: 2–3). Authority can be seen at the individual level as well as the institutional level. Thus, at Pentecost, Jesus' disciples received power "from above" as something gifted to them by God's Spirit (Acts 2). But, as and when they actualized this power "from within" themselves in the course of their ministry, the public began regarding them as Christ's authentic disciples speaking with "authority."

Indian languages derived from Sanskrit distinguish between *satta* and *sakti*. *Satta* is "power" invested in or deputed to someone from an outside agency, hence, referring to political and military might; while *sakti* is regarded as religious-spiritual energy that one inculcates from within. *Sakti*, a feminine noun, can also refer to "divine power" identifiable with the ability, strength and influence of the Hindu deities or the Pentecostal power of God's Spirit (Singh 2006: 60-62). *Sakti* can be said to be roughly synonymous with "authority" in the sense that we are using it. Power decreases with age and can be revoked after a certain period of time, while authority normally increases as one grows older and wiser. It can never be revoked.

We note that power players have perennially forged alliances and found common cause in history. This is especially so in the sociopolitical, economic and religious realms. In India, the top three groups in the hierarchical pyramid—traditionally known as Brahmins (priestly caste), Kshatriyas (warrior caste) and the Vaishyas (merchant caste)—have supported each other in many ways to maintain their stranglehold over the so-called *Dalits*—formerly regarded as untouchables—right up to this day (Teltumbde 2018). Likewise, colonialism in the Indian subcontinent has been fostered through murky alliances between colonial powers, merchants and missionaries—who, though sometimes working against imperialistic designs, were at least shipped by the colonizers into the former colonies to cater to their spiritual needs.

Given this basic distinction between power and authority, let us map some of the conflicts in south Asia, pinpointing the presence and evil effects of Empire, militarization and nuclearization, so as to evolve effective responses against these.

Traces and Trends of Power Play in India, Pakistan and Sri Lanka

Though India, Pakistan and Sri Lanka claim to be free from colonial exploitation, there is little doubt that colonialism has been replaced by neocolonialism—imposed not as a return of the former colonial powers, but from the rich and powerful among its own ranks. This is not to say that foreign, imperialistic powerbrokers are absent from this zone; they are not! The "enemy within" is aligned in sophisticated and subtle ways to the "enemy outside" absorbing those masses within into an imperial complex.

Hindutva Empire and India's Elusive "Acche Din" (Good Days)

Put bluntly, democratic India is being transformed into a "Hindu *Rashtra*"[1] by the proponents of Hindutva.[2] Indians are being brainwashed by the Sarkar to believe that Hindus and Muslims have always been at loggerheads and can never live peaceably together. Dividing communities on religious grounds is simply creating "imagined communities" fired by conflicting nationalisms (Anderson 1996; Kavirai 1992).[3] Historians show that community configurations and cohesion in the Indian subcontinent were determined by location, language, occupation and caste, none of which were necessarily bound together by a common religious identity (Thapar 1989). By contrast, colonial historians like Mill naïvely periodized Indian history in terms of Hindu civilization, Muslim civilization and the British period, which makes Hindu fanatics conclude that the latter two periods were instrumental in destroying a golden, imagined Hindu epoch.[4]

History has recorded heroic struggles of many who strove to free unpartitioned India from the clutches of British colonial oppression. Prominent among these were M. K. Gandhi, B. R. Ambedkar, J. Nehru, S. Radhakrishna, Maulana Azad and others who dreamt of an India with a Constitution respecting diversity, granting special privileges to the weaker sections of society. However, there also arose two communal-radical streams of the *Rastriya Swayamsevak Sangh* (RSS) (Anderson and Damle 2018), with leaders like Hedgewar, Savarkar and Golwalkar (Kanungo 2002; Golwalkar 1947; Vij-Arora 2018), on the one hand, and some Muslim leaders, on the other, who fanned communal feelings among Hindus and Muslims, respectively, eventually leading to a bloody Partition of India at the dawn of Independence in 1947.

Arundhati Roy rightly opines that, "India's freedom struggle, though magnificent, was by no means revolutionary. The Indian elite stepped easily and elegantly into the shoes of the British imperialists" (Roy 2004: 6). Indeed, for decades after Independence, India was almost solely ruled by Congress elites who pampered the corporates with neoliberal capitalist policies and pandered to powerful religious fanatics when deemed expedient. However, Congress imperialism is now replaced with a more virulent variety: Hindutva nationalism that strives to forge homogeneity of creed, stifle dissent, alter the Constitution and destroy democratic systems thereby transforming India into a theocratic state. Hindutva makes believe that India has two enemies: internal and external.

The internal enemies of the Hindutva are allegedly the five "M's": Marxism, Macaulayism, missionaries, materialism and Muslim extremism (Roy 2014). Militant Hindu groups have run riot against the religious minorities in: (a) the demolition of the Babri Masjid on December 6, 1992; (b) the violence against south Gujarat's Christian Adivasis [tribals] and missionaries in 1998-99 (Gonsalves 1999: 11-14); (c) the Gujarat genocide of Muslims in 2002; (d) attacks against Kandhamal's Christian Adivasis in 2008; and many other documented cases of violence.[5]

In May 2014, in the run-up to a most keenly fought national election, Hindutva hardliner and frontrunner Narendra Modi promised the Indian public that "*acche din*" (good days) were ahead. Post-elections, while the Indian public received nothing substantially good, Hindutva Sarkar marches ahead—galvanizing support of those with similar interests and steamrolling over others who question or stall their anti-poor schemes. Sarkar has busied itself with the appointment of RSS *pracharaks* to influential political posts, protection of cows or *gau-rakshan* (resulting in the lynching of Muslims suspected of slaughtering cows or selling beef; Islam 2017), announcing a disastrous demonetization , and burdensome taxation system, gifting huge subsidies to MNCs and other corporate houses, cutting government expenditure on public welfare schemes, contesting the special concessions enshrined in the Indian Constitution, insisting on a Uniform Civil Code, mixing myth with history, lying about development and so on (Kaul 2017).

In addition to "internal enemies" projected as threats to internal security, the Sarkar's aim of defending its public from "external enemies" too (i.e., Pakistani and Chinese infiltrators) provided legitimacy to increased expenditure on militarization and nuclearization. Under BJP rule and the leadership of A. B. Vajpayee on May 11 and 13, 1998, India boasted about conducting successful nuclear tests at the Indian Army's Pokhran Test Range. Not to be outdone, Pakistan reacted soon thereafter on May 28 and 30 by conducting its own nuclear tests to announce that its nuclear capacity cannot be underestimated. This led to heightened tension along the Indo-Pak and Sino-Indian borders with fears that nuclear warheads can be stolen and used by terrorists (Roy 2017). India also entered into a defense contract with the UK to buy Hawk jets (Stavrianakis 2010: 48–49), as well as with France to purchase Rafale fighter aircraft, which, besides raising questions of accountability and corruption, enables the former colonialists to continue interfering in India's internal affairs.

To understand the unexpected success of Hindutva, one must be aware that, in the twenty-first century, corporate globalization, religious fundamentalism, nuclear nationalism and the pauperization of whole populations is impossible to ignore (Roy 2004: 55–56). India, like most south Asian countries, has debunked the "secularization of the world" thesis (Berger 1999), and also the rather skewed Western assumption that with modernity, industrialization and the advances in the InfoTech revolution, religion and nationalisms would weaken their hold over peoples (Sharma 2011: 3). They have not. Conversely, a very powerful form of upper class/caste religiosity fed by corporate finances with solid support from a bought-up media is strengthening the stranglehold of Hindutva nationalism over the public. Furthermore, states that embrace religiously fundamentalist strands have been emboldened by military pacts with the US. Today, the media does not highlight issues like the suicide of farmers, infant deaths, ravage of mother earth, rape of Dalit women, submersion of villages due to the building of dams and incapacity of rural poor to cope with a cashless economy. The living conditions of all these marginal groups has regressed from bad to worse.

Burdens of Nuclearization, Proxy Wars and Militancy in Pakistan

While India largely succeeded until recent times to preserve its secular and democratic character, the ideal of democracy and secularity in Pakistan has been challenged for decades. Islamic fundamentalist strands in Pakistan were groomed by the US in its war against Soviet-backed Afghanistan. An area of perpetual tension between India, Pakistan and China is the state of Jammu and Kashmir, which is the only Indian state with a sizable Muslim majority. The present Indian government has adopted repressive, military measures recently to revoke its "special status." There have been tensions in the sharing of water resources, especially of the Indus River flowing through the two countries. Since Independence, there have been what can be called "water wars" which threaten to escalate and explode in the face of depletion of the earth's resources (Umar undated).

Although there is much similarity in the religiosity and cultures of the Pakistani and Indian publics, the state of siege never ceases and hate spills over, interestingly, even onto the cricket field. Sports is used to showcase one-upmanship and is a weapon to symbolically defeat and shame the "religious other" (Crick 2007: 9–11). Both colonial and neo-colonial factors have molded the masses and fired contexts to their present state, where all forms of militarization, nuclearization and imperialism are sanitized and legitimized (Wolpert 2010). Sadly, studies show that the relationship between economic growth and peace is not positive in Pakistan. In other words, when the country has recorded some growth, due to unequal distribution of resources, such growth has led to further violence, not peace (Niazi 2001).

During the Cold War lines were clearly demarcated between India and Pakistan, with India seeking help from the former Soviet Bloc and Big Brother stepping in to protect Pakistan. However, after the May 1998 tit-for-tat nuclear explosions, international relationships have more complexly soured since Pakistan allegedly approached China for help citing India as a threat, which led to the US and the EU imposing sanctions on Pakistan (Ahmad 2015: 108–109). Not only has Pakistan fought its own wars, but it was turned into a secondary battlefield of the Iran-Iraq war. As mentioned above the situation further deteriorated when the USA initiated a proxy war against the Soviet Union in Afghanistan with the help of Mujahideen who were charged for battle through religious propaganda urging them to wage a holy war to expel the infidels from Muslim Afghanistan (Javaid 2011: 11). All these clashes have spelt disaster for Pakistan's domestic economy, with adverse effects on the public. Specifically, "Pakistan being a small country in comparison to India and spending greater money on defense ultimately put pressure on economy, education and welfare programmes" (Adnan 2014: 48).

In sum, a deadly combination of nuclearization, militancy, US imperialism and fundamentalism has pushed Pakistan to the brink. Consequently, Pakistan suffers from economic disparity, lack of education, unemployment, flourishing militant fundamentalism, poor governance and alignment with United States (Javiad 2011: 17). In addition to the poor who suffer in economic terms, the trauma and psychological effects of violence on Pakistan youth is distressing. This has also led to conflict-induced displacement of unmanageable proportions, extensive brain drain, unemployment, and nationwide insecurity (Ahmed and Zed 2015).

Politicized Buddhism, Military Occupation and Sri Lankan Conflict

To most outsiders, Sri Lanka has always appeared to be an island of beauty and peace—with its scenic settings and the religion of a majority of its citizens, Theravada Buddhism, breeding peace and prosperity. However, this picture has fast been changing with violence first being unleashed against the Tamil community, and more recently directed against Sri Lankan Muslims. As is the case with India and Pakistan, the conflicts faced by the Sri Lankan public are both, internal and external.

In terms of aggression from without, India paid a heavy price for interference into Sri Lankan politics with the IPKF (Indian Peace Keeping Forces) engaging in armed conflict, which eventually led to the assassination of India's former Prime Minister, Rajiv Gandhi in 1991. Later, the Sri Lankan state entered into a formal military agreement with the US government, which resulted in the death and displacement of thousands of Tamils between 2007 and 2009. This was touted to be a resounding military victory of the Sri Lankan Sarkar over the Liberation Tigers of Tamil Eelam (LTTE). In the post-war era, the military buildup in the north and the east of Sri Lanka is unimaginable. There is a heightened level of Sinhalese nationalistic consciousness that not only legitimizes militarization, but also morally justifies it (J. L. Fernando 2018: 94). However, the costs in terms of degradation of human life and destruction of nature is immense. Moreover, in post-war Sri Lanka, the militarization of the entire country continued unabated with state security personnel seemingly wielding influence over every aspect of people's lives.

When the military assumes control over everyday public life, democracy dies a slow death and can simply be called a "phantom democracy" where Empire and Sarkar control everything (Boggs 2011: 1). The armed forces brazenly occupy land, sea and sky as if by birthright, and begin pontificating on what is acceptable and what is not. S. Ratnajeevan H. Hoole, a harassed civilian, reports:

> The Jaffna District today has 93 Naval bases occupying 2,946 acres (exceeding 12 sq. km), 54 Army bases and 1 Airforce base occupying 1,000 acres. These together with the 30 police stations rule us with an iron fist. However, their role is not clear except bullying people at the Casuarina Beach and stopping motorists to make money. Our fishermen have to pass the naval bases into the deeper seas for fishing.
> (Hoole 2018)

After the military victory in 2009 the Sinhala Buddhist nationalists have turned against the Muslim community. This has been accentuated, joined by the Sinhala Christians and some sections of the Tamils, after the Easter Sunday attacks on churches by the Islamic militants in 2019. Cyberspace has been used with lethal effect to create Islamophobia. Thinkers like Bourdieu have spoken about "symbolic violence"[6] by which the dominant group creates a "fictitious integration of society as a whole" and a "false consciousness" among the weaker sections thereby legitimizing the established order (Bourdieu 1991: 167). Muslims are made out to be a threat to the majority Buddhists although the 2001 census showed Buddhists accounting for 76.7 percent of the population while Muslims accounted for just 8.5 percent (Stewart 2014: 241). The internet is being flooded with volatile symbols and hateful messages like: "Any attempts to be tolerant of Islam, and Muslims in general, will only lead to violence and bloodshed. Therefore, attempting to live in tolerance and mutual harmony with Islam is a fruitless exercise" (ibid.: 252).

Having briefly mapped the contours of the conflicts in South Asia, let us establish a biblical-theological framework to help us evolve a Christian approach for responding to Empire, militarization and nuclearization. All the three countries have colonially carved states and religiously supported dominant national identities, which have sown seeds of polarization. The critique of these states should not be seen simply as a critique of dominant religious identities of the region, but also of colonial Christianity and Western imperialism.

God's Option: David's Pebble versus Gigantic Goliath's Armor

In an essay "Gods of War and Wars of God: Religion and Violence in Contemporary Society" written a little before the 9/11 attacks (Gonsalves 2001), I argued that most religions have mythical, mystifying and militant images of the Absolute which, being symbolic, are susceptible to manipulation. For instance, the historical books of the Hebrew Bible are a militaristic history. "From the Exodus from Egypt (c.1440 BCE) onward, the Israelites were a people engaged in conflict both to reach, create, and expand their homeland against opposing forces more powerful than themselves and to fashion themselves into a political nation. War became a way of life for them" (Slattery 2007: 33-34). They experienced God as active in their struggles for a home, land and identity—an anthropomorphic representation of their faith in God's power (Craigie 1986).

The image of the God of war, however, is tempered by alternative images of the God who seeks to exterminate violence (Gen. 6.13), detests both violence (Mal. 2.16) and those who love violence (Ps. 11.5), rejects the offering of the violent (Mal. 1.13), warns the violent of grave consequences (Ezek. 12.19; Joel 3.19; Hab. 2.8,17; Zep. 1.9), saves from violence (2 Sam. 22.3), condemns violence through the words of his prophets (Jer. 22.17; Ezek. 7.11,23; Jon. 3.8; Mic. 6.12) and proclaims that violence will be no more (Isa. 60.18). These images reveal the other side of the picture and bring to the fore the bipolarity present in symbolic language, which requires careful and critical scriptural interpretation.

Scriptural interpretation has often been seen as an apolitical and ahistorical endeavor with God being an isolated and noncommittal deity. Such a depoliticization of the Bible and domestication of Jesus belies Christian belief;[7] for, the God of Jesus was not revealed *per se*, but *in nobis*, experienced as alive and active in human history. This God specially privileged the poor, the younger, the weaker, the underdog and the black sheep. The divine option for the poor, collectively called the *anawim*—comprising widows, orphans and aliens (Ps. 68.5, 146.9, Deut. 26.12)—was premised on the fact that these groups experienced a "lack" without spouses, parents or friends, respectively. This lacuna was seen as a deprivation that required redress, which a just and merciful God responded to.

God's preferential option is first seen at the individual level. Abel is preferred over Cain (Gen. 4.3-5), and Jacob is blessed rather than Esau (Gen. 27.27-29). Joseph and Benjamin—Jacob's youngest sons—find favor with God over their elder brothers (Gen. 37-47). Moreover, God chooses a fleeing murderer, Moses, to lead the chosen Israelites to freedom (Ex. 3) and widowed Moabite Ruth, too, seems blessed with her eventual marriage to Boaz. Apart from special protection of weak individuals, Yahweh protects victims of injustice *as community* because God sees their affliction in slavery, hears their cries and opts to deliver them (Ex. 3.7-8). This option is also reiterated through Israel's prophets by warning those who exploit the needy (Am. 8.4ff). God's defense of the poor does not merely indicate the gratuitousness of God, but is, more appropriately, an ethical imperative and "an option for justice"[8] required for the functioning of a society and world created, and cared for, by God.

One of the finest examples of God's option for the poor is David, the youngest among Jesse's eight sons, who eventually becomes a great leader and hero. David wears many feathers in his cap: shepherd, hunter, fugitive, politician, king, poet, musician, prophet, warrior, friend, lover, father, adulterer, murderer and penitent. He is also prototype of the Christ, since from his lineage is born the Messiah (Ryken, Wilhoit and Longman III 1998). David is a symbol. And, like any other symbol, is bipolar, with potential to evoke different—often divergent—responses from diverse audiences.

The most proverbial picture of David is the shepherd boy face-to-face with gigantic Goliath. Their clash is set in the context of a battlefield with two opposing armies (1 Sam. 17). Battle lines are clearly drawn: Philistines versus Israelites. "Pagans" versus God's People. "Uncircumcised" warriors (1 Sam. 17.26) against "armies of the living God" (1 Sam. 17.27). Both sides are fully armed, ready for battle. A formidable foe, Goliath, is ready to kill. From a context of fear, insecurity, lopsidedness and vulnerability, God intervenes with a "third" force: David!

David is most unqualified and unarmed for battle. Concerned about his safety, Saul tries to equip David with his armor, helmet and sword. Encumbered by these, David says, "I cannot walk with these; for I am not used to them" (1 Sam. 17.39). Then he says to Goliath, "You come to me with sword, spear and javelin; but I come to you in the name of the Lord of hosts, the God of the armies of Israel, whom you have defied" (1 Sam. 17.45). Armed only with God's name, David slays the invincible giant, Goliath.

Jesus's Authority and the Jesus Movement for the Poor the Powerless

David slays Goliath "in God's *name*"; and, God assumes flesh and name through a descendent of David: Jesus of Nazareth. He is born in the violent context of Roman imperialism, on the one hand, and resistance movements against avatars of Empire, on the other.[9] Eschewing tendentious portraits of Jesus as a political revolutionary, social reformer, spiritual guru, religious rebel or economic gamechanger, could adopt a "relational-contextual approach to the historical Jesus' that considers five interrelated aspects, attempting to understand how:

> (1) in the particular historical conditions that had created a crisis for the ancient Judean and Galilean people (2) and working out of the Israelite cultural tradition in which those people were rooted, (3) Jesus emerged as a leader (4) by assuming / adapting particular social roles[s] (5) in interactions with particular people who responded by forming a movement that became historically significant.
> (Horsley 1993: 57–58)

It is beyond the scope of this chapter to highlight every aspect of such a contextual-historical inquiry; nonetheless, let us briefly examine Jesus' ministry that birthed a "Jesus Movement."

Like David appearing as a "third" force to bring about a solution to the Israelite–Philistine warring factions, Jesus, offspring of David, appears in history where, on the one hand, power was held and exercised by the Roman Empire in connivance with the Jewish priestly hierarchs and the wealthy, propertied elite, while, on the other hand, the poor and powerless were victims of the social, political, religious, cultural and spiritual setup (Brown 1985). Aware of the backbreaking burdens which the former alliance imposed upon the latter, in deep spiritual communion with the one he tenderly called *Abba* and banking upon the internal *Shakti* he experienced, Jesus embarks upon a multipronged approach with a clearly-proclaimed mission manifesto:

> The Spirit of the Lord is upon me, because he has anointed me to bring good news to the poor. He has sent me to proclaim release to the captives and recovery of sight to the blind, to let the oppressed go free, to proclaim the year of the Lord's favor.
>
> (Lk. 4.18-19)

Against the might of Empire, then, Jesus seems to draw his inspiration from and focus his attention upon three entities: (a) Abba-God, (b) Shakti-Spirit, and, (c) Public, especially the poorest and powerless among them. "Not by might, nor by power, but by my Spirit, says the Lord of hosts" (Zech. 4.6) seems to be the principle operative in Jesus' life and mission. God's Spirit empowers him to preach the empire he seems obsessed with: the reign of God and to surrender to its only emperor: God. Anybody armed with his charism would have surely sped to Rome or Jerusalem; for, that was where power prospered. But, Jesus, born in nondescript Bethlehem, begins his ministry in Galilee—moving from one polis to another, through villages and tiny towns (Mk. 1.38,39,45) "precisely where no politician would ever tread, where no religious leader would ever head" for his privileged friends would be "those who were marginalized, those who were possessed by demons, people who were not in control of their lives, people who had to fear for their lives, people who could not walk upright because they were under so much pressure and oppression.... He believed that there is no chance for any liberation or development to succeed until the hearts and minds of people in remote areas are reached" (Raheb 2018: 104–105).

During his ministry, Jesus sets himself up against many foes: rich landowners of the feudal classes, the Pharisees, the scribes, the priests thriving on temple treasures, and Herod, whom he called "fox" (Lk. 13.32). He wages battle against these *sine vi humana, sed verbo*—without human power, simply by the word (Hengel 1977: 16–18). His word is authoritative since the public is "astounded at his teaching, for he taught them as one having *authority* and not as the scribes" (Mk. 1:22). At his Last Supper, he performs a prophetic, symbolic action of washing his disciples' feet—announcing a new order of relationships based on love, service and sacrifice, while denouncing all forms of hierarchical power (Gonsalves 2015: 126–128).

Jesus' power shines brightly at his passion. He rejects the power of the sword with a rebuke to his unnamed disciple: "Put your sword back into its place; for all who take the sword will perish by the sword" (Mt. 26.52). Then, before Pilate, Jesus' authority is pitted against the brute power of Empire. Pilate symbolizes Roman *power*—strong, armed, and invested with the reins of governance by the Roman Empire, while Jesus, apparently Pilate's victim, truly stands tall before Empire since his *authority* comes from within. Hence, when slapped by a guard, he protests: "If I have spoken wrongly, testify to the wrong. But if I have spoken rightly, why do you strike me?" (Jn. 18.23). Bowing to Empire, after renewing friendship with an old foxy friend, Herod, Pilate raises a yet-to-be answered question: "What is truth?" (Jn. 18.38). Then, he washes his hands in a vain attempt to absolve himself of his guilt.

The Cross, Church Built on Martyrs' Blood, and Unholy Christendom

Jesus' gruesome crucifixion is the epitome of powerlessness and shamefulness to both, religious and political hierarchies. Yet, in its wake we have the sowing and stirrings of a Jesus movement. Paul says: "We proclaim Christ crucified, a stumbling block to Jews and foolishness to Gentiles" (1 Cor. 1.23); for, in the cross of Christ, Jesus' followers experience power, not weakness; life, not death; and sublime, endless love. That is precisely what they dared preach even unto their own crucifixions and deaths.

In the early Christian centuries, amidst violence and bloodshed, Jesus' disciples echoed his Sermon on the Mount teaching: "Blessed are the peacemakers!" Later, Church Fathers wrote about peace, as Justin Martyr (100–165 CE) writes to his opponent Tryphon:

> We who were filled with war, mutual slaughter, and every form of evil have everywhere transformed our instruments of war, fashioning our swords into ploughshares and our spears into farm tools. We are now cultivators of piety, justice, generosity, faith and the hope which comes from the Father through him who was crucified.
>
> (Quoted in Swift 1983: 18)

The birth and growth of the Church in the first three centuries of Christianity is marked with persecutions and bloodshed as Tertullian attested: "The Church is built on the blood of martyrs." These early martyrs were not weaklings who fearfully submitted to those in power. Rather, mindful of their mission to preach the kingdom of God and to live as children of the God of that kingdom, they made options for the poor and against despotic rulers, sacrificing their own lives when required. There were also "military martyrs" like Marinus, Maximilian and Marcellus who, despite earlier being enrolled in the emperors' armies, refused to take up arms since warfare went against their Christian values and conscience.[10]

Among the early Church Fathers, on the one hand, we see the development of strong pacifist arguments in the writings of Tertullian, Origen and Lactantius while, on the other, thinkers like Ambrose and Augustine espoused just war, arguing for the legitimacy of war under certain conditions. With the reign of Constantine (312–337 CE) and the "*cuius regio, eius religio*" at work, Christians—especially influential thinkers like Eusebius of Caesarea (*c*.260–340 CE)—began preaching that, with the advent and advance of Constantine's Empire, God's Kingdom had finally arrived (ibid.: 82–89). The conflation of Church and State, God and Mammon, soon led to a politicization of Christianity, the imposition of the Pax Romana, and the evolution of various forms of Christendom forming unholy alliances with Empire and Mammon. Ironically, when Christendom's imperial power peaked, the authority of the Christian hierarchy was at its lowest ebb.

Post-Constantine, popes and bishops would often become direct bearers of political power. The most striking example of usurping political power by the church is Pope Boniface VIII's bull *unam sanctam* of 1302, directed against Philip the Fair of France, which claims that both swords mentioned in Luke 22.38—the secular as well as the spiritual—are in the church's hands, thereby insisting that the secular authority must be subservient to the spiritual (i.e., the Roman pontiff; Hengel 1977: 66). The protests of the Reformation would serve as an antidote against the then-church's tendency to grab political power resulting in a perversion of that power which Christ desired his disciples to be outstanding in: the power of love, service and self-sacrifice.

South Asian Jesuit Initiatives among Jesus' Least Sisters and Brothers

We have briefly proposed the God-versus-Goliath narrative as being paradigmatic of the exercise of divine power, reiterated by Jesus who with the authority of God's word and impelled by God's Shakti-Spirit, becomes trailblazer of a peaceful "Jesus movement," which has found universal acceptance not only by Christians, but by all those seeking peace and prosperity of all peoples. We now chart three *margas* or pathways that we can tread to be faithful to Jesus. Some of these have been adopted by south Asian Jesuits, a Catholic religious congregation of which I am a member for close to four decades.

The Way of Knowledge—Jñana Marga—Lex Credendi

Cases for reflection: Two Indian Jesuit priests—Alphonse Aind and Stan Swamy—were jailed and placed under house arrest, respectively, on fabricated charges of Sarkar. In June 2018, Fr. Aind—committed to nonformal education and tribal welfare—was jailed for allegedly raping five tribal women who were performing a *nukkad* (street play) in his school (Chacko 2018), while Stan Swamy, aged 81, is accused of being an "Urban Naxal" for his work among poor Adivasis and for publicizing the pitiable plight of prisoners (Narayaran and Debmalya 2018). Even after nabbing the actual culprits who raped the five women (Sarkar 2018), it is shocking that Fr. Aind still lingers in jail (Week 2018). The knowledge which Fr. Aind and Fr. Swamy have acquired is truth, and it is dangerous for Sarkar.

In the encounters against Empire, true, relevant and up-to-date knowledge is needed. Military and nuclear powers perpetuate their stranglehold through peddling falsehood, camouflaging facts and repeating lies. To Pilate's hitherto unanswered, "What is truth?" let truth be told! Plain and simple. Every half-truth is a half-lie. Thus, there is urgent need for organic-public intellectuals who fearlessly expose "everyday orientalism" (Krishna 2009: 133) to come together for what Roy (2004: 29) calls the "globalization of dissent." Philosophers, journalists, theologians, media-persons, semioticians, artists, poets, filmmakers, dramatists and street-performers who express revolutionary viewpoints, club together ideas, evolve evocative symbols and provocative slogans to strip and shame Empire must unite to fight.

The Western mind is obsessed with anthropocentric, bipolar dualisms seeking black-vs-white clarity. Either–or, right–wrong, good–bad dichotomies are privileged over pluralistic harmony, multipolar wisdom and cosmic communion. The Asian mindset, contrastingly, is comfortable with pluralism, multipolarity, cosmic connectedness and an Advaitic (nondual) worldview. Such knowledge is neither anthropocentric nor dualistic, but holistic and what Panikkar terms *"cosmotheandric"*—seamlessly harmonizing the divine, human and cosmic.

Holistic theological knowledge is God-talk that seeks to evolve an Asian "God of our soil" made flesh (Gonsalves 2010), who struggles in solidarity with us. Kaufman writes:

> Christian theology is completely free—indeed, theology is under the imperative—to become fully indigenous in every respect in each culture in which the Christian believes, lives and works, so long as the Principle of God's absoluteness and the Principle of God's humanness are maintained. The central task of theologians in every culture is to work out, to construct, an image/concept of God appropriate to contemporary life.
>
> (Kaufman 1981: 278–279)

Theology—and all the fields of knowledge, as well—must powerfully retrieve the prophetic memory of the Messiah who lived, was crucified and raised by God for standing in solidarity with God's poor and powerless children while vehemently resisting the Western theological imperialism. We must distinguish between "memory as *prison*" and "memory as *prophesy*" (Rafiq Khoery quoted in Raheb 2018: 20). The former leads to a mummified and paralyzing regression into the past, while the latter stimulates and impels one out to imagine that another world—a *mother-world*—is possible (Gonsalves 2004).

Over and above the need for indigenous God-talk, we ought to retell stories,[11] and rewrite narratives of the joys and hopes, dreams and visions of the public for "public theology" (Doak 2004). Moreover, with interdisciplinary perspectives, the silent ravaging of mother earth must be exposed. Pope Francis' *"Laudato Si"* is a commendable document that calls for "dialogue on the environment in the international community" (Francis 2015: 164–175). All these ventures will entail reading and reflecting upon the "signs of the times" and the "signs of the place"[12] in an age of globalization where it is not always easy to decipher the deceitful designs of unholy alliances.

The Way of Prayer (Devotion)—Bhakti Marga—Lex Orandi

Cases for reflection: Some Sri Lankan Tamils reclaimed their lands after praying together in church. They were initially afraid, but decided that they would reclaim what was rightfully theirs. According to Ruki Fernando (2018), they said to the Naval officers occupying their island:

> We have come to our lands, our church. We have had enough of displacement, and we plan to stay here. We have legal documents. You (Navy) can also stay in the islands, but not on our lands, and you should not disturb or obstruct our lives.

Fernando, a lay collaborator with the Sri Lankan Jesuits, reports how he was initially afraid to accompany these victims on this protest. He writes: "With me on the boat was a long-time friend and Catholic Priest from Pesalei, and we recalled the fire power of the Navy, and how they had even attacked and killed and injured people inside the Pesalei church" (R. Fernando 2018). But prayer empowered the public to successfully reclaim their island despite grave risks.

Indian Jesuit priest Alexis Premkumar, my former student who headed the Jesuit Refugee Service (JRS) in Afghanistan, was kidnapped by Taliban militants in Sohadat and spent eight months and twenty days locked up or chained for most of the time. He confesses:

> In the first few weeks I thought even Jesus did not have to suffer this much. That must have been spiritual arrogance! Soon I realized that no one could suffer as much as He [Jesus] did. I tried to unite my sufferings with His. I offered them for people who suffer all over the world in so many ways. I prayed all the time.

Such a creative response to suffering does not warrant vilification of the tormentor. In this context it totally prohibits Islamophobia. Both Islamic militancy and Islamophobia are constructs of the Empire which aims to divide Christians and Muslims. If we are to combat the powers and principalities "not by might, nor by power, but by God's Spirit," then disernment and prayer are indispensable. Resistance is an act of faith that needs discernment and prayer. Pope Francis repeats that every Christian is gifted with God's Spirit, which enables us to discern and decide on the "Yes" and "No" of protest and resistance. "All is *not* fair in love and in war!" says the Christian dissenter; for, Empire sees everything and everyone as mere handy tools to occupy land, eject public, rob resources, stifle dissent and expand empire. The resister is called to overcome this deadly rationale.

Nouwen rightly says, "Resistance does not stand in contrast to prayer, but is in fact a form of prayer itself ... We will fully grasp the meaning of peacemaking only when we recognize not only that prayer is a form of resistance but also that resistance is a form of prayer" (Nouwen 2009: 83). It is heartwarming to see publics in silent prayer, reading God's word, collectively discerning Spirit-powered avenues for action, at the Eucharist, or praying the "way of the cross" before engaging in prophetic action against Sarkar and Empire. Prayer emboldens, empowers, and enables dissenters to protest and resist. Prayer also equips protesters and dissenters not to be consumed by hatred, but to forgive foes through what a newly-canonized Salvadoran saint Archbishop Oscar Romero called "the violence of love" (Romero 1988: 12).[13]

In a deeply religious context like south Asia, any liberative action must be interreligious (Hardawiryana 1989). It could be difficult to come together on an interfaith platform since different religions pray in very diverse ways. However, there is a sacramental dimension of *bhakti* that involves creative use of symbols. Activists and Adivasis who resisted eviction from their villages during the NBA (Narmada Bachao Andolan) resorted to *jal-samadhi* (water-immersion ritual); and, south Koreans have had "candlelight protests" to oust a corrupt regime and "hundred bows" of meditation to block the construction of the Naval base in Jeju.

The Way of Action—Karma Marga—Lex Vivendi

Cases for reflection: Indian Jesuit Stanislaus Jebamalai has been coordinator for JESA (Jesuits Engaged in Social Action) for six years and has spent more than four decades campaigning for the rights and resources of Adivasis. He says, "There is no greater force on earth than people's power." He founded and coordinates an Indian national network called Lok Manch (literally, "People's Platform") which can be called a "Jesus Movement" working in tandem with many other secular, social movements in south Asia. He says:

> The current goal of *Lok Manch* is to develop a vibrant network to help improve the quality of life for up to 300,000 households. The process is guided by thousands of community leaders, 50% of whom are women. More than 3,000 leaders have already been trained to provide local communities with up-to-date information on food and other rights under the law, on how to access these rights, and on what measures to take when failures in the system are encountered.
>
> (Jebamalai 2018)

Another massive movement actively supported by JESA is the "National Alliance of Peoples Movements" (NAPM) which, on October 2, 2018, the birthday of Mahatma Gandhi, embarked upon a *"Samvidhan Samman Yatra"*—literally, "Respect the Constitution March." This literal "movement of people" will journeyed 25,000 kilometers through 26 Indian states in 65 days holding meetings, discussions, public events, supporting struggles, sharing grief of victims of the violence and hate and spreading the message of plurality, love, peace and social justice. The *Yatra* culminated in Delhi on December 10, 2018, the "International Human Rights Day" to publicize and protest against Sarkar's divisive hate-agenda, looting of resources and abuses against the Constitution.

The JESA has networks not only in India, Sri Lanka and Pakistan, but collaborates and networks throughout south Asia. Collaboration and networking is of utmost importance. Indeed, whether it be supporting the "Mothers' Front" in Sri Lanka, or protesting against the Koodenkulam nuclear plant in south India, or blocking the building of the Netarhat Field Firing Range (NFFR) in Jharkhand, central India, need to build horizontal solidarity. If they are to be truly effective, the *margas* of knowledge (*jnana*) and prayer (*bhakti*) must fructify in action (*karma*) against all forms of subjugation and silencing of the poor. Arundhati Roy (2004: 26) rightly says, "Radical change cannot and will not be negotiated by governments; it can only be enforced by people. By the *public*. A public who can link hands *across* national borders." She adds, "Wars will be stopped only when soldiers refuse to fight, when workers refuse to load weapons onto ships and aircraft, when people boycott the economic outposts of Empire that are strung across the globe" (ibid.: 39). All this must be the agenda of peacemakers who Jesus calls "blessed" (Mt. 5.9).

Conclusion: Building Asian Churches of Prophets, Priests and Pastors

Today, Empire not only heightens offensives and governs us from land, seas and skies (Hippler 2017), but has also vitiated every bit of cosmic reality and megabytes of cyberspace with its vile presence. For the Empire's violations, vitiations and victimizations to cease, we, the public, must ensure that our prophetic, priestly and pastoral policies and programs, too, continue unabated *in God's name* so as to defeat imperialistic designs and deeds.

The God-versus-Goliath and Jesus-versus-Pilate motifs are not only typical of Judaism and Christianity, but have parallels in other religious traditions.[14] Ultimately, people emerge victorious not by power but by authority, not by military might but by Spirit, not by subjugating people but by submitting to God. Different creeds, like the religions of the publics we discussed here—namely, Hinduism, Islam, Buddhism and Christianity—endorse different beliefs and perform divergent rites and rituals. Therefore, though the *margas* of *jñana* and *bhakti* may sometimes seem unfamiliar or even unacceptable, we can surely meet and move along the *karma marga* of selfless action.

Does it really matter whether one joins what we call "Jesus movements" because one feels inspired by the *shūnyatā* and compassion of Buddhism (Mitchell 1991),[15] or is moved by *kenotic* love of Christ, or considers this as an act of *karuna* (mercy) or *tyaga* (sacrifice) enjoined by Hinduism, or opts for a *weak ontology*[16] amid poverty, war and violence, out of concern for suffering humanity? Ultimately, aren't we all actively playing out our eco-human responsibility in that wondrous, cosmic cycle of birth, death and life to protect life and guarantee the continuity of life believing that there is an alternative world beyond empire?

Francis Gonsalves is the dean of theology of Jnana-Deepa Vidyapeeth, Pune, India. He was the former principal of Vidyajyoti Theological College, New Delhi for 18 years. He is the executive director of the Commission for Theology and Doctrine of the Conference of Catholic Bishops of India, and the author of many articles and books on contextual theologies.

Notes

1. The Hindi word "*Rashtra*" simply means "nation" or "country."
2. One must distinguish between "*Hindutva*" and Hinduism. The former refers to the militant brand of Hinduism aggressively propagated by the Hindu Right; the latter, to the normal practice of Hinduism. V. D. Savarkar writes: "Hindutva is not a word but a history. Not only the spiritual or religious history of our people as at times it is mistaken to be by being confounded with the other cognate term, Hinduism. Hinduism is only a derivative, a fraction, a part of Hindutva ... Hindutva embraces all departments of thought and activity of the whole being of our Hindu race" (Savarkar 1969: 3–4). Also, see Sharma (2011).
3. Benedict and Kaviraj propose that nationalisms are often constructed by tenuous use of constructs like the census, map, museum, etc.
4. James Mill's work, "A History of British India" proved useful for communal ideology. See Thapar (1998: 7-8) for a brief critique of this approach.
5. Dayal and Hashmi (2015) offers many cases of violence a year after election of the BJP.
6. "Symbolic violence" is a term used by Bourdieu (quoted in Painter 2000: 246). See also Lele (1995).
7. Horsley (2003) argues against this approach, which is popular in North American Christianity.

8. Vigil (2004) criticizes the "softened" stand of Gutiérrez and other Latin-American liberation theologians who now interpret "option of the poor" to mean mere "gratuitousness of God." Vigil argues that this option is God's option for justice in favour of "victims of injustice."
9. Horsley (1993) calls for abandoning the unhistorical quest for an apolitical Jesus, arguing that Jesus was deeply committed to all critical issues of his times since they concerned groups which God had opted for.
10. See Swift (1983: 71–79) for details of their lives and martyrdom.
11. The First Asian Mission Congress held in Thailand in October 2006 had as its theme "Telling the Story of Jesus in Asia," encouraging Asian theologians to adopt a story-telling form of theologizing.
12. Felix Wilfred (2003: 186) adds that, besides the *chronos* (time), listening to the *topos* (place or context) is vital especially since Christianity must strive to be an active interlocutor in the public realm of civil society in a global world.
13. Romero was canonized saint in Rome on October 14, 2018.
14. For instance, in the Kurukshetra, when warring Arjuna is asked to choose between the Lord Krishna, on the one hand, and his whole army, arsenal and armory on the other, he chooses the Lord. Contrastingly, Duryodhan, like Goliath, depended on arms and ammunition.
15. Chapters 1, 3 and 4 of Mitchell (1991) show points of convergence between Christianity's *kenosis* and Buddhism's *shunyata*.
16. Agnostic philosopher Vattimo (1999: 65) sees "weak ontology" of *kenosis* as an antidote to godlessness of the present.

References

Adnan, Mubeen. 2014. "Nuclearization of South Asia 1998: Pakistan's Domestic Constraints." *South Asian Studies* 29(1): 41–60.

Ahmad, Sajjad. 2015. "The Nuclearization of India and Pakistan and the Quest for Peace in South Asia: Response and Apprehensions of the West." *Journal of European Studies* 31(2): 101–113.

Ahmed, Zahid Shahab, and Khan Zeb. 2015. "Impacts of Terrorism-Related Violence on Pakistan and its Youth." *Journal of People's Studies* 1(2): 40–49.

Andersen, Walter K., and Shridhar D. Damle. 2018. *The RSS: A View to the Inside*. Delhi: Viking Penguin.

Anderson, Benedict. 1996. *Imagined Communities: Reflections on the Origin and Spread of Nationalism*. New York: Verso.

Berger, Peter L. (ed). 1999. *The Desecularization of the World: Resurgent Religion and World Politics*. Grand Rapids, MI: William B. Eerdmans Publishing Company.

Boggs, Carl. 2011. *Empire versus Democracy: The Triumph of Corporate and Military Power*. New York: Routledge. https://doi.org/10.4324/9780203834176

Bourdieu, Pierre. 1991. *Language and Symbolic Power*, trans. Gino Raymond and Matthew Adamson. Cambridge: Polity Press.

Brown, John Pairman. 1985. "Techniques of Imperial Control: The Background of the Gospel Event." In *The Bible and Liberation: Political and Social Hermeneutics*, edited by Norman K. Gottwald, 357–377. New York: Orbis Books.

Chacko, P. A. 2018. "Jharkhand Gangrape and Jesuit's Arrest." Retrieved from http://mattersindia.com/2018/06/jharkhand-gangrape-and-jesuits-arrest (accessed October 3, 2018).

Craigie, Peter C. 1986. *The Problem of War in the Old Testament*. Grand Rapids, MI: William B. Eerdmans Publishing Company.

Crick, Emile. 2007. *Cricket and Indian National Consciousness*. Research Paper. New Delhi: Institute of Peace and Conflict Studies.

Dayal, John, and Shabnam Hashmi (eds). 2015. *A Report–365 Days: Democracy and Secularism under the Modi Regime*. Delhi: Anhad.

Doak, Mary. 2004. *Reclaiming Narrative for Public Theology*. Albany, NY: State University of New York Press.

Fernando, Jude Lal. 2018. "Prophetic Imagination and Empire in Asia: In Search for Peace Theologies in Korea and Japan." *International Journal of Asian Christianity* 1(1): 91–116. https://doi.org/10.1163/25424246-00101006

Fernando, Ruki. 2018. "Iranaitheevu: A Community Reclaims their Island Home from the Navy." Retrieved from https://groundviews.org/2018/04/25/iranaitheevu-a-community-reclaims-their-island-home-from-the-navy (accessed October 2, 2018).

Golwalkar, M. S. 1947. *We, or, Our Nationhood Defined*. Nagpur: Bharat Prakashan.

Gonsalves, Francis. 1999 "Grisly Christmas for Christians in Gujarat." *Communalism Combat* 6(50): 11–14.

Gonsalves, Francis. 2001. "Gods of War and Wars of God: Religions and Violence in Contemporary Society." *The Yearbook of Contextual Theologies*, 33–59. Aachen: Missionswissenschaftliches Institut Missio.

Gonsalves, Francis. 2010. *God of Our Soil: Towards Subaltern Trinitarian Theology*. Delhi: ISPCK/VIEWS.

Gonsalves, Francis. 2015. *Feet Rooted, Hearts Radiant, Minds Raised: Living Sacraments in India*. Anand: Gujarat Sahitya Prakash.

Hardawiryana, R. 1989. "Asia's Quest for Peace: A Challenge to the World Religions." In *Towards a Theology of Peace*, edited by Stephen Tunnicliffe, 152–178. London: European Nuclear Disarmament.

Hengel, Martin. 1977. *Christ and Power*, trans. Everett R. Kalin. Philadelphia, PA: Fortress Press.

Hippler, Thomas. 2017. *Governing from the Skies—A Global History of Aerial Bombing*, trans. David Fernbach. London: Verso.

Hoole, S. Ratnajeevan H.. 2018. "Jaffna: No Democracy when People Live Under Military Rule." Retrieved from http://srilankabrief.org/2018/09/jaffna-no-democracy-when-people-live-under-military-rule (accessed October 2, 2018).

Horsley, Richard A. 2003. *Jesus and Empire: The Kingdom of God and the New World Disorder*. Minneapolis, MN: Fortress Press.

Horsley, Richard A. 1993. *Jesus and the Spiral of Violence: Popular Jewish Resistance in Roman Palestine*. Minneapolis, MN: Fortress Press.

Islam, Shamsul. 2017. "Cow and Hindutva: Myths and Facts." Retrieved from www.academia.edu/33854298/In_the_Name_of_Cow_Lynching_and_More_Lynchings (accessed September 28, 2018).

Javaid, Umbreen. 2011. "Thriving Fundamentalism and Militancy in Pakistan—An Analytical Overview of their Impact on the Society." *South Asian Studies* 26(1): 8–19.

Jebamalai, Stanislaus. "Lok Manch." Retrieved from www.canadianjesuitsinternational.ca/projects/india-lok-manch (accessed October 4, 2018).

Kanungo, Pralay. 2002. *RSS's Tryst with Politics: From Hedgewar to Sudarshan*. Delhi: Manohar Publications.

Kaufman, Gordon D. 1981. *The Theological Imagination: Constructing the Concept of God*. Philadelphia, PA: Westminster Press.

Kaul, Natasha. 2017. "Rise of the Political Right in India: Hindutva-Development Mix, Modi Myth, and Dualities." *Journal of Labor and Society* 20: 523–548. https://doi.org/10.1111/wusa.12318

Kaviraj, Sudipta. 1992. "The Imaginary Institution of India." In *Subaltern Studies VII—Writings on South Asian History and Society*, edited by P. Chatterjee and G. Pandey, 1–39. Delhi: Oxford University Press.

Krishna, Sankaran. 2009. *Globalization and Postcolonialism: Hegemony and Resistance in the Twenty-first Century*. New Delhi: Rawat Publications.

Lele, Jayant K. 1995. "Hindutva as Pedagogic Violence." In *Hindutva: The Emergence of the Right*, 81–103. Madras: Earthworm Books.

Mitchell, Donald W. 1991. *Spirituality and Emptiness: The Dynamics of Spiritual Life in Buddhism and Christianity*. New York: Paulist Press.

Narayanan, Rajendran and Debmalya. 2018. "Father Stan Swamy, Children and the Unholy State." Retrieved from https://thewire.in/rights/stan-swamy-jharkhand-adivasis-undertrials-pesa-uapa (accessed October 3, 2018).

Niazi, Tarique. 2001. "Economic Growth and Social Violence in Pakistan." *International Journal of Contemporary Sociology* 38(2): 171–192.

Nouwen, Henri. 2009. *Peacework: Prayer, Resistance, Community*. Bangalore: Asian Trading Corporation.

Painter, Joe. 2000. "Pierre Bourdieu." In *Thinking Space*, edited by Mike Crang and Nigel Thrift, 239-259. New York: Routledge.

Pieris, Aloysius. 1996. *Fire and Water: Basic Issues in Asian Buddhism and Christianity*. Maryknoll, NY: Orbis Books.

Raheb, Mitri. 2018. *Faith in the Face of Empire: The Bible through Palestinian Eyes*. New York: Orbis Books.

Romero, Oscar. 1988. *The Violence of Love*, trans. James R. Brockman. Farmington, PA: Plough Publishing House.

Roy, Arundhati. 2004. *Public Power in the Age of Empire*. New York: Seven Stories Press.

Roy, D. N. 2017. *South Asia on Short Fuse: Nuclear Politics and Disarmament*. New Delhi: Gaurav Books Centre.

Roy, Siddharthya. 2014. "On Hindutva and the 'Five Ms' that Pose A Threat To It." Retrieved from www.newslaundry.com/2014/12/02/on-hindutva-and-the-five-ms-that-pose-a-threat-to-it (accessed September 30, 2018).

Ryken, Leland, James C. Wilhoit and Tremper Longman III, eds. 1998. *Dictionary of Biblical Imagery*. Leicester: InterVarsity Press.

Sarkar, Debashish. 2018. "Pathalgadi Masterminds Arrested in Kochang Gang Rape of 5 Tribal Girls." Retrieved from www.hindustantimes.com/india-news/pathalgadi-masterminds-arrested-in-kochang-gangrape-of-5-tribal-girls/story-iTwScm2D0eytFNkZgrXQdJ.html. 22 July (accessed October 3, 2019).

Savarkar, V. D. 1969. *Hindutva*. Bombay: Veer Savarkar Prakashan.

Sharma, Jyotirmaya. 2011. *Hindutva: Exploring the Idea of Hindu Nationalism*. New Delhi: Penguin Books.

Singh, Niranjan S. 2006. *"Sakti": Gems from India*, edited by George Gispert-Sauch. Delhi: ISPCK/VIEWS.

Slattery, Michael W. 2007. *Jesus the Warrior? Historical Christian Perspectives & Problems on the Morality of War and the Waging of Peace*. Milwaukee, WI: Marquette University Press.

Stavrianakis, Anna. 2010. *Taking Aim at the Arms Trade: NGOs, Global Civil Society and the World Military Order*. London: Zed Books.

Stewart, James John. 2014. "Muslim-Buddhist Conflict in Contemporary Sri Lanka." *South Asia Research* 34(3): 241–260. https://doi.org/10.1177/0262728014549134
Swift, Louis J. 1983. *The Early Fathers on War and Military Service*. Wilmington, DE: Michael Glazier, Inc.
Sykes, Stephen. 2006. *Power and Christian Theology*. London: Continuum.
Teltumbde, Anand. 2018. *Republic of Caste: Thinking Equality in the Time of Neoliberal Hindutva*. New Delhi: Navayana Publishing.
Thapar, Romila. 1989. "Imagined Religious Communities? Ancient History and the Modern Search for a Hindu Identity." *Modern Asian Studies* 23(2): 209–231. https://doi.org/10.1017/S0026749X00001049
Thapar, Romila. 1998. "Communalism and the Historical Legacy: Some Facets." In *Secular Challenge to Communal Politics: A Reader*, edited by P. R. Ram, 6–24. Mumbai: Vikas Adhyayan Kendra.
Thapar, Romila. 2000. *History and Beyond*. New Delhi: Oxford University Press.
Umar, Mohammed Baba. Undated. "The Water Wars: Pakistan, India Hostility over Kashmir Waters." Retrieved from www.academia.edu/27470540/The_Water_Wars_Pakistan_India_hostility_over_Kashmir_waters (accessed 1 October 2018).
Vattimo, Gianni. 1999. *Belief*, trans. L. D'Isanto and D. Webb. Cambridge: Polity Press.
Vigil, José M. 2004. "The Option for the Poor is an Option for Justice, and not Preferential: A New Theological-Systematic Framework for the Option for the Poor." *Vidyajyoti Journal of Theological Reflection* 68(7): 509–520.
Vij-Arora, Bhavna. 2018. "HQ, Nagpur." *Outlook* 58(36): 28–32.
Weber, Max. 1968. *Economy and Society*, edited by Günther Roth and Claus Wittich. New York: Bedminster Press.
Week. 2018. "Bail Plea of Father Alfons Rejected in Kochang Gang-Rape Case." *The Week*, September 11. Retrieved from www.theweek.in/wire-updates/national/2018/09/11/lgc3-jh-court-kochang.html (accessed 4 October 2018).
Wilfred, Felix. 2003. *Asian Dreams and Christian Hope: At the Dawn of the Millennium*. Delhi: ISPCK.
Wolpert, Stanley. 2010. *India and Pakistan: Continued Conflict or Cooperation?* Berkeley, CA: University of California Press.

11

The Empathetic Power of Suffering: The Memories of Killing and Feminist Interfaith Spiritual Activism

Keun-Joo Christine Pae

I am the twelve-year-old girl, refugee on a small boat,
who throws herself into the ocean after being raped by a sea pirate,
and I am the pirate, my heart not yet capable of seeing and loving.

I am a member of the politburo, with plenty of power in my hands,
and I am the man who has to pay his "debt of blood" to my people,
dying slowly in a forced labor camp.

My joy is like spring, so warm it makes flowers bloom in all walks of life.
My pain is like a river of tears, so full it fills the four oceans.

Please call me by my true names,
so I can hear all my cries and laughs at once,
so I can see that my joy and pain are one.
    —Thich Nhat Hanh, *Please Call Me by My True Names* (1999: 72–73)

Introduction: Between a Politics of Killing and a Politics of Love

War is about killing. As postcolonial theorist Achille Mbembe bluntly states, "war is as much a means of achieving sovereignty as a way of exercising the right to kill" (Mbembe 2003: 12). Mbembe's concept of necropolitics accentuates sovereignty's exercise of its right to kill by controlling the mortality of the population and by defining life as "the deployment and manifestation of power." Hence, sovereignty does not wage war or militarize its population for the sake of fostering life or security. Rather, to eliminate certain populations, sovereignty declares war, and justifies the need of the institutionalized military.[1] Necropolitics, or sovereignty's right to kill, is complex. Just as there is a population to eliminate who is often called the enemy, there is also a group of people such as soldiers who should carry out the deadly labor of exterminating the targeted population, although that action risks their own lives.

Sovereignty does not simply kill the targeted population but also maims them. The maimed population may eventually succumb to death, marginalized from society and debilitated. What Jasbir Puar calls "the right to maim" is "a right expressive of sovereign power that is linked to, but not the same as, 'the right to kill'" (Puar 2017: xviii). Maiming is "a source of value extraction from populations that would otherwise be disposable" and leads to further perpetuation of debilitation (ibid.: xviii–xix). Sovereignty can maim many populations beyond the enemy—soldiers, civilians, military prostitutes, and those who challenge its legitimacy. Puar's concept of the right to maim is similar to what Korean American cultural theorist Jin-kyung Lee calls "necropolitical labor" which means the extraction of labor from those who are condemned to death is limited to serving the labor demands of the state or empire (Lee 2010). Necropolitical labor, as the most disposable form of labor, highlights an intermediate stage where "the extraction of labor is related to and premised on the possibility of death, rather than the ultimate event of death itself." Both soldiering and prostitution are considered forms of necropolitical labor because both constantly expose the laborers to deadly violence, the possibility of death, and ultimate disposability. When they are not in use or cannot be in use, they may experience physical, social, and psychological debilitation.

Mbembe, Puar and Lee all point out "a politics of killing" as the core practice of any war, no matter how politicians justify war through the language of love, protection, peace, and security. Since a politics of killing has been normalized in history, we may not know where to begin to tell the stories of killing. Among the countless stories of killing during wartime, this chapter tells of America's genocide of Korean civilians during the Korean War (1950–1953). I argue that America's mass killings have transnationally and transgenerationally haunted those who live the effects of the war. Along with memories of genocide, the chapter analyzes prostitution industries around US military bases in South Korea. US military prostitution, as the affective site of the war, has existed in South Korea for more than seven decades, constantly reminding people of America's genocide of Korean civilians. Military prostitution is the example of the racialized, sexualized, and gendered debilitation of a targeted population. Hence, this chapter argues that genocide and military prostitution are the two characters of the US military empire in East Asia.

Subsequently, I map out a politics of love, informed by Christianity, Buddhism, and transnational feminism. Based on imagined dialogue between Dorothee Soelle and Sister Chan Khong, I delineate "feminist spiritual activism" as a political form of love that counters a politics of killing. These two religious women's non-violent peace activism, built upon Christian mysticism and Zen Buddhism, will show how empathy with the sufferers becomes a powerful tool in healing "us" from the haunting memories of war and courageously moving toward peace. Spiritual activism further searches for the possibility to create solidarity among diverse groups of people who live with different memories and effects of war. Feminist interfaith activism as constructed in this chapter should not be considered a direct remedy for the never-ended Korean War. Just as I use the Korean War as a site to show the US military empire's brutality during the early Cold War period and its legacy, I delineate interfaith activism as a present praxis for healing of past wars and for preventing future wars.

Korean War: A Palimpsest of Genocide

Due to the US–North Korea summit in Singapore on June 12, 2018, many Americans and Koreans may refrain from talking about the historical animosity between the two countries. Their hostile relationship can be traced back to 1945, when the US military occupied the southern part of the Korean peninsula, replacing Imperial Japan's thirty-five-year occupation of the region.[2] Since the Korean War, which is casually called "the Forgotten War" in America, North Korea has become a perpetual enemy to America. Although the Korean War is willfully forgotten in the American public, the war has always been alive in the Korean diaspora beyond time and space.

How can we retrieve the traumatizing memories of American troops' genocide during their forgotten war? As I will unpack later in this chapter, story-telling is an important tool in creating empathetic understanding of people's suffering caused by war. "How" to tell the story is as crucial as "what" and "whose" stories to tell. Here, I borrow the idea of a palimpsest from transnational feminist scholar M. Jacqui Alexander. According to Alexander, "time is neither vertically accumulated nor horizontally teleological" (Alexander 2005: 190). Hence, she frames time as a palimpsest—"a parchment that has been inscribed two or three times, the previous text having been imperfectly erased and remaining therefore still partly visible" (ibid.). A palimpsest brings the past into the present and the future, and the future into the present and the past simultaneously. It leads one to consciously look at what has been erased and what will leave traces. The concept of a palimpsest enables us to look at the fragments and remains of the war more consciously, so that we can grasp the partialities of mass killing in the remains of the war ruins. The palimpsestic stories of killing from the Korean War appear familiar and unfamiliar, historically specific and transcendental, visible and invisible, and after all, ambiguous.

The brutal Korean War officially claimed 1.5 million people's lives, although arguably as many as four million people might have been killed and seven million people maimed by the war. Mass killings, massacre, or what Korean Sociologist Dong Choon Kim calls "genocide," is the character of the Korean War (Kim 2004: 529).

Despite the official denials of the United States, the US attacks on Korean civilians started at the beginning of the war. One of the early civilian massacres happened at Nogeun-ri, the central part of South Korea, between July 25 and 29, 1950. The Nogeun-ri massacre was rarely known to the public until 1999, when the Associated Press started uncovering the US army orders to shoot approaching refugees. The press also released the interviews conducted with the Korean survivors of the massacre and the 7th Calvary veterans, who were ordered to shoot the refugees (Cho 2008: 59–60).

At the beginning of the Korean War, the US and South Korean troops could not stop the North Korean advancement while countless refugees passed through the US–South Korean lines. The US Eighth Army was worried about the possible presence of North Korean spies among the refugees. On July 25, 1950, one month after the outbreak of the Korean War, the US Eighth Army announced "the Stop Refugee Order" that considered "any refugees leaving the war zone as the enemy" (Shin 2014: 216–217).[3]

Defeated in Daejeon, the US 7th Calvary troops retreated to Youngdong, seven miles north of Nogeun-ri. On July 25, 1950, the troops evacuated the nearby villages, gathered about six hundred refugees, and herded them to Haga-ri, where the refugees spent the night by a stream. The next morning, the refugees discovered that the American soldiers had disappeared. Some of the refugees went back to their villages while the majority of them continued to walk southward. On July 26, 1950, the refugees again met American soldiers who ordered them to walk along the railroad tracks. Soon, US warplanes started shooting the refugees, instantly killing more than one hundred. The survivors hid inside the twin underpass of the railroad. For the next three days, American soldiers would gun down about three hundred civilians hidden inside of the underpass.

The Nogeun-ri massacre was neither the beginning nor the end of American troops' genocide of Korean civilians. More than sixty cases of US troop-involved mass killings were reported in the aftermath of the news of Nogeun-ri. A week before the Nogeun-ri massacre, about one hundred refugees were killed by napalm and machine gun when they tried to cross the river at Cheongwon, not far from Nogeun-ri. In early August and September 1950, a few weeks after the Nogeun-ri massacre, about eight-hundred refugees were killed in Pohang by bombs simply because they stayed near the military line (Shin 2014: 214, 217, 219). Similar stories of civilian massacres by US soldiers are found across Korea.

Besides direct shootings, America's use of napalm brought massive destruction to the lives of Koreans. The US army used 32,357 tons of napalm. Of this, 4,313 tons were dropped during "Operation Strangle" between August 1951 and June 1952 (Kim 2006: 152–153). Operation Strangle refers to the carpet bombing in North Korea done by the US, whenever the truce talks between North Korea/China and the United States/United Nations were at a stalemate. Korea was the testing site for napalm, a newly developed weapon of mass destruction at that time. Several years later, based on its testing and observation of napalm in Korea, the United States used napalm more systematically along with Agent Orange during the Vietnam War to scorch jungles and forests where Vietcong guerillas were believed to be waiting in ambush. During the Rolling Thunder Operation in Vietnam alone, the US dropped 34,261 tons of napalm bombs (ibid.: 153).

Napalm spreads jellied gasoline everywhere, when it explodes, turning the bombing area into a "hell of fire" (Kim 2006: 154). Thus, napalm cannot target particular military or industrial facilities but scorches the areas where the possible human and non-human targets reside. The photos taken by American soldiers during the Korean War proved that the majority of napalm bombs were dropped in small rural villages filled with hay-roofed houses (ibid.). Although the United States justified its use of napalm even in small villages for dismantling enemy lines or killing communists waiting in ambush, they knew that they were killing civilians. American soldiers often received the order to kill refugees even after they reported no presence of enemies to military authorities (ibid.: 156).

According to Korean American sociologist Grace Cho, the Nogeun-ri massacre evokes the future My Lai massacre in Vietnam in 1968 (Cho 2008: 57–58). The Nogeun-ri massacre also reveals the palimpsest of the genocide of American Indians at Wounded Knee on December 29, 1890. On that day, the US 7th Cavalry, the same regiment later responsible for the Nogeun-ri massacre, slaughtered as many as three hundred mostly unarmed and defenseless Lakota men, women, and children (LaDuke 2012: 8). Since the present moment of militarized violence happens too quickly to be perceived, it is accessible to conscious experience only through its palimpsests. The trauma of militarized violence can traverse the boundaries of time and space from Wounded Knee through Nogeun-ri to My Lai only to open the temporality in which past and future collide.

Race, Gender and Sexuality of Genocide

One might wonder why American soldiers showed such a high level of cruelty toward ordinary Koreans in the war while they claimed to protect them from communist enemies. In the broader context of Cold War politics, America saw North Korea as a proxy of Stalin. "Korea" was insignificant to the United States, but from an American perspective, the prevention of Soviet expansion was crucial for the rest of the world (Kim 2007: 144). Hence, the protection of Korean civilians was the rhetoric to justify US intervention in the Korean War. In this context of Cold War politics, the mass killings by American soldiers were related to the combination of their deep racism against Koreans and the relative isolation of the incidents. The Korean War was the first war where the United States to participate in nation-building in a post-colonial Third World country without understanding the country's historical complexities or its people's desires. A lack of knowledge of Korea and an unwillingness to learn about the country inevitably led Americans to treat all the Koreans as potential Reds or communists. Through an American eye, Koreans were "gooks" without history. America's accumulated racism through the Pacific War was unleashed in Korea. On the other hand, the US government controlled the Western media tightly at the peak of McCarthyism. As a result, ordinary American citizens rarely knew what really happened on the Korean peninsula and did not question US responsibility for civilian deaths (Kim 2004: 531).

The genocide of Korean civilians was sexualized. During the first few months of the three-year Korean War in 1950, 875 women were reported raped by US soldiers stationed in Seoul (Cho 2008: 67). No one knows how many women were raped by the American soldiers or by any soldiers. Since the Confucian society of Korea highly valued female chastity, many rape cases might have been unreported, many rape victims might have been killed by their rapists, or they committed suicide. Female family members of communists or female communists were especially vulnerable to sexual violence. The systematic rape and forced marriage of these two groups of women was the most visible during the Jeju Massacre (1948–1953), the precursor of the Korean War that killed one tenth of the population of Jeju island. In response to the Jeju people's uprising for economic justice and the unification of North and South Korea in 1948, the US army and the Korean police labeled them as "Reds" and wiped out many mountain villages in the island (Pae 2016: 203).

Furthermore, during the Korean war, the Korean government and the US military systematically ran brothels in the designated areas to control venereal disease and keep up morale among soldiers. Although public prostitution became outlawed in Korea in 1947, the Korean government adopted the Imperial Japanese institution of "comfort stations" during the Pacific War to serve UN Allied Forces and Korean soldiers in the name of "protecting respectable women and rewarding soldiers for their sacrifice" (Moon 2010: 41).

Since their arrival on Korean soil, the US military had fought two wars: one against communism and the other against venereal disease. While venereal disease threatened the soldiers' readiness to fight in the war, the US military could not properly control the soldiers' sexual behaviors (Moon 2010: 51). To control VD among the soldiers, both the US military and the Korean government regulated prostitution rather than abolish it. The effort to control VD failed because the soldiers could take sexual advantage of poor Korean women, mostly war widows and orphans who had multiple dependents (Hong 2007: 181). Although the US Armed Forces restricted the soldiers' contact with local Korean women, the soldiers' attitudes toward the women resembled those of white European colonialists toward the colonized women of color, who were seen as sexually exploitable. Prostitution for American soldiers stationed in Korea was systematized after the Korean War, and has further spread the hypersexualized images of Korean women among Americans. Regardless of their affiliation with any political ideologies, all Korean women during the War were treated as Reds, female enemies, who were sexually available to or to be conquered by American soldiers.

Military prostitution is not different from military rape. Based on the patriarchal assumption that male soldiers' sex drives are uncontrollable, the politicians secretly look for safe commercialized sex to avoid diplomatic conflict caused by military rape and to control VDs among the soldiers simultaneously. In the meantime, systemic rape against enemy women has been the most insidious military tactic to instill fear among enemies and destroy the culture and land of the targeted population because women have been considered the carriers of culture, people, and land through their procreative power. Genocide usually accompanies the systemic rape of women whose bodies turn into battlefields as we have seen in various wars in Germany, Rwanda, the Republic of Congo, Bosnia-Herzegovina, and so forth. In the case of the Korean War, American soldiers' rape of local Korean women and use of military prostitution were interwoven with the soldiers' fear and anxiety, and the otherization of the Korean women as the enemy. Namely, the women's bodies were used to appease the soldiers' fear in the war and perceived as those of the enemies or as warriors' booty.

Race, gender, and sexuality are important tools in analyzing genocide. In the case of the Korean War, civilian massacres were possible because American troops racially and sexually otherized Koreans. Even the term "Red" for a communist is a quasi-racist term to dehumanize communists. Once the civilians are racially and sexually otherized, they become a target to eliminate.

Genocide as a Colonial Legacy

The mass killings of civilians during the Korean War were a learned behavior of military brutality intertwined with colonialism. Considering America's long history of the genocide of American Indians, one would find a parallel between massacres in Korea and those in the United States. Like European settlers in North America, American soldiers in Korea identified with the conquerors rather than with the protectors of civilians. A similar logic applies to the Korean soldiers who mercilessly killed their fellow Koreans labeled as Reds. For instance, Deok-sin Choi, the commander of the Republic of Korea Army's Eleventh Division, initially devised the mission of exterminating guerillas while serving under Chinese General Chiang Kei Shek's corps. Choi's army indiscriminately killed several thousands of unarmed civilians, including babies, women, and elderly people, during the operations entitled "Keeping the Position by Cleansing the Fields." These operations, which were titled as the "three-cleans-all" operations (kill all, burn all, loot all), had been developed by Japanese imperial forces fighting against anti-Japanese leftist rebels in China (Kim 2004: 532).

The horror of civilian massacres did not end with the Korean War. Fifteen years later, Korean troops entered the Vietnam War and used the same tactic of the "three-cleans-all" against Vietnamese civilians (ibid.: 534). The villages were burnt down and looted out. Women had been raped before being killed. Until these days, many Vietnamese remember the cruelty of Korean soldiers. It is not a coincidence that during the Vietnam War, South Korea was ruled by the military dictator Jeong-hee Park, who had been a soldier of the Japanese Imperial Army, fighting against Korean nationalists and Chinese leftist rebels against Japan rule in Manchuria. His regime was willing to send troops to Vietnam and condone Korean soldiers' atrocities toward civilians.

All these stories of genocide cannot be retrieved linearly because future, present, and past wars collapse in the narratives of genocide. This insight gives us the reason that we have to stop any war before it begins because war solves nothing but only to perpetuate the vicious cycle of mass killings.

Genocide: Sovereignty's Right to Kill and Right to Maim

The pile of dead bodies left behind genocide is the spectacular display of sovereignty's necropower. Labeling Korean civilians as Red, American troops controlled the mortality of the Korean population. War and genocide do not merely leave the pile of dead bodies behind but also maimed and psychologically wounded bodies. Namely, the opposite of biopolitics is not necropolitics manifested through death but also maiming that further perpetuates "debilitation," the status of moving toward neither life nor death (Puar 2017: xviii). The dead bodies left by genocide may provoke immediate reactions among bystanders. However, maimed bodies that escaped death but might eventually succumb to death are often neglected after the event of genocide, although maimed bodies are the living palimpsest of genocide.

Furthermore, debilitation was the collective experience of the survivors and their family members of the massacres committed by American troops during the Korean War. Since the victims of American genocide were collectively labeled as Reds, they had been debilitated to speak about their experiences publicly. The Red label has insidiously weakened the Korean public's moral capacity to interrogate the countless deaths of civilians during the Korean War. Since maiming has longer-term effects than death itself, genocide should be understood more broadly as including not only sovereignty's right to kill but also its right to maim the population.

Christian Triumphalism: The Religious Root of America's Militarized Violence

The genocide committed by American troops is linked to the American version of Christian triumphalism. As an ideology, Christian triumphalism, by definition, is "an appeal to the victory over sin, evil, and death by Jesus Christ," and that "Christians share this victory with Christ" (Townes 2006: 90). The Christian rhetoric of triumphalism translates to America's mission as God's chosen nation to save the world. This rhetoric was visible when President Truman declared a national emergency on December 9, 1950. In response to China's entry into the Korean War, Truman proclaimed that if the goal of communist imperialism were achieved, Americans could no longer worship their God or enjoy God's blessings of freedom. He urged Americans to make every possible sacrifice for America's triumph over communism, specifically in the Korean peninsula (Truman 2012: 1938). Truman's declaration shows how he interpreted Christian triumphalism as America's physical and ideological victory over communism.

Since World War II, the United States has been an economic and military hegemon in world politics, participating in almost every armed conflict across the globe. America's global wars would have been impossible without ordinary American citizens' patriotic support. The understanding of patriotism for many Americans has been cast in religious terms: America is God's chosen nation to be the example to the world (Cook 2014: 182). The danger of Christian triumphalism infused with American politics is that ordinary Americans refuse to see the complexities of America's global wars but fall into simple solutions: killing and maiming the enemy.

If America has known its wars through triumphalism, now, the American public should interpret wars through the genocide of civilians and military prostitution. America has carried out its global wars at the cost of the unbearable suffering of civilians, especially in the third world. At the heart of Christianity, as many liberation theologians and ethicists argue, is God's justice, peace, and liberation, the values precisely opposite to sovereignty's right to kill and maim. America's genocide is unstoppable as long as Christianity ideologically feeds America with triumphalism. The American public, especially American Christians, should not allow the smallest part of the Christian doctrine of triumphalism to take over Christianity or America's foreign policy.

Toward a Politics of Love

Genocide makes up many palimpsests of America's war stories. These palimpsests can connect the survivors and bystanders of genocide transgenerationally and transnationally who can, in return, create a power of resistance against sovereignty's right to kill and maim. The future study of genocide and war needs to read historically specific genocide stories across the world more holistically, questioning how their palimpsests communicate with one another traversing time and space.

In search of transnational and transgenerational solidarity for global peace, I propose feminist spiritual activism as a counternarrative to a politics of killing. Feminist spiritual activism will be considered at three stages: first, empathy through a feminist story-telling method, second, interconnectedness with independence, and third, shared political goals for peace as a guideline for interfaith resistance against militarism. These three stages correspond to my imaginative dialogue between Dorothee Soelle and Sister Chan Khong.

Dorothee Soelle was a German theologian who theologized human suffering, caused by unjust social structures such as war and callous capitalism. Her childhood memories of World War II motivated her to denounce war and militarism and appreciate non-violent peace activism found both in Christianity and Buddhism. Sister Chan Khong is Zen Master Thich Nhat Hahn's beloved disciple. With Nhat Hanh, she was involved in the Buddhist peace movement in South Vietnam before the Vietnam War, the anti-Vietnam War movement during the war, and the resettlement of Vietnamese refugees, known as "Boat People." Although Soelle and Chan Khong did not meet in person, their faith-based peace activism shares similar visions and strategies.

Empathy and a Story-telling Method

Women's experiences of militarized violence such as military prostitution, wartime rape, and genocide should be stopped. However, in what way can these experiences inform interfaith dialogue for peace? In other words, how can we read the palimpsestic stories of women's resistance to militarism, denouncement of military rape and military prostitution, and courageous activism for peace? These question lead me to first revisit a story-telling method integrated in Dorothee Soelle's and Sister Chan Khong's peace activism.

The story-telling method used by Dorothee Soelle and Sister Chan Khong has two purposes: (1) to empathize suffering with the sufferers; and (2) to invite empathic empowerment from Christian and Buddhist mystics, teachers, and peace activists. These particular aspects of the story-telling method allude to human experiences of suffering as the ground for interfaith dialogue for peace. The stories of human suffering reveal the brutality of war and subsequently create counternarratives to the stories that glorify war. The stories of concrete human beings who survived genocide and military prostitution expose the realities of militarized suffering and thus, create an interfaith dialogue without reducing human beings of flesh and blood into the grand narratives of war or the doctrines of war and peace (i.e., America's military triumph over communism in the Korean Peninsula and its military presence in South Korea for peace and security in East Asia). By listening to others' stories, we actively respond to human suffering rather than become numb to suffering (Soelle 1975: 154). Namely, not only the pile of dead bodies left behind the war but also the survivors' will to life reveal human suffering, and, more importantly, the power of life itself.

Second, the story-telling method does not attempt to find commonality or universality among people with diverse religious backgrounds and experiences. Rather, the method from a feminist perspective highlights the particularities and diversity of people's experiences of suffering and liberation. For instance, the suffering of Korean women caused by the Korean War is not perfectly aligned with that of Vietnamese women whose bodies remember rape and genocide during the Vietnam War. These two groups of women, however, can empathetically understand each other's suffering. Their stories can be read together as the palimpsests of America's wars in Asia. Recently, the Korean Council for the Women Drafted for Military Sexual Slavery by Japan visited Vietnam and met the female survivors of rape by Korean soldiers during the Vietnam War. Through multiple meetings with Vietnamese female survivors, the Council searched for possible reconciliation between Vietnam and Korea, the Korean government's official apology for its soldiers' systemic rape of Vietnamese women, and reparations for the victims. Although their perpetrators and war contexts are different, both Korean and Vietnamese women denounced military rape by sharing their stories of suffering and survival wisdom (Park 2017).

Third, the story-telling method can create a space where religiously diverse people empathetically embrace one another's suffering and experience healing and transformation. Through this process, those who participate in interfaith dialogue may experience Dorothee Soelle's notion of the "mystical sense of becoming one," namely, "difference is acknowledged but not absolutized in the destruction of community" (Soelle 2001: 262).

Interdependence

Both Soelle and Sister Chan Khong can practice "empathy," thanks to their contemplation of interconnectedness, interdependence, or inter-being among all living beings. However, a heartfelt understanding of interconnectedness needs feminist constructive criticism. According to Gloria Steinem,

> Talking about interdependence is almost dangerous for women because it is easy to believe that connectedness, the empathy we treasure is so easy to confuse dependence, empathy sickness. We know others' feelings better than our feelings. It is bred so much in us. How important it is that we celebrate independence first. We can't get to interdependence until we experience independence.
> (Steinem 2004: 77–79)

Solle and Chan Khong put their spiritual understanding of interdependence into interfaith peace activism. And yet, they articulate *independence* of human beings as their discerning will to practice their respective religious teachings of resistance to militarism.

The Buddhist teaching of interconnectedness enables Sister Chan Khong to play an active part in peace activism with Christians rather than only talk about religious dogmas, which would not save the dying people in Vietnam. For her, religions are interdependent on one another for their existence, enlightenment, human suffering, and ultimately peace of the world. Sister Chan Khong accentuates that religious peace comes through interfaith peace activism. As Christians and Buddhists work together for peace, they practice their respective religious teachings of love and compassion as well as experience the deeper meanings of those teachings living here and now. Her activist approach to interfaith dialogue comes from her experience of Buddhist-Christian conflict that escalated in post-colonial Vietnam (Chan Khong 2006: 77-79).

Soelle's articulation on resistance to violence as the heart of mysticism grew out of her interfaith dialogue. Taking Thich Nhat Hanh's teaching of interconnectedness seriously, Soelle emphasizes that the root of violence is the "dissociation of the I" (Soelle 2001: 263). Therefore, violence is overcome when the belief in the I is expanded and transposed until one finally lives "recognizing oneself in everything." This particular quote from Soelle can apply to the social healing of the survivors. If due to fear among people, genocide debilitates not only the survivors of genocide and brutal military violence but also society to publicly speak about their experiences or against militarized violence, "recognizing oneself in everything" can enable the society to break down the fear and silence fed by the military power. The radical recognition of the I in everything breaks down the separation between bystanders and victims.

Furthermore, both Sister Chan Khong and Dorothee Soelle suggest the power of interconnectedness as resistance to the dualistic boundary between us and them as well as the oppressed and the oppressors (Chan Khong 2006: 82-92; Soelle 1975: 178). This does not mean that we ignore oppression or blindly forgive oppressors. We must name and analyze oppression. Naming and resisting oppression come from one's inner power, one's discerning will not to cooperate with the existing world's status quo. In addition, empathy of suffering is the Bodhisattva path or an active form of resistance to "apathy of suffering" (Soelle 2006: 104). Soelle writes that through empathy, one mystically experiences the oneness of joy and suffering which shines forth from the agony present in many experiences of suffering free of numbness (ibid.: 106). In order to resist the destructive power of suffering, one must nurture inner peace and strength, which is possible through their faiths. This active action would be continuously renewed and refreshed if we courageously let other people's suffering flow into our hearts and vice versa; we must let their hope and dreams flow into our hearts even in the midst of suffering and vice versa. The process of courageously embracing others' suffering challenges us to rememorialize the suffering of history's victims (e.g., victims of genocide) who left the fragments, whispers, and palimpsests of the ruins of war.

Feminist Spiritual Activism: A Politics of Love

These two religious women's spirituality and peace activism lead me to propose feminist spiritual activism as an active form of a politics of love. Feminist spiritual activism first assumes that one's inner peace and global peace through social transformation are not mutually exclusive. Therefore, religious faith and dialogue for peace do not function, as Dorothee Soelle says, "within a depoliticized, privatized piety" (Soelle 2001: 285). In our excessively militarized world led by the United States, feminist spiritual activism resists privatized and commercialized spirituality, which only aims to make one feel good about oneself without being aware of suffering present in millions of people's lives. Feminist spiritual activism makes one feel agonized by others' suffering but simultaneously allows one to experience joy and inner-peace through resisting militarized violence, the cause of human suffering. For this reason, interfaith dialogue must be aware of and agonized by women's particular suffering caused by military violence and yet it also must send out a global invitation to joy and inner-peace in resistance to militarism.

Second, feminist spiritual activism rooted in interconnectedness approaches peace in a holistic way. Peace is present among us when we attempt to eliminate the roots of oppression, such as patriarchal militarism, which denies women's full humanity. Both Christian and Buddhist feminists understand that women's true liberation comes only when the roots of oppression are eradicated. Here, we may consider Christian and Buddhist feminist solidarity for peace. Solidarity is not created upon the assumption of an enforced commonality of oppression, but on the shared political goal to eradicate the roots of oppression. Both Soelle and Sister Chang Khong demonstrate that solidarity does not come from our same experiences of suffering, but rather from empathy with sufferers, and our choice to eradicate oppression (i.e., militarism).

Interfaith dialogue which is attentive to women's particular suffering from military violence should utilize the power of empathy so that people of faiths can share politicals goals for peace. For this, we should continue to analyze the gendered assumptions within interfaith dialogue for peace and its impact by asking how this dialogue will affect the relationships between women and men globally or locally or on both levels.[4] A gender conscious approach to interfaith activism for peace is important in the face of Christian triumphalism. Christian triumphalism which emphasizes "winning" over the enemy, including non-Christians, is a highly masculinized ideology, marked with aggression, competition, and rationality. In contrast, empathy-based interfaith peace activism invites vulnerability into our lives by sharing one another's suffering, and navigates the uncertain future (not victory) through shared wisdom. Hence, religious feminists continue to challenge their respective traditions to overcome the gender biases embedded in religious teachings and practices. Gender-based military violence such as military rape and prostitution is intertwined with women's status in their respective societies and cultures. Once war breaks out, discrimination and dehumanization of women become escalated, unless we filter sexism in our religions, societies, and interfaith dialogue.

Finally, feminist spiritual activism as a politics of love can be manifested through multiple forms, just as Dorothee Soelle and Sister Chan Khong utilize narratives, poetry, silent meditation, peace rallies, and eating and living with others in their interfaith peace activism. The various religious forms of celebrating life can further create activism against the destructive power of militarism as well as overcome the verbal communication-dominated interfaith dialogue for peace.

Conclusion

Taking America's war and military presence in the Korean Peninsula as a case study, this chapter delineates how interfaith peace activism or a politics of love can overcome a politics of death manifested by war. The genocide of civilians and military prostitution are considered the two characteristics of America's transnational militarism particularly in the Korean peninsula. How to retrieve the haunted memories of racialized and sexualized war and how to resist militarized violence are the main objects of this chapter. African postcolonialist Achille Mbembe's idea of "necropolitics," and transnational feminist M. Jacqui Alexander's concept of time as a "palimpsest" offer the theoretical lens in retrieving and analyzing the haunted memories of war. An imagined interfaith dialogue between Christian feminist theologian Dorothee Soelle and Zen Buddhist peace activist Sister Chan Khong suggests the feminist praxis of peacemaking, or a politics of love, counteracting war and militarism.

Today feminist spiritual activism is necessary because of the amount of violence, and thus suffering, affecting so many people worldwide. Currently there are approximately thirty major conflicts happening in nineteen countries including Afghanistan, Iraq, and Syria (Murray 2008: 135–136). The majority of civilian victims killed and maimed in these wars are women and children. They also make up 80 percent of those who have fled their homes because of conflict and human rights violations. Although women are major non-combatant victims in all forms of warfare, be it international, internal, religious, ethnic, or nationalistic they remain invisible. Gender-based sexual violence has increasingly become a weapon "of warfare and one of the defining characteristics of contemporary armed conflict" (United Nations 2002: 3). I hope interfaith feminist spiritual activism or a politics of love will bring concrete hope for peace in these women's lives and make them visible before it is too late.

Keun-Joo Christine Pae is associate professor and chair of the Religion Department in Denison University, Ohio, USA. Taking social ethics as a discipline, Pae researches and teaches ethics of peace and war, feminist peacemaking, interfaith spiritual activism, transnational militarism, military prostitution, and Asian/Asian-American ethics.

Notes

1. War can be defined in various ways. This chapter considers war only in terms of the state power, namely, the state's authorized violence against a certain group of people or other nation.

2. Korea won independence over Imperial Japan on August 15, 1945. On September 8, 1945, the US Twenty-Fourth Army Corps, consisting of some 72,000 soldiers, who were led by Lieutenant-General John R. Hodge, commanding general of the US Armed Forces in Korea, arrived to transfer power from the Japanese colonial empire. Due to the sudden surrender of Japan, General Douglas MacArthur selected the units to deploy from Okinawa to South Korea on the basis of availability and transport, but not expertise. The main purpose of this deployment is to stop the Soviet Union from expanding its power to Northeast Asia of which armies were already present in the north of the 38th parallel of the Korean Peninsula, disarming Japanese soldiers. Differently from the Soviet Union that did not attempt to establish its occupant government in North Korea but led North Koreans to take the class revolution, the United States immediately founded its military government and would rule over the southern part of the Korean Peninsula officially until 1948 (Moon 2010: 40–41; Rose 1976: 98–101).
3. Among an estimated 300,000–430,000 prostitutes during the war, 150,000–200,000 were widows.
4. Modified from Enloe's gender impact analysis. Cynthia (Enloe 2007: 13).

References

Alexander, M. Jacqui. 2005. *Pedagogies of Crossing: Meditations on Feminism, Sexual Politics, Memory, and the Sacred*. Durham, NC: Duke University Press. https://doi.org/10.1215/9780822386988

Chan Khong. 2006. *Learning True Love*. Berkeley, CA: Parallax.

Cho, Grace. 2008. *Haunting the Korean Diaspora: Shame, Secrecy, and the Forgotten War*. Minneapolis, MN: University of Minnesota Press.

Cook, Martin L. 2014. "United States I." In *Religion in the Military Worldwide*, edited by Ron Hassner, 181–195. Cambridge: Cambridge University Press. https://doi.org/10.1017/CBO9781139583428.013

Enloe, Cynthia. 2007. *Globalization and Militarism: Feminists Make the Link*. Lanham, MD: Rowman & Littlefield Publishing.

Hong, Seong-cheol. 2007. *YuGawkUi YeokSa* [*History of YuGwak*]. Seoul: Paper Road.

Kim, Dong Choon. 2004. "Forgotten War, Forgotten Massacres: The Korean War (1950–1953) as Licensed Mass Killings." *Journal of Genocide Research* 6(4): 523–544. https://doi.org/10.1080/1462352042000320592

Kim, Gi-jin. 2006. *The Korean War and Mass Killings* [*HanGukJeonJaengGwa JipDanHakSal*]. Seoul: PuReun Yeoksa.

Kim, Jodi. 2007. *Ends of Empire: Asian American Critique and the Cold War*. Minneapolis, MN: University of Minnesota Press.

LaDuke, Winona. 2012. *The Militarization of Indian Country*. Ann Arbor, MI: Michigan State University Press.

Lee, Jin-kyung. 2010. *Service Economies: Militarism, Sex Work and Migrant Labor in South Korea*. Minneapolis, MN: University of Minnesota Press.

Mbembe, Achille. 2003. "Necropolitics." *Public Culture* 15(1): 11–40. https://doi.org/10.1215/08992363-15-1-11

Moon, Seungsook. 2010. "Regulating Desire, Managing the Empire: US Military Prostitution in South Korea, 1945–1970." In *Over There: Living with the US Military Empire from World War Two to the Present*, edited by Maria Hohn and Seungsook Moon, 39–78. Durham, NC: Duke University Press. https://doi.org/10.1215/9780822393283-003

Murray, Anne Firth. 2008. *From Outrage to Courage: Women Taking Action for Health and Justice*. Monroe, ME: Common Courage Press.

Pae, Keun-Joo Christine. 2016. "Faith-Based Popular Resistance to the Naval Base in Gangjeong of Jeju: Transforming US-Korea Relations for Peace and Justice." In *Critical Theology against US Militarism in Asia: Decolonization and Deimperialization*, edited by Nami Kim and Wonhee Anne Joh, 199–226. New York: Palgrave Macmillan. https://doi.org/10.1057/978-1-137-48013-2_9

Park, Sujin. 2017. "The Korean Council for the Women Drafted for Military Sexual Slavery by Japan Apologizes to Vietnamese Women for Korean Soldiers' Raping Women during the Vietnam War." *HanGyeoRei News Paper*, September 14. Retrieved from www.hani.co.kr/arti/PRINT/811073.html (accessed September 18, 2019).

Puar, Jasbir. 2017. *The Right to Maim: Debility, Capacity, and Disability*. Durham, NC: Duke University Press. https://doi.org/10.1215/9780822372530

Rose, Lisle. 1976. *Roots of Tragedy: The United States and the Struggle for Asia, 1945–1953*. Westport, CT: Greenwood Press.

Shin, Gi-cheol. 2014. *Gukmineun Jeogi Anida* [*The People Are Not the Enemy: Searching for the Missing Connection between the Korean War and Civilian Massacres*]. Seoul: Hertz 9.

Soelle, Dorothee. 1975. *Suffering*. Philadelphia, PA: Fortress Press.

Soelle, Dorothee. 2001. *The Silent Cry*. Minneapolis, MN: Augsburg Fortress.

Soelle, Dorothee. 2006. "Oneness of Joy and Suffering." In *Dorothee Soelle: Essential Writings*, selected by Dianne Oliver, 99–106. Maryknoll, NY: Orbis Books.

Steinem, Gloria. 2004. "Declaration of Interdependence." Retrieved from http://eomega.org/popups/wi_videos.html?file=WAP_Steinam.flv (accessed September 20, 2019).

Thich Nhat Hanh. 1999. *Please Call Me by My True Names*. Berkeley, CA: Parallax Press.

Townes, Emilie. 2006. *Womanist Ethics and the Cultural Production of Evil*. New York: Palgrave Macmillan. https://doi.org/10.1057/9780230601628

Truman, Harry. 2012. "A Declaration of National Emergency, December 16, 1950." In *Almanac of American Military History*, edited by Spencer Tucker, vol. 3, pp. 1938–1939. Santa Barbara, CA: ABC-CLIO.

United Nations. 2002. *The Impact of Violent Conflict on Women and Girls*. New York: United Nations.

12

The Qur'an, the Bible, and the Indigenous Peoples of Canaan: An Anti-Colonial Muslim Reading

Shadaab Rahemtulla

It is Our Will to bestow Our grace upon the downtrodden of the Earth, and to make them the leaders and to make them the inheritors of the Earth. And to establish them securely on the Earth, and to let Pharaoh and Haman and their hosts experience through them (the Israelites) the very thing against which they sought to protect themselves.

—Qur'an 28.5-6

Introduction

The Exodus—the story of the liberation of the ancient Israelites from Egyptian bondage—is a central point of reference in Christian liberation theology. The Peruvian priest Gustavo Gutiérrez, a foundational figure in Latin American liberation theology, considered the Exodus a "paradigmatic" experience, representing a radical lens with which to reread both the Old and New Testaments (Gutiérrez [1971] 1973: 159–160). What is so compelling about the Exodus to liberation theologians is its ability to capture the justice and compassion of a deity who intervenes in human history to stand in solidarity with the oppressed. Consider the following passage from the Book of Exodus:

> I have seen the miserable state of my people in Egypt. I have heard their appeal to be free of their slave-drivers. Yes, I am well aware of their sufferings. ... And now the cry of the sons of Israel has come to me, and I have witnessed the way in which the Egyptians oppress them (Exod. 3.7,9).
>
> (Boff and Boff [1986] 1999: 44)

To be sure, all Christian liberation theologies, as *Christian* theologies, are based principally on the figure of Jesus Christ, whose suffering presence is found, it is argued, not in the affluent center of society but among the poor, the outcast (Rowland 2007: 12). Yet it is difficult to overstate the prominence of the Exodus. In their introduction to liberation theology, the Brazilian theologians Leonardo and Clodovis Boff provide a listing of scriptural texts "most appreciated by liberation theology," and it is telling that the Book of Exodus tops that list, preceding even the Gospels (Boff and Boff [1986] 1999: 34–35). The Exodus has been as significant a paradigm in Black Theology, which is intuitive, of course, given the American context of slavery. Paralleling his Latin American counterparts, James Cone—the pioneering scholar of Black Theology—emphasizes that the Exodus reflects God's participation in human history. Indeed, it is nothing less than "a revelatory event" in which God disclosed Him/Herself not just to humankind in general but to the oppressed group in particular (Cone [1970] 2010: 48–49), thereby displaying a preferential option for that group. According to Cone, the Exodus constitutes "the most significant revelatory act in the Old Testament" and the "history of Israel is a history of God's election of a special, oppressed people" (Cone [1969] 2011: 64). The Exodus can also be found in Asian liberation theologies, such as Minjung Theology in Korea. Here, the Exodus became a "revolutionary paradigm," attaining such influence among Korean Christians that the occupying Japanese forces actually banned the Book of Exodus (Wielenga 2007: 63–64).

Indigenous thinkers, however, have challenged the liberative character of the Exodus. The Native American scholar Robert Warrior points out that the depiction of the Exodus as an act of divine solidarity with the oppressed is incomplete (Warrior 1989: 262), leaving out a large chunk of the story: namely, the Israelite conquest of Canaan and the ensuing destruction of its indigenous inhabitants. To quote Warrior's words:

> As a member of the Osage Nation of American Indians who stands in solidarity with other tribal people around the world, I read the Exodus stories with Canaanite eyes. And, it is the Canaanite side of the story that has been overlooked by those seeking to articulate theologies of liberation. Especially ignored are those parts of the story that describe Yahweh's [God's] command to mercilessly annihilate the indigenous population.
>
> (Warrior 1989: 262)

To clarify, in his critique of the Exodus, Warrior is not dismissing liberation theology or Christianity as a whole. Instead, he stresses that (liberation) theology needs to be done from the vantage point of indigenous peoples and their lived experiences (ibid.: 264). To use the phrasing from the above passage, theology needs to be reread through "Canaanite eyes." The Palestinian intellectual Edward Said has also challenged the Exodus paradigm, focusing on the work of the Jewish American political theorist Michael Walzer. The Exodus, according to Walzer, represents a "paradigm of revolutionary politics" (Walzer 1985: 7) that has exerted a formative impact on Western political thought. Indeed, he even goes so far as to claim that, in the political history of the West, "revolution has often been imagined as an enactment of the Exodus" (ibid.: ix). Paralleling Warrior, Said lambasts Walzer for his selective engagement with the Exodus, glossing over God's commandment to destroy the local inhabitants of Canaan (Said 1986: 91).[1] It is this glaring omission that allows Walzer to portray the Exodus in such a progressive light. The underlying problem with the Exodus narrative, Said points out, is its sectarianism: the justice of God seems to be reserved for the Israelites alone, while the Canaanites stand outside the moral purview of the text (ibid.: 92–93).

And this is where I come in as a Muslim liberation theologian and scholar of the Qur'an. I am following Warrior's and Said's anti-colonial critique and, all the while, reflecting on my own scripture. The Israelites' liberation from Pharaoh, after all, is also an influential trope in Islamic liberation theology, most notably in the writings of the South African anti-apartheid activist Farid Esack.[2] A pioneering voice in the field, Esack argues that the Exodus is a model not simply of social liberation, but also of religious pluralism, for in the Qur'an God stands in solidarity with the oppressed Israelites despite their continuous displays of disbelief (Esack 1997: 98–99, 195). In other words, this is a deity who makes a preferential option for the oppressed simply by virtue of being oppressed, irrespective of their faith. But what, I wondered, does the Qur'an have to say about the *other* side of the Exodus: the Israelite encounter with the land of Canaan and its inhabitants? Does the Qur'anic account mirror the biblical one? Did a mass genocide take place and, if so, was this a result of divine sanction? That is, did the God of justice become the God of empire? By unpacking and contrasting the biblical and Qur'anic accounts, I will demonstrate that the narrative of a military conquest is, significantly, absent in the Qur'an: at no point does God command the Israelites to attack the indigenous people of the land. Furthermore, I will show how the Old Testament narrative profoundly shaped Muslim understandings of the Qur'anic account, as various Muslim commentators drew on the *isra'iliyat* (biblical) literature when expounding the Qur'an. In so doing, they basically produced a narrative of conquest and dispossession where it did not previously exist.

Method and Terminology

Critical textual analysis is my prime methodology, carefully examining what exactly the scriptural texts say and, just as importantly, do *not* say, that is, their silences. Textual silence matters; it cannot be taken for granted.[3] The Qur'an and the Bible are the two key texts that I examine. As a believing Muslim, I approach the Qur'an as the Word of God (*kalamallah*). Its words are authoritative and binding. I do not approach the Bible in such a manner. But while the Bible does not carry any religious authority for me, I devote attention to it because, as stated earlier, the Bible has deeply shaped Muslim understandings of what transpired in the Holy Land. The *tafsir* tradition (the millennium-old tradition of Qur'anic commentary) is crucial in fleshing out these understandings. I have drawn on a number of leading commentators, from pre-modern and contemporary times. These include the Meccan 'Abdullah ibn 'Abbas (d. 687), one of the earliest commentators and a revered cousin of Prophet Muhammad; the Persian Abu Ja'far al-Tabari (d. 923), arguably the most influential commentator in the entire tradition; the Syrian Isma'il b. Kathir (d. 1373), who lived in the Mamluk era; the Egyptians Jalal al-Din al-Mahalli (d. 1459) and his student Jalal al-Din al-Suyuti (d. 1505), who collectively produced *Tafsir Jalalayn* (literally, the Commentary of the Two Jalals); the leading Islamist thinkers Sayyid Qutb (d. 1966) from Egypt and Abul A'la Mawdudi (d. 1979) from Pakistan, whose commentaries on the Qur'an have attained mass readerships in the contemporary Muslim world (Zaman 2002: 39); the Iranian Muhammad Husayn al-Tabataba'i (d. 1981), coming from a Shi'a Twelver background; and, finally, the Austro-Hungarian convert Muhammad

Asad (d. 1992), whose famous English translation of the Qur'an is, in fact, a substantial commentary in its own right, including copious notes and reflections on the Qur'an. To clarify, this article is not about the commentarial tradition. In select parts, I draw on these commentaries—that is, where they have something to say about the Israelite encounter with the Holy Land—in order to explore how Muslims have historically understood certain verses. Moreover, I do not view these commentaries as authoritative or binding, since their ontological character is fundamentally different from the Qur'an. These are works produced by fallible (however insightful) human beings, and therefore reflect limited horizons and contextual realities. For me, it is the Word of God—not the words of humans—that ultimately and authoritatively defines what is *Islamic*, and what is not.

But I am no different, of course, from other Qur'anic commentators: as a human being, I too have limited, contextual horizons. It is only fitting, therefore, that I unpack the "baggage" that I bring to the interpretive table. Firstly, I do not subscribe to the myth of neutrality, since no reader can exist in a social vacuum. As a reader, I bring various subjectivities rooted in my own lived realities of race, religion, class, and gender, among other factors. Secondly, I have been deeply influenced by liberation theology, which (re)conceptualizes theology as "critical reflection on historical praxis," seeking not simply to reflect on religious texts for the sake of reflection alone but to do so as part of a broader liberationist project of societal transformation (Gutiérrez [1971] 1973: 15). It is this manifestly political commitment to social justice (*praxis*) that becomes the framework, the point of departure for interpretation. Thirdly, I am an anti-colonial reader. As a Muslim of Indian descent, I have been shaped by the exploits of empire, especially Euro-American imperialism in the global South—of which the Muslim world is a significant component—and popular, grassroots resistance to it. My own anti-colonial activism has focused on resisting settler colonialism, specifically the Israeli occupation of Palestine. Simultaneously, as a Canadian from Vancouver/Coast Salish Territories, I stand in solidarity with the struggles of the indigenous peoples of Canada, and of indigenous peoples across the world. So when I look at the Israelite (not to be confused with the modern-day *Israeli*, as there is no connection between the two, their distance spanning thousands of years) encounter with the Holy Land, I am asking if the Qur'anic representation, produced in late antiquity, is compatible with my own anti-colonial sensibilities as a contemporary reader?

Finally, a note on terminology: what exactly is "settler colonialism"? Settler colonialism is a specific form of colonialism, seeking not merely to dominate another people's territory from without but "to replace the original population of the colonized territory with a new society of settlers (usually from the colonial metropole)" (LeFevre 2015). This process of replacement is often achieved through genocide. Article II of the UN Convention on the Prevention and Punishment of the Crime of Genocide (1948) defines genocide as including any of the following acts targeted at a particular group, whether religious, ethnic, racial or national:

(a) Killing members of the group;

(b) Causing serious bodily or mental harm to members of the group;

(c) Deliberately inflicting on the group conditions of life calculated to bring about its physical destruction in whole or in part;

(d) Imposing measures intended to prevent births within the group;

(e) Forcibly transferring children of the group to another group.

(UN 1948)

To be sure, the settler colonial project of replacing the indigenous population is a complex one. Settler colonialism's "logic of elimination" (Wolfe 2006: 387)—as the scholar Patrick Wolfe calls it—can entail outright genocide but also extends to more institutionalized forms of domination. These include forced religious conversion; deploying the (settler) legal system to seize indigenous land, breaking it down into individual freeholds for sale; separating indigenous children from their families and resocializing them in boarding schools (a tactic alluded to in the above UN definition); and officially promoting interbreeding between groups in order to dilute their ethnic identities, thereby assimilating them into the wider settler population (ibid.: 388).

The Bible and the Conquest of Canaan

Before unpacking the conquest of Canaan in the Bible, it is important to clarify, at the very outset, that the biblical narrative does not line up with the archaeological evidence of what historically transpired. In his classic study—*The Tribes of Yahweh: A Sociology of the Religion of Liberated Israel, 1250-1050 BCE* (1979)—the American biblical scholar Norman Gottwald argued that a conquest did not take place and that early Israelite society was actually comprised largely of indigenous Canaanites (Gottwald 1973: xxiii). According to Gottwald, a small group of former slaves from Egypt arrived in Canaan, bringing with them a radical theology of Yahwism, premised on a singular deity who promises deliverance to the oppressed. As the existing society in Canaan was sharply hierarchal, this Yawhist theology naturally spoke to the marginalized Canaanite classes based in the rural highlands, who then coalesced with the Yahwist group and rebelled against their urban overlords (ibid.: 214). In other words, Israel emerged from a social rupture *within* Canaanite society (ibid.: xxiii). While the thesis of an alliance between an incoming band of radical Yahwists and the existing Canaanite underclass is debatable, there is now an established consensus among biblical archaeologists—based on housing, clothing, pottery, and linguistic evidence from the time—that the population of early Israel (that is, between 1200 and 1000 BCE) was "overwhelmingly indigenous"; that it emerged from civil strife within Canaanite society; and that early Israel can be viewed as "a rural group of Canaanites" (Brett 2008: 4). This suggests that the conquest narrative was constructed, as a founding mythology of the Israelite state, at a much later point in that state's history. For instance, the text Deuteronomy 20, in which the Israelites are instructed to invade and exterminate the indigenous population of Canaan, was actually produced in the 600s BCE (ibid.: 4),[4] and thus centuries after the state's founding.

That being said, the biblical narrative *matters,* as it has been deployed to legitimate imperial conquest, especially in the modern era. Warrior, while acknowledging the historical value of Gottwald's revisionist scholarship, has pointed out that the Canaan narrative has taken on a powerful, colonial afterlife of its own, exerting lasting consequences on indigenous peoples:

> ... scholarly agreement should not allow us to breathe a sigh of relief. For, historical knowledge does not change the status of the indigenes in the narrative and the theology that grows out of it. ... People who read the narratives read them as they are, not as scholars and experts would like them to be read and interpreted. History is no longer with us. The narrative remains.
>
> (Warrior 1989: 262)

Consider the title of the "first epic poem" of the US colonial period: *The Conquest of Canaan* (1774), composed by Reverend Timothy Dwight, who would later serve as president of Yale College (Schechla 2005: 328). This eleven-volume poem reflects the extent to which the conquest narratives influenced the early American colonists, representing indigenous Americans as "fiendish, wolflike Canaanites," England as Pharaonic Egypt, and the American colonies as Israel (ibid.: 337–338). Indeed, it was commonplace for Christian preachers at the time to refer to the indigenous peoples as Canaanites and Amalekites (Warrior 1989: 264). The American colonies are just one example of how the biblical narrative of Canaan has been used to justify European imperial projects across the world. Michael Prior's comparative study—*The Bible and Colonialism: A Moral Critique* (1997)—is worth highlighting here, as he examines the role of the Canaan narrative in colonial discourses in Latin America in the fifteenth century, South Africa in the seventeenth century, and Palestine in the twentieth century (Prior 1997: 43–44).

So what, precisely, is the biblical narrative? Following the Exodus from Egypt and the revelations on Mount Sinai, the Israelites journey to the edge of the land of Canaan. In preparation for an invasion, God commands Moses to send twelve men (one from each Israelite tribe) to spy out the land and its inhabitants, and to report back with their findings (Num. 13.1-2).[5] The spies survey the land for forty days (Num. 13.25). On their return, they report that the land is fertile and rich, flowing with "milk and honey" (Num. 13.27). They also discover that the inhabitants are "strong, and the cities are fortified and very large" (Num. 13.30). With the exceptions of Caleb the son of Jephunneh and Joshua the son of Nun, whose belief is unshaken by God's command to invade Canaan, the spies are disillusioned by the manifest strength of the Canaanites. This is not a fight they want to start. In order to ensure that the rest of the Israelites agree with them, they exaggerate their findings. In their words: "[Canaan is] a place that devours its inhabitants, and all the people that we saw in it are of great height ... we seemed to ourselves like grasshoppers, and so we seemed to them" (Num. 13.32-33). The spies are successful in their endeavor. The report leads to an uproar among the Israelites, who adamantly refuse to enter the land that God promised them. They go so far as to exclaim that they would have preferred to die in Egypt, and they even consider appointing another leader to replace Moses and returning to Egypt (Num. 14.2-3). In light of the numerous miracles that Moses had performed, through God's will, for the Israelites in Egypt—from the ten plagues to the parting of the sea—God is enraged by the Israelite response and wants to destroy them for their lack of faith and gratitude, but Moses swiftly intervenes on behalf of his people, seeking God's mercy (Num. 14.12-19). Fortunately for the Israelites, God accepts Moses' plea. Instead of destroying them, He condemns them to wander in the wilderness for forty years—basically, one for each day that the spies surveyed the land of Canaan (Num. 14.34). In other words, the punishment of wandering in the wilderness is actually a form of divine mercy. The idea is that that insolent generation (and only that generation) who witnessed the miraculous events of Egypt and yet still grumbled and lost faith at the border of Canaan, will live out their days in the wilderness, while the next generation will eventually enter the Promised Land (Num. 14.29-31), the sole exceptions being Caleb and Joshua (Num. 14.30),[6] who remained true to God all along.

Canaan thus re-emerges in the narrative after the passing of the mandated forty years. The new generation of Israelites are given permission to return to the border of Canaan and are commanded to conquer the land. They hear and obey. The narrative catalogues a series of military victories, first in the East Bank of the Jordan River and then the West Bank. To be sure, there are some discrepancies within the biblical texts: in the Book of Joshua, for example, the conquest is portrayed as a "Blitzkrieg," as a rapid and efficient military expedition, while in the Book of Judges we get a more gradualist story, shifting between successes and failures (Prior 1997: 32-34). But, by and large, the Old Testament books paint a picture of a bloody massacre, in which the natives of the land are wiped out. This process begins with the East Bank, including the defeat of King Og—the King of Bashan—and the killing off of his people "until he had no survivor left" (Num. 21.33-35; Deut. 3.3), and the defeat of Sihon, King of the Amorites (Num. 21.34). With regard to the latter, the Israelites "devoted to destruction every city, men, women, and children, leaving no survivors" (Deut. 2.33-34). Upon crossing the Jordan River into the West Bank, Jericho is the first city to fall. Here, the Israelites "devoted all in the city to destruction, both men and women, young and old, oxen, sheep, and donkeys, with the edge of the sword. ... And they burned the city with fire, and everything in it" (Josh. 6.21-24).

Ai is the next city to fall, with the Israelites killing "both men and women" (Josh. 8.25), and refusing to lay down their swords until they had "devoted all the inhabitants of Ai to destruction" (Josh. 8.26). This pattern of carnage continues as Israel sacks various cities in Southern Canaan, such as Libnah, Lachish, Gezer, Eglon, Hebron, and Debir, massacring everyone in these cities (Josh. 10.29-40). This is followed by the fall of cities in northern Canaan, including Hazor, Madon, Shimron, and Achshaph, whose people are also massacred (Josh. 11.11-15). Under Joshua, Israel defeats a total of thirty-one kings (Josh. 12.7-24).[7] Following the conquest, the land is allotted to the twelve Israelite tribes. The Book of Joshua, in exhaustive detail, lays out the different "inheritances" that each tribe receives, devoting a lengthy section to each tribe's land allotment: 9½ tribes inherit in the West Bank and 2½ tribes inherit in the East Bank (Josh. 13.8-21.45).[8] The narrative begins and ends with the land; it is settler colonialism at its best. It is important to add here that the Israelites did not just seize land, but also gold and silver—which they never destroyed but stockpiled—as well as livestock. They only killed the livestock in select cities, such as Jericho. Following the conquest of Canaan, here is what Joshua says to the tribes of Reuben, Gad, and the half-tribe of Manasseh, who had, early on in the conquest, expressed their preference for land in the East Bank but still crossed the Jordan to fight for Israel in the West Bank: "Go back to your tents with much wealth and with very much livestock, with silver, gold, bronze, and iron, and with much clothing. Divide the spoil of your enemies with your brothers" (Josh. 22.8).

What is perhaps most disturbing within the biblical narrative is that these acts of violence are divinely sanctioned. God explicitly commands the Israelites to drive out the inhabitants of the land and/or to destroy them outright. With regard to the former, God states in the Book of Numbers: "you shall drive out all the inhabitants of the land before you" (Num. 33.52), warning that if the Israelites fail to heed this command and allow the local inhabitants to live alongside them, they will become like "barbs in your eyes and thorns in your side" (Num. 33.55). In the Book of Deuteronomy, God orders the Israelites to "devote them to complete destruction" (Deut. 7.1) and to "save alive nothing that breathes" (Deut. 20.16). The reasoning offered is that if the Israelites show mercy and let the indigenous inhabitants remain, their pagan belief systems will steer the Israelites away from monotheism (Deut. 7.4, 20.18). Indeed, the Canaanites, as a people, are demonized from the very beginning of the Old Testament, which claims that God cursed them from the time of Noah (Gen. 9.18-27; Pitkänen 2010: 400).[9] It is important to point out, moreover, that in the conquest narrative God is portrayed as being intimately involved in the battles themselves. For instance, God gives detailed military instructions to the Israelites in terms of how to defeat the peoples of Jericho and Ai (see Josh. 6 and Josh. 8.1-23, respectively). Notably, just before the siege of Jericho, Joshua encounters the Commander of the Lord's Army, who clarifies that he has come to fight alongside the Israelite forces (Josh. 5.13-14). Within the narrative, then, the Israelites are not fighting alone. A cosmic army of God's soldiers fights with them.

The Qur'an and the Conquest of Canaan

Before embarking on the Qur'anic account, two points of clarification are in order. Firstly, the word "Canaan" (*kan'an*) is never used in the Qur'an. Instead, the text simply refers to the land as "the Holy Land" (*al-ard al-muqaddasa*), such as in Q. 5.21. Hence, when engaging the Qur'anic account I will use this latter term. Secondly, there is a difference in the Qur'anic representation of the Holy Land as a "Promised Land." In the Bible, the Promised Land is portrayed as a primordial vow made to Abraham about the land of Canaan. In the Book of Genesis, God explicitly promises Abraham, when he arrives in Canaan, that God will give the land of

Canaan to his offspring (Gen. 12.5-7), and this is precisely why the Israelites, as the children of Abraham through Isaac and Jacob, refer to Canaan *as* the Promised Land. Later in Genesis, God repeats this promise to Abraham but this time, curiously, describes a considerably larger stretch of land, extending "from the river of Egypt to the great river, the river Euphrates" (Gen. 15.17-18). No such promises are made to Abraham in the Qur'an. Instead, God vows to make Abraham a leader (*imam*) of humankind, and when Abraham asks about whether this promise will extend to his offspring, God clarifies that it will extend only to those who are not oppressors (*al-zalimin*) (Q. 2.124). The text has much to say about God's gifts to Abraham. It mentions that God gave Abraham what was "good" (*hasana*) in this world (*al-dunya*) and in the Hereafter (*al-akhira*) (Q. 16.122); that Abraham was given Isaac (perhaps as a reward for being willing to sacrifice Ishmael) and Jacob, and made them both righteous (Q. 21.72); and that Abraham and his nephew Lot were delivered, by the mercy of God, to a land blessed "for all the worlds" (*lil-'al-amin*, Q. 21.71).[10] But, again, nowhere in the Qur'an is Abraham promised ownership of the Holy Land, whether to himself or to his offspring. This is a distinctly biblical notion.

To be sure, in the Qur'an the fleeing Israelites are assured that God has "written" (*kataba*) the Holy Land for them (Q. 5.21). The Qur'an also makes a number of generalized statements about land, and these statements do reflect a promise to the Israelites. Consider Q. 28.5-6:

> It is Our Will to bestow Our grace upon the downtrodden of the Earth, and to make them the leaders and to make them the inheritors of the Earth. And to establish them securely on the Earth, and to let Pharaoh and Haman and their hosts experience through them (the Israelites) the very thing against which they sought to protect themselves.[11]
>
> (Qur'an 28.5-6).

Furthermore, in Q. 7.128-9, Moses addresses the Israelites in Egypt, pointing out that "the earth indeed belongs to God, and He gives its inheritance to whomever He wishes of His servants." Later in the same chapter, the Qur'an states that God made "the people who were oppressed the inheritors to the east and west of the land, which We had blessed, and your Lord's best word [promise] was fulfilled to the Israelites" (Q. 7.137). The verse that directly follows this one—Q. 7.138—relates how the Israelites crossed the sea to escape Pharaoh. A couple of themes stand out in the above verses. Firstly, they emerge in a particular context: that of Pharaonic domination. The promise of inheriting the earth/land is made in a context of unequal power relations, and God, as a just deity, is taking sides with the oppressed group *as* oppressed group. This is a promise of social liberation. This is not a covenant made with a powerful force—an army awaiting orders to invade new territory—nor is this a primordial covenant made with the Israelites *as* Israelites, that is, through their ancestor Abraham. Secondly, the Qur'an emphasizes that true dominion / ownership of the land, and by extension everything in it, belongs not to the powerful (Pharaonic) status quo, however entrenched and permanent its foothold may seem, but to God, the All-Powerful, who chooses to bequeath it to whomever S/He wills. The way in which "inheritance" is being used in these verses is clearly figurative, not literal. The underlying point is that God exercises ultimate ownership and will stand in solidarity with the oppressed group, providing for them in their time of need.

Given the Qur'an's keen interest in the Israelites, the text is remarkably silent when it comes to their encounter with the Holy Land. Moses' name occurs roughly 140 times, making him the most mentioned prophet in Muslim scripture (Esack 2005: 154). We are provided with a detailed (albeit spread out) account of his life. This includes his early years, when his mother leaves him in a chest on the sea (Q. 20.37-40); its discovery by Pharaoh's wife, who adopts Moses and raises him in her own household (Q. 26.18); and Moses' killing of the Egyptian solider as a youth and his subsequent flight to Midian (Q. 28.15-28) (Shöck 2003). Considerable attention is paid to Moses as Prophet, beginning with his being directly addressed by God (Q. 20.9-16); his performance of various miracles in front of Pharaoh and his elites, including the nine signs (Q. 17.101, 27.12); Moses' dividing of the sea and the delivery of the Israelites from Pharaoh, who subsequently drowns (Q. 26.63-66; 27.12); the revelation of the Holy Tablets at Mount Sinai (Q. 7.144-145); and the Israelites' worshipping of the Golden Calf in Moses' absence (Q. 7.148-149, 20.85-91) (Shöck). Later Israelite prophets are also discussed in the Qur'anic text, including David (Q. 2.129-151; 4.163; 17.55; 34.10-11; and 38.17-26) and Solomon (Q. 27.15-44; 34.12-4; 38.30-40). Yet despite the extensive attention devoted to the Israelite prophets, the Qur'an is curiously silent in its treatment of the Israelite encounter with the Holy Land: essentially, the text gives us two snapshots of that encounter. This section will unpack each of these snapshots, contrasting what exactly the Qur'an says with how Muslim commentators have expounded these passages.

The first snapshot—found in Q. 5.20-6—is of the newly liberated Israelites' arrival at the edges of the Holy Land. The Qur'anic passage reads:

> When Moses said to his people, "O my people, remember God's blessing upon you when he appointed prophets among you, and made you kings, and gave you what none of the nations were given. O my people, enter the Holy Land (*udkhulu al-ard al-muqaddasa*) which God has written (*kataba*) for you, and do not turn your backs, or you will become losers." They said, "O Moses, they are a mighty people in it. We will not enter it (*lan nadkhuluha*) until they leave it. But once they leave it, we will go in (*anna dakhilun*)." Said two men from among those who were God-fearing and whom God had blessed: "Enter upon them through the gate! (*udkhulu 'alayhim al-bab*). For once you have entered it, you will be victorious (*fa-idha dakhaltamuhum fa-annakum ghalibun*). Put your trust in God, should you be faithful." They said, "O Moses, we will never enter it so long as they remain in it. Go ahead, you and your Lord, and fight! (*fa-idhhab anta wa rabbuka fa-qatila*) We will be sitting right here." He [Moses] said, "My Lord! I have no power over anyone except myself and my brother, so part us from the transgressing lot." He [God] said, "It shall be forbidden them for forty years: They shall wander about in the earth. So do not grieve for the transgressing lot."

So this episode is similar to (though, as we will shortly see, also different from) the biblical account of the spies. The Israelites discern that a powerful people already live in the land and refuse to enter it, despite God's commandment to do so. This leads, as a divine punishment, to the land being forbidden to them for forty years, during which time they must wander through the wilderness. It is crucial to examine the precise wording of the Qur'anic passage. Observe that God does not, at *any* place in the passage, command the Israelites to attack or fight the indigenous inhabitants. The divine command is simply to "enter" (*dukhul*). This is the Arabic verb that is used in various forms (as imperative, active participle, future tense) throughout the passage. Significantly, it is the Israelites, not Moses or God, who introduce the notion of fighting (*qital*) when the Israelites tell Moses to fight while they stay behind: "Go ahead, you and your Lord, and fight" (*fa-idhhab anta wa rabbuka fa-qatila*). In other words, the Israelites make a core assumption: that entering the land must necessarily entail attacking the inhabitants of that land. But the Qur'anic text itself makes no such assumption. What is clear in the passage is that God is presenting a test of faith to the Israelites, ordering them to enter the land, in full view of the manifest strength of its local inhabitants. Do the Israelites genuinely believe in God and His/Her protection? The locals are clearly strong, but why should such strength translate into antagonism and hostility? Perhaps the locals will welcome the Israelites—battered refugees fleeing Pharaoh's Egypt—taking them into their homes and giving them sanctuary? While this divine commandment to "enter" may seem like an unreasonable, dire test, clearly opening up the Israelites to vulnerability, recall that this commandment is being issued shortly after their liberation from Pharaonic Egypt and the countless miracles that accompanied that victory. By this point, surely it should be clear that God is on the Israelites' side. This is why Moses reminds them, at the beginning of the passage, of God's blessing upon them and how God had given them what none of the other nations had been given. The two men of faith, who seem to be fellow Israelites, have no doubt that God will protect them and that they will indeed emerge victorious (*ghalibun*) from this divine test. In fact, they urge the Israelites to not simply obey by entering the land, but to do so right through its main gate, that is, in plain view and in broad daylight. God walked with them in Egypt; God will walk with them now.

There is a second assumption that the Israelites make. Note the sharply dichotomous thinking that frames their discourse. For them, only one group can reside in the land: an ascendant group, a dominant group. The possibility of actually co-inhabiting the land—the indigenous people as the respected locals, they as sanctuaried refugees/migrants—is inconceivable in their exclusivist "us" versus "them" logic. That is, the Israelites assume that since the land is written for them, it must *only* be written for them; the land cannot be written for multiple peoples. To quote their own words, "We will not enter it until they leave it. But once they leave it, we will go in," and again, "We will never enter it so long as they remain in it. Go ahead, you and your Lord, and fight!" This last part is telling, as it shows that it is precisely this dichotomous logic that leads them to assume that attack/invasion is the only mode of entry.

Various Muslim commentators have expounded this Qur'anic passage through a biblical lens, thereby creating a narrative of conquest where it does not exist.

Al-Tabari (d. 923), arguably the most influential figure in the commentarial tradition, is a compelling example. He interprets Q. 5.20-6 as "the command of God to fight the mighty people" (*amr Allah fi qital al-jabbarin*) (al-Tabari undated: vol. 3 p. 65) and "to attack them in their land" (*wa hujumihim 'alayhim fi ardihim*) (ibid.: 67). In his commentary, al-Tabari subscribes to exactly the same type of binary, Israelite thinking that I discussed in the above paragraph: that only one group can reside in the land, a dominating group. Earlier in this section, we discussed the (figurative) notion of the Israelites inheriting the land. Al-Tabari's line of thinking is acutely dichotomous, assuming that the inheritance of one must entail the *disinheritance* of the other: "And his Majestic Grace says *awrathna* [We gave to inherit] because He has given it to the Children of Israel to inherit that [land] by the destruction of those who were from the giants" (*bi-mahliki man kana fiha min al-'amaliqa*) (ibid.: 491).[12] Furthermore, al-Tabari is explicit about his usage of *isra'iliyat* literature (that is, biblical accounts) in his interpretation of Q. 5.20-26. For instance, he writes that the two righteous men referred to in the passage are Joshua son of Nun (*yusha' bin nun*) and Caleb son of Jephuna (*kalib bin yunfa*), adding that he took these names directly from the Torah (al-Tabari undated: 68). Al-Tabari reproduces biblical assumptions/narratives not only in his famous Qur'anic commentary, but also in his (equally famous) historical compendium: the History of al-Tabari. The History is interesting because here al-Tabari misunderstands the very biblical texts that he draws upon, taking the spies' description of the inhabitants of Canaan *literally*. Recall that, in the Old Testament narrative, while the local inhabitants of the land are clearly strong, the spies grossly exaggerate their strength, portraying them as towering giants in order to sow fear and disillusionment among their fellow Israelites. To quote the Book of Numbers: "all the people we saw in it are of great height ... we seemed to ourselves like grasshoppers, and so we seemed to them" (Num. 13.32-33). Referring to Q. 5.20-23 in his History, al-Tabari writes that when Moses dispatched the twelve spies:

> One of the giants, who was called Og, met them. He seized the twelve and placed them in his waistband, while on his head was a load of firewood. He took them off to his wife and said to her, "Look at these people who claim that they want to fight us." He flung them down in front of her, saying, "Shouldn't I grind them under my foot?" But his wife said, "No, rather let them go, so they will tell their people what they have seen."
>
> (al-Tabari undated: vol. 3, 80–81)

It is important to appreciate that al-Tabari is not picking such myths out of a vacuum. He is drawing on existing Muslim accounts that were clearly influenced by the *isra'iliyat* literature. For instance, when mentioning that the "base of Og's head was eight hundred cubits high" (ibid.: 83), al-Tabari cites a chain of Muslim scholars. In other words, early Muslim readers were keenly familiar with the biblical narrative, and this exposure inevitably effected how they read the Qur'an. Indeed, these stories seemed to have had a formative impact on the Arabic language itself, as the words for "giant" ('*imlaq*; pl: '*amaliqa*) and "Amalekite" ('*amaliq* / pl: '*amaliqa*) are derived from the same grammatical root.

Other Qur'anic commentators, too, have been deeply influenced by the biblical narrative. Paralleling al-Tabari, there is a general consensus among the commentators (Ibn 'Abbas, Ibn Kathir, al-Mahalli, al-Suyuti, Mawdudi, al-Tabataba'i, and Asad) that Joshua and Caleb are the two men referred to in the Qur'anic passage (Ibn 'Abbas 2007: 116; Ibn Kathir 2003: 144; al-Mahalli and al-Suyuti 2007: 117; Mawdudi 2018; al-Tabataba'i 2001: 115; Asad 2003: 170). This is a claim that can be corroborated only by referring, directly or indirectly, to the biblical account, as the Qur'an does not specify their names. Interestingly, al-Mahalli and al-Suyuti add that the giants whom the Israelites encounter are "those remaining of the people of 'Ad, who were very tall and mighty" (Al-Mahalli and al-Suyuti, 117). This is similar to the biblical claim that the Canaanites were cursed since the time of Noah (Gen. 9.18-27), for by connecting the Canaanites to the people of 'Ad, whom God destroyed in the Qur'an for their faithlessness and oppressive rule (Q. 7.65-72; 11.50-60), al-Mahalli and al-Suyuti are implicitly linking the Canaanites to disbelief and tyranny, thereby justifying their killing. A number of commentators are explicit, like al-Tabari, that Q. 5.20-26 is a call to war. Ibn Kathir writes that Moses "ordered the Children of Israel to enter Jerusalem and fight their enemy" (Ibn Kathir 2003: vol. 3, 143).[13] He then juxtaposes the Israelites' fear of fighting, with the Muslims' enthusiastic response to Muhammad at the Battle of Badr (624 CE). Here, Ibn Kathir cites the *hadith* (prophetic report) that when Muhammad asked the Muslims about whether they would support him by fighting the mighty Quraysh, the Muslims responded:

> We will never say as the Children of Israel said to Moses, "So go, you and your Lord, and fight you two, we are sitting here." By He who has sent you with the Truth! If you took the camels to Bark Al-Ghilmad (near Makkah) we will follow you.
> (Ibn Kathir 2003: vol. 3, 145-146).[14]

Ibn Kathir's commentary thus tries to contextualize Q. 5.20-26 in terms of the Qur'an's revelation in seventh-century Arabia. This also shows, as I noted earlier, that the early Muslims were acutely aware of biblical stories and this shaped how they interpreted—and, in the case of the above *hadith* report, evoked—Qur'anic passages. Mawdudi also interprets Q. 5.20-26 as a call to war, commenting that "God allotted this land to them [the Israelites] and commanded them to conquer it" (Mawdudi 2018). Mawdudi actually *quotes* Old Testament texts in his commentary of Q. 5.20-26, specifically the Book of Numbers. While Qutb echoes Ibn Kathir's contextualization of the Qur'anic passage, citing the same *hadith* report about the Muslim response at Badr (Qutb undated: 6), Qutb is the sole voice among the surveyed commentators who reflects on the wider principle of the passage. He is uninterested in speculation over details, such as who the two men are. Instead, he reflects on the qualities, the faith of these two men:

> They wanted to show what it meant to fear God alone at times when people fear each other. God does not combine the two feelings of fear in any one man's heart: fearing Him and fearing human beings. A person who fears God fears no one else.
> (Qutb undated: 62)

To be sure, Qutb is unable to escape a battle-based exposition of Q. 5.20-26. Like other commentators (and the Israelites), he presumes that entry into the land entails attacking its inhabitants. But this assumption aside, Qutb does discern the wider point of the Qur'anic passage: namely, the immense test of faith being presented to the Israelites.

The second Qur'anic snapshot fast-forwards to the Israelites' actual entry into the Holy Land forty years later, having completed their term of punishment in the wilderness. This snapshot is found in Q. 2.58-59 and Q. 7.161-162, which are almost identical passages:

> And when We said, "Enter (*udkhulu*) this town and eat thereof freely when you wish, and enter prostrating (*sujjadan*) at the gate, and say 'Relief!' [that is, relieve us of our sins], that we may forgive your mistakes, and we will increase the doers of good (*al-muhsinun*)." But those who oppressed (*alladhina zalamu*) changed the saying with other than what they were told. So We sent down on those who oppressed a punishment from the sky because of the transgressions they used to commit (*bi-ma kanu yafsiqun*).
>
> (Q. 2.58-59)
>
> And when they were told, "Dwell (*uskunu*) in this town and eat thereof when you wish, and say, 'Relief!' [that is, relieve us of our sins], and enter prostrating (*sujjadan*) at the gate, that We may forgive your mistakes, and we will increase the doers of good (*al-muhsinun*)." But those who oppressed (*alladhina zalamu*) changed the saying with other than what they had been told. So we sent against them a punishment from the sky because of the oppression they used to commit (*bi-ma kanu yazlimun*).
>
> (Q. 7.161-162)[15]

There are a number of themes that emerge in these verses. Firstly, the discourse here is squarely one of entry (*dukhul*), just like God's commandment forty years earlier. There is no mention whatsoever of fighting (*qital*) or attacking (*hujum*). In the case of Q. 7.161-162, the Arabic verb used is the imperative form of *sakana*, which means to live / to dwell. Interestingly, *sakana* also means to become calm/ tranquil, with the noun *sukun* denoting tranquility and peace of mind.[16] Secondly, the Israelites are ordered to enter the town "prostrating" (*sujjadan*), that is, in humility and worship, seeking God's forgiveness. To enter a town through its gate, as mentioned earlier, is to enter it in plain sight of everyone, and that entry, according to the Qur'anic text, must be humble and pious—a rather different image than the triumphalist parade of an arrogant, conquering force. This is supposed to be an entry of faith, just like the entry commanded forty years past. Notably, it is the "doers of good" (*al-muhsinun*), a Qur'anic term referring to those who undertake righteous works, who are praised in these verses. Thirdly, it is evident that something—what exactly we do not know—has gone terribly wrong. A group of Israelites changed the words of God and acted in an oppressive manner (again, what exactly they said and did we do not know) and this rebellion was so severe that it led to a swift punishment (*rijz*) from the sky. It is telling that the verb *zalama* ("to oppress")—the noun form being *zulm* ("oppression")—is used to describe the actions of this wayward group of Israelites.

Muslim exegetical engagement with these verses has tended to speculate over details that cannot be conclusively known. One point of discussion has been the specific town being referred to, the two candidates being Jerusalem (*bayt al-maqdis*) and Jericho (*ariha*). Al-Tabari and Qutb support the former (al-Tabari undated: vol. 1, 219; Qutb undated: 76), while Ibn 'Abbas, Ibn Kathir, al-Mahalli, and al-Suyuti consider both towns as possibilities (Ibn 'Abbas 2007: 12; Ibn Kathir 2003: vol. 1, 237–238; Al-Mahalli and al-Suyuti, 11). The commentators also speculate over which specific word the Israelites used to replace "Relief!" (*hitta*), which they were commanded to say when they entered the gate. A number of commentators (Ibn 'Abbas, al-Tabari and Ibn Kathir) maintain that the Israelites changed *hitta* to *hinta* ("wheat") (Ibn 'Abbas 2007: 12; al-Tabari undated: vol. 3, 513; Ibn Kathir 2003: vol. 1, 240). What this implies precisely—switching the word "relief" with "wheat"—is unclear, but the word-switch seeks to convey the sense of Israelite rebellion, of mocking God's commandments. Ibn Kathir clarifies this when he writes: "They were commanded to enter the city while bowing down, but they entered while sliding on their rear ends and raising their heads!" (Ibn Kathir 2003: vol. 1, 240). There has also been speculation over what exactly the punishment (*rijz*) was that God meted out. Al-Tabari suggests that this was a plague, an outbreak of "boils" (al-Tabari undated: vol. 1, 221). To corroborate this claim, he cites a *hadith* report stating that various nations before the Muslims were punished by the plague (ibid.: vol. 1, 221).[17] To be sure, al-Tabari is also reflective here of the limits of his own exegetical knowledge. He acknowledges that "there is no evidence manifest in the Qur'an, and nor is there any concrete trace from the Prophet, of what precise type it [the punishment] was," concluding that what we do know is that a punishment was sent down due to the sinful actions of the Israelites (ibid.: vol. 1, 221).

More significantly, despite the absence of any call to war in this second snapshot, Muslim commentators have superimposed a biblical narrative onto the Qur'anic text. Ibn Kathir, in his interpretation of Q. 2.58-59, maintains that, with God's grace and under Joshua's leadership, the Israelites were able to successfully "conquer" the land on a Friday, during which the sun was delayed from setting so that the Israelites could win the battle (Ibn Kathir 2003: vol. 1, 238). Al-Mahalli and al-Suyuti echo Ibn Kathir's reading, claiming that Joshua "was commanded to fight against the giants" (that is, the local inhabitants) and, on the day of Friday, the sun stood still for an hour until the fighting had finished (al-Mahalli and al-Suyuti 2007: 117). This miraculous image of the sun standing still is noteworthy for three reasons. Firstly, it positions God as supporting a military campaign against the indigenous people, thereby providing divine sanction for war and conquest. Secondly, it reflects the lasting impact of the Bible on their readings of the Israelite entry into the Holy Land, as this imagery comes straight from the Old Testament. In the midst of fighting the Amorite kings in the West Bank, Joshua, seeking God's help, exclaims:

> "Sun, stand still at Gibeon, and moon, in the Valley of Aijalon." And the sun stood still, and the moon stopped, until the nation took vengeance on their enemies... The sun stopped in the midst of heaven and did not hurry to set for about a whole

day. There has been no day like it before or since, when the Lord heeded the voice of a man, for the Lord fought for Israel.

(Josh. 10.12-14)

Thirdly, the sun trope reveals the critical role of the *hadith* corpus in acting as a conduit, a bridge between the *isra'iliyat* literature and the Qur'anic commentarial tradition, transferring key assumptions, narratives, and themes from the former to the latter. In their commentary of Q. 2.58-59, al-Mahalli and al-Suyuti do not consult the Bible directly. Instead, they draw on the following *hadith* report, which was clearly influenced by the biblical account: "The sun was never detained for any human, except for Joshua during those days in which he marched towards the Holy House (of Jerusalem)" (al-Mahalli and al-Suyuti 2007: 117).[18] Alongside Muslim commentarial works, the biblical narrative has shaped Muslim historical scholarship on the so-called conquest of Canaan. Al-Tabari's History, for example, draws extensively on the biblical narratives, explicitly referring to the accounts of "the people of the Torah" (al-Tabari 1991: vol. 3, 96). Like Ibn Kathir, al-Mahalli, and al-Suyuti, al-Tabari claims that "God had commanded him [Joshua] to fight the giants," reproducing the same story of the sun standing still on a Friday. The similarities between al-Tabari's account and that of the Old Testament are striking, especially his description of the falls of Jericho and Ai, which basically replicate the biblical narrative (ibid.: 96). Paralleling Josh. 6, al-Tabari writes that the Israelites surrounded Jericho, blew their trumpets, gave a single shout in unison, and the walls of Jericho swiftly fell.[19] After the defeat of Ai, al-Tabari claims that Joshua "slew twelve thousand men and women" (ibid.: 96)—a number taken directly from Josh. 8.25. By not questioning the reliability of such a claim, al-Tabari not only plays into the assumption of a military conquest, but also a bloody genocide of the indigenous inhabitants, including women, men, and children.

Conclusions

In this chapter, I undertook an anti-colonial reading of the Qur'an, expounding the sacred text in the light of my own political commitments to indigenous rights and liberation. By contrasting the biblical and Qur'anic accounts of the Israelite entry into the Holy Land, I have highlighted fundamental discrepancies between the two. The biblical account, to put it plainly, is unapologetically genocidal, with God explicitly commanding the Israelites to destroy the indigenous population, to "save alive nothing that breathes" (Deut. 20.16). But the Qur'an has a rather different discourse. This chapter has shown that in the Qur'an the "Conquest of Canaan" does not actually exist and that no subsequent genocide of the indigenous people took place. Despite the extensive attention that the Qur'an gives to the Israelite prophets, especially Moses, the text is remarkably silent when it comes to the Israelite encounter with the Holy Land. We are basically given two snapshots of that encounter—at two different points in Israelite history—and a careful analysis of the text's wording shows that, at no point, does God order the Israelites to attack the indigenous inhabitants. The command is simply one of entry (*dukhul*), humbly and respectfully walking into the land in which they seek sanctuary and trusting that God will protect them, just as S/He did in their liberation from Egypt. In fact, the only way a commentator can arrive at a violent, conquest-driven understanding of the Qur'anic passages is *if* there is already biblical baggage in place, *if* there is an existing meta-narrative framing (however unconsciously) her/his reading of the Qur'an. And this is precisely the problem. Qur'anic commentators have been unable to think, to expound beyond a colonizing framework, as they have been deeply influenced by the biblical account, which has made its ways into the commentarial tradition through the *isra'iliyat* and *hadith* literature. This demonstrates the lasting impact that the Bible has exerted on Muslim (mis)understandings of their own scripture, and its wider ethical implications in terms of human rights and social liberation.

Shadaab Rahemtulla is lecturer in Islam and Christian–Muslim relations at the School of Divinity, University of Edinburgh. Trained in Islamic thought at the University of Oxford, his primary interest lies in how religious texts can be (re)read to challenge contexts of social marginalization, such as patriarchy, poverty, racism, and empire. Rahemtulla is the author of the book *Qur'an of the Oppressed: Liberation Theology and Gender Justice in Islam*, published by Oxford University Press.

Notes

1. While there are clear parallels between Warrior's and Said's arguments, it is important to appreciate that they are speaking to very different audiences. Warrior is speaking to comrades in struggle, that is, liberation theologians and Black theologians who are committed to social justice. This is an internal critique within progressive circles. Said, on the other hand, is critiquing Walzer: someone who built his career in the corridors of power and is an outspoken supporter of the State of Israel and its policies in Palestine.
2. For a comparative analysis of Islamic liberation theologies, see Rahemtulla (2018).
3. Women's readings of the Qur'an have underlined the importance of textual silence, questioning entrenched Muslim assumptions of what the Qur'an says and contrasting these assumptions with what the text actually states. For instance, Riffat Hassan and Amina Wadud have shown that the assumption of woman as being created from Adam's rib is absent in the Qur'an, having been taken from the Old Testament (Gen. 2.21-23). Instead, they point out that, in the Qur'anic text, humankind was created from a single soul (*nafs wahida*) (Q. 4.1; see Hassan 1990: 98; Wadud 1999: 19–20).
4. Deuteronomy 20.16-17 reads: "But in the cities of these peoples that the Lord your God is giving you for an inheritance, you shall save alive nothing that breathes, but you shall devote them to complete destruction, the Hittites and the Amorites, the Canaanites and the Perizzites, the Hivites and the Jebusites, as the Lord your God has commanded." In this article, I have taken all biblical quotations from *Holy Bible: English Standard Version, Anglicized Edition* (London: Collins, 2007).
5. There is a slightly different account in the retelling of these events at the beginning of Deuteronomy. In this account, the Israelites themselves suggest sending spies out to Canaan, to which Moses agrees (Deut. 1.21-23).

6. To be sure, the spies themselves (again, with the exception of Caleb and Joshua) are not pardoned for their role in inciting the Israelite rebellion against Moses. They are killed by a plague (Num. 14.36-38).
7. It is worthwhile noting that not all of the land was conquered under Joshua (Josh. 13.1-6). Furthermore, it seems that in the post-Joshua conquests—that is, the conquest of the remaining land following his death—the Israelites generally did not massacre the inhabitants (perhaps due to inability but also choice), allowing them to live alongside them, albeit in forced servitude (see, for instance, Judg. 1.27-30).
8. The tribe of Manasseh decided to split their "inheritance" between the East and West Bank.
9. While the Canaanites have become synonymous with the indigenous inhabitants of the land, it should be clarified that when the Old Testament books refer to the inhabitants of Canaan, they are actually referring to a cluster of seven communities: namely, the Canaanites, Hittites, Amorites, Girgashites, Perizzites, Jebusites and Hivites. See, for instance, Deut. 7.1.
10. Q. 21.71 reads: "We delivered him and Lot to the land which We have blessed for all the worlds" (*wa najjaynahu wa lutan ila al-ardi allati barakna fiha lil-'alamin*).
11. In terms of the Qur'an, I have drawn on a number of English translations, supplemented by my own knowledge of Qur'anic Arabic. The translations include Qara'i (2004), Ali (1993) and Asad (2003).
12. To clarify, here he is commenting on Q. 7.137.
13. See also Ibn Kathir (2003: vol. 1, 237).
14. As Ibn Kathir notes, this *hadith* report can be found in the collections of Ibn Hanbal and al-Nisa'i.
15. The difference between these two occurrences of the passage seems to be *intent*. Q. 2.58-59 appears within a wider passage the function of which is to recall the favors that God bestowed on the Israelites. Q. 2.47 begins this wider passage, stating: "O Children of Israel, remember My favor that I have bestowed upon you and that I preferred you over the worlds." The text then goes on to talk about the Israelite story: God saving them from the oppression of Pharaoh, their taking of the Golden Calf—after which God forgives them so that they may become grateful (Q. 2.52)—and God giving them manna and quails as sustenance in the wilderness. It is at this point that Q. 2.58-59 appears. The textual context of Q. 7.161-162 is slightly different: here the lesson of the wider passage is that people bring punishment upon themselves through their own actions, the implication being that God is just. So the punishment inflicted on the Israelites in this verse is due to their own actions (disobeying God's commandments) and the verses that immediately follow this one convey the same lesson: they speak about a group of Israelites who fished on the Sabbath, and, due to their own sinfulness, were turned into apes.
16. The verb *sakana* is also used in the imperative form in Q. 17.104: "We said, after him [Pharaoh], 'Dwell in the land' (*uskunu fi al-ard*)." In another verse—Q. 10.93—the verb *bawwa'a* is used, meaning to provide accommodation for someone / to settle someone down in a place: "Indeed, we settled the Israelites in an honorable dwelling (*laqad bawwa'na bani isra'ila mubawwa'a sidqin*)." Hence, like *sakana*, *bawwa'a* does not carry connotations of violence or conquest.
17. This *hadith* report, he adds, can be found in the collections of Muslim, Bukhari, Malik, Ibn Hanbal, and al-Tirmidhi.
18. They add that this report is found in the *hadith* collection of Ibn Hanbal.
19. Al-Tabari claims that the siege of Jericho lasted six months, with the city falling in the seventh month, whereas the Book of Joshua claims that the siege lasted six days, with

the city falling on the seventh day (Josh. 6.15-17). This is another example, then, of how al-Tabari simultaneously draws on the biblical narrative while also misreading it.

References

Al-Mahalli, Jalal al-Din and Jalal al-Din al-Suyuti. 2007. *Tafsir al-Jalalayn* [*The Commentary of the Two Jalals*], translated by Feras Hamza and edited and introduced by Ghazi bin Muhammad bin Talal. Amman: Royal Aal al-Bayt Institute for Islamic Thought.

Al-Tabari, Abu Ja'far. Undated. *Tafsir al-Tabari: Min Kitabihi, Jami' al-Bayan 'an Ta'wil al Qur'an* [*The Commentary of al-Tabari: From his Writings, the Collection of the Statements on the Exegesis of the Qur'an*]. Revised and edited by Bashar Ma'rouf and 'Isam al-Harastani.

Al-Tabari, Abu Ja'far. 1991. *The History of al-Tabari* (vol. 3), translated by William M. Brinner. Albany, NY: State University of New York Press.

Al-Tabataba'i, Muhammad Husayn. 2001. *Al-Mizan: An Exegesis of the Qur'an* (vol. 10), translated by Sayyid Saeed Akhtar Rizvi. Tehran: World Organization for Islamic Services.

Ali, Ahmed. 1993. *Al-Qur'an: A Contemporary Translation.* Princeton, NJ: Princeton University Press, 1993.

Asad, Muhammad. 2003. *The Message of the Qur'an.* Bristol: The Book Foundation.

Boff, Leonardo and Clodovis Boff. [1986] 1999. *Introducing Liberation Theology.* Maryknoll, NY: Orbis Books.

Brett, Mike G. 2008. *Decolonizing God: The Bible in the Tides of Empire.* Sheffield: Sheffield Phoenix Press.

Cone, James. [1970] 2010. *A Black Theology of Liberation.* New York: Orbis Books.

Cone, James. [1969] 2011. *Black Theology and Black Power.* New York: Orbis Books.

Esack, Farid. 1997. *Qur'an, Liberation, and Pluralism: An Islamic Perspective of Interreligious Solidarity Against Oppression.* Oxford: Oneworld.

Esack, Farid. 2005. *The Qur'an: A User's Guide.* Oxford: Oneworld.

Gottwald, Norman. 1979. *The Tribes of Yahweh: A Sociology of the Religion of Liberated Israel, 1250–1050 BCE.* Maryknoll, NY: Orbis Books.

Gutiérrez, Gustavo. [1971] 1973. *A Theology of Liberation: History, Politics, and Salvation.* Maryknoll, NY: Orbis Books.

Hassan, Riffat. 1990. "An Islamic Perspective." In *Women, Religion, and Sexuality: Studies on the Impact of Religious Teachings on Women,* edited by Jeanne Becher. Philadelphia, PA: Trinity Press International.

Holy Bible: English Standard Version, Anglicized Edition. 2007. London: Collins.

Ibn 'Abbas, Abdullah. 2007. *Tanwir al-Miqbas min Tafsir Ibn 'Abbas* [*Illuminating the Ember from the Commentary of Ibn 'Abbas*], translated by Mokrane Guezzou. Amman: Royal Aal-Bayt Institute for Islamic Thought.

Ibn Kathir, Isma'il. 2003. *Tafsir Ibn Kathir* [*The Commentary of Ibn Kathir*] (vols. 1–10), abridged under the supervision of Shaykh Safiur-Rahman Mubarakpuri. Riyadh: Darussalam Publishers.

LeFevre, Tate A. 2015. "Settler Colonialism." Retrieved from www.oxfordbibliographies.com/view/document/obo-9780199766567/obo-9780199766567-0125.xml (accessed August 15, 2018).

Mawdudi, Abul A'la. 2018. *Tafhim al-Qur'an* [*Understanding the Qur'an*]. Retrieved from www.englishtafsir.com (accessed 15 July 2018).

Pitkänen, Pekka. 2010. "Dr. Jekyll and Mr. Hyde? Deuteronomy and the Rights of Indigenous Peoples." *Political Theology* 11(3): 399–409. https://doi.org/10.1558/poth.v11i3.399

Prior, Michael. 1997. *The Bible and Colonialism: A Moral Critique*. Sheffield: Sheffield Academic Press.

Qara'i, Ali Quli. 2004. *The Qur'an, with a Phrase-by-Phrase Translation*. London: Islamic College for Advanced Studies Press.

Qutb, Sayyid. Undated. *Fi Zilal al-Qur'an* [*In the Shade of the Qur'an*], vols 1–14. Translator and publication date unknown. Retrieved from https://tafsirzilal.wordpress.com (accessed August 15, 2018).

Rahemtulla, Shadaab. 2018. *Qur'an of the Oppressed: Liberation Theology and Gender Justice in Islam*. Oxford: Oxford University Press. https://doi.org/10.1093/acprof:oso/9780198796480.001.0001

Rowland, Christopher ed. 2007. *The Cambridge Companion to Liberation Theology*. Cambridge: Cambridge University Press. https://doi.org/10.1017/CCOL0521868831

Said, Edward. 1986. "Michael Walzer's 'Exodus and Revolution': A Canaanite Reading." *Grand Street* 5(2): 86–106. https://doi.org/10.2307/25006845

Schechla, Joseph. 2005. "A Covenant of Dispossession and Genocide." In *The Endangered Planet in Literature: Select Proceedings*, edited by Barry Tharaud and Elizabeth Pallito. Istanbul: Doğuş University.

Schöck, Cornelia. 2003. "Moses." In *Encyclopaedia of the Qur'an*, vol. 3, edited by Jane D. McAuliffe. Leiden: Brill.

UN. 1948. "Convention on the Prevention and Punishment of the Crime of Genocide." Retrieved from www.un.org/en/genocideprevention/documents/atrocity-crimes/Doc.1_Convention%20on%20the%20Prevention%20and%20Punishment%20of%20the%20Crime%20of%20Genocide.pdf (accessed December 6, 2019).

Wadud, Amina. 1999. *Qur'an and Woman: Rereading the Sacred Text from a Woman's Perspective*. Oxford: Oxford University Press.

Walzer, Michael. 1985. *Exodus and Revolution*. New York: Basic Books.

Warrior, Robert. 1989. "Canaanites, Cowboys, and Indians: Deliverance, Conquest, and Liberation Theology Today." *Christianity and Crisis* 49(12): 261–265.

Wielenga, Bastiaan. 2007. "Liberation Theology in Asia." In *The Cambridge Companion to Liberation Theology*, edited by Christopher Rowland. Cambridge: Cambridge University Press. https://doi.org/10.1017/CCOL0521868831.005

Wolfe, Patrick. 2006. "Settler Colonialism and the Elimination of the Native." *Journal of Genocide Research* 8(4): 387–409. https://doi.org/10.1080/14623520601056240

Zaman, Muhammad Q. 2002. *The Ulama in Contemporary Islam: Custodians of Change*. Princeton, NJ: Princeton University Press.

13

Counter-imperialistic Features in Biblical Israel

Youngseop Lim

> Yet throughout the Bible, with the exception of the Exodus, the God in whom the people of Palestine put their faith appears to be silent. He sees the Assyrians resettling his people and does nothing. He watches the Babylonians desecrate his temple, and doesn't move an inch. His capital is destroyed by the Romans, and he appears not to care. Even when his only beloved Son is hung on the cross, he is *absconditus* and hides (Mk 15: 34). This has been the experience of the people of Palestine throughout history, irrespective of their religious affiliation.
> —Mitri Raheb (2014: 69)

Introduction: The Bible as a Bridge between Past and Present

Considering the characteristics of biblical Israel, Palestine may be currently closer to biblical Israel than to present day Israel despite the latter's claim to have solid historical roots in biblical Israel. Continuity between biblical and current Israel is theologically controversial in terms of identity and attribute. Current Israelis believe that they are the descendants of Abraham and, as such, God's chosen people. On that basis, the occupation of Palestinian land is not a takeover but recovery of a lost land. God had said to Abraham that God will give the land to Abraham's descendants forever, even though the Canaanites were living in the land at that time (Genesis 12.6-7). Moreover, many Christians around the world believe that the use of armed force by Israelis against the Palestinians can be justified on biblical grounds. Historically, military conquest in the book of Joshua has been recognized as historical fact and the fulfilment of promise. Biblical Israel, surrounded by empires, built up military power to ensure survival, which can be regarded as an essential factor in keeping a chosen people on a promised land.

These biblical grounds, even if they do not currently work under international law, have influence in establishing the modern Israeli identity and supporting encroachment on Palestinian land through military means. The Bible has, for instance, played a key role in Jewish nationalism as a bridge between the past and the present. Since the national movement required a genealogy, the biblical story served to retrieve a mythological past, the glorious days when biblical Israel was formed, from oblivion. This created the primordial experience that gives the legitimacy required to give the present nation its own place. Ever since modern Zionism emerged in the late nineteenth century, Aliyah immigrants, particularly the second immigration wave, 1904–1918, felt a strong bond to the Bible, as a bridge between the promised land they had imagined, and the land in which they arrived, as fulfilment of that promise. They could identify sites, plants, and animals on the basis of biblical descriptions, and because the Bible spanned the centuries, could feel a sense of direct continuity between their biblical ancestors and themselves as present-day descendants re-establishing a foothold in the land. After all, the Bible, particularly the Exodus, the settlement in the land of Canaan, and the Return to Zion in the Persian era, endowed Jewish nationalism with mythological–theological–historical foundations to strengthen distinctiveness around ancestral lands (Shapira 2012: 17).

However, we need to theologically analyze this continuity between biblical Israel and current Israel in terms of ethnic identity, historicity of occupation and legitimacy of the use of violence. Since the twentieth century, biblical criticism has led people to set forth a counterargument to the above biblical basis. With the introduction of various methodological approaches to the Bible, although biblical Israelites had generally been deemed as the descendants of Abraham, it turns out that they were not simply related by blood. The Israel community, which was formed through the Exodus, consisted of vulnerable, so-called "Hebrews," who had diverse racial, religious, and cultural backgrounds. The important motive that bound them as a community under the Yahweh faith was liberation. They were not only those who were chosen by God, but also those who chose God, for liberation. In addition, the theory of military conquest during the settlement in Canaan was found to be uncertain in recent excavations and studies. Rather, archaeological research shows that Israel settled in the land of Canaan peacefully. In recent years, many scholars no longer regard the accounts of the book of Joshua as historical fact, but rather as a message of ideological desire and the recovery of a people who had lost their promised land because of the Babylonian empire (Carr 2010: 142).

The most characteristic features of biblical Israel revealed by biblical criticism are counter-imperialistic. Biblical Israel had been a geopolitical bridge between ancient Egypt and Mesopotamia; most maps of the ancient Middle East show Canaan/Israel at the center. The rise and fall of biblical Israel was not only internal, but was also connected to neighboring nations and societies. Biblical Israel was influenced by surrounding empires such as Egypt, Assyria, Babylonia, Persia, Greece and Rome. Ironically, there has also been the tremendous ramification of "modern empires" such as the Ottoman Empire, France including Napoleon's empire, the Russian Empire, the Nazi empire, Great Britain and the United States, in the process of Israeli occupation of Palestinian land in the twentieth century.

Historical events that have changed the course of history were related to empire, and, whether ancient or modern, empires have been a variable in determining the identity and destiny of Israel. Although biblical Israel was affected by empires in many ways, they, nevertheless, kept their identity by putting distance between particular characteristics of the Yahweh faith and imperialistic values. Above all, I will look at the counter-imperialistic features of biblical Israel; who the Israelites were, how they occupied the land, and what kind of community they pursued to build. Christians who tend to equate themselves with "new Israelites," also attempt to link biblical stories to the reality, and for them it raises an unconscious homology with present-day Israel and a consensus about what the Israeli state is doing in Palestine. At times, this creates somewhat biased opinions, and influences political decisions by Western societies today. Therefore, this chapter will discuss whether these features of biblical Israel also apply to current Israel and "new Israelites," in their relationship to modern empires.

A People Who Escaped an Empire

When we attempt to define the early Israel community, we need to be mindful that ethnicity is a slippery concept, and that, even today, we use ambiguous and ill-defined terminology in referring to diverse groups of peoples. The purity of blood for Israelites is more likely to be ideology rather than historical fact. Israel has been considered a homogeneous nation, who are descendants of Abraham. In the biblical narrative, the Israelites are often described as proud of being a chosen people, related by blood, and rejecting people, socially and religiously, who destroyed the purity of blood. Following their return from Babylonian exile, for example, if an Israeli man had married a Gentile, he had to divorce his Gentile wife (Ezra 10.1-17). As is well known in the Gospels, the Samaritans, who had married Assyrians following the fall of northern Israel to the Assyrian Empire, were discriminated against up to the period of Roman Empire (John 4.9). Since then, in the relationship between Jew and Gentile, including Christians, which alternates between conflict and coexistence through the Middle Ages to the modern times, the attitude of Jews toward Gentiles was often conditioned by the Bible, which provided a historical record to account for the distinctiveness of Jewry from other nations (Shapira 2012: 6).

However, the history of the formation of biblical Israel reveals that this prejudice and discrimination are not biblical. In the early Israel community, religious, political and social characteristics were stronger than ethnicity. The exodus group, which later developed into the state of Israel, is depicted in the specific term *ereb* in Hebrew. This term indicates "ethnic mixture," which does not refer to a single blood group, but might have included many foreigners living among the Israelites (Exodus 12.38). Some stories during the exodus showed non-Israelites travelling with Israel (Numbers 11.4; Deuteronomy 29.10; Joshua 8.35; Propp 1999: 414). Since Israelites were allowed to marry foreigners, non-pure blood descendants of Israelites could also become members. Hellenistic Egyptian historians also suggest that many Egyptians including those who were disabled and diseased accompanied the Israelites in the exodus procession (ibid.: 415).

The reason foreigners were able to participate in the community, known to be exclusive, was that the purpose of the exodus was not a preservation of ethnicity but a new community of covenant with God. The law of God applied both to native Israelites and to foreigners without conditions relating to race. In the case of the instructions for Passover, if foreigners wanted to celebrate Passover, they could join in the meal if they were circumcised, as were Israelites (Exodus

12.48-49). Another example is the people of Gibeon, who were able to become part of the Israeli community by taking a vow in the name of God (Joshua 9.27). Thus, although the community was highlighted as descendants of Abraham, there were many people of various ethnic groups, and diverse religious backgrounds (Exodus 1.1-7; 12.38). From the beginning of the Israel community, anyone could become an Israelite through faith, if not through biology.

Another important aspect is the term "Hebrew." Israelites were often referred to as Hebrew and their God also was called the God of the Hebrews (Exodus 3.18; 5.3; 7.16; 9.1, 13; 10.3). However, Hebrew and Israelite were not used as synonyms at that time. The term Hebrew historically refers to a social class, rather than to any particular ethnic group. As William Foxwell Albright (1968) suggested, Hebrew could mean the noun "dust" or the adjectives "hungry," "thirsty," "barefoot." Above all, it can be found as "*Apiru/Habiru*" in Akkadian texts, and it was considered to be the lower classes, such as transients, minorities, rebels and outlaws, around the 2nd Millennium BCE (Miller and Hayes 2006: 113–114; Anderson 1986: 47). The term Hebrew and its relevance to the Israelites are consistent with the context in the Old Testament. More to the point, this social background of Israelites is an important basis for the understanding of major events and features of Israelite history.

We need to pay attention to the historical geographical direction of important biblical events, such as the calling of Abraham, the Exodus, and the Return to Zion. Abraham, for example, is described as an immigrant from Ur of the Chaldeans, which was the main stage of world civilization (Genesis 11.31; 12.1-5). He was a settled city dweller who suddenly became a nomad, wandering the wilderness and backward regions. Due to a more highly developed infrastructure, Mesopotamia would have been much more efficient than Canaan for the spread, and impact, of the Israeli religion. It is similar to the Israelites escaping Egypt, which was the most advanced civilization at that time, and returning to a land which had been ruined in the Persian era, despite living in the developed culture of empire. The reason for leaving the empire to establish a new religion and community was that the values of the community did not match with imperialism and the link to a past shaped by Hebrew slavery.

Moreover, the connection between biblical Israel and the term Hebrew provides a clue to the settlement in the land of Canaan, which is a very controversial issue. If the Hebrew were Israelites, the historical feasibility of military conquest of stronger nations, as described in the Book of Joshua, is in doubt. Therefore, some scholars hypothesize that the narratives of settlement in the land of Canaan were actually rebellions against the city-states of Canaan, which at the time were ruled by vassal princes appointed by the Pharaoh in Egypt. This theory is based on the view that the early Israelites, as the Hebrew, were oppressed and disenfranchised peasants, farmers, pastoralists, outlaws, wanderers and mercenaries (Anderson 1986: 47).

In addition, in the flexible political system during the era of Judges, a negative evaluation of monarchy, and the ideal of fairness and justice in the days of David can also be understood from a Hebrew background. The motive for the Exodus was the repression and discrimination that the Israelites had to suffer as slaves. For them, a monarchy based on domination and subordination would not have matched the ideals of the Hebrews and would have been the reason for pursuing a comparatively equal social system. The assembly of diverse members that continued into the days of David was sufficient reason for the social ideal of fairness and justice. These features were strongly counter-imperialistic, distinguishing them from surrounding nations.

Military Conquest or Peaceful Infiltration

The common biblical view on the settlement in Canaan is that of military conquest. As the Bible emphasizes in the conquest of Jericho and Ai, the occupation of Canaan by armed forces of Israelites was not only granted by God, but was also a war that God carried out directly. It is not merely a human war or the military superiority of Israel, but a Holy War or the Divine Warrior's overwhelming victory, and, thus, has theological significance for Christians beyond simple historical authenticity. People have used biblical justifications for military action, or have stood on the Marcionist view that the Divine Warrior was a separate and lower entity than the all-forgiving God of the New Testament. However, the wars depicted in the Old Testament are neither a basis for allowing the use of violence, nor to be underestimated. To later theological reflections on the particular way in which Israelite faith presented history, the wars illustrated in the Exodus and settlement of Canaan have distinctive features, such as the sole kingship of Yahweh, cultic celebration of liberation, and defensive war (Ee-kon 1989: 153–156).

For example, the Song of the Sea in the Book of Exodus, which contains Yahweh's military victory, has a cultic setting of a worshipping community, does not emphasize war or violence, but the sovereignty and glorification of Yahweh (Exodus 15.1-21; Durham 1987: 205). War, described as being defensive and to liberate the vulnerable, is carried out by Yahweh, and the role of man is so limited that the skills and strategy for warfare do not affect the outcome of a war (Exodus 14.13-14). It is for this reason that the victory and glory of war was given to Yahweh only, and the Israelites were not allowed to take possession of the spoils (Exodus 15.6-11; Joshua 6.17). This emphasizes reliance on Yahweh rather than on a strong army or superior diplomacy. Therefore, attempting to justify violence in the narrative of war in the Bible is theologically disputable, as found in the discoveries of biblical archaeology.

Jericho and Ai, for example, have been archaeologically proven not to have fallen to Israel. W.F. Albright first suggested a connection between the destruction of the city, found to be in the Late Bronze Age strata (thirteenth century BCE), and conquest by the Israelites, but additional archaeological data has shown this theory to be flawed. The biggest problem is that it is impossible to reconstruct a history of Jericho later than 1560 BCE. The only evidence of any occupation related to the Exodus is the remnant of one corner of a mudbrick house, which seems to have been destroyed in approximately 1560 BCE. Settlements in Jericho had not been reoccupied, and there are no artefacts from the period. Thus, we find little archaeological evidence of Jericho, despite the highly descriptive account of conquest by the Israelites in the biblical tradition (Callaway 1963: 39–40; Shanks 1999: 65–66). Similarly, there is no evidence to support the conquest of Canaan in cities such as Arad, Heshbon, Hormah, Jeremoth, and little or no archaeological evidence of being inhabited during the thirteenth century BCE (Shanks 1999: 68–69). Consequently, mainstream biblical scholars and archaeologists alike have dismissed ideological arguments of a military conquest.

According to A. Alt, the central highlands of Canaan, where biblical traditions locate the initial settlement, were sparsely settled at the time of the infiltration by semi-nomadic Israelites. Because there was little resistance to be encountered in the wide gaps between cities, Israelites were able to acquire this region. Existing landowners would not have been harmed by the Israelites, so the peaceful transition and development by the Israelites who were initially nomadic, would have been possible. Most importantly, an approach of gradual peaceful settlement corresponds with the available archaeological evidence that some two or three hundred small settlements were established in almost empty hills. Therefore, it is reasonable to assume that the Israelites settled in a relatively peaceful manner, rather than through military conflict, as described in Joshua 1-12 (Weippert 1971: 5–6; Shanks 1999: 72–73).

Thus, it is not reasonable to justify war or violence based on the Book of Joshua. In addition to the lack of archaeological evidence, there are several problems such as anachronism, contradiction and doublets. Scholars generally agree that the Book of Joshua was an oral tradition in Joshua's time, written, rewritten and edited later on, with several theological revisions of historical events (Gottwald 1987: 230; Butler 1983: xx–xxvii). Furthermore, the characteristics of biblical literature may lead us to misunderstanding, because biblical writers ignored historical fact and used literary exaggeration to illustrate theological meaning. We can find that biblical writers also preserved and handed on contradictory traditions of the settlement. In the Book of Joshua, the Israelites conquered and occupied the land of Canaan through all-out war, without great difficulty, as if this scenario had been predetermined. In the Book of Judges, however, the battles were local and defensive, the Israelites were sometimes defeated in battle, and had to slowly infiltrate and coexist to settle in the land. We should note that the Israelites had settled in Canaan in a relatively peaceful way, and this is clearly different from the conquest wars by an invincible military force pursued by other countries, even though the church and Christians prefer a story of conquest by divine authority and dramatic content.

What Happens When People Get a King?

For more than 200 years, from the Exodus to the beginning of David's reign, the early Israeli political regime was markedly different from monarchy. In the ancient Middle East, the birthplace of biblical Israel and its culture, the king was regarded as part of creation and in close connection with the gods. The Pharaoh of Egypt was himself a god or the son of the sun god. In Mesopotamian texts, the king who was described as the agent or mediator between the gods and men, stood next to the gods in the hierarchy. The human kingdom existed to serve the needs of the gods. It was perceived that the king's reign was to be as part of human existence and embodied a god's will and grace. We can find similar features in the Old Testament, influenced by the ancient Middle Eastern cultures, which are the link between the king and the deity (Johnson 1958: 207-208; Whitelam 1992: 40-43; Gerbrandt 1986: 123).

For example, Saul, the first king in the history of Israel, and later David and his descendants were chosen, elected and anointed by God. The king was chosen to be ruler of God's people (1 Samuel 10.1), and was given sacred status in that God would punish anyone who killed his chosen king and gave divine wisdom to the king to practice justice in his kingdom (1 Samuel 26.9; 2 Samuel 8.15). God also had a special relationship with the king as offspring, and this relationship is described as father and son, namely, God was the king's father and the king was God's son. When the king did wrong, God would see that the king was corrected, just as children are corrected by their parents (2 Samuel 7.14; Amit 1999: 43-44).

However, we should note that biblical Israel, from its formation, had features distinct from the surrounding empires. Biblical writers criticized the strong military-based monarchies and hierarchical societies contradictory to the ideal of the Exodus. In general, political and religious stability were achieved through a strong centralized regime, but Israel had maintained a very flexible political system for a long time. As well as being a religious leader, Moses was a leader in dealing with war and administrative procedures. Most judges, from Othniel to Samuel, played the roles of warrior, tactician, or even king, but their roles were tentative and temporary. Furthermore, they had their own jobs and played a judge's role only when the community was at risk. Even Saul, the first king in the history of Israel, at the beginning of his reign had his own occupation and no royal palace or standing army (1 Samuel 11.5; 13.2). This characteristic also extended, to some extent, to David.

Despite the advantages and disadvantages of this political system, it was appropriate for applying the ideals of the Exodus community. Monarchy was inevitably accompanied by repression, exploitation and violence, through the ruling class, taxation and war. From the biblical point of view, the criteria for the rise of biblical Israel was, accordingly, not the expansion of territory and accumulation of wealth through military power, but through the establishment of justice and peace. Biblical writers identify the need for a monarchy, but nonetheless, also illustrate the negative aspects and the importance of restricting its power. It is certain that the monarchy was denigrated because of the absolute gap between the single almighty God and a king, which was emphasized by biblical writers. In particular, God was considered to be the one true king to rule the whole world (Exodus 15.18; Numbers 23.21; Jeremiah 8.19; 10.7-10; Szikszai 1962: 14). This is why the early leaders of biblical Israel were not kings but judges who were chosen by God. These leaders were criticized whenever they acted like a king or sought hereditary monarchy. Thereby, when people asked the judge Gideon to be king, he answered: "I will not be your king, and my son will not be king either. Only the Lord is your ruler" (Judges 8.23). The Book of Judges also reiterated the negative stance toward the kingship of Abimelech, calling it useless and even harmful (Judges 9.1-15; Horsley 2008: 18).

Criticism of the Israelite monarchy is mainly through prophetic tradition and the Deuteronomistic History in the Old Testament. The Book of Samuel, in particular, prominently depicts criticism and derision toward monarchy: the people were warned that it was evil to ask for a king (1 Samuel 8.17). When people preferred a flesh and blood king, it meant they rejected the divine rule they had promised to follow in the Exodus. The Israelites were motivated by covetousness, not necessity, because they were not content with their reality. When the elders of Israel wanted a king for a leader, similar to the surrounding nations, God replied flatly: "I am really the one they have rejected as their king" (1 Samuel 8.6-7; Tsumura 2007: 242-243, 250-252). Even when God showed Israel that Saul would be king, God criticized the Israelites who rejected the God who rescued them from their troubles and hard times. In his farewell speech, Samuel mentioned that even though God is the king of Israel, Israelites wanted a king to rule them. It was emphasized that asking for a king is no different than rejecting God (1 Samuel 10.19; 12.12; cf. Judges 8.22-23). For those people who demanded a king, God also warned them about how a king would treat people and listed the negative aspects of monarchy (1 Samuel 8.9-18).

Interestingly, the evils of monarchy are described in *mishpat hamelech* ("justice of the king" or "the rights and duties of the king"; 1 Samuel 8.9b, 10), and the word *shapat* is emphasized repeatedly (1 Samuel 8.1, 2, 3, 5, 6, 20). The Hebrew word *mishpat* means "justice," as do *tsedeq* or *tsedaqah*. These words can also be translated into "righteousness," "right," "judgment," "punishment," "sentence," "law," "regulation," "ordinances." A verb form of *mishpat* is *shapat*, interpreted mainly as "to judge" and only on occasion as "to avenge," but can be also translated to "rescue," "deliver," "free," "save." It was used where God saved someone from their enemies, paid attention to their cries for help, and did justice for the orphans and the oppressed (2 Samuel 18.19, 31; Ps. 10:17, 18; Enns 2013: 17–18). It can be interpreted that God directly intervenes in human history on behalf of vulnerable people (Psalms 96.12, 13; 98.9; Ezekiel 34.22). Therefore, it is intentionally ambiguous to use *mishpat hamelech* and *shapat* as wordplay for the consequences of a monarchy (Tsumura 2007: 252–254; McCarter 1980: 157). These words have both positive and negative meaning and remind us of the Exodus and the ideals of the community. These words warn that although people expect justice, monarchy would bring the tyranny of power; if people demand rescue, they would also experience judgement and revenge. The advocacy of God towards the vulnerable, which *mishpat* and *shapat* indicate, actually turned into oppression and exploitation by a class society, the negative meaning of these words, when the royal system was introduced.

Notably, the great mischief monarchy inflicts on people is related to military power. A king would take their possessions and force people to join his standing army. Some of them would have to ride in his chariots, serve in the cavalry, and run ahead of the king's chariot. Under a royal regime, people would have an obligation to farm the king's land, harvest his crops for military provisions, or make weapons. Above all, strengthening royal authority would bring class differentiation to Israeli society, removing the equal rights which were provided by God; people would have to submit to the rule of a king and become the king's slaves (1 Samuel 8.11-20). This warning shows the two-facedness of monarchy with regard to the relationship between monarchy and militarism. What the Israelites expected of a king was to carry out juridical justice, instead of the evil that Samuel's sons committed, and to do battle to ensure their safety (1 Samuel 8.3, 20b). However, the monarchy inevitably brought social inequality, tax collection and conscription for the military. In principle, the king of Israel must be chosen by God but, in reality, royal authority was hereditary, with accompanying power struggles. Thus, there was contradiction between the expectations for monarchy and reality from the time that monarchy was introduced (cf. 1 Samuel 12.13; 22:7; 1 Kings 5.13, 16; 9:23). It is very important to note that the military confrontations occurred in the eleventh century BCE, when the tribes were beginning to coalesce into a monarchy, rather than in the thirteenth century BCE, when they first entered Canaan (Weippert 1971: 5-6).

The Influx of Imperial Values and the Degeneration of Israel

In reality, this ominous warning soon proved prophetic. First of all, the state system, which was influenced by other cultures, came to a great turning point in Israelite society (Shanks 1999: 85-86). From the time of Solomon, the cause of the conflict and division of the monarchy was strongly related to the ramification of neighboring empires. Solomon also reorganized the administration of the kingdom, by dividing Israel into twelve administrative districts or provinces to centralize power (1 Kings 4.8-19). There was a strong Egyptian influence at Solomon's court, which was evident in the royal cabinet, administrative organization, and the administrative districts. These changes, triggered from the outside, invoked resistance at many levels of Israelite society. This was particularly so among the northern tribes because of the burden of the new state administrative structures. Equal relations between tribes collapsed through Solomon's forced labor and conscription policies, resulting in hostility between Israel and Judah, which eventually led to the division of the kingdom (Shanks 1999: 104-108).

As ramification from foreign states became more prominent, a superstructure of commerce and industry in the agricultural and pastoral society developed. Solomon's business policies caused many people to migrate from rural to urban areas, and with the economic boom, an urban culture was created. The growth of a wealthy class increased the gap between the rich and the poor. There were proletarians, hired laborers, and slaves, and a nobility with a sense of entitlement began to emerge (Bright 2000: 223). International marriage (1 Kings 11.1-3; 14.21), military reinforcement (1 Kings 9.19, 25; 10.26), building operations (1 Kings 6.37; 7.1-8; 10.16, 21), the flowering of culture (1 Kings 3.4-28; 4.29-34; 10.7, 23), trade policy and economic prosperity (1 Kings 9.26-28; 10.1-10, 13, 15, 22), which are essential elements in maintaining monarchies in most countries, brought negative consequences to biblical Israel. These changes, which made Israel a status society, caused the decline of the egalitarian community which had been the ideal of the Exodus community. Factors that historians evaluate positively, such as economic growth, political stability, diplomatization, and strong military power did not enter into the biblical writers' calculations. Any king who deviated from egalitarian criteria, abused their power or violated the commandments, received a harsh appraisal from biblical writers, even if the king had great accomplishments.

To use Omri, who was a king of northern Israel as an example, he built his distinctive policies and created a heyday for Israel. According to the Mesha Stone, Omri militarily subdued the Moabites and made them Israelite vassals, and this continued during the time of Ahab, his son. He moved the capital from Tirzah to Samaria and established cordial relations with neighboring states through international marriages. Above all, he granted economic concessions to Damascus and gave Syrian traders permission to operate shops in Samaria's bazaars, which brought impressive economic development (1 Kings 20.34). According to Assyrian records, he was so famous that Israel was referred to as "the land of the house of Omri" long after Omri's dynasty vanished (Shanks 1999: 139–40). However, not only are his achievements severely scaled down in the Old Testament, but the biblical writer asserts that "Omri did what was evil in the sight of the Lord; he did more evil than all who were before him" (1 Kings 16.25). A similar case can be found in Jeroboam II, who had been harshly evaluated by prophets in the eighth century BCE. He made northern Israel wealthy using methods he had learned from the empires. There was a bit of resurgence under Jeroboam II, he was able to capture territory ranging from Lebo-hamath in north to Arabah Creek in the south, and pushed enemies out of Israel. His achievements compared with David-Solomon, but he did not receive a positive evaluation due to severe economic polarization and oppression of the weak (cf. 2 Samuel 8.1-14; 1 Kings 4.21; 2 Kings 14.23-29; 17.22-23).

As a result, the history of Israel has theologically, as well as historically, been a series of the failings, rather than the achievements, of kings. Most of the descriptions of the Old Testament Israeli kings exposed the human weaknesses and failures of kingship. Since the rise of the monarchy, the lives of the people were placed under the rule of the kingship, and the practical basis of social obligations shifted to the state. As commercial activities burgeoned, a privileged class was created; the ties of tribes were weakened, and the solidarity feature of tribal society was destroyed. Even though the Yahweh faith remained the state religion, the law of the covenant with God became virtually irrelevant. Thus, there was no longer a pure form of Yahwism in Israel, which led to religious social corruption (Bright 2000: 260).

Theological Reflections and Messianic Hope

Realistically, the negative viewpoint of Deuteronomist historians and prophets on the monarchy would have been partial and limited to the early days of the monarchy. Since the monarchy became a stable political system, the criticism of prophets was about the side-effects of kingship rather than monarchy itself. However, biblical traditions that negatively evaluate royal regimes are theologically worthy of notice. This historical assessment was a theological diagnosis and prescription about why the Israelites were destroyed and what nation they could be in the future.

Looking back at the threat of Assyrian Empire and the rule of Babylonian Empire, Israelites did not think they should have armed themselves with stronger military power or achieved economic prosperity. The desire of Israel to become a nation through monarchy, just like the surrounding nations, led to centuries of war and violence (1 Samuel 8.5). Justice and peace, which had been ideals of the community since the Exodus, were nowhere to be found in Israel. However, the future proposed by Isaiah was that God would settle arguments between nations, swords and spears would be pounded into rakes and shovels, and people would never make war or attack one another (Isaiah 2.4). The ultimate goal of God for Israel, that they would be the center of the world in the future, was entirely unrelated to nationalistic ideals. God's role is described as adjudicating among the nations, His reign is universal, harmonious, and peaceful, despite the remaining demonic threat of a return to war (Childs 2001: 30–31).

Another Messianic prophecy, which was born under crisis from the empires, Isaiah 9, describes the Messianic hope as follows: "The people who walked in darkness have seen a great light; those who lived in a land of deep darkness – on them light has shined" (Isaiah 9.2). Here, darkness refers to the Syro-Ephraimite War, and the subsequent invasion by Assyria during the eighth century BCE. When observing northern Israel in a crisis of destruction by Assyria, the prophet envisioned a new kingdom through God's intervention. The brutal violence of imperialism and by Ahaz, king of Judah, who blindly followed the Assyrian Empire, reminded the prophet of the identity of the Israelites, and this historical introspection and hope were reflected in the Messianic prophecy. For this reason, the preface of prophecy is drawn from the judgment of Yahweh against the injustice and violence of oppressors: "For the yoke of their burden, and the bar across their shoulders, the rod of their oppressors, you have broken as on the day of Midian" (Isaiah 9.4, NRSV). However, the Messiah will remove the elements of war, and will establish a new governance of peace with justice and righteousness (Isaiah 9.6-7; Childs 2001: 80–81). "For all the boots of the tramping warriors and all the garments rolled in blood shall be burned as fuel for the fire" (Isaiah 9.5). In particular, the Messiah comes as a Prince (*sar*) of Peace, not a king (*melek*), to remind Israel of their identity as an egalitarian community (Isaiah 9.6; Hanson 1984: 350–351).

These features are found in other Messianic prophecies in Zechariah. Yahweh neutralizes the power of oppressors and destroys those who incited Israel to war (Zechariah 9.3-4, 8, 13). As in Isaiah, Yahweh will take away war chariots and horses, bows that were made for war will be broken (Zechariah 9.10). The new king Messiah is poor and suffering like the remnants in Micah, and will remove the military weapons of which the great powers boast, and will proclaim peace, similar to the Messiah in Isaiah (Micah 1.1-2.13; Zechariah 9.10). Consequently, the Messianic hope, as a historical reflection and alternative to monarchy contains the following features:

1. This hope and expectation came from the threat of great powers and imperialism.
2. The Messiah is not just the arrival of a new political leader but a judgment on the existing oppressors.
3. The Messiah is not a ruler over the people, but a poor and suffering servant of God.
4. He does not build a new kingdom by violent revenge, but pursues absolute peace through justice, abolishing all military weapons.

To sum up, as a result of pondering the problems and alternatives of the Israel community in national crisis, their hope for the Messiah was far from imperialistic monarchy, and this expectation was revived through the Jesus movement in the time of the Roman Empire.

Forming Resistance to Empire and Militarization

Imperialism has existed since the birth of civilization, and most nations have tried to push aside other nations to become the world center. Centralized groups or nations sought to create empires in order to rule the nations on their periphery. Considering the political-economic leverage, strong military force, and subsidies by the United States and Europe for Israeli occupation and, in particular, seeing oppression towards the Palestinians, current Israel can be considered to belonging to empire (Raheb 2014: 24). For thousands of years since the Exodus, the land of Canaan/Israel has been a battlefield, a buffer zone and crisscrossing paths of war and peace, where these empires or world powers have struggled (ibid.: 50–2). Until modern Israel encroached upon Palestinian land, the Israelites were on the side of victim of empires, and they, who longed for liberation, had a motto and a historical confession to keep in mind: "Remember that you were a slave in Egypt and the Lord your God redeemed you from there" (Deuteronomy 24.18). "My ancestor was homeless, an Aramean who went to live in Egypt" (Deuteronomy 26.5). However, this primordial experience as Hebrew does not hold anymore. Rather, just as many modern readers interpret the Bible literally, and accept the war and violence described in the Old Testament, biblical literalism was used to justify Israel's military victory in 1976 and the subsequent occupation of the West Bank. Christians, particularly, those who base themselves on mainstream evangelical culture, have been supporting a victorious God, who resembles empire, and His people (Raheb 2014: 24–25).

Notably, the Israelites, most of whom were slaves as Hebrews, attempted a radical two-dimensional change from imperial reality. This was the break from the religion of static triumphalism and from the politics of oppression and exploitation. The Egyptian religion and gods, which were dismantled by an alternative religion, community and politics of justice and peace, were creatures of the imperial consciousness and immovable lords of order. The reality emerging out of the Exodus was not only a new religion, but also, a new social community that had to create laws, patterns of governance and norms of right and wrong (Brueggemann 2001: 6-9). The early Israel community, as a new social reality, was divergent from Egypt. Yahweh, the name of God, was not static but a phenomenal-functional concept who responded to the groans of the suffering and oppressed for liberation.

However, by the time of Solomon a radical shift, which meant the abandonment of the radicalness of the Exodus, happened in the foundation of Israelite society and religion. This radical shift, which was in the opposite direction from the radical break from Egypt, resulted in political marriages (1 Kings 11.1-3), systems of tax districts (1 Kings 4.7-19), elaborate bureaucracy (1 Kings 4.1-6; 9.23), standing armies (1 Kings 4.4; 9.22), fascination with wisdom (1 Kings 4.29-34; 10.1-5, 23-25; Proverbs 1.1; 10.1) and conscripted labor from the villages (1 Kings 5.13-19; 6.1-7.51; 9.15-19, 26). All these things were an imitation of the larger empires and great regimes, that are "paganisation of Israel" (Brueggemann 2001: 23-25). The possibility of an alternative community with counter-imperialistic features was removed from Israel in Solomonic times. Instead, he achieved a highly developed material civilization, which was, in part, made possible by an oppressive social policy (1 Kings 4.20-23; 5.13-18). God and temple became part of the royal landscape, and the sovereignty of God was completely subordinated to kingship (1 Kings 8.12-13). He countered the economics of equality with the economics of affluence, the politics of justice with the politics of oppression, and the religion of liberation with the religion of eminence (Brueggemann 2001: 26-37). To make matters worse, the subsequent history of ancient Israel could hardly escape from these problems, despite the warning of the prophets and the destruction of Israel and Judah.

As mentioned above, if we think of the members of biblical Israel, the descendants of Abraham, as those who journeyed to be liberated from oppression and exploitation, Christians, Muslims and Jews today should identify themselves with the oppressed on earth. They are asked to make hermeneutical choices to establish an identity somewhere between the Exodus and the monarchy of Solomon. In particular, this choice affects individual economic activities, the formation of public opinion and policy decisions. As Mitri Raheb suggests, it is not only the "hardware," such as military equipment and advanced technology, that provides the fuel to maintain an occupying power, but it is also the "software," such as culture, narrative, and theology that helps to power the modern state of Israel which has been built totally opposing the liberative spirit of biblical Israel (Raheb 2014: 24). Consequently, forming resistance to empire and militarization can be started from an awareness of the counter-imperialistic features of biblical Israel. Although Israelites achieved prosperity and military power in the 8th century BCE, God said to the Israelites at the time; "you are not my people and I am not yours" (Hosea 1.9), certain eligibility rules that have identity of justice and peace were required to be an Israelite, as God's people, and this is valid still today.

Youngseop Lim is a biblical scholar and a PhD candidate at the School of Religion, Trinity College Dublin and his primary research revolves around faith, empire, division, and the peaceful unification of the Korean Peninsula.

References

Albright, William Foxwell. 1968. *Yahweh and the Gods of Canaan*. Winona, MN: Eisenbrauns.
Amit, Yaira. 1999. *History and Ideology: An Introduction to Historiography in the Hebrew Bible*. Sheffield: Sheffield Academic Press.
Anderson, Bernard W. 1986. "Mendenhall Disavows Paternity: Says He Didn't Father Gottwald's Marxist Theory." *Bible Review* Summer: 46–50.
Bright, John. 2000. *A History of Israel*, 4th ed. Louisville, KY: Westminster John Knox Press.
Brueggemann, Walter. 2001. *The Prophetic Imagination*, 2nd edition. Minneapolis, MN: Augsburg Fortress.
Butler, Trent C. 1983. *Joshua*. Nashville, TN: Thomas Nelson Publishers.
Callaway, Joseph A. 1965. "The 1964 'Ai (et-Tell) Excavation." *Bulletin of the American Schools of Oriental Research* 178: 13–40. https://doi.org/10.2307/1356277
Carr, David M. 2010. *An Introduction to the Old Testament: Sacred Texts and Imperial Contexts of the Hebrew Bible*. Oxford: Wiley-Blackwell.
Childs, Brevard S. 2001. *Isaiah*. Louisville, KY: Westminster John Knox Press.
Durham, John I 1987. *Exodus*. Nashville, TN: Nelson Reference & Electronic.
Ee-kon, Kim. 1989. *A Theology of Suffering in the Book of Exodus*. Seoul: Korea Theological Study Institute, 1989.
Enns, Fernando. 2013. "Toward an Ecumenical Theology of Just Peace." In *Just Peace: Ecumenical, Intercultural, and Interdisciplinary Perspective*, edited by Fernando Enns and Annette Mosher. Eugene, OR: Pickwick Publications.
Gerbrandt, Gerald Eddie. 1986. *Kingship According to the Deuteronomistic History*. Atlanta, GA: Scholars Press.
Gottwald, Norman. K. 1987. *The Hebrew Bible: A Socio-Literary Introduction*. Philadelphia, PA: Fortress Press.
Hanson, Paul D. 1984. "War and Peace in the Hebrew Bible." *Interpretation* 38(4): 341–362. https://doi.org/10.1177/002096438403800402
Horsley, Richard. A. (ed.). 2008. *In the Shadow of Empire: Reclaiming the Bible as a History of Faithful Resistance*. Louisville, KY: Westminster John Knox Press.
Johnson, Aubrey R. 1958. "Hebrew Conception of Kingship." In *Myth, Ritual and Kingship*, edited by S. H., 204–235. Oxford: Clarendon Press.
McCarter Jr., P. Kyle. 1980. *1 Samuel: A New Translation with Introduction, Notes and Commentary*. Garden City, NY: Doubleday.
Miller, J. Maxwell, and John H. Hayes. 2006. *A History of Ancient Israel and Judah*. Louisville, KY: Westminster John Knox Press.
Propp, William H. C. 1999. *Exodus 1-18*. New York: Doubleday.
Raheb, Mitri. 2014. *Faith in the Face Empire: The Bible through Palestinian Eyes*. Maryknoll, NY: Orbis.
Shanks, Hershel (ed.). 1999. *Ancient Israel: From Abraham to the Roman Destruction of the Temple*, revised and expanded edition. Upper Saddle River, NJ: Prentice Hall.
Shapira, Anita. 2012. *Israel a History*. London: Weidenfeld & Nicolson.
Szikszai, Stephen. 1962. "King, Kingship." In *The Interpreter's Dictionary of the Bible 3*, edited by George Arthur Buttrick and John Know, 14. New York: Abingdon Press.

Tsumura, David Toshio. 2007. *The First Book of Samuel*. Grand Rapid, MI: Wm. B. Eerdmans Publishing Co.
Weippert, Manfred. 1971. *The Settlement of the Israelites Tribes in Palestine*. London: SCM Press.
Whitelam, Keith W. 1992. "King and Kingship." In *Anchor Bible Dictionary 4*, edited by David Noel Freedman, 4–47. New York: Doubleday.

Part II
Africa, Latin America, The Caribbean and The Pacific Islands, and Beyond

14

Colonialism Still Matters: Militarization and Imperial Grand Strategy in the Era of US versus China

Andy Higginbottom

When two elephants fight, it is the grass that gets trampled.

—African proverb

Today it is a case of the grasshopper pitted against the elephant. But tomorrow the elephant will have its guts ripped out.

—Le Loi/Ho Chi Minh (Hsiao and Lim 2016: 14)

Introduction

This chapter will take a critical geopolitical approach concerning the militarism of contemporary imperialism. US strategists address the world with the imperialist mindset of making sure that their country stays the only global super-power. I make three general propositions:

(a) The US is still the leading imperialist power, it relies heavily on huge military capacity to retain that position. US imperialism is a highly weaponized elephant, ready to trample with great force anywhere in the world.

(b) Linked to this, the US in concert with the UK acting as junior partner bolster their global leadership by means of a network of alliances with militarized regimes of a neo-colonial type. These regimes rule through forms of internal repression backed up externally as required.

(c) Despite US victory in the Cold War against the Soviet Union, its domestic manufacturing industry has since stumbled, such that preserving forms of monopoly combined with intensified methods of exploitation overseas are crucial to maintaining US corporate super-profits in most industrial sectors.

The above three factors combine to fuel US hostility to any state representing significant independent economic power, an aggressive agenda that is rationalized as defending US national security interests. The US political leadership currently frames their global military strategy in terms of responding to a triple threat to

US hegemony: control over the Middle East; from a non-compliant Russia; and above all, from China's continuing rise (Department of Defense 2019). This threat complex is the principal driver of global militarization, and is the reason for the US strategic "pivot to Asia."

The pivot was announced by Obama's Secretary of State, Hilary Clinton in 2010 but, as we will see, was already well under way with catastrophic consequences. For example, these general propositions were the over-determining geopolitical drivers of the war in Sri Lanka that culminated in that state's genocidal massacre of 70,000 or more Tamil people in 2009, as exposed in Chapter 5 by Athithan Jayapalan and Gajendrakumar Ponnambalam. This raises the question of how exceptional is the Eelam Tamil case, or whether it can be considered an indicator of a broader pattern of neo-colonized peoples sacrificed at the altar of Washington's grand strategy to control the entire Indo-Pacific region. The chapter concludes that US imperialism has built a huge military advantage for a reason, and it is prepared to use it across the continents. In contrast to the capitalist state-centered alliances implementing militarization, we call for a renewed internationalism, the anti-imperialist unity of all oppressed peoples.

Global Picture: US Military Pre-eminence

According to the Stockholm International Peace Research Institute (SIPRI), military expenditure as a proportion of the world's GDP declined from 6 percent at the height of the Cold War in the 1960s to just over 2 percent by 2016. This measure, suggesting a real "peace dividend" needs to be tempered by the ratio of military expenditure to total central government spending, which rose sharply from 5 percent in 1996 to peak at 7 percent in 2006 and still runs at over 6 percent (SIPRI 2018). In 2018, the US spent $649 billion on the military, China spent $250 billion. These two giants were followed in declining order by Saudi Arabia, India, France, Russia, UK, Germany, Japan and South Korea, all in the $40–70 billion expenditure range (statistica.com 2019a). The figures indicate the overwhelming predominance of the US in military expenditure, with China running second in the decade since 2008, but only spending a third as much. The aggregate military spend of the EU states is on a par with China's, but this prompts the question of their cohesion or not as a military power.

Where the US focuses its military effort is indicated by the breakdown of its expenditure. For the decade after 9/11, US military budgets were heavily committed to the wars in Iraq (2002–2012), peaking at $150 billion in 2008; and Afghanistan (2007–2016), peaking at $120 billion in 2011. The ongoing US occupation of Afghanistan costs around $50 billion a year as of 2018, around 8 percent of its total military spend (Crawford 2018). In what theatres is the US military now putting its resources? A major clue is given by the pattern of US arms exports, as in Table 14.1, which indicates a clear regional focus on its allies in the Middle East region ($5.9 billion) and in East Asia ($2.2 billion).

The huge concentration of US arms sales to Saudi Arabia and other countries in the Gulf is notable. These regimes are dependent on the support of the US to keep

Table 14.1 US arms exports, by country in 2018 (US$ million).

Exported to	Export value
Saudi Arabia	3,353
Australia	918
United Arab Emirates	799
Japan	675
South Korea	612
Israel	480
Qatar	423
Norway	346
Morocco	333
Turkey	293
Italy	241
Afghanistan	206
Egypt	197

Source: statistica.com (2019b)

control of the region, which remains a crucial fulcrum in the balance of world power (Hannieh 2011: 101).

Post-World War II Militarized US/UK Neo-colonialism

The resurgence of US militarization post 9/11 has taken place through multiple new forms: the mushrooming of private security from the Iraq occupation; an international system of rendition and torture operating with impunity; a global network of forward operating bases; enhanced surveillance capacities; drone warfare; the militarization of space. We need to synthesize these different elements with a critical approach that captures the underlying international power relations and the contradictions that drive them.

While there are debates on the terminology, "militarization" is used to mean the expansion of a state's armed forces in generalized preparation for war, especially an increasing degree to which industrial production is geared to their demands (Gillis 1989). "Militarism" is the ideology that accompanies militarization, and pushes it even further to involve the mass of the population in the military project; it is the domination of the military over all other spheres and a heightened "disposition to use force" (Mabee and Vucetic 2018: 98). This recent typology of militarism identified "nation state militarism" and "neoliberal militarism," but had no category for neo-colonial or imperialistic militarism, which we see as central organizing concepts, as will be explained in what follows.

The US and UK emerged victorious at the end of World War II operating a partnership at the center of the global order. They were the principal architects of the Bretton Woods international financial institutions and the undemocratically structured UN. Without discarding language, common heritage and culture, what underpins their "special relationship" is the convergence rather than clashing of their imperialist interests.

Mark Curtis explains the changes in this partnership, which passed through moments of deep tension, adjustment and ultimately deepening on new terms with clearly the US as the stronger partner (Curtis 1998: 24–32). The public US–UK partnership took on a specific diplomatic *modus vivendi* with the creation of the UN. For decades the basic play, one that Curtis illustrates worked time and again, was that the US proposes and an apparently independent UK disposes through endorsement, encouragement, alliance building to rally support for the US position (ibid.: ch. 7). Curtis expresses this neatly by the formula "2 + 2 = 5." Diplomacy through the UN was however the tip of the iceberg, alongside was the more private deep collaboration between the military establishments in constructing joint approaches, and of the respective intelligence services in spying and related dirty war operations. More than any other, the region in which the realigned American-Anglo power duo has been both fundamental and successful is the Middle East, most especially the states around the Persian Gulf, where the basic design of the state order rests on neo-colonial regimes that are dependent on US–UK military assistance to maintain themselves in power, broadly in exchange for priority access to the primary sources of the world's oil supply.

The Persian Gulf

The post-World War II construction of state power in the Middle East built a further level on the foundations already laid by the UK and France in the midst of World War I. The main element of the post-World War II Gulf settlement was the entry of the US into the power alliance, closely linked to Saudi Arabia as its major interest (Sampson 1975). The result has not been an absolute US/UK monopoly of international oil supplies, but significant control as well as huge profits, and a deep understanding of mutual self-interest between the Western powers and the highly anti-democratic and repressive dynastic regimes sitting on the oil reserves. This convergence of interest gets thrown whenever a national government shows independence and steps out of line with the Western powers' agenda; whereupon the US and UK have intervened militarily to enforce regime change, as in their coup in Iran 1953 and the wars against Iraq in 1991 and 2003–2007. The military, economic and political dimensions are all closely inter-related in this combined expression of imperial power, wealth extraction and dependency of corrupt regimes (Curtis 1998).

The US and UK have for decades worked in concert to arm the reactionary regimes that benefit from and control huge oil resources of the Persian Gulf region. There are multiple connections between London and a chain of the most anti-woman, anti-democratic *rentier* state regimes that are kept in power. The UK has a dirty history of implementing a torture regime in Oman, for example (Takriti 2013: 75–81). UK arms exports to the Gulf states amounted to nearly $5 billion year in the early 2010s (Raphael and St. John 2016). As well as the sale of warships and aircraft, since used by Saudi Arabia to bomb Yemen, the UK supplies a range of technologies and training for internal repression, and has a new military base in Manama, Bahrain, opened by Prince Andrew in 2018 (Stubley 2018). "Our Armed Forces are the face of Global Britain and our presence in Bahrain will play a vital role in keeping Britain safe as well as underpinning security in the Gulf," said defense secretary Gavin Williamson, perhaps too frankly. An example of pure imperial chutzpah to claim a military base some three thousand miles away has any defensive purpose. "Keeping Britain safe" translates into keeping British oil company profits safe, as the base is positioned close to the shipping lane that passes through the Strait of Hormuz, and is designed with facilities for the UK's two new aircraft carriers, the Queen Elizabeth and the Prince of Wales. This sequence demonstrates joined up thinking that has put in place serious and rapid land, sea and air power projection.

As this chapter is being finished, the "tit for tat" crisis of oil tankers being seized in Gibraltar by the UK, and in the Hormuz Strait by Iran, unfolds. The claim by UK Foreign Secretary Jeremy Hunt that his decision to seize an Iranian super-tanker were implementing EU policy and backed by international law, while Iran's seizure of vessels are not, is tissue thin and belied by the report that UK action was not the result of consultation with fellow EU members, but at the prompting of US National Security Advisor John Bolton, after his urgings had failed with Spain (Sabbagh and Burgen 2019). Despite UK promptings, Germany has refused to join a US led naval patrol force that risked war with Iran (Sabbagh 2019). In a tilt away from the attempt at European cooperation, the Boris Johnson government has committed the UK to joint naval patrols in the Hormuz Strait and the adjoining Gulf of Oman under the aegis of US Operation Sentinel (Wintour 2019).

Africa

Rita Abrahamsen writes in general terms concerning Africa at the time of independence, militarization "as in all newly independent regions, was externally dependent and fueled by external actors ... This was particularly the case in terms of the hardware that made militarization possible" (Abrahamsen 2018: 21). In the context of the Cold War, arms supplies, and with that training and funding, was a way of keeping client relations between the new rulers and global powers. Maintaining institutional military links were strategically vital:

> For Africa's Western allies, functioning militaries were not only seen as part of building the modern nation-state, but also regarded as naturally conservative institutions that could be relied upon to temper and contain the social pressures and dislocations arising from rapidly changing societies.
>
> (Abrahamsen 2018: 22).

Militarization was a normal condition of dependent state power that became heightened into militarism, defined in this context as "the constant readiness for war" (ibid.: 22). In Africa the *coup d'état* was deployed repeatedly, to the extent that it became the norm. This "domestically oriented militarism," saw the generals targeting internal enemies, not only against corrupt politicians as Abrahamsen notes (ibid.: 23), but against leaders like Patrice Lumumba who were headed in too progressive a direction and, as was also the case in Latin America in the 1970s and 1980s, the physical elimination of large sections of the population. Nor did the Middle East and Asia escape the tendency to dictatorship by armies trained and armed by the West (Blanchard 1996).

The general condition of these authoritarian forms of government and social control is a mutual agreement between the Western powers and domestic elites, that was coined neo-colonialism by Kwame Nkrumah. According to Nkrumah:

> The essence of neo-colonialism is that the state which is subject to it is, in theory, independent and has all the outward trapping of international sovereignty. In reality its economic system and thus its political policy is directed from outside.
> (Nkrumah 1965: ix)

While this terminology has fallen out of academic fashion, and we do not have space to retrieve its full ramifications, neo-colonialism remains the most useful concept to explain the multiplicity of voluntary pacts that keep nominally independent states in an economically subordinate position.[1]

The end of the Cold War saw a shift in policy as well as in the dominant framing narrative:

> Freed from the constraints of bipolarity, Western states abandoned their long-term, often authoritarian allies and demanded multiparty elections and free market economics in return for continued development assistance.
> (Abrahamsen 2018: 23)

Abrahamsen traces how development and security became enmeshed in a common reform agenda, that itself came under critique. This is one side of the story, for the undoubted shift to development discourse was matched by the open endorsement of military solutions justified by the "war on terror." In other words, there was a complex variation in the terms of the neo-colonial condition, rather than its termination. Post-Cold War soon became post-9/11, once again bolstering US military solutions, a new round of interventionism and its active seeking out of authoritarian solutions as, which has witnessed under so called "security cooperation" the rapid expansion of the US Africa Command, a military network of forward bases with emphasis on rapid deployment and special forces (H. Campbell 2017). The occupation of Libya was pushed for by France and the UK as much as the US (Elliott 2011). Their aerial bombardment was less to do with human rights under Gadaffi or even to secure access to the country's oil, for Tony Blair had already anointed a huge contract between Libya and BP, than it was to secure access on more profitable terms (Macalister 2011) and, as Horace Campbell (2013) demonstrates, to extend NATO's reach into Africa.

Latin America

Since Hugo Chávez electoral victory in Venezuela in 1998, there emerged a bipolar pattern in Latin America of leftist governments brought into office with support from popular movements; in tension with continuing right-wing neoliberal regimes. The contrast was particularly sharp in the Andean region with Bolivia, Venezuela and rather equivocally Ecuador seeking to strike an alternative path; in contrast to Chile, Colombia and Peru whose governments remained closely aligned with imperialism, embracing for example the misnamed US, Canadian and European "free trade agreements." There is evidence of divergence between these two groupings, especially in terms of efforts to escape the profit drain by multinational corporations (Higginbottom 2013).

Ecuador's Rafael Correa government invited new investment from China but without breaking from the extractivist model, and turned on its own original popular base, especially the indigenous movement which remains a real signifier across the region as shown by Napoleón Saltos Galarza and Luis Arizmendi in chapters fifteen and sixteen of this work respectively. Even with the continuing goodwill of most social movements, the governments of Bolivia and Venezuela have not escaped the dilemmas of their structural legacies (Gudynas 2018). Presidents Evo Morales and Nicolás Maduro are resisting escalating destabilization and economic warfare from Washington; defense of the national sovereignty of Bolivia and Venezuela against imperialist intervention by the US and its allies is again an immediate and urgent issue. Meanwhile the authoritarian and neo-colonial character of Colombia and Chile has returned to international view with massacres of the indigenous movement (Democracy Now 2019) and assassination, disappearances and torture of working class youth protestors in Chile (Aguilera 2019); both by repressive state apparatuses fashioned and trained by the US military.

The region's two biggest countries Mexico and Brazil have swapped the ideological allegiances of their governments but, whether reluctantly in the case of social-democrat AML Obrador in Mexico (Carlsen 2019), or willingly as with neo-fascist Bolsonaro in Brazil (Phillips 2019), they too are caught in the logic of internal repression to enforce external extraction in the service of empire. In this regard, it is important to trace the deeply institutionalized military connections: as demonstrated by sociologist Martha Huggins (1999); the more human rights training Brazilian police received from the US, the more violations they committed.

Imperialist Grand Strategy at the End of the Cold War

There are two models of international relations that are significant for framing the current headlong rush to US imperialist militarization of the Indian and Pacific Ocean regions, known as the "pivot to Asia," a term first coined in 2010 but in reality well in motion in the preceding decade (K. Campbell 2016). The first model, the Brzezinski Doctrine, emerged in the final phase of the Cold War, as a strategy for the US to manage the collapse of the Soviet Union in its interests: the fall of the Soviet Union opportunity model. The second model is the rise of China model, in which China is portrayed as the new imperial power akin to the USA's own eruption as a global power at the beginning of the twentieth century. Both models are the inventions of US strategists with the common aim of maintaining

US supremacy, and in this regard share certain delusional aspects; and yet we have to consider them seriously for these strategies of domination are the main drivers of militarism in the world.

The Brzezinski Doctrine: control Eurasia, control the World

The fundamental premise argued by Brzezinski is that to control the world, an imperial power must have control of the Eurasian land mass, but since the US is located on another continent it has to find a way of overcoming this structural impediment to consolidating its global leadership as "the world's paramount power" (Brzezinski 1997: viii). The question was addressed with some urgency at the end of the bi-polar dynamic of the Cold War. Brzezinski's answer was for the US to pay special attention to the conflicts in countries on the rim of the former Soviet Union, and take control of them as far as possible and so construct a network of pro-US states. Brzezinski highlighted the outer boundaries of the former Soviet Union and China, where he posited three central strategic fronts of emerging conflict that the US should seek to control: one being between eastern and western Europe; the second the southern Soviet Union's interface with the Middle East from Turkey to Afghanistan; and thirdly the line across the seas of East Asia between China and North Korea on the one side, and their capitalist neighbors stretching from Japan to Indonesia. It is by controlling these three peripheries, ran the argument, that the US would be able to control the vast Eurasian hinterlands (ibid.: 39).

This was geopolitics on a grand scale, the world reduced to a chessboard on which the US would move its pieces. Brzezinski had been a key adviser to President Jimmy Carter, often portrayed as the most liberal of US presidents, and yet the imperialist underpinnings are undeniable, as for example:

> the three grand imperatives of imperial geostrategy are to prevent collusion and maintain security dependence among the vassals, to keep tributaries pliant and protected, and to keep the barbarians from coming together.
>
> (Brzezinski 1997: 40)

What we have here is a frank admission from a grand master of informal empire of seeing relations with other nominally independent states solely in terms of domination, subordination and manipulation that we have already identified as neo-colonial, as the best critique pointed out at the time (Gowan 1999).

Brzezinski's influence persists, his predictive approach provides an identifiable thread running through the course of military conflicts in the last quarter century, in which the US has conducted wars of occupation in Iraq and Afghanistan to keep control of the southern rim; but also with an adjustment to take account of the surprise economic turn, the shift of production to China and its consequences. Without losing its concern to thwart Russia as a possible super-power the US has, according to the logic of its over-weaning imperial ambition, had to give ever more of its attention to the lines connecting the Middle East and the Far East, and this has in turn led to a shift in the locus of its global military strategy.

The geopolitical concept of a rim of land based conflicts had to be extended and shifted south to include the struggle for power over the Indian Ocean and Western Pacific.

The Mahan/Roosevelt Precedent

The opening of the twentieth century saw the US join in the fight between seaborne powers for dominance over oceans and continents. Brzezinski agrees with Lenin that to analyze modern imperialism the 1898 Spanish-American War is an appropriate starting point. For such opposed analysts to converge on this one point, probably the only thing they could agree on, deserves reflection. Lenin and Brzezinski's commentaries bracket the birth and then subsequent fall of the Soviet Union (1917–1991), the former to call it into being as an act of resistance to World War I, the latter to celebrate its demise. For all their ideological difference both writers had a keen grasp of world politics and a rare capacity to situate their living moment in the *longue durée* of history; both analysts sought to analyze the drivers of imperial strategies that were rapidly changing the international order in order to thwart or advance them respectively. Lenin cited the Spanish-America conflict along with the Anglo-Boer War and the Russo-Japanese War at the beginning of the twentieth century as signaling the start of the period of modern imperialism characterized by wars between a handful of industrial powers seeking to carve up the rest of the world between them (Lenin 1916). The US used its occupation of the Philippines as the launch pad for the dispatch of 2,500 troops to Beijing where they joined the European powers in suppressing the Boxer Uprising (Paterson et al. 2014: 26–27). For Brzezinski the significance of "America's first overseas war of conquest" is that is marked a great leap forward in US imperial ambitions to police the Western Hemisphere and use its newly built naval power to dominate both the Atlantic and Pacific, in short the beginning of "US Century" (Brzezinski 1997: 1).

US triumphalism at the collapse of the Soviet Union proved to be short lived, and has required a rethought global military strategy. The decline of US imperial power (to what degree is for evaluation) and the rise of China as challenger (likewise subject to evaluation) puts world politics at a similar pivotal moment as at the beginning of the twentieth century. Is there such a major shift in the locus of industrial power that we are already on the cusp of China's century? Not the same configuration, for sure, as the beginning of the twentieth century but certainly one that sees the return of themes inter-imperial rivalries, protectionism and trade wars turning into currency wars, technology wars, that beg the question of whether the increasing across spectrum tensions will spill over into proxy wars and even full scale war. But within this headline story, there is another that Lenin at least was aware of, and is best exemplified by the insistence the Spanish-America war was actually a triangular fight in which the Cubans rose in arms for their independence, as Philip Foner ([1972] 2005) records comprehensively. In terms of the proverbs with which we open this chapter, the Cubans were already by 1898 the grasshopper and not the grass; and yet despite the Cubans' resistance there was an ambivalent outcome. Cuba got rid of Spanish colonialism only to be burdened by US neo-colonialism, it would take another two generations before they rose again to push the US elephant fully out of their island.

The rapid burst US naval power was the fruition of a ship building program put in place some fifteen years earlier by Alfred T. Mahan; and enacted by President Theodore Roosevelt, see Chapter 17 by Kyle Kajihiro. Both are celebrated figures for today's US strategists, who draw attention to the need for a system of ships complimented by well-placed bases, with special attention to the capacity to concentrate battle power on strategic control points (Kaplan 2014: 44–50). This sums up the Mahanian logic informing current US geo-political strategy. The US repositioning of its military capacities into Asia was a double movement of forces to the Indian Ocean's western edge to control the Middle East, and to the Pacific's Ocean's western edge to contain China. The Obama strategy put imperative emphasis on controlling the maritime routes, especially the vulnerable choke points, the Hormuz Strait and the Malacca Strait:

> We will not permit conditions under which our maritime forces would be impeded from freedom of maneuver and freedom of access, nor will we permit an adversary to disrupt the global supply chain by attempting to block vital sea-lines of communication and commerce.
>
> (Cited in Bradford 2011: 185)

The Malacca Strait is a critical choke point, narrowing to under 3 kilometers at its narrowest off Singapore, it is nonetheless the main shipping between the Indian and Pacific Oceans (Emmerson and Stevens 2012). Shipping through the passage carries three quarters of China's oil and gas imports, rising to over 90 percent for Japan and South Korea; and the Strait is the main conduit for raw materials from Africa and imports from Western Europe (ERIA 2016). In 2003 China's government identified Malacca as a vulnerability to US intervention, to be offset by building its own naval capacity on the one hand and seeking alternative routes on the other (Lanteigne 2008). Beijing's determination to construct an intercontinental infrastructure to secure its massive flow of imports and exports is a significant factor in the truly vast and much commented upon One Belt One Road initiative, launched in 2013. Opening an Arctic route to Europe is also projected (Arctic Institute 2013). The "maritime silk road" could have several threads if all these ambitions are fulfilled, but for now the straits at Hormuz and Malacca remain crucial geo-political nodes.

Modes of Militarization

The *mode* of global militarization and the manner of its organization as significant as location. In Brzezinski's reading, the Soviet Union "the world's leading land power, paramount on the Eurasian heartland" (Brzezinski 1997: 6), was pitted against the USA as "the world's leading maritime power," to which we add air power, as the new dimension of the twentieth century. Command of the air became the *sine qua non* of military strategy. Thomas Hippler shows convincingly how the European powers (UK, France, Italy) first used aerial bombing as a means to target and terrorize civilian populations in their Middle East and African colonies, before similar strategies were adopted by the UK and US against the populations of Germany and Japan in World War II (Hippler 2017).

How to maintain capacity to dominate militarily any corner of the world without vast standing armed forces? Informatics and communications have become another dimension. When leaders speak of full spectrum capabilities they mean it literally. Today we have a synthesis of modes of warfare combining the mercantile naval empires with twentieth century aerial and informatics power. Air strike capacity is not limited any more to airplanes, the full spectrum includes missiles and drones as delivery mechanisms (Medea 2012; Manson 2018). In terms of efficiency the US military have developed a global system of aerial monitoring and rapid deployment power projection. On land this is advanced by a network of forward operating locations (Vine 2017), and at sea by the formation of naval/aerial battle groups.

The re-organization of the military along neo-liberal lines has seen a new chapter in the military industrial complex. The US/UK occupation of Iraq gave a huge boost to private military and security companies, that were encouraged by particularly lax regulatory regimes, and in any case developed various tactics to disguise and offshore their operations (Raphael 2016). The sector is worth hundreds of billions, and includes major multinationals such as G4S and a myriad of medium sized outfits (securitydegreehub.com 2019). The mega-corporations of the extractive industries, Big Oil and Big mining, are major clients of private military and security services, as are big ports (Raphael 2016: 6–7). Privatized, para-state repression against local populations is an auxiliary function of export oriented growth. Imperialism, neocolonialism and neoliberalism all come together in this web of privatized repressive services, whose removal from democratic accountability is useful to both the Western powers and neo-colonial clients.

China's Rise from Savior to Rival—from Trade Wars to ...?

How to analyze US rivalry with China in a way that satisfactorily combines the political-economic with military analyses?

Political-Economic Considerations

Critical political economy analysis is polarized between two contrasting evaluations that summarize a complex and contradictory totality quite differently: does China's continuing rise since 1980 mean the beginning of the end for the US; or does the opposite interpretation hold, that we are at the end of the beginning of what will be another American century? It is common ground that China avoided the worst of the 2008 crash, and that the strength of its boom helped alleviate the depth of the crisis in the US and the rest of the capitalist world. The picture according to national production and exports appears as significantly different to that from the perspective of corporate profits. Using data and other figures on imports, monetary reserves and capital exports Caputo and Galarce conclude that by 2014 *China had already surpassed the US as the world's leading economic power* (Caputo and Galarce 2014).

Caputo and Galarce do note that US multinationals were able to claim a substantial part of the profits from production in China, and viewing through this lens gives a different landscape of economic power. First, Sean Starrs identifies the leading and most profitable companies globally, finding that in 2013 US corporations lead in eighteen out of twenty five industrial sectors (Starrs 2014: 87). Second, and more than is supposed, US corporations supply China's domestic markets in high tech sectors such as civil aviation and computer software. Third, the role of off-shored manufacture in boosting profits of US multinationals; which has been widely exemplified in the case of Foxconn and Apple. Harsh forms of labor exploitation are a constant condition of the coercion of daily life, a syndrome or structural violence for the many under imperialist globalization. The analysis of this is by John Smith (2016) explores the general pattern of unequal exchange through which value is produced at one pole and captured at another. The basis of the relation is the super-exploitation of labor, more often than not of female workers, that occurs more widely than China and is extending across the global South.

Of the world's top 100 multinationals, ranked by foreign assets, 20 are US corporations, 14 are UK, 12 are based in France, and 11 each Germany and Japan. Corporations from these five countries count for 70 percent of the foreign assets of the top 100 multinationals (UNCTAD 2018: 29). At 16.7 percent, the accentuated strength of the UK by this last criterion is because London is the platform for several of the super-majors, the world's biggest oil and mining corporations. These figures point to the concentration on particularly profitable operations, super-profits in Lenin's terms, drawn from abroad in a parasitic manner. They also point to the economic motive for a particular type of state military, with the capacity for various forms of imperial power projection as the need arises. Starrs argues that China is still inhibited by a junior relation with the US. "China is the first major country to rise in the era of globalization, with its development driven to a large extent by foreign capital" (Starrs 2015: 14). He concludes that we have just arrived at the end of the first phase US hegemony, the end of the beginning. We are only now entering the full "American Century" (Starrs 2018).

The pace of Chinese capitalism's rise means that the picture is fast moving. Its positioning in the global mining industry is instructive. In the previous super-cycle much of the profits from commodities boom went to mining majors based in the UK and its white settler close allies: Canada, Australia, and South Africa. To a large extent the shares in these majors were held by US based entities, 56 percent for example in the case of the world's richest mining corporation BHP Billiton (Starrs 2017: 655). Chinese state supported enterprises bought up mining assets in 2016 at the bottom of the cycle and have now begun to enter into the global top 40. These Chinese companies are moving into the earlier points in the supply chain. They do not yet lead worldwide mining, but they have a significant and growing presence (Higginbottom 2018).

There are two further problems with Starr's interpretation: Chinese state capitalism is of a different type to the capitalism of the traditional imperialist powers, so the measures of its overall strength are not the same. Specifically the modality of capital export is different, and is in the form of state sponsored loans backing large infrastructure projects, rather than direct foreign investment. The more general objection to Starrs's interpretation is quite obvious, if US multinationals and finance are doing so well out of China's boom, then why are there so many tensions and growing hostility to China's rise from the US state? Is the US program of escalating military pressure on China a colossal mistake, a misunderstanding of its own interests, or otherwise a lack of internal cohesion within the US ruling class between its economic actors and state military institutions? Indeed, were there such separate logics of economic benefits versus military competition, it is hard to conceptualize a coherent ruling class at all.

Will US–China Competition Lead to War?

The contradictions underlying the 2007/8 crash have not gone away, and will sooner or later reassert themselves, and in recession capitalist powers tend to lurch towards protectionism and zero-sum solutions. China's trade surplus with the US has been converted into monetary reserves, which in turn are converted in US state treasury bonds as a safe haven investment, with the result that China holds much of US public debt. Rather than a mitigating factor, tensions have moved onto the terrain of the exchange rate between the *renminbi* and the US dollar, that is from a "trade war" to "currency wars" (Szalay 2019).

The dominant debate in the US establishment is whether war with China is inevitable. For one example of many, see (Holmes and Yoshihara 2017). Under Trump the language is sharply belligerent, verging on the drive to a self-fulfilling prophecy (Department of Defense 2019). Yet, despite the change in presidential tone there is considerable continuity in US policy. Jude Woodward largely succeeds in showing that under Obama US was aggressive in pushing towards a conflict that China has been seeking to avoid. Woodward (2017) concludes that the US does not want full scale open war, but models its objectives in a similar way to how it managed the decades-long competition with the Soviet Union. In other words, Cold War with China was the Obama agenda. Woodward pinpoints Hillary Clinton's claim in Hanoi on July 23, 2010 that the South China Sea is in the US sphere of "national interest" as the real indication of what the pivot to Asia indicated, the US will actively intervene diplomatically, step up its naval challenge in China's immediate environs and even prepare for possible war through what is euphemistically termed a "pre-emptive build-up" (Woodward 2017: 72, 174–175). Her analysis also shows how important it is for Washington to present China as bullying its neighbors, and so bring into play a "coalition of the willing" against Beijing. The view from the Chinese leadership is that Clinton's declaration was itself an aggressive disruption, seeking to inflame differences into international law breaking *casus belli*. China and the south-east Asian countries had established their own regional process which emphasizes common aims and projects while recognizing competing claims. Woodward provides a different context on the disputed islands in the South China Sea to that prevailing in the Western media. China's historical claim to the area within the "nine dash line" was acknowledged by the US at the end of World War II, and on her account Taiwan, Malaysia, Vietnam and the Philippines all have their own airstrip islands (ibid.: 177).

"What does America want?" The answer Woodward gives is to get as much benefit as possible from the reintroduction of capitalism in China, which means in broad terms keeping China's growth in channels that also benefit the US, a subordinate capitalism that does not challenge US strategic monopolies. The US wants China to open its public sector, especially state sponsored banking, to private US finance capital. But the US has not been able to lever a split in the Chinese political leadership with a Yeltsin figure emerging to implement this program. Consequently the US is seeking to lever its superior military power to supplement political-economic measures to "persuade China to change course." (Woodward 2017: 8–18). It is exactly this return to a subordinate role in the world division of labor that China is seeking to escape, and is already on the cusp of doing so. However the only means to do this *on a capitalist basis* is for the Chinese state itself to move in the direction of a new imperialist power in its own right. In a remarkably prescient speech over forty years ago, Deng Xiaoping (1974) warned precisely against this outcome.

After making his initial moves, Trump's core policy towards China has more continuity with Obama than is often supposed (Kauikan 2017). Trump broke long held convention and make direct contact with Taiwan, and he withdrew the US from Obama's Trans-Pacific Partnership (TPP) project, moreover he implemented campaign promises to put tariffs on Chinese imports to the US. The underlying consensus assumption between Republicans and Democrats is that the US must maintain "leadership" (i.e. domination) in the Asia-Pacific. The parties have their distinct preferred ways of doing international politics, the much vaunted multilateralism versus unilateralism made so much of in the international relations discipline, but again there is not so much substantive difference when it comes to focusing on bolstering connections with key allies and the wooing of others. The underlying reason for the original pivot to Asia has become more transparent, competition with China and full spectrum effort to channel its rise in a direction most advantageous to the US.

From US Militarization to Imperial Militarism?

In this chapter we have argued that the interventionist Brzezinski doctrine illuminates US military strategy, which has nonetheless shifted to the Indo-Pacific region in order counter the rise of China perceived as a global threat. Militarism is the ideology that accompanies militarization, and pushes it even further to involve the mass of the population in the military project; as we have noted, it is the domination of the military over all other spheres and a heightened "disposition to use force" (Mabee and Vucetic 2018: 98). In the neo-colonial condition, the imperial powers are able to sub-contract militarism to the local elite's more rooted ability to mobilize class or ethnic hatred, as the case of Sri Lanka exemplifies. Social militarism has only erupted in the imperialist countries on occasion, as a response to heightened inter-imperialist rivalries leading to war. Contemporary US militarism expresses the *strong preference for war* as the means to resolve conflicts of interest.

We see a shift from militarization to militarism in the US with Trump's supposedly "populist," but actually imperial-nationalist, mobilization around "America First." Under the Trump presidency the move from tariffs on imports *from* China, to naval blockades to stop imports *into* China, is quite believable. Indeed, the US military has for the last decade been preparing for battle operations centered on control of maritime routes at their chokepoints; Hormuz and Malacca Straits, Taiwan, Korea, South China Sea, and now Hong Kong. Although nowhere near the US global dominance, China has itself built up considerable military capacity with a regional deterrence factor which is probably sufficient to hold off the most flagrant US aggression. But the build-up of tensions is a structural contradiction that could sharpen radically, especially so with any return of the underlying tendency to economic crisis.

We have sought to argue that militarization and militarism are the deadly companions of imperialism. However, the missing link in state-centered approaches to militarized imperialism is the potential for agency of oppressed peoples and workers, for in the end the only way to ensure peace and security of the poor is through the fight to destroy imperialism. This spirit of enduring resistance is the unmarked legacy of the tragically massacred Eelam Tamils, as well as of so many other oppressed peoples. These contributions must be seen as the bedrock of a new humanity of the oppressed. Recognizing their sacrifice for world peace is a step on the road to recovering internationalism for the twenty-first century, and a genuine dialogue leading to cooperation that we sincerely hope this volume contributes to.

Andy Higginbottom is associate professor in Kingston University and a senior fellow of Higher Education Academy in the UK. He is an international solidarity campaigner in support of social movements in Colombia, South Africa and Tamil Eelam. He teaches modules on international political economy, slavery and emancipation, and crimes of the powerful.

Note

1. Singapore is one clear example of how the US and UK worked in concert to intervene to snuff out the threat of radical nationalism against their imperial interests. Nominally independent since 1965, the city state of Singapore epitomizes what we term neo-colonialism. Singapore has been locked into an authoritarian mode of governance, with generations of prisoners detained without trial under the Internal Security Act. The repeating pattern of the controlled neo-colonial transition was to promote the moderates and defeat the militants (Poh 2016: 113–116). Today the US has taken over what was the UK Royal Navy base in Singapore, which operates as the logistics center for the entire US 7th Fleet, with close cooperation with Australian and New Zealand forces (Brooke-Holland 2018). With his left-wing political rivals removed from the

scene, Lee Kuan Yew rose to international stardom as a pro-Western Asian leader with special insight into the geo-politics of his northern neighbor, China.

References

Abrahamsen, Rita. 2018. "Return of the Generals? Global Militarism in Africa from the Cold War to the Present." *Security Dialogue* 49(1–2):19–31. https://doi.org/10.1177/0967010617742243

Aguilera, Juana. 2019. *Del 17 al 27 de octubre 2019: los 10 días en que el Terrorismo de Estado vuelve a campear por Chile*. Santiago, Chile: Comisión Ética Contra la Tortura.

Arctic Institute. 2013. "The Future of Arctic Shipping: A New Silk Road for China?" Retrieved from www.thearcticinstitute.org/wp-content/uploads/2013/11/The-Future-of-Arctic-Shipping-A-New-Silk-Road-for-China.pdf?x62767 (accessed October 15, 2019).

Blanchard, William. 1996. *Neocolonialism American Style, 1960–2000*. Westport CT: Greenwood Press.

Bradford, John. 2011. "The Maritime Strategy of the United States: Implications for Indo-Pacific Sea Lanes." *Contemporary Southeast Asia* 33(2): 183–208. https://doi.org/10.1355/cs33-2b

Brooke-Holland, Louisa. 2018. "Royal Navy: A Return to the Far East?" Retrieved from https://ukdefencejournal.org.uk/royal-navy-a-return-to-the-far-east (accessed October 10, 2019).

Brzezinski, Zbigniew. 1997. *The Grand Chessboard: American Primacy and its Geostrategic Imperatives*. New York: Basic Books.

Campbell, Horace. 2013. *Global NATO and the Catastrophic Failure in Libya*. New York: Monthly Review Press.

Campbell, Horace. 2017. "The United States and Security in Africa: The Impact of the Military Management of the International System." *Africa Development* 42(3): 45–71.

Campbell, Kurt. 2016. *The Pivot—The Future of American Statecraft in Asia*. New York: Twelve.

Caputo, Orlando and Graciela Galarce. 2014. "China Desplazó a EEUU Como Primera Potencia Económica Mundial." Retrieved from www.rebelion.org/docs/184347.pdf (accessed October 12, 2019).

Carlsen, Laura. 2019. "Mexico's Transformation in the Shadow of Trump." Retrieved from www.sheffield.ac.uk/slc/news/mexicos-transformation-shadow-trump (accessed October 15, 2019).

Crawford, Neta. 2018. "United States Budgetary Costs of the Post-9/11 Wars Through FY2019: $5.9 Trillion Spent and Obligated." Retrieved from https://watson.brown.edu/costsofwar/files/cow/imce/papers/2018/Crawford_Costs%20of%20War%20Estimates%20Through%20FY2019.pdf (zccessed October 15, 2019).

Curtis, Mark. 1998. *The Great Deception: Anglo-American Power and World Order*. London: Pluto Press.

Democracy Now. 2019. "Five Indigenous Leaders Massacred in Colombia: New Wave of Violence Feared as 2,500 Troops Deployed." Retrieved from www.democracynow.org/2019/11/1/cristina_bautista_colombia_indigenous_leaders_killed (accessed October 16, 2019).

Deng Xiaoping. 1974. "Speech By Chairman of the Delegation of the People's Republic of China, Teng Hsiao-Ping, At the Special Session of the UN General Assembly." Retrieved from www.marxists.org/reference/archive/deng-xiaoping/1974/04/10.htm (accessed October 19, 2019).

Department of Defense. 2019. *Indo-Pacific Strategy Report: Preparedness, Partnerships, and Promoting a Networked Region.* Retrieved from https://media.defense.gov/2019/Jul/01/2002152311/-1/-1/1/DEPARTMENT-OF-DEFENSE-INDO-PACIFIC-STRATEGY-REPORT-2019.PDF (accessed October 19, 2019).

Elliott, Michael. 2011. "Viewpoint: How Libya Became a French and British War." *Time*, March 19. Retrieved from http://content.time.com/time/world/article/0,8599,2060412,00.html (accessed 20 October 2019).

Emmerson, Charles and Paul Stevens. 2012. *Maritime Choke Points and the Global Energy System: Charting a Way Forward.* London: Chatham House. Retrieved from www.chathamhouse.org/publications/papers/view/181615 (accessed October 22, 2019).

ERIA. 2016. "Sea Lane Security in the Selected EAS Countries." In *Sea Lane Security of Oil and Liquefied Natural Gas in the EAS Region*, edited by S. Kimura, T. Morikawa and S. Singh, 41–55. Retrieved from www.eria.org/RPR_FY2015_No.14_Chapter_4.pdf (accessed October 19, 2019).

Foner, Philip. [1972] 2005. *The Spanish-Cuban-American War and the Birth of American Imperialism*, 2 vols. New York: Monthly Review Press.

Gillis, J. R., ed. 1989. *Militarization of the Western World.* New Brunswick: NJ: Rutgers University Press.

Gowan, Peter. 1999. *The Global Gamble: Washington's Faustian Bid for World Dominance.* London: Verso.

Gudynas, Eduardo. 2018. "Extractivisms, Tendencies and Consequences." In *Reframing Latin American Development*, edited by Ronaldo Munck and Raúl Delgado Wise, 61–76. New York: Routledge. https://doi.org/10.4324/9781315170084-4

Hannieh, Adam. 2011. *Capitalism and Class in the Gulf Arab States.* New York: Palgrave Macmillan. https://doi.org/10.1057/9780230119604

Higginbottom, Andy. 2013. "Foreign Investment in Latin America: Dependency Revisited." *Latin American Perspectives* 40(3): 184–206. https://doi.org/10.1177/0094582X13479304

Higginbottom, Andy. 2018. "A Self-Enriching Pact: Imperialism and the Global South." *Journal of Global Faultlines* 5(1–2): 49–57. https://doi.org/10.13169/jglobfaul.5.1-2.0049

Hippler, Thomas. 2017. *Governing from the Skies: A Global History of Aerial Bombing.* New York: Verso Books.

Holmes, James R. and Toshi Yoshihara. 2017. "Taking Stock of China's Growing Navy: The Death and Life of Surface Fleets." *Orbis* 61(2): 269–285. https://doi.org/10.1016/j.orbis.2017.02.010

Hsiao, Andrew and Audrea Lim, eds. 2016. *The Verso Book of Dissent.* London: Verso.

Huggins, Martha. 1999. *Political Policing: The United States and Latin America.* Durham, NC: Duke University Press.

Kaplan, Robert. 2014. *Asia's Cauldron: The South China Sea and the End of a Stable Pacific.* New York: Random House.

Kauikan, Bilahari. 2017. "Asia in the Trump Era: From Pivot to Peril?" *Foreign Affairs* 96(3): 146–153.

Lanteigne, Marc. 2008. "China's Maritime Security and the 'Malacca Dilemma'." *Asian Security* 4(2): 143–161. https://doi.org/10.1080/14799850802006555

Lenin, Vladimir. 1916. *Imperialism and the Split in Socialism.* Retrieved from www.marxists.org/archive/lenin/works/1916/oct/x01.htm (accessed 10 July 2019).

Mabee, Bryan and Srdjan Vucetic. 2018. "Varieties of Militarism: Towards a Typology." *Security Dialogue* 49(1–2): 96–108. https://doi.org/10.1177/0967010617730948

Macalister, Terry. 2011. "So, Was This a War for Oil?" *The Guardian*, September 2.
Manson, Katrina. 2018. "Robot-Soldiers, Stealth Jets and Drone Armies: The Future of War." *Financial Times*, November 16.
Medea, Benjamin. 2012. *Drone Warfare: Killing by Remote Control*. New York: OR Books.
Nkrumah, Kwame. 1965. *Neocolonialism—the Last Stage of Imperialism*. New York: International Publishers.
Paterson, Thomas G., Garry Clifford, Robert Brigham, Michael Donoghue, Kenneth Hagan, Deborah Kisatsky and Shane J. Maddock. 2014. *American Foreign Relations: A History, Volume II: Since 1895*. Stamford, CT: Cengage.
Phillips, Dom. 2019. "Brazil: Tortured Dissidents Appalled by Bolsonaro's Praise for Dictatorship." *The Guardian*, March 30.
Poh, Soo Kai. 2016. *Living in a Time of Deception*. Singapore: Function 8 Limited.
Raphael, Sam. 2016. *Mercenaries Unleashed: The Brave New World of Private Military and Security Companies*. London: War on Want.
Raphael, Sam and Jac St. John. 2016. *Arming Repression: The New British Imperialism in the Persian Gulf*. London: War on Want.
Sabbagh, Dan. 2019. "UK Calls Meeting with US and France to Discuss Hormuz Plan." *The Guardian*, July 30. Retrieved from www.theguardian.com/world/2019/jul/30/uk-us-europe-shipping-strait-of-hormuz (accessed 10 August 2019).
Sabbagh, Dan and Stephen Burgen. 2019. "Ex-military Chief Urges Iran to Seize UK Ship in Gibraltar Tit-for-Tat." *The Guardian*, July 5. Retrieved from www.theguardian.com/world/2019/jul/05/spain-to-lodge-complaint-over-british-seizure-of-oil-tanker-gibraltar (accessed September 14, 2019).
Sampson, Anthony. 1975. *Seven Sisters: Great Oil Companies and the World They Made*. London: Coronet.
securitydegreehub. 2019. "30 Most Powerful Private Security Companies in the World." Retrieved from www.securitydegreehub.com/most-powerful-private-security-companies-in-the-world (accessed September 20, 2019).
SIPRI. 2018. "Military Expenditure (% of General Government Expenditure)." Retrieved from https://data.worldbank.org/indicator/MS.MIL.XPND.ZS (accessed September 20, 2019).
Smith, John. 2016. *Imperialism in the 21st Century*. New York: Monthly Review Press.
Starrs, Sean. 2014. "The Chimera of Global Convergence." *New Left Review 2* 87: 81–96.
Starrs, Sean. 2015. "China's Rise is Designed in America, Assembled in China." *China's World* 2: 9–20.
Starrs, Sean. 2017. "The Global Capitalism School Tested in Asia: Transnational Capitalist Class vs Taking the State Seriously." *Journal of Contemporary Asia* 47(4): 641–658. https://doi.org/10.1080/00472336.2017.1282536
Starrs, Sean. 2018. "The Rise of Emerging Markets Signifies the End of the Beginning of the American Century." In *American Hegemony and the Rise of Emerging Powers: Cooperation or Conflict*, edited by Salvador Santino F. Regilme J and James Parisot, 77–101. New York: Routledge.
statistica.com. 2019a. "The 15 Countries with the Highest Military Spending Worldwide in 2018, in Billion US Dollars." Retrieved from www.statista.com/statistics/262742/countries-with-the-highest-military-spending (accessed September 20, 2019).
statistica.com. 2019b. "US Arms Exports in 2018, by Country, in TIV Expressed in Million Constant 1990 US Dollars." Retrieved from www.statista.com/statistics/248552/us-arms-exports-by-country (accessed September 20, 2019).

Stubley, Peter. 2018. "UK Opens Permanent Military Base in Bahrain to Strengthen Middle East Presence." *The Independent*, April 6.

Szalay, Eva. 2019. "Currency War Fears Bolster Demand for Havens." *Financial Times*. 7 August 2019.

Takriti, Abdel. 2013. *Monsoon Revolution: Republicans, Sultans, and Empires Oman 1965–1976*. Oxford: Oxford University Press. https://doi.org/10.1093/acprof:oso/9780199674435.001.0001

UNCTAD. 2018. *World Investment Report 2018*. Retrieved from https://unctad.org/en/PublicationsLibrary/wir2018_en.pdf (accessed September 20, 2019).

Vine, David. 2017. *Base Nation: How US Bases Abroad Harm America and the World*. New York: Skyhorse Publishing.

Wintour, Patrick. 2019. "US and Britain Could Sign Sector-by-Sector Trade Deals, Says Bolton." *The Guardian*, August 13. Retrieved from www.theguardian.com/politics/2019/aug/12/us-and-britain-could-sign-sector-by-sector-trade-deals-says-bolton (accessed September 20, 2019).

Woodward, Jude. 2017. *The US versus China: Asia's New Cold War?* Manchester: Manchester University Press. https://doi.org/10.7228/manchester/9781526121998.001.0001

15

New Imperialisms and Struggles for Peace

Napoleón Saltos Galarza

> To know the empire is part of fighting it.
> —Alex Callinicos, "El imperialismo y la economía política hoy" (2011: 161)

> War looks but to the frontage, the appearance.
> —Herman Melville, *Billy Budd* (2016: 309)

Introduction

This text addresses the transmutations of late capitalism from two perspectives: structural changes in inter-imperialist contradictions, and the domination of peoples. On the first perspective, we are not in a transition phase, but in a stage prior to that transition, marked by the decline of world capitalism in the absence of an alternative utopian horizon. We can locate antisystemic seeds, nevertheless, in people's resistance. We are facing extreme forms of liberal modernity, which conclude the process of estrangement of the individual subject, now himself in a posthumanist phase, whose dystopian horizon is marked by artificial intelligence and cynical rationality. The paradox is the existence of "ultraimperialism" with extreme concentration of wealth and new forms of poverty, exclusion and disposability of towns and continents; but with the intensification of inter-imperialist contradictions. We are facing imperialism in the plural. The expectation of the "end of history" and the triumph of the West was not fulfilled after the fall of the Berlin Wall, but we entered into a phase of wars and conflicts on a different scale. This is not a repeat of the "Cold War" between two poles, but a complex process: the contradiction between the North–South axis, led by US imperialism in relation to the traditional powers US–EU–Japan and the East–West axis, led by China–Russia alliance in connection with the BRICs; and the presence of contradictions within each pole, contradictions between dynamic globalist-financial sectors and nationalist/post-industrial sectors. The end of the Westphalian order and weakening of nation states is combined with the emptiness of a world state, which is being taken over by US imperialism as a global custodian, based on a warmongering strategy and strengthening a trend towards a new arms race.

In relation to the peoples of the South, the main modification is the new imperialism's "accumulation by dispossession" and the delegation of civil wars framed by geopolitical disputes, while nation states are progressively emptied of substance. Thus, the boundaries of wars and conflict hot spots are located at the intersection of three dynamics. First, control of the five strategic monopolies, particularly linked to traditional technological income. Second, civilizational and religious-ethnic confrontations and geopolitical disputes. Third, the ways of peace from the people and from the South: negotiations or surrender, resisters and disconnections, ethical and political struggles.

A Complex New Turn in History

Following the illusory "end of history" (Fukuyama 1992), which was proclaimed after the USSR's implosion, we did not enter into a new century of "pax Westerner" based on the triumph of capital. Neither did we enter into a unilateral hegemony headed by the triad USA–EU–Japan. What we experienced was a multilateral decentralization under two main dynamics: the structural hegemony of liberal capital, in a post-humanist form (Ramas and Tamames 2018) and in a decadent phase; and a multilateral order with diverse nodes, influenced not only by geopolitics, but also by a return to ethnic, national and religious identities. This is not just about a new cycle of struggles for hegemony between the traditional powers led by the US and the emerging powers gathered around the BRICs, and led geo-economically by China, in the sense that Giovanni Arrighi (2014) understood, as a new version of the "Cold War," with two poles ordering the confrontation. We are rather witnessing the internal transmutation of each of these poles, modifying the borders of disputes and alliances, externally and internally.

In the West, we have a schism between the "nationalist-pragmatists," represented by Trump and the Brexiteers, as they move towards strengthening internal markets and they re-orient the capitalist process; and the "globalist-geopolitical" tendencies, represented by the establishment and the multilateral technocracy, who are trying to consolidate the structural tendency towards the domination of capital, in a local version of "progressive neoliberalism," while they work as an empire on the global level. But also among the BRICs there are dynamics of rapprochement and differentiation. The China–Russia Alliance brings order in the confrontation with the traditional powers, but it risks conflicts in the Euro-Asian area they are trying to consolidate. In China, the dispute is between two political models on the internal as well as on the external level: the existence of a continental China, with a strong peasant-agrarian society and traditional ways of life, more conservative and nationalist; and a coastal, globalizing China, oriented towards liberal capitalism. But there are also situations specific to other emerging economies such as India or Brazil. They dispute control in their own regions while oscillating between distancing and approaching the Western axis and the Euro-Asian axis.

Thus, in the world order we need to identify the intersection of these various dynamics, which constitute a kind of cross with four main poles. This is a structure in constant mutation, in an uncertain environment. We still cannot talk of a post-capitalist/post-patriarchal transition stage; we are not in a new "Renaissance"; we are possibly in the phase prior to this, a phase marked by the decadence and complexity of the capitalist world order, which lingers in extreme economic-cultural-political forms, and the emergence of the seeds of resistance and alternatives, which are nonetheless unable to proclaim with certainty their utopian horizon. We have movements of resistance, partial, local and temporary attempts to overcome the capitalist-patriarchal world, but often they are re-absorbed by the general-structural dynamics of capital and patriarchy. Therefore, to understand the current stage of capitalism-imperialism, we need both to analyze the structural tendencies of late capitalism, identify the contradictions and the struggles for hegemony, for the orientation rather than the direction of the world. We need to analyze the new imperialisms to know the location and alignment of the peoples and countries of the South.

Economic Transmutations

Under the logic of the globalization of capital, current imperialism has been transmuted. We are witnessing, in the economic dimension, the increasing monopolistic centralizations of capital accumulation by a handful of financial-rentier multinational corporations, so we have a centralized capitalism. But the inter-imperialist contradictions and the world order and its relationship to the periphery have also been modified.

Kautsky's premonition about "ultra-imperialism" is apparently becoming real, not in the sense that he foresaw it, as the pacific stage to previous socialism (Kautsky 1914), but rather, as the decadent centralization of capital, without a transition in sight. The financial flows within multinational corporations and their branches, and between dominant multinational corporations, prevent the destruction of inefficient capital. On the contrary, it amplifies criminal and speculative tendencies in the expanded reproduction of global capital. So, the crisis of economic over-accumulation which started in the 1980s has not been overcome; successive bursts of financial bubbles are part of the capital accumulation flux from the periphery to the center. Particularly since the dot.com crisis in 2001, the preferred route of US capital is the development of the classical boom of speculative credit, through all sorts of deceitful and untrustworthy financial "innovations" (collateral debt obligations, structured investment means and so on and so forth) and a flow of company purchases by private capital companies through cheap credit, their main effect being that, when the boom inevitably came to bust, they spread the toxic debts throughout the financial system, causing a paralysis which led to a massive world recession (Callinicos 2011: 141).

As Dierckxsens and Fomento explain:

> 80% of the world trade is trade among multinational corporations and 50% of the trade is intra-multinational corporations' trade. 48% of the social wealth produced/assembled by multinational corporations is based in tax havens (London-Delaware-Hong Kong, etc.) ... 48% of it is circulating in the so-called "tax havens" and 52% is circulating in nation-states, that means, this 52% is visible for the administrative institutions of these countries. 97% of the profits and annual rents produced

socially end up in the so-called tax havens. These tax havens are part and parcel of the new global financial architecture emerging as an extra-territorial system (extra-national states).

(Dierckxsens and Fomento 2019: 91–92)

According to Oxfam, in 2017,

> [T]he number of people whose wealth was above a billion dollars reached a historical maximum, with a new billionaire every second day. Today, there are 2043 billionaires in the world. Nine out of ten are men. The wealth of these billionaires has experienced a massive increase, enough to end hunger even seven times. 82% of the world's wealth growth during the last year ended up in the hands of the richest 1%, while the poorest 50% of the world population did not experience the slightest increase in their wealth.
>
> (Oxfam International 2018: 9)

Research from Zurich University, based on an analysis of 37 million companies in the world, established that there is a super-nucleus of 147 multinational corporations, intimately linked to one another, controlling 40 percent of the world economy. The vast majority of these corporations are financial institutions from the USA and the UK (Coghlan and MacKenzie 2011). The director of the IMF, Christine Lagarde, declared at the start of October 2018 that "since 1980, the richest 1% have doubled their profits in relation to the economic growth of the poorest 50%" (Elliot 2018). This is not just about wealth distribution; it is about the monopolist capture of the key areas of the economy. The evolutionary tendencies of current capitalism are articulated around "five monopolies" which exemplify the polarizing globalization of current imperialism: (i) monopoly of the new technologies; (ii) control over the world financial movements; (iii) control of the access to the planet's natural resources; (iv) control of mass media; (v) monopoly of weapons of mass destruction.

The endogenous transnational *modus operandi* of global capital makes the crisis spiral, in a permanent leap forward, without a clear way out of its ascending circle and without the prospect of a final crisis. The issue here is not just about economic social relations or the monopolistic concentration of property and wealth; it is about the material support for the appropriation of new productive forces resulting from the third and fourth scientific-technological revolution, particularly of the IT, genetic and management revolutions. The main contradiction on this point is that humanity, for the first time, is in a position to overcome scarcity and to create the basis for a world civilization; but that potential has been captured by capitalist modernity and transmuted into new forms of control and domination. Power transmutes into biopower, and becomes the lord deciding life or death not only of individuals and peoples, but of entire continents, the final frontier in humanity's survival. Climate change, more than a hazard for mother-nature, signals the alarm for human survival. Thus, we are entering the latest phase of capitalism, a phase which has not been understood in its own terms, for it is thought of as post-capitalism, post-modernism, as a transition thought of in terms of its own past. Late capitalism appears not only as anti-humanist, but as post-humanist, constructing a naked *homo*, bare even of references to itself, in the search for a dystopia in a post-positivist thought which hopes for salvation in artificial intelligence and robotics, in a society without workers. The communist utopia of the classless society is transformed into the dystopia of the ordering Matrix. In this dystopian view we also find the seductive militaristic games and the entrenchment of securitization, symbolized in the right to own and carry weapons for self-defense, and the securitization of politics and the creation of the "securitized state."

As Jaramillo (2013) states, "the prefix "post" indicates something that (often) is no longer, but which lacks an understanding of what it has actually become." Although there too we find a state of transition, the moment prior to the rebirth, in which it is easier to identify the decadent world than the emerging world on the horizon. The failure of the three attempts during the twentieth century to find a way out of capitalist domination—real socialism, liberation struggles and the social-democrat project—dissipates the global utopian horizons. I do not want to give as an alternative the apocalyptic choice between barbarism or socialism, but rather to locate the tendencies towards global control, this kind of Matrix operating through autopoiesis. The material basis of this is the real subsumption of consumption to capital. The material structure of use-values is determined to such a degree so as to respond to the needs of exploitation and surplus accumulation. Therefore, the subjection of human beings it is not only about politics and economics, nor merely ideological and cultural, but also physiological; now, the capitalist mode of production is shaping our lifestyles and political subjection is also psychosocial, and in consequence, sexual (Veraza 2008).

Modern capital and the state have colonized all of the spheres of life with the logic of accumulation and profit. In this process, late capitalism is mixing mechanisms belonging to the cycle of financialization of accumulation with mechanisms from the primitive accumulation and variations such as accumulation by dispossession; that is, financial-rentier capital dominates society and nature at the global level. When it comes to its rentier component, it monopolizes the new technological rent, while the exploitation and control of the traditional rent of land and strategic natural resources remains in place. According to this logic, the excesses of financial over-accumulation is not operating only at the level of the excess in exchange-values, but it has developed several strategies to curtail the life of use-values, from the technological manipulation of the programmed obsolescence of commodities, the strategies to promote consumerism and fashion, to the maintenance of a state of permanent warfare and of various forms of protracted localized wars and arms races, with an eye to accelerate the circulation of exchange-values and the strengthening of the conditions of accumulation. At the top of this competition between transnational monopolies and geopolitical powers there is an alliance between financial capital and military business; this is not merely the industrial-military complex for which Trump yearns, but a financial-rentier-military complex.

The Implications for the Peoples of the South

For the South, it is above all about discovering the cracks in this totalitarian form of control, to identify the anti-systemic seeds of new forms of life, announcing the possibility of alternatives. This is a door through which we can understand the situation from our own identity and difference:

> In order to clarify the whole, is not a useless exercise for us to think of ourselves as a point of comparison. This is probably the most important point here: we are finding ourselves as part of what we consider as a radical comparison.
> (Dumont 1987: 22)

There is a modification of the nature of the contradictions in the framework of imperialist workings, not as a phase, but as the very nature of world capitalism. The contradiction between the North–South axis, led by the USA, in a triad with Japan and the EU: and the East–West axis, led by China–Russia in the BRICs bloc. "Any understanding of current imperialism which does not take into account the tensions and potential cleavages among the main powers is perilously unilateral" (Callinicos 2011: 151). The existence of China, "as the main territory for world capital surplus to be based and obtain benefits, as well as the main export market for raw materials, as well as for the producers of capital goods" (Hung 2008: 170, quoted in Callinicos 2011: 142), provides a temporary way out to the global crisis. China has had a dramatic growth over the last four decades, in a strategy of mutual agreements with the US economy. This strategy has reached its limit now that Trump has shifted his attention to the reconstruction of the military-industrial complex as the backbone of his "nationalist" proposal for economic growth; this, plus the economic war against China and the displacement of the scenario of conflict from the axis of evil and war on terror to the confrontation against the expansion of the emerging powers, which is witnessing a movement of the conflict axis to the Pacific.

In the Obama period, this contradiction was dealt with by geopolitical strategy, led by financial capital and multilateral organizations, the axis of conflict was on terror and securing military domination. With Trump and the Brexiteers, the idea is to recover the logic of the military-industrial complex. Therefore, this strategy expresses in terms of an economic war, an increased belligerence against China, and the acceleration of the arms race. This war is not only about economy, tariffs, global currency, market control—it is also militaristic. "The US strategy in Asia implies, specifically, to keep Japan in a strategically subordinated position, and more generally, to create a coalition of states with a capacity to contain China" (Callinicos 2011: 152).

One of the conflict fronts opened between Chinese expansionism and the US strategy of contention, is the South China Sea, in the Asian far south-east. It is a Western extension of the Pacific Ocean, connected to the Indian Ocean through the Malacca strait. It covers vast extension of sea from Southern China to Indonesia, and from the Philippines to Indochina's peninsula and Malacca. Because it is a connection between the Pacific and the Indian oceans, the Southern

Sea of China is a zone of great importance in terms of naval transit, allowing the communication between Eastern Asia and Southern Asia and the Middle East. Daily, hundreds of cargo ships replete with containers of manufactured merchandise from East Asia and Southeast Asia sail towards South Asian, Middle Eastern and even European markets. This sea is also sailed, in the opposite direction, by tanker-ships bringing oil from the Persian Gulf to the industrialized countries of Eastern Asia and Southeast Asia, such as China, the Republic of Korea, Philippines, Japan, Singapore and Taiwan. On top of this, this sea is rich in natural resources, for it is estimated that there are oil and natural gas fields, and much fish for the fishing industry. This is a sea of great importance to the world economy as a whole, and for the countries in East and Southeast Asia, who are intimately linked to the Western markets thanks to their condition as export economies producing a good portion of the manufactured goods that we consume on a daily basis (Hernández 2018). War drills and joint exercises in this theatre of conflict are multiplying, in order to keep China "trapped in the region" and to prevent global competition. The presence of India and other regional powers is behind this objective.

This scenario is closely related to the triad's strategy to contain Russia with an economic-military wall, with hot spots in the Ukrainian conflict and the creation of a series of military bases on this geographical border. However, the strategic response of the Russian–Chinese alliance has displaced these conflicts towards the wars in the Middle East, where Syria appears like a space of geostrategic re-ordering. The policies of Trump against Iran, are intending to bring conflict to the arrangements reached in the Obama period.

The arms race

News of a new arms race, of increased military spending, of new types of wars, denunciations of agreements of arms control, are daily occurrences. Trump just announced that he will put an end to the 1987 Gorbachev-Reagan agreement about the elimination of mid- and short-range nuclear missiles. He has also announced his intention to block the New Star Treaty, signed up with Russia in 2010 and which will expire in 2021. The calculation behind the arms race is not only geopolitical, it is also geoeconomic.

According to the latest SIPRI report (2018), military expenditure in 2017 represented 2.2 percent of the world GDP, that is, $230 per person. Chinese expenditure in relation to the global military expenditure increased from 5.8 percent in 2008 to 13 percent in 2017; whereas Russian military expenditure for 2017, $66.3 billion, was 20 percent lower than 2016.

The US remains the country with the highest military expenditure in the world. It showed no changes between 2016 and 2017, staying at $610 billion. It remains, also, the biggest military power: it concentrates 35 percent of the global military expenditure. US expenditure equals the combined expenditure of the next eight countries.

US hegemony is facing many challenges; and the new world order is de-centering into an unstable multilateralism. The limits of US hegemony are to be found in the "disconnection between its military might and its decreasing economic power and its ailing solvency in the geopolitical plane" (Katz 2011). Again, "The US remains the dominant capitalist power, but they still hold this position as a result of the considerable efforts they do in order to keep their hegemony in three key regions—Europe, Eastern Asia and the Middle East" (Callinicos 2011: 158). After the fall of the Berlin Wall, US imperialism tried to consolidate its hegemony resorting to military means. During the first Iraq war,

> the mechanism of control ... was still open to capital, commodities and exchange between many states and companies. This could not be regarded as a merely economic strategy, as part of a predatory form of hegemony. On the contrary, the US used its military might to design a geopolitical order in line with their most favoured model of world economy: that is, an increasingly open liberal world order. The US policies aimed at creating an open international oil industry, in which markets, dominated by big multinational corporations, allocate capitals and raw materials. US might was used not only to protect the particular interests and consumption needs of the US companies, but in order to create the general preconditions of an open world oil market, hoping that as the leading economy it would be in a position to satisfy all of its needs through trade exchange.
>
> (Bromley 2005: 253–254, quoted in Callinicos 2011: 115)

The military backbone of the US strategy is a sign, not of its strength, but of the decline of its hegemony.

> The recent shift towards more of an open imperialism, backed by the US military power can be understood as a sing of the decline of its hegemony in the face of serious threats posed by generalised recession and devaluation in the country, in sharp contrast with the various devaluation attacks inflicted previously to other countries.
>
> (Harvey 2003: 64)

The US imperialist strategy of domination resorts to its military might to counter its weaknesses in other areas. "The US enjoys today of an unprecedented military supremacy, but the (second) Iraq war has exposed the limits of this supremacy" (Callinicos 2011: 122). With Trump's arrival to power, we can foresee an increasing military expenditure for the next decade, and an increase in the trends already mentioned, see Table 15.1.

The predictions were already conservative. On December 12, 2017, Trump approved the military budget for 2018 of over 700 billion dollars: 626 billion for basic operations, plus 66 billion for missions abroad, like Afghanistan and Syria (EFE 2018). This increase is causing an arms race and the dispute on advanced technologies. The SIPRI report (2018) indicates that in 2017 "there was a substantial increase in military expenditure in Asian and Middle Eastern countries." The main focus of this expenditure is shifting from the Atlantic to the Pacific.

Contradictions with the peoples and the countries of the Global South: "accumulation by dispossession."

"The idea ... that capital is freed from the straightjacket of geography is a sheer myth" (Callinicos 2011: 131). This tendency is accentuated particularly after the

Table 15.1 US military expenditure projections 2018–2027.

Fiscal year	Previous proposal (billion USD)	Current proposal (billion USD)
2018	549	603
2019	562	616
2020	576	629
2021	590	642
2022	605	655
2023	620	669
2024	636	683
2025	652	697
2026	668	712
2027	685	727

Source: White House Office of Management and Budget (2017)

2008 crisis which articulated financial and rentier capital. Neoliberalism not only gave the capitalists and state managers the ideological cohesion and the self-confidence to push back organized workers. It also legitimated the deregulation and global integration of the financial markets; and a generalized tendency to open markets provided capital, whether industrial, commercial or financial, in order to search for every opportunity to make a profit; at the start of the neoliberal era, Fredric Jameson (1984: 78) stated that this was "a new and historically original penetration and colonization of Nature and the Unconscious."

"But neoliberalism wasn't successful in bringing profits to the same levels as with the great boom" (Callinicos 2011: 136). On the contrary, it created new contradictions. Between the two sources of commodities, rents of nature or labor, in Latin America the predominant source has been rent. Colonial and neo-colonial domination have created this situation. The distinctive characteristic of the "new imperialism" according to David Harvey is "accumulation by dispossession," which takes the form primarily of dispossession of strategic resources, of communal territories, and of public goods. It is this which creates the new geopolitical battlefields, particularly over Venezuela and the Amazon.

In order to solve this crisis of capital over-accumulation,

> if system-wide devaluations (and even destruction) of capital and of labour power are not to follow, then ways must be found to absorb these surpluses. Geographical expansion and spatial reorganization provide one such option.
>
> (Harvey 2003: 63)

But, since the successive crises from the 1970s on, these "spatio-temporal fixes … failed even in the medium run." Financial crises, particularly after the dot.com crisis in 2001, continued to hit the center and especially the US economy. Harvey concludes that "the inability to accumulate through expanded reproduction on a sustained basis has been paralleled by a rise in attempts to accumulate by dispossession. This … is … 'the new imperialism'" (Harvey 2003: 64).

Accumulation by dispossession has a main scenario in the South, in our continent, and in the Amazon. A sign of this is the galloping increase in deforestation in this new millennium. The tendency of the Latin American economies is to be primary economies once again, and for the extractive model to expand, in articulation with the primacy of financial capital. The extractive invasion takes different forms: mining in areas of biodiversity and in indigenous lands, global tolls, biofuels, genetically modified monocrops for export. The appropriation of the traditional rent over land and strategic natural resources is combined with the technological rent, and the appropriation of traditional knowledge. There is a substantial change at work,

> Imperialism is a change in the essential relations of capitalist production in the extraction of surplus-value, and not only the forms of its distribution. The drive to extra-surplus value through the super-exploitation of labour-power is a general and necessary tendency of capitalism that becomes predominant in the imperialist stage of capitalism.
>
> (Higginbottom 2012: 264–265)

Wars: The New Frontiers

Two changes were the starting point for the new world order: the implosion of the USSR was the reason to declare the "end of history" and the "Western triumph" (Fukuyama 1992); and the decline of the nation-state together with the emergence of a new form of global sovereignty, laying down the foundations of a new political world order which adopts imperialist-empire forms. For Hardt and Negri, the "basic hypothesis is that sovereignty has assumed a new form, with national and supranational organizations united under a single command logic. This new form of sovereignty is what we call Empire. The declining sovereignty of the nation-state and its progressive incapacity to regulate economic and cultural exchanges is, in fact, one of the clearest signs of the arrival of Empire" (Hardt and Negri 2000: xii). Nonetheless, this Matrix is unable to erase internal contradictions or the presence of national dynamics.

The crisis of the Westphalian world order and the subsequent decline of the nation-state, have affected the "monopoly to legitimate physical violence" within territories and regions. On the other hand, after the fall of the Berlin Wall, the absence of a world state and the weakness of multilateral organizations, including the UN, are countered by the power of the US state, as a hegemon within the international community; this is to the detriment of the monopoly of legitimate physical violence at a global level, thus opening a period of dispute and armed violence in various regions. According to SIPRI, in the first decade of the twenty-first century (2001–2010) there were 69 armed conflicts,[1] representing a quantitative reduction if compared with the Cold War period. There was also a reduction of high intensity conflicts, that is, those with more than 1,000 deaths a year (SIPRI 2012). The majority of the victims are civilians: today 90 percent of the mortal victims of conflicts are civilians, compared to 10 percent of military deaths. We also need to take into account mass displacement: in 2012, according to the UN High Commissioner for Refugees, there were 45.2 million displaced people, the highest figure since 47 million in 1994 (García 2013).

The vast majority of conflicts are civil wars (80%), but they are often linked to geoeconomics (wars for oil, water, coltan) and to geopolitical wars, particularly in Central Asia and the Middle East. These figures do not record new forms of violence, linked to "social fascistization" and to the "mafia-inclinations" of politics, which often leave behind more victims than war. In Latin America, the permanent state of war in Colombia for over 60 years has left some 60 thousand mortal victims, more than six and a half million internally and externally displaced people. The US–Mexico border is one of the most violent places in the world. The frontier of wars occurs in the intersection between three factors: strategic natural resources, mostly oil–water–coltan; civilization–religious–ethnic; geopolitics.

Territorial and ideological motivations which were typical of Cold War conflicts are losing ground, and those based on religious, ethnic, racial, tribal, national identities become prominent. "Between 2001 and 2010, 60% of the non-State conflicts were fought between ethnic or religious communities" (SIPRI 2012). These identity motivations, however, can be the spark or a subterfuge for geopolitical and geoeconomic disputes, mostly for the control of strategic resources, such as Middle Eastern wars and the forgotten wars of Africa. At the same time, there is a process of privatization of wars and armies:

> [P]rivatisation of security modifies too the dynamics of armed conflicts. It also influences management: the existence and "normalisation" of a security market conditions conflict resolution. In this market, military and private security companies, secure their business through the creation of fresh needs. The main task of these companies is not to convince about the technical competence of their services, but to create needs, that is, to convince their clients (States, international organizations, non-governmental organizations, companies, etc.) that they need their services.
>
> (García 2013: 11)

Thus, we are experience a transmutation of the modern capitalist state, which is transitioning from the rule of law to security state and securitized politics, both locally and globally:

> The "reasons of security" have replaced what before was called "reasons of State." There is interest in keeping a generalised state of fear, to depoliticise citizens, to renounce to the certainty of law: these are three features of the security State … This state of Security were plunged into, does exactly the opposite to what it promises, for—if security means lack of worries (*sine cura*)—it keeps people in fear and terror. … On the other hand, this is a form of police State, for the decline of the judicial power increases the space for police discretion, which in this normalised state of emergency, acts increasingly as a sovereign.
>
> (Agamben 2015)

In this process, the citizens are gradually turned into potential terrorists. This is not the Leviathan of early modernity, but an absolute control structure invading desire and taking violence even into our most intimate lives. Despite this, we are not in a closed system. This matrix has internal cracks. The wars against the nation-states and communal territories, end up in mass mobilizations, migrations spurred by various economic, political, belligerent and environmental forms of violence, which end up storming the walled center and bringing imbalance to the security state.[2] The face of the absolute Other, from its negative perspective, raises questions about the alternatives.

The Roads to Peace

At the extreme we find the possibility of a way out. The signs are confusing and partial. Anti-imperialism, even against the US domination, is not enough for a just struggle. We need to understand the geopolitical conflicts, and also the internal democratic and ordering processes. In the Middle East, the frontiers of conflict stop, for the time being, at the Syrian war, with the resistance of the nation-state to an offensive of the North–South alliance, backed by the Russian military who are trying to keep war as far as possible from its actual borders. Trump's offensive against Iran, is trying to plunge the East into war again. Amidst this scenario, autonomist attempts such as those of the Kurdish people in Rojava, are at risk of being captured by the dominant geopolitical game. A cruel example of this paradoxical situation is Sri Lanka's conflict. The civil war led to the genocide of Tamil people in May 2009. However, because of geopolitical alignments, there has not even been an independent enquiry by the UN on government and army responsibilities. In Latin America, Venezuela represents this geopolitical clash between the interests of US imperialism for the control of strategic resources, particularly in the Orinoco, and the failure of the Bolivarian project to find a democratic and national alternative.

An idea for a peace strategy could have, as its starting point, transgression of this systemic limits beyond the state and the construction of projects grounded in communities. The struggle for peace is, above all, an ethical struggle, and only then comes politics. Extreme forms of exploitation and violence in late capitalism make this struggle for peace into a civilizational issue. In those periods of belligerent explosion, we come back to the same question faced at the time of the emergence of fascism in the 1930s—was this an anomaly or a result of capitalism? We can recall the answer of the Frankfurt School about the nature of capitalist modernity based on the imperialism of instrumental reason, and use this argument about cynical reason and vital violence, about the emergence of Thanatos-power as a form of domination. The peace alternative is based on the critique of capitalist modernity. We can also recall the ethical thesis of Levinas, born out of the extreme experience of concentration camps, about desire as a creative drive, until we discover in the extreme Other, in the victim, the possibility of human responsibility, the transcendence which brings together enjoyment with freedom:

> That being who *expresses himself* imposes himself, calling me from his misery and nudity in a way in which I can't ignore this call ... *That there are human beings suffering from hunger is a fault that no circumstance can attenuate, without distinction of*

> *the voluntary from the involuntary* ... In the face of human hunger, responsibility can be objectively measured ... So the unveiling of the being in general (Heidegger), as the basis of knowledge and as the meaning of being, *pre-exists* in relation to the being who expresses himself (the Other); the ontological level (precedes) the ethical level.
>
> (Levinas 1977: 175; quoted in Dussel 1988: 363)

"Ethical reason—the only sustainable reason—is the fruit of the other's responsibility" (Dussel 1998: 367). Levinas finds there the rationality of peace:

> Res-ponsibility[3] about the other, or communication, is the adventure which contains all science or philosophy's discourse. Thus, this res-ponsibility is the very rationality of reason or its or its universality, *the rationality of peace*.
>
> (Levinas 1987: 203; quoted in Dussel 1988: 367)

The belligerent strategy and arms race implies an ontological problem which nullifies our life. The alternative starts by recognizing the precariousness of life, "implying a social life, that is, the recognition that our life is at all times, in a sense, in the hands of others," many of whom we don't know and can't name. "The social implications of this idea is, precisely, interrupted by alterity, as said by Levinas, and therefore the obligations that 'we' have are those which dismantle any established notion of 'we'" (Butler 2010: 30–31).

This road has conjuncture landmarks, in response to concrete circumstances. The first step is a self-critical look at the causes of defeat. Currently in Latin America, in relation to the "rationality of peace," the most pressing question is about democracy. "Democracy and human rights have been militarized" by imperialism (Suh 2014; CWM 2018). However, "progressive governments" too have been unable to strengthen democracy, even under the guise of the liberal-representative form, in order to peacefully solve conflicts, and the consolidation of authoritarian forms of control and institutionalized corrupt practices, which have created a legitimacy deficit for various governments, thus paving the way for the return of far-right governments. This, however, is not a circumstantial debate, but it is a debate about the roots of the failure of alternatives to capitalism, about the trap of understanding the state as the only solution, and the renunciation of bottom-up forms of power.

Conclusion: The Strategy of Peace at the Border

On April 13, 2018, Ecuador's president, Lenin Moreno, confirmed the death of three workers of newspaper *El Comercio*, the reporter Jorge Ortega, the photographer Paul Rivas and the driver Efraín Segarra, who were kidnapped on March 26 by a dissident group of the FARC, led by Guacho. Their murder came on top of the murder of four soldiers in Mataje, also killed in an ambush by the dissidents, at the border with Colombia. This wave of violence started on January 27, with the explosion of a car-bomb in the police station of San Lorenzo. These events, opened up a debate on response strategies. The dilemma was about the wisdom of applying an anti-terror, anti-guerrilla, anti-drugs militaristic approach in line with Plan Colombia, with its counter-productive results and the perpetuation of a permanent state of warfare. The government inclination, although there is talk of an integral response to attend the needs of regions forsaken by both states, is clearly towards asymmetrical warfare.

Some voices demanded a different response. Msgr. Eugenio Arellano, president of the Bishop's Conference of Ecuador and Bishop of Esmeraldas, claimed that "peace is a difficult road, but a necessary one for the progress of the peoples." He warned "the border of Ecuador, where these things take place, is not an alive border but a very poor one." "There's a few villages, education and health services are in a sorry state, and there are no opportunities for the youth." Therefore, the "temptation to join the guerrillas or drug cartels is huge." He added, "now that these people are dead, the temptation of the government is for a strong military intervention." But he said "peace is not born from fire, but is a fruit of the tree of justice." An observation which, according to this priest, derives from the example of the neighboring country: "Colombia has spent 40 years investing on arms and they have been unable to smother violence." "It is time to give opportunities to the youth, with decent work, it is time to give them a chance by promoting development in the region." In line with encyclical *Populorum Progressio*, written by Paul VI, the Bishop said: "development is the new name for peace." From this perspective, Msgr. Arellano tried to mediate in a prisoners' exchange, but the hesitations and the interference of military operatives both sides of the border, precipitated their deaths (Arellano 2018).

On April 16, 2016, an earthquake with a magnitude of 7.8 M_w affected Manabí and Esmeralda provinces. Muisne, in the south of Esmeraldas and close to the epicenter, was one of the worst affected urban centers: although there were no deaths recorded, 803 houses collapsed and the basic services were interrupted for several days. The people, in the initial absence of state support, assumed the care of the victims, and their own survival in precarious conditions.

The state's intervention was limited to offering the people to move out from their ancestral home on an island, moving them 2.5 kilometers to a "safe" new ground. The engineer Susana María Dueñas de la Torre, government secretary in risk management, decreed resolution no. SGR-073-2016, on June 21, 2016, in which is claimed that "all of the island is at risk of being affected by the Tsunami according to the flood document 080350-Muisne, Esmeraldas province" (Art. 2). Also, "by virtue of this decree, human settlements in the zone of risk are forbidden, in line with the Fourteenth General Disposition of the Organic Code of the Territorial, Autonomy and Decentralisation Organization" (Art. 3).

Important segments of the population defended the right of the people to remain in their ancestral home, particularly since the resolution was taken without any previous consultation and without a clear technical basis. Eventually, all of the people re-settled in the island. Then, it became increasingly evident that the attempt to empty the island of its people had more to do with the interest of tourist companies moving into the island. The problems of Muisne island are not a tsunami, but the lack of state intervention and the crisis of the local institutions.

This is one of the areas worst affected by poverty, in its different manifestations: unemployment, uncleanliness, inappropriate housing, illiteracy, etc. It is, also, an area affected by the presence of national and transnational drug mafias, also involved in the trafficking of weapons and people.

The defence of the right to their territory by the people, with the support of the church and the social movements, in the face of the state and organized violent crime, it's part of a broader strategy of peace under permanent attack. Líder Góngora, the main popular leader in the area, now mayoral candidate, proposed a peace approach which aimed at allowing the coexistence of everybody and the integral development of the area. When we asked him what is to be done with the mafia, he said:

> our people are used to living at risk. We want to negotiate an agreement for our area to be a zone of peace, free of production and processing of drugs, which doesn't induce youth to consume drugs, and which progressively normalizes life. We do not fear them, but we have to talk to them. And we need that the State, instead of a policy of violence, develops a policy that erases the conditions why the youth and the people of the community are tempted by the offers of drug traffickers. We have great potential, mostly on agriculture and tourism, to leave behind our dependency on drug trafficking.

We insisted, "your life may be at risk." He simply replied movingly, "I am not a hero, nor a martyr. I did not want this responsibility, but the people gave it to me. It is our responsibility, not to accept it means to condemn us to death. Despite the risk, we need to give life a chance. I am not alone, I am part of the community, our alternative comes from the strength of our people and their organization."

Maybe it is only a desperate cry in defense of life, something similar to what Levinas describes in his experience of the concentration camp. "Biopolitics is legitimated by its rejection of all social links, of all common law, condemning the majority of the people to an economy limited to a mere *conservatio vitae*" (Bustelo 2007: 94). The road back to connecting the individual as a subject of a community, to connecting human rights as a question of wealth and power, to connecting negative rights to the right to a dignified life, can be the departing point towards an alternative.

In Levinas's view:

> The "other" in his dimension of absolute alterity demands an ethics of infinite responsibility ... Human experience is such because of the possibility of being human in the sense of "being for others," in an ethical relationship which demands the absolute questioning of the self.
>
> (Quoted in Bustelo 2007: 102)

Against absolute violence, we propose absolute ethics: "the critique does not reduce the Other to the Self as in ontology, but it questions the exercise of the Self. A questioning of the Self—which cannot be made by the spontaneous selfishness of the Self—is made by the Other. The questioning of my spontaneity by the very presence of the Other is what we call ethics" (Dussel 1998: 361). There is the contribution from another viewpoint, from the native peoples of Latin America, the sense of a community as being-with-us-other, *ser-con-nos-otros*. This does not imply renouncing the self, but the creation of a new field of sharing, us-other, *nos-otros*.[4]

Napoleón Saltos Galarza is the director of the School of Sociology of the Central University of Ecuador, whose main expertise is in the study of changing dynamics of modern empires. He is one of the leaders of the Coordinating Committee of Social Movements in Latin America.

Acknowledgements

Translated from Spanish by Jose Antonio Gutierrez. Editor's note: I am grateful to Andy Higginbottom from Kingston University, UK, for his assistance in editing this chapter.

Notes

1. According to the SIPRI, armed conflicts are all those in which two parties resort to the use of force to solve a particular incompatibility. At least one of these parties needs to be a government of a state, and there needs to be at least 25 deaths per year.
2. "It is estimated that in 2015 there were 244 million international migrants all over the world (3.3% of the world population), representing an increase from the 155 million of migrants estimated in 2000 (2.8% of the world population). Internal migration is even more prevalent: the most recent global estimates indicate that 740 million people have migrated within their own country of birth."
3. Translation note: the device of spelling "responsibility" as "res-sponsibility" is in the original Spanish. It implies an objectification of responsibility by highlighting "res," which in Latin is the thing, as in "res-publica," public things.
4. Translation note: the Spanish original *nos-otros* in implies a meaning that would be lost in the more literal translation our-self; *nos-otros* rendered as "us-other" is an appeal to empathy.

References

Agamben, G. (2015). "Del Estado de derecho al Estado de seguridad." Retrieved from http://artilleriainmanente.blogspot.com/2015/12/giorgio-agamben-del-estado-de-derecho.html?spref=fb (accessed November 24, 2018).
Arellano, E. (2018). "La paz es un fruto que nace del árbol de la justicia." Retrieved from www.revistaecclesia.com/monsenor-arellano-ecuador-la-paz-es-un-fruto-que-nace-del-arbol-de-la-justicia (accessed November 24, 2018).
Arrighi, G. 2014. *El largo siglo XX. Dinero y poder en los orígenes de nuestra época*. Madrid: Siglo XXI.
Bromley, S. 2005. "The United States and Control of World Oil." *Government and Opposition* 40: 225–255. https://doi.org/10.1111/j.1477-7053.2005.00151.x
Bustelo, E. 2007. *El recreo de la infancia: Argumentos para otro comienzo*. Buenos Aires: Siglo XXI Editores Argentina.
Butler, J. 2010. *Marcos de guerra: Las vidas lloradas*. México: Paidós.

Callinicos, A. 2011. "El imperialismo y la economía política hoy." In *Cuadernos del Pensamiento Crítico Latinoamericano* 45: 111–166. Retrieved from http://biblioteca.clacso.edu.ar/clacso/se/20120510114140/cuadernos45.pdf (accessed December 11, 2019).

Coghlan, A. and D. MacKenzie 2011. "Revealed—the Capitalist Network that Runs the World." *New Scientist*, October 19. Retrieved from www.newscientist.com/article/mg21228354-500-revealed-the-capitalist-network-that-runs-the-world (accessed November 25, 2018).

CWM. 2018. "Reclamando el carácter sagrado de vidas, tierras y mares. Un proceso de estudio para la mejora de la resistencia y la solidaridad." Mimeo.

Dierckxsens, W. and W. Fomento. 2019. "Un agónico final de la globalización: ¿Cambio Civilizatorio?" In *Diálogos con el pensamiento de Francois Houtart*. Bogotá: Ediciones Desde Abajo.

Dumont, L. 1987. *Ensayos sobre el individualismo: Una perspectiva antropológica sobre la ideología moderna*. Alianza: Alianza Universidad.

Dussel, E. 1998. *Ética de la liberación en la edad de la globalización y la exclusión*. Madrid: Trotta. https://doi.org/10.7202/401177ar

EFE. 2018. "Presupuesto militar de Trump: 700.000 millones de dólares." Retrieved from www.elpais.com.uy/mundo/presupuesto-militar-trump-millones-dolares.html (accessed November 20, 2018).

Elliot, L. 2018. "Don't Believe the World Bank – Robots Will Steal Our Wages." *The Guardian*, October 14.

El Tiempo. 2018. "¿Qué países tienen el mayor gasto militar?" Retrieved from www.eltiempo.com/mundo/gasto-militar-en-el-mundo-aumenta-en-2018-273678 (accessed November 28, 2018).

Fukuyama, F. 1992. *The End of History and the Last Man*. New York: Free Press.

García, C. 2013. *Las "nuevas guerras" del siglo XXI. Tendencias de la conflictividad armada contemporánea*. Working paper 323. Barcelona: Institut de Ciències Polítiques i Socials.

Hardt, M. and T. Negri. 2000. *Empire*. Cambridge, MA: Harvard University Press. https://doi.org/10.2307/j.ctvjnrw54

Harvey, D. 2003 "The 'New' Imperialism: Accumulation by Dispossession." In *Socialist Register 2004*, edited by Leo Panitch and Colin Leys, 63–87. London: Merlin Press.

Hernández, F. 2018. "Escala la tensión en el mar de China Meridional." Retrieved from http://revistafal.com/escala-la-tension-en-el-mar-de-china-meridional (accessed November 30, 2018).

Higginbottom, A. 2012. "Structure and Essence in Capital: Extra Surplus-Value and the Stages of Capitalism." *Journal of Australian Political Economy* 70: 251–270.

Hung, H.-F. 2008. Rise of China and the global overaccumulation crisis. *Review of International Political Economy* 15: 149–179. https://doi.org/10.1080/09692290701869654

Jameson, F. 1984. "Postmodernism, or the Cultural Logic of Late Capitalism." *New Left Review* 2(146): 53–92.

Jaramillo, P. 2013. "Etnografías en transición: escalas, procesos y composiciones." Retrieved from https://revistas.uniandes.edu.co/doi/pdf/10.7440/antipoda16.2013.02 (accessed November 30, 2018). https://doi.org/10.7440/antipoda16.2013.02

Katz, C. 2011. *Bajo el imperio del capital*. Buenos Aires: Ediciones Luxemburg.

Kautsky, K. 1914. "Ultra-imperialism." Retrieved from www.marxists.org/archive/kautsky/1914/09/ultra-imp.htm (accessed December 12, 2019).

Levinas, E. 1977. *Totalidad e infinito*. Salamanca: Sígueme.

Levinas, E. 1987. *De otro modo que ser o más allá de la esencia*. Salamanca: Sígueme.

Melville, H. 2016. *Billy Budd, Sailor and Other Stories*. London: Penguin Books.
Oxfam International. 2018. *Informe anual 2018. Premiar el trabajo, no la riqueza*. Oxford: Oxfam GB.
Oxfam International. 2018. *Reward Work, not Wealth*. Oxford: Oxfam GB. Retrieved from www-cdn.oxfam.org/s3fs-public/file_attachments/bp-reward-work-not-wealth-220118-summ-en.pdf (accessed December 12, 2019).
Ramas, C. and J. Tamames. 2018. "Trump es un paso hacia nuestro objetivo, pero es insuficiente." Retrieved from https://ecuadortoday.media/2018/11/28/trump-es-un-paso-hacia-nuestro-objetivo-pero-es-insuficiente (accessed November 23, 2018).
SIPRI. 2012. *Year Book 2012: Armaments, Disarmament and International Security*. Estocolmo: SIPRI.
SIPRI. 2018. "Global Military Spending Remains High at $1.7 Trillion." Retrieved from www.sipri.org/media/press-release/2018/global-military-spending-remains-high-17-trillion (accessed December 12, 2019).
Suh, B. 2014. "La militarización de los derechos humanos coreanos: una perspectiva peninsular."*AsianStudies*46(1):3–14.https://doi.org/10.1080/14672715.2014.863575
Veraza, J. 2008. *Subsunción real del consumo al capital*. México: Itaca.
White House Office of Management and Budget. 2017. *A New Foundation for American Greatness*. Washington, DC: White House Office of Management and Budget. Retrieved from www.whitehouse.gov/wp-content/uploads/2017/11/budget.pdf (accessed December 12, 2019).

16

Necropolitical Capitalism, the State of Exception and Accumulation by Dispossession

Luis Arizmendi

Greco-Roman slavery was revived in a different world; to the plight of the Indians of the exterminated Latin American civilizations was added the ghastly fate of the blacks seized from African villages to toil in Brazil and Antilles. The colonial Latin American economy enjoyed the most highly concentrated labour force known until that time, making possible the greatest concentration of wealth ever enjoyed by any civilization in the world history.

The whole process was a pumping of blood from one set of veins to another: the development of the development of some, the underdevelopment of others. Could the sadism of the repression and the ferocity of the war be explained clinically? Were they the result of inherent evil in the protagonists?...the horror of all the violence merely exposed the horror of the system.
—Eduardo Galeano, *Open Veins of Latin America* (1997: 38, 83, 104)

Introduction: Necropolitical Capitalism and Ayotzinapa

Ayotzinapa evokes Auschwitz. This powerful formulation, expressed by Elena Poniatowska, establishes a parallel that is not an allegory. It should not be taken lightly. Ayotzinapa is not simply Ayotzinapa; it is the window to an era. The murder of 43 college students in 2014 reveals, in all its horror, the new configuration that is traversing Mexico; one of the most violent configurations in the history of world capitalism that can be called *necropolitical capitalism.*[1] It discloses the politics of death as the basis for accelerating and decadent forms of accumulation by dispossession. In this sense, Ayotzinapa has awakened a peculiar protest: the first national struggle against necropolitical capitalism.

If one attempts to critically periodize Mexico's history in recent decades, it emerges that this is the outcome of a trajectory that has passed through the stages of cynical capitalism and global subordination. At the end of the last century, capitalist mundialization said farewell to the liberal state. The historical configuration of capitalism was characterized by the intervention of the state as a counterweight to the deployment of the anonymous economic violence immanent to the accumulation of capital. This operated throughout the twentieth century, first in the Global North and, after World War II, also in the Global South, in an effort to control what Wallerstein calls the "dangerous classes" by means of a rise in living standards, periodic electoral processes, and the promotion of national sovereignty (Wallerstein 1996: 231–241).

Between 1982 and 1988, Mexico became part of a new tendency, taking the same tact as had been unleashed slightly earlier in Argentina through its military dictatorship: accumulation by dispossession of the wages of the nation as a source of revenue to pay the foreign debt. In less than six years, decades of social development were harshly reversed. By 1987, the real minimum wage was at its lowest level since 1951. Huge masses of wealth that had originally made up the social consumption fund were now redirected to capitalist accumulation. A configuration of capitalism emerged that cannot be called "neo-liberal," but might rather be called cynical. Cynical capitalism is a configuration in which the state stops intervening as a counterweight to the anonymous economic violence immanent in accumulation, but continues its intervention in the economy to guarantee the transfer of control over accumulation to private capital. The establishment of the politics of accumulation by dispossession cynically jettisoned the promise of progress for all. Instead, the capitalist market determines the wounded and the dead. That is the real meaning of *laissez faire et laissez passer.*

Between 1988 and 2006, being the only country in which the Washington Consensus was applied to the letter and in an uninterrupted way, Mexico gave birth to the foundation of a new kind of North/South power relations: global subordination. To defend against the monopoly over state-of-the-art technology that Northern capitals use as a weapon to extract revenue through technological rents and unequal exchange, many Southern states (among them, Mexico in Latin America) defended and exercised their national sovereignty. As a result of the tremendous outflow of revenue due to technological rents and the servicing of the external debt, representing the exemplary defeat of Mexico by this consensus, the state has since granted to private capital (especially transnational private capital but also Mexican private—but anti-nationalist—capital) control over strategic points of all economic sectors. The state has intervened in oil, gas, water, biodiversity, minerals, food, banking and even the education system to impose an unprecedented form of North/South domination in the short-, medium- and long-term: global subordination as the foundation of a new form of accumulation by dispossession in North/South power relations (Arizmendi and Welty 2014).

From this unprecedented form of capitalist subordination, the criminal economy, which has always been present throughout the history of capitalism, grew through an increasingly wide range of modalities to establish linkages between various elements of the political class and the criminal economy: from 2006 onwards, necropolitical capitalism emerged as a new configuration of accumulation by dispossession based on decadent violence. In the beginning, in some places, it engaged in activities (such as building schools or roads) that had been abandoned by the state. As the UN reported in the early 2000s, Mexico imported ephedrine in such quantities that all Mexicans must have been sick with the flu all year round (OAS 2010: 33). Despite this information provided by the UN, the federal government took no action to intervene in narcopolitical structures. By 2005, as evidence of its global expansion, the Mexican criminal economy already had factories and contracts in Asia.

From 2006 onwards, the shift to necropolitical capitalism occurred. The transition had germinated over the previous decades. The politics of death as the basis for new forms of accumulation by dispossession expanded: the enslavement of migrants on the southern border, trafficking and forced prostitution, the depopulation of areas with strategic natural resources and their subsequent repopulation with more docile communities. In places like Michoacán, taxes were imposed on the circulation of goods, the movement of persons, on the area of housing up to per square meter, as well as on the black market for weapons, organs or children—all of which became sources of a new type of capitalist rent: the criminal rent. A tremendous concentration of private wealth, which would be impossible if not for the establishment of decadent political violence, has been generated by an aggressive form of accumulation by dispossession imposed by necropolitical capitalism. Undoubtedly, its most sordid expression is that Mexico was turned into a country full of clandestine mass graves.

The criminal economy had never before been as significant in the structural corridors of national and global accumulation. Its scope is such that Edgardo Buscaglia (2009), director of the International Centre for Legal and Economic Development, has estimated that the clusters of capital income derived from criminal rent, intersecting with legal businesses, correspond to 40 percent of national GDP and are moving around the world economy through a network operating in 47 countries. The criminal economy operating from Mexico is among the most powerful in the twenty-first century.

Ayotzinapa has enabled a struggle, unprecedented in Mexican national history, to have an international impact. Its pain reflects an ominous and unacceptable time. The growing historic bloc which it summons could change the future. The movement around Ayotzinapa is highly pluralistic. It represents an open convergence of the most diverse groups: students from public and private universities, workers, peasants, artists, feminists, Catholics, nuns, Hare Krishnas, agnostics and indigenous peoples. Its just claims have motivated demonstrations in dozens of cities in Europe, South America and Europe. The parents of Ayotzinapa have their counterparts in Argentina and Bolivia, including the Mothers of the Plaza de Mayo. The struggle must be peaceful to maintain cohesion and the ongoing development of the historic bloc that is emerging in opposition to necropolitical capitalism. The narrative of twenty-first-century Mexico deserves an historical alternative; it calls for the democratization of the country and its institutions.

The Neo-authoritarian Tendency and the Shift towards a State of Exception

In the context of a risky but invariably unstable transition, of unpredictable outcomes due to the radicalization of the relationship between capitalism and devastation, a dangerous trend has been expanding and consolidating in the effort of the planetary power to determine its reconfiguration in the face of the epochal crisis of twenty-first-century capitalism. This is the most serious crisis in the history of world capitalism, before which, in constant conflict with liberal tendencies which press for the intervention of the state system as a counterweight to the destructive effects of capitalist accumulation, the prevailing trend is the tendency towards neo-authoritarianism; a trend that sees an intersection, in an increasingly threateningly way, between anonymous economic violence and destructive political violence.

Now that it is responding to the intensification of the dispute over world hegemony, the trend towards neo-authoritarianism seeks to reverse the peculiarity of Latin America as the only region that has tried to offer certain kinds of counter-hegemonic resistance to "neoliberalism" in the new century. 2030 is a crucial date in the fight for global power, since, according to calculations of the Pentagon, China could exceed the GDP of the US by 250 percent and even surpass its military power. The attempt to reverse this future scenario provides the context for the current multidimensional (economic, political and military) offensive of the US against the triple Eurasian alliance between China, Russia, and Iran. It represents the tendency to stop, impede and reverse the almost inescapable collapse of American hegemony.

In order to impose a regional geopolitics based on accumulation by dispossession in all its violent proportions, and to subordinate Latin America as a key element in the dispute for global hegemony, the neo-authoritarian tendency has broken the alliance built by Brazil with the eastern powers in the form of the BRICs, attacked Venezuela for being a counterhegemonic state, and longed to subordinate the entire subcontinent to global domination, as we saw in 2019 with the IMF offensive and the imposition of the state of exception in Ecuador.

If we start by updating the core critical content from the concept of the authoritarian state inherited from Max Horkheimer (2006) (which provides a critical alternative to the liberal notion of "totalitarianism" elaborated by Hannah Arendt, who posited an illusion that Nazism struck as a kind of extra-historical lightning which ended up interrupting, if only in a temporary way, the march of capitalist modernity that represents the promise of unstoppable economic-political progress, above all from American modernity), we could say that what characterizes the neo-authoritarian trend first and foremost is the growing radicalization of the permanent relation between capitalism and violence in an effort to integrate decadent configurations of capitalism that interlaces anonymous economic violence and destructive political violence in increasingly threatening ways. Without hesitation, the neo-authoritarian tendency abandons the promise of universal progress and its offer of a better standard of living for all as an absurd whim of the past, and assumes that the radicalization of an increasingly violent configuration of capitalism constitutes an indispensable way to guarantee access to comfort and opulence for a very few.

Capitalism itself constitutes a permanently violent historical system, but it produces highly divergent configurations, and even those counterposed to the organization and administration of the exercise of its systemic or structural violence. Placing the modern dominated at structural risk of death, starting with the daily expropriation of livelihoods, and converting this danger into the basis of a generalized commodification of labor power and wage labor. The threat of rendering the modern dominated part of a surplus population that can be sacrificed, and even attacking the process of vital reproduction for those who are part of the active workers' army, constitutes the socio-historical platform that makes capitalism a modernity based on the simulacrum of a ceasefire. It makes capitalist modernity an economic system that throws out the wounded and the dead (Echeverría 1995: 176–179).

As Marx clarified in *The Civil War in France*, redefining the concept of civil war beyond a clash of two national projects within the same state or two state projects inside the same nation, a "civil war" silently but effectively and permanently governs modern capitalism (Echeverría 2006: 97–98). The devastation of social life that derives from the general law of capitalist accumulation constitutes the world of a civil war that takes the form of contrasting historical modalities according to the balance of forces in the class struggle. In its strictest sense, a properly historical-liberal configuration of this simulacrum of peace or, if preferred, the state of pax capitalist-modernity occurs when the state intervenes in a limited but effective way as a counterweight to the anonymous economic violence immanent to the destructive power of accumulation. Instead, we move towards a properly historical-authoritarian configuration where that state of pax is torn to pieces: when the civil war, even without having been formally declared as such, takes the form of an open war through the growing deployment of destructive political violence by capital and the state, which is added to the devastation emanating from anonymous economic violence of capitalism (Arizmendi 2018: 9–13). In this sense, insofar as the epochal crisis of twenty-first-century capitalism has emblazoned its historically most aggressive form on the general law of capitalist accumulation, we can say that (to paraphrase Walter Benjamin 2010 conceptually to arrive at his current relevance), as a rule, the State of Exception constitutes an epochal trend of our time.

Undoubtedly, twenty-first-century capitalism is pushing for the reissue (not a mere repetition, but subject to a historical metamorphosis) of the rupture of the simulacrum of peace that was in play around a hundred years ago by the Hitlerian state and World War II. In contemporary capitalist mundialization, the group of states that are moving towards scenarios of coup d'état and states of exception are not minor expressions of this trend. With the imposition of a political reconfiguration that already has transcontinental support in the US (Bellamy Foster 2017; Giroux 2015) and Europe (Rügemer 2017), where a deep crisis of the social democratic governments that dominated the post-war period has led to their displacement by far right parties, Latin America (the only region in the world that offered resistance to "neoliberal politics" at the turn of the century) is now subject to a strong offensive through a new kind of coup d'état; that is, one deployed through an articulation between the mass media and judiciary.

Mexico: Prototype of the Neo-authoritarian Tendency in Latin America

Mexico has experienced a drastic transition from the prototypical state characterized by defensive nationalism during the twentieth century, to one marked by the neo-authoritarian tendency of the twenty-first century South. It is the country in which accumulation by dispossession has gone further without a military dictatorship or armed invasion. Hence, it epitomizes the paradigm of *global subordination* that the United States now intends to expand geopolitically in Latin America, through the new-style coups and tendency towards states of exception.

If we look at Mexican history from the turn of the century, we can identify the successive deployment of three forms of accumulation by dispossession, which superimpose themselves one upon another as they emerge so that the dispossession achieved in a latter phase does not itself displace previous phases, but rather adds new dimensions to the domination achieved in earlier moments. From this point of view, it can be said that Mexico has imposed:

1. from 1982 to 1988, accumulation by dispossession of the national wage;

2. from 1988 to 2006, global subordination as a form of accumulation by dispossession based on the total defeat of the nationalist state in the Global South; and

3. from 2006 onwards, necropolitical capitalism as an extremely violent and decadent form of accumulation by dispossession, based on a politics of death intended to impose an unchecked range of sources of a new type of rent, criminal rent.

Between 1982 and 1988, the configuration of accumulation by dispossession just imposed over the previous six years by Videla in Argentina was re-introduced in Mexico, but without a military dictatorship; one which linked the explosive growth of the foreign debt to an unprecedented fall in national wages. As one of the countries that experienced one of the biggest falls in wages in the history of world capitalism, Mexico imposed what can be called accumulation by dispossession of the national wage fund: a form of accumulation characterized by the dispossession of an enormous share of the national consumer wage fund, only to convert it violently into a spurious fund for accumulation. This reveals that the external debt operates as an essential complement to the power of technological rent (i.e., the tribute that the Global South must pay to the Global North for its technological supremacy). By 1982, Mexican external debt had reached a practically unpayable point when it reached an amount equivalent to 134.19 percent of GDP, its highest point in the modern economic history of Mexico. After the minimum wage reached its maximum level of 120.77 pesos in 1978, it fell precipitously from 66.04 in 1982, to 28.65 pesos in 1987. That is to say, in only five years, three and a half decades of development with regard to the minimum wage were reversed by placing it well below its historically-lowest level (35.46 pesos in 1951).

Undoubtedly, accumulation by dispossession did not create labor overexploitation—which constitutes, as Marini (1973) demonstrated, a regular process imposed by the impact of power relations within world capitalism on dependent capitalism—but it did lead to a new and more violent historical modality. The capitalist anonymous economic violence combined with accumulation by dispossession brought forth what can be defined as cynical or brutal over-exploitation; a mode of over-exploitation that places even workers in the active army at risk of being unable to access the basket of basic consumer goods. Not only is cynical or brutal over-exploitation imposed in sectors like mining, but this has also now become the general foundation of accumulation by wage dispossession. Cynical or brutal over-exploitation makes use and abuse of anonymous economic violence as a platform, imposing the expropriation of the wage fund in such magnitudes that it endangers the vital process of reproducing the work force.

The prolonged persistence of cynical or brutal over-exploitation, which imposed a violent downward trend on the wage rate along with the accelerated growth of the big capitals, saw the integration of Mexican capitalism as an economy that offers one of the cheapest workforces in the capitalist world. For this reason, Mexico currently has the longest working day and lowest wage among OECD countries. The minimum wage gap between Mexico and the US is brutal: Mexican and US minimum wages are $0.5 and $7.2 per hour respectively. If wages in the manufacturing sector are taken into account, while China tripled its wages between 2005 and 2016, reaching $3.60 per hour, and in South African wages fell from $4.30 to $3.60, and Brazil from $2.90 to $2.70, in Mexico they sank from $2.20 to $2.10. The measure of household income and its material bases does not take into account the historical-moral or historical-cultural conditions necessary for social-national reproduction; in this context, 80 percent of the population is in a situation of poverty and 50 percent in extreme poverty (Boltvinik 2013: 68–71).

Cynical or brutal over-exploitation has left twenty-first-century Mexico with a working day that represents a subtle historical retreat with respect to the eight-hour workday, conquered internationally following the Chicago struggles at the end of the nineteenth century. Currently, the Mexican average working day is almost 9 hours. Within the OECD countries, the average annual work time is 1763 hours. The US is above average with an annual total of 1783 hours; Russia has an average of 1974. Among the Latin American countries, Chile, like Russia, registers at 1974 hours. But Mexico surpasses all other OECD countries, with the longest annual working hours at a global level: placing itself above a small country like Costa Rica, which registers 2212 hours, the average Mexican working time is 2255 hours a year. This rate has not declined, even as many other countries are approaching the OECD average. At the other extreme, Germany has an annual working time of 1363 hours (OECD 2017). This means that Mexico has a working day equivalent to 165.44 percent of the German and 127.90 percent of the average annual working time of the OECD.

Accumulation by wage dispossession is thus accompanied by one of the highest, most extensive rates of absolute surplus value in the world. It combines violation of international labor law with a regressive neo-authoritarian right, enacted in the labor counter-reform of 2017. Accumulation by dispossession of the national wage has not only made Mexico a prototype for the de facto violation of the law of value underlying the capital/labor relation; starting from the labor counter-reform, it has turned it into a prototypical state of the *de jure* violation (i.e., with legal recognition) of the law of value underpinning the capital/

labor relation. The minimum wage violates international agreements signed by the Mexican government, such as the Universal Declaration of Human Rights or the International Covenant on Economic, Social and Cultural Rights; but, at the same time, the new labor constitution legalizes the transgression of the law of value in the world of work. It legalizes *outsourcing* (which was used previously even though illegal) and the disappearance of conciliation and arbitration boards, granting new offensive powers to private capital to impose layoffs and wage/labor flexibility.

One of the mainstays of wage dispossession has been the offensive for the privatization of pensions. In an in-depth essay on the advance of pension privatization across the American continent, James Russell (2014) has shown that this offensive was first launched after the Pinochet's coup Chile. It was taken further by 401(k) schemes in the US. However, whereas Bolivia under Evo Morales and Argentina under the Kirchners returned to the state management of retirement pension funds, Mexico implemented the most aggressive privatization program. While the average wage replacement ratio (that is, the percentage of a salary received after retirement) is 65.9 percent within the OECD, and the average in Holland and Argentina surpasses 100 percent, in Mexico it corresponds to 31.5 percent. And Mexican neo-authoritarian capitalism plans to go even further. Mexico represents the historical trajectory of a future for Argentina that Macri sought to conceal as he imposes a harsh counter-reform on pensions. The "middle classes" will by no means be spared that regressive impact in the near future.

Between 1988 and 2006, without armed invasion or military dictatorship, Mexico became the prototype for an unprecedented configuration of the power relations between the North and the South: global subordination. A form of subordination created at the turn of the century, global subordination entails the direct subordination of all strategic nuclei of the national economy to private capital, imposed by the state. First, the national economy was subordinated to transnational private capital, although this also occurred for the benefit of sectors of national but anti-nationalist private capital which jumped on the bandwagon of an aggressive and accelerated dispossession of key public goods. In this period a profound recomposition of the ruling class took place, definitively extinguishing any remnant of a nationalist business class. Technological development, oil, gas, mining, water, food, agriculture, biodiversity, banking and education became dominated internally by private capital as never before. With the destruction of the Liberal state, Mexico's subordination to the dynamics of "globalization" became radical. In other words, the material infrastructure that a state must govern in a sovereign way during a state of war became controlled by private capital. Or if preferred, the pillars on which national economic sovereignty depend became subordinated in practical terms in their entirety, giving shape to an unprecedented form of subordination by the US over Mexico, built to become a form of long-term global subordination.

Accumulation by dispossession with global subordination gave rise to an expected dispossession of *public goods*, as Mexico became the first state of the South to privatize (without war and invasion, as in Iraq) the totality of strategic parastatal companies (Fernández 2002): a radical dispossession of *common goods*, in so far as more than half the national territory has been handed over to mining operations (above all to transnational corporations) which devastate the reproduction of indigenous and peasant communities (Geocomunes 2017); and a general dispossession of *generic goods*, as Mexico has become the number one country in the world in terms of water commodification (La Jornada 2005).

Accompanying the defeat of state-level defensive mechanisms regarding the reproduction of the national workforce, the state monopoly over strategic natural resources as an essential source of natural resource rent in service of national income was broken. An enormous transfer of value is, in a spurious way, taken away through the cynical intervention of the state, blocking it from operating as a lever of economic and social development, and instead, making it to metamorphose into extraordinary natural rent and profit in service of powerful private (and above all, transnational) capital. Mexico has the fourth largest gas reserves in the world and one of its largest oil reserves in the Gulf of Mexico. Since the tragic definition of the maritime borders surrounding Bermeja Island, which previously appeared on the CIA maps and now as such no longer exists (Barbosa 2003), for the United states, dominance over Mexican energy reserves in the Gulf of Mexico is of strategic important in its dispute for global hegemony.

The strategic or programmed deindustrialization of PEMEX (the state-owned petroleum company) began the process of reconverting natural rent into what can be called spurious transnational rent. Currently, there are 681 refineries in the world. The US has 149, giving it the largest refining capacity globally. It is followed by China and Russia. Japan, which does not have oil reserves, has almost 50. Venezuela has 24 (although, among them, there is the second largest refinery in the world). With PEMEX acting as an example of the strategic deindustrialization to which the country has been subjected, Mexico is the only oil state counting on only six refineries, which also operate below their operating capacity. While in the twenty-first century more refineries are being built in Asia Pacific and the Middle East, Mexico is going in the opposite direction, falling further and further behind. Exporting cheap oil in order to import more expensive gasoline from the US, for up to 75 percent of national consumption requirements, makes this circuit of techno-energy subordination the source of an enormous spurious differential rent. Truly sabotaging national income, the state has imposed the reconversion of natural rent (derived from oil and gas) into an enormous mass of extraordinary profits in the form of artificial or spurious transnational rent.

Accumulation by dispossession goes even further. Starting with the most recent energy counter-reform of 2014, the direct exploitation of Mexico's most important energy deposits has been made available to private capital for the first time. Prior to this, the various contracts signed to allow the private servicing or exploitation natural gas reserves in the Burgos Basin, or of national oil reserves, were unconstitutional. The counter-reform transformed this illegal accumulation into de facto dispossession, into accumulation by de-possession of gigantic masses of national income based on natural resources. Since 2015, 19 Mexican and foreign companies have mapped the energy resources of the Gulf of Mexico based on 54 permits that have been granted, without going to public tender or auction. Transnational corporations from the US, Norway and Australia will be able to conduct geological studies until 2027 in areas with ample hydrocarbon potential, without paying a single peso to the Mexican state. Worse still, and in stark contrast to the counter-hegemonic policy exercised by Evo Morales in Bolivia (who, since becoming president, has demanded that gas transnationals reverse the relation between spurious differential rent and national revenue, so as to leave the country 80 percent rather than 20 percent of gas revenue, as they previously did), the undersecretary of finance Miguel Messmacher told the foreign press that the Mexican government would ask transnational corporations that benefitted from the 2014 energy reform to pay only 10 percent royalties on each barrel produced. In fact, not even this ridiculous rate of 10 percent royalties is guaranteed, given that the National Hydrocarbons Commission did not establish any mechanism to monitor or register the oil extracted from Mexican territorial and marine subsoil. Not even in "neoliberal" Bolivia was the subordination of natural income so extreme.

Far from marking the end of the "goose that laid the golden egg," Mexico's qualification as part of the "new Middle East" in the twenty-first century is due to enormous oil reserves in the Gulf, for which the US has the best studies for each of its quadrants. Nineteen of 29 blocks have already been tendered to transnational corporations, including BP, ExxonMobil, Shell, Total, Enil, and CNOOC. This is the largest deep water tender in Mexican history, with licenses granted for up to half a century. From being a prototype of national energy sovereignty during the last century, Mexico has become a prototype of total energy subordination to the United States. At the same time, also in the context of global subordination, from being an exemplary country in terms of the exercise of food sovereignty in the twentieth century, Mexico has gone on crudely to be the prototype of artificial food subordination in the twenty-first century. Under the "neoliberal" pretext that it was economically better to import than to self-produce, global subordination has taken Mexico from importing 10 percent of its food requirements to 46 percent. By 2020, the import of hard grains (corn, sorghum, barley, rye and oats) could reach more than 60 percent. According to the FAO, Mexico ranks third in the importation of cereals. In the twentieth century, Mexican capitalism made food sovereignty an effective counterweight to labor over-exploitation; where there might have been poverty, there were few deaths from hunger. Now that global subordination has shattered Mexican food sovereignty, labor over-exploitation is accompanied by chronic malnutrition and deaths due to hunger in marginal areas of Mexico.

Despite the enormous financing set aside for its bailout, the banking sector has been practically denationalized and operates as the private property of foreign capital, that is, as a means of doubling the accumulation by dispossession of the national wage fund. The sector by no means operates as a development bank. It constitutes a means of transferring huge volumes of value expropriated from the national wage fund for consumer-credit interests to the headquarters of foreign banks. They operate in Mexico with much higher interest rates than those of their countries of origin.

Accumulation by dispossession through the debt contracted in a false bailout of the banking sector will impact the whole lifespan of millennials. In 1999, FOBAPROA was re-established to service the public debt, which it calculated would have an impact for three decades, and require an average rate of GDP growth of over 4 percent. Since Mexico has been growing at around 2 percent annually, FOBAPROA may end up covering the debt until 2076 or beyond. Millennials may leave this spurious debt as a legacy to their grandchildren. In order to rescue the banks, in 1998, the Mexican government issued a loan corresponding to US$60 billion, that is, 18 times higher than the income obtained from privatizing the banks in the first place. The result can be evaluated: in 1988, at the end of the first phase of accumulation by dispossession, the external debt decreased to correspond to 60 percent of GDP; by 2018, having done away with the discourse that justified the sale of all strategic state enterprises and the entire offensive march of wage dispossession, the debt still amounted to 51 percent of the GDP. Mexico has privatized everything and yet remains the state with the largest foreign debt in Latin America.

The tragedy has not stopped there. From 2006 on, consolidating a form that was drafted in the 1990s, Mexico has imposed a historical-decadent configuration of accumulation by dispossession: necropolitical capitalism. This form makes use and abuse of a politics of death as the foundation for violent and accelerated forms of accumulation by dispossession,[2] which has led to the multiplication of different sources of a new type of rent: criminal rent. The criminal economy has accompanied capitalism throughout its history, but it has never played such a role in global accumulation and power. Where narcopolitical capitalism is characterized by a growing linkage between various power groups of the political class and the criminal economy, so that the cartels attempt to fulfil social provisioning functions abandoned by the federal government (including building carriers, schools, churches and even giving away toys in bulk, sometimes with dedications), necropolitical capitalism is defined as the radical intertwining of anonymous economic violence and decadent, destructive political violence. The illegal revenue (i.e., extraordinary profits) produced through the circulation of drugs, the movement of migrants, trafficking, black markets for weapons, organs or babies, by businesses established in the formal and informal economy or in the housing market, by the sale of gasoline stolen from PEMEX pipelines (or worse yet, its refineries), even through the enslavement of labor power (including that of women, girls and boys), comprise many of the sources of a kind of revenue which would be impossible were it not for the politics of death underpinning this accelerated form of decadent accumulation by dispossession: criminal rent.

Evoking Auschwitz, Ayotzinapa (Grecko 2016)[3] has provided a window onto the world of what Mexico means by the historical concretion of *necropolitical capitalism*. Without a doubt, Mexico has been one of the countries with the greatest numbers of human rights violations worldwide. The politics of death is the foundation of a decadent form of accumulation by dispossession, creating spaces of criminal government in parallel to the state but allowed by it. Strictly speaking, this form of capitalist domination cannot be sufficiently understood as a "power vacuum" (Buscaglia 2013), as painfully revealed by the discovery of more than 3000 clandestine graves in Mexico.

Contrary to the ignominious Iron Wall project proposed by Trump, necropolitical capitalism in Mexico would be simply impossible without its deep articulation with the American economy. As acknowledged by the UN Office on Drugs and Crime, along the US–Mexico border alone operates a huge black market with an annual flow of approximately 730,000 illegal weapons. The magnitude of the accumulation by dispossession by necropolitical capitalism is so enormous that it would be impossible for it to operate without multiple links between the legal and illegal economy. As such, the classification of the Mexican state as the most corrupt within the OECD is correct. Corruption has played an essential role in making Mexico the country that most quickly embraced global money laundering (Buscaglia 2015). Without the slightest doubt, this is a mirror of the future, towards which the neo-authoritarianism tendency, with its project to expand accumulation by dispossession geopolitically, is aiming to take Latin America. The "middle classes" supporting this tendency are called to a historical pedagogy of solidarity out of self-interest. However, there is no way that they will not be deeply impacted by this labyrinth.

The state project represented by Andrés Manuel López Obrador, beginning in late 2018, must be evaluated first and foremost as a response to the integration of one of the most violent historical configurations of world capitalism. In that sense, it is fitting to define the project of the new Mexican government as that for a liberal state of peace. López Obrador's attempt to position oil extraction as a lever for national development is an expression of an effort to recover natural rent in the service of national income. There is no way for Southern states to defend themselves in the context of current power relations in the planetary economy and the system of technological rent without making use of this natural rent.

However, the arrival of López Obrador to the presidency also revealed that the complicity of the state is a crucial condition of the enormous theft of gasoline (a practice known as *huachicoleo*), which is not only siphoned in large quantities from pipelines, but also stolen using ships that have been directly loaded from PEMEX refineries. As such, what is known as the land-based *huachicol* is actually a window to something even greater: the maritime *huachicoleo*. This massive theft of fuel to sell illegal gasoline in Central America, South America and the US would be impossible without the participation of transnationals.[4] The new Mexican government has started a very important fight against *huachicoleo*, and has managed to block this source of criminal rent to a great extent.

While the government has proven to be strategically minded on this theme (for example, with a project to build the Dos Bocas refinery to counteract PEMEX's technological subordination to the US), there are two outstanding challenges which have yet to arise: the need to renegotiate the distribution of differential rent from oil with the multinationals that won tenders in the Gulf of Mexico; and more importantly, the strategic need for a project to move towards a post-fossil fuels transition. In the context of the globalized environmental crisis, the energy transition is a crucial outstanding challenge. Likewise, while price guarantees have been designed to ensure that the national production of basic grains is carried out in the country, it is essential to aim to overcome food subordination. The food economy needs to attend to national sovereignty and to stop being a great channel of accumulation for foreign capital that creates vulnerability around social reproduction in the nation. The US positioned itself as a hegemon of the world food market at the turn of the century, imposing a long-term power relationship on the nations of the South.

It is very important that, given the risk of a US military invasion of Venezuela, which has the largest reserves of oil and thorium (a strategic mineral which will replace plutonium in the production of nuclear weapons in the twenty-first century), Mexico stays firm in defending its position of respect for international law and non-intervention. Its promotion of a peaceful solution to the conflict in Venezuela seeks to prevent South America from being converted into a new Middle East. The project for the liberal state of peace personified by López Obrador must confront the accumulation by dispossession imposed on Mexico, in all its complexity, at the turn of the century. The liberal state is a mediation in the struggle against both necropolitical capitalism and the dangerous period into which the neo-authoritarian tendency is propelling Latin America. At the same time, the liberal state of peace faces the challenge of taking on the development of a more far-reaching project: the counter-hegemonic state as alternative to the epochal crisis of twenty-first-century capitalism.[5]

The Contemporary Crossroads of Latin America

It is not just the crisis of progressive governance that is at stake in this socioeconomic cycle. The period has challenged the very ability of a popular government to attempt to increase the living standards of the middle class. This runs the risk that this class will then later reject the redistribution of national income to all sectors and instead throw its support behind neo-authoritarian right-wing parties, which in turn will negatively impact the middle class standard of living. The support of the impoverished middle class will then return one again to a progressive government, and the whole cycle starts again. Without an end to the first half of this cycle, it cannot be assumed that history will inevitably return progressive governments to the executive branch of the state in any predestined way. The triumph of neo-fascism under Bolsonaro in Brazil serves to confirm that this cycle is not destiny.

Latin America is at an inescapable and increasingly radical crossroads: tension is growing between the neo-authoritarian tendency, which struggles to extend accumulation by dispossession in all its aspects, and a counter-hegemonic tendency, which tries to resist but is unable to break through, relying purely on the project of a liberal state to act as a counterweight to violent planetary accumulation and the epochal crises of twenty-first-century capitalism. Beyond successfully imposing accumulation by dispossession, the neo-authoritarian tendency has managed to co-opt important blocs of the Latin American ruling class by creating a deep convergence of interests: the huge dispossession of public goods (like the strategic state enterprises), common goods (such as oil and gas deposits) and generic goods (such as the genetic codes of biodiversity and water) has greatly benefited the ruling classes of the North, while recomposing the ruling classes of the South. In Mexico, accumulation by dispossession has generated radical polarization. It has made the country a factory for the creation of the poor and, at the same time, a factory for billionaires who are among the richest in the world (Zepeda 2007).

Now, in order to spread throughout Latin America, the neo-authoritarian tendency is driving the creation of a convergence of another order, this time around the interests of the "middle classes." This tendency seeks to provide social support for the violent clash against workers, peasants and social movements, installing a *bellum omnium contra omnes* from below. Assuming that natural rent at the service of national income is nothing more than a progressive past fiction that must be left behind (meaning that economic and political progress for all is an impossibility, and therefore, that comfort and a higher standard of living can alone remain for the middle classes, if it is guaranteed that they—but not other subaltern classes—have access to natural rent and income derived from strategic natural resources), the capitalist crisis has thus propagated a political culture that, with this exclusion, aims to promote: racism and xenophobia, the deployment of anonymous economic violence and destructive political violence against the bulk of the modern dominated classes. In this way, not only the dominant class but also the middle class of the South end up converging around the current neo-authoritarian tendency.

In this sense, transnational capital, the political class and the ruling class not only manipulate the middle class using the mass media; they are also exploiting the generation of a historical convergence. Brazil and Argentina have become a breeding ground for the radicalization of a xenophobic culture that is now absorbed into the neo-authoritarian trend. However, it is Mexico, more so than Colombia, which provides a mirror of the region's future. Accumulation by wage dispossession, global subordination and necropolitical capitalism constitute real threats to the totality of Latin American national societies. But accumulation by dispossession also leads towards an authentic cul-de-sac for the middle classes of Latin America. Paradoxically, it is from this danger that a new period of opportunity, for the construction of anti-systemic alternatives, emerges. But to take advantage of it requires learning from the limitations experienced previously. In *Nuestramérica* (Our America) at the beginning of the twenty-first century, a polarity emerged between state-centered and autonomous movements, which is simultaneously counterproductive and practically inevitable. It was this form that the classical polarity between reform and revolution took in contemporary regional history.

The negation and even clash between autonomous anticapitalistic movements and state-centric political forces invariably ends up weakening the social bases of the latter. Moreover, in the context of an historical project reduced to seeking a Liberal state in the new century, the middle classes (which includes sections of the working class with better living standards) remain politically uneducated; thus, the premise of their support for the neo-authoritarian tendency. Without at least tactical agreements and a strategic perspective, the rejection of and antagonism from autonomous movements towards state-centered forces opens up the risk of leaving the historical need to accommodate the diverse needs of the multiple nationalities and social forces within the same state at *solum nihil*. The polarization in which local needs collide with the use of natural resources as a source of national income, and the national need for economic and social development to counteract the destructive effects of labor over-exploitation, are to a certain extent, materially inevitable. Both local and national needs are legitimate, but we require the urgent construction of historical pacts to answer them.

The Latin American left is struggling to forge an effective articulation between these two dimensions as it confronts the dangers posed by the neo-authoritarian tendency: between the project for a counterhegemonic state, which cannot confront planetary power without the support of autonomous social forces; at the same time, autonomous movements require, one way or another, counter-hegemonic projects to be propagated to fight for the integrity of "self-determination in the country," to borrow a phrase from Rosa Luxemburg. By promoting social recognition of the deep interconnection between accumulation by dispossession and barbarism, it may be that the anti-systemic left will generate conditions for the most open and plural convergence of social movements, from the conception of an essential but common agenda aimed at creating an effective counter-power that will allow us to confront the neo-authoritarian tendency of the twenty-first century.

Luis Arizmendi is lecturer at the National Polytechnic Institute for 30 years and is the director of the international magazine *Mundo Siglo XXI*. He holds a Doctor Honoris Causa from the Alva Edison University, Mexico. He was an author of many articles and books on the global crisis of capitalism, both in English and Spanish, and lecturer in Universidad Nacional Autónoma de México.

Acknowledgments

Translated from Spanish by Jacqueline Díaz. Editor's note: I am grateful to Amanda Latimer from Kingston University, UK for her assistance in editing this chapter.

Notes

1. The debate around necropolitics was initiated in a foundational way by Achille Mbembe, political science researcher at the University of the Witwatersrand in Johannesburg. Seeking to decipher the exercise of a policy of death which unfolded in settings like apartheid in South Africa, the Gaza Strip in Palestine and the Kosovan war, Mbembe created the term necropolitics to investigate the specificity of these configurations of violence that, without simply duplicating Nazism, evoke the violence of Mussolini's black shirts or Hitler's SS. He also analyses the way in which necropower operates illegally by imposing areas controlled by an "indirect private government" based on the territorialization of violence, in which local technocrats and foreign

traffickers are articulated in a government that overflows the state (Mbembe 2011: 79-107). The immediate discussion is meant to question the tendency towards Nazism. Within the postmodernist horizon, however, to the degree that necropolitics is defined as a necropower within Mbembe's framework, it at the same time suggests greater possibilities: that is, from a conception that does not position the critique of capitalist domination as its foundation. The refusal to establish an authentic dialogue with Karl Marx's critique radically weakens the author's conception of necropolitics, as it introduces a rotating platform: instead of deciphering necropolitics as a historical configuration that radicalizes the violence immanent in capitalist modernity, producing the collapse of its simulacrum of peace, Mbembe treats necropolitics as an expression of the exercise of biopower. And, without a doubt, while biopower is meant to investigate the politics of population control, it is power. Biopower is one of the multiple "technologies of power" of Foucault. It is a term full of ambivalence in so far as it takes the exercise of power relations away from the state, beyond forms of control deployed by local technocrats, to define it as form of dominance immanent to all sociality. Finally, power is inescapable because it is inherent in subjectivity. To be a subject means to exercise subjection. Hence, Mbembe ended up hesitating at his own perspective, in so far as he consistently fails to introduce visible alternatives. The concept of necropolitical capitalism follows the path that Mbembe refused to: it shows that necropolitics, without duplicating Nazism, radicalizes the violence immanent in capitalist modernity by adding to the anonymous economic violence the deployment, increasingly decadent, of political-destructive violence. In fact, we must insist, paradoxically, that while it is not simply a repetition of Nazism, necropolitical capitalism only reveals its full scope when it is identified as a historical configuration inserted into the neo-authoritarian tendency with which world capitalism is trying to respond to its epochal crisis. In this way, the concept of necropolitical capitalism questions the contemporary concretion of the capitalism/barbarism binomial.

2. The connection between capitalist barbarism and accumulation by dispossession in the spoliation of land and territory, mining and hydrocarbon extraction, the plundering of the countryside and the peasants, as well as over those who live on the urban borders, is investigated in Carlos Rodríguez and Ramses Cruz (2013).
3. See the documentary "The Army in the Night of Iguala" by Témoris Grecko: https://vimeo.com/338606003 (password: letmesee).
4. The word *huachicol* comes from the Latin "*aquati*," which means watered down. Throughout the nineteenth century, sellers of tequila and brandy who diluted the drinks with water to obtain more profits began to be called *guachicoleros* or *huachicoleros*. In the twenty-first century, the term is used in Mexican Spanish to denote people and companies dedicated to the theft, illegal transfer and sale of hydrocarbons that integrate a huge network of criminal rent created from the extraction of resources from PEMEX. The rent extracted is of such enormous magnitude that these actors become competitors both with the Mexican economy and in international markets, including Central America and at least the south of the US. By far surpassing the theft of hydrocarbons from PEMEX pipelines is that which has taken place using ships that come to load fuel directly from the largest PEMEX refineries, to sell on both the black and formal markets, generating a mass of criminal rent of such magnitude that members of the Zetas drug cartel have become *huachicoleros* because of the tremendous extraordinary profits. One of the main achievements of the López Obrador government is that it has practically stopped and almost entirely reversed the *huachiocoleos* economy (Pérez 2011, 2017).

5. The epochal crisis of twenty-first-century capitalism is a concept that, while including the most far-reaching crisis of over-accumulation in modern history (that is, the first major capitalist crisis of a truly planetary scale), surpasses it at the same time, as it also contains the globalized environmental crisis and its secular trend, which endangers the world of social-natural life. As this crisis will have an impact at least throughout this century, it is epochal, itself constituting an entire era (Arizmendi and Welty 2014; also Arizmendi 2016).

References

Arizmendi, Luis. 2018. "Capitalismo y violencia: A 150 años del Libro I de *El Capital*." *Observatorio del Desarrollo* (Universidad Autónoma de Zacatecas) 6(18): 5–15.

Arizmendi, Luis. 2016. "Baroque modernity and peasant poverty in the 21st century." In *Peasant Poverty and Persistence in 21st Century*, edited by Julio Boltvinik and Susan Archerman. London: Zed Books.

Arizmendi, Luis and Gordon Welty. 2014. "Latin America and the epochal crisis of capitalism." In *The Global Capitalist Crisis and its Aftermath*, edited by Berch Berberoglu. London: Ashgate.

Barbosa, Fabio. 2003. *El petróleo en los hoyos de dona y otras áreas desconocidas del Golfo de México*. Mexico City: Miguel Ángel Porrúa.

Bellamy Foster, John. 2017. "Neofascism in the White House." *Monthly Review* 68(11). Retrieved from https://monthlyreview.org/2017/04/01/neofascism-in-the-white-house (accessed October 20, 2019). https://doi.org/10.14452/MR-068-11-2017-04_1

Benjamin, Walter. 2010. *Tesis sobre la historia y otros fragmentos*, edited and translated by Bolívar Echeverría. Bogotá: Ediciones Desde Abajo.

Boltvinik, Julio. 2013. "Para reformar la reforma social neoliberal." *Estados y Comunes: Revista de Política y Problemas Públicos*. Quito, Ecuador: Instituto de Altos Estudios Nacionales.

Buscaglia, Edgardo. 2015. *Lavado de dinero y corrupción política*. Mexico City: Debate Editorial.

Buscaglia, Edgardo. 2013. *Vacíos de poder en México*. Mexico City: Debate Editorial.

Buscaglia, Edgardo. 2009. "La economía infiltrada por el narco." *El Universal* (Mexico), November 15. Retrieved from https://archivo.eluniversal.com.mx/nacion/172966.html

Echeverría, Bolívar. 2006. "El sentido del siglo XX." In *Vuelta de siglo*. Mexico City: Ediciones Era.

Echeverría, Bolívar. 1995. *Las ilusiones de la modernidad*. Mexico City: UNAM/El Equilibrista.

Fernández, John Saxe. 2002. *La compra-venta de México*. Mexico City: Plaza Janés.

Galeano, Eduardo. 1997. *Open Veins of Latin America: Five Centuries of the Pillage of a Continent*. New York: Monthly Review Press.

Geocomunes. 2017. *Amenaza neoliberal a los bienes comunes*. Mexico City: Fundación Rosa Luxemburgo.

Giroux, Henry. 2015. "Fascism in Donald Trump's United States." *Truthout*, December 8. Retrieved from www.truth-out.org/news/item/33951-fascism-in-donald-trumps-united-states (accessed October 20, 2019).

Grecko, Témoris. 2016. *Ayotzinapa, mentira histórica. Estado de impunidad, impunidad de Estado*. Mexico City: Ediciones Proceso.

Horkheimer, Max. 2006. *Estado autoritario*. Mexico City: Itaca Editorial.

La Jornada. 2005. "Agua." Special issue. *La Jornada*, December.

Marini, Ruy Mauro. 1973. *Dialéctica de la Dependencia.* Mexico City: Ediciones Era.
Mbembe, Achille. 2011. *Necropolitica.* Mexico City: Siglo XXI Editores.
OAS. 2010. *Evaluación del progreso del control de drogas.* Washington, DC: OAS.
OECD. 2017. *OECD Employment Outlook 2017.* Paris: OECD Publishing.
Pérez, Ana Lilia. 2011. *El Cártel Negro.* Mexico City: Editorial Debolsillo.
Pérez, Ana Lilia. 2017. *PEME RIP.* Mexico City: Editorial Grijalbo.
Rodríguez, Carlos and Ramses Cruz. 2013. *El México bárbaro del siglo XXI.* Culiacán, Mexico: Universidad Autónoma de Sinaloa.
Rügemer, Werner. 2017. "Donald Trump, Presidente de EU: la visión desde Europa." *Mundo Siglo* XXI(41). Retrieved from www.mundosigloxxi.ipn.mx/pdf/v12/41/02.pdf (accessed October 20, 2019).
Russell, James W. 2014. "La expropiación capitalista de los ahorros de jubilación en América Latina y EU." *Mundo Siglo* XXI(32). Retrieved from www.mundosigloxxi.ipn.mx/pdf/v09/32/02.pdf (accessed October 20, 2019).
Wallerstein, Immanuel. 1996. *Después del liberalismo.* Mexico City: Siglo XXI Editores.
Zepeda Patterson, Jorge. 2007. *Los amos de México.* Mexico City: Editorial Temas de Hoy.

17

Hawai'i: A Pivot of Empire or Piko of Aloha 'Āina?

Kyle Kajihiro

The breath in man is the breath of Papa (the earth). Man is merely the caretaker of the land that maintains his life and nourishes his soul. Therefore, 'āina is sacred. The church of life is not in a building, it is the open sky, the surrounding ocean, the beautiful soil.
—George Helm, "Personal Statement," January 30, 1977[1]

Introduction

Aloha mai kākou. Warm greetings from the US-occupied territories of the Hawaiian Kingdom, which are the ancestral lands of Nā Kānaka Maoli (Native Hawaiians). I want to recognize the Mexica and other indigenous peoples of this region, on whose territory we are gathered. Thank you to the Council of World Mission for organizing these urgent conversations on Resisting Empire And Militarization: Reasserting The Sacredness Of Seas, Lands And Lives, and for the invitation to be a part of the conversation.

I am a fourth-generation descendant of Japanese migrant-settlers in Hawai'i. My ancestors originally immigrated to Hawai'i from the Japanese provinces of Hiroshima, Kumamoto, and Yamaguchi in the late nineteenth century in search of work on Hawai'i's sugar plantations. They faced racism and economic exploitation, and endured martial law during World War II. Yet subsequently, like many Japanese in Hawai'i, my family has since enjoyed relatively upward social and economic mobility, but this socio-economic improvement for Asians in Hawai'i has come at the expense of Kanaka Maoli dispossession, whose stolen lands, exploited culture, and usurped sovereignty are the foundation of the American settler state in our islands.

In my previous work as a program coordinator for the American Friends Service Committee in Hawai'i, I have accompanied Kanaka Maoli in numerous struggles for land and sovereignty and against the destructive force of settler militarism and capitalism. But I am also mindful of my positionality as a non-indigenous person who is constantly discerning and negotiating my responsibilities. I am currently completing my PhD in Geography at the University of Hawai'i at Mānoa and working in the Ethnic Studies Department. The main focus of my scholarly and activist work since 1996 has been to understand and challenge the United States military impacts on the land and people of Hawai'i and the broader consequences of US military policies. As a non-indigenous co-conspirator with Kanaka Maoli in Hawaiʻi, I believe that my kuleana, a Hawaiian word encompassing responsibility as well as privilege, includes working to dismantle the oppressive apparatus of the settler state which oppresses Kanaka Maoli and uses Hawaiʻi to inflict imperial violence against other peoples and lands. I have had the privilege to visit and learn from other communities struggling against similar problems, including Vieques, Puerto Rico, Manta, Ecuador, San Antonio, Texas, Yakima, Washington, the Marshall Islands, Guåhan (Guam), Okinawa, Jeju, Pyongtaek, and Maehyang-ri, South Korea, and Iwakuni and Yokosuka, Japan. There I saw the devastating effects of the global empire of US military bases and was invigorated by the creative resistance by local communities.

As early as 1837, the Kanaka Maoli historian David Malo saw it coming, "If a big wave comes in, large fishes will come from the dark Ocean which you never saw before, and when they see the small fishes they will eat them up" (Malo 1837). What are these "large fishes" to which Malo refers in his prophesy? Here is one example. In 1900, Indiana Senator Albert Beveridge said:

> The Pacific is our ocean ... And the Pacific is the ocean of the commerce of the future. Most future wars will be conflicts for commerce. The power that rules the Pacific, therefore, is the power that rules the world. And ... that power is and will forever be the American Republic.
>
> (Beveridge 1900)

So when US Secretary of State Hillary Clinton and President Barack Obama unveiled the United States' so-called "Pacific Pivot" in 2011 at the APEC Summit in Honolulu, many of us who know the historical geography of this region understood that this was not something new, but simply the most recent iteration of an imperial process stretching back more than a century.

This chapter examines a paradox of contemporary United States imperial power as seen through the case of Hawaiʻi. I argue that Hawaiʻi is a fulcrum of the United States pivot towards becoming a global empire and yet is largely overlooked by scholars and activists as a problem of empire. This paradox exemplifies what some geographers have called the "lost geography" of United States empire (Smith 2004). Further, this occlusion of US imperial power characterizes the shape-shifting abilities of imperial formations. However, Hawaiʻi also is a piko—a center or source—of a more just and alternative future.[2] By confronting the militarization of Hawaiʻi we begin to dismantle the apparatuses of imperial control and capitalist exploitation that wage endless war on the earth. For this reason I am grateful to have a chance to discuss militarization and resistance in Hawaiʻi in the context of ongoing, contemporary imperialism and to be in conversation with other sites of liberatory struggle.

Imperial Formations

First, I would like to clarify my understanding of empire. Rather than engage in taxonomic debates over the proper definitions of "empire" or of types of empire or whether or the United States fits any of these definitions, I prefer Ann Laura Stoler's concept of *imperial formations* which are macropolitical formations and "relations of force" that rely on variegated, shifting, and gradated forms of sovereignty marked by "sliding and contested scales of differential rights": "Imperial formations are defined by racialized relations of allocations and appropriations. Unlike empires, they are processes of becoming, not fixed things" (Stoler 2008). In this chapter, I use both terms—imperial formations and empire—to express this more flexible concept in describing the contemporary United States.

Through the lens of imperial formations we can see that the US has employed a variety of shifting, and sometimes even contradictory, modalities of imperial power in Hawai'i. First, the settler colonial assemblage of territorial expansion, environmental transformation, transfer of settler populations, and the military extermination and removal of indigenous peoples and their juridical and physical enclosure, has made the transit from North America to Hawai'i and through Hawai'i to other parts of the world. Chickasaw scholar Jodi Byrd argues that the spectral figure of the Indian, as the eternal savage Other haunting the outside of imperial sovereignty, makes the transition of empire from the frontier of early US expansion, to the overseas colonial frenzy of the late nineteenth century, to the subsequent wars and counterinsurgencies around the world from World War II up to the Global War on Terror (Byrd 2011).

A second imperial modality that made the transit through Hawai'i is the Monroe Doctrine. In 1842, the year before the Hawaiian Kingdom signed treaties with Great Britain, France, and the United States recognizing its independence and sovereignty, President Tyler proclaimed the Tyler Doctrine which extended the terms of the Monroe Doctrine 2400 miles across the Pacific Ocean to unilaterally include Hawai'i as part of the US sphere of influence (Tyler 1842). As China Miéville argues, the Monroe Doctrine inaugurated a new imperial modality whereby the United States exercises imperial sovereignty through the formal recognition of independent, yet subordinate states (Miéville 2006). This turned into the aspiration, beginning with President Wilson, to extend the Monroe Doctrine globally through the creation of a US-administered international order (Smith 2004). With the formation of the United Nations and other apparatuses of international governance, the United States has engineered a kind of global Monroe Doctrine, an imperial apparatus initially devised to subjugate Latin America and extended to Hawai'i, and through Hawai'i to the rest of the world.

A third modality of US imperial formation concerns the production of variegated colonial and semi-colonial formations. With the United States victory in the Spanish American War in 1898, it acquired new overseas colonies in Puerto Rico, Guam, and the Philippines and proceeded with an occupation-disguised-as-annexation in Hawai'i. Later American Sāmoa was added to this collection. But this created a contradiction whereby the United States, an ostensibly anti-colonial republic, suddenly possessed overseas colonies which it had to justify in some way. The US Supreme Court ruled on a series of cases collectively known as the "Insular Cases," which juridically assigned these colonies to a new category of colonial status known as "non-incorporated territories," possessions that belong to but are not internal to the United States; in the words of the Court, they are "foreign in a domestic sense" (Burnett and Marshall 2001). But Hawaiʻi and Alaska were exceptions, classified as "incorporated territories" which are eligible to become full states of the United States. According to Lanny Thompson (2010), the key factor that made statehood a possibility for Hawaiʻi was the long-standing presence and influence of white US settlers. In the case of Hawaiʻi and Alaska, the putative "civilizing" effect of white settler colonialism was the pivot upon which the assimilability of these new colonies was judged and became the condition that modulated between the foreign and the domestic.

Fourth, Hawaiʻi was also the pivot of the United States' shift from a continental territorial imperial formation to a sea-based and archipelagic imperial formation. In 1893 Captain Alfred Mahan theorized the importance of sea-power for the continued vitality of the United States and argued for the speedy annexation of Hawaiʻi (Mahan 1897). With Frederick Jackson Turner's declaration of the closing of the frontier in 1893, anxious US leaders looked westward across the Pacific Ocean to the potential riches of China as a fix for its economic and political crises (Turner 1893). At that time, US leaders clamored for the military occupation and annexation of Hawaiʻi in order to secure command of the seas for the United States.

Thus, Hawaiʻi was a site where shifting modalities of imperial power have produced a complex legal and political landscape. Settler colonialism's constitutive imaginaries of frontiers and savage Others made its transit from the North American continent through Hawaiʻi to the wider Pacific. Similarly, the new imperial sovereignty of the Monroe Doctrine made its way from Latin America, through Hawaiʻi to the world. The United States used Hawaiʻi as a stepping stone from which to extend its new Mahanian concepts of sea power. And Hawaiʻi also acted as a switch to modulate between different degrees and variations of coloniality and gradations of rights. The lost geography of Hawaiʻi is produced in part by this shape shifting ability of US imperial formation, which conceals the ways that Hawaiʻi is both a casualty of and an accessory to the crimes of imperialism.

The First Regime Change

The United States has long viewed Hawaiʻi as an object of geopolitical desire and of military strategic calculus. As early as the 1842 United States Exploring Expedition led by Commodore Charles Wilkes, US military planners sought to control Ke Awalau o Puʻuloa, otherwise known as Pearl Harbor (Wilkes 1844: 85). In 1872–1873, under the cover of a diplomatic mission, General John Schofield led an expedition to conduct a secret military survey of the Hawaiian Islands. He reported back "It is the key to the Central Pacific Ocean, it is the gem of these islands, valueless to them because they cannot use it, but more valuable to the United States than all else the islands have to give" (quoted in Linn 1997: 6–7).

Of course, Schofield was talking about Ke Awalau o Puʻuloa (or Puʻuloa for short). But his representation of this site as valueless could not have been further from the truth. For centuries, Puʻuloa, a broad estuary draining watersheds from twelve *ahupuaʻa* (traditional land divisions) and two mountain ranges, was a vital food producing region for Kānaka Maoli on Oʻahu. The abundance of freshwater provided for cultivation of a variety of Hawaiian crops, especially wetland kalo/taro, and the mixing of fresh and saltwater in the shallow inlets were extremely productive to a complex web of marine life. The waters of Puʻuloa produced the greatest variety of mollusks and crustaceans, and attracted a wide variety of fish, including certain pelagic species that ventured into the shallows to feed. Kānaka Maoli constructed an elaborate complex of fishponds and fish traps in this region, which once contained the highest concentration of aquaculture sites on Oʻahu. This is to say that Ke Awalau o Puʻuloa was a very important resource for Hawaiians.

The Civil War created an opportunity for Hawaiʻi's *haole* (white foreigner) sugar planters to increase their sales to the United States, but by 1875, the sugar planters clamored for a free trade agreement between the Hawaiian Kingdom and the United States to sustain favorable terms for their Hawaiʻi-grown sugar. While some suggested that the Hawaiian Kingdom should offer the United States access to Puʻuloa in exchange for the Treaty of Reciprocity, due to the strong native opposition, King Kalākaua removed this clause from the Treaty and was still able to win approval.

However, by 1885, with negotiations under way for a renewal of the Treaty of Reciprocity, opposition to a second treaty made passage tenuous. US sugar growers were organizing to kill the Treaty as were Hawaiian nationals who saw the Treaty as weakening Hawaiʻi's sovereignty. In 1887, the haole sugar planters, afraid that the Treaty might die and their profits shrink, staged the first act in a series of actions that culminated in the US occupation and annexation of Hawaiʻi through belligerent and illegal means. They forced King Kalākaua, under threat of violence, to sign a new constitution drafted by the haole settlers. This illegitimate document, which today is commonly known as the "Bayonet Constitution," weakened the monarchy and strengthened the haole-controlled cabinet. It imposed property requirements for voting, which disenfranchised the majority of Kanaka Maoli. And it barred the naturalization of Asian immigrant laborers, most of whom at that time were from Japan. One of the first acts of the haole leaders of this coup was to rush approval the second Treaty of Reciprocity, which contained new language granting the United States exclusive rights to use Puʻuloa for a naval coaling station. This was the beginning of the dismemberment of Hawaiian sovereignty.

In January 1893, when Kalākaua's successor Queen Liliʻuokalani attempted to rescind the Bayonet Constitution, the haole settlers conspired with US Minister Stevens to land US Marines to depose her, which was the first time the United States carried out a "regime change" against another sovereign state (Kinzer 2006). Liliʻuokalani yielded to the US military forces but did not surrender to nor recognize the legitimacy of the conspirators. Rather she appealed to the US President Cleveland to rectify the situation since it was the United States military intervention that enabled this small group of haole men to seize the government. Cleveland sent Senator Blount to Hawaiʻi to investigate. Blount concluded that the overthrow was not a genuine revolution but was an illegitimate coup d'état backed by the US military. He described the US military's role in backing the coup an "act of war" and called for the restoration of Liliʻuokalani as the rightful monarch. But despite promising to do so, Cleveland failed to follow through.

The leaders of the coup attempted twice to negotiate a treaty of annexation with the United States, failing both times. In 1893, Cleveland refused to sign the Treaty. Then, in 1897, with an expansionist President McKinley in the White House, the coup leaders tried again. This time a massive organizing campaign by Hawaiian nationals produced two anti-annexation petitions representing almost ninety percent of the Kingdom's population. These petitions helped to defeat ratification by the US Senate of the second Treaty of Annexation in 1897.

However, the outbreak of war with Spain in 1898 created an opportunity for the annexationists to push through a joint resolution of Congress which purported to seize Hawaiʻi as a military necessity. At the time, in a secret session that remained sealed until 1969, members of Congress acknowledged the questionable legality of the resolution and the international legal jeopardy it created for the United States by violating the recognized neutrality of the Hawaiian Kingdom (Honolulu Star-Bulletin 1969). This act, known as the Newlands Resolution, is the flimsy basis on which the United States has staked its claim to sovereignty over Hawaiʻi, and one of the main points of contention raised by the Hawaiian independence movement.

Mapping the Heʻe

In order to sketch the current situation of the US military in Hawaiʻi, I will utilize an oceanic metaphor coined by Kanaka Maoli scholar and activist Kaleikoa Kaeo. In 2003, he delivered the Hawaiʻi country report to the delegates of the 9th Nuclear Free and Independent Pacific movement in Nukualofa, Tonga. Kaeo asked the assembly to imagine the US military in Hawaiʻi as the head of a monstrous *heʻe* (octopus).

The brain of this heʻe, Kaeo continued, is the United States Indo-Pacific Command (USINDOPACOM), with supercomputers and fiber optic cables as its nervous system. Hawaiʻi is the headquarters of several major military commands: under USINDOPACOM the other subordinate commands headquartered in Hawaiʻi include the US Army Pacific (USARPAC), US Pacific Fleet (USPACFLT), US Marine Corps Forces Pacific (MARFORPAC), US Pacific Air Forces (PACAF), US Special Operations Command Pacific (SOCPAC). USINDOPACOM, the oldest and largest of the unified military commands, is based at Camp Smith. Its area of responsibility encompasses more than half of the area of the planet and a majority of the Earth's population.

The US military has approximately 142 military sites in Hawaiʻi, which occupy 224,897 acres of land (US Department of Defense 2016). In 2016, the military population of Hawaiʻi was 112,075 (47,733 active duty service members and 64,342 dependants) or 7.8 percent, out of a total population of 1,428,557 (Department of Business, Economic Development, and Tourism 2017).

Hawaiʻi is a central hub for US military forces in the Pacific. The Army maintains two brigade combat teams of the 25th Infantry Division based at Schofield Barracks. The Navy has cruisers of Naval Surface Group Mid Pacific, three attack submarine squadrons, and a destroyer squadron homeported at Joint Base Pearl Harbor-Hickam (JBPHH). The Air Force maintains the 15th Air Wing with one fighter squadron, one air refueling squadron, and two airlift squadrons based at JBPHH. And the Marine Corps has an infantry regiment and Marine Air Group stationed at Marine Corps Base Hawaii (MCBH), Kaneohe Bay. There are numerous battalions and squadrons of the Army and Air Force Reserve and National Guard within this hub.

The "eyes" and "ears" of the heʻe can be imagined as the various sites involved in radar, electronic communications, remote sensing, and optical tracking. Many of these occupy the peaks of Hawaiʻi's sacred mountain tops, such as the Air Force Maui Optical and Supercomputing (AMOS) observatory on Haleakalā on Māui, or the radar facilities at Kaʻena Point on Oʻahu, both of which are implicated in missile testing programs. They are also arrays of underwater acoustic sensors or underground complexes only visible by the white satellite dishes on the surface, such as the Naval Computers and Telecommunications Master Station (NCTMS) or the National Security Agency (NSA) Regional Signals Intelligence Center, where the US government conducts surveillance of all electronic communications.

The excrement of this heʻe consists of the various deleterious effects of militarization in the islands. While supporters of US military bases argue that they provide protection and economic benefits, these reports typically overlook the social and environmental costs associated with the bases which are sources of conflict with local communities. The social, cultural, environmental, and economic costs of militarization are distributed unequally, where some sectors profit handsomely, while other pay the price in the form of land dispossession, negative social indicators, and environmental racism. Here are a summary of some of the military's negative impacts in Hawaiʻi.

The US military produces major environmental impacts in Hawaiʻi. In 2015, the US military listed 995 contamination and munitions cleanup projects on active and former military sites in Hawaiʻi (US Department of Defense 2015). Ke Awalau o Puʻuloa, once an important indigenous food system for Oʻahu, is now a high risk contaminated site from which seafood consumption is restricted. The Navy's Red Hill Underground Fuel Tanks—there are 20 tanks, each 250 feet tall by 100 feet diameter with a 12.4 million gallon capacity—have leaked hundreds of thousands of gallons of jet fuel near a major drinking water source for Honolulu. Despite significant improvements in the military's conservation programs in the region, ecological destruction continues to be a serious environmental impact of military bases. Large scale construction projects and training activities, especially those involving live-fire munitions, frequently destroy or damage sensitive ecosystems and endangered species.

Closely related to the military's environmental impacts are its negative impacts on the ancestral lands and the cultural sites, resources, and practices of Kanaka Maoli. In Hawaiʻi, most of the land occupied by the military are public trust lands that derive from the lands of the Hawaiian Kingdom lands which were seized by the United States after 1898. Military activities frequently destroy, damage, or desecrate Kanaka Maoli cultural sites, sacred landscapes, and burials and are an ongoing source of conflict.

Military spending is a major economic factor in Hawai'i. Defense spending accounted for an estimated $7.8 billion or 9.8 percent of the gross domestic product (National Conference of State Legislatures 2018), making the military Hawai'i's second largest industry behind tourism. Proponents of the US military presence typically cite these economic benefits as the main rationale for a continued military presence. However, these economic reports typically ignore the true costs associated with the military economy, such as externalized environmental, social services, and cultural costs, opportunity costs for human resources, land and infrastructure used by the military, and the economic dependency, inefficiency, and distortion created by military economies. An example of the military's negative economic impact in Hawai'i is the inflationary effect of military housing allowances on the overall cost of housing and the uneven advantages created by these subsidies, which contributes to high rates of poverty and homelessness. Another negative economic impact is the cost of public services and infrastructure such as schools and roads for non-resident military personnel and their dependants stationed in Hawai'i, who are not taxed on their military pay.

There are numerous negative social impacts related to the presence of large military bases, some of which include accidents, physical violence between military personnel and local residents, and crime. Military bases around the world are known drivers of sexual exploitation of women and children through sex abuse, prostitution, and sex trafficking.

Many residents of Hawai'i see the US military as a foreign occupier and an obstacle to self-determination. By facilitating settlement by military-connected populations in these islands, the military drives changes in the ethnic composition and political demographics of the population. For example, in Hawai'i's case, military personnel voted in and influenced the outcome of the 1959 statehood referendum.

And the tentacles of this he'e are the network of military bases in other locations such as Okinawa, Guam, the Marshall Islands, American Sāmoa, Japan, Korea, Australia, Palau, and the Philippines. Each of these locations experience negative impacts from these bases including environmental damage, socioeconomic impacts, crime and accidents, and violations of local sovereignty. And like a real octopus, if tentacles are cut off, this monstrous he'e can regrow them. Despite the ouster of Clark Air Base and Subic Naval Base from the Philippines in 1992, US military forces have returned, first in Mindanao under the guise of advising in the fight against Islamist terrorists, and now in multiple joint-use bases throughout the Philippines to counter China's aggressive military expansion in the South China Sea.[3] As Kaeo reminded his Oceanic colleagues in Tonga, to neutralize a he'e a fisher person would usually bite its head. If there is to be a substantial reduction in US militarization of the Asia and Pacific Region, there would need to be a reduction in the militarization of Hawai'i.

Kahoʻolawe and Aloha ʻĀina

While Kanaka Maoli have continuously resisted US imperialism since the nineteenth century, a crucial modern turning point was the 1970s emergence of the movement to protect Kahoʻolawe Island from Navy bombing. For many centuries, Kahoʻolawe, also known as Kohemālamalama o Kanaloa (the southern beacon or shining birth canal of Kanaloa, deity of the sea and voyaging), the smallest of the main Hawaiian Islands, was considered a sacred place by Kanaka Maoli, especially for practitioners of voyaging and traditional navigation and fishing. Kahoʻolawe was an ancient *piko* (navel or umbilicus) of Polynesian voyaging and navigation. In 1793, British Captain Vancouver gifted goats to Kahekili, ruler of Maui, Molokaʻi, Lānaʻi, and Kahoʻolawe. The goats were released on Kahoʻolawe, but as their numbers multiplied, they quickly denuded the fragile dry-forest landscape, generating massive erosion and desertification. This led to the widespread perception that Kahoʻolawe was desolate wasteland for all eternity. From 1826 to 1853, the Hawaiian Kingdom utilized Kahoʻolawe as a penal colony. Opium smugglers also found it convenient for hiding their goods. Later, a series of entrepreneurs tried to establish ranching on the Island, but most of these failed. However, one rancher, Angus McPhee, got a long-term lease from the Territory of Hawaiʻi in 1918 and began to cull the goats, restore vegetation, and raise cattle on the Island. His efforts eventually began to stem the environmental degradation, and his venture started to turn a profit.

However the December 7, 1941 Japanese bombing of Pearl Harbor ushered in dramatic social changes in Hawaiʻi. Within hours of the Pearl Harbor attack, the territorial governor declared martial law and ceded control of all aspects of life in Hawaiʻi to the US military. The war sparked what some have called a military industrial revolution by displacing the hegemony of the haole oligarchy, which had ruled the islands since the turn of the century and beginning a transformation of the plantation economy into a service oriented economy. The government interned more than 1300 persons of Japanese ancestry while ruling the islands as if the entire archipelago were a concentration camp. Under this wartime emergency, the military seized hundreds of thousands of acres of land by executive order. Kahoʻolawe was one such place. The McPhee's lost their ranch as the military bombarded and practiced amphibious assault on the Island. The military claims that training on Kahoʻolawe was key to winning the Pacific War. But the devastation was so extreme that Kahoʻolawe became known as the "target island" or the "island of death."

After years of growing resentment among Maui residents towards the training, there was a convergence of factors in the 1970s that created fertile conditions for the emergence of a Kanaka Maoli movement to protect Kahoʻolawe and seek its return as a site of Hawaiian cultural reserve. A rapidly changing political economy in the wake of World War II and statehood raised expectations of upward social mobility while simultaneously fueling anger and resentment at the disruptions and inequalities these changes were producing. It was a recipe for political unrest. The sugar and pineapple industries were overtaken by tourism. Growing foreign investment heralded the more intensive integration of Hawai'i into the global economy. These economic changes fueled encroachment of urban development into rural areas which threatened to eliminate rural and indigenous lifeways and gave rise to a number of land struggles beginning in the early 1970s. Public sentiment had grown cynical of the federal government after the Watergate scandal and the United States' war in Vietnam. And the growing political ferment of the 1960 and early 1970s, including the anti-war movement, the Black Panther Party, the American Indian Movement, the Environmental Movement, and international anti-colonial revolutions, inspired a wave of protest movements and new organizations in Hawai'i.

On January 4, 1976, a loose coalition of groups set out from Maui on fishing boats to stage a symbolic occupation of Kaho'olawe to draw attention to the historical wrongs committed against Kanaka Maoli by the United States. It was to make a statement like the American Indian occupations of Alcatraz and Wounded Knee. Although most of the group were turned back by the US Coast Guard, one boat managed to land nine people on the Island. These activists were profoundly affected by their encounter with the devastated landscape and the wealth of Kanaka Maoli cultural sites. The experience awakened a sense of Hawaiian identity and inspired them to organize to save the Island. They formed a group that would later become known as the Protect Kaho'olawe 'Ohana. The 'Ohana organized a series of daring landings on the Island to disrupt Navy exercises and sued the Navy over violations of various environmental and cultural protection laws. They lobbied politicians, coordinated with international movements, and conducted broad public education and mobilization for their cause. In 1980, their lawsuit resulted in a consent decree that put restrictions on military training, required the Navy to complete environmental and cultural studies of the Island, and permitted monthly Kanaka Maoli cultural access to the Island organized by the 'Ohana. Even with the tragic loss of two of the movement's leaders at sea in 1977, the Protect Kaho'olawe 'Ohana helped to revitalize a number of cultural practices such as the Makahiki ceremonies honoring Lono, the god of agriculture, storms, and growth.

After 14 years of activism, in 1990, President George H.W. Bush ordered the bombing halted. Congress then created the Kaho'olawe Island Conveyance Commission to study and decide the fate of the Island. The Commission recommended an end to the bombing, that the navy clean up the unexploded munitions, and that Kaho'olawe be returned to the State of Hawai'i as a cultural reserve. In 1993, Congress passed legislation which appropriated $400 million for the clean-up, transfer, and governance of the Island. In April 2004, the Navy completed its clean-up operations and turned over control of the Island to the Kaho'olawe Island Reserve Commission, a state entity created in 1993 to govern the Island as a trustee until it can transfer the Island to a Hawaiian nation. Approximately 75 percent of the Island was surface cleared of unexploded ordnance, but only 10 percent was cleared to a subsurface level. None of the underwater munitions have been removed. Today restoration efforts on Kaho'olawe continue under both the Kaho'olawe Island Reserve Commission and the Protect Kaho'olawe 'Ohana.

Thousands of volunteers have made the pilgrimage to Kahoʻolawe for cultural ceremonies and environmental and cultural restoration work.

The Kahoʻolawe movement popularized the slogan and concept of *aloha ʻāina*, an expression meaning love of the land and people, and love of country.[4] It revives a nineteenth-century slogan of the Hawaiian pro-independence movement. And the concept has spread to include almost any project or campaign dedicated to the protection of Kanaka Maoli cultural sites and practices and the environment. In the age of catastrophic anthropogenic global warming, ecosystem collapse, and the slow violence of environmental toxins, aloha ʻāina is more important than ever. And Kahoʻolawe, a site that was once forsaken as a wasteland, has become a modern piko of Kanaka Maoli cultural and political resurgence and of the environmental ethic of aloha ʻāina. This concept was a guiding theme of the 2014 to 2017 "Mālama Honua" (take care of the Earth) round-the-world voyage of the Hōkūleʻa, the modern replica of a double-hulled Polynesian voyaging canoe which in 1976 proved that Polynesians were able to navigate to Hawaiʻi without instruments. The Hōkūleʻa has inspired the revitalization of indigenous voyaging traditions throughout Oceania. And today, as in ancient times, the spiritual piko of voyaging is Kahoʻolawe.

Mākua Valley

Kahoʻolawe inspired other struggles against militarization in Hawaiʻi. One site where the spirit of aloha ʻāina spread is Mākua Valley in the Waiʻanae district of Oʻahu, where the Army has occupied and used the valley for training since 1942. Mākua, which means parents in Hawaiian, was believed to be place where Wākea (the god of the sky) and Papahānaumoku (the goddess of the earth and creation) created life in the islands. There are numerous sacred sites and an extensive complex of archaeological sites that indicate a thriving community once inhabited the valley and lived off of the abundance of offshore fisheries and ʻuala (sweet potato) and other dry land crops. There are approximately 40 endangered endemic species that live in the upper reaches of the valley. But hundreds of fires from military activity have destroyed the dry land forest and replaced it with alien shrubs and grasses. Soon after the declaration of martial law in Hawaiʻi during World War II, President Roosevelt issued an executive order seizing Mākua Valley for military training. The residents who farmed, ranched, fished, and tended the railroad station and church, were evicted. Their homes and church were bombed for target practice. But the unfulfilled promise that the government would return the land 6 months after the war has fueled the hope that someday this land would be restored and returned to the community. A few weeks after the first protest landing on Kahoʻolawe in 1976, a solidarity rally was held at Mākua. The activists from Waiʻanae agreed to support Kahoʻolawe first before intensifying the push for Mākua's return.

In addition to the conflict over the military occupation of the valley, Mākua was the site of numerous anti-eviction struggles of Kanaka Maoli houseless[5] communities on the beach. The most recent eviction occurred in 1996 when the state forcibly removed more than 200 people living in a community on Mākua beach, who called their village a puʻuhonua (a place of refuge or sanctuary). In a highly militarized multi-agency police operation where media was excluded, 16 people were arrested for refusing to leave. The juxtaposition of military occupied land and a predominantly Kanaka Maoli houseless community starkly illustrates the contradictions and hidden violence of the US military presence in Hawaiʻi. The military's seizing of land and removal of native inhabitants are related to the skyrocketing statistics of houselessness in Hawaiʻi. A majority of the houseless in rural areas such as the Waiʻanae district, are Kanaka Maoli; they are Hawaiʻi's indigenous people landless in their own homeland.

In 1992, when the Army applied for a permit from the Environmental Protection Agency to operate an open burn/open detonation disposal site in Mākua, the community jumped into action. Mālama Mākua, which was formed to counter this threat, defeat the disposal site. Later, joining forces with leaders of the houseless beach community, Mālama Mākua turned its attention to challenging the Army's activities in the valley. In 1997, the day after thousands of mourners scattered the ashes of beloved musician Israel Kamakawiwoʻole in the waters off Mākua Beach, the Marine Corps announced plans to conduct amphibious assault training there. The community mobilized to resist and stopped the amphibious training plans. This incident intensified efforts to stop the bombing altogether.

In 1998, the Mālama Mākua sued the Army under the National Environmental Policy Act (NEPA) for failing to conduct an environmental impact statement for Mākua. A settlement agreement reached in 2001 allowed a limited amount of military training within prescribed areas, required the Army to surface clear unexploded ordnance from approximately a third of the valley and complete an environmental impact statement with additional studies of impacts on cultural resources and marine resources, and permitted Mālama Mākua two day-long cultural accesses per month, plus overnight accesses for Makahiki ceremonies twice a year. After the Army failed to complete its environmental impact statement within the allotted time, the court imposed an injunction on live-fire training in 2003.

Stryker Brigade and Pōhakuloa

Shortly after the September 11, 2001 Al-Qaeda attacks on the Pentagon and World Trade Center, the Army announced plans to install a new Stryker Brigade Combat Team in Hawaiʻi. It planned to station in Hawaiʻi approximately 230 Strykers, which are 20-ton fast armored combat vehicles. Training this new Stryker Brigade would require an expansion of 23,000 acres on Hawaiʻi Island and 2000 acres on Oʻahu, the largest military land grab since World War II. Opponents of the plan pointed out the hypocrisy that as the Navy was returning the 28,000-acre Kahoʻolawe island after a lengthy struggle to stop the bombing and a decade-long cleanup project, the Army intended to seize almost the equivalent amount of land.

A network of groups called DMZ-Hawaiʻi/Aloha ʻĀina mobilized against the Stryker Brigade threat. Numerous protests and lawsuits ensued. While the courts found that the Army violated the National Environmental Policy Act by failing to consider alternatives before selecting Hawai'i, the expansion was finally approved to proceed. The emergence of depleted uranium and chemical weapons as well as newly uncovered Kanaka Maoli cultural sites at Schofield Barracks and Pōhakuloa delayed construction, and in some cases, forced plans to be modified. But the Stryker Brigade construction proceeded. Then in 2014, with the so-called sequestration of the Army's budget, the Pentagon decided to move the Strykers out of Hawai'i, citing an argument that opponents had articulated all along, that stationing an armored brigade on an island made no sense even from a military perspective. In 2016, the Army moved the Stryker Brigade to Washington State, but its land acquisitions remained intact.

The military has adapted to growing opposition on Kaho'olawe and O'ahu by shifting much of its training activities to Pōhakuloa on Hawai'i island. This 133,000-acre range is the largest training area outside of the continental United States. All service branches use this area for all manner of training from simple maneuver and surveillance activities to heavy artillery and aerial bombardment. B-2 Bombers have flown from Guam to drop bombs on Pōhakuloa.

In 2015, there was a surge of Kanaka Maoli protest against the University of Hawai'i's construction of a giant Thirty Meter Telescope (TMT) on Mauna Kea, which many consider to be the most sacred temple in Hawaiian spiritual traditions. Although opposition to the TMT had continued for many years in the courts and various administrative venues, when the threat of actual construction became apparent, there was a powerful mobilization led by young people to block construction on the mountain through non-violent direct action. The Kū Kia'i Mauna movement grew via social media and attracted many people to the mountain. Movement leaders also built bridges of solidarity with the Standing Rock water protectors, which was occurring at the same time. This new wave of Kanaka Maoli activism has spilled over into growing opposition to the military activity at Pōhakuloa, which sits at the foot of the mountain and lies within the same ahupua'a.

In 2015, two Kanaka Maoli kūpuna (elders) sued the State of Hawai'i for failing to enforce the terms of a lease with the US Army for large parts of Pōhakuloa. The Army leases 7371 acres from the State of Hawai'i on O'ahu and 22,971 acres on Hawai'i Island. These leases run 65 years from 1964 to 2029, each for the cost of one dollar. The lawsuit holds the State accountable for ensuring that its tenant, the US Army, stop destroying the natural and cultural environment. The court ruled that the State was derelict in its duties and halted negotiations for the renewal of this lease at Pōhakuloa until satisfactory measures were taken to ensure the protection of the environment. The State has appealed the court decision.

Weaving A Net of Solidarity

Since the 1970s, activists from Hawai'i have been working in solidarity with other groups to counter militarization. In the late 1970s, members of the Protect Kaho'olawe 'Ohana traveled to Culebra and Vieques to support those struggles.

Between 1999 and 2004, a number of Hawaiʻi activists went to Vieques to support their resurgent and ultimately successful fight to remove the Navy. Hawaiʻi activists participated in international networks against foreign military bases, traveling to Japan, Korea, the Philippines, the Marshall Islands, Guam, Okinawa, Brazil, and Ecuador. In 2007, the International Conference for the Abolition of Foreign Military Bases convened in Quito and Manta, Ecuador. Shortly thereafter, Ecuador removed the US military from Manta. But other military bases have sprung up or expanded, including bases in Honduras and Panamā.

One international effort I would like to highlight is the International Women's Network Against Militarism. Shortly after the 1995 rape of a 12-year-old Okinawan girl by three US Marines, Okinawan anti-bases protests surged. The group Okinawan Women Act Against Military Violence did a speaking tour in the United States, which led to the formation of the International Women's Network Against Militarism. The Network, which includes women's organizations in Okinawa, Japan, Korea, the Philippines, Puerto Rico, Guam, Hawaiʻi, and the United States, has convened in different locations over the years to build relationships and collaboration between women in these military-affected communities. One of their most important contributions is their critique of militarized notions of "national security," which brings violence, dispossession, environmental destruction, and insecurity for people living in so-called "host" communities. Instead the Women's Network calls for *genuine security*, which consists of four elements:

1. The physical environment must be able to sustain human and natural life;
2. People's basic needs for food, clothing, shelter, health care, and education must be guaranteed;
3. People's fundamental human dignity should be honored and cultural identities respected;
4. People and the natural environment should be protected from avoidable harm (Women for Genuine Security 2018).

This reframing of security shifts the ground from the zero-sum geopolitical calculus of imperial formations to a relational understanding of security based on an ethic of care. And this is precisely the spirit of aloha ʻāina.

Conclusion

Hawaiʻi and numerous other islands in the Pacific have been weaponized by the United States to form an archipelago of sites crucial for projecting its military power over the earth. And yet, these sites remain hidden in most discussions of the costs and consequences of America's wars. Attending to this "lost geography" of US empire in the Pacific, and Hawaiʻi's crucial role in it, I have argued that dismantling the US imperial infrastructure of island military bases is necessary for improving the prospects for peace and for advancing self-determination and social and environmental justice for peoples of these military-occupied islands. As the Oceanic scholar Epeli Hauʻofa has argued, Oceania is not a vast emptiness peppered with remote and insignificant specks; rather it is a region with epic histories and visionary futures, deep cultural wisdoms about more sustainable ways of living with limited and fragile resources, and the potential to help us reimagine what international politics could be through a global ethics of care (Hauʻofa 1995). Hauʻofa's challenge, like that of the Nuclear Free and Independent Pacific movement and other indigenous Pacific struggles, unsettles the imaginative geography of the Pacific as an "American Lake," and instead opens the space for reimagining the region as Moananuiākea, the great ocean that connects rather than divides us. The late Banaban scholar Teresia Teaiwa said, "We sweat and cry salt water, so we know that the ocean is really in our blood" (Hauʻofa 2000: 113). And Hawaiʻi as a piko within Oceania can be one source for this transformation. But we must remove the monstrous heʻe that greedily holds our islands hostage to a vision of empire and endless war.

Around 2000, as I was heading out to a Mālama Mākua meeting, I got a call from Atwood "Maka" Makanani, a veteran of both the Protect Kahoʻolawe ʻOhana and the Hōkūleʻa. He wanted to catch a ride to the meeting. As we drove to the west side of Oʻahu, Maka told me many stories and gave me one bit of advice that stuck with me. "You gotta haku," he said. Haku means to compose something, like a song or a flower lei. It implies arranging different elements into something new and meaningful. But his statement was cryptic, and being too intimidated to ask for clarification, I just nodded. Today, I extrapolate from his words. Like Oceanic peoples who could haku fragile plant fibers into cordage strong enough to lash together great canoes that withstood voyages of thousands of miles across the sea, let us haku the strands of our particular struggles and communities into a great net that is big enough, and strong enough to restrain the monstrous fishes that threaten to devour the earth.

Kyle Kajihiro is a Ph.D. candidate at the University of Hawaiʻi at Mānoa. He was born and raised a fourth generation Japanese in Hawaiʻi. His current work involves research, education and action for the demilitarization of Hawaiʻi and solidarity with the native Hawaiian movement for sovereignty and human rights. He is a board member for Hawaiʻi Peace and Justice.

Notes

1. George Helm is one of the leaders of the Protect Kahoʻolawe ʻOhana which stopped the bombing of that island considered sacred by Kānaka Maoli. Helm was one of two members of the group who mysteriously died at sea in 1977. See Helm (1977 [1984]: 54–55).
2. "Piko" is the Hawaiian word for the navel or umbilicus; it also refers to sources of life, ancestral or cultural inspiration, and procreation.
3. The US will have rotational deployments to Antonio Bautista Air Base, Basa Air Base, Fort Magsaysay, Lumbia Air Base, and Mactan-Benito Ebuen Air Base (Military Times 2016).

4. "Aloha ʻĀina" is a philosophical and political concept that means literally "love of the land," but it has more capacious meanings which include love of all human and non-human relations in the environment, and an expression of political commitment to Hawaiian independence.
5. The term "houseless" rather than "homeless" is commonly used especially by Kanaka Maoli who say that their home is Hawaiʻi, but what they lack is access to a house.

References

Beveridge, Albert J. 1900. "In Support of an American Empire." Retrieved from www.teachingamericanhistory.org/library/index.asp?documentprint=639 (accessed November 18, 2018).

Burnett, Christina Duffy, and Burke Marshall, (eds). 2001. *Foreign in a Domestic Sense: Puerto Rico, American Expansion, and the Constitution.* Durham, NC: Duke University Press. https://doi.org/10.1215/9780822381167

Byrd, Jodi. 2011. *The Transit of Empire: Indigenous Critiques of Colonialism.* Minneapolis, NC: University of Minnesota Press. https://doi.org/10.5749/minnesota/9780816676408.001.0001

Department of Business, Economic Development, and Tourism. 2017. "2016 State of Hawaiʻi Data Book: A Statistical Abstract, November 2017 Update." Honolulu, HI: State of Hawaiʻi.

Hauʻofa, Epeli. 1995. "Our Sea of Islands." In *Asia/Pacific as Space of Cultural Production*, edited by Rob Wilson and Arif Dirlik. Durham, NC: Duke University Press.

Hauʻofa, Epeli. 2000. "The Ocean In Us," in *Voyaging Through the Contemporary Pacific*, edited by David Hanlon and Geoffrey White. Lanham, MD: Rowman & Littlefield.

Helm, George. 1977 [1984]. "Personal Statement: Reasons for Fourth Occupation of Kahoolawe." January 30. In *Hoʻihoʻi Hou: A Tribute to George Helm and Kimo Mitchell*, edited by Rodney Morales. Honolulu, HI: Bamboo Ridge Press.

Honolulu Star-Bulletin. 1969. "Secret Debate on US Seizure of Hawaii Revealed." *Honolulu Star-Bulletin*, February 2.

Kinzer, Stephen. 2006. *Overthrow: America's Century of Regime Change from Hawaii to Iraq.* New York: Times Books.

Linn, Brian McAllister. 1997. *Guardians of Empire: The US Army and the Pacific, 1902-1940.* Chapel Hill, NC: University of North Carolina Press.

Mahan, Alfred Thayer. 1897. *The Interest of America in Sea Power Present and Future.* London: Sampson Low, Marston & Co.

Malo, David. 1837. "Auhea Oe e Kaahumanu 2, a Me Mataio?—Letter to Kaʻahumanu 2 (Kīnaʻu) and Mataio." 18 August, Chronological File, 1790—1848. Honolulu, HI: Hawaii State Archives.

Miéville, China. 2006. *Between Equal Rights: A Marxist Theory of International Law.* Chicago, IL: Haymarket Books.

Military Times. 2016. "The US Military is Moving into these 5 Bases in the Philippines." *Military Times*, March 21.

National Conference of State Legislatures. 2018. "Military's Impact on State Economies." Retrieved from www.ncsl.org/research/military-and-veterans-affairs/military-s-impact-on-state-economies.aspx#table1 (accessed November 18, 2018).

Smith, Neil. 2004. *American Empire: Roosevelt's Geographer and the Prelude to Globalization.* Berkeley, CA: University of California Press.

Stoler, Ann Laura Stoler. 2008. "Imperial Debris: Reflections on Ruins and Ruination." *Cultural Anthropology* 23(2): 191–219. https://doi.org/10.1111/j.1548-1360.2008.00007.x

Thompson, Lanny. 2010. *Imperial Archipelago: Representation and Rule in the Insular Territories Under US Dominion after 1898.* Honolulu, HI: University of Hawai'i Press. https://doi.org/10.21313/hawaii/9780824834012.001.0001

Turner, Frederick Jackson. 1893. "The Significance of the Frontier in American History." Retrieved from www.historians.org/about-aha-and-membership/aha-history-and-archives/historical-archives/the-significance-of-the-frontier-in-american-history (accessed November 18, 2018).

Tyler, John. 1842. "Special Message to Congress (Tyler Doctrine)." Presidential message to Congress, December 30. Retrieved from www-rohan.sdsu.edu/dept/polsciwb/brianl/docs/1842TylerDoctrine.pdf (accessed November 18, 2018).

US Department of Defense. 2015. "Table 5—Status of Active Installations, BRAC Installations, and FUDS Properties by State as of Sept 30 2015." Retrieved from www.denix.osd.mil/derp/fy2015tables (accessed November 18, 2018).

US Department of Defense. 2016. "Base Structure Report Fiscal Year 2015 Baseline (A Summary of DoD's Real Property Inventory)." Retrieved from www.acq.osd.mil/eie/Downloads/BSI/Base%20Structure%20Report%20FY15.pdf (accessed December 20, 2019).

Wilkes, Charles. 1844. *Narrative of the United States Exploring Expedition during the Years 1838, 1839, 1840, 1841, 1842.* 5 vols, with an atlas. Philadelphia, PA: US Navy, commissioned by the US Congress. https://doi.org/10.5962/bhl.title.61621

Women for Genuine Security. 2018. "What is Genuine Security?" Retrieved from www.genuinesecurity.org/aboutus/whatisGS.html (accessed November 18, 2018).

18

Existential Threats to the Pacific Islands: Oceania Resists the Long Reach of Empire

Vanessa Griffen, Gordon Nanau, and Maureen Penjueli

> Learn to love the land and the people, and then you will know what you are fighting for.
>
> —Belau Roman Bedor (cited in de Ishtar 1994: 236)

Introduction

The Pacific Ocean area covering the north and south Pacific referred here, is the area containing 26 Pacific Island countries, which includes independent and self- governing territories. There are several colonies of France in the region (French Polynesia, New Caledonia, Wallis and Futuna Islands, for example) and self-governing but not fully autonomous countries connected to New Zealand (Cook Islands, Niue). The United States has ongoing special Compacts of Free Association with its former Trust Territory countries (now Federated States of Micronesia, Marshall Islands, Palau) but it retains Guam as a military base. The US compacts of free association with the above countries, retain economic dependence and certain political controls. The Pacific Island Forum Secretariat (PIFS), originally set up for independent states as decolonization occurred, lists 16 independent and self-governing members, but has recently included, for example, French Polynesia, which is still a colony of France.

For the purposes of the discussion in this chapter, the analysis in all the sections refers to the Pacific Island region as a whole, including all Pacific Island countries regardless of political status that have a shared Pacific cultural and social identity as Pacific Islanders. On Pacific Island responses to militarization, land grabs, and sea bed resource exploitation, the chapter concentrates on the options of resistance and desistance. In the case of land grab legislation, independent states where there is legal recognition of those countries' formal rights of control over their lands, seas and natural resources the state has full jurisdiction over its territory and governance. This is to recognize that Pacific Island states do have powers of resistance and their leaders can use such powers.

The chapter is an exploration of three different areas of colonial and post-colonial impacts shared by many in Pacific islands and raises questions on what forms of resistance now and in the past, can be used by Pacific Islanders in response to globalization.

The Pacific Island Region: Cultural and Ethnic Sub-regions

Three broad groupings of the Pacific Islands into sub-regions of Micronesia, Polynesia and Melanesia are often applied as categories delineating ethnic, social, and cultural similarities and differences between Pacific Island countries and peoples. These divisions are part of the empire, originally based on distinguishing types of Pacific islanders and their societies for anthropological analyses. These divisions also were used for administrative purposes and are still used today for organizing, by government and non-government organizations, aid donors, UN and development agencies and other groups, including religious organizations. The divisions of countries and peoples into Micronesia, Polynesia and Melanesia are entrenched and have certain usefulness, in allowing groups to find common ground, organize and commit to acting together based on similar conditions, social structures and/or related political positions. However, these divisions are not used in this chapter in reference to the Pacific Island region.

Micronesia, Melanesia and Polynesia collectively belong to the political grouping of "the Pacific Island states." Australia and New Zealand are included in the Pacific region for their location, but for most intents and purposes, are clearly with distinct power, interests and political status unequal in comparison to the independent small island states of the Pacific. Australia and New Zealand, while not always presenting a similar front, are united in their military alliance with the United States, and recently unequivocally presented their united security, defense and military interests regarding the Pacific Island states, against their fears of China's growing influence with Island states.

In this chapter, we refer to the Pacific Ocean where the majority of the Pacific Islanders reside and their countries as the Pacific region. For reviewing actions Pacific Island states can take to protect Pacific resources and peoples, we are specifically referring to Pacific Island countries *with independent political status*, which can act collectively and nationally on behalf of their peoples. The collectivity of Pacific Island countries include independent, self-governing, non-self-governing associative islands and colonized countries. The following 12 countries have full membership status in the United Nations: Federated States of Micronesia, Fiji, Kiribati, Marshall Islands, Nauru, Palau, Papua New Guinea, Samoa, Solomon Islands, Tonga, Tuvalu and Vanuatu. In historical use, knowledge, traditional folklore, the Pacific Ocean has no boundaries for islanders, but is a connecting resource and part of their livelihood, life, and spirituality.

American Samoa, Northern Marianas and Guam are under United States control; the latter is a military base. Tokelau is under New Zealand control, as is the semi-dependent countries of Cook Islands and Niue. Wallis and Futuna, New Caledonia, French Polynesia, are colonies of France. Papua New Guinea has the largest Pacific Island population. On nuclear tests and militarization, French Polynesia was the area of French nuclear tests for 30 years. The Marshall Islands, to the north Pacific, is the site of United States' nuclear tests in the 1950s when it was part of its Trust Territory, a wider territory that included present-day Palau, Federated States of Micronesia and Marianas Islands, in a UN mandated territory under US control. The Pacific Island Forum (PIF) is the key regional institution for policy making for the independent Pacific Island states. It has other members and partners that participate in the PIF in different capacities. However, Australia and New Zealand, as key donors, often refer to the Pacific Island region and states as "our back yard."[1] They can assert assumptive "leading" rights in the islands, based on their dominant economic, trade and aid relationships with the Forum and most Pacific Island states. The ANZUS military alliance is a key feature of their security and defense interests, allied with the United States in the Pacific Ocean and including Island countries.

Nuclear Testing

The worst form of militarization of the Pacific region which has had long lasting, damaging effects on peoples' lives, health and the environment across the region, was its use by the United States, United Kingdom, and France, with the collaboration of Australia and New Zealand, in testing nuclear weapons. After the first atomic bombs were dropped on Hiroshima and Nagasaki in Japan in 1945, the Marshall Islands was used for the United States' tests of atomic and hydrogen bombs, from 1946 to 1958. The Atomic Energy Commission conducted 67 atmospheric tests. The first hydrogen bomb was exploded in 1952. Impacts on Pacific lives were immediate and long term, existing until today. Marshallese inhabitants were relocated to other islands with the false information that they would eventually return home. In Micronesia, people on surrounding islands were also affected by the tests. In 1954, the notorious Bravo atmospheric test resulted in nuclear fallout scattering over a wider area than expected, including the inhabited islands of Rongelap and Utirik. Marshallese men, women and children experienced direct radioactive fallout. In terms of the environment, atolls were vaporized and became uninhabitable forever, due to levels of radioactivity on test sites; food sources were contaminated. Health impacts included deaths from radioactive burns, cancers and birth defects; health impacts from nuclear tests continue even today and to future generations. This applies to the tests in French Polynesia (see below), and in Kiritimati (Kiribati) and in Australia (tests impacting on service personnel and indigenous peoples).

Genetic and reproductive impacts were immediately experienced. Women reported giving birth to "jelly fish" babies; forms of life not recognizable as human. Marshallese were often transported to the United States for tests, examined, kept under observation then returned to the islands, with little or no medical treatment offered. Marshallese believe they were used as guinea pigs so the United States could study the impacts of radiation on humans; evidence in documentary film footage shows the Atomic Energy Commission was doing this— as victims were examined clinically but returned home untreated. Today, Runit dome on Enewetak Atoll, Marshall Islands, contains radioactive materials left behind by the United States. The dome is a major concern for Marshall Islanders, including the next generation, who are vocal on its risks of cracking and releasing radioactivity into the sea and food chain. The United Kingdom conducted nuclear tests on Kiritimati Island and Malden Island, part of its colony of Gilbert and Ellis Islands, now the independent states of Kiribati and Tuvalu. The UK tests at Kiritimati Island affected Fijian and British servicemen present; many suffered and died from cancers, and their children have also experienced cancers (Ruff 2016; Maclellan 2017).

France conducted nuclear tests from 1966 to 1996 in Maohi Nui (French Polynesia). It is still a colony of France. Its economy, people, culture, population, composition and government, have been completely affected by the nuclear test program. A total of 193 tests were conducted on Mururoa and Fangataufa Atolls for 30 years. This included atmospheric and underground tests. Tahitians protested the use of their lands and atolls for nuclear tests; France denied any risks from its testing program. Tahitian leaders were denied full information on the tests and also threatened with military takeover by President de Gaulle unless the nuclear tests were accepted. Pouvanaa a Oopa, a much revered Tahitian independence and anti-nuclear leader, protested France's decision but was jailed and sent to France for many years of exile. The churches, particularly the Maohi Protestant Church, led a strong peoples' opposition to the nuclear tests, participated in by Maohi communities and leaders, test site workers, trade unions, and party leaders. The test site atolls of Bikini and Fangataufa remain under French military control and are contaminated and the test shafts threaten to collapse. Moahi Nui activists are concerned about the damage the resulting tsunami of radioactive material will cause across the Pacific Ocean and to their islands. Across the Pacific, an anti-nuclear protest and resistance movement has been formed that spanned 30 years.

The Pacific-Wide Nuclear Free and Independent Pacific Movements

Unlike in the period of the US tests in Marshall Islands in the mid-1940s to late 1950s, there was greater publicity and information available on the effects of the French nuclear tests in Mururoa which began in 1966. For the rest of the Pacific Islands, some still dependent states, the nuclear tests were an outrage to Pacific peoples. Scientists in the new University of the South Pacific shared information on radioactivity and its human consequences. Pacific Island countries were united in protesting French nuclear tests, joined by people and movements in Australia and New Zealand and beyond.

A regional meeting in 1975 organized by ATOM (Against Testing on Mururoa), church groups (Pacific Conference of Churches) and women's organizations (Fiji YWCA, National Councils of Women), brought together activists and organizations from across the Pacific Islands, including from Micronesia, the site of the United States' tests decades earlier. A Pacific-wide collaboration of peace, environmental, independence, indigenous, women's and anti-nuclear movements later grew out of this meeting. It led to the formation of the Pacific Peoples' Action Front and later the Pacific Concerns Resource Centre which served for many years as the hub for acts of resistance, advocacy, information sharing, lobbying and representation of the Pacific Island region in CSO, NGO and governmental gatherings, on issues of militarization, nuclear testing, missile testing and use of the Pacific Island region for the security interests of external states.

In opposition to the French nuclear tests, a unique Pacific Islander solidarity was formed across the region, on upholding the humanitarian, health and human rights of Pacific peoples. France did not cease its tests for 30 years. Nuclear racism is a word used by the late Roland Oldham, President of the Maohi Nui victims' assistance group, Mururoa e Tatou, to describe an element of the Pacific nuclear test history.[2] Many Pacific Islanders, including newly independent states' national leaders, spoke strongly against the use of the Pacific Islands at global level. The Pacific Island Nuclear Free and Independent Pacific (NFIP) movement was unable to stop French nuclear testing which continued with impunity until 1996. However, states' and peoples' memories and solidarity with Pacific nuclear test victims of Marshall Islands' Moahi Nui and Kiritamati tests, continue. This was and is evident in the Pacific Island states strong commitment to the campaign to abolish nuclear weapons and the humanitarian initiative which gained international support leading up to the historic adoption of the Treaty on the Prohibition of Nuclear Weapons (TPNW) on July 7, 2017.

The Campaign to Abolish Nuclear Weapons

The Pacific nuclear test history has resurfaced in the Pacific states' support for the International Campaign to Abolish Nuclear Weapons (ICAN), Nobel Peace Laureate 2017 and other states that led a drive to re-orient the view of nuclear weapons, from a defense and security issue, to one of humanitarian impacts. In this, Pacific Island states needed no introduction, to the many impacts of nuclear weapons, which they experienced through nuclear testing. The ICAN consisting of hundreds of partner organizations and working with states, achieved a treaty banning nuclear weapons. In the UN General Assembly, on July 7, 2017, 122 states voted for the Treaty on the Prohibition of Nuclear Weapons (TPNW); nine were Pacific Island states (Naidu 1988). Efforts are now focused on bringing the Treaty into force, which requires 50 ratifications; currently (October 2019) there are 32 ratifications, and 79 signatories; 5 Pacific region states have ratifed (New Zealand, Palau, Samoa, Vanuatu and Kiribati) and six Pacific Islands states signed the TPNW.

The nuclear tests produced one of the greatest resistance movements the Pacific Island region has seen—the NFIP movement. There is less information or action by non-governmental organizations now, across the region, on nuclear issues and no concerted people's movements on militarization of the Pacific Islands, at the level that existed in the past, which included awareness of military bases, missiles testing, and security issues applied to the Pacific region. This gap of information, awareness and alertness need to be overcome as the intergenerational effect of radiation sicknesses, evident in both places of nuclear tests lingers on in Marshall Islands, Kiritimati, and Moahi Nui (French Polynesia).

Land: Alienation and Dispossession

Remnants of imperial laws in selected post-colonial Pacific states continue to be used by Pacific governments to the disadvantage of their own citizens. Colonial and neo-liberal perceptions of land as a commodity with economic value (exchange value) are currently being pushed by multilateral organizations and donors in the Pacific at the expense of local understandings of land as a provider of life. Individual ownership with "paper titles" as evidence of land ownership is promoted and supported by multilateral organizations and governments, ostensibly to meet the requirements of the neo-liberal economies. A consequence of private ownership of land being prioritized over communal, egalitarian customary ownership has been bloody crises in Bougainville, Papua New Guinea and Solomon Islands. Fears of land loss by customary owners were also part of the first of four coups in Fiji and Samoa's debates on the likely consequences of its 2008 Land Titles Registration Act (LTRA) pushed by the Asian Development Bank (ADB).

Most Pacific societies practice communal ownership of land that ensures that all people have some rights to land on either their mother or father's side of the family. The right to make food gardens, collect building materials, plant fruit trees, cash crops and other livelihood activities were assured under customary tenure. Societies looked after each other and there was security and social safety networks for people through their local land tenure system, which ensured that no member of society was ever left landless. Individual or corporate ownership of land was promoted by the introduced land system. It verifies the land in question and the owner of it. A process to identify indigenous land owners and get them to sign papers purporting to give consent for land use or "legal" land transfer was instituted by colonial administrations throughout Oceania. In many instances, part of the new system of land tenure was the appointment of colonial-designated "trustees"—individuals identified to represent whole landowning groups—a move that contributed to numerous problems among customary owners over rights of sale or alienation occurring later in Pacific states.

In indigenous tenure, records were not written down but kept as oral history and recalled as cherished and treasured historical records, transferred only to members of the same landowning group. The imperial powers that colonized the Pacific Islands imposed a centralized administrative record, keeping of all land and establishing institutions to keep land records, that were divorced from the people's social, cultural, group relationships with land. In Fiji, under the British colonial rule, Sir Author Gordon established the Native Land Trust Board (NLTB) that identified Fijian land owning groups (*mataqali*) and recorded them in a central recording office. This was next linked to establishing a birth register on all Fijians, to ensure continuity of the land records of members of the land owning group or in some cases, the non-continuation of a land owning group, whereby land reverted to the crown. The colonial state became the custodian of indigenous peoples' records and made decisions on their behalf in relation to land development. In Fiji, after a laborious effort at registering land, the British chose a unitary model of *mataqali* (group ownership) and applied it across the Fiji islands. Plantation agriculture (mainly for sugar production) was set up. With labor imported from Melanesia and later India, Fiji embarked on a colonial economy, creating ethnic and land use differences in status between Indian indentured laborers and customary land owners who were incorporated into the native land lease system set up by the colonial administration. This imperial approach

Table 18.1 Percentage of customary and alienated land in five Pacific Island countries.

Country	Total land area (km²)	Alienated land/ freehold (%)	Customary/native land (%)
Fiji	18,274	17.0	83.0
PNG	462,800	3.0	97.0
Samoa	2,842	14.7	85.3
Solomon Islands	28,400	19.7	80.3
Vanuatu	12,189	0.0	100.0

Source: Ministries of Lands and Town Planning Offices for respective countries above, 2018

resulted in the problems with land and ethnic relations in contemporary Fiji. Table 18.1 indicates the existence of the two land ownership systems in selected Pacific Island countries.

Although the percentage of land under freehold or leasehold (alienated) in these countries may appear to be small, alienated land usually represents the most fertile and resource rich areas in the countries concerned. Some of the conflicts in the Pacific over land are discussed below, to demonstrate the legacies of empire.

Land Crises: Bougainville, Papua New Guinea

Only 3 percent of land in PNG is alienated while 97 percent is under customary tenure. This means that most development projects in PNG are on customary land. The fundamental problem here is not land tenure but rather the expectations of investors using the modern land tenure and laws, which are often opposed to the worldview and values of customary landowners. The Bougainville conflict that claimed the lives of an estimated 10,000 to 20,000 people had its roots in the late 1960s when the Bougainville Copper mine was established (Allen 2018: 39). Over the years, Bougainvillians felt that they as landowners were not benefitting from the returns of the mine. The establishment of the mine and its associated problems, occurred when PNG was under colonial control and the land was leased for mining activity—a decision made by the then Australian administration—to an Australian-controlled multinational mining company.

Over the years, through the activities of mining in Bougainville, one of the largest open-cut mines in the world, the land and environment which the local people rely on for their subsistence livelihoods, was destroyed. In 1988, the landowners demanded for reparation from the mining company and the PNG government for damages and for a more equitable share of mining incomes. The PNG government and the mining company were unwilling to meet the demands of the landowning groups and population. A conflict lasting 10 years and closure of the mine, ensued. The current situation in Bougainville is a division of the island into leaders of the Autonomous Bougainville Government (ABG), landowners of the old Panguna mine who want it to reopen and those not from the mining area, in the Me'ekamui Government of Unity (MGU), who do not want the mine reopened and if it is, they want all Bougainvilleans to benefit from it. The current question after this long history of the Bougainville crises, is on the fundamental appropriateness of the use of the title holders model (Allen 2018: 60). The history behind alienation and transfer of customary land for the Panguna mine, resulted in this severe dispute of a civil war, vulnerability, insecurity and armed conflict between indigenous landowners and peoples in the newly created Papua New Guinea independent state.

Solomon Islands

The first colonial regulations that facilitated the alienation of customary land in the Solomon Islands was the Queen's Regulation No. 4 of 1896. This regulation ensured that native landowners could transfer their customary land as either leasehold or freehold (Foukona 2007: 67). By 1900, Queen's Regulation No. 3 allowed the occupation of vacant land if a Certificate of Occupation was issued by the colonial administration (ibid.). The regulation declared all lands that were not occupied or vacant as waste land which would therefore be declared land that is owned by the Crown. The history of the disputes and tensions in the Solomon Islands can be traced back to the relocation of the capital town from Tulagi to Honiara on Guadalcanal after World War II, which used alienated lands in Honiara previously used for plantation development. It was these land ownership transfers since the colonial times until recently, that contributed to the inter-*wantok* tensions on Guadalcanal in 1998 that subsequently led to a total breakdown of law and order and an Australian peace keeping force taking over policing of Solomon Islands for decades, until police control was finally handed back to Solomon Islanders. Land and its transfer of ownership were behind this armed conflict, which caused a disruption of independent political life and sovereignty and caused loss of lives for Solomon Islands.

Vanuatu

The independence constitution of Vanuatu stipulated that all land in Vanuatu is customary. Under the condominium rule, huge areas of land were alienated and so the process of "nationalization" of land was the post independent government's preoccupation. Vanuatu's history of the push for independence shows that this policy was appealing because it promised the return of land to customary owners. These provisions were intended to put right the wrongs done to customary landowners that occurred in the colonial era, but this provision has not stopped continued alienation of land through lease arrangements (Haccius 2009). Land leasing and sub-leasing for longer periods of time for development activities have resulted in the marginalization and dispossession of Ni-Vanuatuans from their customary land.

The alienation of land from customary owners to people from other islands and foreigners continues in Vanuatu. It is a worrying trend, particularly for the island of Efate where the capital Port Vila is situated. During the Land Conference in Vanuatu in 2004, Chairman of Vaturisu Council of Chiefs, Mr. Mormor, indicated that more than 70 percent of the land area on Efate is owned "by expatriates, naturalised citizens, or people from other islands in Vanuatu" (*Vanuatu Daily*, November 5 2004). Customary land is now also being converted into formal titles leased to international companies for very long periods of time, making land inaccessible to its original landowners. This is regarded as land grabs. Land grabs are developments of lands and conditions relating to their use, that make it difficult for customary owners to get their land back at the end of the leases. This is happening on the island of Efate, with the state encouraging tourism. Foreign investors leased large plots of land for hotel development have sometimes built hotels and resorts while others further subdivided the leased plots and subleased land to other interested parties, making fortunes in the process, with little going to original landowners. There is no protection of indigenous customary land rights by the state. Under Vanuatu law, at the end of the lease period, if the landowners wish to get their land back, they can do so, but must first also repay the cost of any land improvements (Stefanova 2008: 2). In Papua New Guinea, similar situations are occurring in leases of land facilitated by the state.

Pacific Island States Facilitating Land Grabs

In the Pacific Islands, new forms of legislation by independent Pacific states to release their own lands to foreigners for extraction or creation of wealth, encourages land grabs and marginalization of customary landowners. The economic system has not changed after independence and indigenous political leaders of the state are doing the same thing to customary landowners, that colonial administrations did in the period of empire in order to facilitate the functions of private enterprises. States in the Pacific are enacting "temporary release of land" measures, to allow business to extract, profit from and exploit land. After independence, citizens and customary landowners are still not receiving the economic benefits from their land resource as owners, but receiving rent from leases made by the state and under state control, often without customary owners participating in decision making.

In the Solomon Islands, the process of converting customary land into registered land is encouraged and promoted by successive governments since independence. The state can also compulsorily acquire land from customary land owning groups for development purposes. A good example of this is the current Tina River Hydro Project on Guadalcanal, where the state acquired land and registered the title in the landowning clans' names. The biggest threats for titled land in the Solomon Islands include the incomplete record of lease lands and the lack of any guarantee by the state of a safe return to customary owners when leases end.

In Samoa, there is a debate on the role of the Asian Development Bank's (ADB) push for land reforms and registration of land using the Torrens system. Due to the ADB's pressure to access government land and customary land for development, the Samoa government changed the law in 2008 to The Land Titles Registration Act (LTRA). Critics of the LTRA fear it will contribute to the further alienation of customary land. Iati Iati states, "all chiefly titles are attached to customary lands"

(Iati 2016: 67). Changes to customary land titles will also affect Samoan social relations and customary leadership.

The use of legal mechanisms to formally access and lease both customary and titled land for big businesses and companies is evident. What we now commonly refer to as land grabs in the Pacific Island countries is the situation where post-colonial states are allowing foreign and local enterprises access to possess and own customary land through the modern land tenure system. The unlawful acquisition of land through corrupt processes by post-colonial political leaders also alienates land from customary owners. Logging licenses and mining permits are issued without the free, informed prior consent of local people.

Reclaiming the Sacredness of Land for Pacific Islanders

The whole economic and political system is tied to one dominant view of the world of neo-liberal economics and politics. It promotes individualism and a minimalist state. Private property and individual ownership of land are part and parcel of this capitalist world order. In this new wave of imperialism, land grabs and dispossession of land and resources stem from laws and policies that are made by governments but pushed and funded by bilateral and multilateral organizations. How can nation states in the Pacific reclaim the sacredness of land in the face of this capitalist mode of globalization?

It is important that Pacific governments and peoples cease the privatization of customary lands undermining cultural values and equal access to resources for livelihoods. The peoples' relationship with land, especially customary land, and the associated community-based worldview need to be revitalized in the process of development. To this end balancing needs of the modern economy (not neo-liberal) and people's needs in a sustainable and equitable manner while redistributing resource revenues is necessary. There should be a recognition of landowning units as owners of land in perpetuity and all its members should also be shareholders in any business undertakings on their leased land. A good example is the Guadalcanal Plains Plantations Limited (GPPOL), where landowning clans (*mamata*) also own shares in the company.

Blue Colonialism: Industrialization of Ocean, the Final Frontier up for Grabs

Global powers including Pacific Island nations are in a race to divide up the last frontier of the world including the ocean's seafloors for exploitation of resources, using a narrative of Blue Economy or Blue Growth. Advancement in technology means that depths once considered unfeasible are increasingly accessible, allowing multinational corporations to plunder oceanic resources in a race to secure food security for countries external to the region and to provide them with alternative sources of minerals and energy. The Pacific Ocean, one of the last remaining healthy oceans, is set to be the new contested space for resources including fisheries and deep-sea minerals. Already Pacific Island governments, without the consent of their peoples, have issued commercial as well as exploration licenses to significant parts of their territories for experimental mining of deep-sea minerals.[3]

The concept of the Blue Economy has its origins in the broader green growth economy definition.[4] Due to the capitalist dictates that have dominated exploitation of the oceans for decades, particularly in international but also national territorial waters, there is a growing concern and recognition now of the heavy damage wrought on ocean ecosystems, the blue heart of our planet. The damages include overfishing, habitat destruction, marine pollution, ocean acidification and climate change. Understanding the science behind the health and resilience that the oceans provide in order to sustain human activities now and into the future is an outstanding, urgent and compelling task. For the Pacific peoples who have a spiritual relationship with the ocean the industrialization of the ocean will see a return of the colonial powers and takeover of resources in new ways by transnational corporations and multilateral financial institutions. Such a move must be resisted not just for the benefit of the Pacific peoples, but for all of human habitation of this planet.

Significance of the Oceans

The oceans are the "blue heart" of the planet. Their importance to the planet's stability and its ability to sustain life is underscored by the oceans' contribution to global climate regulation. Oceans provide 50 percent of atmospheric oxygen and absorb 25 percent of human induced carbon dioxide emissions while its circulation dynamics of ocean currents make our planet habitable. Oceans are home to extraordinary biodiversity and unique ecosystems providing a global service to the functioning of our planet. The Pacific Ocean is the largest of all oceans. Covering approximately 59 million square miles and containing more than half of the free water on earth, the Pacific is by far the largest of the world's ocean basins and is home to the Pacific Island countries and its peoples.[5] The vastness of the Pacific Ocean is illustrated by the fact that all of the world's continents could fit into the Pacific basin!

The Pacific Island science, mythology and understanding of the oceans is a mixture of profound inherited knowledge of sea currents, winds and marine life based on livelihood use, ancient history of oceanic currents through migrations and traditional fishing. The Pacific scientists have contributed to marine and oceanic studies over the past few decades based in Pacific regional and national institutions. They have also documented sea level rise and climate change. However, their knowledge of mineral resources in their own territorial waters are non-existent or just being done, and insufficient to keep up with the implications of the rapid plunder of the ocean which will have a destructive impact on Pacific Islands and peoples.

New Plans for Turning the Oceans into a Wasteland

The ability of humans to harness the power of the oceans is once again evolving in important ways. Ocean resources have been the foundation of global trade and economic activities, a major source of food, energy and livelihood. Measuring the value of the ocean economy gives only part of an understanding of its significance. Updated figures from the European Union, estimates the value of new ocean industries at 5.4 million jobs and gross added value of €500 billion (European Commission undated). The Organisation for Economic Co-operation and Development (OECD) suggests that the ocean economy is likely to outpace the global economy in the next 15 years. Clearly the oceans and their resources are a valuable commodity although some commentators caution that the true value of oceans is undervalued. Framed as perhaps the last untapped, under-explored and under-exploited region in the world, the Pacific Ocean is set to be a contested space. The contest for Oceania can be likened to the nineteenth-century "scramble for Africa." The economic gains Pacific states' leaders are courted with are a minute fraction of the value of the ocean resources that will be extracted. The case of Pacific fish stocks after years of licensing to allow uncontrollable commercial fishing extraction is a case in point.

The depletion of land based minerals and associated devastating impacts on ecology and communities caused by mining coupled with advancements in technology and consumer demand for electronic minerals and infrastructure (Hein et al. 2013), is set to make the ocean floor the next frontier for exploitation of minerals such as copper, lithium, rare earth minerals, cobalt, and manganese nodules.[6] The exploitation of minerals on the sea floor by transnational corporations and governments in depths of around 400 to 6000 meters below sea level is set to take place in the Pacific Ocean, the Indian Ocean and the Clarion Clipperton Area. In total, the amount of area covered under the licenses is astonishing—covering over 1.3 million square kilometers of seabed. Deep sea mining is perceived as an imminent venture with countries like Cook Islands, Fiji, Kiribati, Nauru, Papua New Guinea, Solomon Islands and Tonga are seen as some of the first takers. Despite the experimental nature of the industry exploration has already begun within the territorial waters of these countries with PNG issuing the world's first commercial license set to start exploitation by 2019. Model legislation for Pacific Island countries funded by the European Commission signaled the readiness of the Pacific.[7]

Proponents supporting deep sea mining argue that ores on the sea floor are exceptionally rich and that deep sea mining takes place in smaller areas is considered more environmentally friendly than land based mining. They have long argued that nothing lives there, but the very opposite is true. This framing of low risk and high return ignores several pertinent realities. We do not know the full impact on the deep seabed and the waters. There is increasing evidence that deep sea mining poses a grave threat to the vital planet balance functions. Several studies have found that there would be immediate adverse impact on the ocean ecosystem health, species abundance and biodiversity (Dando and Juniper 2000). Most scientific studies also found that there will be little to zero recovery of biodiversity in the mined sites. More disturbing is that industrial scale operations (both in terms of size, intensity and duration) would have devastating and irreversible effects covering large areas of the ocean floor. In New Ireland and East New Britain in PNG people are already experiencing the negative impact of the exploratory mining and drilling occurring 30 to 50 kilometers from their communities. Villagers have reported an increase in frequency of dead fish washed up on shore, including a number of deep sea creatures hot to the touch as well as excessively dusty and murky waters. There is brutal irony here. In this era of global climate change, the Pacific peoples who have contributed the least to the causes of climate change and are acknowledged to be already bearing a disproportionate burden in terms of effect are also now facing an underwater attack of equivalent if not greater proportion.

Resistance to Desecration of the Sea

In the new era of oceans' exploitation, the Pacific Island states are in an uncharted territory. In that, if they do not have traditional wisdom and new information available to them in confronting and negotiating with the exploitative powers there will be irreversible consequences. Seabed mining is the crucial case challenging Pacific Island leaders and states. Will they make the right decisions involving the peoples? The prevailing position upheld by many Pacific thinkers and writers is that smallness in terms of land size has meant Pacific Island countries to be forever vulnerable. Lacking in agency and dependent on the former colonial powers and developed states or any country with technical resources or new and emerging development partners it is argued that the islanders have no other choice, but to be subservient for their survival. This conformist mentality betrays the deep relationship that the communities have with the ocean. In this age of climate change, we are forced to critically review our political positions, attitudes and actions that contribute to destruction of life and its continuity on the planet.

There are no more suitable people on this planet to be guardians of the world's oceans than those who call it home. Realizing this responsibility, in 2011, a collective which included feminists, community groups, regional non-governmental organizations and a faith based organization organized research and analyses to better understand implications of exploitation and desecration of deep sea minerals for the Pacific peoples and the ocean. In 2012, the collective mobilized over 8,000 signatures to caution Pacific Island Forum leaders over deep sea mining while in 2014 the Lutheran church issued a signed petition representing over a million of its members to the PNG government over growing concerns over impacts of deep sea mining.[8] In Vanuatu, working closely with the Vanuatu Council of Churches and the Vanuatu Kaljoral Senta, the collective persuaded the government to review the 140 licenses issued without the prior knowledge of previous governments. Globally, activists from PNG and Fiji made an appeal in Europe in 2014 to garner support for a ban in seabed mining. It took 3 years of lobbying and advocacy by the European partners before the European Parliament supported a moratorium on deep sea mining (European Union 2012). Palau has placed a ban on commercial activities including fisheries and mining. Fiji's Director of Mineral Resources announced that Fiji will not be issuing any further new licenses for exploration of seabed minerals.

Conclusion: Reclaiming the Sacredness of Lives, Lands, and Seas

For ages the Pacific islanders have been living lives that uphold the sacredness of lives, land and seas. As ocean-going peoples who travelled far and over many routes at different times, to settle and populate the Pacific region they do not forget their rich community-based cultural heritage, the power of the ocean and the preciousness of land. Islands and ocean are part of their lives and worldview without which they have no existence. Egalitarianism and making sure no one is without land are features of customary land tenure that in the past, were in place to "ensure no one was homeless" and without means of living. This beautiful region where people cherished a communal life of sharing and closeness to land and sea has come under an immense onslaught since colonial times, which has been intensified, in our neo-colonial era. Their land and seas have been desecrated by nuclear testing, deep sea mining, privatization of land and commodification of their culture by the tourist industry forcing many of them to fight for their survival or conform to the dictates of the empire. Moreover, some are facing the threat of disappearance of their whole countries like Tuvalu and Kiribati under climate change. In the areas closer to nuclear test sites, particularly Marshall Islands, Maohi Nui (French Polynesia) and Kiritimati, people continue to suffer from the destructive intergenerational, genetic, health, environmental, political and social impact. Yet, many continue to resist the onslaught with great resilience by maintaining a strong sense of place and obligation to protect their homeland and sea. They have been a formidable force that brought about the Treaty on the Prohibition of Nuclear Weapons. Networking among the islands in building a common Pacific identity that proclaims the sacredness of lives, lands and seas is a necessary step towards reclaiming the common good of the Pacific region and beyond. The cosmovision and coordinated actions of the islanders for the protection of land and sea are not only for their region, but also for the whole planet. The communities of islanders may appear to be small in number, but their resistance will have a global resonance in an age where both human beings and nature have been turned into exploitable objects by the empire.

Vanessa Griffen is a Fijian political scientist, researcher, writer, gender and development specialist, and women's rights advocate. She helped form Nuclear Free and Independent Pacific Network and is currently a campaigner with the International Campaign to Abolish Nuclear Weapons (ICAN).

Gordon Nanau is currently senior lecturer in the School of Government, Development and International Affairs at the University of the South Pacific in Suva, Fiji and is from the Solomon Islands. His work focuses on land tenure and extractive development in the Pacific Island countries.

Maureen Penjueli is coordinator of Pacific Network on Globalization, based in Suva, Fiji. She was formerly a team leader with Greenpeace. Her advocacy and published writings focus on trade justice, seabed mining, investment and decolonization.

Notes

1. See recent statements by Australia and New Zealand's Foreign Ministers (September 2018) on new aid for the Pacific region to counter the growing concern about China's aid and security influence.
2. Speaking in New York, at the United Nations side event during the negotiations for a treaty banning nuclear weapons, which was adopted on July 7, 2017.
3. Almost all PICs with the exception of Samoa and Palau have issued exploration licenses to transnational corporations while Papua New Guinea is the first country in the world to have issued a commercial license.
4. Green Economy definition: Green economy is an economy that results in improved human wellbeing and social equity while significantly reducing environmental risks and ecological scarcities. While the Blue Economy (developing definition) as a sustainable ocean economy emerges when economic activities are in balance with the long term capacity of ocean ecosystems to support this activities and remain resilient and healthy.
5. There are 26 Pacific island countries of which 16 are sovereign states, while 8 are still territories including disputed colonial territories of France (New Caledonia, French Polynesia, Wallis and Futuna Islands), Indonesia (disputed—West Papua), USA (Guam, Hawaii, CNMI, American Samoa). Altogether, these countries represent a population of close to 20 million people.
6. The Copper Alliance argues that every mobile phone needs 0.02 kg of copper; for cobalt it is estimated that Volkswagen will need at least one third of the current entire global supply by 2025 for its energy efficient cars; geologists suggest that if all European cars are electric by 2040 (using Tesla Model 3), they would require 28 times more cobalt than is produced now (see Shukman 2018).
7. The SPC-EU Deep Sea Minerals Project has 15 Pacific Island Countries: The Cook Islands, Federated States of Micronesia, Fiji, Kiribati, Marshall Islands, Nauru, Niue, Palau, Papua New Guinea, Samoa, Solomon Islands, Timor Leste, Tonga, Tuvalu, and Vanuatu (see Pacific ACP States 2011).
8. See updates on the role of Pacific peoples resistance in www.pang.org.fj.

References

Allen, Mathew G. 2018. *Resource Extraction and Contentious States: Mining and the Politics of Scale in the Pacific Islands*. Singapore: Palgrave Pivot.

Dando, P. and Juniper, K. 2000. *Management and Conservation of Hydrothermal Vent Ecosystems*. Victoria, Canada: Institute of Ocean Sciences.

De Ishtar, Zohl. 1994. *Daughters of the Pacific*. Melbourne: Spinifex Press.

European Commission. Undated. "Blue Growth." Retrieved from https://ec.europa.eu/maritimeaffairs/policy/blue_growth_en (accessed October 20, 2019).

European Union. 2012. "EU Integrated Maritime Policy." Retrieved from https://ec.europa.eu/maritimeaffairs/sites/maritimeaffairs/files/docs/body/limassol_en.pdf (accessed October 20, 2019).

Foukona, Joseph. 2007. "Legal Aspects of Customary Land Administration in Solomon Islands." *Journal of South Pacific Law* 11(1): 64–72.

Haccius, Justin. 2009. "Coercion to Conversion: Push and Pull Pressures on Custom Land in Vanuatu." *Jastis Blong Evriwan* 3(1).

Hein, James R. et. al. 2013. "Deep-Ocean Mineral Deposits as a Source of Critical Metals for High and Green Technology Applications—Comparison with Land-Based Resources." *Geology Review* 51: 18–19. https://doi.org/10.1016/j.oregeorev.2012.12.001

Iati, Iati. 2016. "The Implications of Applying the Torrens System to Samoan Customary Lands: Alienation through the LTRA 2008." *Journal of South Pacific Law* 1: 66–88.

Maclellan, Nic. 2014. "Banning Nuclear Weapons—A Pacific Islands Perspective." Retrieved from www.icanw.org/wp-content/uploads/2014/01/ICAN-PacificReport-FINAL-email.pdf (accessed October 20, 2019).

Naidu, Vijay. 1988. "The Fiji Anti Nuclear Group: Problems and Prospects" In *Peace, Security and the Nuclear Issue*, edited by Ranganui Walker and William Sutherland. London: Zed Books.

Pacific ACP States. 2011. "SPC-EU DSM Deep Sea Minerals Project." Retrieved from http://gsd.spc.int/dsm (accessed October 21, 2019).

Ruff, Tilman A. 2016. "The Humanitarian Impact and Implications of Nuclear Test Explosions in the Pacific Region." Retrieved from www.cambridge.org/core/journals/international-review-of-the-red-cross/article/humanitarian-impact-and-implications-of-nuclear-test-explosions-in-the-pacific-region/1FDB0D26842BEA5621F33A0B53FCD7F9 (accessed October 20, 2019).

Shukman, David. 2018. "Nautilus Minerals Forecasts that in Copper Alone, Seabed Mining Could Be Worth $30bn a Year by 2030." Retrieved from www.bbc.co.uk/news/resources/idt-sh/deep_sea_mining (accessed October 20, 2019).

Stefanova, Milena. 2008. "The Price of Tourism: Land Alienation in Vanuatu." *Justice for the Poor* 2 (1).

19

Knowledge Militarized in Africa: On Crushing Ubuhlanti to Advance Pseudo-democratic and Economic Imagination in the Context of Empire

V. S. Vellem

One writer makes the point that in an effort to destroy completely the structures that had been built up in the African Society and to impose their imperialism with an unnerving totality the colonialists were not satisfied merely with holding a people in their grip and emptying the Native's brain of all form and content, they turned to the past of the oppressed people and distorted, disfigured and destroyed it. No longer was reference made to African culture, it became barbarism. Africa was "the dark continent." Religious practices and customs were referred to as superstition. The history of African Society was reduced to tribal battles and internecine wars. There was no conscious migration by the people from one place of abode to another. No, it was always flight from one tyrant who wanted to defeat the tribe not for any positive reason but merely to wipe them out of the face of this earth. No wonder the African child learns to hate his heritage in his days at school. So negative is the image presented to him that he tends to find solace only in close identification with the white society.

—Steve Biko, *I Write What I Like* (2017: 31–32)

Introduction

In South Africa during the State of Emergency, townships where black people lived were turned into war zones. Apartheid had literally become a military state, using massive power and force against its own citizens and with legions "dwelling" among the people. At a deeper level though, the Apartheid State, towards its end in the 1980s, had adopted a military strategy called "low-intensity conflict" (LIC), described as "winning the hearts and the minds of the people," to penetrate the psyche and spiritual dispensation of the oppressed masses. By its very nature, LIC is a military use of soft power as opposed to physical power. The ubiquity of military forms of violence in South Africa and Africa after the demise of Apartheid is palpable. For example, in post-1994 South Africa, universities became military zones during the #FeesMustFall and #AfrikaansMustFall campaigns. Think about Patrice Lumumba's demise and his betrayal by his own friend, Mobuto Seseko. What about Darfur in Sudan? Most recently, the death of South African soldiers in Central Africa, the on-going but less spoken of Cameroonian situation neighboring Nigeria's opprobrious Boko Haram related violence? The USA has had closer cooperation with some African countries, including Botswana and Uganda, examples of the penetration of the military in the democratization of that country. With these examples, an illustration of the ubiquity of militarization and *knowing* is intended and this chapter will in the main examine how the continuation of the LIC strategy and tactics are manifest in the vast projects of democratization and economic management. The underlying thesis is that since the violent conquest and colonization of the African continent, militarization on the African continent does not only sustain the superiority of the Eurocentric system of democratic knowledge, but also does so by all means including the destruction of *zoesophia*—the wisdom of life which we examine through the heuristic device of *ubuhlanti* (the kraal), in the arena of human participation for life. Stated otherwise, militarization in the context of Empire, is tantamount to the militarization of knowledge, the destruction of epistemologies of life through forms of knowledge that prize conquest.

Militarized Knowing

The subject of this chapter is about an idea about forms of knowledge that are militarized—*militarized knowing* if you like. Militarized knowing is in our view written on the bodies of black African people in South Africa and the continent at large. It is difficult to imagine an epoch in the history of our continent that is not affected by military violence. To deepen this notion of militarized knowing, we by analogy argue that our life is made up of different spheres, politics, economics, religion and so forth. There is a sphere therefore of inter-subjective knowledge among human beings, which entails the formulation of knowledge through continuous discourse, without violence and any form of coercion so as to develop norms and values for life. The penetration of this sphere by imperatives of power and economics has been the subject of the twenty-first century. In this chapter, it is the penetration of this very sphere by the military that is the subject of our discussion, the colonization of the inter-subjective sphere of life by militarized forms of knowledge.

Written within the context of Empire,[1] this chapter posits that no one in our world today can underestimate the levels of self-destruction and self-killing humanity has attained. Even more shocking in this context is the capability of creating human beings, yes, the manufacture of human consciousness and spirituality by Empire. Albert Nolan postulates that one of the worrying signs of the twenty-first century is spiritual hunger, yet hunger spiritual that cannot be satisfied—we add, in the context of Empire (Nolan 2006: 3–14). This is so because Empire manufactures its own religion and thus creates its own forms of consciousness and spirituality, while its ultimate goal is to destroy and kill life. Therefore we argue that it is something else to manipulate ideographic science[2] as the military industry complex vividly suggests on the physical side of things, but another to manipulate the nomothetic,[3] to sustain supremacy and hegemonic control of the world. This is the crux of our discussion in this chapter, namely that the military has come to manipulate the nomothetic so as to sustain the superiority and supremacy of one race in the world as argued from a black perspective.

It is also important to highlight the fact that this chapter is contemplated at a time when liberal democracy is in crisis.[4] Arguably, neoliberalism has succeeded to create a black man who can kill blacks within the law for the maintenance of an order that merely benefits a few. Remember that from our perspective, neoliberal democracy and economics became part of the end of history, *a la* Francis Fukuyama. The neoliberal ideology undergirding democratic and economic imagination has been up to this day defended militaristically. During #FeesMustFall in South Africa, it simply became clear as many university campuses literally became military zones, with maximum violence used against students, that in essence, the defense of liberal politics and capitalism is nothing but military violence. More importantly, in this conjuncture, is the fact that the executor of this violence, is black against black while the white beneficiary of colonialism is invisible.

Indeed, at this moment, what we used to call "buffer zones," residential places occupied by blacks in between the white residential places and those savage red blanketed ones occupied by the uncivilized has now become a legalized zone politically and economically to protect the white power structure, or the white man's burden. Stated otherwise, democracy has in itself become a buffer zone for the white power structure. During Apartheid South Africa, whites themselves had to kill to protect their interest; today blacks can do it for them within the glamour of the law. This is what we experience as democracy in South Africa: the Marikana Massacre, the killing of Andries Tatane, the burial of Mlotshwa in a coffin alive, militarization of the police, cancerous corruption dubbed as state capture, a devastating resurgence of cultic worship, eating of grass and drinking of petrol and proximity between white and black which cannot be tolerated anymore even at global level. Yes, see an olive tree from Palestine that embellishes and consigns a façade of beauty and aesthetics to the settlement of the Israeli state. Deception at the core in the world turned into a religiosity of supremacy. This, the chapter argues, is Low Intensity Warfare at its best, with democracy itself as a project of war that still continues by other means in the twenty-first century to sustain the superiority of one race or a monologue of history and knowledge in the world.

The *problematiek* is what Amilcar Cabral suggests as return, a return to home in the intricacies of the continuous arrest of liberation and life affirming cosmovisions. The struggle to return labor, faith, people, animals, the environment and land to home, or at least embers that could invigorate the struggle to return for Africa and global South to win the war. Thus our thesis that militarization on the African continent does not only sustain the superiority of the Eurocentric system of democratic knowledge—the authority of whiteness, or the white power structure—but that is also does so by all means including especially the destruction of *zoesophia* (i.e., the wisdom of life as seen through the heuristic device of *ubuhlanti*). The colonial matrix of power which continues to the present, significantly left Africa and the global South with colonial woundedness, the destruction of the *being, power* and *knowledge* of the black African people. This dismantlement of the black African cosmovision(s) of life, as demonstrated in the Statement produced by black theologians within EATWOT in the 1990s, traces this problem to 1492, *ipso facto*, the *longue durée* of sixteenth-century Eurocentric modernity. The indivisibility of military science and violence to sustain this lust for superiority is thus palpable if not obstinate in the twenty-first century. Importantly, this project of the dismantlement of black African's lives, the black African *zoesophia*, first deployed theological sources, faith before it resorted to secular philosophical and natural sciences. Through the examination of the military strategy of LIC, the thesis argues, the continuation of this war by other means in the twenty-first-century ethos of Empire could be unraveled.

To elucidate our thesis, we first say something about the military dogma of Empire. Second, we illustrate how pervasive and ubiquitous military violence has been in the history of our continent. Third, we explore the meaning of ubiquitous warfare on the continent, the pervasive presence of violence in the invention of Africa. Following a catalogue of ubiquitous violence in Africa comes the theme of Low Intensity Conflict and the Crushing black African *Zoesophia : Ubuhlanti.* The link we make with LIC seeks to suggest that there is a clear military strategy to crush the knowledge systems of black African people in what we regard the zenith of Eurocentric civilization, Apartheid. We discuss our last point, *Ubuhlanti*: Resistance and the Remaking of *Isizwe*, to assert that after physical defeat of the black African people, nonetheless, they still have a way to return home when they smell out the dung carpet of their forebears in *ubuhlanti*. Our un-concluding closing remarks indicate the very intent of this chapter, a tentative on-going discussion on the perplexities of military violence and the civilization of affirming life in our times.

Military Dogma in the Context of Empire

With regard specifically to the United States of America (USA), in discerning what the military doctrines of the Empire are, Ninan Koshy says the dogma of the USA is simply " a mandate for the pursuit of permanent military superiority" (Koshy 2006: 341). This is a shocking state of affairs, permanent military superiority with shocking trends too. This dogma entails among others, the building of permanent bases by the USA across the length and breadth of the globe and the decisive use of ferocious, lethal power such as readiness to use nuclear power. One example we can cite, which speaks to this travesty, is the military power exuded by the Israeli state and the plight of Palestinians. Admittedly, the vision for military superiority is a religious cult of many states, even on the African continent too.

As already stated though, our focus is not really on the physicality of warfare in relation to this dogma, but its religiosity if not spirituality of military superiority. It is now common knowledge that countries that are even struggling to feed their own citizens will have astronomical budgets for their military expenses and projects. These traumatic shifts in our imagination of life today, explicitly speak to our theme of knowledge militarized- a traumatic shift about life imagination, which Mark Lewis Taylor describes in this way: "even a minimum budgetary Iraq war cost of US$1.2 trillion 'is 10 times the world's annual official development assistance to all developing countries'" (Taylor 2006: 415). We do not need to labor the point if we simply remember how much Donald Trump is keen on spending in erecting a wall that divides his country from Mexico, let alone the cost to a child from Mexico. The choice to use resources for life in glaring neglect of need and assistance to pursue an ideal that threatens life itself is a traumatic defining moment of our time.

The *Global Kairos Faith Stance* issued by the Oikotree Global Forum in 2013 puts this matter as a faith question in this manner:

> People all over the world (could tell stories) in terms of how the dominating international economic, political and military system is waging war against people and the earth. This is why concerned Christians all over the world are convinced that we as churches and faith communities must urgently respond to this global systemic crisis.
>
> (Oikotree Global Forum 2013: 2)

For the sake of emphasis, our crisis in the world derives from the military system that wages war against people, stated otherwise, it is war against the existence of human beings for as long as those who regard themselves superior are secure. Indeed, this systemic crisis is a crisis of systems of knowledge, a ruthless onslaught against knowing, an epistemic crisis. The existence of a traumatic vision of permanent war in the world and the priority shifts in human imaginaries about life quintessentially suggest a wholesale *epistemicide* with glaring episodes of genocides going on to this day, let alone *spiritualicides* in pursuit of permanent military superiority.

Steve Biko saw this many years as our opening quotation of this chapter suggests. Writing from a black perspective, a Black Theology of Liberation (BTL) and the philosophy that Biko represents, Black Consciousness (BC), our opening insights point to a traumatic, devastating anthropological and existential distortion colonialism has stemmed upon us as black African people. The project of colonialism has been about emptying the black brain of all form. The intellectual doubt of blackness is a challenge up to this day. This project has also been about eroding the past of the oppressed people by distorting, disfiguring and destroying it. Reference made to African culture in our public life today remains tokenistic with the indigenous religious heritage of black Africans still outside the mainstream imaginaries of religious thought imposed by the colonizer. In the context of democratization, as in our case in South Africa, democracy is not framed and shaped by indigenous knowledge systems of polity rather its core is Western and Eurocentric. More pertinent for our conversation in this chapter without excluding the anthropological and existential distortion and disfigurement of black lives, is the reduction of black lives and the African continent to internecine wars. The creation of war against self, while war waged by others continues, now as a dogma and ethos of Empire. The military dogma of the pursuit of superiority is experienced as war among black Africans, internecine war through the manufacture of human consciousness by the powerful.

Ubiquitous Militarization: The Seed for Black Africans Fighting among Themselves

It is said that the Roman Empire, during Caesar's reign was among the first to enlist a permanent military force. Before this, warriors often would be gathered when it was necessary, during war, getting disbanded thereafter when war came to an end. That we now live in a permanent state of war is an unimaginable truth. Why do we in our world keep permanent forces and military formations? In our country South Africa, the then-Apartheid leader and President, PW Botha, literally succeeded to build a security state, a garrison state not in anticipation of war, but a garrison state to safeguard white superiority and to wage war against blacks, the indigenous people of that country. During his tenure, the country was in a state of emergency and saw the introduction of the military strategy LIC, through the help of the United States of America. Well, for now our focus is on the ubiquity of military violence not only in South Africa but on the African continent as whole.

The ubiquity of the military on the African continent is inseparable from the "invention"[5] of Africa. The story of Africa, therefore is a quintessential appropriation of colonialism, the erosion of charisma, intellect, skill, humanness and visionary ambition among black Africans. It is existence simultaneous with violence. See, within six days of the independence of the Democratic Republic of Congo, one army general, Emile Janssens, a Belgian, called his men to inform them that independence might bring changes to politicians and the civilians, but no change for the structure of the army.

> And then, to underline this message, Janssens turns around, takes a piece of chalk, and writes in large letters across the blackboard, BEFORE INDEPENDENCE = AFTER INDEPENDENCE.
>
> (Kenyon 2018: 18)

South Africa is the last country on the African continent to achieve its independence or better, political liberation. "Before political liberation = After political liberation" is written not merely by chalk on the blackboard nor even by Janssens, yet the pattern remains the same. How true, that the structure of the colonial army does not change before and after independence? Well even if it might change, the mind-set of conquest does not. Even after democracy, the structure or logic of conquest does not change. In fact, the army controlled by black faces in democracy continues to protect the ideals of the colonizer.

Is it not an enigma that most African countries that struggled for political liberation and obtained it continue to depict a picture of "under-development" decades long after the departure of colonial administrators and governors? Countries such as South Korea for example that were ravaged by war just as a few of the African counterparts were proclaiming their liberation have made tremendous advancements that a question about the failures of Africa becomes truly inevitable. A comparison between Ghana and Malaysia is but one example as these two countries obtained their political liberation almost at the same time. When one thinks about how many years it took for Nkrumah, the first President of Ghana after its independence to have a decent burial, the intriguing question of the historical arrest of black African liberation, *a la* Cabral, becomes unavoidable—the historical arrest of liberation thought through military knowledge and strategies. Before and after political liberation on our continent simply remains the same.

Zakes Mda's work, *Little Suns* (2015), albeit a novel, threads the story of lost love between Malangana and Mthwakazi through the events of the war that amaMpodomise had to wage against a British magistrate, Hamilton Hope, who attempted to subjugate these people and the kingdoms of the Eastern Cape under British rule. Yes, the defeat of amaXhosa is impossible to imagine without a story of what has been termed "Seven Frontier Wars"—boundary wars as the white establishment was pushing into the interior of the country from the Cape—with South Africa in 1910 becoming a Union between the Boers and Britons, together sealing their victory over black South Africans in the proclamation of the opprobrious 1913 Land Act. Even amaZulu were defeated, baPedi of Sekhukhune, with Moshoeshoe of Basotho apparently losing a huge territory we now call the Free State, a province of South Africa. Antjie Krog on Moshoeshoe and some negotiations with the colonizers along the Caledon River, *Mohokare* in Sesotho, says:

> The debate about land began. Brand stood up and suggested that the land the Free Staters were occupying had been bought from a Bushman. Moshoeshoe, seated to the left of the Governor, became so agitated that he could hardly wait his turn. He jumped up and demanded to know the name of the Bushman. Brand withdrew the remark. Thereafter Moshoeshoe gave a constructive speech explaining the difference between providing hospitality and giving away land permanently after a *pisto* agreement.
>
> (Krog 2009: 191-192)

This story is known well among us black Africans in South Africa, the affront of black African hospitality and their own cultural views and cosmovision by the white power structure. Land sold by a Bushman? Land is not a commodity among Africans. The insights cited above depict a context when the Boers, the Afrikaner had established their own republic, with President Brand their leader then. There were wars and Basotho prevailed partly because of the mountain called Thaba-Bosiu. Krog reminisces: "[President of the Afrikaner republic of the Free State] Brand joined the long succession of leaders whose men had failed to conquer the Mountain of the Night [Thaba-Bosiu]: Matiwane, Sekonyela, Mzilikazi, Cathcart and Boshof" (Krog 2009: 193). In vain we must state.

> Although everything had been thrown into the battle for survival against overwhelming forces, Moshoeshoe's set-up was vulnerable to the coarse competition and sweeping appropriation of colonialism. The society that he and his people had built through immense energy and charisma, intellect and skill, humanness and visionary ambition, accommodating a variety of groups and cultures, found itself eroded and fragmenting. Uprooted, dislodged, bereft and sensing Moshoeshoe's end, the Basotho began to fight among themselves.
>
> (Krog 2009: 194).

Here is our point: Kings Shaka, Moshoeshoe, Sekhukhune, Hintsa, all black South Africans were defeated. Theirs was a vulnerable battle of survival against overwhelming forces. Blacks were uprooted, dislodged, bereft and fighting among themselves to this day. This is the architecture of colonial power. Novels by Mda, Achebe and arts in our continent mirror this ubiquitous existential reality. What then ensued after our defeat as Africans were political and ideological strategies designed to maintain this colonial architecture of military violence. A few examples might be helpful to explain the point. Mahmood Mamdani's assertion is helpful an example for us:

> The policy of legal integration was shaped by both the long history of colonial wars and the eventual defeat and dispersal of the natives. The background of armed resistance had stiffened the resolve of the masters of the Cape—proverbially once bitten, twice shy—in favour of the policy of nonrecognition of native institutions. At the same time, defeat and dispersal made it possible to integrate and dominate natives within a single legal order.
> (Mamdani 1996: 66)

The more black Africans waged wars of resistance, the more obstinate the colonial masters such that policies such as non-recognition of the black African institutions are lock, stock and barrel, a part of the obstinate resolve of the white power structure to defeat the black Africans. It is the perpetuation of the integration of black African people within a single "civilizing" order to defeat and disperse them not so much through physical violence, but more so through the destruction of their imagination and memory with forms of knowing, "colonial alienation" to employ Mamdani's term that became the mantra of colonization after the defeat of blacks. Ngungi wa Thiong'o says:

> Berlin of 1884 was effected through the sword and the bullet. But the night of the sword and the bullet was followed by the morning of the chalk and the blackboard. The physical violence of the battlefield was followed by the psychological violence of the classroom.
> (Ngugi wa Thiong'o 1986: 9)

Ngungi wa Thiong'o explains that colonial imperialism knew how to kill with efficiency not so much with the bullet and physical subjugation, but also through spiritual subjugation. The "morning of democracy" on the African continent—political liberation—is the same as the darkness and night of colonial sword. Low-intensity conflict as an explicit military strategy seals and weaves together both the night and morning of the single colonial order of the conquest and defeat of the black African. Indeed, how possible is it to tell the story of Africa without the ubiquity of the military forces of the West and Eurocentric civilization? It is not necessary to repeat some of these painful moments and wounds that have afflicted a continent known as the cradle of humankind. What has up to this day been portrayed as unassailable cannons of knowledge is a product of the military power of the West. "Decentralized despotism" (Mamdani 1996: ch. 3), Mahmood Mamdani argues, is a colonial form of state which the British called indirect rule.

> Direct rule was the form of urban civil power. It was about the exclusion of natives from civil freedoms guaranteed to citizens in civil society. Indirect rule, however, signified a rural tribal authority. It was about incorporating natives into a state-enforced customary order.
>
> (Mamdani 1996: 18)

State-enforced customary order is a deep sentiment about the militarization of customary knowledge, the attack on the cultural dispensation and heritage of black African people through decentralized despotism. Mamdani argues that the whole continent was ruled in this manner, the inhabitants of the continent being excluded from civil freedoms while subjected to an enforced order of customary law. Right now in Ethiopia there is a coup d'état. In Sudan, Eritrea, the Democratic Republic of the Congo there is no word that one can choose to describe the experience of women, young children and the powerless in such situations of war. The story of Africa is one of guns and blood. Our being and our knowing as black African people is simply intertwined with our conquest, colonization and what the role of Eurocentric Christianity continues to be in the story of Africa. It might not be farfetched to describe Eurocentric Christianity as a religion of guns and war from the perspective of the lived experiences of the black African.

What is important now is that Africa is now facing what is defined as Empire. For a number of years since the publication of the Accra Confession in 2004, the concept of Empire has influenced our thinking in many ways. If Empire is about "the coming together of economic, cultural, political and military power today" (Boesak, Weusmaan, and Amjad-Al 2017: 2), how can we then know if culture itself comes together with military power? Indeed Empire is a spirit of lawlessness, all-encompassing to protect and defend the interest of the powerful therefore knowledge is militarized by this pervasive spirit and more importantly, a spirit that "colonizes consciousness, values and notions of human life by the imperial logic" devoid of compassion and justice. It is this spirit that shades our being and our knowing in this context, yet with a long and protracted history on the continent. This convergence of military power and the colonization of consciousness, values and notions of human life is unprecedented. The story of Africa is one that begins with the ubiquity of military violence, threaded even in novels through war, the architecture of colonial power right into the climax of Empire.

Low Intensity Conflict and the Crushing Black African Zoesophia: Ubuhlanti

By the 1980s at least in South Africa, the white power structure had understood that the component of physical violence in war constituted only 30 percent of total war. A substantial component (70%) constituted issues of the heart and the mind. To win the war then a coarse and sweeping appropriation of the resources of the white power structure had to focus on the DNA of black African *Zoesophia*. We use *Ubuhlanti* as a short hand for this DNA, the sacredness and sacramentality of life, thus cultural and spiritual dispensation of black African people. In the context of Empire, and the capabilities of Empire to manufacture its own religion, economics, politics, aesthetics, all spheres of life continue to be destroyed by a convergence unprecedented that valorizes an ideology and a monologue of reading history, if not the worship of one history in the world, heavily if not ferociously defended militaristically.

Ubuhlanti often translated as the kraal, is a sacred space in African homes. In *ubuhlanti* rituals of worship are performed, political matters are discussed, economics, the relationship to nature, liturgies of life and the entire rhythm of life as understood by Africans would be found. This space, *ubuhlanti*, is rightly understood as an ecclesial symbol of the cosmovision of black African people. It is this space that is the target of the 70 percent strategies of war against black African people, a target of the epistemicide and spiritualicide of the heritage and memory of black African people. Nathan Wright Jr. offers helpful insights to further clarify this space we elucidate through the heuristic device of *ubuhlanti*, especially if we understand this as an aggregation of the power of life among black Africans. Wright says:

> All men need the power to become, Indeed the Greek words for power (*bia*) and life (*bios*) reflect the essential interrelationship of power and life, Power is basic to life. Without power, life cannot become what it must be.
>
> (Wright 1979: 48)

In *ubuhlanti*, nothing but a power enhancing field for black African lives must be seen. Power and life come together in *ubuhlanti*, the power of ancestors, the power of economics, the power of faith, the power of nature, the power of people all with the lives of the people now living come together. *Ubuhlanti* is the power of the memory of black African people. To kill black African people, crush *ubuhlanti*. Our key point is that power is life-giving or better, life-affirming. *Ubuhlanti* in African *Zoesophia* as a heuristic devise, a sacred space in an African home as an aggregation of the cosmovision of black African people, is appropriated as a communication of the efficacy of *bia*—a power space for the re-making of life (*bios*). Colonial alienation and the destruction of the consciousness of black African people can only be attained thought the crushing of this DNA.

Ubuhlanti: Resistance and the Remaking of Isizwe

Have the colonizers including the intrusions of Empire succeeded to completely destroy and crush *ubuhlanti*? Amilcar Cabral says:

> Within the indigenous society the action of the liberation movement on the cultural plane entails creation of a slow but solid cultural unity, symbiotic in nature, corresponding to the moral and political unity necessary to the dynamics of the struggle. With the opening up of hermetic groups, tribal or ethnic racist aggressiveness tends gradually to disappear and give way to understanding, solidarity, and mutual respect among the various horizontal sectors of society, united in struggle and in a common destiny in face of foreign rule. These are sentiments which the mass of the people imbibe readily enough if the process is not hindered by the political opportunism peculiar to the middle classes.
>
> (Cabral 1972)

As colonial alienation creates a massive number of black Africans who have forgotten who they are, becoming enticed by the foreign intrusions of Empire and the white power structure, in defense of their cultural heritage, black African people protect their *ubuhlanti* and form solid cultural unity. The struggle for liberation as it were, becomes rooted in the history and the culture of black African people and this is true in many of the communities across the African continent. *Isizwe*, people defend their cultural heritage and being by appropriating it to the struggle dynamics. This is exactly what Allan Boesak says about this struggle and his deployment of the concept of *isizwe*:

> It is always the people, the *sizwe*, the struggling *sizwe*, the sacrificial *sizwe*, the hopeful sizwe that make the difference. They, through the darkest days, believed and knew with Isaiah that it would be only a little while, and the tyrant would be no more. They believed with Jesus as he assured the seventy upon their return from their mission where they saw "even the demons" submitting to them, that even though there were to be extraordinarily difficult times ahead, ultimate victory is assured, because he had already "seen Satan fall like lightning from the heaven.
> (Boesak 2017: 11)

There is no other place that offers the possibility for the remaking of the struggling *isizwe* but *ubuhlanti*. The defense of the cultural integrity of black Africans by holding on to the cosmovision of their value system in contexts of defeat and oppression transmutes into a repository of the power to be to undermine Empire. Furthermore on the struggle of (*i*)*sizwe*, Boesak says:

> These are the voices of the determined, hopeful *sizwe*. It is they who make me believe that despite all its awesome power, despite the relentless viciousness of the violence, and despite the arrogance of the Israeli state because it feels secure in the uncritical support of world powers, the occupation will be ended, that wall, more and more the solidification of all the tyranny of oppression and the Palestinian people shall be free. Indeed, the words of our prophetic graffiti artist remain: "This Wall May Take Care of the Present, but it Has No Future." They, like Jesus, have seen Satan fall like lightning from heaven, and they, like Isaiah, know that despite the present and the realities of the politics of oppression, occupation and indifference, "it is only a little while, and the tyrant shall be no more."
> (Boesak 2017: 30)

Certainly the sentiments above allude to the struggle by Palestinians against the Israeli government. We however borrow the same sentiments to express the determination of *isizwe*, the people in subverting the military violence of the West perpetrated against *ubuhlanti*. Despite it awesome power, its relentless viciousness and arrogance, the white power structure and its antics against the *zoesophia* of black Africans is sure to be defeated.

What a contradiction in terms, I hear the voice of the critique! How can the very same *ubuhlanti* that is crushed by the white power structure be the locus of the struggle of *isizwe*? Well, we need to remember that Empire as a form of power and ethos that assumes totality does not render the beneficiary of this ethos as the oppressed. The experience of oppression is unique to those that are on the receiving end of this ethos. There is, *à la* Enrique Dussel an "exteriority" to the totality of Empire and Eurocentric logic. There is logic of wounded-ness, wretchedness if you like or even blackness that is uniquely felt by those excluded and oppressed by this totality of this Satanic logic and ethos. Furthermore we should remember, resistance to this logic (i.e., the crushing of *ubuhlanti*, is simultaneous). Resistance to the colonization of knowing by black Africans is simultaneous to any of the antics to crush the wisdom of life enunciated in *ubuhlanti*.

Ubuhlanti a heuristic device of black African Zoesophia, evocatively demythologizes false security attained through the fragmentation and crucifixion of the spheres of life. It is a restorative instrument that points to the plenitude of life, the harmony and salvation of existence against forces of death. It is the habitus of the living dead who hold all spheres together responsible for the satiation and security of all living beings. As a generative, evocative design, with the circular dimension of time brought to mind, it is in the kraal where a demythologization of modern economic discourses in the ethos of Empire that distort how we image God takes place. It is the crushing, ridiculing and denial of the humanity of blacks since 1492 that we explain through the heuristic device of *ubuhlanti*. It is the continuation of the war on *ubuhlanti* that is our subject in this chapter, the crushing of a cosmovision of life at least in Wars of Dispossession, the project of Apartheid, a zenith of Eurocentric modernity or the colonial matrix of power and now the deification of democracy we seek to unravel.

Un-concluding Remarks

In the 1980s, during the struggle against apartheid, the Apartheid government, assisted by Ronald Regan then, adopted a strategy of "low-intensity war," aiming towards "winning the hearts and the minds of the people." At the heart of this strategy, we reiterate, is the understanding that physical war constitutes only 30 percent of victory. The strategy goes on to argue that for total victory to be attained, 70 percent of the war is psychological and spiritual or nomothetic as we have argued. During the days of Apartheid, religion was deployed to achieve the total defeat of black people. Let us put this matter in the following way, as captured in a well-known anecdote of the liberation paradigm of doing theology:

> When the white man came to our country he had the Bible and we [blacks] had the land. The white man said to us, "let us pray." After the prayer, the white man had the land and we [blacks] had the Bible.

This anecdote simply suggests the relationship between land and the Bible, or land and Eurocentric Christianity in South Africa. A lot has been written in this regard. Our take now is that the formulation of this anecdote should go something like this:

> The Bible we had in our hands to struggle for liberation in now snatched away by Empire, meaning, the very spiritual dispensation we used to fight for our land, our cosmovision or *ubuhlanti*, is now being snatched out of our hands.

Empire is an ethos, it deploys its resources of religion, knowledge and culture to fill the 70 percent space of total victory against the oppressed. During the #FeesMust Fall, we saw how some churches were used to derail and to infiltrate the students. Harrowing signs of faith and harmful religious practices in South Africa have become common. The killing of people is the killing of their cultural dispensation and such is the destruction of humanity and the creation of people for the sake of maintaining and sustaining privilege for some. Low Intensity Warfare attacks the religion of liberation and distorts faith to create virtual spiritualities that make drones out of people. This is what we mean by pseudo democracy and pseudo economics today. It is deeper. The Western Code uses the very systems of knowledge it deployed to enunciate a civilization that commodified and rendered black lives dispensable as forms of religion such as democracy and its relationship with Protestantism. What is important for our theological thinking is to grasp that the pursuit for permanent military superiority is a faith and spiritual matter to sustain the myth of the superiority of one race in the world.

We have also attempted to show how ubiquitous military violence is in the lives of black African people. In South Africa for example, our democracy resonates with what has been termed the arms Deal. Billions of rands were wasted in Arms when millions of South Africans still live in harsh conditions of poverty more than two decades after the demise of Apartheid. In our public life, the use of security organs of the state to fight political battles is rampant. Simply stated, military knowledge in South Africa and the democratization of the country are inseparable. The ubiquity of military violence and the penetration of military antics into the discourses that shape our values and norms in the democratization process of this country are simply real. Ubiquitous violence in Africa suggests more about time and space and thus historiography. Colonial violence and its zenith in the ethos of Empire is simultaneous with the invention of Africa by the white power structure.

Where do we find the coals for our struggle when people are being turned into drones? Empire is attacking this notion, people. This is our greatest challenge perhaps that is going to be worsened by the Fourth Industrial Revolution. We have argued that it is in *isizwe* that the subversion of military antics and the colonization of *ubuhlanti* finds expression, a hopeful *isizwe*. It is in the zones of non-being, in the exteriority of *isizwe*, where we can harness coals, our embers for building up power, power to life. Obedential politics is probably the route and millions of struggling people are the power repositories of a new *pistis* and commitment to an alternative vision of life. Lessons for dying, to learn to die and to live in contempt of Empire, are in the zone of non-being.

V. S. Vellem was lecturer in the Department of Systematic Theology and Ethics, and the Director of the Centre for Public Theology, at the University of Pretoria. He was a social commentator on faith-related issues with a specific focus on spirituality, power, and economics, and the co-editor of *A Prophet from the South: Essays in Honour of Allan Aubrey Boesak, Bible and Theology from the Underside of Empire* (2015).

Acknowledgements

Editor's note: V. S. Vellem worked on this text immediately after he recovered from a critical illness. Janet Joyce of Equinox kindly gave an extension to me to submit the manuscript so that Vellem could complete his chapter. The following is one of the last emails he wrote to me: "Hi Jude, Let me say thanks soooo much. I was two days to concluding the paper when I got ill. Am going to try harder to have it sent to you at least earlier so that you can have your time to read it before we submit it. Thanks for prayerful support. So far the worst is over. Am slowly regaining my strength and will call you by Skype this week. I will let you about times but am suspecting Friday afternoon. Kindest regards, VV" (October 15, 2019). Sadly, Vellem fell ill again after he completed this chapter. He could not see the copy-edited version. He passed away on December 4, 2019, in Pretoria, South Africa, his native country. V. S. Vellem was one of the most articulate black theologians of our times, who defined faith in God as a subversive activity that challenges tyrannical forms of power. This is his last published article. May his untiring prophetic voice continue to inspire us.

Notes

1. We shall say a little more about this concept in due course. For now suffice it to say it is a concept related to the Accra Confession to designate the main forms of power that undermine life or at best a life killing.
2. The term "ideographic science," according to Walter Mignolo, citing Wilhem Dilthey, refers to natural sciences (Mignolo 2011: xii; see also Vellem 2018: 284).
3. This term, in the same manner as the note above in terms of sources, means human sciences.
4. One of the best works that critique the neoliberal ideology in relation to democracy is Cornel West's *Democracy Matters* (2004). See also Vellem (2012: 76–93).
5. I have in mind Valentin Mudimbe's work, *The Invention of Africa* (1988). Within African and Black Theologies, the use of the construct Africa is not without any qualification as an invention of the colonizers.

References

Biko, Steve. 2017. *I Write What I Like.* Johannesburg: Picador Africa.
Boesak, Allan Aubrey. 2017. *Pharaohs on Both Sides of the Blood-Red Waters: Prophetic Critique of Empire: Resistance, Justice, and the Power of the Hopeful Sizwe—A Transatlantic Conversation.* Eugene, OR: Cascade Books.
Boesak, Allan, Johann Weusmaan, and Charles Amjad-Ali. 2010. *Dreaming a Different World: Globalization and Justice for Humanity and the Earth: The Challenge of the Accra Confession for the Churches.* Retrieved from http://academic.sun.ac.za/theology/downloads/Globalisation%20report%202010%20proof%203.pdf.
Cabral, Amilcar. 1972. "The Role of Culture in the Struggle for Independence." Paper presented at the United Nations Educational, Scientific and Cultural Organization Meeting of Experts on the Concept of "Race," "Identity" and "Dignity." UNESCO, Paris, July 3–7. Retrieved from https://unesdoc.unesco.org/ark:/48223/pf0000001749 (accessed October 30, 2019).
Kenyon, Paul. 2018. *Dictator Land: The Men who Stole Africa.* London: Head of Zeus.
Koshy, Ninan. 2006. "The Global Empire: An Overview." *Reformed World* 56(4): 335–347.

Krog, Antjie. 2009. *Begging to be Black.* Cape Town: Random House Struik.
Mamdani, Mahmood. 1996. *Citizen and Subject: Contemporary Africa and the Legacy of Colonialism.* Princeton, NJ: Princeton University Press.
Mda, Zakes. 2015. *Little Suns.* Cape Town: Umuzi.
Mignolo, Walter. 2011. *The Darker Side of Western Modernity: Global Futures, Decolonial Options.* Durham, NC: Duke University Press. https://doi.org/10.1215/9780822394501
Mudimbe, Valentin. 1988. *The Invention of Africa. Gnosis, Philosophy, and the Order of Knowledge.* Bloomington, IN: Indiana University Press.
Nolan, Albert. 2006. *Jesus Today: A Spirituality of Radical Reform.* Cape Town: Double Story Books.
Oikotree Global Forum. 2013. *Global Kairos Faith Stance.* Johannesburg. WCC.
Taylor, Mark Lewis 2006. "Theology and Global Empire Today." *Reformed World* 56(4):415–432.
Ngugi wa Thiong'o. 1986. *Decolonizing the Mind: The Politics of Language in Literature.* Nairobi: James Currey.
Vellem, Vuyani. 2012. "The Opiate of neoliberal Globalization and the Dawn of Democracy in South Africa." *Theologia Viatorum* 36(1): 76–93.
Vellem, Vuyani. 2018. "Cracking the Eurocentric Code: A Battle on the Banks of the New Blood Rivers." *Missionalia* 46(2): 284. https://doi.org/10.7832/46-2-313
West, Cornel. 2004. *Democracy Matters.* London: Penguin Books.
Wright, Jr, Nathan. 1979. "Black Power: A Religious Opportunity." In *Black Theology: A Documentary History, 1966–1979,* edited by Gayraud Wilmore and James Cone, 48–61. Maryknoll, NY: Orbis.

20

Resistance, Peoples' Rights and the Role of the Churches in Latin America

Javier Giraldo Moreno

> I believe that the revolutionary struggle is appropriate for the Christian and the priest. Only by revolution, by changing the concrete conditions of our country, can we enable men to practice love for each other.
> —Camilo Torres, *Revolutionary Priest* (1973: 334)

Introduction

All countries of Latin America have suffered from imperial policies, first under colonial empires and then under the hemispheric domination of the USA. Both forms of domination were backed by military force. I want to mention specifically some paramount moments in the consolidation of the imperial domination of the USA over Colombia, my country, in the course of the last century. After World War II, the USA was determined to create a zone protected from the possible influence of the USSR in Latin America. Therefore, the Mutual Security Act of 1951 authorized the US government to provide military aid to Latin America for the defense of the Western Hemisphere. Sixteen bilateral treaties were signed in 1952 and 1953 between the USA and Latin American countries. Colombia was the first country to sign up to a Military Assistance Program with the USA, in April 1952. Already in 1947, in Rio de Janeiro, the Inter-American Treaty of Reciprocal Assistance had been signed up, and in 1950 Colombia was the only Latin American country to send troops to fight in the Korean War, 3,089 soldiers who fought with the US troops, of which 210 died and 570 were wounded (Prada 2010: 23).

Colombia was the first country to send military personnel to be trained in the US schools, first in the Panama Canal region in 1946, later in Fort Benning, Georgia, from 1984 onwards. It is estimated that 12,000 Colombian soldiers were trained in these schools. The Colombian officers in the highest hierarchy of the army were all trained in those schools. In the diplomatic communications between the Colombian and US governments in the period 1952–1959, there is a certain opposition of the US government for the military aid, as military purchases were used in Columbia to repress internal enemies or in the context of the internal conflict. However, from 1959, the US government accepted that the Colombian government used this military aid in the internal conflict, with the argument that communism was a hemispheric enemy (Prada 2010: 22ff.). In 1962 the US government sent to Colombia a military mission which left a secret directive for the Colombian government. According to this, in the struggle against communism it was necessary to engage civilians in war activities, and to create armed structures which brought together civilians and soldiers (Kennedy Library Archives, quoted in McClintock 1992: 222). Later, the paramilitary structures in Colombia became one of the most powerful mechanisms to repress social movements, which were regarded by the governments as agents of international communism and therefore legitimate military targets, which should be exterminated and brutally repressed.

In the 1980s, the US government created the term "narco-guerrilla" so as to allow all of the economic and military aid to the struggle against drug trafficking in Colombia, to be used against the social movements and alternative political movements, based on the fictitious identification of drug trafficking with the social and political insurgencies. According to Stephen Ambrose:

> On the eve of the Second World War, the United States had an army of 185,000 men, with an annual budget of 500 million dollars, with few military agreements and without troops stationed abroad. 50 years later, it had a military force of over 1 million soldiers, a budget of 300 billion dollars, military agreements with 50 countries, soldiers stationed in over 100 countries and a military capacity to destroy many times the planet.
>
> (Quoted in Hernández 2006: 26)

In 2002 it was denounced through the media that the proliferation of private military companies were used by the USA to intervene in many conflicts around the world, mostly in places where the laws prevent the direct presence of the Pentagon. At that time, it was mentioned there were ninety companies, managed by retired army officers, earning incomes above those of the Pentagon, with headquarters in fifteen countries and operations in one-hundred and ten. They had signed up 3,061 contracts for military training in war zones, logistical support, military equipment maintenance and security studies, with the Defense Department since 1994 (Wayne 2002). In 2008, some military bases were closed down in Latin America. Colombia signed up an agreement with the USA on October 30, 2009, according to which they can keep seven military bases with the purpose of controlling South America, the Caribbean and Western Africa, mentioning explicitly the containment of "anti-US governments" (Prada 2010: 70ff.).

The imperialist nature of the USA is based on the fact that its relations with the rest of the world, and particularly with the Latin American subcontinent, are defined according to its own interests. As in the (in)famous 1956 quote by John Fuster Dulles, Secretary of State under President Eisenhower, "the USA have no friends, only interests." The fact that its decisions are based on interests, suppresses radically the possibility of having international relations based on ethical principles, or political and ideological principles, grounded on a universal ethic. This allows it to act in open violation of the rights of the people at so many levels. This chapter will show how these violations are intrinsic to the USA's imperialism while examining the ambiguous role of the churches in Latin America and the sites of people's resistance to such violations.

Imperialism and Disregard for the Rights of the Peoples

It is evident that after the World War II the main concern of the USA, which had already attained a high economic power, was to contain the communist ideology, which was represented in a rival economic and political power (first, the Soviet Union, then communist China), from gaining a foothold in its immediate area of influence, Latin America. It is this fear and concern, which is behind many of its major strategic decisions, leading the USA to modify and violate basic principles of coexistence among nations, of international law, and of basic and universal political ethics. The first of these disregarded principles, is the self-determination of peoples.

Several military interventions to overthrow governments or to impose governments and military juntas, both in Latin America and elsewhere, are testimony to this illegitimate strategy of the USA. The conviction that the ruling powers need to be backed by the coercive power of armed forces, lethal weapons thus becoming the decision-making mechanism, reveals well-seated anti-democratic notions in the USA. These notions are concealed behind a rhetoric about formal electoral democracy, which in spite of all kinds of fraud as well as media, economic and judicial pressure, still resorts to armed force. For this purpose, the USA has military training schools in its territory; various Latin American coup-mongers and the military hierarchy of this continent have attended these schools.

Another ethical-political and judicial principle disregarded by the USA in terms of its international policy, is the professionalization of armed bodies. As a matter of fact, the secret directives imposed on Latin American states through their hemispheric security missions, have rather promoted their de-professionalization by insisting on the need to engage the civilians in warfare through paramilitary bodies. They have done this in disregard of one of the basic principles of International Humanitarian Law, which demands the precise distinction of combatants from non-combatants. The reason behind this de-professionalization is, perhaps, their adherence to war theories in which terror plays a fundamental role, such as that of Clausewitz. The aim of these paramilitary structures, as recognized in their very directives, is to engage in some of the most inhumane actions, actions that professional soldiers cannot engage in at risk of radically delegitimizing the state.[1]

When those states in the area of influence (or of "hemispheric security") of the USA consolidate these principles mentioned above, they develop a friend–foe culture, which is first developed in internal conflicts, and later in the justice apparatus, and in the ideology—including religion—in education, and in the mass media. Such a process leads to the disappearance of some elemental features of justice, such as its independence and impartiality; features of democratic freedoms, such as freedom of information and opinion (press freedom) and of a really democratic education. Everything then becomes biased, aligned to and at the service of the war machine, of polarization, and of inclusion/exclusion patterns.

Anti-communist ideology is at the heart of the US international relations and the fundamental determinant of them, as well as of the definition of their area of influence, or hemispheric security zone. The Cold War polarized the world between a Capitalist West and a Communist East, each bloc having their respective ideology (individualist/collectivist) and economic-political system. The USA shut down through military means the possibility to choose between them to the Latin American peoples. It also blocked, through stigma or demonization, the communist option in its broader sense, while at the same time it covered its own system with a sacred veil under the "democracy" fiction. In this sense, it co-opted religions, giving its anti-communist ideology religious overtones.

The politics of anti-communism ignore the various schools and the pluralist versions of the collectivist ideology and its economic models. Thus, it exploited some elements of particular collectivist schools which were ideologically atheist, turning this particular feature into something essential, in order to co-opt religions and bring them in line with their militant anti-collectivism. Therefore, anti-communism became an articulating space for political, ideological and religious sentiments, even before the Cold War. Religions and churches have, consequently, played an important role in the violation of the rights of the peoples and in promoting a polarized and discriminatory view of global society. The Western bloc, having a well-seated Christian tradition rooted very deep in history, even went as far as defining its identity in the context of this polarization in terms of "Western Christian Civilization," in opposition to the "International Communist Movement," the latter being, by definition, anti-religious.

This is why it becomes paramount to examine in detail the role of the churches in the reproduction of imperialist practices and in the subsequent violation of the rights of the people, as well as in the creation of a world which has sunk into inequality, violence and exclusion for millions of people prevented from having a truly dignified life.

Catholic Anti-communism

Although in different religions anti-communist ideology may have had specific effects, I want to deal specifically here with its impact in Catholicism, for the latter has an undeniable historic importance in Latin America. When we consider in retrospect the conflicts that have plagued the Latin American peoples over the decades, it is fair to recognize that the source of much demonization, exclusion, blame, attacks and sometimes aggressions and violence with the intention to exterminate, had been papal documents which censored and condemned ideological positions and worldviews considered as alien, contrary or even harmful to the practice of the Christian faith.

It cannot be denied that in many Latin American countries the militants of liberal political parties and the members of socialist and communist movements and tendencies were fought against by Catholic masses, under the guidance of their pastors, in a veritable moral panic. This was true in particular against many of those who resorted to the right to rebellion through insurgencies. The condemnation and demonization, in many ways reminiscent of the Crusades and of the Inquisition, fanned the flames of hatred, dogmatism and fanaticism, leaving a deep scar in our Christian tradition, posing a formidable obstacle for national reconciliation today.

Already at the time of the French Revolution, Pope Pius VI, in the papal document *Quod Aliquantum*, on March 10, 1791, not only condemned the civil constitution of the clergy, but also attacked its source, which was no other than the Declaration of the Rights of Man and the Citizen, demanding ecclesiastical principles that were used by the monarchies for their legitimization. But Pope Leo XIII went even further in his encyclical *Libertas*, dated June 20, 1888. In his theological view of freedom he censored and condemned all forms of liberalism, whether radical or moderate, and stated that human rights, which were already being consolidated in liberal and democratic states, were contrary to the Christian tradition and dogma, in particular rights such as the freedom of cult, freedom of opinion, freedom of education, and freedom of conscience. This encyclical was widely quoted by the Colombian bishops in their pastoral letters attacking liberal parties and ideologies.

In the century from 1846, with Pius IX as pope, and 1958, with pope Pius XII numerous documents attacking socialist and communist political and ideological currents were issued. This demonization goes in crescendo until pope Pius XI makes the radical statement in *Divini Redemptoris* (March 19, 1937) that "Communism is intrinsically wrong, and no one who would save Christian civilization may collaborate with it in any undertaking whatsoever" (§58). The Decree of the Holy Office of July 15, 1949, under pope Pius XII, reserves excommunication to any Catholic who joins a communist party or adheres to their doctrines. It is important to mention that this changed with pope John XXIII, whom with his encyclical *Pacem in Terris*, April 11, 1963, leapt over the abyss of misunderstandings with the cultural and political world at the time, incorporating the human rights declarations of the United Nations into the so called Social Doctrine of the Catholic Church. However, to many conservative strands and to those who defend a radical form of capitalism, all of that anti-communist doctrine consecrated in those documents is still valid, and their arguments are still used by those who want to scare away the Christian masses from alternatives to capitalism.

It is undeniable there was a strong tension between the historical movement which progressively conquered the political and civic liberties of the people, which consolidated human rights and the rights of the people through the generations, and institutional and traditional Christianity. The benefit of hindsight allows us to recognize the frailty of their arguments, which nonetheless cannot be considered under any circumstances as fundamental tenets of the Christian faith. The Chilean Jesuit Arturo Gaete, in his minute and detailed analysis, published in various issues of the journal Mensaje (Message) between 1971 and 1972, in Santiago de Chile, exposes the roots of this tension. First of all, the papal documents reflect a lack of knowledge about the theoretical developments in socialism and communism which circulated widely in Europe around that time. Their understanding is vulgar and unrefined, a caricature. There is no nuance about the various strands of socialism advocated by several authors, and they are often put in the same bag with liberal strands which were also demonised. Fr Gaete asserts that Pius IX, under the rubric of socialism and communism, is really condemning the utopian socialists; Leo XIII, under the same rubric, condemns anarchism. Pius IX is the first to mention Marx by his name, but he too addresses only one particular variant of Marxism: its Bolshevik interpretation (Gaete 1972a: 330; see also Gaete 1971a, 1971b, 1972b).

He demonstrates in these articles that the increasingly radical anathema against communism and socialism was not based on a deeper understanding or study of the incompatibility of the doctrine with the various Marxist theoreticians and tendencies, but on the political power that these movements conquered in countries of a Christian tradition, in which the church was in league with the traditional powers. Therefore, the passing mentions to socialism and communism in Pius IX's writings were a response to the ascendancy of these movements in Europe, often hand in hand with the liberal uprisings. The explicit condemnation of Leo XIII was a response to the effects of the First International Workingmen's Association; the more radical statements about its alleged absolute incompatibility with Christianity in Pius XI's documents were a response to the Russian and Mexican revolutions, and their often relentless persecution against the Church; and the Decree of the Holy Office of 1949 which excommunicated the Catholics with links to any communist party or who adhered to its ideology, was a response to the massive participation of Catholics in communist parties, and to the proposals of some of these parties, such as the Italian, of forming alliances with Catholics in order to achieve social reform, which they called the policy of the open hand, viscerally rejected by the Vatican.

In some other analysis, Fr. Gaete addresses the central arguments of the papal documents to condemn socialism and communism, arguments which really deal with the most vulgar versions of these strands: the rejection of the right to private property; class struggle; the egalitarian philosophy; the materialist and atheist philosophy; and the collectivist economy. Every single one of these arguments was confronted with a much discredited version of theology which understood human institutions as part of a natural and divine order. Today it is very rare for a theologian to argue that private property or the existence of states, or that the free market economy, are of divine origin or are based on natural rights. Similarly, it is unlikely for them to argue that egalitarianism or collectivism are in fundamental opposition to the natural proclivities originated by the Creator. Few theologians today would deny the reality and the facts of class struggle. On the charges of atheism, it was the Vatican Council II which stated that the causes of modern atheism lay in a critical reaction against the institutionalized religion, of which the community of believers is responsible in no small measure for concealing rather than revealing the true face of God (Concilio Vaticano II, *Constitución Gaudium et Spes*, no. 19)

But the deepest aspect of Fr. Gaete's analysis of the tension between the Christian and the Marxist worldviews, as can be perceived from the papal documents condemning it, is the discussion on the philosophical systems in which each of these positions is grounded on. The Church argues from a neo-Thomistic position, a thought centered on substance and which gives little importance to accidents; it is a thought centered on being, without much thought for action. On the contrary, Marxism is essentially a historical and dialectical thought, according to which human beings are historical products and do not pre-exist but in a most rudimentary form. Reality is a contradictory process, which can only be captured through a thought of movement, or a strategic-tactical thought. Therefore, while the papal documents describe "class harmony" as a natural and divine law, while "class struggle" happens "per accidens" (accidentally, or as Pius XI argues, "as the work of tormented and cunning men"), according to Marxism, class struggle is a reality of paramount importance throughout history, and a fact which determines who concrete human beings are, although this is not cast in stone but is part of our history as alienated beings who demand to structurally bring that struggle to an end in order to suppress the existence of classes , something that today from the perspective of progressive Christians, we can regard as closer to the Christian ideal of the Kingdom of God.

Another feature of the neo-Thomistic thought prevalent in the papal documents, is its unidimensional character, which does not factor in the distance between reality and its theoretical expression. On the contrary, for Marxists, and also for psychoanalysis and for Nietzschean philosophy, there is a great deal of distance between reality and its theoretical expression, for they can often conceal or distort reality. As such, they are bidimensional discourses which attempt at unveiling the proportions and nature of what is concealed by economic or power interests, or by trauma and emotions which avoid being made explicit. Arturo Gaete ends one of his articles with the following reflection:

> At the end of the last century, the working class had two serious advocates: social Catholics and socialists. But these advocates came from different galaxies, so when they met one another, all they could do was to excommunicate each other. Each regarded the other monolithically as bad. Therefore, there was nothing that one could learn from the other. The working class, in the end, paid the price.
> (Gaete 1972: 716)

It is important to point out that in Colombia this tension was experienced in a most tragic and dramatic way. The Constituent Assembly called by the military dictatorship of General Rojas Pinilla in 1954 decreed, in its Legislative Act No. 6, any activity inspired by communism unconstitutional and illegal. This was clearly an extension of the excommunication decree of the Holy Office in 1949. This tendency becomes even clearer if we compare those activities that the Holy Office considers as sinful to those which the Decree 434 of 1956, regulating Legislative Act No. 6, considers to be criminal: there are 13 offences by which the perpetrator would be submitted to a Martial Court under Military Justice. There is little doubt that one of the inputs for the demonization of the communists, which eventually led to violent persecution, came from the Catholic hierarchy at the time.

It is possible to assert that for nearly two centuries the predominant religious ideology in Latin America, which was adopted by the Christian hierarchies, has been closely linked to the dominant political ideology, intersecting on a primordial anticommunism which takes the form of an implicit, and often very explicit, acceptance of capitalist culture, which in Latin America can't be divorced from the submission to US imperialism and to its military might. This has had many consequences, perhaps the most serious one is the development of a brand of Christianity which is deeply individualistic and adapts people's mentality to capitalist culture, through education and the media.

Churches' Resistance to Imperialism

The Vatican Council II (1962–1965) marked, for the Catholic Church, a moment of opening to the world's reality as well as of renewal, transforming some of its traditional doctrines, mainly in the relations of the Church with the world. For the Protestant churches, something similar happened at the Uppsala Synod (1968). In both gatherings reflections on social injustice, on poverty, and the misery in which the majority of the world's population lives; on violence and the power of weapons; had a deep impact on the churches and had important effects in the following years. For the Latin American Catholics, the general ideas of the Vatican Council II had a much more tangible expression in the Latin American Bishops' Conference which took place in Medellín, Colombia, 1968. The first effect of Medellín was the irruption of Christians in politics from the perspective of denunciation, protest and revolution, forming groups and movements, promoting activities and demanding justice and structural change. The existence of military dictatorships around that period provided a context for that gathering, with much brutal repression, armed insurgency and ideological radicalization.

Immediately after Medellín, the Latin American churches went through a period of intense martyrdom: priests, bishops, nuns and lay people were murdered, arrested, tortured, disappeared, demonized. The book *Praxis del Martirio* (Praxis of Martyrdom), written by various authors, which was published in Colombia in 1977,[2] provides details on many cases all across Latin America (Autores Varios 1977). One of the results of Medellín was the birth of priesthood movements; already in August 1967, 17 Third World Bishops (Asia, Africa and Latin America) made a document public in which they took a clear preference for socialism and denounced the ills of capitalism as anti-evangelical. In response and in solidarity with that document, a group of Argentinian priests promoted adherence to it. Thus, the movement Sacerdotes para el Tercer Mundo (Priests for the Third World) was created, bringing together more than 500 priests in 1968. That same year (1968) the Movimiento Iglesia Joven (Movement Young Church) was created in Chile, which later evolved into the "Group of the 80," and later into the "Group of the 200," and then into the even broader movement Cristianos por el Socialismo (Christians for Socialism) during the government of Salvador Allende (1970–1973). In February 1968 the Oficina Nacional de Información Social (Social Information Bureau), ONIS, was created in Peru, led by Fr. Gustavo Gutiérrez, one of the initiators of Liberation Theology, which had a great impact on the clergy and even on some bishops. Around the same time in Colombia the Golconda group was created, led by the bishop of Buenaventura, Monseigneur Gerardo Valencia Cano. After his death, the Sacerdotes para América Latina (Priests for

Latin America) group was formed. In 1972, the Sacerdotes para el Pueblo (Priests for the People) movement was created, which later evolved into the movement Iglesia Solidaria (Solidarity Church).

The proliferation of priesthood movements taking a stand for the change of social structures and for the preferential option for the exploited classes in the name of their Christian faith, can be appreciated in the compilation of Juan J. Rossi in his book *Iglesia Latinoamericana, protesta o profecía?* (Latin American Church, Protest or Prophecy?) (Rossi 1969). There he collected 65 manifestos up to 1969. All of these documents were the expression of a genuine reflection on faith having as a starting point the concrete situation in which their authors lived, which in all cases was highly conflictive. There we find the earliest expressions of a truly Latin American Theology. The origins of Liberation Theology are to be found in these documents, many of which were not even more than a leaflet, but they all reflect the same commitments.

An important referent for Liberation Theology took place in Colombia with the testimony of Fr. Camilo Torres Restrepo. During his brief but fruitful evangelical mission, first as the chaplain at the National University (1959–1962) and then as a social and political leader (1962–1966), Camilo always emphasized as the core of the Gospel love towards the neighbor, but love had to be effective. This took him to assume very critical positions against some understanding of the Christian way of living which centered in rites, in folkloric devotion, and in collaboration with oppressive powers. Once in the National University he declared that "those who love lack faith, and those who have faith lack love," this being both a paradox and a challenge which moved him to give a radical U-turn to the role of the Christian evangelical mission. His proposal consisted in having as a fundamental criterion for Christian identity concrete and real social commitment in the struggle against injustice and in the construction of a more just society based on solidarity. Whoever demonstrated that commitment could advance towards their Christian maturity through the Catechism and through ritual celebrations deeply immersed in their commitment to the social transformation towards a just world. The convulsions of the times of Camilo led him to opt for joining a guerrilla movement: the Ejército de Liberación Nacional (National Liberation Army). Four months after joining (February 15, 1966), he encountered death amidst an armed confrontation with the state army.

When Liberation Theology was fully developed some years after Camilo's death, becoming a proposal to turn commitment into the first action, and the reflection on this commitment under the light of the Gospel as the second action, it was really following with Camilo's intuitions. At the end of the 1980s and 1990s, when the military dictatorships started to mutate into "restricted democracies" according to the language of the Trilateral Commission (USA, Western Europe and Japan), a strong movement advocating for the rights of victims and their right to know the truth, to justice and reparation, developed. The instrument for this was the project Nunca Mas (Never Again), which developed across many countries, in the majority of which the most committed sectors of the Church engaged enthusiastically. This started in Argentina with the *Sábato Report* on the disappeared, in

September 1984, and this consecrated the name of the Never Again movement. Then, in January 1985, the World Council of Churches and the Archdioceses of Sao Paulo published a book, *Brasil: Nunca Mais*, which brought together the work of a study group which had examined 707 processes of Brazilian military justice between 1964 and 1979, which dealt with crimes against humanity. Two years before, on September 26, 1983 the legal civic group Tortura Nunca Mais (Torture Never Again), whose aim was to denounce and find out the truth about crimes against the people, assuming a firm position against impunity.

In February 1989 the Servicio Paz y Justicia (Peace and Justice Service) in Uruguay made public their report *Uruguay Nunca Más*, which analysed and recounted state terror in Uruguay (Servicio Paz y Justicia 1989). By making explicit their motivations in the introduction, they stated that "beyond the basic demand for justice on behalf of the victims, we have the obligation to prevent by all means that the same happens again." In May 1990, the Comité de Iglesias del Paraguay (Committee of Paraguay Churches) made public a three-volume report *Nunca Más*, about the dictatorship of Stroesner and human rights. In the introduction they stated as their objective "not to re-open wounds which have healed or which remain open, but to prevent the collective memory to easily slip into oblivion, with the hope that the people will never allow again this reign of terror which paralysed and mutilated them over many decades." In May 1993, the Asamblea Permanent de los Derechos Humanos de Bolivia (Bolivia's Permanent Assembly for Human Rights) made public their report *Nunca Más para Bolivia* (Aguiló 1993), which collects occurrences during the period of military governments. In their introduction they make clear their objectives:

> we want to address the Armed Forces of the Nation, we do not deny this, but we do this from the loyal perspective of the staunch defence of human rights which means, concretely, the defence of the dignity of the Bolivian people in their totality... we want to tell the people that they were not wrong to resist. History will take them on board... it is important to heal the wounds of the past, but it is also important to have guarantees this will NEVER HAPPEN AGAIN.

On April 24, 1998, the Human Rights Office of the Archbishop of Guatemala presented publicly the four volume report *Guatemala Never Again* (Arzobispado de Guatemala 1998), written in 1994 as the Proyecto Interdiocesano de Recuperación de la Memoria Histórica, REMHI (Inter-diocesan Project to Recover Historical Memory). On the back cover it can be read, "Each story is a trajectory of much suffering, but also of great willingness to live. Many people came to us to let us know their story, saying "believe me." In the introduction, it can be read that

> the work of searching for the truth is not over with a report, it has to go back to its origins and support, through the elaboration of resources, ceremonies and other means, the use of memory as a mechanism of social reconstruction ... Facts ought to be remembered in a shared fashion and expressed in rituals and monuments; the devolution process needs to help to explain and clarify what happened to the best of our ability, learning the lessons for the present; devolution shouldn't be about recreating the horror or attaching a stigma on the victims, but it ought

to emphasize positive aspects for the sake of the victims' dignity and collective identity.

There were many other such processes which could be added to the list, with some gaps: the Comisión Nacional de Verdad y Reconciliación (National Truth and Reconciliation Commission) in Chile (Decree 335, April 25, 1990) and its three-volume final report of March 1991. In Colombia this process started in 1997, organized according to the territorial space of the Military Brigades, but only 3 volumes were published in the year 2000; the process has followed a slow course, because the number of victims in Colombia is many millions.

The words NEVER AGAIN synthesize and symbolize movements which had deep repercussions in many countries, movements which articulated a heinous past with a future which cannot be conditioned by the consequences of that past. These words, at the same time, refer to the impunity which some pretend to use in order to conceal the truth, to prevent the perpetrators to face justice, and to make sure that the moral and social damage caused by these crimes remains in place. These words reflect a social movement which emerged in many countries and where many Christians found a fertile ground to turn their commitment with the Gospel values into a reality. Intimately linked to this, we have to mention the commitment of many Christians, not only in Latin America but also elsewhere, to the promotion of human rights through organizations, groups, movements, denunciation work, publications, protest actions, often at great personal and collective risk and confronting resolutely the powers to be.

However, the language of human rights in international treaties is exceedingly centered on the individuals as subjects of rights. This led many socialist tendencies to denounce them as an instrument of capitalism and neoliberalism. In any case, this has been a legal instrument for the defense of oppressed communities from an individual angle, with some collective provisions, such as the concept of genocide and the systematic character inherent to the crimes against humanity. On July 4, 1976, various lawyers with an expertise in international law, together with representatives of various national liberation movements, proclaimed the Universal Declaration of the Rights of Peoples. Thus, a non-governmental instrument to promote, develop and defend the collective rights of the victims, was created. This was the origin of the Permanent Peoples Tribunals (PPT), which has created a non-state jurisdiction grounded on the ethical-political field, which has created awareness of the rights of peoples and which has denounced their violation on the international level. In Colombia, the PPT has held two sessions: in 1991 it held the final session of hearings on the impunity in which crimes against humanity remained, which were held in twelve Latin American countries. Then, between 2006 and 2008 they examined through a number of expert hearings on Multinational Corporations and the rights of the peoples of Colombia, which concluded in a final session in July 2008. The PPT practice of inviting personalities of ethical and scientific merit to examine violations against the rights of peoples, independently of any state judicial structure and irrespective of the lack of a capacity to punish or to repair, has been also used in other occasions, such as the Opinion Tribunals, which also have an important participation of Christian movements and groups.

The Churches and Peace Processes

In various Latin American countries, as well as in other parts of the world, there have been peace processes in order to overcome protracted internal armed conflicts, civil wars, and military dictatorships. It's worthy of mention the paradigmatic cases of South Africa, the Balkans, Chile, Argentina, El Salvador, Guatemala.[3] Nonetheless, none of these processes can be considered as satisfactory, for the main objective of any peace process should be to suppress the root causes of the conflict, which was achieved in none of the above cases, although some progress was made towards the possibility of a non-violent coexistence.

One of the challenges typically faced by any peace process is to discern between strategies to remember and strategies to forget. Many religious leaders, psychologists, sociologists and social activists opt for policies to help forget about the past, arguing the danger of re-opening the wounds, of perpetuating suffering, and of agitating hatred and conflict. But from another perspective, forgetting is of use to the projects and designs of the surviving powers, who typically are the perpetrators, thus silencing the dreams and designs of the victims who were eliminated and excluded from history. On the contrary, those who advocate for the strategy of memory, argue that the recovery of memory, of the dreams, of the thought of the victims is intimately linked to the restoration of their dignity. It is also linked to a public debate on the repressive policies and mechanisms used to destroy people's lives and to the clarification of responsibilities in the adoption of these criminal and anti-democratic methods to destroy lives and ideas. This has to be clarified in society's consciousness, so that the root causes of these crimes can be identified to prevent them from happening again in the future, in order to achieve a more humane coexistence.

In the context of the recent peace process in Colombia, a group of a thousand Catholics, supported by thousands of others, have come to the conclusion that in order to restore peace it is necessary to recognize the mistakes and inhumane behavior which made it possible for so much injustice and violence to take place. Among those mistakes and perverse behaviors, it is necessary to recognize the responsibility of the Catholic Church which condemned liberal and collectivist ideas, while supporting repressive governments and the establishment, who were responsible for the murder, massacre, torture and forced displacement of those who participated in social movements and in alternative parties.

Between September 2017 and August 2018 various public rituals were conducted, in which representatives of this Catholic movement asked symbolically for forgiveness from representatives of the groups, social movements and political parties who had been victimized the most, for in their repression and extermination the Catholic church played a conspicuous role, because of its ideological support to governments and social actors who victimized them, a support which was based on its visceral anti-communism. A document, signed by a thousand

Colombian Catholics between July and September 2017, asking for forgiveness was sent to Vatican and circulated in Colombia among many communities. This was organized by several base communities. Although it was proposed to the Bishops Conference of Colombia to adhere to this document, or to draft another one on this topic from their own perspective, or to call for a day of forgiveness, the Bishops Conference rejected all of these options and shunned this initiative. One of the paragraphs of the document stated the following:

> In the most intense periods of our social conflict, the problem of those lethal weapons which destroy life, has been a heavy burden testing permanently the sound nature of our Christian consciousness. To some, including bishops and priests, to kill liberals, communists or guerrillas, not only doesn't pose a moral problem, but are actually commendable actions. The Bishop of Pasto, Ezequiel Moreno, who asked to be marked over his grave headstone that "liberalism is a sin," invited openly to confront liberals with weapons in hand, and he even sold sacred chalices in order to buy weapons for the conservatives. His canonisation was deeply offensive to many Catholics in Colombia and the world, and it moves us to ask for forgiveness, even for past events, from the historical victims of that violence which has been illegitimately sanctified. Generally speaking, our church hierarchies supported the republican armed institutions from the very start, in spite of the violence of their methods and the perverse bias of those social groups and causes which they defended, thus impacting decisively the structures of exclusion, of elitism, of injustice which were progressively consolidated. From the '50s our armed forces adopted the principles and directives of the Cold War focusing on the struggle against an internal enemy which coincided with the oppressed layers of society yearning for justice. And from the '60s they adopted a paramilitary strategy imposed by the United States, which involved many civilians in the war, turning them into objectives of military attacks when their ethical and political options made them adopt anti-system positions, and into a RESERVOIR of auxiliary troops in the paramilitary hordes. The collaboration of our church with an armed force engaged in such perverse strategies, first through the Military Religious Service and then through the Military Dioceses, has produced a deep consciousness crisis in many Colombian Catholics. It is for this reason that we ask for forgiveness from the masses of Colombians victimised by this long-term military and paramilitary repression which had truly criminal dimensions, engaged in the most horrible crimes against humanity. We make a commitment to ask pope Francis to order the suppression of the Military Dioceses and to order our hierarchy to take distance from the repressive and armed institutions which have been involved systematically in such horror.

> This movement is backed by the sincere conviction that if we don't recognize our mistakes and if we don't have the will to consciously eradicate them from our practice, it will be impossible to overcome conflict and to commit ourselves to a future of peace and non-repetition of these crimes. It is this very conviction which has led many groups in Colombia to demand from the government and its armed forces to make public the manuals in which the perverse counterinsurgent military doctrine was designed, for them to reject this doctrine, recognizing their mistakes and taking concrete measures to eradicate those ideas, and to design concrete norms to avoid the repetition of the crimes which were stimulated by those manuals. This, however, has not been possible so far.

Javier Giraldo Moreno is a Jesuit priest known for his defense of human rights in Colombia and Latin America. He is particularly known for working with poor marginalized communities and for spearheading social movements involving indigenous, black, and peasants in Colombia. In 2015, he was invited as one of the historical experts to the peace talks between the Colombian government and the FARC.

Acknowledgements

This chapter was translated from Spanish by Jose Antonio Gutierrez.

Notes

1. This is mentioned in a secret document given to Colombia in February 1962 by the Special Warfare Military Training Team, or Yarborough Mission, which demanded the creation of military-civic structures in order to conduct "paramilitary terrorist actions against the adherents of Communism."
2. Numerous cases from all over Latin America are mentioned in this book. In Colombia, in 1992, the book *Aquellas Muertes que hicieron resplandecer la Vida* was published informally by various Christian movements.
3. See my book about the cases mentioned here (Giraldo 2004).

References

Aguiló, Federico. 1993. *Nunca Más para Bolivia*. Cochabamba: APDHB—IESE—UMSS.
Arzobispado de Guatemala. 1998. *Guatemala Nunca Más*. Guatemala: Arzobispado de Guatemala, Human Rights Office.
Autores Varios. 1977. *Praxis del Martirio*. Bogotá, Colombia: CEPLA Editores.
Comité de Iglesias del Paraguay. 1990. *Nunca Más: La Dictadura de Stroessner y los Derechos Humanos*. Asunción, Paraguay: Comité de Iglesias para Ayudas de Emergencia.
Gaete, Arturo. 1971a. "Socialismo y Comunismo: historia de una problemática condenación." *Mensaje* 200: 290–302.
Gaete, Arturo. 1971b. "Catolicismo Social y Marxismo en el Siglo XIX: un diálogo imposible." *Mensaje* 205: 588–602.
Gaete, Arturo. 1972a. "Los Cristianos y el Marxismo: de Pio XI a Paulo VI." *Mensaje* 209: 328–341.
Gaete, Arturo. 1972b. "Catolicismo Social y Marxismo en la Primera Mitad del Siglo XX: aún no es posible el diálogo." *Mensaje* 215: 706–716.
Giraldo, Javier S. J. 2004. *Búsqueda de Verdad y Justicia: Seis experiencias en posconflicto*. Bogotá: CINEP.
Hernández, Saúl Rodríguez. 2006. *La influencia de los Estados Unidos en el Ejército colombiano, 1951-1959*. Medellín, Colombia: Ediciones La Carreta.
McClintock, Michael. 1992. *Instruments of Statecraft*. New York: Pantheon Books.
Prada, Diego Otero. 2010. *El papel de los Estados Unidos en el conflicto colombiano*. Bogotá: Ediciones Aurora.
Rossi, J. J. 1969. *Iglesia Latinoamericana, ¿protesta o profecía?*. Avellaneda, Argentina: Ed. Búsqueda.
Servicio Paz y Justicia. 1989. *Uruguay Nunca Más*. Montevideo, Uruguay: Servicio Paz y Justicia.

Torres, Camilo. 1973. *Revolutionary Priest: His Complete Writings and Messages*, edited by John Gerassi. Harmondsworth: Penguin Books.
Wayne, Leslie. 2002. "Ejército Secreto Americano con Ánimo de Lucro." *New York Times*, 13 October.
World Council of Churches and the Archdioceses of Sao Paulo. 1985. *Brasil: Nunca Mais*. Petrópolis, Brazil: Vozes.

21

Empire, the Caribbean Church and the Gospel of Resistance

Garnett Roper

I would like to make a special appeal to the men of the army ... Brothers you come from our own people. You are killing your own brother peasants when any human order to kill must be subordinate to the law of God which says, "Thou shall not kill." No soldier is obliged to obey an order contrary to the law of God. No one has to obey an immoral law. It is high time you recovered your consciences and obeyed your consciences rather than obey a sinful order ... In the name of God, in the name of this suffering people whose cries rise to heaven more loudly each day, I implore you, I beg you, I order you in the name of God: stop the repression.
—Oscar Romero (cited in Dear 2010)

Introduction

The purpose of this chapter is to critique the role that the church has played in the protection of the rights of the people in the Caribbean. However, the purpose is more so to make a case for a more activist church where the pursuit of the rights of the people is concerned. To make this case, it will be necessary to ground the arguments in biblical exegesis. The intention is to make use of accounts of exorcism in Mark's Gospel as the locus of the argument. The hypothesis of this chapter will be that the accounts of demonization in Mark's Gospel are in part about the victims of the military occupation of Galilee and Judea by the Roman Empire. Galilee and Judea were occupied territories. It is being argued further that accounts of exorcisms in the Gospel are both about the disorientation caused by occupation and the push back and resistance against empire and also, as such, they define the role of the church in relation to empire and its minions.

This discussion must begin by celebrating the beatification and canonization of Oscar Romero by the Roman Church in 2018. Oscar Romero was the murdered Salvadorian Archbishop who was known for his commitment to the pursuit of social justice and a progressive theology. He was martyred while he served mass in 1976. Oscar Romero has been canonized as a saint recently, by Pope Francis, the Roman pontiff. In the 1970s, Archbishop Romero had been the personification of the church's role in response to the violation of rights. He had been a conservative theologian until it became self-evident to him that murder and assassinations had become political strategy in El Salvador during the 1970s. Ultimately, Archbishop

Romero fell victim to an assassin's bullet. Over the last 40 years since his assassination, the Roman Church or more precisely the Vatican has been less than unequivocal in its endorsement of this modern Christian martyr. However, the Roman Church has now saluted him for his missional life and for his paying the ultimate price. No one is surprised that it is the Papal authority of Pope Francis that has made Saint Oscar's canonization a reality.

The question that ought to be raised is whether or not Saint Oscar is a one off? Is there an ethos of advocacy and protest by the church in the region? Does the church have an institutional response of advocacy and protest in the spaces where rights are violated within the Caribbean and Central America? The history of the church in the region provides answers that are rather equivocal. When the Universal Declaration of Human Rights was made in 1948, it was the climax of a process that began with Pope Leo XIII and Pius XI. However, this matter of the protection of rights has generally been left to the determination of governments, NGOs and courts of law. This chapter will suggest that the work of advocating for one's own rights and protesting against the violation of the rights of others finds its antecedent in the Gospel of Jesus Christ. Seven decades after the Universal Declaration has been made, the demand for activism on the part of the collective Christian presence, including for both protest against rights violations and advocacy in the defense of rights, could not be more urgent.

On the one hand, this discussion of the resistance to human rights violations and the role of the church in the Caribbean is framed in the context of militarization as the new face of empire. The numbers speak for themselves in US Border enforcement, the budgetary allocations have moved from US$1.8 billion in 2008 to more than US$3.5 billion in 2017 (Rajkumar 2010). With the end of the Cold War, the domestication and mass distribution of military arsenals has grown exponentially, especially in the global South in places like the Caribbean and Africa. Militarization is only one of the ways that empire has found to make victims of people. The impact of global warming and climate change is another. While also impacting the people of the North Atlantic, global warming resulting in climate change, has disproportionately affected places like the Caribbean. Available scientific data indicate that carbon dioxide and greenhouse gas emissions from the Industrial North have accelerated global warming. The increasing frequency and intensity of tropical cyclones resulting from warmer oceans in the region have revealed deficiencies in the physical infrastructure and housing stock of the small island states of the region, adding to the story of our victimhood. The region has not contributed to global warming nearly to the same extent that it has been adversely affected by the weather systems that have worsened and intensified because of climate change. The region's fragile eco-systems and its vulnerability to economic shocks means that the region needs to make use of the multilateral forums such as the United Nations. The region must rely on elements codified in international treaties of which Caribbean nation-states are signatories in order to give itself a voice and to secure its interests. These are the very institutions that are under threat by the machinations of empire.

On the other hand, the Caribbean has been a space where the rights of the people have been violated. This was the case from the time of the first encounter between the indigenous peoples of the region, the Kalinagos, Tainos and Ciboneys and the European invaders. In some places, not only were their land and culture stolen, but their lives were also taken and they themselves were threatened with extinction. Chattel slavery was a human rights catastrophe (Patterson 2018). The development of Caribbean statehood and the achievement of political independence have rarely treated as national priorities the protection of rights for the people at the base of the population. Indeed, this has been a moot issue in regional politics. Those political ideologies and political parties that have defined the agenda of their political administration as the pursuit and guarantee of social justice for the mass of the population have failed to attract majority support at the polls, particularly after the 1970s. The exceptions to this are Cuba, St Vincent and the Grenadines, Dominica and Barbados which all, at the time of writing, have left-leaning parties as their political administration in charge of their governments.

This is the context in which the role of the church in the region has to be examined. The church in the Caribbean has been kept by various internal contortions from vigorously pursuing rights for the people as a priority. This is despite the fact that in places like Jamaica and Antigua (Ebenezer), to name only two, the Christian church was pivotal to the overthrow of chattel slavery (Roper 2012; Dick 2011). Many of Jamaica's national heroes and heroines were men and women of the church. This is true for various reasons, including the fact that the church in many places has seen itself as a product of the North Atlantic. In other places, the church is blinded or perhaps benighted by bible reading strategies that have handcuffed God into supporting whatever modern Jews in the Middle East do. As far as these reading strategies are concerned, the only rights that God is interested in, and therefore the only rights the church ought to be interested in, are the right of Israel to exist and the right to exert its political force in the Middle East. I would like to explore the options for intervention and the counter narrative constructed in the wake of push back, opposition and persecution in the experience of the Caribbean Church. The chapter contends that the church has a duty to push back through its advocacy and protest when rights are violated.

The Violation of Rights

The Caribbean was spawned as a space in which the only rights that are respected are property rights. For centuries in the Caribbean, during chattel slavery and beyond, the people that formed the majority in the population did not enjoy the right to life. Their lives could be taken away at a whim, and they did not have the franchise of land, nor did they enjoy the right to a just wage and to decent work. Though the Caribbean has gradually become a community of laws, there still remain deficits of social justice, as well as a "dip and fall back" (a throwback to the past) where the defense of human rights is concerned. In regard to the violation of rights, the following matters of context need to be made clear:

1. There are inherited and reinforced structures of marginality, disfranchisement and dispossession. The way Caribbean societies are constructed leave the mass of the population in economic and social circumstances with limited economic mobility. This is evinced in terms of landlessness and, therefore, families being reared in informal and unplanned settlements. In Jamaica, 30 percent of the population lives in squatter settlements (Cummings 2009; Wade 2012; Wilson 2018).

2. Over the last six decades after gaining political independence in Jamaica, use has been made of violence as a tool of social and political control. It has been used to engineer demographic shifts. These include violence being used as a means of ensuring the predictability of electoral results. (This has resulted in what are called political garrisons.[1] These communities are managed and controlled by political goons and henchmen. They use violence and political clientelism as tools for maintaining political uniformity and electoral predictability.) This has also resulted in the rise of criminal gangs around the trading of contrabands (including narcotics), human trafficking and money laundering and the use of extraordinary violence. Homicides (double, triple and quadruple victims) in which the victims are sprayed with bullets and the using extra-ordinary levels of violence has been a tool of trade for these gangs. The rise and use of death squads by the Jamaican Constabulary Force has also developed in response to the extraordinary violence used by these criminal gangs. These death squads mimic and replicate the violence and tactics of urban gangs and carry out targeted assassinations against so-called high value targets. A police commissioner was forced to resign from the Jamaican Constabulary Force (JCF) after his US visitor's visa was cancelled by the US Embassy in Kingston; the use of death squads by the JCF has surfaced as one of the ostensible causes of his forced resignation. Subsequent to the resignation of the former police Commissioner, there have been arrests, trials and convictions secured in murder trials of members of the JCF that are alleged to have carried out these assassinations. Some of those convicted have claimed that they were following the orders from their superiors in the JCF.[2] None of these superiors have been brought to trial.

3. People at the base of the population are treated as disposable things that must be swept away without being consulted, relocated or compensated, all to make way for major economic and infrastructure projects. A national identification law, called the NIDS, was successfully challenged and defeated before the Jamaican Supreme Court. The NIDS was deemed unconstitutional because it required the collection and storage of people's biometric data and no person

living in Jamaica could access services—including medical services—without presentation of a NIDS Identification card. Importantly, the bill was enforced before it was defeated in the courts even though there had been no attempt to consult the people about the NIDS law before it was enacted.

4. As a result of Jamaica's location on the periphery of empire, there has been widespread distribution of guns and ammunition. Jamaica has porous borders and is located along shipping lanes from the Panama Canal to the Eastern Seaboard of the USA. It is therefore ideally located for the transshipment of narcotics. Additionally, because of its proximity to the USA—the world's most significant weapons manufacturing economy with permissive gun laws—Jamaica has an oversupply of guns and ammunition. This is in spite of the fact that Jamaica does not manufacture guns.

The violation of rights not only entails human rights failures, but also means a violation of civil liberties, as well as political, social and cultural rights.[3] In general it is thought that the fundamental contribution of the church, in response to the violation of human rights, has been made by Pope Leo XIII and Pope Pius XII. Leo XIII's *Rerum Novarum* is rightly acknowledged as the *Magna Carta* of socio-economic reconstruction of the modern era.

> Human rights receive forceful vindication in *Quadragesimo Anno*, where Pius XI sets out not merely a positive formulation of human rights but also the general requirements of the common good with the duty of public authority to ensure proper development of social and economic conditions as the pre-condition for the actual realization of the variety of human rights.
> (Pontifical Commission 2011)

The Resistance to Legion

For the sake of this chapter, however, I would like to lay a foundation in respect of the struggle against the violation of rights from within the Gospels. In particular, I would like to suggest some things that we learn from the Gospel account of exorcism in Mark's Gospel. The first is that in the account of demonization of Mark, we see a connection between the violation of rights (the denial of the full humanity of people in the socio-cultural economic and political situation created by empire) on the one hand, and, on the other hand, militarization. Secondly, in the Gospel account of Legion, it is made plain that the real struggle arises not so much prior to liberation/exorcism but in the pushback afterwards by empire. It arises from palace guards and gatekeepers, after attempts have been made to humanize those victimized by the actions and excesses of empire. Thirdly, the legion narrative in Mark's Gospel calls attention to an implied relationship to three factors at play: there is the military occupation by the Roman legion, there is the instance of large corporations (evinced by the large farm with 2000 pigs) and the role of the cultured despisers who, by promoting a particular narrative, lead the charge to evict Jesus from the region. Fourthly, the account highlights the task of the church in resisting oppression, in relieving distress and in deconstructing the infrastructure that supports and effects repression. It is also profoundly the task of the church to tackle the interiorization of the systems of oppression (my name is legion) and the valorization of the circumstances and the means of their distress by the victims themselves. This is the most recalcitrant and difficult task of all; to root out the self-abnegation, self-flagellation and self-doubt of oppressed peoples in the region is neither easy nor immediately rewarding. The majority black population in the region exists in an environment in which they have no real narrative of their own, but they are a footnote to the narrative of others. They imbibe image of themselves that ascribe them roles, rendering them as nothing more than mimic men and women, minstrel performers of their own song.

The case that demonization as presented in the Gospel of Mark is a way of speaking about the victims of militarization remains to be made in the eyes of many. I believe, however, that I have made the case in Roper (2012: 93). I assert that references to demons and evil spirits throughout Mark's Gospel are a part of the hidden transcript—which is a way of speaking about empire and a way of betraying the oppression by evil forces upon the lives of the people in the far-flung places of empire. The use of the word "legion" at the time when Mark wrote his gospel inevitably invoked dread and terror, deepening the sense of trauma among the peoples of Galilee. Legions were the strike force of Roman imperialism.

The relationship between imperial Rome and its subjects in places like Galilee was simple: the taxes and tributes extracted from the people maintained and fed the legions occupying the land—the most visible face of Roman empire and Roman oppression. The revenue taken on the backs of the people sponsored the elaborate games at the center of the empire that were the circus for the oppressed classes. Any failure to comply with their obligations to pay tributes, revenues, duties and taxes was met with firm, resolute and brutal measures, of which crucifixion was the most extreme punishment. From the point of view of these actions to stamp out rebellion and quell dissent, legions were seen as the prime enforcers.

The general view that the legion narrative is about derangement and schizophrenia would not adequately explain the presence of the details that Mark provides in the miracle account. It is also argued that legion is a representation of many like him that are affected by the disorder disintegration and the same derangement throughout the land. The issue however is not what the man was but how the writer uses the account of legion. Demon possession in the Gospel of Mark seems to have a wider reference than simply to schizophrenia or madness. The encounter with legion is being used, at least in part, to speak about the encounter of the people of the land with the occupying force. This is why the narrative is suffused with military language. However, while the occupying force is the representative of the evil that has brought disorientation, disorder, life diminution and destruction, the occupying force does not exhaust the evil in the land; evil always has a surplus dimension.

One of the outcomes of the legion narrative is that it encourages the liberating witness of the church in the context where people are made victims by empire with its life diminishing and life destroying capacity, and it is to cause the church's own praxis to evolve in close proximity to Jesus's praxis. The real lesson from the legion narrative of Mark 5 is the point made by the denouement of the dramatic parable. In the resolution, Jesus is asked to leave the region by the self-appointed gatekeepers of the region.

Mark, in setting out the Gospel of Jesus as the Son of God from the *locus imperium*, is reflecting on the nature of the powers. In this respect, his work is similar to the treatment by the Ephesian correspondence and by the Apocalypse of John. Like them, Mark sets out the powers as a parody of the Trinity. In Mark 3, there is a triad of forces: they are Satan, Beelzebub and the demons. In the exorcism of the Gerasene demoniac, and in particular in the denouement of the narrative, three representatives of the powers are shown. Among these, "legion" is the name of the Roman military force stationed in Galilee that has wreaked havoc in the region whenever there have been protestations and rebellions against Roman rule. There is also the substantial commercial interest represented by the pig farm with two thousand pigs. Finally, there are the representatives of civil society, the cultured despisers who appoint and present themselves to speak on behalf of the people of the land.

Mark uses linguistic parallels to establish the link between legion, the vanquished and exorcised forces of evil, and those who came to plead with Jesus to leave the region. The demons pleaded earnestly (*kai prekalai auton polla*) for Jesus not to banish them from the land. The spokespersons and gatekeepers pleaded with (*kai erxanto parakalein auton*) Jesus to leave their region. The narrative sets out the common design between the demonic host (legion) and the civic and commercial interests. One is cause, but the other is complicit. One is vanquished, but the other mounts a rearguard action for the sake of legion. One is imperial and hegemonic, but the other is cultural and ideological. One is the oppression that is defeated in the revolution to bring about liberation, but the other is the counter-revolution to keep imperial interests in their place (Roper 2012: 112–113).

Fighting the Legion in the Caribbean

All of the above must be taken into account in terms of what is seen of the church's response to a context where the violation of rights is common place. In the Caribbean, decisions do not privilege ordinary citizens. Their rights are often abrogated in favor of what are thought to be long-term economic goals that benefit the already privileged. I refer to two sets of incidents in which the rights for ordinary Jamaicans have been imperiled.

The first has to do with the vendors in the Constant Spring Market in St Andrew. The Constant Spring Market was built in 1965 and many of those who ply their wares there have been there since that time. Altogether, some seventy eight persons are vendors and service providers at the Constant Spring Market. In January of 2018, all the vendors at the market were given notice to quit the market by

March 2018. The notice was not provided in writing. This was the case despite the fact that all the vendors had been duly licensed by the Kingston and St Andrew Municipal Corporation, the body responsible for markets. The vendors were also up to date with the payments of all market dues and fees. The KSAMC indicated that the market needed to be demolished in order to facilitate the widening of the Constant Spring Road. The road widening project is a US$21 million project that is itself part of broader modernization and gentrification program for the Kingston Metropolitan Region.

What makes this a matter of rights rather than simply a matter of the privity of contract include a number of factors. First, the vendors were entitled by law to receive written notice. In all the circumstances, the notice ought to be for a period sufficient to permit them to be able to make other arrangements for themselves. No written notice was given at the time. Secondly, since this matter has to do with their livelihoods that were being lost, the least that could be expected from the governing authorities was the offer (if not the provision) of reasonable compensation for the loss of their livelihoods. Thirdly, as the vendors have contended from the very beginning, only thirteen feet of the present market building is needed for the widening of the road. The land on which the market is situated along with the market itself is 262 feet wide. Therefore, space is sufficient to both widen the road and relocate the vendors on the present plot of land. This would be important because accommodating the market in that location would allow the vendors to continue to serve their customers and clients that they have served for many years. Fourthly, the reluctance of the government to consider and pursue this option betrays the real intention. Since the Constant Spring Market is adjacent to the very opulent Manor Park Plaza and generally high-end real estate, the road widening project is a ruse to get rid of the market and the vendors from that area. In this respect, the displacement of the Constant Spring Market vendors is not dissimilar to what was done in Durban South Africa during the heady days of Apartheid to displace Indian villages to make space for white people. It is also similar to what Ahab and Queen Jezebel in the Dynasty of the Omrides in Israel did to Naboth when he needed to make space to build a palace garden in an Ahab gentrification and palace beautification project (Roper 2018). In this respect, there is a moral imperative that arises from the way in which this matter is addressed. The matter of the Constant Market vendor is also similar to any reading of how Palestinians are treated in their own homeland. There is a common issue there. In all of these instances, it is to give cause to the idea that development is meant to be for some members of society but not for others.

Another set of issues to which this chapter alludes is the operations of death squads within the JCF. This matter is not new and is not peculiar to Jamaica. Both Trinidad and Tobago and Guyana make similar allegations about the operations of death squads in those jurisdictions. In the case of Guyana, the assassination of the late Professor Walter Rodney has been attributed to the work of a death squad many years ago. Recently corporal of police Colin Chucky Brown was convicted on all three counts of murders and attempted murders committed in Clarendon between 2009 and 2012. In his evidence, Brown indicated that he was recruited (and specially selected) for this purpose, instructed by his superiors and resourced to carry out these assassinations (Star 2018; Loop News 2018). The assertion that we can make without fear of contradiction is that it is a part of policing strategy in Jamaica to use targeted assassination. This is a further deterioration from even what happened before, when there was the disproportionate use of force, and there was evidence of high numbers of victims of police homicide that were merely extra-judicial killings. The evidence before the court was that members of the JCF mimic gang activity by carrying out the killing of persons of interest as it they were gangland killings. In one instance, for which Chucky Brown was convicted, the first attempt was incomplete and the police returned to the hospital bed and assassinated the target while he was recovering from his wounds. The police were confident that the gullible public would merely assume that this was reprisal for the set of gang activities.

What both the situation of the vendors of Constant Spring Market and the police death squad in Clarendon have in common is the lack of advocacy or protest and solidarity on the part of the church. On behalf of the vendors, I have managed to mobilize a team of lawyers including attorneys at law Bert Samuels and Daynia Allen (who is also my executive assistant). They filed an injunction against the first deadline which was set for March 30, 2018. This injunction was granted and extended until June. When the court lifted the injunction to allow the parties to continue discussions in June, the KSAMC immediately gave the vendors written notices to quit by September 30, 2018. We have however continued the negotiation and protest until we have come to a position in which the government is offering to pay compensation. It would rather pay compensation than have vendors remain in the opulent Manor Park District. Negotiations are ongoing and, as they say, *alutha continua*: the struggle continues.

The silence by the church and the absence of solidarity, advocacy and protest in the face of the violation of rights is the result of the relationships that the church has forged for itself because of how the church wishes to position itself. The reasons for the somewhat insular approach by the church in the region in response to the violation of rights are many. To begin with, the majority church in the region is the American church. A census of Jamaica's population has revealed that Seventh Day Adventists, Pentecostals and members of the Church of God are the most populous religious groups in Jamaica. These are followed in the census by Jamaica Baptist Union. Roman Catholics, Anglicans and other churches from Europe follow behind. Ashley Smith, a retired elder statesman of the Caribbean, pointed out in a 1982 unpublished paper that "American hegemony is manifest not only in the spheres of politics, economics and culture but also in religion. He has argued further that in fact it is mainly through religion that the Americanization of the region has been effective and is being perfected" (Smith 1982).

Smith has pointed out that the affinity of new line churches to American hegemony is resonant with the experiences among the poorer classes that see the USA as a place of opportunity, where one can get a start, get a break and achieve educational aspirations for themselves and their children. Smith's writing echoed English and Scottish views about the deficiencies in everything that was

American. This was especially the case in areas of dogmatics, liturgics, and evangelism. According to Smith, during the 1940s most Pentecostal churches emerged in the region with the support of American evangelists and American capital. This period has been followed on by an acceleration of the Americanization of evangelization of the under-class, which has also been accompanied by assistance to the under-class for self-expression and economic advancement. Despite the justifiable criticism by mainline churches that American approaches to evangelism were deemed to be coercive and contributory to an inauthentic Christian experience, churches with American origin and support have grown exponentially in the region. In fact, in some instances, the American connection has proven to be a key point of appeal and is credited as the reason they succeed and grow. This is in part why the churches come complete with an American accent to boot. The net effect, therefore, is that the churches originate in the USA, are supported by the USA (by way of donations, a supply of educational resources for schools and capital grants for church buildings), and frequently are facilitating of pathways to migration to the USA (Smith 1982).

The significance of this for the agenda of the church is quite predictable. There is no surprise that he who pays the piper calls the tune. It is therefore unsurprising that the agenda of this section of the church in the region is completely aligned with the agenda the evangelical right in the USA. The culture wars against those with minority sexual orientation and against those seeking abortion indicate that this section of the church in the region has been completely coopted by the emissaries of the North Atlantic. First, this section of the church is prepared to ignore (or at least make no public comment against) any atrocity in the social context, but are on high alert when it has to do with homosexuality and abortion. Beyond that, the church has been befuddled in its response to the violation of rights in the context in which it finds itself. The paradigm that the church wishes to follow is the separation of church and state, which is the model in the USA. Neither law nor precedent in the region requires the separation of church and state. This is the reason that advocacy and protest against the violation of rights has been left to governments and NGOs, with the church feeling no obligation to be a moral leader in this regard. Still another limitation on the effective ministry, which reveals itself in the failure to respond to these issues, is that the American extract church in the region promotes a privatized gospel. The reading strategy employed by this section of the church is a dispensational one. It is ambivalent about the future of the world. As far as it is concerned, the earth is going to be destroyed. If the building is going to be demolished, why change the wallpaper? The violation of rights is par for the course—the church's business is to save souls, and such matters will attend to themselves. At the same time that it promotes this privatized approach in response to demands for social action, this section of the church is quite activist in money matters. There has been an alliance both with the agenda of capital, and with political parties that offer it certain guarantees and allow it to enjoy power by proximity to the sources of power. Where those things are concerned, the church has been quite overt in the offer of its political support and the making of political pronouncements. This is the case in

Jamaica, with Seventh Day Adventists that overtly support the governing Jamaica Labour Party, which is proud of its affinity to the Republican Party in the USA. It has also been the position taken by Pentecostal denominations, such as the New Testament Church of God.[4]

The majority church is at worst co-opted by empire and at best confused by the agenda of empire. The only issues that the church in the region is fired up about are culture wars issues like the supposed "gay agenda" and matters related to abortion. The church has pursued with zeal its protest against any potential for an amendment of the buggery law or the law to legalize abortion. Ironically, both of these matters put the church in the region at odds with the pursuit of certain rights. In some instances, the church pursues these matters because it is sponsored. In other instances, its outrage is orchestrated by the agenda of others. As long as the church is bogged down in the fight to chase the gays out of town, it has no time to see anything else. This is not the only way it works, but, in this instance, the church has remained loyal to the agenda of the evangelical right in the metropoles to the north of the Caribbean. The issues there that have led to the galvanizing, mobilizing, internationalization of certain culture wars relate to ruses to make America white again. It has nothing really to do with us, or anything to do with morality.

The majority church lacks the hermeneutical lenses to read both text and context. This is not by accident, but theological problems are hermeneutical problems. Additionally, the church is a victim of its own inertia and insularity where mission and ecumenism are concerned. Churches in the global South need to rediscover each other. This is the reason that fora, such as the DARE conferences, are essential to the way forward. This allows us to compare notes and share paradigms pastoral practices. It is the strategy of empire to keep us distracted and divided. Our conversations with each other, such as these fora are our push back and resistance.

The Caribbean as a postcolonial space has been marked both by a steady push back against the violation of rights, and by processes to ensure the enfranchisement of the masses of the people at the base of the population. In that regard, those who participated in and contributed to that struggle have included the Jamaican government, including through engaging political administrations from both sides of the aisle. These include the work of the Parliament under the Nettleford Commission (1997-2002) that changed the meaning of the color black in the Jamaica flag. (The Jamaican flag is black, green and gold. The color black hitherto meant hardship. The Nettleford Commission changed it to mean resilience.) This was part of a larger project to lift the self-confidence of the majority black population. The commission also resulted in the annual public holiday of August 1 in order to commemorate our emancipation from chattel slavery. It also resulted in the building of the Emancipation Park within the capital city of Kingston. While the Nettleford Commission was the work of the People's National Party, it was under the watch of the Jamaica Labour Party that the Charter of Rights was enshrined in the Jamaican constitution in 2011. This has given legal and constitutional backing to the civil liberties and rights of all Jamaican people.

This work has also included the contributions of civil society. The work of the Jamaican Council for Human Rights in the period beginning in the 1970s has been absolutely foundational. They were succeeded by a much more flamboyant media darling called, Jamaicans for Justice. Their success was to turn the searchlight on, among other things, the high rate of homicides at the hands of the police. Perhaps the most stellar (if underrated) contribution has been made in this regard by the combination of individual churchgoers and individual congregations. I name Father Hugh Sherlock, a Methodist Minister who also penned the words to Jamaican National Anthem and who developed Boys Town in the western end of the capital city in a tough urban neighborhood. Among other things, Sherlock used sports as a vehicle to re-socialize youth and to create a pathway to mainstreaming them. Of much more recent vintage is the work of Bethel Baptist Church, which has used holism in ministry and literacy initiatives aimed at street boys and the offer of a shower to the homeless as a way of rescuing people absolutely on the edge. The Jamaica Baptist Union has been singular in the struggle to enhance dignity and to create possibilities for Jamaicans within and outside of their congregation. They are not alone in this. The Anglicans may also wish to state their claims in terms of their work in education.

Conclusion

My own work in the 1980s and 1990s, while I served as a pastor in the tough urban ghettos of inner Kingston, confronted me with the violation of rights, largely through the interface between inner city youths and actors of the Jamaican state. I defined the role of the church then as one in which the ministries of the church supplement and complement provisions of the state for vulnerable populations, one in which the church pioneers and innovates ministries to minorities and the excluded, one in which the church advocates for the voiceless and spoken against. At that time, I worked with Tyrone Reddie from the Anglicans and Brian Massie from the Roman Catholics to get the then-Minister of Justice Karl Rattary to reinstate the Board of Visitors for correctional institutions, including for maximum-security facilities. I served for almost 20 years as chairman of the Board of Visitors of the Tower Street Adult Correction facility, the largest maximum-security facility in the island. Through the work of Board of Visitors, we ensured the protection of rights of inmates and gradually saw an improvement in the quality the circumstances of their incarceration. We did this with the goal of decreasing recidivism and facilitating the rehabilitation of inmates. That work of the board of visitors has since largely been taken up by very activist lay magistrate associations across the island. When it comes to the violation of rights, the more things change the more they remain the same. Those in whose interest the rights of the people are violated will find new ways to serve their interest. Therefore, eternal vigilance is the first and last duty. The church needs to bring all hands on deck in order to make Jamaica and the Caribbean a space where human beings flourish.

Garnett Roper is the president of Jamaica Theological Seminary (JTS), who has pastored three congregations over a period of 35 years in Jamaica. He has been a radio preacher on *Grace Hour* for more than forty years, and published works such as *Caribbean Theology as Public Theology* (2012), *Who God Bless No Man Curse* (2016), and *Thus Says the Lord: Responding to the Resurgence of Empire* (2018).

Notes

1. There have been developments in Jamaican law that have annulled the results of political elections where it has been demonstrated that violence was used in a manner that influenced the outcome of those elections.
2. This has a history going all the way to Back O Wall in West Kingston that was demolished in 1966 in order to build the Tivoli Gardens community, which resulted in the dispersal of the residents of Back O Wall to create communities like Sufferers' Heights and Bull Bay. More recently there was the dislocation of the Constant Spring Market vendors when the market in which they earned their livelihoods was demolished in order to widen the thoroughfare. The vendors, some of whom have been earning a living by selling in the market for more than 50 years were never compensated.
3. The matter of sporting dreadlocks (the hairstyle that is grounded in Rastafarian religious belief but is also sported by non-Rastafarian) is moot because the dreadlocks hairstyle is not permitted for persons in certain public sector jobs, most notably within the security forces. There are matters presently being litigated in the Jamaican courts in which children bearing dreadlocks have been barred from school.
4. The present Jamaican head of state, the Governor General, Sir Patrick Allen is a former head of the SDA in Jamaica and the current Prime Minister Andrew Holness and his wife Juliet Holness MP as well as other members of his cabinet are members of the SDA faith. In 1980, in a previous JLP administration, Bishop Herro Blair of the Deliverance Centre and the NT COG made very public their endorsement of the Edward Seaga led administration. Such public political endorsements were at that time completely counter-posed to what they had preached about partisan political engagements.

References

Cummings, Victor. 2009. "The Problem of Squatting in Jamaica." Retrieved from http://mobile.jamaicagleaner.com/20090524/news/news1.php (accessed October 3, 2019).

Dear, John. 2010. "Romero's Resurrection." Retrieved from www.ncronline.org/blogs/road-peace/romeros-resurrection (accessed September 20, 2019).

Dick, Devon. 2011. *The Cross and the Machete: Native Baptist in Jamaica, Identity, Ministry and Legacy*. Kingston: Ian Randle Publishers.

Loop News. 2018. "Police Commissioner Issues Statement on "Chucky" Brown's Conviction." Retrieved from www.loopjamaica.com/content/police-commissioner-issues-statement-chucky-browns-conviction (accessed October 1, 2019).

Patterson, Orlando. 2018. *Slavery and Social Death*. Cambridge, MA: Harvard University Press.

Pontifical Commission. 2011. *The Church and Human Rights*. Retrieved from www.clerus.org/clerus/dati/2011-07/23-13/The_Church_and_Human_Rights.pdf (accessed October 4, 2019).

Rajkumar, Peniel. 2010. *Dalit Theology and Dalit Liberation: Problem, Paradigms and Possibilities*. Farnham: Ashgate.

Roper, Garnett. 2012. *Caribbean Theology as Public Theology*. Kingston: Jugaro Publishing House.

Roper, Garnett. 2018. "Constant Spring Market the New Naboth's Vineyard." *Gleaner*, August.

Star. 2018. "Killer Cop Convicted! Constable 'Chucky' Brown Found Guilty of Murder." Retrieved from http://jamaica-star.com/article/news/20181115/killer-cop-convicted-constable-%E2%80%98chucky%E2%80%99-brown-found-guilty-murder (accessed September 3, 2019).

Wade, Barry. 2012. "Landlessness, Squatting and Environmental Refugees in Jamaica: A Role for Environmental Professionals." Retrieved from http://jiep.org/drupal/sites/default/files/ENVIRONMENTAL%20JUSTICE%20-%20B%20Wade%20paper%20dec32012.pdf (accessed October 5, 2019).

Wilson, Nadine. 2018. "Ministry to Spend Big on Squatting Census." Retrieved from http://jamaica-gleaner.com/article/lead-stories/20180603/ministry-spend-big-squatting-census (accessed October 3, 2019).

Index

Abe government, Japan 82–83, 84–87, 88, 92
abortion 378, 379
Abu Ghraib 57–59
accumulation by dispossession 277–279, 288–305
ADB *see* Asian Development Bank
aerial warfare 27–28
Afghanistan 54, 60, 132, 183
Africa 70, 255–256, 339–353
Afro-descendants 77
agency 7
alienation 103, 104, 110, 327–332, 349
alliances
    China-Russia 270, 271, 275
    neo-colonial 251
    Pacific Islands 324
    South Asia 180
    structural genocide 98
    territorial boundaries/ inter-European rivalries 29–30
    UK–US alliances 30–31, 104–105, 253–257
America *see* United States of America
America First 265
American-European-Japanese trilateral hegemony 64–65
ancestral lands 312–313
Anglo-American factors 26, 30–31, 32, 36, 64–65
anti-base movements 16, 88–91
anti-collectivism 357
anti-colonialism 13–14, 26, 30, 35, 213–232
anti-communism 64–65, 356–361
anti-imperialism 64–80
anti-nuclear campaigns 17
anti-terror self-protective Atlantic Liberalism 67
anti-violence stances 133, 135
Apartheid 17, 339, 341, 342, 344, 350
apathy to suffering 208
APDP *see* Association of Parents of Disappeared Persons

Arab Spring 59–60
archaeological evidence 217, 234, 237–238
Argentina 362–363
armed conflicts 115–117, 279–281
    see also war
armed forces 34–37, 38, 105–107, 114–126, 128
arms trade 36, 252–253, 276–277, 351, 373
Asia 252, 257, 258–259, 263, 264, 291
    see also South Asia
Asian decedents 77–78
Asian Development Bank (ADB) 331–332
Asian liberation theologies 214
Association of Parents of Disappeared Persons (APDP) 118, 121, 123–124
Assyrian Empire 235, 242, 243
asylum-seekers 36–37
atheism 359
Atlantic Charter 65
Atlantic hegemony 64
Atlantic Liberalism 10, 66, 67–68
atolls 325, 326
Australia 324, 325
Ayotzinapa, Mexico 15, 288, 290, 298–299
Azadi rallies 115

Bahrain 255
Bangladesh 32
banking sector 297–298
Baptist Church 380
Bayonet Constitution 310
Bethel Baptist Church 380
biblical narratives 1, 13–14, 213–232, 233–247
biblical-theological frameworks 184–193
Biko, Steve 339, 343
billionaires 273
Birzeit student group 161, 169–171
black people 339, 341–342, 343, 347–349, 374, 379
Black Theology 213–214
blood of martyrs 188–189

Blue Colonialism 17, 332–335
Bolivia 257, 363
border peace 282–283
Bougainville, Papua New Guinea 329–330
Brazil 257, 363
Britain *see* United Kingdom
British colonialism 9–10, 29–30, 34–35, 98–100
  see also colonialism
Brzezinski Doctrine 257, 258–259, 264
Buddhism 130, 183–184, 208, 209
Bush administration 53–55, 56, 58, 315

Canaan conquest/settlement 213–232, 233, 236–238
capital 50–51, 262, 272, 273, 278–279
capitalism
  globalization 10, 45, 46–49
  modernity 2, 15, 26, 98–99
  neocolonialism 251–305
  soft power 58
capitalist-patriarchal world 272
Caribbean islands 18–19, 369–382
Carnatic wars 99
Catholic Church 357–361, 369–370, 373
CCK *see* Christian Council of Korea
Chamber of Princes 38
chattel slavery 371, 379
Chile 257, 361, 364
China 32, 36, 37, 69–72, 84, 251–269, 275–276, 324
China-Russia Alliance 270, 271, 275
Chinese Occidentalism 68
Christian Council of Korea (CCK) 134–135
Christian triumphalism 205, 209
Christianity
  Africa 347
  anti-colonialism 13–14, 213–232
  anti-communism 357
  conscientious objection 134–136
  Israel 235
  low intensity conflict 350
  oppression 209
  South Asia 179–180, 184–193
civil society 375, 380
civil wars 280, 292
class 164–165, 166, 168, 172, 300, 301–302, 360
client states 84, 88–89, 91

climate change 17, 335, 370
Cold War 3, 4, 10–11, 32–33, 128, 257–261, 263
  see also new Cold War; post-Cold War
collective approaches
  OBOR project 71–72
  Okinawan struggle 142–143, 153, 154
  Pacific Ocean 335
  rights 364
  structural genocide 97, 98
  women 119–120, 120–122
Colombia 18, 257, 282–283, 354–355, 360–366
colonialism
  alienation 349
  alliances 180
  black African people 339, 343
  blue 332–335
  ethno-national conflicts 25–44
  expansion 69–72, 99–100
  genocide 97–98, 204
  governance 33–34
  imperial grand strategy 251–269
  land tenure 328–329, 330
  legitimate conquest 218
  necropolitical capitalism 288
  settler 216–217, 220
  state formations 29, 308–309
  treaties 28–29
  war on terror 32
colonization 102–104, 108–110, 340, 348–349
common goods 296, 301, 336, 373
communal land ownership 328
communism
  containing 30–31
  demonization of 357, 358–360
  Korean War 202, 203, 205
  Latin America 354, 355, 356
  South Korea 131
community level 119–120, 180, 281, 284
Compacts of Free Association 323
compulsory military service 12
the Concert of Vienna, 1815 29, 37
conflicts 10, 25–44, 275
  see also war
conformist mentality 335
Congress of Vienna, 1815 99
conquest 13, 213–229

conscientious objection 127–140
conscription *see* mandatory military service
Constant Spring Market, Jamaica 375–376, 377
Constantine's Empire 188
corporate mercantilism 46
cosmovision 2–3, 8, 17–18, 347–350
Council of World Missions (CWM) 6
counter-hegemony 132, 137, 291, 297, 300, 302
counter-imperialism 13–14, 233–247
counter-insurgency 7, 17, 100, 104–105
coup d'état 310–311
crimes against humanity 102, 363, 364, 366
criminality 15–16, 136, 289–290, 298, 372
critical textual analysis 215–217
critically self-reflective practice 7–8, 143
crown colonies 33, 100
crucifixion 188
Cuba 259–260
cultural aspects
    hegemony 58–59
    low intensity conflict 347–349
    OBOR project 71–72
    Okinawan struggle 153
    Pacific Islands 312–313, 315, 320, 324–325
cultural-ideological offensive 52–53
cultured despisers 373–374, 375
currency markets 46–48, 263
customary land tenure 328–332, 336
CWM *see* Council of World Missions
cynical capitalism 289, 294

David and Goliath 185–186
de-cold war 128
de-imperialization 178–247
de-professionalization of armed bodies 356
death squads 372, 376–377
debilitation 204–205
debt 46, 293, 298
decentralized despotism 346–347
decision making 145, 147, 154–155
deep sea mining 332–333, 334–335
defense agreements 33
defense budgets 82–83, 128, 313
defensive nationalism 292–293
dehumanized enemies 54, 55

deindustrialization 296
democracy
    buffer zones 341
    ethics 15
    imperialism 357
    indigenous peoples 17, 343
    participatory 153, 155
    peace 282
    restoring 4–5
    social solidarity 52
demonization 19, 60–61, 107–108, 158, 220, 357–360, 369, 373–374
denuclearization 69
dependent militarization 81, 82
dependent state powers 255–256
deployment 35, 38, 66
deregulation 45–46, 49
derivatives trade 47
development
    inequality and rights 376
    land acquisition 103, 104, 110, 150–151, 155, 329, 331
    neo-colonialism 256
    OBOR project 70–72
    peace 283
    post-independence 344–345
dialogue for reconciliation 64–80
direct action 141–157
disappeared people 114–126, 362–363
displacement 151–153, 183–184, 190–191, 279–280, 376
disposable populations 372–373
dispossession, accumulation by 15, 270, 274, 277–279, 288–305
dispossession of land 306, 327–332
divide-and-rule strategies 144
divine
    commandment 220, 223, 224, 228–229
    power 178, 179–180, 189
    punishment 219, 223, 227
DMZ-Hawai'i/Aloha 'Āina 317–318
domestic manufacturing industry 251
domestic roles 114–126
domestically oriented militarism 25, 255–256
domination 223, 224, 270–271, 274, 354
dominion status 34
DPRK *see* North Korea
drug trafficking 355

earthquakes 283
East Asia 11, 13, 81–96
East Asian Occidentalism 65–66
East–West axis 270, 275
eco-human rights 75
eco-humanity 19
economic factors
   accumulation by dispossession 288–302
   Blue Colonialism 333, 334
   concessions 105
   conscientious objection 136
   development 150–151, 242
   disappearances 117–118, 120
   growth 84, 182–183
   imperial grand strategy 251–252, 261–263
   knowledge militarization 339–353
   military bases 313
   mobility 372
   political unrest 314–315
   women's movements 168
   see also financial factors
Ecuador 257, 282–283
education 166
Eelam Tamil, Sri Lanka 11, 97–113, 252
El Salvador 369–370
elections 85, 169–170
emerging economies 271
empathy 3, 198–212
employment 166, 168
empowerment 158–177
encirclement of China 36, 37
end of history 52, 53, 270, 271, 279
endemic intervention 49–51
endogenous collective development 71–72, 72–73
endogenous human rights 73–74, 76
enemies 54, 55, 127–140, 180, 181, 181–182, 203
energy deposits 296–297
enforced disappearances 114–126
environmental factors 312, 315–317, 325–326, 333, 334–335
ethnicity 35, 235–236, 280, 324–325
ethno-national conflicts 10, 25–44
Eurasia 258–259, 291
Eurocentrism 341–342, 347
evangelism 378, 379
everyday struggle 114–126

everyone is a representative of the struggle 147, 148, 149–155
evictions 316–317, 376, 377
exchange-traded derivatives 47
existential threats 323–338
the Exodus 213–215, 218, 234, 235, 236–237, 245
exogenous human rights 76–77
exorcism 369, 373–374
exploitation 10, 332–335
express rail links 86–87
extractive invasion 279
extraordinary rendition 55
extreme Other 281–282

factional loyalties 165
family organization 114–126
Far East Occidentalists 67–68
fascism 281
female Hamas activists 158–177
feminism 158–177, 198–212
Fiji 328–329
financial factors 46–49, 274, 277–278
   see also economic factors
fishing 110, 150–151
food subordination 297, 300
forgiveness 365–366
forgotten war *see* Korean War
forward deployment 66, 261
fourth generation human rights 76–77
France 326, 327
free trade agreements 257
free-market logic 107, 110
freedom fighters 60
French Revolution 358
friend-foe culture 356
fuel theft 299
Fukushima 86
fundamentalism 3–5, 7, 8, 12, 182, 183

gambling law 86
gang mimicry 377
garrison states 36, 344
Gaza, Palestine 12, 158–159
gender 161, 167, 170–171, 173, 202–203, 209
General Assembly, United Nations 37–38
General Union of Palestinian Women (GUPW) 164
generic goods 296, 301

Geneva Convention 54
genocide 38, 97–113, 199, 200–202, 204, 216–217, 219, 228
  see also massacres
genuine security 319
geopolitics 29–30, 32–33, 36, 81–113, 234, 251–269, 271, 281
  see also politics
giants of Canaan 224–225
Global Financial Network 47
global level 5, 53–54, 64–65, 252–253, 291, 293, 295, 296
  see also international level
global warming 370
globalist-geopolitical approaches 271
globalization 10, 23–80, 272, 273, 295
GMEP *see* Greater Middle Eastern Project
God 220, 228–229, 233, 237, 239, 242, 249
God versus Goliath 178–197
goods 34, 295–296, 301
Gospel of resistance 369–382
governance 25–26, 33–35, 50, 58
grassroots organizations 109
grassroots participatory democracy 147–148
Greater Middle Eastern Project (GMEP) 58
Guatemala 363–364
GUPW *see* General Union of Palestinian Women
Guyana 376

half-widows 116, 117–119, 121–122
Hamas 158–177
Hawai'i 16, 306–322
headscarves 158–159, 161, 169, 174
hegemonic masculinity 12, 132, 136–138
hegemony
  counter- 132, 137, 291, 297, 300, 302
  cultural 58–59
  global 53–54, 64–65, 291, 296
  Islam 172
  US 53–54, 68, 81–82, 98, 205, 251–252, 262, 276–277, 377–378
  see also power
Henoko Bay, Okinawa 142, 143–149
heretics of the church 127–140
hijab 158–159, 161, 163, 174
Hindutva Empire 180–182
Hiroshima and Nagasaki 26–27, 65–66

historical contexts 164–166, 233–247, 270, 271–272, 293, 339, 343
holistic knowledge 189–190
the Holocaust 26, 27
the Holy Land 220, 222
homosexuality 378, 379
houseless communities 316–317
human development 48
human rights
  accumulation by dispossession 295
  fourth generation 76–77
  humanitarian intervention 10, 38–39, 67
  imperialism 356–357
  indigenous 73–74
  OBOR project 70–71
  Occidentalism 67–68
  religion 362–363, 364
  sanctions 5
  violation of 371–373
  women's movements 166–167, 172
  see also rights
humanitarian interventions 10, 38–39, 67
humanity 273–274
Hussein, Saddam 53, 57

ICAN *see* International Campaign to Abolish Nuclear Weapons
identity 130–132
ideology
  anti-communist 356–357
  national security critique 131–132
  New World Order 52–53
  orientalist knowledge production 100–101
  politics of death 18
  student group 169
  warfare 27, 28
  women's empowerment 162, 163–164
illiteracy 164, 165
imagined communities 180
imperialism
  churches' resistance to 361–365
  colonialism 251–269
  counter- 241–242
  definition 2
  ethno-national conflicts 25
  geopolitics 30–33, 97–113
  globalization 45–61, 49–50

human rights 356–357
legitimate 218
nuclearization of 64–80
peace 3, 4, 5–6, 270–287, 306–338
post-war 26–29
state structures 9–10
terrorism 54
US-Japanese 12
imprisonment 129, 135
incorporated colonies 309
independence 31, 181, 324, 344
independent Pacific movement 326–327
India 31–32, 35–36, 70, 71, 179–182
Indian Ocean 11, 107
indigenous communities
    African cosmovision 17, 348–349
    Canaan 213–232
    creative power 12
    displacement 152
    global emergence 74–76
    human rights 73–74, 371
    island states 16
    land tenure 328–332
indirect rule 33–34, 346–347
industrial sector 251
industrialization 332–335
inheritance 221–222, 224, 239–240
inquisition justice 56–57
insurgencies 357–358
integration of the state 26–27
intelligence services 27
intensive actions 143–149
inter-European rivalries 29
inter-imperialist contradictions 270, 272
interconnectedness 19, 207–208, 209
interdependence 207–208
interfaith spiritual activism 198–212
intergenerational radioactive impacts 17
International Campaign to Abolish Nuclear Weapons (ICAN) 327
international level 28–29, 37–39, 47–48, 51, 107, 364
    see also global level
International Women's Network Against Militarism 319
internet 184
internment camps 151
interreligious aspects 7, 12, 178–247
interventions

capitalism 288, 289
endemic 49–51
humanitarian 67
international 38–39, 107
liberalism 288, 289, 291
regime change 310–311
state-centric 37
invention of Africa 344
Iran-Iraq war 183
Iraq 53, 56, 57–59, 132, 133, 183, 277
irrigation development 103, 104
ISIS *see* Islamic State of Iraq and the Levant
isizwe 348–349
Islam 13–14, 158–177
Islamic Bloc 169, 173
Islamic State of Iraq and the Levant (ISIS) 60
Islamophobia 4, 60, 158, 184, 191
island states 16, 141–146, 306–338
Israel 13–14, 233–247, 341, 342, 349
Israelite state 13–14, 216, 217–229

Jamaica 371, 372–373, 375–377, 379
Japan 11, 65–66, 70, 76, 81–96, 141–157, 306
Japanese Occidentalism 68
Jehovah's Witnesses 128–129, 130, 134, 135
Jeju uprising 202–203
Jesuits 178, 189–193
Jesus 135, 186–188, 375
Jesus movement 13, 186–188, 189, 192, 193, 244
Jewish nationalism 233–234, 242
joint military bases 91
Book of Joshua 219–220, 230–231, 233, 234, 236, 238

Kaho'olawe Island movement, Hawai'i 314–316
Kanaka Maoli, Hawai'i 306, 310–311, 314–316, 318
Kandyan kingdom 99–100
Kashmir 11–12, 114–126
Ke Awalau o Pu'uloa 309–310
killing 198–199, 204–205
Kim Jong-un 68–69
Kin Bay movement 150–151
kingship 238–241, 242–243, 245
Kiritimati Island 326
knowledge 189–190, 339–353

Korea 64, 81–96
Korean Occidentalism 68
Korean Peninsula 11, 12, 13, 18, 69, 79, 82, 127–139
Korean War 199, 200–202, 207
Kuwait invasion 53

labor 34, 199, 262
land
    acquisition 103, 104, 110, 314, 317–318, 323, 327–332, 376
    dispossession 306
    occupation 108–109
    post-independence 345–346
    reclamation 150, 336
    tenure 328–332, 336
landfill operations 143–149
large corporations 373, 374
late capitalism 273–274
Latin America 14–15, 18, 73–74, 76, 278–279, 280, 288, 354–368
Law of Intervention 51
lay siege to empire 1, 20
League of Nations 38
leftist government 256–257
legal aspects 28–29, 38–39, 50–51, 167–168, 331–332
legion narrative 373–380
liberal democracy 341
liberal state of peace 299, 300
liberalism 66, 67–68, 288, 289, 291, 358–359
liberation
    Africa 344–345, 348–349
    Jewish nationalism 234
    low intensity conflict 351
    movements 14–15
    theology 213–214, 361–362
Liberation Tigers of Tamil Eelam (LTTE) 183–184
Libya 107, 256
LIC *see* low-intensity conflict
life imagination 342–343
linear super express rail 86–87
lost geography 307, 319
love, politics of 199, 206, 209–210
low intensity conflict (LIC) 17, 339–340, 342, 344, 346, 347–349, 350
loyalty oath 127
LTTE *see* Tamil Tigers of Eelam

MAD *see* mutually assured destruction
mafia 280, 284
Mahan/Roosevelt precedent 259–260
maimed populations rights 198–199
maiming 204–205
Māakua Valley, Hawai'i 316–317
Malacca Strait 260, 275–276
mandatory military service 127–139
Maohi Nui, French Polynesia 326
market vendors 375–376, 377
Mark's Gospel 369
Marshall Islands 324, 325, 326
martial law 55, 306, 314, 316
martial races 35
Marxism 359–360
masculinity, hegemonic 12, 132, 136–138
mass displacement 279–280
massacres 105, 200, 204, 219
    see also genocide
media 5
Melanesia 324
memorials 108–109
memory strategies 365
Messianic hope 242–244
Mexico 15–16, 257, 288–302
Micronesia 324, 325
Middle East 53–57, 254
migration 72–73, 77–78
militarism 2, 253
military
    deployment 35, 38, 66
    dictatorships 360, 362–363
    expenditure 252–253, 276, 313, 342–343
    martial races 35
    occupation 373
    presence 109, 110
    total war 27
military bases/training
    Colombia 355
    expansion 31
    forward deployment 66
    Hawai'i 312, 314, 315, 316, 317–320
    international law 28
    islands 141–146, 323, 324
    Japan 82, 84, 87–89, 88–91
    Persian Gulf 254–255
    South Korea 128
    Sri Lanka 105–107, 184
military-administered zones 98

military-industrial complex 275
mining activities 262, 329, 332–333, 334–335
minimum wage 289, 293, 294–295
Ministry of Women's Affairs, Palestine 163–164, 171
minority groups 181
Miyamori Elementary School jet crash 148
modernity 2, 10, 15, 26, 29–33, 98–99
Modi, Narendra 181
monarchy 238–243
monetarist counter-revolution 45–46
Monroe Doctrine 308, 309
monuments 123–124
Moritomo and Kake affairs 86
Moses 185, 218–219, 221–225, 228, 229, 230
Muisne island 283–284
multi-culturalism 72–73
multinational corporations 262, 272, 273
Mururoa 326
Muslim liberation theologies 213–232
Muslims 180, 181, 184
mutual distrust 143–144
Mutual Security Act, 1951 354
mutually assured destruction (MAD) 68
Myanmar's Occidentalism 68

napalm 201
Napoleonic wars 99
narco-guerrilla 355
national identification law (NIDS) 372–373
national interests 151, 263, 355
national security 3, 4, 54–55, 127–139, 181–182, 319
 see also security
nationalism 99, 100–104, 180, 181, 184, 233–234, 242, 292–293
nationalist-pragmatism 271
nationalization of land 331
natural rent 296, 299, 301
natural resources 296, 302
naval forces 105–107, 260, 312
Nazism 55, 291
necropolitics 15, 198, 199, 210, 251–305
necropower 204–205
neo-authoritarianism 290–301, 302
neocolonialism 2, 3–5, 17, 180, 251–305
neoliberalism 74, 271, 291, 341

neo-Thomist positions 359–360
Nettleford Commission (1997-2002) 379
networks 192, 318–319
Never Again movement 362–364
new Cold War 64–80, 75
 see also Cold War; post-Cold War
new imperialisms 270–287
New World Order (NWO) 48–49, 50–51, 53, 61
New Zealand 324, 325
Newlands Resolution 311
NFIP see Nuclear Free and Independent Pacific movement
NGOs see non-governmental organizations
NIDS see national identification law
Nogeun-Ri massacre 200–202
nominally independent states 256, 258
non-governmental organizations (NGOs) 165, 167
non-incorporated colonies 308–309
Non-Proliferation Treaty 84
North Korea (DPRK) 68–69, 127–140
North-South axis 270, 275, 289
nuchi du takara 141
Nuclear Free and Independent Pacific (NFIP) movement 326–327
nuclear imperialism 64–80
nuclear technology 17, 26–27, 83, 83–84, 85–86, 181–182, 324–327, 336
nuclearization 10, 182–183
Nunca Mas 362–364
NWO see New World Order

Obama administration 60, 252, 260, 263, 264, 275, 307
OBOR see One Belt One Road project
Occidentalism 65–66, 67–68
occupation 16, 167, 183–184, 223–247, 374
ocean protection 143–149, 153
oil
 reserves 254, 255, 296, 297, 299–300
 stockpiling 148, 150–151, 153
 tanker crisis 255
Okinawa, Japan 12, 87–91, 141–157, 319
One Belt One Road (OBOR) project 66, 69–72, 260
online right-wingers 143
open spaces 116
Operation Strangle, Korean War 201

oppression
    Africa cosmovision 349–350
    Canaan conquest 221, 226
    China 265
    church resistance of 374, 375
    collective hope 19
    imperial peace 5
    India 180–181
    interconnectedness 208, 209
    Israeli occupation 244, 245
    Jesus movement 187
    Korean reunification 64
    the Qur'an 215
    religious majoritarianism 12–13
    speaking truth to 6–7
    Tamil 101, 102, 104–108
organic dominance 58
orientalist knowledge production 100–101, 108
Orientalist–Occidentalist discourses 68, 77
the Other 127, 131, 203, 208, 281–282, 284–285, 308
Oura Bay, Japan 88–91
over-accumulation 274, 278–279
over-exploitation 294

Pacha Mama 73, 75
Pacific Island Forum (PIF) 325
Pacific Pivot 307–309
Pacific region 16–17, 323–338
Pacific/Indian Ocean 70–72, 74–76, 306–322
pacificism 82, 136, 188
Pakistan 31–32, 181–182, 182–183
Palaikarrar (Polygar) rebellion 99
Palestine 12, 158–177, 233–247, 341, 342, 349, 376
Palestinian Liberation Organization (PLO) 165–166
Papua New Guinea 335
Paraguay 363
participatory democracy 153, 155
partition of India 31–32, 35–36, 181
patriarchal heroism 137
Patriot Act, US 2001 54–55
patriotism 205
PCOR *see* People's Congress of Resistance
peace
    biblical Israel 243
    capitalist accumulation 292

    co-existence 71
    ethno-nationalist conflicts 10, 26–29
    feminist spiritual activism 209–210
    geopolitics 81–113
    human rights 73–74
    imperial 3, 4, 5–7, 270–287, 306–338
    Korean Peninsular 138
    mandatory military service 133–134
    religion 188, 191, 365–366
    see also security
peaceful infiltration 237–238
Pearl Harbor attack 314
pension privatization 295
people-centered regional frameworks 39
People's Congress of Resistance (PCOR), US 72
permanent state of war 280, 283, 344
Permanent Tribunals of the People (PTP) 364–365
Persian Gulf 53, 57, 254–255, 276
personal experiences 148–149, 151–153, 154, 155, 206–207
Peru 361
PIF *see* Pacific Island Forum
pivot to Asia 252, 257, 263, 264
Pledge of Allegiance, South Korea 127
PLO *see* Palestinian Liberation Organization
pluralism 15–16, 73, 215
Pōkakuloa 317–319
politicization of Christianity 188
politicized Buddhism 183–184
politics
    of family 125
    imperial geopolitics 30
    killing 198–199, 369–370, 371
    of love 206, 209–210
    post-World War II 3
    religion 360–361, 378–379
    role of the king 238–241
    US and China rivalry 261–263
    women's movements 165, 172, 173
    see also geopolitics; necropolitics
Polynesia 324
post-9/11 256
post-Apartheid society 17
post-capitalism 273–274
post-Cold War 64–78, 107
    see also Cold War; new Cold War
post-modernism 10–11, 72–73

post-World War II 3, 81, 154, 253–257, 354
poverty 1, 48, 185–186, 186–188, 294
power 15
    Africa 348, 349–350
    capitalism 273
    China 261–263, 291
    concepts of 179–180
    criminal economies 15
    fundamentalism 3, 4
    independent economic 251–252
    interconnectedness 208
    knowledge 189, 340, 341
    monarchy 240–241, 242
    multinational corporations 273
    North/South 289, 295
    peace and security 6
    religion 188–189, 359, 375, 378–379
    sea-based imperial formations 309
    soft 339
    South Asia 178, 179, 180–184
    United Nations 37–38
    US 14, 251, 261–263
    see also hegemony; sovereignty
prayer 190–191
priesthood movements 361–362
prisoners 167, 168, 380
private capital 15
private military companies 355
privatization 279, 295–296, 332
privatized gospel 378
professionalization of armed bodies 356
progressive governments 15, 282, 300
progressive neoliberalism 271
the Promised Land 219, 220–221, 234
property rights 371
prophecy 190, 243
prostitution 13, 199, 203, 209
protectorate systems 33–34
proxy wars 30, 32, 182–183, 259
pseudo-democracy 339–353
PTP *see* Permanent Tribunals of the People
public goods 295–296, 301
public spaces 170–171, 173
psychological warfare 2, 28

the Qur'an 213–232

racism 202–203, 210
radioactivity 325–326
rape 88, 142, 202, 203, 209

rational philosophy 144
rationality of peace 282
reactionary regimes 254
Reaganomics 45–46
reclamation of land 88, 89
reconciliation dialogue 64–80
Reds 202, 203, 204
refugees 5, 72–73, 200–201
registration of land 331–332
relational capacities 168
religion
    conscientious objection 128–130, 134–136
    demonization 18–19
    fundamentalism 3–5, 7, 8, 12, 182, 183
    indigenous civilizations 75–76
    interreligious 7, 12, 178–247
    majority domination 12–13
    socio-political analyses 8
    theologies of resistance 339–382
religiosity of superiority 341, 343
rendition 55
rent, criminal 290, 298
representatives of struggles 147, 148, 149–155
repression 10, 365
reservoir armed forces 129
resident movements 153–155
resilience 6
responsibilities 154, 281–282, 284, 307, 335, 365
restricted democracies 362
retirement pension funds 295
revolutionary Tamil militant organizations 104
right-wing neoliberal regimes 257
rights
    land 328
    religion 354–368, 369–382
    territory 283–284
    to kill and maim 198–199, 204–205
    to rebellion 357–358
    women's movements 166–167
    see also human rights
rivers 75
road widening 376
Roman Catholic Church 18, 357–361, 369–370, 373
Russia 276

Saleh, Dr. Mariam 160, 162, 163–164, 166–169, 171, 172
Samoa 331–332
San Francisco Treaty, 1951 81–82, 92
sanctions 5
Saudi Arabia 252–253, 254
scientific innovations 27–28
scientific laws 340–341
scriptural analysis 178–193, 215–217
sea beds 142, 332–335
sea sacredness 336
sea-power 309
sectarianism 214
secularism 8, 158, 160, 168, 169, 172, 182
securitization 274
security
   cooperation 14, 256
   global 5
   India and US 33
   Latin America post-World War II 354
   national 3, 4, 54–55, 127–139, 181–182, 319
   people's 73
   reframing 319
   states 280–281
   see also national security; peace
self-defense forces 82, 83
self-determination 101–102, 302, 356
self-protective Atlantic Liberalism 67
separate gender spaces 162, 170–171, 173
settlement practices 103–104
settler colonialism 216–217, 220
   see also colonialism
Seventh Day Adventists 129, 377, 379
sexual violence 202–203
sexualization of war 210
shipping 260, 275–276
Sikh nation 36
silk roads OBOR project 69–72
Sinhala, Sri Lanka 99, 100–104, 108–110, 111, 184
sit-in 147–149
Siyam, Amal 160, 163, 166–169, 171
slavery 214, 288
social aspects
   armed struggle 116
   capitalist accumulation 292
   liberation 221
   militarism 265
   military bases 313

   movements 15–16, 362–364
   peace 282
   the right to peace 76–77
   solidarity 51–53
   women's movements 172
socialism 358–360, 364
socio-political organization 25
soft peace 82
soft power 58, 339
soldiering 199
solidarity
   beyond borders 14
   groups 16
   Kashmir uprisings 123
   networks 318–319
   Pacific Islands 326–327
   religious 192, 361–362, 377
   spiritual activism 199
   transnational and transgenerational 206
Solomon Islands 330, 331
South Africa 17, 339, 344, 345–346, 350, 351
South Asia 9–10, 25–44, 178–197
South China Sea 263, 264, 275–276
South India 99
South Korea 12, 127–139
South peoples 270–271, 275–279
sovereignty
   Eelam Tamils 99, 101–102
   globalization 50–51
   imperial formations 308
   Japan 84–87
   Mexico 289
   military bases 313
   nation state decline 279
   post-Cold War rivalry 107
   right to kill and maim 198, 204–205
   see also power
Soviet Union 30–31, 32, 257, 260–261
spaces 162, 348
Spanish War (1969) 311
Spanish–American War (1898) 259–260
speculation 45, 47, 49, 272
spirituality 8, 17–18, 340, 346
Sri Lanka 11, 36, 68, 97–113, 183–184, 190–191, 252, 265
state of exception 288–305
state level
   administrative structures 241
   church separation 378

conscientious objection 133
ethno-national forces 25–26, 35
immigration 72
imperialism 9–10, 97, 98
interventions 37
militarism 253
national interests 151, 263, 355
national security 3, 4, 54–55, 127–139, 181–182, 319
security 280–281
South Asia 29–33
structural genocide 97–113
weakening of 270–271, 279
see also nation states
state-aided colonization 102–104
state-enforced customary order 347
status societies 242
stigmatization 134, 136
story-telling methods 1, 206–207
strategic interests
asylum-seekers 36–37
imperialism 257–261
independent economic power and US 251–252
locations 17, 98, 255, 309–310
Sri Lanka 105–107, 110, 111
structural adjustment 46
structural genocide 97–113
structural violence 291–292
Stryker Brigade Combat team 317–319
student groups 161, 169–171
sub-regional empire 33
subordination 289, 295–297
suffering 191, 198–212
sugar plantations 310
sun standing still 227–228
super-exploitation of labor 262
superiority 341–342
supremacy, religiosity of 341
Syrian civil war 59–60

Tahiti 326
Taiwan 264
Taliban 60
Tamil *see* Eelam Tamil, Sri Lanka
Tamil Tigers of Eelam (LTTE) 102, 104–105, 107, 108
tax havens 272–273
technological factors 27–28

technological subordination 296, 299
telescope construction 318
territorial boundaries 29
terrorism 54, 60, 108
see also war on terror
theology 8, 178–197, 339–382
three-cleans-all operations 204
torture 55, 363
total war 27–28
tourism 283
trade 98–99, 263
transgenerational solidarity 206
transnational capital 301
transnational corporations 297
transnational rent 296
transnational solidarity 206
treaties 28–29, 310
Treaty of Reciprocity 310
trilateral hegemony 64
Trincomalee harbor, Sri Lanka 105–106, 110
triumphalism 205
Trump administration 66, 68–69, 83–84, 263, 264, 265, 276, 277–278
truth 6–7, 189, 363–364
Tyler Doctrine, 1842 308

ubiquitous militarization 344–347
ubiquitous violence 351
ubuhlanti 17–18, 347–349
ultra-imperialism 270, 272
unemployment 48
unholy Christendom 188
unified Korea 138
unitary states 97–113
United Kingdom (UK) 26, 30–31, 32, 36, 64–65, 254–255, 325–326
UK–US alliances 30–31, 104–105, 253–257
United Nations 37, 102, 254
United Nations Charter 28–29, 34, 37–38
United States of America (US)
anti-communism 356
arms race 276–277
Atlantic Liberalism 67–68
China rivalry 251–269, 275–276
colonialism 218
conscientious objection 132–133
Hawai'i 306–320

hegemony 53–54, 68, 81–82, 205, 252, 262, 276–277
humanitarian interventions 10
imperialism 107, 111, 257–261
Japan relations 11, 12, 81, 84–85, 87–89
Korean War 199, 200–203, 204, 210
Mexico border 299
military bases 128, 141–157, 199, 260, 311–312
military expenditure 252
military pacts 14
military superiority 342
military aid 354–355
national security 54–55
neo-colonialism 253–257
nuclear policy 66, 68–69, 325
post-modern left 72–73
religion 377–378
South Asia 31, 32
structural genocide 98
total war 27
US–UK alliances 30–31, 104–105, 253–257
Vietnam Syndrome 56–59
war on terror 53–57
Universal Declaration of Human Rights 370
Universal Declaration of the Rights of the Peoples 364
university violence 341
unworthy victims 5
Uruguay 363
USSR 3, 4, 18, 98, 271, 279, 354

Vanuatu 330–331
venereal disease 203
Venezuela 256–257, 281, 291, 300
veto countries 37–38
victims 5–6, 114–126
Vietnam syndrome 56–57
Vietnam War 132–133, 204, 206, 207
violence
  accumulation by dispossession 291–292, 293–294, 298–299
  Africa 342, 346
  Canaan conquest 223, 227–228, 237
  conscientious objection 133–134, 135
  dissociation of oneself 208
  divine sanction 220

low intensity conflict 350, 351
monopoly of legitimate 279
neoliberalism 341
religion 185, 220, 361
social and political control 372
wars 279–281
women's experiences 206–207

wage dispossession 289, 293, 294–295
war
  Africa 346
  experiences 151–152, 154, 155
  heroes 102
  imperialism after 26–29
  killing 198–199
  militarized prostitution 13
  new imperialisms 279–281
  permanent state of 280, 283, 344
  post 3, 81, 154, 253–257, 354
  trauma 148–149
  see also armed conflicts; Cold War
war on terror 3, 10, 11, 32, 53–56, 65–66, 105, 256
  see also terrorism
wealth 48, 273, 274, 289, 290
weapons of mass destruction 56
Western triumph 279
Westernization 65
Westphalian system of state 15, 64, 66, 72, 76, 270, 279
women 11–12, 114, 115–122, 142, 158–177, 319
Women's Work Committees (WWC) 164–165
working day length 294
world recession 272–273
World Social Forum 72
world wars 26–29, 30–31
worship sites 109, 110
worthy victims 5
WWC *see* Women's Work Committees

Yahweh 237, 243–244, 245
Yongsan Tragedy 133
youth 159

Zapatista movement, Mexico 74–75
Zionism 233–234

www.ingramcontent.com/pod-product-compliance
Lightning Source LLC
Chambersburg PA
CBHW050832230426
43667CB00012B/1974